15.99

D0414310

ns

This book is to be returned on or before
the last date stamped below.

1 2 JUN 1992	THIS BOOK CANNOT BE RENEWED UNLESS FOR SPECIFIED COURSE NO:	CANCELLED
2 3 APR 1993	1 5 MAY 1998	CANCELLED
	1 & JUN 1998	
1 0 DEC 199~	3 JUL 1998	
	2 4 JUN 1998	-7 MAR 2008
1 7 FEB 1995	2 2 APR 1999	
	2 8 MAY 1999	2 3 MAY 2008
2 4 MAR 1995	1 2 JUN 2000	
2 6 FEB 1996	0 3 JUL 2000	CANCELLED -8 AUG 2008
2 5 OCT 1996		CANCELLED
1 5 NOV 1996	2 4 JUL 2000	
-6 DEC 1996		
-6 JAN 1997	-7 DEC 2000	2 8 MAY 200~
3 1 JAN 1997	5 1	CANCELLED
1 0 APR 1998	2 9 MAY 2002	LIBREX

This is the first t
problems and thei
has been specifica
qualified, and for

The contributors r
variety of clinical
alcohol problems,
lar clinical proble
gives an up-to-dat
peutic interventior

Windy Dryden is
sity of London, wh

Adult clinical problems

A cognitive-behavioural approach

Edited by
Windy Dryden and
Robert Rentoul

London and New York

First published in 1991
by Routledge
11 New Fetter Lane, London EC4P 4EE

Simultaneously published in the USA and Canada
by Routledge
a division of Routledge, Chapman and Hall Inc.
29 West 35th Street, New York, NY 10001

Typeset in Times by Michael Mepham, Frome, Somerset
Printed in Great Britain by
Mackays of Chatham PLC, Chatham, Kent

British Library Cataloguing in Publication Data
Adult clinical problems: a cognitive-behavioural approach.
1. Clinical psychology
I. Dryden, Windy   II. Rentoul, Robert *1939–*
616.89

Library of Congress Cataloging in Publication Data
Adult clinical problems: a cognitive-behavioural approach/edited by
Windy Dryden and Robert Rentoul.
p.   cm.
Includes bibliographical references.
Includes index.
1. Cognitive therapy. I. Dryden, Windy. II. Rentoul, Robert Reid.
[DNLM: 1. Behavior Therapy. 2. Cognitive Therapy. 3. Mental
Disorders. WM 100 2415]
RC489.C63A37   1991
616.89'142—dc20

DNLM/DLC

90–9119
CIP

ISBN 0–415–01136–1
      0–415–01137–X (pbk)

Contents

Figures and tables

FIGURES

TABLES

Editors and contributors

EDITORS

Windy Dryden is Senior Lecturer in the Department of Psychology, Goldsmiths' College, University of London. He has authored or edited thirty-eight books in the field of counselling and psychotherapy. He is editor of the *Psychotherapy Handbook series*, Open University Press and editor of the *Counselling in Action* series, Sage Publications.

Robert Rentoul is Lecturer in Psychology at Goldsmiths' College, London University, specializing in Abnormal Psychology. After graduating from Queen's, Belfast with a first, he did post-graduate research at University College, London and as a British Council scholar in Warsaw, Poland. He became a Lecturer in Physiology at Edinburgh University, before moving to his present post. He has written a number of textbooks; including a contribution to a psychiatric nursing textbook, and is the author of *Explanations in Psychology* (in preparation). His research is directed at the evaluation and modification of NHS health care provision.

CONTRIBUTORS

Alastair Ager is Senior Lecturer and Head of the Department of Psychology, Chancellor College, University of Malawi, where he is researching applications of Clinical Psychology in developing nations. Current research interests include tropical health psychology, the psychological status of refugees and the provision of services for the developmentally disabled. He has published widely within the field of mental handicap, and is the recent author of *The Life Experiences Checklist*, Windsor: NFER/Nelson.

Max Birchwood is Top Grade Clinical Psychologist with West Birmingham Health Authority. His main professional and research interests centre upon the application of psychological principles and techniques to the management of schizophrenia. He has published work in the area of family interventions, the control of auditory hallucinations, early prediction of relapse, informing patients and their families with schizophrenia. He is co-author of a recent book *Schizophrenia: An Integrated Approach into Research and Treatment* published by Longmans.

Nicola Bradbury Following the completion of her Clinical Psychology training in Leeds, she moved to the West Midlands to join the Walsall Psychology Department. She has developed a particular interest in working with elderly people, and moved to Bromsgrove and Redditch to establish a district-wide psychology service for older adults. Her primary interests are continuing care services, the development of models of evaluation and evaluation of services. She is currently an Honorary Lecturer at Birmingham University and is author of 'Geriatric Medicine' in A. Broome (1989) (ed) *Health Psychology: Processes and Applications*, London: Chapman & Hall.

Martin Cole is Director of the Institute for Sex Education and Research in Birmingham; he also practises sex therapy privately. He has been actively involved in sex education and therapy for over twenty-five years and has many publications in this field including a series of films. He is author of a critical review of sex therapy in the *British Journal of Psychiatry* (1985) and also co-edited *Sex Therapy in Britain*, Open University Press (1988).

Norman Epstein is Associate Professor in the Department of Family and Community Development, University of Maryland, College Park, Maryland, USA. He has published numerous articles and chapters describing his research and clinical work regarding cognitive and behavioural factors in marital and family problems. He is co-editor of the volumes *Cognitive-Behavioral Therapy with Families* (Brunner/Mazel) and *Depression in the Family* (The Haworth Press), and co-author of *Cognitive-Behavioral Marital Therapy* (Brunner/Mazel).

Gerry Kent is Lecturer in Medical Psychology in the Department of Psychiatry, Sheffield University Medical School. He is the author of two books on the psychological aspects of medicine and dentistry and has published numerous papers on the cognitive aspects of anxiety.

Celia McCrea is a Clinical Psychologist, lecturing in the Department of Psychology, Leicester University. Her main interest concerns the therapeutic usefulness of videofeedback for weight loss and improvement of body image in the treatment of obesity.

Robert Newell is a Lecturer at the Institute of Nursing Studies, University of Hull. His main areas of research and clinical interest have been cognitive-behavioural interventions with irritable bowel syndrome and premenstrual syndrome. He is the author of several journal and magazine articles.

Martin Preston is District Clinical Psychologist with West Birmingham Health Authority. He has extensive experience developing rehabilitation services for people with schizophrenia and is closely involved in the planning and implementation of community focused services. He has published work concerning the psychological management of auditory hallucinations and is co-author of a recent book: *Schizophrenia: An Integrated Approach into Research and Treatment* published by Longmans.

Stephen E. Schlesinger is a Clinical Psychologist in independent practice in Chicago and Oak Park, Illinois, USA. He is an Assistant Professor in the Department of Psychiatry at Northwestern University Medical School in Chicago. He is co-editor of *Cognitive-Behavioural Therapy with Families* and co-author of both *Taking Charge: How families can climb out of the chaos of addiction ... and flourish* and *Stop Drinking and Start Living*.

Jan Scott is a Consultant and Senior Lecturer at the University Department of Psychiatry, Newcastle upon Tyne. She is the author of articles on depression and cognitive therapy and has recently co-edited *Cognitive Therapy in Clinical Practice*. She is associate editor of the *British Journal of Clinical and Social Psychiatry*.

Peter Trower is Head of Psychology Services for Rehabilitation, Solihull Health Authority and formerly Lecturer in Clinical Psychology, Leicester University. He has published extensively in the areas of social skills training, social anxiety and cognitive psychotherapy.

Ron Tulloch is currently Top Grade Psychologist and Clinical Programme Director at Stanley Royd Hospital, Wakefield, Yorkshire. He is currently researching the effectiveness of cognitive therapy with personality disorders, schizophrenia and violent men. He has published in the field of personality disorder and cognitive therapy for anger problems.

Vivien Twaddle is a Principal Clinical Psychologist in the Department of Clinical Psychology, Royal Victoria Infirmary, Newcastle upon Tyne. She is currently involved in organising a Post Qualification Training Course in Cognitive Therapy in the Northern Region.

Richard Velleman is Lecturer in Psychology at the University of Bath and Principal Clinical Psychologist with the Bath Health District. His main research interests centre on alcohol and drug problems, especially the families of people with drug and alcohol problems, the evaluation of services, and the use of volunteer counsellors. Publications include a number of book chapters (e.g. in the *Handbook of Counselling in Britain*, 1989) and papers in the *British Journal of Addiction, Journal of Studies on Alcohol, British Journal of Clinical Psychology*.

Preface

Most texts on abnormal psychology which are written for advanced undergraduates in psychology and beginning postgraduate students in clinical psychology, rely heavily on the third edition of the Diagnostic and Statistical Manual of Mental Disorders (DSM-111-R) framework, first developed in 1980 and revised in 1987 by the American Psychiatric Association. In our opinion, what these texts lack is a systematic in-depth coverage of adult clinical problems and their treatment from a cognitive-behavioural perspective. Furthermore, these texts tend not to draw heavily upon representative research evidence and as such, do not meet the educational needs of advanced undergraduates in psychology and beginning postgraduates in clinical psychology.

Informal discussions with colleagues throughout Britain convinced us that there is a need for a text which systematically covers the conceptualization and treatment of adult clinical problems from a cognitive-behavioural perspective, and which in doing so, draws upon the available research literature.

The structure of the present text is as follows. After an introduction to the cognitive-behavioural approach, contributors deal with the following adult clinical problems: anxiety, depression, anger and violence, eating disorders, alcohol and drug problems, schizophrenia, problems of elderly people, mental handicap, interpersonal problems, marital and family problems, and sexual problems.

To maintain consistency throughout the book, authors were encouraged to use a specified chapter structure to guide their work. Each chapter is divided into three sections. In the first section, *Conceptualization*, authors show how the clinical problem under consideration is conceptualized from a cognitive-behavioural perspective, to include an up-to-date review of the relevant empirical literature and discuss the most commonly used assessment measures. Then they consider the development and maintenance of the clinical problem from a cognitive-behavioural perspective, again including a review of relevant and current empirical research.

In the second section, *Treatment*, authors present an up-to-date review of research findings on cognitive-behavioural interventions, with relevance to the clinical problem under discussion. In particular they detail the most important therapeutic ingredients that have been found in both process and outcome research studies conducted in their given area.

In the final section, *Future Developments*, authors briefly outline needed developments in conceptualization and treatment. In particular, they consider how a cognitive-behavioural approach to the clinical problem under consideration could be enriched by drawing upon work emanating from outside of cognitive-behaviour therapy.

We hope that this book provides readers with a thorough grounding in the cognitive-behavioural approach to clinical problems, and would like to thank our contributors for their sterling work.

Windy Dryden
Robert Rentoul
London, March 1991

Abbreviations

APA	American Psychiatric Association
BDI	Beck Depression Inventory
BMI	body-mass index
CT	cognitive therapy
DAI	Dyadic Attributional Inventory
DAS	Dysfunctional Attitude Scale
DRDT	Daily Record of Dysfunctional Thoughts
EE	expressed emotion
EEG	electroencephalogram
FBI	Family Beliefs Inventory
GAD	Generalized Anxiety Disorder
IBS	irritable-bowel syndrome
MAS	Marital Attitude Survey
PTSD	post-traumatic stress disorder
RBI	Relationship Beliefs Inventory
RET	rational-emotive therapy
RO	Reality Orientation
SADQ	Severity of Alcohol Dependence Questionnaire
SIT	self-instructional training
SST	social-skills training
STAI	State–Trait Anxiety Inventory

Chapter 1

Clinical problems

An introduction to the cognitive-behavioural approach

Robert Newell and Windy Dryden

WHAT IS A COGNITIVE-BEHAVIOURAL APPROACH?

When students of psychology first examine therapeutic approaches to clinical problems, they may experience bewilderment at the sheer number of approaches on offer. In addition, they may have difficulty in getting to grips with the concepts put forward concerning the processes of development, maintenance and recovery in the course of client difficulties, particular to each school of thought. These concepts are often accompanied by different research methods and even different uses of language, all of which add to the confusion, as the student attempts to understand the often contradictory and competing approaches, and to evaluate their claims to provide accurate accounts regarding the nature of client problems.

Additionally, the various traditions of therapeutic intervention are themselves often heterogeneous in composition. Within each discipline, there are points of divergence and convergence. Thus, it is probably inaccurate to speak of psycho-dynamic therapy, client-centred therapy, behaviour therapy, cognitive therapy and so on, as though each were a single entity. It may be more appropriate to regard such descriptive terms as indicative of general approaches in psychotherapy, within each of which numerous more specific formulations of client problems exist, each related to equally numerous specific assessment and intervention strategies.

This heterogeneity is particularly true of cognitive-behavioural approaches, reflecting several historical influences and the considerable recent growth of interest in the field from both clinicians and researchers. Therefore, the chapters in this volume reflect the wide range of cognitive-behavioural approaches, with some authors adopting an approach more linked to traditional behavioural theories, while others pursue more cognitive accounts of client distress and treatment. Of these latter accounts, some spring from the empirical observations of leading clinicians in the field, whilst others have more explicit connection with modern information-processing accounts of human cognition. Finally, some chapters offer accounts of client difficulties and their treatment which stress equally the cognitive and behavioural aspects of cognitive-behaviour therapy. Throughout, the aim of this volume is to offer clear descriptions of recent endeavours to conceptualize and treat a broad range of adult client problems using cognitive-behavioural interventions, and by doing so to arrive at an integrated picture of the current status of cognitive-behavioural interventions with regard to such problems.

This chapter attempts to orientate the reader by covering a number of broad issues relating to cognitive-behaviour therapy, and thus creating a framework for understanding the more specific information offered about specific client problems in later chapters. The cognitive-behavioural approach is set within the context both of clinical psychology as a whole and of research in behavioural and cognitive psychology. In addition, the distinctions and similarities between the cognitive, behavioural and cognitive-behavioural approaches are outlined, beginning with a discussion of historical aspects of the various approaches, so that by the end of the chapter, the reader should have a clear idea of which kinds of approach to client difficulties may be reasonably referred to under the general rubric of 'cognitive-behaviour therapy'.

HISTORICAL CONTEXT OF BEHAVIOUR THERAPY

The roots of behaviour therapy lie in the investigative strategy of behaviourism and in conditioning theories of learning. Both these traditions stretch back to the early years of this century. Behaviourism was intended by its proponents to be a philosophy of psychological investigation which would free psychology from 'mentalistic' notions of human experience, perception and behaviour and the attendant methodological difficulties involved in investigating covert occurrences such as thought and emotion. The investigation of learning was to be achieved by the use of laboratory experimentation involving only observable, measurable phenomena, with the intention of making psychology an objective natural science (Watson 1914/1967). The two major types of learning in behavioural formulations of human motivation and behaviour are classical and operant conditioning.

Classical-conditioning accounts are based on the work of Pavlov and involve the pairing of an artificial (conditioned) stimulus with a natural (unconditioned) stimulus, with the resulting occurrence of a (conditioned) response in the presence of only the conditioned stimulus. Classical-conditioning approaches emphasize the antecedents of an event, exercise close control of subject behaviour in the experiment and principally affect automatic processes (for example, salivation, heart rate, bowel motility).

The other main strand of learning theory, operant conditioning, involves, first, the consistent and contingent application of reward (positive reinforcement) and withdrawal of aversive stimuli (negative reinforcement), in order to increase the frequency of desired behaviours; and second, punishment, by administration of aversive stimuli or withdrawal of a reward, to decrease the frequency of undesired behaviours. Unlike classical conditioning, operant conditioning allows the introduction of new behaviours into the subject's repertoire, through the process of shaping (the differential reinforcement of successive approximations to the desired new behaviour), and is thus regarded as a more complex form of learning. The approach emphasizes the consequences of an event, allows considerable freedom of experimental subject behaviour and principally affects motor behaviour. It should be noted, however, that these are general descriptions of the two types of learning, and that there is evidence for the existence of, for example, operant conditioning of automatic processes, classical conditioning of motor behaviour and 'backward' learning, where the conditioned stimulus is presented after the unconditioned stimulus. Nevertheless, these are all weak effects when compared with the more characteristic classical- and operant-conditioning paradigms (Walker 1987).

Early experiments led to the observation of the conditioning of fear. The example of an 11-month-old child taught to fear white rats (Watson and Raynor 1920) has now passed into behaviour therapy folklore. A loud noise was sounded whenever the previously unafraid child reached for a rat. The child showed fear when the noise sounded, and eventually came to display this response in the presence of the animal, but without the application of the noise. This example of classically conditioned fear is offered by behaviour therapists to account for a variety of anxiety-based responses. Thus, the dental phobic is assumed to have had some unpleasant experience (for example, pain) at the dentist, and to have associated this with its antecedent events (sight of the dental drill, dentist, surgery door), which themselves trigger anxiety as a conditioned response on subsequent occasions. Even comparatively complicated fears such as social anxiety are conceptualized in this way by strict behaviourists, who assume that some unpleasant experience is paired with numerous social situations, which then become conditioned stimuli.

Fear responses are then maintained by means of operant conditioning, through avoidance of and escape from the feared situations. By escape, the fearful person obtains relief from anxiety, which acts as negative reinforcement for the escape, thus increasing the likelihood of escape on subsequent occasions. Entry into feared situations is punished by the arousal of the physiological symptoms of anxiety, leading to a decrease in approach behaviour to such situations. This explanation of learning as a combination of operant and classical conditioning was described by Kornorski and Miller (1937) as two-factor theory, applied by Mowrer (1960) to the acquisition and maintenance of fear, and revived and revised by Gray (1975) as two-process theory.

From such observations of conditioned fear responding, it seemed reasonable that such fear might be deconditioned, either through extinction (repeated presentation of the conditioned fear stimulus without the unconditioned stimulus), or through counter-conditioning a more adaptive response to the fear stimulus, by pairing it with some powerful pleasant occurrence. The most significant step in offering effective treatment for client problems based on behavioural theories came with the development of systematic desensitization, a set of procedures which has survived in some areas of behaviour therapy to the present day. Wolpe (1958) proposed the possible use of counter-conditioning involving sexual behaviour, feeding behaviour or muscular relaxation. These activities were to be engaged in during exposure to the fear stimulus, in the belief that they were incompatible with fear responses.

Wolpe opted for the use of progressive relaxation (Jacobson, 1938) as the response incompatible with fear in desensitization. Clients were presented with a ladder or hierarchy of increasingly anxiety-evoking situations, while always maintaining a sufficiently powerful state of relaxation to ensure the absence of fear. Hawton *et al.* (1989) note that systematic desensitization is no longer widely used, particularly since the introduction of the 'exposure'-orientated therapies (Marks 1987), and that reciprocal inhibition is rarely supported as a theory of anxiety reduction. However, they grant that Wolpe's influence in behaviour therapy has been vast, owing to his methodological rigour and descriptions of treatment based upon his methods across a wide variety of client problems. Wolpe himself has remained sceptical of many recent developments, dismissing advocates of exposure therapy, multimodal therapy and the cognitive therapies as 'malcontents' (Wolpe 1976), yet at the same time stating that systematic desentitization has always been a cognitive treatment strategy (Wolpe 1978).

Nevertheless, behaviour therapy today is far more heterogeneous than in the 1950s and 1960s. The field contains so great a variety, that it is most appropriate to regard behaviour therapy as an orientation rather than a theory or set of theories. This orientation is characterized by a clear focus on presenting complaints, the selection of specific interventions to suit these complaints (following rigorous individual assessment), the brevity of these interventions, their systematic and rigorous appraisal (Garfield and Bergin 1986) and by the use of interventions with varying rationales.

Although there is general agreement as to the usefulness and wide applicability of behaviour therapy (Rachman and Wilson 1980), the approach still leaves several issues unresolved. First, behaviour therapy is not always successful in those difficulties for which it is the treatment of choice. Second, there are numerous client difficulties for which observable behaviour is absent, or a minor component (for example, obsessional ruminations). Third, insufficient attention is paid to issues of client compliance (Hawton *et al.* 1989). Finally, the theoretical underpinnings of behaviour therapy have faced continuing criticism. Behavioural explanations are simply not powerful enough to explain complex human (or animal) behaviours. For example, it seems unlikely that reinforcement principles alone can successfully account for language acquisition, as Chomsky's (1959) critique of Skinner's (1957) account of verbal behaviour demonstrated. If behavioural accounts of human learning are incomplete, then those treatment interventions based upon such accounts must be equally so.

HISTORICAL CONTEXT OF COGNITIVE THERAPY

Partly because of this difficulty in using stimulus–response models to account for complex behaviours, behavioural models in academic psychology had long recognized the need to postulate covert processes in attempting to understand behaviour. Early attempts to revise such stimulus–response accounts included Tolman's (1932) concept of 'purposive' behaviourism, which, using behavioural methodology in animal experimentation, sought evidence for internal representations. This led to the development of the concepts of cognitive mapping and expectancy in animals, both of which terms clearly describe mediating variables determining animal behaviour. In a later attempt to defend behavioural formulations of complex behaviour from increasing criticism, Skinner (1969) proposed the notion of rule-governed behaviour. This essentially extends the concept of operant reinforcement to allow humans to follow rules which have never been specifically reinforced, through a process of generalization from a specific instance of a rule, once this has been sufficiently reinforced. Although the model remains a simple reinforcement-based account, much of the reinforcement takes place at a covert level. Thus, by the time attempts were being made to depart from a behavioural approach to therapy which concerned itself only with observable acts, and denied the usefulness of considering internal covert processes, cognition was already respectable again in psychological research.

More recently, computer models of human cognition have departed radically from behaviourist notions, and begun building a coherent information-processing account of human cognition. Such models now represent the most significant area of psychological research in perception (Marr 1982), memory (Baddeley and Hitch 1974), problem solving (Newell and Simon 1972) and many other aspects of human performance (Johnson-Laird 1988). Despite the general agreement that cognition was an acceptable, and, indeed essential, area of study in experimental psychology, behaviour therapists remained reluctant to depart from their reliance on observable behaviour and conditioning accounts of human difficulties. In part, this is under-standable in terms of the philosophical opposition of behaviourism to psychoanalysis, with its almost exclusive concentration upon internal processes and lack of emphasis on measurable change. Cognition had likewise received little attention from psychoanalysts themselves, and was not accepted as a central aspect in the mediation of client difficulties until the development of the cognitive therapies.

Cognitive therapy is at least as diverse in its theoretical underpinnings as behaviour therapy. In the early 1980s, Rachman and Wilson (1980) identified three major schools of thought in cognitive therapy: Ellis's (1962) rational-emotive therapy (RET), Beck's (1976) cognitive therapy (CT) and Meichenbaum's (1977) self-instructional training (SIT). These approaches continue to enjoy considerable support, and there are numerous less well-known variants (see Dryden and Golden 1986). Ellis and Beck began their professional lives within the psychoanalytic movement, while Meichenbaum was one of a number of therapists working in the behavioural tradition who sought to expand the discipline's conceptual framework and clinical efficacy. All the cognitive approaches are, however, united by the following assumptions: (a) there are cognitions; (b) these cognitions mediate client problems; (c) such mediating factors are available for scrutiny and subsequent change by the client; and (d) cognitions are the primary targets for change in attempting to address clients' cognitive, affective and behavioural difficulties.

Of the three major variants, Ellis's RET is the oldest, and remains influential, particularly in North America, although some commentators (for example, Hawton *et al.* 1989) give pre-eminence to Beck's cognitive therapy. RET formulates client difficulties according to an ABC model, where (A)ctivating events are mediated by (B)eliefs which give rise to emotional, behavioural and cognitive (C)onsequences (Ellis 1977). It is the irrational appraisal of activating events which gives rise to client difficulties. Therapy involves the training of the client in identifying, challenging and modifying these beliefs, and is accomplished by a variety of strategies including self-monitoring with feedback, direct challenging of irrational beliefs by the therapist, cognitive rehearsal of more rational statements and behavioural testing of both the validity of irrational beliefs and the efficacy of more rational thinking, by means of homework tasks.

Beck's cognitive therapy developed independently of RET, but makes somewhat similar assumptions about the genesis and maintenance of client problems. Beck was dissatisfied with the inability of psychoanalysis to account for the characteristic thinking patterns of his clients, noticed that analysis of their dreams demonstrated that they frequently saw themselves in the role of victims, and evolved a treatment which focused upon the modification of what he took to be their faulty thinking patterns. Kendall and Bemis (1983) describe the treatment process as involving: monitoring of automatic thoughts, recognizing their relationship to behaviour and mood, testing their validity, generating alternative thoughts and identifying and modifying dysfunctions underlying assumptions which predispose the client to such thoughts.

Wessler (1986) describes a critical difference between the cognitive interventions of Beck and Ellis as the tendency of the latter to focus on the irrational nature of the appraisal of a particular thought, rather than the distorted nature of its content. Thus, the practitioner of CT might ask the agoraphobic with fears of fainting what evidence they had to suppose that they were likely to faint during their next visit to the supermarket, while the practitioner of RET might ask for evidence that it would be catastrophic if they did so. Although both Ellis and Beck advocate the use of behavioural tasks as part of the restructuring process, the purpose of these tasks is often different in the two approaches. While behavioural tasks are used in CT mainly to help clients to challenge their distorted inferences (for example, about the probability of negative events occurring), such tasks are used in RET chiefly to help clients in challenging their catastrophic evaluations of these negative events.

Meichenbaum's self-instructional training involves six phases (Kendall and Bemis 1983): problem definition and approach, attention focusing, coping statements, error correction and self-reinforcement. More specifically, treatment tactics will involve the identification and modification of negative self-statements, with coaching and reinforcement from the therapist, and possibly with training in a range of coping and problem-solving skills. SIT grew both from the influence of Ellis's work in RET, and from Meichenbaum's (1969) work on operant instruction with schizophrenics. He observed that those clients who engaged in covert self-instruction demonstrated superior task performance. He related this occurrence to the work of Luria (1961) regarding the gaining of covert control of behaviour in children, a process with similarities to the Skinnerian notion of rule-governed behaviour (Skinner 1969).

Thus, Meichenbaum's cognitive-behavioural interventions are closely linked to the mainstream of behaviour therapy and to notions of covert reinforcement. Meichenbaum intended that SIT be a flexible, broadly applicable set of interventions, and has demonstrated a particularly strong commitment to empirical studies of treatment packages derived from SIT (Dobson and Block 1988). This commitment, coupled with the closeness of SIT to the behavioural tradition, has led to a great deal of popularity for the method among clinicians (Hawton *et al.* 1989). In summary, SIT is a skills-acquisition model of therapy.

Apart from the importance of cognitions as central both to the development and maintenance of client difficulties and to attempts to alleviate those difficulties, cognitive therapies share a common philosophical standpoint which conforms broadly to the Stoical view that humans are disturbed by the views they hold about events rather than the events themselves (Mahoney *et al.* 1989). Equally, the cognitive therapies hold that human beings are responsible for their actions and are therefore capable of internally mediated behaviour change. This reflects a classical humanistic tradition which Woolfolk and Sass (1989), in analysing the philosophical foundations of RET, distinguish from the romantic humanism of the so-called 'third force' psychology of Rogers and Maslow. The classical humanism of cognitive therapy pre-dates romantic humanism and asserts that science is superior to other methods of enquiry and knowledge. Classical humanism eschews the extreme responses of romanticism but shares with romantic humanism an emphasis on human desires, rights and capabilities. Thus, in all forms of cognitive therapy, the client is regarded as being capable of becoming an equal partner with the therapist in problem definition and in the selection, implementation and evaluation of therapeutic strategies. For example, in behaviour therapy, administration of reinforcers is usually in the hands of the therapist and colleagues. Reinforcement is often used in cognitive therapy, but clients are encouraged to identify the situations where reinforcement is appropriate, and to administer such reinforcement themselves.

DEVELOPMENT OF THE COGNITIVE-BEHAVIOURAL APPROACH

The above cognitive approaches all contain behavioural elements (for example, in the use of homework tasks), but tend to emphasize the primacy of cognition in influencing client difficulties and to stress the importance of modifying cognitions in any attempt to deal with such difficulties. While these approaches continue to recognize the role of the mediating effect of cognitions in determining behaviour, and, therefore, in influencing the development and maintenance of client problems, they now stress equally the importance of other response systems (for example, physiological) and the reciprocal nature of the interaction between these response systems and the environment. These approaches are now generally referred to as cognitive-behaviour therapies (CBTs). As has been noted, cognitive psychology represented a significant challenge to the assumptions of behaviourism, and cognitive-behaviour therapy was an equal challenge to the assumptions of behaviour therapy, at a time when therapists were beginning to examine problematic issues such as treatment failure and client compliance.

The proposition that three separate response systems (Lang 1971) mediate human activity was influential in turning the attention of behaviour therapists towards the importance of cognitive variables. Lang suggested that inappropriate responding in one or more of the physiological, behavioural or cognitive systems, as accessed by physiological measurement, observation and client self-report, was responsible for client difficulties. Intervention could be addressed to any of the three systems. This three-systems model gave rise to ideas of synchrony and desynchrony between the systems, which state that the physiological, behavioural and cognitive systems are only loosely linked, and that changes in these systems may or may not co-vary. Thus, clients might show increased avoidance behaviour, while stating that they knew the avoided situation was not harmful (desynchrony between the behavioural and cognitive systems), or a pain sufferer might describe pain experience in the absence of physiological indices of pain or pain behaviours (desynchrony between the cognitive system and the physiological and behavioural systems). From the notions of synchrony and desynchrony numerous predictions were derived regarding treatment outcome in behaviour therapy (Rachman and Hodgson 1974). For example, interventions directed primarily at the behavioural system (for example, response prevention in compulsive ritualization) are predicted to cause greatest and most rapid changes in that system. The three-systems model also encouraged a more focal approach to psychotherapy outcome research, emphasizing the need for specific measurement directed at areas of potential dysfunction within the three systems, rather than global appraisals of improvement or deterioration.

The social-learning theory of Bandura (1977a), and his work on the use of modelling in behaviour therapy, provided a further impetus for the acceptance of cognitions as a mediating force in client difficulties. The role of vicarious learning (the increase in frequency of behaviour following observation of that behaviour being reinforced when performed by another) received vigorous support in the research literature (Rachman and Wilson 1980), and the effectiveness of modelling as a treatment strategy was largely inexplicable in purely operant terms. Indeed, the occurrence of vicarious learning is difficult to account for using any non-mediational approach (Rosenthal and Zimmerman 1978). Nevertheless, modelling was absorbed into the framework of behaviour therapy at a comparatively early stage in the history of the discipline, and generally described as a behavioural technique, despite owing its theoretical basis to cognitive social-learning theory, rather than to classical or operant theory (Rosenthal and Bandura 1978). This tendency to marginalize the degree to which new effective techniques departed from conditioning theory was characteristic of early responses by behaviourists to such innovations (Mahoney 1988).

Additionally, Bandura (1977b) proposed the concept of self-efficacy as a major determinant of human behaviour. He argued that, in any given situation, humans and animals consider not only outcome expectancies (the probability that a particular course of action will be reinforced), but also self-efficacy expectancies (beliefs about one's own performance). These self-efficacy beliefs are representations of the perceived difficulty of the task to be performed (magnitude), the confidence of the performer in his or her ability to perform the task (strength), and whether or not success in a given task is likely to generalize to success in other tasks (generality). Judgements regarding magnitude, strength and generality contribute to the person's overall self-efficacy. Such judgements are based on experience, vicarious experience, verbal persuasion or physiological information, and rely on perceived, rather than actual, reinforcement. As self-efficacy rises, it increases the likelihood of a person persisting at the task under consideration.

This formulation resembles closely the three-systems model, but allows greater co-operation between the systems, stresses the importance of mediating factors and is echoed in the integrative approach of the CBTs. As an explanatory theory, self-efficacy has predicted the behaviour of phobics in behavioural tests with considerable accuracy (Bandura 1982). Social-learning theory also stresses the importance of the individual's goals and values in determining behaviour (Bandura 1977a), a further respect in which this influential theory represented a most significant break with behavioural accounts of the treatment of client difficulties, and facilitated greater acceptance of cognitive-behaviour therapies, such as Beck's CT, which sprang from traditions other than that of behaviourism.

The term cognitive-behaviour therapy currently encompasses a wide range of models of human distress and an equal diversity of treatment interventions. Nevertheless, there are clear lines of demarcation which separate the CBTs from other forms of therapy, and clear lines of connection among the CBTs. Behavioural therapies which allow no role for cognitions are clearly not CBTs, and nor are forms of therapy which concentrate solely upon altering physical components of distress (for example, relaxation training). Similarly, therapies which rely on the evocation of intense emotion are not CBTs (Dobson and Block 1988). Techniques derived from therapies other than CBTs may, however, be fairly regarded as CBT interventions when the therapeutic procedure involves consideration of cognitive variables. Thus, relaxation training with the aim of offering clients a skill to enhance their judgement of self-efficacy in anxiety-provoking situations becomes a CBT intervention, since the CBTs are defined by their emphasis on the interaction between the cognitive, behavioural and physiological systems, and their readiness to target any or all of these systems both for intervention and eventual change.

The CBTs are not, therefore, sets of techniques, but sets of orientations and models of human experience. They articulate general goals in the modification of that experience. CBTs share a common view of human response which describes that response as being based on 'reciprocal determinism' (Bandura 1978), a process whereby human cognitive structures, processes and contents, behaviours and antecedents and consequences of those behaviours in the environment are intimately related in a multidirectional fashion. Thus, cognitions and behaviours are not only shaped by the environment, but shape it, giving to the client an active role in creating future outcomes (Turk *et al.* 1983). The goals of the CBTs are linked to this concept of reciprocal determinism, and involve the client's becoming aware of the interaction between dysfunctional cognitions and behaviours (and the possibility of changing this interaction) through a combination of cognitive, behavioural and physiological interventions.

COGNITIVE-BEHAVIOUR THERAPY AND INFORMATION PROCESSING

The CBTs stress the importance of cognitions as mediating factors in human behaviour, and thus subscribe to a view of humans as processors of information. Particular dysfunctional forms of thinking give rise to client difficulties. For example, Beck and Emery (1985) suggest that structures in long-term memory (schemata) represent informational rules which are applied to external situations. These schemata may be divided into subsystems ('modes'), relating to smaller elements of cognitive content (for example, depressive or anxious modes) which, if overactive, give rise to specific client difficulties. Thus, overactivity of the anxious mode might give rise to activation of schemata relating to anxiety, in response to situations of threat in the environment, but inhibit cessation of such activation once such threats have passed (Brewin 1988). Beck (1967) proposes a similar set of subsystems in depression: the so-called 'cognitive triad' of negative thoughts about the self, the rest of the world and the future. As has been noted earlier, much of this speculation regarding the cognitions of people experiencing dysfunction is derived from clinical practice and the application of various cognitive techniques designed to modify dysfunctional thinking.

This speculative approach to the role of cognitions in client difficulties can be traced back to the earliest stages in the development of the cognitive-behaviour therapies, and is reminiscent of the emphasis on the derivation of theory from clinical practice embodied in the psychoanalytical tradition of which Beck and Ellis were part. However, although the considerable success enjoyed by the CBTs in addressing client difficulties adds to the face validity of these conceptualizations, until recently there has been relatively little attempt to link cognitive-behaviour therapy to the mainstream of cognitive-psychology research, other than the kind of speculation described above. Some aspects of cognitive theory may prove highly problematic for the CBTs. For instance, Brewin (1988) notes that numerous cognitive theorists have argued that humans have little or no access to cognitive acts or processes. If this is so, the process whereby cognitive-behaviour therapies achieve client improvement may have little to do with modification of supposed cognitive structures, unless these may be supposed to be modifiable without the client's having access to them.

Clinical research into cognitive therapy seems to have added little to our understanding of cognitive processing more generally. More recently, however, attempts have been made to integrate the cognitive therapies with information-processing theories of cognition. Research has involved the development and evaluation of specific information-processing models to account for the dysfunctional thinking processes observed in clinical practice and to clarify some speculative aspects of CBT theories (for example, Alloy and Abramson's (1982) investigation of the existence of depressive schematic processing). Such attempts should both allow an increase in our understanding of cognitive processing, and provide a cogent general rationale upon which to base clinical practice.

Brewin (1988) identifies a number of roles for cognitions in client difficulties. Cognitions may act as precipitating factors, vulnerability factors or factors in recovery. For example, in an investigation which embraces all these factors, but concentrates on notions of vulnerability to depression, Bradley and Mathews (1988) reported the occurrence of selective memory bias in recovered depressives. These subjects recalled more negative than positive other-person-referent material, showing the opposite pattern to depressed subjects and controls. More negative than positive self-referent items were recalled by depressed Ss. However, since retrieval processes remained affected in recovered subjects, Bradley and Mathews argued for the existence of more enduring cognitive structures than mood (for example, the content or structure of negative information in memory) in response bias. Their results were generally consistent with their self-schema model of depression, which suggests that depressives have a memory bias particular to information regarding the self, recalling more negative than positive information (Bradley and Mathews 1983).

Teasdale and Dent (1987), in a recall experiment using a slightly different methodology from that of Bradley and Mathews (1988), observed enduring negative bias in recovered depressives. Both these findings are consistent with Clark and Teasdale's (1985) differential-activation hypothesis, which contends that it is the nature of the processes and constructs which become accessible in depression that determine the progression of the complaint. This theory is influenced by Bower's (1981) suggestion that activation in an associative neural network spreads from a node in that network in accordance with prevailing mood, and activates those areas of the network which had previously been activated in association with that particular mood.

Teasdale (1988) notes that the differential-activation theory is not dependent upon acceptance of Bower's ideas, being rather more general in its assumptions. Nevertheless, in the differential-activation hypothesis, we have a theory regarding the interaction of mood and cognition which is coherently linked to current thinking in cognitive psychology. Similar studies have been undertaken into schematic thinking in other emotional disorders (for example, Mathews and Macleod 1985). Such recent studies share with experimental psychology not only theory, but also methodology, often employing traditional psychological tasks (for example, recall tasks, tachistoscope presentation) in highly controlled conditions, and often using non-clinical populations.

BEHAVIOURAL AND COGNITIVE-BEHAVIOURAL RESEARCH METHODS

In the experimental-psychology literature, similarities as well as differences emerge between the behavioural and cognitive traditions of investigation. These similarities are even more marked when we examine the literature relating to behaviour therapy and cognitive-behavioural therapy.

Behaviourism was a challenge to earlier, mentalistic notions of human experience, and represents an early step in integrating psychology into the mainstream of research using scientific method. Although a social science, psychology has followed the physical sciences in relying on precision of observation and method (Hersen and Bellack 1984). Modern cognitive psychology shares with behaviourism this emphasis on precise measurement, quantitative rather than qualitative analysis and parsimonious interpretation of data. Behaviourism, however, has a research tradition with its historical basis in the use of analogue populations, often animals, often in highly artificial situations with tight experimental control. It has tended to confine itself to the investigation of extremely simple processes.

Although this framework possesses numerous advantages (for example, less stringent ethical requirements, accuracy of the investigation, high confidence in the internal validity of the experiment), there are also problems. The use of animal subjects, in early conditioning experiments, led to scepticism about the generalizability of behavioural research findings to the human species. Few behaviour therapists or behaviourally orientated psychologists today suggest that human learning and animal learning are directly comparable, yet animal models of distress, albeit more sophisticated than early behavioural models, still have influence (for example, Eysenck and Martin 1987; Gray 1982). Walker (1987) notes, however, that animals and humans may share physical or psychological characteristics along certain critical dimensions, and that, in such cases, the use of animal models of human behaviour is permissible.

Tight experimental controls are often desirable, and are by no means confined to behaviourist approaches, but decrease the degree to which experimental findings may be generalized to clinical populations as a whole, since task description and conditions in the experimental situation may vary greatly from clinical practice. (Howell 1987).

In clinical research into behaviour therapy, many of the early conceptualizations of client problems were derived from research into learning in non-clinical and animal populations. With regard to the use of human populations, many of the problems being investigated, such as specific phobias of unusual animals and test anxiety, were of subclinical severity and not identified by the subjects as problematic. The human samples were often drawn from a highly selected group, generally university students. This gave rise to criticism that early behaviour therapy studies were unlikely to generalize to clinical populations. Mathews (1978), in a review of the fear-reduction literature, found important and systematic differences between the responses to treatment of clinical and non-clinical subjects. However, this source of error may be less important if subjects can be matched according to crucial characteristics (for example, intensity of fear) (Bandura 1978). Other dissimilarities between analogue and clinical studies (for example, brevity of treatment, lack of realism of the experimental situation, inexperience of therapists) represent further criticisms of this aspect of behavioural research, but more recent studies in behaviour therapy have addressed these difficulties by the use of subjects from clinical populations, treatment interventions equivalent to those found in clinical practice and appropriately experienced therapists.

Similarly, the early emphasis on behavioural changes as the sole indices of improvement, which led to suggestions that behaviourism was a mechanistic approach, ignoring the richness and diversity of human behaviour, has gradually shifted. Nevertheless, observable behaviour and conditioning models (albeit more complex than those of early behaviour therapists) have been retained by many behaviour therapists as the main elements of behavioural intervention. Thus, though Eckert (1983) accepts that operant conditioning is not the sole factor in determining outcome in treatment of anorexia nervosa, the bulk of her paper consists of a comparison between different schedules of reinforcement for weight gain. More recently, in a single case-study of smoking cessation, Self (1989) describes the entire process of cessation in terms of extinction, with little discussion of possible cognitive factors contributing either to cessation or its maintenance, a factor which, as the author notes, is a major issue in interventions with smokers. This degree of concentration upon purely behavioural explanations is, however, unusual in present-day behaviour therapy. For example, Mineka's (1987) primate model of phobias, while strongly based in conditioning theory, nevertheless draws upon notions familiar to cognitive-behavioural therapists, such as Lang's (1971) three-systems model of fear, and clearly accepts the importance of cognitive mediation. Finally, even stern critics of cognitively orientated interventions such as Marks (1987) recognize the interaction of behaviour and cognition (for example, Marks and Mishan 1988).

Although the focus on observable behaviours has helped psychologists avoid over-ambitious mentalistic theorizing, and provided therapists with a source of reliable indices of clinical improvement, this focus excludes a good deal of information which is of interest to researchers and clinicians – that information which is principally cognitive. Furthermore, as we suggested earlier, conceptualizations of learning which take no account of mediating processes are insufficiently powerful to account for complex behaviours.

By contrast with behaviourism, the cognitive tradition has typically employed a broader range of investigative strategies. The tendency is towards an emphasis on human research, investigating complex psychological processes using a variety of research designs, including innovative use of single-case experiments (Kazdin and Wilson 1978), and towards the use of computer models of human cognition.

The clearest advantage of cognitive research is its ability to examine and account for covert events, in contrast to the exclusively external focus of early behaviourism. Furthermore, the use of a wide range of experimental paradigms allows researchers and clinicians to have greater confidence in the applicability of experimental findings to human cognitions and their mediating influence on client difficulties.

Despite these considerable advantages, there are problematic areas in the cognitive approach to psychological research. First, there has been sustained criticism of the information-processing models which underly much experimentation in cognitive psychology (for example, Marr 1982), and in particular, of artificial-intelligence approaches to information processing. Prominent difficulties are the inherent remoteness of the likelihood that computers (whose 'thinking' is implemented in completely different hardware) will think in the same way as humans, the lack of intentionality of computer processing (Searle 1980) and the inability of computers to solve comparatively trivial human cognitive problems (Dennett 1984). Since information-processing accounts inform much current therapeutic intervention, we may ask whether these accounts accurately model the covert processes thought to mediate client difficulties.

Second, despite many innovative attempts, cognitive psychology and cognitive-behavioural therapy have yet to solve fully the difficulties inherent in dealing with covert material. Investigators are often reliant upon self-report information alone. To illustrate this, let us take the example of intrusive thoughts, a phenomenon of interest both to the cognitive theoretician and the cognitive-behaviour therapist. Even if we take the simple index of thought frequency as a measure of such thoughts, there are immediate methodological difficulties. How does the subject decide what constitutes an intrusion, and how may the investigator have confidence in the reliability of the subject's recording of thought frequency, or evaluate the comparative importance of frequency and severity in deciding the level of intrusion?

An increasing number of researchers have attempted to depart entirely from the self-report as a method of investigating cognitions. England and Dickerson (1988), for example, used a signal-detection paradigm to investigate the difference between pleasant and unpleasant intrusive thoughts in terms of controllability. However, by contrast, much of the work in this field continues to reply upon methodologies which ultimately necessitate a form of self-report. An influential paper (Sutherland *et al.* 1982) investigated the relationship between mood and intrusive thoughts, using a procedure in which subjects were asked to signal the experimenter when a particular thought was dismissed from the mind. Leaving aside any technical considerations, there are significant difficulties in conceptualizing how a subject decides that a thought is in the mind, and, more importantly, when it has been dismissed. Some efforts have been made to standardize self-report techniques, although the problem of accurate investigation of covert phenomena remains largely unresolved.

This emphasis on the importance of covert factors, with the attendant difficulty of measurement, is equally present in studies of cognitive-behaviour therapy. The cognitive variables thought to underly client difficulties and their resolution are, by their nature, not available for direct scrutiny. Even in the case of phobic problems, where approach to the feared object may be seen in successful treatment, cognitive therapy still has difficulty, since the observer may not presume that such behaviour occurs because of changes in subject cognitions. In the clinical literature, fewer methods have been devised of avoiding these difficulties than in the theoretical studies mentioned above. The major strategy in accessing client cognitions in the therapeutic situation remains by means of self-report, although many of the scales designed to assist in this measurement have proved reliable. For example, Simons *et al*. (1984) used the Dysfunctional Attitude Scale (Weissman and Beck 1978), a scale which aims to access underlying assumptions by asking clients to rate their agreement with a series of evaluative statements, to assess the impact of antidepressants and Beck's cognitive therapy on mechanisms thought to mediate depression. Alternative approaches to the measurement of assumptions include Fennell and Campbell's (1984) Cognitions Questionnaire, which presents clients with a series of scenarios, in which they are asked to judge how they would think. Furthermore, considerable debate has taken place regarding the conditions which result in the most accurate use of self-reports (Ericsson and Simon 1980).

Two further difficulties in the cognitive-behaviour therapy methodology relate to the accurate definition of what constitutes cognitive-behaviour therapy, and of what constitutes an appropriate trial of such therapy. These issues are also present in behaviour-therapy research, but are particularly important in cognitive-behaviour therapy for several reasons. First, cognitive-behaviour therapy has always contained a number of widely diverging approaches, focusing on cognitive restructuring, problem solving, coping-skills acquisition and many combinations of these approaches (Mahoney and Arnkoff 1978). Therefore, to examine clinical studies of cognitive-behaviour therapy is to examine a wide range of extremely different interventions, which have less in common than behaviour therapy had at the same stage in its development.

Second, the early research involved the use of many poorly trained therapists. Again, this was also a problem for early behaviour-therapy literature, but was less critical since the behaviour therapy of that time was a much simpler, procedure-based therapy than is current cognitive-behaviour therapy, addressed a narrower range of client difficulties, and was in competition with a far less potent opponent. Since therapeutic interventions along psychoanalytical lines showed little or no advantage over placebo (Eysenck 1952: Eysenck and Wilson 1973), it was relatively easy to demonstrate an advantage for behavioural treatments over psychoanalytic interventions. By contrast, cognitive-behaviour therapy has frequently been compared with behaviour therapy, a treatment orientation of considerable proven efficacy. For a therapy in the early stages of its development, demonstrating efficacy over and above that of a well-developed (albeit limited) set of interventions is a difficult task, which is rendered more problematic by poor definition of the treatment tactics employed, and the use of inexperienced or inappropriately trained therapists. More recently, however, these two difficulties have largely been addressed. (See Williams (1984) for a review of recent treatment studies of cognitive-behavioural interventions in depression.)

OUTCOME RESEARCH IN COGNITIVE-BEHAVIOUR THERAPY

Much of the material in the ensuing chapters will concern the current status of numerous treatment interventions in different fields of cognitive-behaviour therapy, and it is not the intention of this chapter to describe in detail findings relating to the general efficacy of cognitive-behavioural approaches when compared with other treatments of any particular client difficulties. (For a comprehensive review of the early literature, see Rachman and Wilson (1980); for more recent, selective reviews, see Marks (1987) and Teasdale (1986).) Nor will any attempt be made to compare different cognitive-behavioural approaches, a task which is beyond the scope of this volume (see Dryden and Golden 1986). It is important, however, to describe the general structure of CBT outcome research, which currently includes a wide range of investigation strategies.

Since the cognitive-behavioural approach strongly emphasizes outcome measurement, the structure of much therapy conducted outside formal research settings corresponds to the conventions of single-case experimental design (Kazdin 1982), and single-case designs are numerous in the literature. Such designs include the statistical treatment of quantitative data drawn from case-study material, and are characterized by the use of objective data, planned comparison involving careful specification of the independent and dependent variables, relatively standardized intervention procedures, repeated measurement and long-term follow-up with continuing measurement. Single-case design experiments are contrasted with treatment case-studies, in that a far greater degree of inference may be drawn from the results of such experiments (Kratochwill et al. 1984).

The single-case experiment involves numerous strategies, including treatment comparison, dismantling and process investigations. In outcome literature, the single-case experiment may yield information regarding intervention which suggests a direction for future, more rigorously controlled research. Where an unusual client difficulty is addressed, quantitative as well as qualitative data are available, thus giving more precise information regarding the problem. Such data may, in turn, lead to further speculation regarding the causation and maintaining factors of such cases. Additionally, in the single-case experiment, results obtained remain closer to the level of the individual client than in any other form of evaluation. Although the single-case experiment is limited by the considerable possibility of order effects and other unwanted interferences with the unambiguous interpretation of its results, it remains an important tool in outcome research, particularly in the early stages of developing and validating a therapeutic intervention. Thus, in the treatment of epilepsy, for example, a good deal of the literature consists of single-case experiments (for example, Dahl et al. 1987; Daniels 1975). Both these studies offer considerable information regarding novel treatment interventions, and suggest directions for further study.

Turning to group-outcome studies, these may be hierarchically ordered from small uncontrolled studies, where a comparatively low level of inference may be made from the results, to large controlled studies conducted in clinical settings, where, if the methodological problems associated with conducting such studies have been adequately addressed, the level of inference is comparatively high. Analogue studies, using non-clinical subjects and, often, interventions which correspond poorly to clinical treatments, are also generally group studies, and often concern treatment-outcome issues. The level of inference that can be made from such studies depends upon how far the experimenters have been successful in overcoming the potential difficulties associated with such studies and discussed earlier. For further discussion of the use of analogue studies, and a description of several such studies used to construct a coherent cognitive-behavioural model of fear based on animal subjects, see Mineka (1987).

Small, uncontrolled studies represent the next stage of research reliability and complexity from the single-case design, and are, in essence, the application of the principles of systematic manipulation of the independent variable, with planned measurement, across a group of subjects. These studies have the advantage of allowing the experimenter to control, to some extent, for order effects in the administration of treatment interventions, and diminish the likelihood of chance favourable results. Nevertheless, the uncontrolled study does not prevent the experimenter from mistakenly ascribing successful client outcome to the chosen intervention, rather than to such non-specific factors as therapist variables, client variables and spontaneous remission over time. Studies of this kind represent further attempts to ascertain the therapeutic efficacy of particular interventions which have been identified at the single-case level.

In order to address such issues, some form of control is introduced into the experimental design. These 'controlled studies' represent a reasonably stringent test of the effect of the independent variable (usually treatment type), and fall into a number of categories. First, the client may be assigned to a treatment or no-treatment condition. In the case of research settings, where clients are recruited specifically for the trial, this is unproblematic, but in clinical settings, it is often ethically impractical. As a compromise, clients in the control group may remain on a waiting-list for a given length of time before receiving treatment, while the experimental group receive treatment immediately. Unfortunately, this often has the effect of making the treatment and control groups different, since the control group will have had a comparatively long wait before commencing treatment, and will not have received the same attention as the treatment group. Additionally, the waiting-list group may seek and receive intervention elsewhere. So, while waiting-list controls can lessen the effect of time as an intervening variable, studies employing such controls are still vulnerable to the effect of attention and non-specific therapist variables (Bergin and Lambert 1978).

An alternative is to offer some placebo treatment, though this will again give rise to ethical difficulties in the clinical setting. One solution is to offer some non-specific or minimally effective intervention which is nevertheless often administered in clinical practice, and numerous studies compare specific interventions with 'general hospital management' (Rachman and Wilson 1980). However, to do so is simply to avoid the ethical question, since such management strategies may be of limited effectiveness. Against this it is sometimes argued that the experimental strategy is itself of comparatively poorly validated efficacy, a test of such efficacy being the point of the proposed study. Paradoxically, the offering of a 'best-available' treatment as an alternative to the experimental treatment is also ethically problematic, since the control treatment is, at least in an ideal world, in receipt of greater empirical support than the experimental treatment. Such considerations are generally overcome by the careful explanation to potential participants of the nature of the experiment, though such explanation may itself change subject expectations in a systematic way which influences the results of the trial (Beck *et al.* 1984).

In spite of these difficulties, the controlled study, conducted in a clinical setting, using treatment interventions which are similar to those practised outside the research context, is regarded as a rigorous test of the effectiveness of a treatment method, and it is considered a major achievement for an intervention to demonstrate a significant result in such a context. This is particularly so if there is random allocation of subjects to the experimental conditions, and extended follow-up of subjects, with assessment of outcome by independent raters who are unaware of the experimental status of subjects ('blind raters'), since such allocation and rating procedures reduce the likelihood of experimenter bias in evaluation (Rosenthal 1966). Typically, controlled trials are conducted after an intervention has received considerable support in smaller, uncontrolled studies. Thus, in the areas of phobic and obsessive-compulsive disorders, cognitive-behavioural interventions have received considerable support under controlled conditions using varied control groups, including attention placebo, waiting-list, relaxation. 'anti-behaviour therapy' and others (see Marks (1987) for a review).

Evaluations of cognitive-behavioural interventions using all the above strategies are described in this volume, with, as might be expected, an emphasis on controlled studies in those areas where the cognitive-behavioural approach is firmly established (for example, depression and anxiety). However, CBT is a relatively new approach to client difficulties, and there are, therefore, numerous areas where research is at too early a stage for any great body of controlled outcome research to have been established. Indeed, in CBT as a whole, there is a continuing need for controlled outcome studies (Golden and Dryden 1986), particularly those which expand the areas of intervention of cognitive-behavioural approaches, or enhance our knowledge both of the effective components of treatment, and of the cognitive processes being affected by such components (Brewin 1988).

THE COGNITIVE-BEHAVIOURAL APPROACH AND OTHER TRADITIONS

Although the need for systematic outcome research continues, the cognitive-behavioural approach is, nevertheless, in a position of considerable influence in the field of psychological approaches to client difficulties. Furthermore, cognitive and behavioural research have become the fastest-growing areas of psychotherapy

research (Hoon and Lindsley 1974) and have had significant impact on psychotherapy training programmes (Brady and Wienckowski 1978) during the past two
decades. We have described how cognitive-behavioural approaches originally
grew from, on the one hand, dissatisfaction with the apparently mechanistic and
over-simple stimulus–response accounts of early behaviour therapy, and, on the
other, an equal dissatisfaction with the neglect of cognition as a factor in determining client difficulties in the psychoanalytic therapies. Although psychoanalysis has
continued as a trend in psychiatry and psychology, its influence has greatly
diminished (Busfield 1986). The same can also be said of the 'humanistic' methods
of therapy (for example, Rogers 1965).

In part, the comparative decline of psychodynamic and humanistic techniques
may be attributed to the increased emphasis placed by behaviour therapists and
cognitive-behaviour therapists upon adequate outcome studies. Despite many years
of investigation, unequivocal support for the psychoanalytically orientated psychotherapies remained extremely scarce, while the CBTs were becoming accepted
through the amassing of a vast literature of empirical studies. In a survey of over
300 published articles in psychoanalytic journals, Rachman and Wilson (1980)
found only one that described a treatment outcome study. In their review of the
psychoanalytic outcome literature more generally, they found that few outcome
studies met scientific criteria for the conduct of research to a sufficient degree to
allow meaningful conclusions to be drawn from them, and of those that did meet
their criteria, the vast majority showed no effect of psychoanalysis on client
difficulties.

A later review (Lambert *et al*. 1986) found some evidence for the general
efficacy of psychotherapy, but this review was marred by a failure to specify which
types of psychotherapy were being considered, and a reliance on many of the older
studies already considered and criticized on methodological grounds by the Rachman and Wilson review. Of the newer studies considered, most were
meta-analyses, which aimed to evaluate quantitatively the body of outcome literature. While these were generally favourable to psychotherapy, the status of
meta-analysis in psychotherapy outcome research is highly controversial. Meta-
analysis is intended to be a more accurate alternative to the literature review. It
generally involves the calculation of the 'effect size' (mean difference between the
treatment and control groups on each dependent measure) over a large number of
controlled studies and the averaging of this effect size between studies to give an
overall quantitative indicator of therapeutic efficacy. Three major difficulties of
the meta-analysis approach are: (a) the comparability or otherwise of the data under
consideration; (b) the inclusion of diverse therapies under a general rubric (for
example, inclusion of psychoanalytical psychotherapy and biofeedback in the same
category); and (c) the evaluation of data from studies regardless of their individual
quality in methodological terms. Fuller discussions of the strengths and weaknesses
of meta-analysis are given by Rachman and Wilson (1980) and Kazdin (1986).
Eysenck (1987) reviews a small number of the most influential studies which
support the general efficacy of psychotherapy, and notes weaknesses similar to

those suggested above. He concludes that there is no reason to depart from his original (Eysenck 1952) assertion regarding the lack of efficacy of psychoanalytic forms of psychotherapy.

Many advocates of psychoanalysis denied that the kind of change their therapeutic interventions generated was amenable to empirical investigation, following the precepts of Freud himself (Freud 1973).

By contrast, Rogers was greatly concerned with the experimental investigation of his proposed 'necessary and sufficient' conditions for successful psychotherapy (Rogers 1957) and contributed greatly to research into psychotherapy outcome. Thus, the desire for treatment evaluation was not confined to the cognitive and behavioural traditions, but was a significant part of client-centred therapy. Nevertheless, research has generally failed to find evidence for the necessity or sufficiency of warmth, empathy or genuineness on the part of the therapist (Lambert *et al*. 1978). It is therefore suggested that the current pre-eminence of CBTs in clinical psychology is due not only to their commitment to methodological rigour, but more particularly to the failure of both analytical and humanistic approaches to withstand examination under such conditions.

It would be a mistake, however, to dismiss entirely the links between the CBTs and psychoanalytic and humanistic interventions. Although the latter two tend to discount the importance of cognition and behaviour, they certainly take account of the existence of covert phenomena in mediating human distress, and therefore formed a counterpoint to orthodox behaviourism. Furthermore, there has long been recognition of the existence of similarities between behavioural and psychodynamic accounts of psychological problems (French 1932), which some therapists have sought to use as the basis of an eclectic therapeutic intervention employing elements of both disciplines (Feather and Rhoads 1972). Most recently, the technical eclecticism of Lazarus's (1973) multimodal therapy would not rule out the use of psychodynamic techniques, provided that these possessed demonstrable efficacy, although the use of such techniques would not imply acceptance of their underlying rationale.

The humanistic approaches have tended to emphasize the importance of therapist characteristics to the virtual exclusion of consideration of the importance of specific techniques or client variables, two issues which have received much study in cognitive-behavioural research. We noted above that behaviour therapy, and to an extent the CBTs, had been regarded as impersonal, mechanistic interventions. While it is certainly true that cognitive-behavioural approaches emphasize treatment technique, even to the extent of offering computer-directed interventions (Carr and Ghosh 1983), cognitive-behaviour therapists are united in stressing the need for the construction of a successful therapeutic alliance with the patient, and often stress the importance of the same therapist variables as the humanist approaches. Where the cognitive-behavioural approaches differ from the humanistic perspectives is in the denial by the former that particular therapist traits (as opposed to skills such as the ability to conduct appropriate assessment and construct appropriate interventions) are either always necessary or ever sufficient in addressing client difficulties.

Cognitive-behaviour therapy, therefore, of the three current trends in the psychological management of client difficulties, has achieved its current position of pre-eminence through a continuing commitment to evaluation of treatment efficacy and to theoretical research into the psychological processes underlying both its procedures and the development and maintenance of clinical problems. Cognitive-behaviour therapy places far greater importance than either psychodynamic or humanistic accounts on the role of both behaviours and cognitions, yet acknowledges the influence of these other disciplines in initially promoting the interest of clinicians in covert phenomena and the nature of the client–therapist relationship.

COGNITIVE-BEHAVIOURAL APPROACHES AND CLIENT PROBLEMS

This book is large in scope, in that it covers a wide range of client difficulties, and a wide range of interventions. However, there are no detailed descriptions of the presenting features of the various difficulties. In part, this is because such descriptions exceed the scale of this volume, but also because it reflects the emphasis in cognitive-behavioural approaches upon the identification of differences between individual clients, rather than the identification of similarities between members of particular diagnostic categories. In this sense, the CBTs, despite their diversity, share a common perspective on client difficulties, which notes both individual differences and the similarities of behaviour and cognition which unite clients with non-clients. This extends from the behavioural rejection of medical models of psychological distress and also of the Freudian model which accepted many of the precepts of the medical view. Cognitive-behavioural models likewise stress the continuum between problematic and non-problematic patterns of thinking and behaviour and set the client within the context of views of human experience which are argued to be true of all humans, rather than either the well or distressed.

In research a classification system is necessary in order to ensure standardization between one group of researchers and another. In the clinical setting, such a system offers general guidelines to the therapist in the application of research findings to the individual client. However, while cognitive-behavioural assessments draw on the theoretical framework offered by medical classification systems, they are not exercises in categorization. Rather, the cognitive-behavioural assessment is an attempt to arrive at an individualized client profile, from which conclusions regarding treatment strategies may be reached. We noted earlier that this book offers a range of cognitive-behavioural approaches to client problems, with the emphasis shifting between the behavioural and cognitive components of therapy. Nevertheless, we suggest that these varied approaches are united by the importance placed by cognitive-behaviour therapists on clients' individual differences, interactions with their environment and ability to shape that environment. It is within the context of this emphasis on the reciprocal nature of human experience that cognitive-behavioural approaches to clinical problems are developed.

REFERENCES

Alloy, L. B. and Abramson, L. Y. (1982) 'Learned helplessness, depression and the illusion of control', *Journal of Personality and Social Psychology* 42: 1114–26.

Baddeley, A. D. and Hitch, G. (1974) 'Working memory', in G. Bower (ed.) *The Psychology of Learning and Motivation*, Vol. 8, London: Academic Press.

Bandura, A. (1977a) *Social Learning Theory*, Englewood Cliffs, NJ: Prentice-Hall.

—— (1977b) 'Self-efficacy: towards a unifying theory of behavioral change', *Psychological Review* 84: 191–215.

—— (1978) 'On paradigms and recycled ideologies', *Cognitive Therapy and Research* 2: 79–104.

—— (1982) 'The self and mechanisms of agency', in J. Suls (ed.) *Psychological Perspectives on the Self*, Vol. 1, Hillsdale, NJ: Lawrence Erlbaum.

Beck, A. T. (1967) *Depression: Clinical, Experimental and Theoretical Aspects*, New York: Hoeber.

—— (1976) *Cognitive Therapy and the Emotional Disorders*, New York: International Universities Press.

—— and Emery, G. (1985) *Anxiety Disorders and Phobias: A Cognitive Perspective*, New York: Basic Books.

Beck, J. G., Andrasik, F. and Arena, J. G. (1984) 'Group comparison designs', in A. S. Bellack and M. Hersen (eds) *Research Methods in Clinical Psychology*, New York: Pergamon.

Bergin, A. E. and Lambert, M. J. (1978) 'The evaluation of therapeutic outcomes', in S. L. Garfield and A. E. Bergin (eds) *Handbook of Psychotherapy and Behavior Change*, 2nd edn, New York: Wiley.

Bower, G. H. (1981) 'Mood and memory', *American Psychologist* 36: 129–48.

Bradley, B. and Mathews, A. (1983) 'Negative self-schemata in clinical depression', *British Journal of Clinical Psychology* 22: 173–81.

—— (1988) 'Memory bias in recovered clinical depressives', *Cognition and Emotion* 2(3): 235–45.

Brady, J. and Wienckowski, L. (1978) 'Update on the teaching of behavior therapy', *Journal of Behavior Therapy and Experimental Psychiatry* 9: 125–7.

Brewin, C. R. (1988) *Cognitive Foundations of Clinical Psychology*, Hove: Lawrence Erlbaum.

Busfield, J. (1986) *Managing Madness: Changing Ideas and Practice*, London: Hutchinson.

Carr, A. C. and Ghosh, A. (1983) 'Response of phobic patients to direct computer assessment', *British Journal of Psychiatry* 142: 60–5.

Chomsky, N. (1959) 'Review of Skinner's *Verbal Behavior*', *Language* 35: 26–58.

Clark, D. M. and Teasdale, J. D. (1985) 'Constraints on the effects of mood on memory', *Journal of Personality and Social Psychology* 48: 1595–608.

Dahl, J., Melin, L. and Lund, L. (1987) 'Effects of a contingent relaxation program on adults with refractory epileptic seizures', *Epilepsia* 28(2): 125–32.

Daniels, L. K. (1975) 'The treatment of grand mal epilepsy by covert and operant conditioning techniques: a case study', *Psychosomatics* 16: 65–7.

Dennett, D. (1984) 'Cognitive wheels: the frame problem of AI', in C. Hookway (ed.) *Minds, Machines and Evolution*, Cambridge: Cambridge University Press.

Dobson, K. S. and Block, L. (1988) 'Historical and philosophical bases of the cognitive-behavioral therapies', in K. S. Dobson (ed.) *Handbook of Cognitive-Behavioral Therapies*, New York: Guilford Press.

Dryden, W. and Golden, W. L. (eds) (1986) *Cognitive-Behavioural Approaches to Psychotherapy*, London: Harper & Row.

Eckert, E. D. (1983) 'Behavior modification in anorexia nervosa: a comparison of two reinforcement schedules', in P. L. Darby, P. E. Garfinkel, D. M. Garner and D. V. Coscina (eds) *Anorexia Nervosa: Recent Developments in Research*, New York: Albert R. Liss.

Ellis, A. (1962) *Reason and Emotion in Psychotherapy*, New York: Lyle Stuart.

——(1977) 'The basic clinical theory of rational-emotive therapy', in A. Ellis and R. Grieger (eds) *Handbook of Rational-Emotive Therapy*, New York: Springer.

England, S. L. and Dickerson, M. (1985) 'Intrusive thoughts: unpleasantness not the major cause of uncontrollability', *Behaviour Research and Therapy* 26: 279–82.

Ericsson, K. A. and Simon, H. A. (1980) 'Verbal reports as data', *Psychological Review* 87: 215–51.

Eysenck, H. J. (1952) 'The effects of psychotherapy: an evaluation', *Journal of Consulting Psychology* 16: 319–24.

—— (1987) 'Behavior therapy', in H. J. Eysenck and I. Martin (eds) *Theoretical Foundations of Behavior Therapy*, New York: Plenum.

—— and Martin I. (eds) (1987) *Theoretical Foundations of Behavior Therapy*, New York: Plenum.

—— and Wilson G. T. (1973) *The Experimental Study of Freudian Theories*, London: Methuen.

Feather, B. W. and Rhoads, J. M. (1972) 'Psychodynamic behavior therapy: I. Theory and rationale', *Archives of General Psychiatry* 26: 496–502.

Fennell, M. J. V. and Campbell, E. A. (1984) 'The cognitions questionnaire: specific thinking errors in depression', *British Journal of Clinical Psychology* 23: 81–92.

French, T. M. (1932) 'Interrelations between psychoanalysis and the work of Pavlov', *American Journal of Psychiatry* 12: 1165–203.

Freud, S. (1973) *Introductory Lectures on Psychoanalysis*, Harmondsworth: Penguin.

Garfield, S. A. and Bergin, A. E. (1986) 'Introduction and historical overview', in S. L. Garfield and A. E. Bergin (eds) *Handbook of Psychotherapy and Behavior Change*, 3rd edn, New York: Wiley.

Golden, W. L. and Dryden, W. (1986) 'Cognitive-behavioural therapies: commonalities, divergences and future development', in W. Dryden and W. L. Golden (eds) *Cognitive-Behavioural Approaches to Psychotherapy*, London: Harper & Row.

Gray, J. A. (1975) *Elements of a Two-Process Theory of Learning*, London: Academic Press.

—— (1982) *The Neuropsychology of Anxiety: An Inquiry into the Functions of the Septohippocampal System*, Oxford: Oxford University Press.

Hawton, K., Salkovskis, P. M., Kirk, J. and Clark, D. M. (1989) 'The development and principles of cognitive-behavioural treatments', in K. Hawton, P. M. Salkovskis, J. Kirk and D. M. Clark (eds) *Cognitive-Behaviour Therapy for Psychiatric Problems*, Oxford: Oxford University Press.

Hersen, M. and Bellack, A. S. (1984) 'Research in clinical psychology', in A. S. Bellack and M. Hersen (eds) *Research Methods in Clinical Psychology*, New York: Pergamon.

Hoon, P. and Lindsley, O. (1974) 'A comparison of behavior and traditional therapy publication activity', *American Psychologist* 29: 694–7.

Howell, D. C. (1987) *Statistical Methods for Psychology*, Boston: Duxbury Press.

Jacobson, E. (1938) *Progressive Relaxation*, Chicago: University of Chicago Press.

Johnson-Laird, P. N. (1988) *The Computer and the Mind: An Introduction to Cognitive Science*, London: Fontana.

Kazdin, A. E. (1982) *Single-Case Research Designs: Methods for Clinical and Applied Settings*, New York: Oxford University Press.

—— (1986) 'Research designs and methodology', in S. L. Garfield and A. E. Bergin (eds) *Handbook of Psychotherapy and Behavior Change*, 3rd edn, New York: Wiley.
—— and Wilson, G. T. (1978) 'Criteria for evaluating psychotherapy', *Archives of General Psychiatry* 35: 407–18.
Kendall, P. C. and Bemis, K. M. (1983) 'Thought and action in psychotherapy: the cognitive-behavioral approaches', in M. Hersen, A. E. Kasdin and A. S. Bellack (eds) *The Clinical Psychology Handbook*, New York: Pergamon.
Kornorski, J. and Miller, S. (1937) 'On two types of conditioned reflex', *Journal of General Psychology* 16: 264–72.
Kratochwill, T. R., Mott, S. E. and Dodson, C. L. (1984) 'Case study and single-case research in clinical and applied psychology', in A. S. Bellack and M. Hersen (eds) *Research Methods in Clinical Psychology*, New York: Pergamon.
Lambert, M., deJulio, S. and Stein, D. (1978) 'Therapist interpersonal skills', *Psychological Bulletin* 83: 467–89.
Lambert, M. J., Shapiro, D. A. and Bergin, A. E. (1986) 'The effectiveness of psycho-therapy', in S. L. Garfield and A. E. Bergin (eds) *Handbook of Psychotherapy and Behavior Change*, 3rd edn, New York: Wiley.
Lang, P. (1971) 'The application of psychophysiological methods to the study of psycho-therapy and behaviour modification', in A. E. Bergin and S. L. Garfield (eds) *Handbook of Psychotherapy and Behavior Change*, New York: Wiley.
Lazarus, A. A. (1973) 'Multimodal behavior therapy: treating the BASIC I.D.', *Journal of Nervous and Mental Disease* 156: 404–11.
Luria, A. R. (1961) *The Role of Speech in the Regulation of Normal and Abnormal Behavior*, New York: Liveright.
Mahoney, M. J. (1988) 'The cognitive sciences and psychotherapy: patterns in a developing relationship', in K. S. Dobson (ed.) *Handbook of Cognitive-Behavioral Therapies*, New York: Guilford Press.
—— and Arnkoff, D. (1978) 'Cognitive and self-control therapies', in S. L. Garfield and A. E. Bergin (eds) *Handbook of Psychotherapy and Behavior Changes*, 2nd edn, New York: Wiley.
Mahoney, M. J., Lyddon, W. J. and Alford, D. J. (1989) 'An evaluation of the rational-emotive theory of psychotherapy', in M. E. Bernard and R. DiGuiseppe (eds) *Inside Rational-Emotive Therapy*, San Diego: Academic Press.
Marks, I. M. (1987) *Fears, Phobias and Rituals: Panic, Anxiety and their Disorders*, Oxford: Oxford University Press.
—— and Mishan, J. (1988) 'Dysmorphophobic avoidance with disturbed bodily perception: a pilot study of exposure therapy', *British Journal of Psychiatry* 152: 674–8.
Marr, D. (1982) *Vision: A Computational Investigation into the Human Representation and Processing of Visual Information*, San Francisco: W. H. Freeman.
Mathews, A. (1978) 'Fear reduction research and clinical phobias', *Psychological Bulletin* 85: 390–404.
—— and Macleod, C. (1985) 'Selective processing of threat cues in anxiety states', *Behaviour Research and Therapy* 23: 563–9.
Meichenbaum, D. (1969) 'The effect of instructions and reinforcement on thinking and language behaviors of schizophrenics', *Behaviour Research and Therapy* 7: 101–14.
—— (1977) *Cognitive Behavior Modification*, New York: Plenum Press.
Mineka, S. (1987) 'A primate model of phobic fears', in H. J. Eysenck and I. Martin (eds) *Theoretical Foundations of Behavior Therapy*, New York: Plenum.
Mowrer, O. H. (1960) *Learning Theory and Behavior*, New York: Wiley.
Newell, A. and Simon, H. A. (1972) *Human Problem-Solving*, Englewood Cliffs, NJ: Prentice-Hall.

Rachman, S. J. and Hodgson, R. (1974) 'Synchrony and desynchrony in fear and avoidance', *Behaviour Research and Therapy* 12: 311–18.

Rachman, S. J. and Wilson, G. T. (1980) *The Effects of Psychological Therapy*, 2nd edn, Oxford: Pergamon.

Rogers, C. R. (1957) 'The necessary and sufficient conditions of therapeutic personality change', *Journal of Consulting Psychology* 21: 95–103.

—— (1965) *Client-Centered Therapy*, Boston: Houghton Mifflin.

Rosenthal, R. (1966) *Experimenter Effects in Behavioral Research*, New York: Appleton-Century-Crofts.

Rosenthal, T. L. and Bandura, A. (1978) 'Psychological modeling: theory and practice', in S. L. Garfield and A. E. Bergin (eds) *Handbook of Psychotherapy and Behavior Change*, 2nd edn, New York: Wiley.

Rosenthal, T. L. and Zimmerman, B. J. (1978) *Social Learning and Cognition*, New York: Academic Press.

Searle, J. R. (1980) 'Minds, brains and programs', *Behavioral and Brain Sciences* 3: 417–21.

Self, R. (1989) 'The effects of cue-exposure response prevention on cigarette smoking – a single case', *Behavioural Psychotherapy* 17(2): 151–60.

Simons, A. D., Garfield, S. L. and Murphy, G. E. (1984) 'The process of change in cognitive therapy and pharmacotherapy: changes in mood and cognition', *Archives of General Psychiatry* 41: 45–51.

Skinner, B. F. (1957) *Verbal Behavior*, New York: Appleton-Century-Crofts.

—— (1969) *Contingencies of Reinforcement*, New York: Appleton-Century-Crofts.

Sutherland, G., Newman, B. and Rachman, S. J. (1982) 'Experimental investigations of the relations between mood and intrusive unwanted cognitions', *British Journal of Medical Psychology* 55: 127–38.

Teasdale, J. D. (1986) 'Non-pharmacological treatments for depression', unpublished manuscript, Cambridge: MRC Applied Psychology Unit.

—— (1988) 'Cognitive vulnerability to persistent depression', *Cognition and Emotion* 2(3): 247–74.

—— and Dent, J. (1987) 'Cognitive vulnerability to depression: an investigation of two hypotheses', *British Journal of Clinical Psychology* 26: 113–26.

Tolman, E. C. (1932) *Purposive Behavior in Animals and Man*, New York: Century.

Turk, D. C., Meichenbaum, D. and Genest, M. (1983) *Pain and Behavioral Medicine: A Cognitive-Behavioral Perspective*, New York: Guilford Press.

Walker, S. F. (1987) *Animal Learning: An Introduction*, London: Routledge & Kegan Paul.

Watson, J. B. (1914/67) *Behavior: An Introduction to Comparative Psychology*, London: Holt, Rinehart & Winston.

—— and Raynor, R. (1920) 'Conditioned emotional reactions', *Experimental Psychology* 3: 1–14.

Weissman, A. and Beck, A. T. (1978) 'The dysfunctional attitudes scale', paper presented at the meeting of the Association for the Advancement of Behavior Therapy, Chicago (cited in Teasdale 1988).

Wessler, R. L. (1986) 'Conceptualizing cognitions in the cognitive-behavioural therapies', in W. Dryden and W. L. Golden (eds) *Cognitive-Behavioural Approaches to Psychotherapy*, London: Harper & Row.

Williams, J. M. G. (1987) 'Cognitive treatment of depression', in H. J. Eysenck and I. Martin (eds) *Theoretical Foundations of Behaviour Therapy*, New York: Plenum.

Wolpe, J. (1958) *Psychotherapy by Reciprocal Inhibition*, Stanford: Stanford University Press.

—— (1976) 'Behavior therapy and its malcontents – II. Multimodal eclecticism, cognitive exclusivism and exposure empiricism', *Journal of Behavior Therapy and Experimental Psychiatry* 7: 109–16.

—— (1978) 'Cognition and causation in human behavior and its therapy', *American Psychologist* 33: 437–46.
Woolfolk, R. L. and Sass, L. A. (1989) 'Philosophical foundations of rational-emotive therapy', in M. E. Bernard and R. DiGuiseppe (eds) *Inside Rational-Emotive Therapy*, San Diego: Academic Press.

Chapter 2

Anxiety

Gerry Kent

CONCEPTUALIZATION

As is the case with many psychological difficulties, there is much disagreement about how anxiety might be best defined and understood. Some psychologists share many ideas, disagreeing on minor details. Others take almost incompatible approaches. It is possible to group certain types of difficulty together under a label of Anxiety Disorders, as does the American Psychiatric Association's DSM-III-R classification (American Psychiatric Association 1987). Here there is little concern with aetiology but mainly with a descriptive classification based on symptoms.

The DSM-III-R Classification

The 1987 *Diagnostic and Statistical Manual of Mental Disorders – Revised* is the most recent in a long line of attempts to classify psychiatric difficulties. It provides descriptions of most problems that a psychiatrist or clinical psychologist is likely to encounter. One of the main advantages is that, by using the specified criteria, there can be reasonable certainty that when one clinician uses a term it will be understood by others. This is especially important in research when the efficacy of one type of therapy is compared with another for a particular group of patients.

There are several categories of difficulty under the general term Anxiety Disorders. There are panic disorders (periods of unexpected intense fear or discomfort where the symptoms can include shortness of breath, dizziness and palpitations), simple phobias (fear and avoidance of specific objects or situations), social phobia (where the fear is specifically of social scrutiny) and obsessive-compulsive disorder (where a person continually ruminates over anticipated calamities or feels compelled to keep checking against possible dangers). Another category, post-traumatic stress disorder (PTSD), was developed with particular reference to American soldiers who, on returning from Vietnam, showed delayed stress reactions. This category has also been used to describe reactions to civilian traumas such as assault and accidents. The final main category is Generalized Anxiety Disorder (GAD), or excessive anxiety and worry about life circumstances.

Although this classification scheme is widely used in both research and clinical work, it is largely descriptive. There is little theoretical justification for the categories, and an individual may often have more than one kind of difficulty.

The three-systems model

The three-systems model provides an alternative approach. It emphasizes the nature of the symptoms of anxiety rather than their classification. The basic notion is that anxiety is not a simple 'lump' experience, but has physiological, behavioural and cognitive components. Lang (1971) developed this distinction on the basis of clinical observations. While most phobic clients showed an improvement in behaviour after treatment, many still felt very anxious. Conversely, other clients reported less fear but nevertheless remained highly aroused physiologically.

It seems that these three components of anxiety do not necessarily relate to each other in any simple way. Not only might physiological measures (for example, heart rate, sweating and visceral responses) be unrelated to behavioural indices (for example, avoidance, restlessness), but they might also be discordant with self-reports. Furthermore, there may be little association between various behavioural or between various physiological measures.

A recent example of this principle is provided by Thyer *et al.* (1984). They sought to determine the extent of the relationship between subjective reports of anxiety and two measures of autonomic arousal – peripheral vasoconstriction and heart rate. Subjective anxiety correlated significantly with hand temperature in fifteen out of twenty subjects, but in only six cases was there a significant relationship between subjective anxiety and heart rate. These results point out that, like the subjective experience of pain, anxiety cannot be considered an objective entity that resides in people as viruses or bacteria might do. How individuals interpret or make sense of their physiological state and behaviour varies widely.

The cognitive component

As it was originally formulated by Lang (1971) the cognitive component was seen as the individual's overall appraisal of their level of anxiety. Thus, the cognitive component was limited to some measure of self-reported anxiety, such as a 'fear thermometer' or a SUD scale. More recently, with the increased interest in the cognitive aspects of anxiety, our understanding of this component has increased considerably. Assessment methods are more sophisticated (discussed shortly) and this has provided a better basis for relating the components to each other.

The nature of the relationship between cognitions and behaviour and between cognitions and physiological arousal is central to the cognitive-behavioural approach. Since it cannot be assumed that responses on the three systems will covary, it is important to show that there is some mutual influence between cognitions and the other components. That is, what a person thinks about ought to have some influence on how they react physiologically and what they do behaviourally.

In order to test the hypothesis that thought content can affect physiological arousal, Rimm and Litvak (1969) asked students to read affectively loaded sentences (for example, 'My grades may not be good enough... I might fail... that would be awful') and neutral sentences (for example, 'Inventors are imaginative... Edison was an inventor... therefore he was imaginative'). As expected, physiological arousal as measured by Galvanic Skin Response (sweating) and respiration rate was higher in the affective condition than in the neutral one. In a similar but more recent study, Orton *et al.* (1983) found significant increases in heart rate when subjects were asked to read anxiety-related statements compared with neutral or depressive statements.

Albert Bandura (1986) has been conducting some of the more important work on the relationship between what people believe and what they do. He argues that when people believe that they are able to exert control over their behaviour and achieve their desired ends, they have a sense of 'self-efficacy'. A potential threat will not be associated with apprehension if a person believes that he or she can deal with it. In a series of studies (for example, Bandura *et al.* 1982, 1985) Bandura has shown that not only behaviour but also physiological changes are related to such beliefs. For example, Bandura *et al.* (1985) asked women with a phobic dread of spiders to indicate how confident they were that they could approach a spider to varying proximities. This measure of self-efficacy was found to be related not simply to their actual behaviour but also to the release of stress hormones and naturally occurring opiods. When treatment designed to increase self-efficacy was provided, the women's behaviour showed improvement and their physical arousal decreased.

The nature of anxious cognitions

There is general agreement (Ingram and Kendall 1987) that anxiety-related cognitions are associated with themes of physical or psychological danger (rather than themes of loss, as in depression). In one of the earliest studies in this area, undertaken by Beck *et al.* (1974), thirty-two patients who suffered either acute panic attacks or high levels of chronic anxiety were given a structured interview. Analysis of the interviews indicated all of the patients reported that they 'consistently had thoughts or visual fantasies, or both, revolving around the theme of danger just prior to or during the onset of exacerbation of anxiety' (p. 320). In each case the patients anticipated being harmed physically (for example, a fear of imminent death) or psychologically (for example, a fear of being rejected). Certain stimuli would trigger or provoke the anxiety (for example, news of accidents or social confrontations) and most of the patients could specify a clear-cut precipitating event such as a near-fatal accident or the death of a close friend.

The severity of the patients' distress was related to the range of events which could trigger the reaction. The most disabled individuals were most likely to report a wide range of triggers, while for the least anxious the triggering events were very circumscribed. Furthermore, anxiety levels were related to the perceived probability of the feared event actually happening. Despite the many occasions when the feared event did not occur, the expectations of harm did not extinguish.

Beck *et al.*'s (1974) paper introduced many of the ideas which have become central to the cognitive-behavioural approach to anxiety and is regarded as seminal. The following sections provide a brief description of some later research on these ideas.

Content

As mentioned above, the cognitions associated with anxiety usually involve thoughts of danger and harm. The greater the severity of the anxiety, the more likely it is that the ideation will be of a 'catastrophic' kind, where the worst possible outcomes are anticipated.

The actual content of the ideation varies with the presenting complaint. One distinction is between perceived physical danger and perceived psychological harm. Research on the types of anxiety experienced by medical and dental patients provides an example of the former. Chaves and Brown (1978) found that anxious dental patients were likely to employ catastrophic thinking styles. While anxious patients would often ruminate on the possibility of sudden and severe pain (for example, 'I feel like any minute I'm going to receive a terrific, horrible pain'), patients with low anxiety attempted to cope with any concerns by distracting themselves or rationalizing their experience. Similarly, Kendall and Hollon (1981) found that cardiac catheterization patients who were rated as being anxious by attending physicians were likely to reflect on how 'the catheter might break off and stick in my heart'.

Patients with panic attacks also perceive danger, but this is associated with catastrophic interpretations of unusual bodily states. That is, there is a tendency to construe bodily sensations as indications of severe illness, such as a heart attack. This misinterpretation can lead to an escalation of worries resulting in the vicious circle of a panic attack (Hibbert 1984).

Such misconstruing has recently been implicated in the aetiology of agoraphobia. Franklin (1987) argues that psychological and/or physical stressors can lead to hyperventilation. This in turn can lead to panic attacks if the resulting physiological changes are interpreted as being indications of a heart attack or loss of control. This can then result in the avoidance of any situation (for example, being alone, especially away from home) in which the person anticipates further attacks may occur. According to this model, then, agoraphobic avoidance is a way of coping with the possibility of harm.

Other individuals are anxious about the possibility of psychosocial rather than physical harm. Here, there are themes of rejection and failure rather than illness and disease. Hibbert (1984) found that patients who reported thoughts concerned with rejection (for example, 'I'll make a fool of myself' or 'They will dislike me') did not experience panic attacks and were generally less disabled by their anxiety than patients who feared physical harm. There appears to be a strong tendency for these patients to compare themselves with others, whether the fear concerns general social situations (Glass and Arnkoff 1983), or more limited situations such as writing exams (Wine 1981).

At this point it should be noted that many people – including those who would not consider themselves unduly anxious – report that they occasionally experience the kinds of negative cognitions reported by patients. But there are two important differences between those who are disabled by their cognitions and those who are not. The first distinction has to do with control. People who are troubled by their ideation find such thoughts, once they begin, more difficult to dismiss (Borkovec *et al*. 1983a; Clark and de Silva 1985; Kent and Gibbons 1987). The second difference is the relative balance between positive and negative thoughts. Most people report that they often have some negative ideation but this is usually balanced by positive thoughts. In people severely troubled by anxiety, though, there is a preponderance of negative thoughts (Schwartz 1986).

Cognitive assessment

There are many self-report measures of anxiety currently in use, the most popular being the State–Trait Anxiety Inventory (or STAI – Spielberger *et al*. 1983). Spielberger makes a distinction between anxiety as a relatively stable predisposition and anxiety as a response to a particular situation. The former is known as trait anxiety and is measured by asking subjects such questions as how often they lack self-confidence or feel like crying. State anxiety, by contrast, is more transitory, depending on feelings at the time of administration. Subjects are asked to indicate their agreement with such items as 'I feel calm' and 'I feel upset'.

This and other self-report measures do not, however, provide a way of assessing the content of ideation. The most straightforward assessment method involves the clinical interview, as used in the Beck *et al*. (1974) and Hibbert (1984) studies mentioned earlier. For example, Hibbert (ibid.) first asked his patients to tell him 'what thoughts have been going through your mind when you have been anxious in the past 3 weeks'. If this request did not elicit any thoughts related to the theme of danger, further probes were made.

There are at least two difficulties with this method. First, there are demand characteristics. Interviewees may become aware of what kinds of responses the interviewer is looking for and supply them, even if the responses have little validity. Second, if the interviewer asks several questions of this kind it seems likely that sooner or later some ideation which could be labelled as related to danger will turn up.

Researchers have attempted to overcome these difficulties in several ways. Sewitch and Kirsch (1984) asked clients to monitor their thoughts over a specified period of time. They instructed their subjects 'Each time you feel a little anxious or uptight during the next 24 hours, try to recall what thoughts you have been having prior to this feeling.' Some researchers have used endorsement approaches. While Kent and Gibbons (1987) provided a list of thoughts which previous research had implicated as important and simply asked subjects to check off any thoughts which they had 'ever' experienced, Kendall and Hollon (1989) also asked their subjects to indicate how frequently each thought occurred.

Other approaches involve placing subjects in the anxiety-provoking situation and asking them to verbalize the content of their thoughts. One such approach is known as thought listing in which subjects are asked to report their thoughts in written form while contending with the situation (Arnkoff and Smith 1988) or just after leaving it (Cacioppo and Petty 1981). In the 'think aloud' or recording approach (Genest and Turk 1981), subjects verbalize their thoughts while performing a task. Another approach is 'sampling', which involves making planned interruptions during the task and asking subjects to record any ideation immediately (for example, Klinger 1984).

There are some studies which have examined the comparability of various assessment methods. Blackwell *et al*. (1985) compared 'think aloud' with thought listing: on average the former procedure provided about twice as many thoughts as the latter. Similarly, Last *et al*. (1985) found that the congruence between the measures they took was modest, even when they were administered in the same situation. Furthermore, the data provided by these measures were not stable over time. Such results are of concern since they indicate that the data collected are determined to some extent by the method of collection. Much further work needs to be done in this area, but it should be remembered that such difficulties are also found with behavioural and physiological indices of anxiety.

The validity of different methods has also been examined, with Arnkoff and Smith (1988) providing a good example of this type of research. They asked students both to list their thoughts and to endorse items from a check-list during a classroom examination. Since the endorsement method showed a higher correlation with Sarason's (1978) Test Anxiety Scale, the authors concluded that endorsement provides greater construct validity than does thought listing. D. A. Clark (1988), in an extensive review of the literature on the validity of various measures of cognitions, came to the conclusion that the endorsement approach has gathered the most empirical support.

Finally, it should be mentioned that the collection of ideation is generally followed by some kind of classification, such as that used by Rimm *et al*. (1977). They employed five categories: (1) thoughts of catastrophic consequences, (2) thoughts invoking avoidance or escape, (3) thoughts indicating awareness of fear, (4) thoughts objectively describing the situation, and (5) thoughts that could not be easily classified. The latter category constituted only about 10 per cent of their sample and inter-rater agreement reached 87 per cent overall, indicating that this categorization scheme has some face validity and acceptable reliability.

The development of anxiety

Thus far, the content and assessment of anxiety-related cognitions has been considered, but there has been no explanation of how or why anxiety develops.

Until recently, Mowrer's (1960) two-stage theory was the most widely accepted. Mowrer argued that anxiety responses originated through classical conditioning – a negative experience is associated in time with an object or situation. The anxiety was said to be then reinforced and maintained through operant means: an individual learns to reduce the fear by subsequently avoiding the situation.

However, with the recognition that people deal with and process information rather than simply reacting to stimuli, Mowrer's formulation has been abandoned by cognitive-behavioural theorists. The question has now become how individuals process information and why this has come about (Williams *et al.* 1988).

Some have adopted an evolutionary perspective. Beck (Beck and Emery 1985) argues that many fears are innate and have served a protective function in evolutionary terms. These fears may continue to be useful in the early years of an individual's development. For instance, it really can be dangerous to approach strangers when young, just as it may have been in our distant past. Similarly, many people complain of intense fears of dogs, cats and spiders – the type of animals which could have posed a physical threat earlier in our species' development.

Thus, symptoms of anxiety can be seen as responses to realistic threats during evolution, and to have some survival value. An organism may be more likely to survive by making many false positive errors (perceiving danger where none exists) than one false negative (not perceiving a real danger). In other words, 'evolution favours anxious genes'. This notion applies most clearly to physical dangers, but may also apply to social anxieties: humankind, being a social animal reliant on others for survival, may have an in-built fear of rejection or disgrace.

In this way the function of anxiety may be similar to pain. Whereas pain motivates the person to do something to terminate or reduce discomfort, anxiety can likewise be seen as a response to perceived threat. Sometimes this response is realistic, but when it is a reaction to an exaggerated or misperceived threat it may become problematic and disabling.

Not only might there be an evolutionary basis for anxiety in general, but humans may also be biologically primed to become anxious about certain objects and situations more easily than others. There is a greater incidence of cat, dog and spider phobias than one would expect by chance, indicating that not all situations are equally likely to become anxiety provoking. Conversely, relatively few people become phobic about driving at high speeds, which is objectively more dangerous. This has led some psychologists to argue for the notion of an innate predisposition to fear certain objects and situations, known as *preparedness* (Seligman 1971).

There is also the problem of individual differences in vulnerability to anxiety. Virtually everyone will have had the kinds of experiences reported by intensely anxious people (for example, the death of a close friend, a bad experience at the dentist) but not everyone develops disabling levels of anxiety. In Beck *et al.*'s (1974) study some of the precipitating events (for example, a mother's death by heart failure, an allergic reaction to a penicillin injection) may have served to sensitize the patients to their own somatic state, but there were several cases where no event could be identified, or else it was not clear how the event (for example, moving to a new job in a distant city) could have had a sensitizing effect.

It may be the combination of a cognitive vulnerability and the occurrence of a particular event which is associated with the development of a particular type of anxiety (Barlow 1988; Beck and Clark 1988). Any such vulnerability may be due to child-rearing practices (perhaps parental use of punishment – Krohne 1980), or to genetic characteristics such as Temperament (especially difficulty in adapting to change, Williams *et al*. 1985) or Neuroticism.

The age of the development of anxiety disorders has received some attention. Thyer *et al*. (1985) found that social phobias tended to develop during adolescence, while simple phobias tended to develop earlier. By contrast, patients with agoraphobia usually reported an onset of their difficulties after the age of 25.

Expectations

Belief in the importance of unrealistic expectations in the development and maintenance of anxiety is shared by most theorists. The mechanisms involved are, however, understood in many different ways. While some place emphasis on the notion of schemata, others rely on biochemical and neurological research.

Neuroanatomy of anxiety

Here Gray's work (Gray, 1982, 1985) is noteworthy. His argument, based on the effects of anti-anxiety drugs, is that subjective feelings of anxiety are essentially a result of activity in the septo-hippocampal system of the brain. The hippocampus is said to act as a comparator, matching expected with actual events. If there is some kind of mismatch between these, the organism reacts with increased arousal, attention and inhibition of ongoing behaviour.

Gray (1982) speculates that it is possible to understand mismatching in two ways. In one, the hippocampal checking system is overactive, checking too many items too frequently or too repetitively. This would correspond to obsessive-compulsive difficulties. Alternatively, the checking system could detect too many mismatches, leading to the excessive inhibition of behaviour displayed behaviourally as a phobia.

This notion that individuals, when anxious, are constantly checking for possible sources of harm is consistent with patients' reports of their experiences. It is clear, for example, that anxious dental patients expect more pain than they are likely to experience (Kent 1984), that agoraphobic patients expect more severe consequences of being unsupported than are likely to occur (McNally and Foa 1987), and so forth. Thus, while everyone is motivated to avoid stimuli that arouse expectations of danger (Reiss and McNally 1985), it seems that these expectations are particularly unrealistic in clinical anxiety states.

Schemata

While, in Gray's theory, the source of unrealistic expectations is rooted in neurological structures, most cognitive psychologists have used the general and hypothetical construct of cognitive set or *schema*. This term has been used in several ways, but in general it refers to a body of knowledge which guides attention, expectations, interpretations and memory search. Stimuli are processed to conform with a stereotype of the environment (Williams *et al*. 1988). Such schemata are particularly relevant when ambiguous information is encountered. Schemata related specifically to anxiety predispose the individual to perceive danger, acting as a kind of 'hyperactive alarm system' which can be sounded by the slightest perceived threat. Thus, 'the anxious patient is so sensitive to any stimuli that might be taken as indicating imminent disaster or harm that he is constantly warning himself... about the potential dangers' (Beck and Emery 1985: 31).

The precise nature of the schemata will very according to the problem. In people who suffer from panic attacks, the expectations often concern death or illness; for social anxiety the theme is rejection; and for test anxiety, failure. However, the general principle of heightened sensitivity to certain aspects of the environment is hypothesized to hold whatever the condition. There are three aspects of the schemata which deserve particular discussion: one concerns the subjective probability of negative events; another, the focus of attention; and the third, memory processes.

Probability

There is always the slight chance that the catastrophic outcomes imagined by anxious people will occur. A person may fail an examination badly, may be rejected and laughed at, and may be having a heart attack. For most people, though, the *perceived* probability of these events actually occurring is low, whereas it is very much higher for those who are anxious (Butler and Mathews 1983; Kent 1985a; McNally and Foa 1987). Subjective probabilities may increase as a person approaches a situation in time or space. For example, Beck and Emery (1985) describe one patient with a phobia about flying whose beliefs about the probability of a crash varied according to the proximity of the flight. When not planning a flight in the near future, the chance of an accident was placed at 1:100,000, but as the time of a flight grew near, the estimated chances increased dramatically. Just as the plane started to take off, the chances were about 50:50 (Beck and Emery 1985: 128).

Butler and Mathews (1987) have recently found similar results with students due to take examinations. The students' expectations of negative outcomes varied with their levels of anxiety and the temporal proximity of the exams. Interestingly, the subjective probability of negative events unrelated to the exams showed a similar change.

It is tempting to conclude that the changes in anxiety were caused by changes in subjective probability, but it is in fact not possible to reach a conclusion regarding causality. Other studies have shown that the subjective probability of an event varies according to whether a person thinks about or ruminates upon that event (Caroll 1978; Sherman *et al*. 1985). Perhaps the perception of increased risk is a consequence of increasing anxiety and rumination, rather than vice versa.

Focus of attention

In recent years, the notion that anxious people inappropriately focus their attention on particular aspects of the environment has become firmly established. This is supported by clinical impressions. It is very noticeable, for example, that during treatment programmes which involve *in vivo* desensitization to animals, phobic patients will show an extraordinary sensitivity to their presence. During walks though city streets, patients with a cat phobia will be able to spot cats sitting in the most unlikely places. As treatment progresses and the phobia lessens, they will sometimes volunteer that 'there don't seem to be as many cats (or dogs, or spiders) around any more'.

The focus of attention varies according to the problem. In clinically anxious individuals with fears of social rejection or panic attacks, attention may be directed internally (for example, on the perceived inadequacy of what they say and how they behave for the former and on somatic state of the latter), whereas for phobic people the focus may be on environmental cues (Sartory 1986). Since our ability to attend to various environmental cues is restricted (i.e. our information processing capacity is limited), any focus of attention on particular stimuli will be at the expense of other tasks. For example, a student who attends to how others are answering examination questions may be distracted from the task at hand – i.e. answering the questions him- or herself – and thus do poorly in the exam (Wine 1981).

Recently there has been much interest in employing some of the techniques developed within cognitive psychology during the 1950s and 1960s to study attention processes in anxiety. One method is the Stroop test. In the original studies, subjects were given lists of words printed in different colour inks and their task was to name the colour of the ink (not to say the word) as quickly as possible. In some lists the words did not refer to colours at all and subjects were able to identify the ink colour quite quickly. In other lists, however, the words were names of colours, so that, for example, the word 'blue' could have been printed in red ink. Under these conditions subjects took significantly longer to identity the ink colour. It seemed as though the meaning of the words which were discordant with the ink colour interfered with the process of colour identification.

This technique was used by Watts *et al*. (1986) to compare the information-processing characteristics of people with spider phobias with those of non-phobic control subjects. To simplify this study somewhat, Watts *et al*. (1986) found that there was no difference between the two groups in how quickly they could name the colour of the ink in the standard Stroop test, but there was a difference when words such as 'creepy', 'hairy', 'legs' and 'spider' were used. In this condition the phobic subjects took significantly longer to name the colours than the non-phobics, indicating that the meaning of the target words interfered with the processing.

Another technique is the dichotic listening task. The subject wears a set of headphones, with different messages being emitted from each side. The subject is asked to attend to one side only, and to repeat immediately the words he or she hears from that side. Because attention capacity is limited, subjects are usually unable to report the message being emitted on the unattended side. However, particularly meaningful stimuli (such as the subject's name) are sometimes heard from the unattended side. Such stimuli seem to 'capture' the subject's attention .

Foa and McNally (1986) used this technique in order to examine the sensitivity of obsessive-compulsive patients for words associated with contamination and dirt. Each patient heard two sets of tapes. The neutral word 'pick' was randomly inserted on both sides of one tape: as expected the patients usually heard the target word on the attended side but heard it much less frequently on the unattended side. On the second set of tapes, however, words associated with contamination (for example, 'urine', 'faeces' and 'cancer') were inserted instead of the neutral word 'pick'. Now the patients were much more likely to report the presence of the words on the unattended side. These results thus indicated a sensitivity for feared stimuli not shown for neutral words.

There has also been interest in the possibility that such attentional processes can operate outside an individual's awareness. Mathews and MacLeod (1986) used the dichotic listening task while at the same time asking subjects to respond on a reaction time task. The hypothesis was that anxious subjects would take longer to react than control subjects when threat words (such as 'injury', 'assault' and 'disease') were being spoken on the unattended side than non-threatening words (for example, 'poetry', 'safety' and 'greetings'). The hypothesis was supported, although neither group could give a report on the listed words.

Memory

Not only do schemata lead people to overestimate the probability of certain events and to focus their attention on them when they do occur; schemata may also influence memory processes. There are at least three ways in which this can occur. First, it seems likely that if an individual is selectively attending to particular stimuli (for example, the presence of cats), then he or she will encode these observations in memory. Second, schemata may be involved in the reconstruction of memories, so that previous encounters with these stimuli may be recalled as being more unpleasant than they were experienced at the time (Kent 1985b).

There is also a third way in which memory processes may be implicated in the development or maintenance of anxiety, based on Bower's (1981) work associating mood and recall. He argued that mood can serve as a context for recall, such that when people are in a particular mood they are more likely to access mood-congruent than mood-incongruent experiences. Thus, when an individual is sad or depressed he or she is more likely to recall sad experiences than happy ones. This is often observed in clinical work: for example, a recently bereaved person may find that other bereavements and losses come to mind.

However, while this idea is now well supported in work on depressive illnesses, there is much less evidence that anxious schemata can act in a similar way. That is, it has proved difficult to demonstrate that clinically anxious patients are more likely to recall anxiety-related material than normal samples (for example, Mogg *et al.* 1987). It may be that the effect is more pronounced for transient state anxiety than chronic state anxiety. Recently, Kent (1989) asked patients about to see their dentist to complete questionnaires measuring their anxiety before and after the appointment. The patients were also asked to describe a previous visit, but half were given this task before the visit – when their state of anxiety was high – and half afterwards – when their state of anxiety had declined. Female patients (but not males) rated the recalled experience as being significantly more unpleasant before the appointment than afterwards, and a blind judge's ratings indicated a similar effect for how vivid the descriptions were. There were indications that these results were not due to differences in actual experiences. Due to the design it was not possible to say whether the results were due to retrieval or reporting biases, but they suggested that similar processes may be operating in anxiety as in depression.

In summary, this section of the chapter has considered some of the conceptual issues which are important for the understanding of the cognitive-behavioural approach to anxiety. The three-systems model considers anxiety to have physiological, behavioural and cognitive components which interact in idiosyncratic ways. Most of the discussion has concerned the cognitive aspects of anxiety: how ideation usually involves thoughts of danger and harm, and the various ways in which cognitions might be assessed. Some cognitive-behavioural theorists argue that anxiety develops as a result of archaic fears which are common to most people and sensitize them to danger. In some people, perhaps because of a combination of life events and biological vulnerability, anxiety develops to unrealistic levels and becomes disabling. Once anxiety has developed, it is maintained since people come to focus their attention on potentially harmful aspects of the environment, the subjective probability of danger is inflated, and memory processes result in selective recall of negative experiences.

TREATMENT

In this part of the chapter, some of the studies which have explored the effectiveness of cognitive-behavioural treatments for anxiety are described. First, however, there is a brief outline of three theorists who place emphasis on slightly different aspects of this approach.

Three approaches to reducing anxiety

Although there are many individual variations in how cognitive principles are applied, most are based on the thinking of Ellis (1962), Beck (Beck and Emery 1985) and Meichenbaum (1977).

Albert Ellis is known as the main proponent of rational-emotive therapy (RET). He emphasizes the maladaptive nature of certain irrational beliefs. These involve a number of absolute 'shoulds' and 'musts', such as 'I should be perfect in everything I do' and 'I must always try my hardest'. Ellis argues that (1) we all carry such irrational beliefs around with us, (2) the beliefs can be triggered by events in a person's life, and that (3) these beliefs are a core component of emotional distress. RET involves a process of discovering the nature of the 'musts' and 'shoulds', and confrontation of these beliefs.

Beck also argues that negative thinking is a central part of emotional distress, but his therapy appears to be less didactic and less confronting than Ellis's. There is also more emphasis on the establishment of a sound therapeutic relationship. Questioning is the main therapeutic method, in which the therapist enquires about alternative ways of interpreting and reacting to events. The aim is for clients to take on this approach in their everyday life, asking themselves questions like 'What do I have to lose?' and 'What can I learn from this experience?'.

Like Ellis and Beck, Meichenbaum attempts to help clients become aware of their negative and irrational beliefs, but concentrates more on how they are a part of an internal dialogue which can serve to maintain anxiety. His concern is with what people say to themselves before entering stressful situations. His aim is to substitute alternative and more positive thoughts which could help them to cope more effectively.

One of the earliest studies was conducted by Meichenbaum (1972), and it provides an example of his Stress Inoculation Training (SIT) approach. He divided students who had requested assistance for their anxiety about taking examination into three groups. One group served as a waiting-list control, a second group received standard systematic desensitization therapy, and the third group was given the SIT programme. This involved two main components. First, the students were helped to become aware of their thoughts and self-instructions which affected their anxiety. Second, they were asked to imagine themselves coping with the anxiety-provoking situation by instructing themselves to remain calm, to relax and to attend to the task at hand.

Several measures pointed to the efficacy of this latter treatment. Subjects in this group showed the most marked improvement in their grades, the most improvement on self-reported anxiety, and their overall levels of test anxiety became similar to those of low-anxiety students.

A second study illustrates a matching of intervention to the individual client. Kendall et al. (1979) compared the efficacy of three approaches for helping patients about to undergo cardiac catheterization procedures. Some patients were assigned to an attention-placebo control group, where they were encouraged to discuss aspects of their job, family and related topics. Other patients were given an educational intervention, where the procedures were described and explained. But for neither group was there any mention of coping methods.

The third group was given the cognitive-behavioural intervention. This involved the therapists disclosing how they coped with events and encouragement for the patients to reflect on theirs. More specifically, the patients were urged to view any anxiety they felt as cues which they could use to prompt coping skills. For example, if a particular patient became anxious about the complicated equipment, the therapist would model coping statements such as 'Science has come such a long way to be able to have and use all this expensive equipment, and the doctors are very skilled in its use' (p. 51). Other patients, with their own individual concerns, were encouraged to develop coping strategies tailored to their particular needs.

There were several dependent measures of adjustment. Only those patients in the third, cognitive-behavioural intervention group showed a consistent reduction in state anxiety. Another set of measures involved ratings of adjustment by attending physicians and attendants. Again, the patients in the third group fared best.

These two studies illustrate the general design of studies in the literature. In the following, a description of further studies concerned with the treatment of panic disorder, agoraphobia, obsessive-compulsive difficulties, generalized anxiety disorder and phobias is given.

Panic disorders

It now seems that the prevalence of panic attacks throughout the general population is much higher than had previously been assumed. For example, occasional attacks may be experienced by about one-third of young adults, and about 2 per cent of this population would meet the DSM-III-R criteria for a clinical disorder.

In developing a cognitive approach to panic attacks, several workers (for example, D. M. Clark 1986) have suggested the following model. First, a situation is perceived as threatening which leads to apprehension and physical arousal. The crucial point is how the individual interprets this arousal. If it can be controlled, or not attended to, or accepted as a normal reaction to the situation, then a panic attack will not develop. However, if the bodily sensations are misinterpreted and seen as an indication of some severe imminent danger (such as fainting in a public place or even death), a vicious circle develops. Now the person becomes anxious not only about the original threat but also about the 'uncontrollable' symptoms as well. The person may overbreathe or hyperventilate, which lowers the CO_2 level in the blood and which in turn causes further physical symptoms.

The role of physiological changes in panic disorders has been investigated several times. Some of these studies have involved experimentally induced changes through such agents as sodium lactate and a CO_2 challenge (see D. M. Clark 1986). These agents produce some of the sensations (such as breathlessness, dizziness and palpitations) associated with panic attacks. When given to people with a history of panic attacks, symptoms are often provoked, but only rarely do they provoke an attack in control subjects.

Such results can be interpreted in at least two ways. On the one hand, they can be taken as an indication that biochemical changes have a panic-inducing effect only for certain vulnerable individuals, and so a researcher might attempt to identify biochemical abnormalities in panic patients (Woods and Charney 1988). However, the alternative psychological explanation, that panic patients misinterpret their arousal, is supported by several studies. For example, van der Molen et al. (1986) induced arousal by sodium lactate in normal subjects. While some were told that the infusion might cause unpleasant bodily sensations similar to those experienced during periods of anxiety, others were told that they would feel pleasantly excited. As predicted, those in the first group reported a significant increase in anxiety, but there was little change in the second group. In another recent study (Ehlers et al. (1988) both patients with a panic disorder and normal controls were given false feedback of an abrupt heart-rate increase. On self-ratings and physiological measures, the patients showed much greater increases in anxiety than the controls.

These latter studies suggest that a cognitive approach, where the focus is on how a patient interprets arousal, may be most appropriate. A cognitive-behavioural therapist will be more interested in what a person thinks will happen as a result of becoming physiologically aroused than in the arousal itself. This *secondary anxiety* or 'fear of fear' becomes the primary target of therapy. There are several question-naires which can be used to measure this type of anxiety (Chambless and Gracely 1989; Reiss et al. 1986).

D. M. Clark (1986) and Clark et al. (1985) described one attempt to alter patients' cognitions. The first step involved asking patients to hyperventilate (overbreathe). The bodily sensations which are produced in this way are very similar to those experienced in naturally occurring panic attacks. Second, patients were given an explanation of the way hyperventilation can induce panic, along with discussion of how a vicious circle could develop. Third, there was training in how to use slow and controlled breathing as a coping technique. There was also training in more appropriate interpretations of bodily sensations and the identification of the stimuli which triggered the attacks. With this treatment package, substantial reductions in attack frequency were reported within the first few weeks of treat-ment, and these gains were maintained at a 2-year follow-up.

Agoraphobia

In recent years, there has been a marked shift in the understanding of agoraphobia. Rather than concentrating simply on the behavioural symptoms of being anxious about leaving home unaccompanied, there have been attempts to ascertain why an individual has developed agoraphobia. Several researchers have noted an associ-ation between agoraphobic avoidance and the fear of unexpected panic attacks. In clinical samples at least, agoraphobia without a history of panic attacks is rare (APA 1987). This has led to the suggestion that the avoidance is usually an attempt to avoid situations (for example, buses and trains, being left alone) where a panic attack may possibly occur. In this model, the condition is thus seen as a further stage in the development of what is essentially an anxiety disorder (Franklin 1987).

Rapee and Barlow (1990) provide a detailed protocol for the treatment of agoraphobia within this approach. The first session consists of an outline of their view of agoraphobia, namely that it involves a fear of experiencing a panic attack and that the avoidance of situations is a way of seeking safety in case of an attack. The major aim of the second session is to introduce the principles of cognitive restructuring, particularly the notion that the interpretation of events and feelings can produce an emotional reaction.

During the second session patients are also encouraged to consider their estimates of the probability of a panic attack, and then challenged about this. How realistic are their estimates that they will faint or even die? Have they ever died before? For homework, the patients are asked to monitor their thoughts when they are feeling anxious and to write down the realistic probability of the occurrence of the feared event.

Other sessions provide training in breathing control, demonstrations of the effects of hyperventilation and discussion of homework assigned between sessions. This homework involves monitoring thoughts at the time of the panics, rehearsing coping self-statements and exposure to situations which had previously been avoided.

Thus, this cognitive-behavioural treatment of agoraphobia closely follows that for panic disorders. There have been some attempts to evaluate this approach using measures other than simply reduction of avoidance. McNally and Lorenz (1987) were interested in the effects of such a therapy programme on patients' fear of their anxiety. On several measures of 'fear of fear', after treatment the patients became less sensitive to any anxiety they experienced, approaching the sensitivity level shown by normal subjects. In another study (McNally and Foa 1987), treated agoraphobics became less likely to exaggerate the probability of unpleasant events and less likely to interpret bodily sensations as threatening.

There has been some interest in the relative efficacy of a cognitive-behavioural approach compared with the more traditional behavioural *in vivo* approach. An early study (Emmelkamp *et al.* 1978) indicated that straight exposure was more effective than cognitive modification alone, and current thinking is that cognitive approaches are best undertaken alongside exposure: since there is a reciprocal relationship between cognitions and behaviour, a graded approach is itself a powerful way of modifying beliefs. Possibly what is necessary during exposure is that the patient experience several occasions, under differing conditions, where the expectations of harm are disconfirmed (Kent 1986).

Obsessive-compulsive disorders

Obsessions are recurrent and persistent ideas, thoughts or images which are involuntarily produced and experienced as being senseless and repugnant. Examples are a parent having repeated impulses to harm a child he or she loves, or a religious person having recurrent blasphemous thoughts. Compulsions are repetitive behaviours which are performed in a ritualistic or stereotyped fashion. These could involve washing, checking or counting. Patients recognize that the obsessions and compulsions are a product of their own minds, and may be deeply ashamed of their thoughts and actions (APA 1987).

Currently there is agreement that obsessions and compulsive behaviour are attempts to prevent the occurrence of some negative event or situation. Thus, they can be seen as ways of reducing anxiety (Emmelkamp 1982). When there are fears of disease or illness the individual may take extensive steps to avoid any possibility of contamination by either repeated cleansing or phobic-like avoidance. Or a person may ruminate on all possible sources of danger in order to 'neutralize' the possibility of being blamed.

Several researchers have commented that obsessional individuals have a very low tolerance for ambiguity and have perfectionist ideals (Rachman and Hodgson 1980). Their feelings of inadequacy make uncertainty threatening and sometimes intolerable. But such descriptions of patients do not explain the psychological processes involved in the problem. There are pharmacological agents which can be used to treat compulsive behaviour, but it seems that these have only a suppressant effect: the rituals often return when the dosage is reduced or stopped (Marks 1983).

For several years the psychological treatment of choice for compulsive behaviour has been exposure and response prevention. As in other anxiety disorders, overestimation of the probability of harm and catastrophic ideation are common (Turner and Michelson 1984). Someone who compulsively checks to see that all possible precautions have been taken to minimize harm (for example, repeatedly checking that a door is locked) would be prevented from doing so, or would not be given any reassurance that the checks had been performed. Someone who compulsively cleans could be contaminated with dirt. The aim here has been to demonstrate to the patient that the imagined catastrophes do not, in fact, occur. Over repeated exposures confidence is gained that the behaviour does not need to be performed.

However, obsessions seem to be more difficult to treat (Rachman and Hodgson 1980), partly perhaps because there is no obvious behaviour to be prevented. Thought stopping (where the therapist asks the patient to concentrate on a particular thought and then shouts 'stop') and habituation (where the patient is exposed to the obsession for an uninterrupted 60 minutes) have had some limited success.

Recently there have been several attempts to understand the processes involved in obsessional thinking. The notion that *control* of intrusive thoughts is important is suggested by studies (Rachman and de Silva 1978; Salkovskis and Harrison 1984) which have found that 80–88 per cent of normal populations experience what can be termed intrusive and unwanted thoughts on occasion. In these studies the difference between the obsessional and normal populations did not concern the content of the thoughts – almost everybody worries about the possibility of harm or that they will be blamed occasionally – but whether the individual found the thought acceptable and how easily the thoughts could be controlled or dismissed when they did arise.

This research suggests that obsessional thinking, which is generally regarded as pathological, may be on a continuum with normality (Salkovskis 1985). There are also therapeutic implications from this work. One suggestion is that if a person could learn to control the presence of certain thoughts through redirection of attention or self-distraction, their obsessional difficulties would decline. This method has been used by Hoogduin *et al.* (1987). They asked their patients to engage in some distracting activity (for example, cycling, visiting a friend) whenever they experienced obsessional thoughts. With this method, 73 per cent of the patients improved and 60 per cent maintained the improvement 12 months after treatment was completed. An alternative method for controlling intrusive thoughts was tested by Borkovec *et al.* (1983b) who encouraged patients to establish a half-hour period in each day in which they would be 'allowed' to worry. Whenever they found themselves ruminating on something at another time, they were to postpone their worrying until the designated 30 minutes. This approach resulted in a significant reduction in the amount of reported ruminating.

However, these methods can be criticized because they only provide the patient with alternative ways of coping with the symptom. Salkovskis (1985) argues for another approach. Because disturbing thoughts occur frequently in normal individuals without leading to serious disturbance of mood, he argues that it is important to explore why some individuals *react* to these thoughts with such distress. From his clinical experience, it seems that obsessional patients find these thoughts unacceptable and evaluate themselves negatively for having them – for example, 'if I have thoughts like this it means that I'm an evil person' (p. 573).

In some ways, Salkovskis's description is similar to the recent 'fear of fear' explanation given for panic disorders and agoraphobia: that it is not the presence of the thoughts which is important, but rather how the individual reacts to these thoughts which determines distress.

The therapeutic question now concerns the meaning that the patient gives to having the thoughts, and the belief systems which give rise to this meaning. Salkovskis suggests that some of the erroneous beliefs include 'having a thought about an action is like performing the action', 'failing to prevent harm is like having caused the harm' and 'one should exercise control over one's thoughts' (Salkovskis 1985: 579).

Generalized anxiety disorder

This difficulty is sometimes referred to as free-floating anxiety. It is characterized by an apparent lack of external anxiety cues and persistent, chronic tension. Many such patients also suffer from panic attacks. Perhaps the most widely used method of treatment in the past has been relaxation therapy, but this seems to have mainly short-term effects. This may be because patients do not practise the relaxation exercises consistently, or because relaxation training deals with only the physiological component of anxiety and not the behavioural and cognitive ones.

A study by Butler *et al.* (1987) illustrates how a cognitive-behavioural approach can be used in the treatment of generalized anxiety disorder. Their treatment package included relaxation training, but it also targeted avoidance behaviour and negative cognitions. Avoidance could be shown in many ways, such as not accepting an invitation to a party because of acute anxiety of being rejected or embarrassed. Avoidance was tackled by graded practice. This involved the patients first choosing a situation which they found slightly anxiety provoking but could be managed. Then they were encouraged to confront this situation several times until they could manage it without any difficulty. The next step was then to work on a slightly more difficult situation, and so on.

The kinds of cognitions reported by patients involves the themes of personal danger and illness reported in the Beck *et al.* (1974) and Hibbert (1984) papers cited earlier in the chapter. In the Butler *et al.* (1987) study, patients were taught to control these catastrophic cognitions by distraction and by questioning how realistic they were.

On a variety of self-report questionnaires and independent assessments, this approach seemed very helpful to the patients involved. Before treatment 46 per cent of the patients were taking regular medication for their anxiety, but this had fallen to only 13 per cent 6 months after the completion of treatment.

There are other studies which have used similar anxiety-management techniques. For example, Borkovec *et al.* (1987) compared the efficacy of cognitive therapy with non-directive therapy. In the latter condition, the patients were provided with an opportunity to express their feelings with a therapist who was warm and concerned, but who did not provide any advice or suggestions on how to manage their anxiety. The patients given cognitive therapy were given a much more structured approach. They were taught to identify any irrational anxiety-provoking thoughts, to question the validity of these thoughts, and to identify and use alternative, more realistic thoughts in their place. There was significant improvement on all of the dependent measures for both types of therapy, but on all but one of the questionnaire measures (which included the STAI and diary accounts) the cognitive therapy approach was significantly more effective.

Phobias

The DSM-III-R classification of phobias includes agoraphobia (discussed above), social phobia (where there is a compelling desire to avoid situations in which the individual may feel under the scrutiny of others) and simple phobia. In the latter the phobic objects are most often animals, and phobic situations frequently involve heights or closed spaces. There is no doubt that the traditional *in vivo* behavioural method, where the client is gradually exposed to the phobic stimulus, is very effective. The question for the cognitive-behavioural therapist is why improvement does occur, and how therapy could be designed to be even more effective.

Perhaps because of the effectiveness of exposure methods, there has been relatively little interest in the cognitive aspects of phobias. Wade *et al.* (1977) examined the cognitions of snake phobics and found that those showing the greatest avoidance reported more negative imagery regarding snakes than did the less-avoidant patients. In another study phobic patients were more likely to endorse such irrational beliefs as 'I must be approved of and liked by all others in order to be worthwhile' and 'If something could possibly go wrong I should dwell on this possibility' (Mizes *et al*. 1987).

While such cognitions seem similar to those seen in people who are anxious but not phobic, Last and Blanchard (1982) argue that there is a qualitative difference here. On the basis of interviews with people with both phobic and moderate anxiety difficulties, they found some specific differences in cognitions. In particular, the phobic patients reported a greater likelihood of thoughts of avoidance and escape and to have thoughts of catastrophic consequences than the patients with less severe difficulties.

The role of such maladaptive thoughts in the maintenance of phobias is far from clear. There is evidence that behavioural treatments affect the frequency and intensity of such thoughts, but whether phobic behaviour can be altered by challenging beliefs remains to be shown. While most cognitive therapists do not claim that cognitive procedures alone are sufficient to alter phobic behaviour, Last (1984) went further than this: she contended from her review of the literature that cognitive therapy adds little to *in vivo* exposure.

There are several reasons why cognitive approaches, by themselves, seem ineffective. One possibility is that phobias, being by definition primarily behavioural in nature, respond best to behavioural treatments. Although cognitions about the phobic stimulus change after treatment, these may be secondary. A second possibility is that there may be different kinds of phobias, some of which are primarily behavioural/physiological in nature, others primarily cognitive. Öst and Hugdahl (1983) and Hugdahl and Öst (1985) have interviewed patients with a variety of phobias in an attempt to distinguish between patients who acquired their avoidance in different ways: 90 per cent of the patients attributed their phobias to conditioning experiences or vicarious learning, but none recalled instruction or information. This suggests that phobias based on cognitive learning are at the very least rare.

A third possibility is suggested by Bandura's (1986) theory of self-efficacy. Bandura argues that people experience anxiety when they perceive themselves to be ill-equipped to manage potentially painful events which will make them vulnerable to harm. When they feel they can control themselves or their environment, then no anxiety will ensue. This feeling of control – the judgement that one is able to perform the necessary tasks – is what is meant by self-efficacy. A person with a snake phobia, for example, may have a high sense of self-efficacy in most areas of life, being able to perform many tasks, but no confidence in his or her ability to approach a snake.

Behavioural treatments such as *in vivo* exposure and modelling have important effects on self-efficacy beliefs. After treatment, patients have more confidence in their ability to approach phobic objects, and this belief corresponds well to changes in their actual behaviour.

Bandura (1983) has developed his theory with particular reference to phobics' behaviour, but he also provides some anecdotal descriptions of their cognitions and self-statements as well. For example, he quoted one patient's comments that 'As I got closer to the [snake's] cage I'd feel the tension spread... if I picked him up I'd lose control of my hands and arms and drop him' (p. 467). This patient's self-statements were reflected by his inefficacious behaviour.

The missing link for Bandura's theory is a demonstration that direct changes in self-efficacy result in a change in behaviour. That is, there is a need for studies in which therapy is aimed at increasing confidence in ability. One possible method is suggested by Dowrick (1983): he edited videotapes of patients to show them the occasions when they succeeded in performing set tasks. If one effect of *in vivo* exposure is to convince patients that they can, indeed, perform tasks that they previously felt unable to perform, such a self-modelling procedure may be very effective.

In summary, cognitive-behavioural treatments focus on the relationship between interpretations and self-statements on the one hand and how people behave on the other. For some problems, such as obsessional difficulties, the emphasis is on ideation, while for phobias the emphasis might be mainly on the behaviour itself. In the case of panic disorders and GAD there is a clear need to consider behavioural, cognitive and physiological manifestations of the problem. But whatever the difficulty it is rare that one aspect is treated to the exclusion of others.

FUTURE DEVELOPMENTS

In this final section, two issues which are pertinent to the future development of the cognitive-behavioural approach are considered. The first is the issue of selecting between various treatment methods, and the second is whether it would be more effective to help patients to try to control the intrusiveness of thoughts or to make more basic alterations in content.

The selection of treatment programmes

There are now literally hundreds of published studies designed to measure the relative effectiveness of various therapeutic procedures. These include comparisons between the recognized forms of behavioural treatment (for example, modelling, systematic desensitization and *in vivo* exposure), the 'insight' psychotherapies (for example, person-centred therapy) and the more recent cognitive-behavioural approaches.

A typical example of one such study is given by Durham and Turvey (1987). They provided either a cognitive-behavioural or a more traditional behavioural treatment to patients with a diagnosis of generalized anxiety disorder. Although both treatment packages included such behavioural strategies as relaxation and exposure, only the cognitive-behavioural approach included attempts to modify thinking patterns and processes.

The results of this study are instructive. On a variety of measures, both treatment groups showed improvement overall: as far as an independent assessor was concerned, 25 per cent of the patients showed no change, 20 per cent were moderately improved and 54 per cent had markedly or completely improved. While there appeared to be no difference in improvement between the groups when they were assessed immediately after the completion of therapy, a very different picture emerged when the patients were again assessed 6 months later. At that time, 60 per cent of the patients who had undergone the cognitive-behavioural programme were considered to be markedly improved, but only 30 per cent of the patients in the behavioural group had maintained this level of improvement.

Although it is possible to cite many similar studies in support of the cognitive-behavioural therapies, it is also possible to find others which contradict this general pattern. Rather than relying on particular studies to settle the issue of relative effectiveness, Shapiro and Shapiro (1982) argue that an overall view should be taken, with studies which have shown a strong effect for one type of therapy being weighted more heavily than studies whose results are more equivocal.

They analysed over 140 studies in this way. Unfortunately many of the reports did not provide adequate descriptions of the therapeutic programmes, nor did many studies include long-term follow-ups of their clients. Nevertheless, Shapiro and Shapiro (ibid.) concluded that there is little to choose between the effects of various therapies overall.

Although patients who underwent therapy fared better than control groups, the effects of the therapies were roughly equivalent. There are several explanations for this equivalence. One possibility is that the various therapeutic techniques have some common factors which are responsible for most of the improvement. These include some kind of rationale for treatment, hope and motivation to get better (Garfield 1971). The opportunity to confide in a trusted and socially sanctioned helper may also be important: Persons and Burns (1985) have shown that when patients are given cognitive therapy, their perceptions of the quality of the relationship with the therapist make a significant contribution to changes in mood.

Another possible reason for this equivalence is that different approaches are appropriate for different problems. As mentioned earlier, in some instances more emphasis needs to be placed on behavioural exposure (such as phobic difficulties – Thyer et al. 1983), while for other patients (such as those suffering from generalized anxiety disorder) greater attention to cognitions is warranted (Woodward and Jones 1980).

Another approach based on the three-systems model of anxiety has also been explored. There is much evidence that multimodal treatment packages, where physiological, behavioural and cognitive components are all targeted (for example, Kleinknecht and Bernstein 1979), are more effective than any one approach taken alone. Perhaps this is because the response system which is most reactive is always being treated for each individual patient.

Taking this a step further, Haug et al. (1987) treated patients with a fear of flying. They were classified as either physiological or cognitive responders, and then were given either cognitive therapy or muscle-relaxation training. The main interest of the study was the relative effectiveness of the two therapy types depending on whether they were consonant with the mode of response (i.e. cognitive therapy for the cognitive responders and relaxation for the physiological responders) or non-consonant (for example, cognitive therapy for the physiological responders). The prediction that consonant therapies would be more effective than non-consonant ones was generally supported.

Evaluation of therapies would also be enhanced by a greater sophistication in assessment. Researchers rarely report long-term follow-ups of their patients which, as shown by Durham and Turvey (1987), can be very different from a short-term assessment. Nor do researchers often measure improvement within the cognitive system, usually relying on behavioural or self-report indices of anxiety. Earlier in the chapter, the notion that anxious individuals show heightened sensitivity to feared stimuli was discussed. One method used to demonstrate this was the dichotic listening task, where obsessive-compulsive patients were shown by Foa and McNally (1986) to be more likely to hear words associated with contamination than neutral words on the unattended side. The next step in their research was to treat these patients with *in vivo* exposure and response prevention. But instead of relying solely on behavioural and self-reported reductions in anxiety, Foa and McNally (ibid.) again asked the patients to take part in the dichotic listening task. Now, after treatment, the patients showed significant reductions in sensitivity to material on the unattended side, indicating that the treatment was effective in altering how the patients processed environmental information. The use of such cognitive assessments would greatly enhance research methodology.

These latter studies suggest that the selection of therapeutic programme might best be made not on the basis of type of disorder (e.g. phobic anxiety or generalized anxiety) but on the basis of the symptoms (physiological, behavioural or cognitive) shown by a particular patient. Such a viewpoint has implications for diagnosis as well: the therapist might be less interested in the classification of symptoms according to the DSM-III-R and more in the system or systems of anxiety response.

Control or restructuring of cognitions?

When the cognitive system has been selected for treatment there are further issues to be considered. One of the basic issues is whether it would be more helpful to assist the patient to gain control over his or her cognitions, or whether it would be more fruitful to attempt a fundamental change in content. In Meichenbaum's (1977) Stress Inoculation Training approach, both strategies are used: clients are taught to cope with their maladaptive cognitions as well as to question the underlying assumptions which lead to them. The coping component is designed to help the patient when he or she is under stress, while the restructuring component is designed to reduce the likelihood that stress will be experienced (Arnkoff 1986).

The support for the importance of being able to control intrusive thoughts comes from many sources. Earlier, Bandura's (1983) description of a phobic person's self-statements that he would be unable to control his reactions as he approached a snake was mentioned – the closer he approached the snake, the more he was overwhelmed by thoughts of his inability to hold the animal. Similarly, you may have noted that as the date of an important examination approaches you find yourself thinking about it more and more frequently. In the final days before it is due to take place it may be difficult to think of anything else. The thoughts become more and more frequent, uncontrollable and, if you are anxious about the exam, unpleasant (Kent and Jambunathan 1989). That is, the thoughts become increasingly intrusive so that on the day of the exam it may be difficult to focus your attention on anything else.

There is the possibility that it is this loss of control over unpleasant thoughts which is the most important aspect of anxiety. In a test of this idea, Kent and Gibbons (1987) asked subjects which of a list of negative thoughts they had experienced about dentistry and also to indicate how much control they could exert over them during the week leading up to a dental appointment. As expected, highly anxious subjects reported both a larger number of negative thoughts and a steeper decline in control than low or moderately anxious subjects. Analyses of covariance indicated that the effect for the extent of negative thoughts was reduced to statistical insignificance when control was partialled out, but differences in control remained significant when the number of thoughts was partialled out. That is, this study indicated that it was the degree of anticipated control the subjects perceived which was important in determining anxiety level rather than the number of cognitions themselves.

This notion has important implications for therapy. If control of cognitions is so important, then it may not be necessary for the therapist to help clients dispute their irrational beliefs and assumptions. Helping them to learn to distract themselves or control their thoughts in some other way would be sufficient.

The argument against this approach is that it is symptom orientated. Although it may affect the intrusiveness of negative cognitions by making it easier to dismiss them (D. A. Clark, 1986), it may not affect the distress the thoughts engender when they do arise. In other words, disputing the irrational beliefs underlying anxiety could mean that there are fewer negative thoughts to control and thus break the cycle maintaining anxiety more effectively.

If this is the aim of therapy then it will be necessary to gain a better idea of the nature of such irrational beliefs (Beck and Clark 1988). Deffenbacher et al. (1986) explored the possibility that specific cognitions and irrational beliefs are associated with specific difficulties. They found that anxiety about examinations and anxiety about negative evaluations from others have many basic similarities, but also some important differences. It seems that the former is associated with the belief that the possibility of negative events must be constantly dwelt upon, while the latter is more closely associated with the belief that it is essential to be approved of by everyone.

Although this distinction between control over versus change in thoughts is important conceptually, it may not make a difference clinically. In her study of treatments for test anxiety, Arnkoff (1986) assigned some students to a coping condition, which taught coping self-statements to be used during examinations, and other students to a restructuring condition, which involved disputing beliefs about examinations. She found that students in both conditions reported similar changes on measures of irrational beliefs and thought content.

Perhaps, as Bandura (1986) suggests, the various therapies are effective because they all increase an individual's sense of self-efficacy. Whether the aim is to control or change cognitions may be less important in the long run than helping patients to become more confident in their ability to deal with situations.

REFERENCES

American Psychiatric Association (1987) *Diagnostic and Statistical Manual of Mental Disorders. Third Edition (Revised)*, Washington, DC: APA.

Arnkoff, D. B. (1986) 'A comparison of the coping and restructuring components of cognitive restructuring', *Cognitive Therapy and Research* 10: 147–58.

Arnkoff, D. B. and Smith, R. J. (1988) 'Cognitive processes in test anxiety: an analysis of two assessment procedures in an actual test', *Cognitive Therapy and Research* 12: 425–39.

Bandura, A. (1983) 'Self-efficacy determinants of anticipated fears and calamities', *Journal of Personality and Social Psychology* 45: 464–9.

—— (1986) *Social Foundations of Thought and Action*, Englewood Cliffs, NJ: Prentice-Hall.

Bandura, A., Reese, L. and Adams, N. E. (1982) 'Microanalysis of action and fear arousal as a function of differential levels of self-efficacy', *Journal of Personality and Social Psychology* 43: 5–21.

Bandura, A., Taylor, C., Williams, S., Mefford, I. and Barchas, J. (1985) 'Catecholamine secretion as a function of perceived coping self-efficacy', *Journal of Consulting and Clinical Psychology* 53: 406–14.

Barlow, D. (1988) *Anxiety and its Disorders*, New York: Guilford Press.

Beck, A. and Clark, D. A. (1988) 'Anxiety and depression: an information processing perspective', *Anxiety Research* 1: 23–36.

Beck, A. and Emery, G. (1985) *Anxiety Disorders and Phobias*, New York: Basic Books.

Beck, A., Laude, R. and Bohnert, M. (1974) 'Ideational components of anxiety neurosis', *Archives of General Psychiatry* 31: 319–25.

Blackwell, R. T., Galassi, J. P., Galassi, M. D. and Watson, T. E. (1985) 'Are cognitive assessments equal? A comparison of think aloud and thought listing', *Cognitive Therapy and Research* 9: 399–413.

Borkovec, T. D., Robinson, E., Pruzinsky, T. and DePree, J. A. (1983a) 'Preliminary exploration of worry: some characteristics and processes', *Behaviour Research and Therapy* 21: 9–16.

Borkovec, T. D., Wilkinson, L., Folensbee, R. and Lerman, C. (1983b) 'Stimulus control applications to the treatment of worry', *Behaviour Research and Therapy* 21: 247–51.

Borkovec, T. D., Mathews, A., Chambers, A., Ebrahimi, S., Lytle, R. and Nelson, R. (1987) 'The effects of relaxation training with cognitive or nondirective therapy and the role of relaxation-induced anxiety in the treatment of generalised anxiety', *Journal of Consulting and Clinical Psychology* 55: 883–8.

Bower, G. H. (1981) 'Mood and memory', *American Psychologist* 36: 129–48.

Butler, G. and Mathews, A. (1983) 'Cognitive processes in anxiety', *Advances in Behaviour Research and Therapy* 5: 51–62.

—— (1987) 'Anticipatory anxiety and risk perception', *Cognitive Therapy and Research* 11: 551–65.

Butler, G., Cullington, A., Hibbert, G., Klimes, I. and Gelder, M. (1987) 'Anxiety management for persistent generalised anxiety', *British Journal of Psychiatry* 151: 535–42.

Cacioppo, J. T. and Petty, R. E. (1981) 'Social psychological procedures for cognitive response systems', in T. T. Merluzzi, C. Glass and M. Genest (eds) *Cognitive Assessment*, New York: Guilford Press.

Caroll, J. S. (1978) 'The effects of imagining an event on expectations for the event', *Journal of Experimental Social Psychology* 14: 88–96.

Chambless, D. L. and Gracely, E. J. (1989) 'Fear of fear and the anxiety disorders', *Cognitive Therapy and Research* 13: 9–20.

Chaves, J. F. and Brown, J. M. (1978) 'Self-generated strategies for the control of pain and stress', paper presented at the Annual Meeting of the American Psychological Association, Toronto.

Clark, D. A. (1986) 'Factors influencing the retrieval and control of negative cognitions', *Behaviour Research and Therapy* 24: 151–9.

—— (1988) 'The validity of measures of cognition: a review of the literature', *Cognitive Therapy and Research* 12: 1–20.

—— and de Silva, P. (1985) 'The nature of depressive and anxious intrusive thoughts: distinct or uniform phenomena?', *Behaviour Research and Therapy* 23: 383–93.

Clark, D. M. (1986) 'A cognitive approach to panic', *Behaviour Research and Therapy* 24: 461–70.

——, Salkovskis, P. M. and Chalkley, A. J. (1985) 'Respiratory control as a treatment for panic attacks', *Journal of Behavior Therapy and Experimental Psychiatry* 16: 23–30.

Deffenbacher, J. L., Zwemer, W., Whisman, M., Hill, R. and Sloan, R. (1986) 'Irrational beliefs and anxiety', *Cognitive Therapy and Research* 10: 281–92.

Dowrick, P. W. (1983) 'Self-modelling', in P. W. Dowrick and S. J. Biggs (eds) *Using Video: Psychological and Social Applications*, London: Wiley.

Durham, R. C. and Turvey, A. A. (1987) 'Cognitive therapy versus behaviour therapy in the treatment of chronic general anxiety', *Behaviour Research and Therapy* 25: 229–34.

Ehlers, A., Margraf, J., Roth, W., Taylor, C. and Birbaumer, N. (1988) 'Anxiety induced by false feedback in patients with panic disorder', *Behaviour Research and Therapy* 26: 1–11.

Ellis, A. (1962) *Research and Emotion in Psychotherapy*, New York: Lyle Stuart.

Emmelkamp, P. M. G. (1982) *Phobic and Obsessive-Compulsive Disorders*, New York: Plenum.

——, Kuipers, A. and Egeraat, J. (1978) 'Cognitive modification versus prolonged exposure in vivo: a comparison with agoraphobics as subjects', *Behaviour Research and Therapy* 16: 33–41.

Foa, E. B. and McNally, R. J. (1986) 'Sensitivity to feared stimuli in obsessive-compulsives: a dichotic listening analysis', *Cognitive Therapy and Research* 10: 477–85.

Franklin, J. A. (1987) 'The changing nature of agoraphobic fears', *British Journal of Clinical Psychology* 26: 127–33.

Garfield, S. L. (1971) 'Research on client variables in psychotherapy', in A. E. Bergin and S. L. Garfield (eds) *Handbook of Psychotherapy and Behavior Change*, New York: Wiley.

Genest, M. and Turk, D. C. (1981) 'Think-aloud approaches to cognitive assessment', in T. V. Merluzzi, C. Glass and M. Genest (eds) *Cognitive Assessment*, New York: Guilford Press.

Glass, C. R. and Arnkoff, D. B. (1983) 'Cognitive set and level of anxiety: effects on thinking processes in problematic situations', *Cognitive Therapy and Research* 7: 529–42.

Gray, J. A. (1982) *The Neuropsychology of Anxiety: An Inquiry into the Functions of the Septo-Hyppocampal System*, Oxford: Clarendon Press.
—— (1985) 'A whole and its parts: behaviour, the brain, cognition and emotion', *Bulletin of the British Psychological Society* 38: 99–112.
Haug, T., Brenne, L., Johnsen, B. H., Berntzen, D., Gotestam, K. and Hugdahl, K. (1987) 'A three-systems analysis of fear of flying: a comparison of a consonant vs a non-consonant treatment method', *Behaviour Research and Therapy* 25: 187–94.
Hibbert, G. A. (1984) 'Ideational components of anxiety: their origin and content', *British Journal of Psychiatry* 144: 618–24.
Hoogduin, K., De Haan, E., Schaap, C. and Arts, W. (1987) 'Exposure and response prevention in patients with obsessions', *Acta Psychiatrica Belgium* 87: 640–53.
Hugdahl, K. and Öst, L. (1985) 'Subjectively rated physiological and cognitive symptoms in six different clinical phobias', *Personality and Individual Differences* 6: 175–88.
Ingram, R. E. and Kendall, P. C. (1987) 'The cognitive side of anxiety', *Cognitive Therapy and Research* 11: 523–36.
Kendall, P. C. and Hollon, S. D. (1981) 'Assessing self-referent speech: methods in the measurement of self-statements', in P. C. Kendall and S. D. Hollon (eds) *Assessment Strategies for Cognitive-Behavioral Interventions*, New York: Academic Press.
—— (1989) 'Anxious self-talk: development of the anxious self-statements questionnaire', *Cognitive Therapy and Research* 13: 81–93.
Kendall, P. C., Williams, L., Pechacek, T. F., Graham, L., Shisslack, C. and Herzoff, N. (1979) 'Cognitive-behavioral and patient education interventions in cardiac catheterization procedures', *Journal of Consulting and Clinical Psychology* 47: 49–58.
Kent, G. (1984) 'Anxiety, pain and type of dental procedure', *Behaviour Research and Therapy* 22: 465–9.
—— (1985a) 'Cognitive processes in dental anxiety', *British Journal of Clinical Psychology* 24: 259–64.
—— (1985b) 'Memory of dental pain', *Pain* 21: 187–94.
—— (1986) 'The typicality of therapeutic surprises', *Behaviour Research and Therapy* 24: 625–8.
—— (1989) 'Memory of dental experiences as related to naturally-occurring changes in state anxiety', *Cognition and Emotion* 3: 45–53.
—— and Gibbons, R. (1987) 'Self-efficacy and the control of anxious cognitions', *Journal of Behavior Therapy and Experimental Psychiatry* 18: 33–40.
Kent, G. and Jambunathan, P. (1989) 'A longitudinal study of the intrusiveness of cognitions in test anxiety', *Behaviour Research and Therapy* 27: 43–50.
Kleinknecht, R. A. and Bernstein, D. A. (1979) 'Short term treatment of dental avoidance', *Behaviour Research and Therapy* 10: 311–15.
Klinger, E. (1984) 'A consciousness-sampling analysis of test anxiety and performance', *Journal of Personality and Social Psychology* 47: 1376–90.
Krohne, H. (1980) 'Parental child-rearing behavior and the development of anxiety and coping strategies in children', in I. G. Sarason and C. D. Spielberger (eds) *Stress and Anxiety, 7*, London: Hemisphere.
Lang, P. (1971) 'The application of psychophysiological methods to the study of psychotherapy and behavior modification', in A. E. Bergin and S. Garfield (eds) *Handbook of Psychotherapy and Behavior Change*, New York: Wiley.
Last, C. (1984) 'Cognitive treatment of phobia', in M. Hersen, R. Eisler and P. Miller (eds) *Progress in Behaviour Modification, 16*, London: Academic Press.
—— and Blanchard, E. (1982) 'Classification of phobic versus fearful non-phobics: procedural and theoretical issues', *Behavioral Assessment* 4: 195–210.
Last, C., Barlow, D. and O'Brien, G. (1985) 'Assessing cognitive aspects of anxiety', *Behavior Modification* 9: 72–93.

McNally, R. J. and Foa, E. B. (1987) 'Cognition and agoraphobia: bias in the interpretation of threat', *Cognitive Therapy and Research* 11: 567–81.

McNally, R. J. and Lorenz, M. (1987) 'Anxiety sensitivity in agoraphobics', *Journal of Behaviour Therapy and Experimental Psychiatry* 18: 3–11.

Marks, L. (1983) 'Are there anticompulsive or antiphobic drugs? Review of the evidence', *British Journal of Psychiatry* 143: 338–47.

Mathews, A. and MacLeod, C. (1986) 'Discrimination of threat cues without awareness in anxiety states', *Journal of Abnormal Psychology* 95: 131–8.

Meichenbaum, D. (1972) 'Cognitive modification of test anxious college students', *Journal of Consulting and Clinical Psychology* 39: 370–80.

—— (1977) *Cognitive-Behavior Modification: An Integrative Approach*, New York: Plenum.

Mizes, J. S., Landolf-Fritsche, B. and Grossman-McKee, D. (1987) 'Patterns of distorted cognitions and phobic disorders: an investigation of clinically severe simple phobics, social phobics and agoraphobics', *Cognitive Therapy and Research* 11: 583–92.

Mogg, K., Mathews, A. and Weinman, J. (1987) 'Memory bias in clinical anxiety', *Journal of Abnormal Psychology* 96: 94–8.

Mowrer, O. H. (1960) *Learning Theory and Behavior*, New York: Wiley.

Orton, I. K., Beiman, I., LaPointe, K. and Lankford, A. (1983) 'Induced states of anxiety and depression: effects on self-reported affect and tonic psychophysiological response', *Cognitive Therapy and Research* 7: 233–44.

Öst, L. and Hugdahl, K. (1983) 'Acquisition of agoraphobia, mode of onset and anxiety response patterns', *Behaviour Research and Therapy* 21: 623–31.

Persons, J. B. and Burns, D. D. (1985) 'Mechanisms of action of cognitive therapy: the relative contributions of technical and interpersonal interventions', *Cognitive Therapy and Research* 9: 539–51.

Rachman, S. J. and Hodgson, R. (1980) *Obsessions and Compulsions*, Englewood Cliffs, NJ: Prentice-Hall.

Rachman, S. J. and de Silva, P. (1978) 'Abnormal and normal obsessions', *Behaviour Research and Therapy* 16: 233–48.

Rapee, R. M. and Barlow, D. H. (1990) 'The psychological treatment of panic attacks and agoraphobic avoidance', in J. R. Walker, G. R. Norton and C. Foss (eds) *Panic Disorder and Agoraphobia: A Comprehensive Guide for the Practitioner*, Chicago: Brooks-Cole.

Reiss, S. and McNally, R. (1985) 'Expectancy model of fear', in S. Reiss and R. McNally (eds) *Theoretical Issues in Behavior Therapy*, New York: Academic Press.

Reiss, S., Peterson, R., Gursky, D. and McNally, R. (1986) 'Anxiety sensitivity, anxiety frequency and the prediction of fearfulness', *Behaviour Research and Therapy* 24: 1–8.

Rimm, D. C. and Litvak, S. G. (1969) 'Self-verbalisations and emotional arousal', *Journal of Abnormal Psychology* 74: 181–7.

Rimm, D. C., Janda, L., Lancaster, D., Nahl, M. and Dittma, K. (1977) 'An exploratory investigation of the origin and maintenance of phobias', *Behaviour Research and Therapy* 15: 231–8.

Salkovskis, P. (1985) 'Obsessional-compulsive problems: a cognitive-behavioural analysis', *Behaviour Research and Therapy* 23: 571–83.

—— and Harrison, J. (1984) 'Abnormal and normal obsessions – a replication', *Behaviour Research and Therapy* 22: 549–52.

Sarason, I. G. (1978) 'The Test Anxiety Scale: concept and research', in C. D. Spielberger and I. G. Sarason (eds) *Stress and Anxiety, Vol. 5*, pp.193–216.

—— (1985) 'Cognitive processes, anxiety and the treatment of anxiety disorder', in A. H. Tuman and J. D. Maser (eds) *Anxiety and the Anxiety Disorders*, London: Erlbaum.

Sartory, G. (1986) 'Effect of phobic anxiety on the orienting response', *Behaviour Research and Therapy* 24: 251–61.

Schwartz, R. M. (1986) 'The internal dialogue: on the asymmetry between positive and negative thoughts', *Cognitive Therapy and Research* 10: 591–605.

Seligman, M. (1971) 'Phobias and preparedness', *Behaviour Therapy* 2: 307–20.

Sewitch, T. S. and Kirsch, I. (1984) 'The cognitive component of anxiety: naturalistic evidence for the predominance of threat-related thoughts', *Cognitive Therapy and Research* 8: 49–58.

Shapiro, D. A. and Shapiro, D. (1982) 'Meta-analysis of comparative therapy outcome studies: a replication and refinement', *Psychological Bulletin* 92: 581–604.

Sherman, S., Ciladini, R., Schwartzman, D. and Reynolds, K. (1985) 'Imagining can heighten or lower the perceived likelihood of contracting a disease', *Personality and Social Psychology Bulletin* 11: 118–27.

Spielberger, L. D., Gorsuch, R., Lushene, R., Vagg, P. and Jacobs, G. (1983) *Manual for the State–Trait Anxiety Inventory*, Palo Alto, Calif.: Consulting Psychologists Press.

Thyer, B. A., Papsdorf, J. D. and Kramer, M. K. (1983) 'Phobic anxiety and irrational belief systems', *Journal of Psychology* 114: 145–9.

Thyer, B. A., Papsdorf, J., Davis, R. and Vallecorsa, S. (1984) 'Autonomic correlates of the subjective anxiety scale', *Journal of Behavior Therapy and Experimental Psychiatry* 15: 3–7.

Thyer, B. A., Parrish, R., Curtis, G., Nesse, R. and Cameron, O. (1985) 'Ages of onset of DSM-III anxiety disorders', *Comprehensive Psychiatry* 26: 113–22.

Turner, S. M. and Michelson, L. (1984) 'Obsessive-compulsive disorders', in S. M. Turner (ed.) *Behavioral Theories and Treatment of Anxiety*, London: Plenum.

van der Molen, G. M., van den Hout, M., Vroemen, J., Lousberg, H. and Griez, E. (1986) 'Cognitive determinants of lactate-induced anxiety', *Behavior Research and Therapy* 24: 677–80.

Wade, T. C. W., Malloy, T. E. and Proctor, S. (1977) 'Imaginal correlates of self-reported fear and avoidance behaviour', *Behaviour Research and Therapy* 15: 17–22.

Watts, F. N., McKenna, F., Sharrock, R. and Treise, L. (1986) 'Colour naming of phobia-related words', *British Journal of Psychology* 77: 97–108.

Williams, J. M. G., Watts, F. N., MacLeod, C. and Mathews, A. (1988) *Cognitive Psychology and Emotional Disorders*, Chichester: Wiley.

Williams, J. M. G., Murray, J. J., Lund, C., Harkiss, B. and de Franco, A. (1985) 'Anxiety in the child dental clinic', *Journal of Child Psychology and Psychiatry* 26: 305–10.

Wine, J. (1981).'Test anxiety and direction of attention', *Psychological Bulletin* 76: 92–104.

Woods, S. W. and Charney, D. (1988) 'Applications of the pharmacologic challenge strategy in panic disorders research', *Journal of Anxiety Disorders* 2: 31–49.

Woodward, R. and Jones, R. B. (1980) 'Cognitive restructuring treatment: a controlled trial with anxious patients', *Behaviour Research and Therapy* 18: 401–7.

Chapter 3

Depression

Vivien Twaddle and Jan Scott

INTRODUCTION

The central features of the syndrome of depression are depressed mood, pessimistic thinking, loss of interest and reduced energy levels. The abnormality of mood is the most consistent and prominent feature. It is differentiated from sadness because it is more persistent, perhaps exaggerated in response to the provoking stress and varies qualitatively from previous experiences of unhappiness. If the disorder is very severe the individual may also complain of biological symptoms such as sleep, appetite and weight disturbance, alteration of bowel functioning and loss of libido.

Traditionally, the disturbance of mood has been seen as the primary symptom of the depressive syndrome with the cognitive, motivational, behavioural and biological changes regarded as secondary phenomena. However, the cognitive revolution in psychology in the 1960s brought with it a number of explanations of depression which accord cognitive phenomena more status in the development, maintenance and treatment of the disorder. This chapter will begin by concentrating on four models of depression which reflect the range of cognitive factors deemed to be important in the cognitive-behavioural analysis of depression.

CONCEPTUALIZATION

Cognitive-behavioural models of depression

Beck's theory (Beck 1976)

Outline of the model

For Beck the salient psychological symptom of depression is the dysfunctional thinking which occurs at three different levels.

The cognitive triad The content of a depressed person's thinking (i.e. thoughts in the stream of consciousness) is dominated by negativity and characteristically forms a negative triad focused on views of self, world and future. These negative cognitions are referred to as automatic as they occur spontaneously and are not necessarily the result of directed thinking.

Systematic logical thinking errors   The depressed person's processing of events shows habitual errors of reasoning. These errors fall into a number of categories:

1 *arbitrary inference* – drawing a negative conclusion in the absence of supporting data: for example, an individual concludes 'my friend has fallen out with me' on the basis that they did not send them a birthday card.
2 *selective abstraction* – focusing on the detail (often negative) and usually at the expense of other more salient information: for example, an employee only notices the bad points in a report about himself and concludes 'they think badly of me'.
3 *overgeneralization* – arbitrarily drawing conclusions about a wide variety of things on the basis of single events: for example, a student who has failed her maths examination thinks to herself 'I'll never pass any of the other exams'.
4 *magnification and minimization* – making errors in evaluating the importance and implications of events: for example, by exaggerating the importance of an error in your day and minimizing all the achievements, you conclude that 'I'm no good at my job'.
5 *personalization* – relating external (often negative) events to oneself where this is not justified: for example, 'if I had warned my friend to stop smoking he wouldn't have died of a heart attack'.
6 *absolutistic dichotomous thinking* – thinking in polar opposites (black and white), something is either all good or a total disaster: for example, 'if my husband leaves me then I may as well be dead'.

Depressogenic schemata   This terms refers to the structural organization of thought such as attitudes, schemata or personal rules. These makes excessive use of directives (shoulds), of rigid quantifiers (always) or of pre-emptive class assignments (either/or). Thus, for example, 'in order to be happy I must be accepted by all people at all times', 'in order to be a worthy person I have to be successful in whatever I undertake'.

Comment

A vast number of studies investigating cognitive aspects of depression have found that depressed individuals do indeed differ from control groups in their thought content and thought processing. Most of these studies are correlational in nature, (i.e. no conclusions can be drawn as to whether the observed cognitive changes are a cause or a consequence of the depression). Weintraub *et al.* (1974), for example, observed that negative bias in thinking correlated significantly with ratings of depression. Nelson (1977) found significant correlations between a self-rating scale that measures the severity of depression, the Beck Depression Inventory (BDI)

(Beck *et al.* 1961), and various depressogenic attitudes. Blackburn and Bishop (1983) found highly significant correlations (p < 0.001) between scores on the BDI and a negative view of self, the world and the future as measured by semantic differential techniques. However, correlations with an observer rating scale, the Hamilton Depression Rating Scale (Hamilton 1960), were only significant for the negative view of self. Giles and Shaw (1987) found that negative views of self, world and future were interrelated and were specific to depression. In their study, low self-concept was a uniform finding in depression, while more negative views of world and future were positively related to the severity of depression.

Of greater interest are the studies which show that mood can be altered by manipulating a person's cognitions. They are important because the main criticism of Beck's theory is that it interprets dysfunctional cognitive phenomena as causal when they may really be *symptoms* of depression. If cognitions are proven merely to be the bi-product of depression then it would throw into question the usefulness of looking for procedures which attempt to change cognitive style and then cast doubt on the whole status of cognitive therapy.

The evidence that cognitions precipitate mood swings is convincing. Experimental manipulation of mood is particularly powerful because these studies have been able to eliminate variables which might otherwise contribute to disturbed mood. Several forms of mood induction procedures have been used (for a review see Williams 1984) and all provide strong evidence that asking subjects to create voluntarily images, thoughts or memories which are unpleasant or unhappy has a negative effect on mood state. The value of having shown this is somewhat debatable: severe mood disturbance is a rather unreliable indicator of depression (Depue and Monroe 1978); ratings of mood alone cannot be used as an indicator of depression as it occurs in other states (for example, anxiety), whereas the diagnosis of a depressive illness is made on the basis of a number of different variables. In addition, a high score on the self-rating scales may be due to a variety of inadvertent factors (see later). However, Williams (1984) suggests that the evidence from mood-induction techniques is not completely redundant. Although the experimental evidence may not tell us anything that is unique to depression, he argues that it should alert clinicians to the possibility that depression may have cognitive antecedents and should not just be analysed in biological terms.

Rational-emotive therapy (Ellis 1970)

Outline of the model

Ellis's approach is similar to that of Beck in so far as maladaptive thoughts are seen as mediators of depressed feelings and behaviours, but there is less emphasis on the subordinate level of thinking such as automatic thoughts and more on basic assumptions and beliefs. The model asserts that emotional change results from discovering and tackling the irrationality of beliefs. The primary psychological disturbance is considered to consist of the tendency to make devout absolutistic evaluations of perceived events. These evaluations are couched in the form of dogmatic 'musts', 'shoulds', 'have to's', 'got to's' and 'oughts'. These 'musts' are considered to form the core of psychological disturbance. However, Ellis (1988) also argues that four types of irrational thinking are derived from 'must' statements: awfulizing; low frustration tolerance (or 'I-can't-stand-it-it is'); global negative evaluation of self, others and/or the world; and always-never thinking.

Comment

In earlier writings Ellis (1962) described a list of particular beliefs considered to be at the root of emotional disturbances such as depression. Since that time the rationale for a finite list of irrational beliefs has been seriously questioned (Arnkoff and Glass 1982). Indeed, Ellis's recent theorizing has focused less on providing *lists* of irrational beliefs and more on emphasizing *types* of irrational beliefs as described above (Ellis 1988).

Far less research has concentrated on this model of depression as compared to Beck's. A number of studies have found correlational evidence that irrational beliefs are associated with depression (LaPointe and Crandell 1980; Thorpe *et al*. 1983; Watkins and Rush 1983). More specifically, Fösterling (1985) indicated a clear relationship between negative emotional states following non-attainment of goals when individuals held irrational beliefs that they 'must' achieve their goals as opposed to when they 'would like to'. Rohsenow and Smith (1982) reported significant correlations between depression and two of Ellis's main irrational beliefs – i.e. 'bad things must not occur and it is awful if they do' and 'one should be thoroughly competent, adequate and achieving in all possible respects if one is to consider himself worthwhile'. Finally, Silverman *et al*. (1984) reported that dysfunctional thinking, including absolutistic demands on oneself and others, was more prominent in individuals during their depressed states but not following recovery. Haaga and Davison (1986) in their brief review argue that while there is some evidence that irrational beliefs correlate with negative disturbed emotions like depression, it cannot be determined from the evidence that irrational beliefs play a causal role in the production of these emotions.

Self-control model of depression (Rehm 1977, 1981)

Outline of this model

Here depression is seen as a cognitive-behavioural deficit in self-control (Rehm 1977, 1981), with its roots in the theory outlined by Kanfer (1970). It attempts to combine behavioural and cognitive formulations of depression. The central premiss is that the control that an individual has over his or her own behaviour can be divided into three processes: self-monitoring, self-evaluation and self-reinforcement. The following deficits are postulated in depression:

1   *Self-monitoring:*
   (a) Depressed individuals attend selectively to negative events in their environment to the exclusion of positive ones.
   (b) Depressed individuals attend selectively to immediate as opposed to long-range outcomes of their behaviour.
2   *Self-evaluation:*
   (a) Depressed individuals tend to set stringent self-evaluative standards for their behaviour.
   (b) Depressed individuals make negative attributions for their behaviour such that they attribute positive outcomes to external factors and negative outcomes to internal factors.
3   *Self-reinforcement:*
   (a) As a result of the above, depressed individuals administer insufficient positive reinforcement to themselves.
   (b) Depressed individuals administer excessive self-punishment to themselves.

Comment

If one removes the behavioural terminology, it then becomes apparent that some of Rehm's concepts are not far removed from Beck's. Self-monitoring and self-evaluation can be seen to be related to systematic logical errors of reasoning.

Evidence consistent with Rehm's formulation comes from a number of sources. The question of distortion in the self-monitoring of events has been addressed in studies that have looked at differences between depressed and non-depressed people in their interpretation of ambiguous stimuli (Finkel *et al.* 1979; Weintraub *et al.* 1974). Depressed individuals have been shown to be more negative in their evaluation of themselves: for example, Young *et al.* (1981) showed an increased tendency to attribute negative personality descriptions to themselves; and Fry (1976) found that, unlike normal subjects, depressed subjects did not describe themselves more positively after success experiences. Not all the literature is consistent, however: Gotlib (1979) found no difference in self-evaluation between normals and depressives. Other studies suggest that it is not so much distortion in self-evaluation that is crucial, but that depressed individuals have much higher aspirations for themselves but not for others, especially in a skilled task (Golin and Terrell 1977). With respect to self-reinforcement, a number of sources have shown that depressed subjects do indeed reward themselves less and punish themselves more than do non-depressed subjects (Lobitz and Post 1979; Rozensky *et al.* 1977). A fuller critical discussion has recently been given by Rehm (1988) himself.

The learned-helplessness model (Seligman 1981)

Outline of the model

Like Rehm's approach this model sees control as an important psychological issue in depression but emphasizes the role of an individual's expectations of it. It proposes that organisms which attempt but cannot achieve control experience motivational (i.e. reduced initiation of voluntary responses), cognitive (i.e. erroneously pessimistic expectations of future contingency) and emotional (i.e. depressed mood) disruption. The initial model was seriously inadequate but has since been reformulated (Abramson *et al*. 1978) to include four basic premisses which, if they co-occur, are sufficient to account for the above deficits of depression:

1 *Expected aversiveness:* Here, the individual expects that high aversive outcomes are probable or that highly desired outcomes are improbable.
2 *Expected uncontrollability:* Here, the individual expects that he or she will be able to do nothing about the likelihood of this state of affairs.
3 *Attributional style:* Here, the individual possesses a maladaptive attributional style so that negative events are attributed to internal, stable and global causes, and positive events to external, unstable and specific causes. (This component of the model states that attributions for an uncontrollable event determine the individual's response to the event. The three dimensions are: *internal–external*, i.e. how far the cause of the event is attributed to factors within or outside oneself; *stable–unstable*, i.e. how changing or unchanging the cause is seen to be; *global–specific*, i.e. how circumscribed or far reaching it is perceived to be. For example, if you fail an examination you might see it as being because you did not have the necessary ability or that you did not try hard enough (both internal attributions, but ability is a more unchanging or 'stable' cause than effort which can be increased next time around). Or you may understand the failure as being due to the stiff examination board (another 'stable' but this time 'external' attribution). Or you may believe that it was just bad luck and next time it will be all right ('unstable', 'external'). On the other hand you may think that you did not have the ability to pass either 'specifically' because you lack ability in this subject, but that this has no bearing on other examinations, or 'globally' in that you are no good at taking formal examinations. (Taken from Williams 1984.))
4 *Severity of motivational, cognitive and emotional symptoms:* Here, the greater the certainty of the aversive state of affairs and the expected uncontrollability, the greater the motivational and cognitive deficits. In addition, the greater the importance to the individual of the uncontrollable event, the greater will be the affective and self-esteem disruption.

Comment

Most studies on the learned-helplessness model have focused on the third premiss, regarding attributional processes, but the results are inconsistent. Klein *et al*. (1976) showed that depressed university students make more internal attributions for failure than non-depressed subjects. However, Abramson *et al*. (1978) could not replicate these results in depressed patient groups. Likewise, comparisons between depressed and non-depressed adults have not shown significant differences in attributions for stability and for those of effort, luck, task difficulty and perceived control (Garber and Hollon 1980; Kuiper 1978). Similarly ambiguous results have been found using the attributional-style questionnaire (Manly *et al.* 1982; Seligman *et al.* 1979). On the other hand, Raps *et al.* (1982) demonstrated a maladaptive attributional style in clinical depressives that was not present in control groups of hospitalized schizophrenics. Heimberg *et al.* (1987) found that stable, global attributions showed both specificity and sensitivity for depression as opposed to anxiety disorder.

Other experiments have attempted to show the link between the shift in expectancy and subsequent behaviour as postulated by the model. Klein and Seligman (1976) demonstrated that in normal subjects the experience of non-contingent failure produces subsequent performance deficits. In these experiments people were asked to solve anagrams as quickly as they could. In fact these word puzzles were insoluble so the subjects failed to solve them despite instigating all their problem-solving skills. The subjects, therefore, came to the conclusion that outcome (non-resolution of the problem) is independent of response (attempts to solve the anagram). This non-contingent failure reduces their motivation to engage in the next task and cognitively engenders a sense of helplessness. Increases in expectation following successful task performance were associated with subsequent increases in performance levels. Other results in a similar population have been inconsistent (for example, Willis and Blaney 1978).

Alloy *et al.* (1988) are very critical of the research strategies utilized to test their hypothesis (which has now been renamed the 'Hopelessness Theory of Depression'). They argue that the ambiguous and inconsistent results are a function of the failure of investigators to comprehend the purported causal relationships specified by this theory (an issue which will be discussed in more detail on page 65). With regard to expectancy, Bandura (1977) has made an important distinction between *outcome* expectancy (i.e. the probability that an outcome will occur, given an appropriate response) and *response* expectancy or self-efficacy (i.e. the probability that the particular individual is capable of performing the necessary response). From this, Davis and Yates (1982) predicted that depression would be induced under conditions where response expectancy (self-efficacy) was low and outcome expectancy high. No depression would occur if both expectancy factors were low. They found evidence for this in males, but interestingly not for females. The distinction between these two types of expectancy is only recently being applied in research and is an exciting development.

Cognitive measures of depression

Integral to any model of depression is the empirical evidence to support it and this can only be collected if there are reliable and valid measures of the cognitive phenomena described. Clark (1988) has discussed in detail the status of measures of cognition and concludes that cognitive assessment is still at an exploratory stage. Most of the procedures devised for depression are of the self-statement type and the best known are shown in Table 3.1.

Table 3.1 Measures of depressive cognitions

Name of measure	What it measures
Automatic Thoughts Questionnaire (Hollon and Kendall 1980)	Frequency of negative automatic thoughts
Crandell Cognitions Inventory (Crandell and Chambless 1986)	Frequency of negative automatic thoughts
Self-verbalization Questionnaire (Missel and Sommer 1983)	Frequency of negative automatic thoughts
Cognitions Check-list (Beck *et al.* 1987)	Frequency of negative automatic thoughts
Hopelessness Scale (Beck *et al.* 1974)	Expectations of hopelessness/ irritability to overcome aversive situations or explain values
Cognitive Style Test (Wilkinson and Blackburn 1981)	Differential cognitions to given situations
Attributional Style Questionnaire (Seligman *et al.* 1979)	Causal attributions
Learned Helplessness Scale (Rosenbaum 1980)	Locus of control and associated concepts of self-reinforcement, self-efficacy, problem-solving strategies
Dysfunctional Attitude Scale (Weissman 1979)	Beck-type underlying depressive assumptions/schema
Distressing Thoughts Questionnaire (Clark 1986)	Frequency, emotional intensity, controllability and unacceptability of anxious and depressive cognitions
Irrational Beliefs Test (Jones 1968)	Ellis-type irrational beliefs
Frequency of Reinforcement Questionnaire (Heiby 1982)	Self-control variables – Self-reinforcement, positive self-attitudes
Self-control Questionnaire (Fuchs and Rehm 1977)	Self-control variables – self-monitoring, self-evaluation and self-reinforcement

Self-statement questionnaires have inherent problems. The majority attempt to measure frequency of cognitions. However, an individual may endorse a cognition because of its importance to them rather than its regularity. Alternatively, they may be endorsing an item on the questionnaire because of its similarity to their own thoughts or again due to the personnel relevance they put upon it.

The very nature of self-statement questionnaires relies upon recognition of, rather than on recall of, thought processes, and as such they are susceptible to processes of selective memory bias, social desirability, post-performance rationalization, inconsistent responses and demand characteristics. Several procedures have been devised which rely upon recall processes – for example, the cognitive response test (Watkins and Rush 1983). These methods are also not without criticism, as the assessment strategy itself can interfere with cognitive functioning, only a portion of the cognitions may be reported, and with simultaneous cognitions subjects might report those of low importance or personal relevance (for example, Mavissakalian *et al*. 1983) or cognitions of low frequency but high relevance may be missed. Limitations aside, it has been argued that open-ended recall is a more accurate procedure than closed fixed choice (Coyne and Gotlib 1983). This is a serious indictment of cognitive-behaviour therapy since most of its empirical support has been based on the latter. However, Clark (1988) is optimistic about the validity of such measures and points out that fixed-choiced procedures can over-come some of the difficulties that a depressed individual has in accessing specific memories. Because fixed-choice procedures rely on recognition rather than recall they can overcome the problem of concentration and memory impairments seen in depression.

Over and above the issue of recall and recognition, however, Clark (1988) criticizes the present over-reliance on the self-endorsement technique which still tends to focus on the frequency of cognitions at the expense of other dimensions like emotional impact, degree of belief and self-control (Kendall and Hollon 1981; Linden and Simons 1983; Wilson *et al*. 1983). The distressing-thoughts question-naire (Clark 1986) is his attempt at a more content-valid measure which attempts to distinguish between frequency, emotional intensity, controllability and unaccep-tability of depressive and anxious cognitions.

Clark (1988) argues that the validity of measures of cognition relies on a number of additional factors: the degree to which it can differentiate between functional and dysfunctional groups; its capacity to demonstrate concurrent and discriminant validity (i.e. high correlations with corresponding measures and low correlations with measures of other dysfunctional states); its sensitivity to treatment interven-tions; and its capacity to access relevant thought content.

Measures of depressive cognitions do very well on the issue of concurrent validity (for example, Crandell and Chambless 1986; Dobson and Shaw 1986; Ross *et al*. 1986). Fewer studies have investigated discriminant validity; exceptions here are the unequivocal findings of Beck *et al*. (1987), using the cognitions check-list, and the equivocal ones of Clark (1986), with the distressing-thoughts question-naire. Studies of treatment sensitivity are at early stages (for example, Dobson and Shaw 1986; Eaves and Rush 1984; Simons *et al*. 1984).

Reliability is of course relevant in any discussion of validity. The implications of schemata-based cognitive models such as Beck's are that cognitive structures (attitudes) are relatively stable and enduring, while cognitive products (automatic thoughts) are more transient and mood dependent. Theoretically, measures of underlying beliefs and assumptions (for example, the Dysfunctional Attitude Scale (DAS) – Weissman 1979) should show more temporal stability and hence greater reliability coefficients than self-statement inventories. (For a review of DAS see Segal and Shaw 1988.) The evidence so far is not encouraging as the reliability coefficients are in fact comparable over similar time periods (for example, Beck *et al*. 1987; Clark and de Silva 1985). This issue clearly requires more research.

Development and maintenance of depression

It has long been recognized that the occurrence of certain types of negative life events precede the onset of most clinical depressions (Brown and Harris 1978). However, only a minority of those who experience such events become clinically depressed; most do not (Scott 1988a). Of those who *do* become depressed, some recover rapidly, whereas others fall into a pattern of chronic or recurrent depression. Any credible cognitive model of depression needs to be able to answer the following questions adequately:

1 What underlines the vulnerability of some people to becoming clinically depressed after a life event?
2 What determines whether depression will be transient or more persistent?

The two models which have been the centre of dialetic debate on these questions are Beck's model and the hopelessness theory (previously the learned-helplessness model). They each propose a different cognitive diathesis (predisposition) to stress explanation: in the hopelessness theory this is a depressogenic attributional style while Beck's model focuses on the negative schemata laid down in childhood. The rest of this section will focus on these two theories. The key to understanding these diathesis–stress models lies in, first, the type of causal pathways they espouse and, second, the type of depression upon which they focus.

Both models are *sufficiency* and not *necessity* models. (Sufficient causal factors are those that, once present, assure manifestation of a set of symptoms. Necessary causal factors are those that must be present in order for a set of symptoms to become manifest.) Both models also acknowledge either explicitly (the hopelessness theory) or implicitly (Beck's theory) that there is a heterogeneity of depressive disorders and that people become depressed for reasons other than those stated in cognitive theories. It is due to a misunderstanding of these key issues that research efforts have so far been inconclusive.

There have been major advances in the hopelessness model to the extent that the original learned-hopelessness thesis is hardly recognizable. Alloy and co-workers (1985, 1988) have contributed the key theoretical papers in this field. The latest (Alloy *et al.* 1988) suggests that 'perceived negatively' rather than 'controllability' is the first link in the causal chain resulting in the theoretical subtype 'hopelessness depression'. The key to understanding this chain is in the different causal concepts: 'necessary', 'sufficient' and 'contributory'. They assert that there are several contributory factors which serve to increase the probability that an individual will respond to a negative event with an expectation of hopelessness.

Some of these contributory factors are proximal and include the causal attributions made for the event, the degree of importance attached to the event and situational information about the event (consensus, consistency and distinctiveness). Typically, individuals would tend to attribute an event to internal, stable and global causes if the event is low in consensus (for example, failing a maths examination while others do well), high in consistency (for example, typically

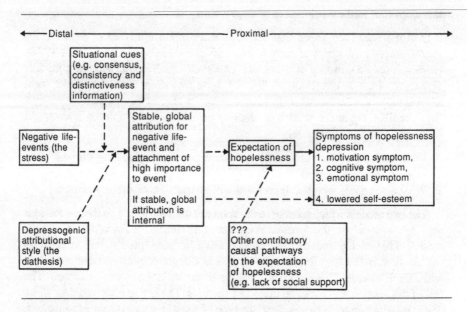

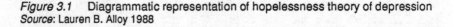

Causal chain specific in the hopelessness theory of depression → sufficent causes;--→, contributory causes

Figure 3.1   Diagrammatic representation of hopelessness theory of depression
Source: Lauren B. Alloy 1988

failing in maths) and low in distinctiveness (typically failing exams in other subjects as well as maths). Thus, situational cues have a constraining effect on attributions. In their 1978 reformulation Abramson *et al*. identified a more distal factor that may also constrain the attributional process and thereby influence the content of causal attributions for an event – individual differences in attributional style. This remains an important element in the latest model – i.e. that some individuals exhibit a general tendency to attribute negative events to internal, stable, global factors and to view these events as very important. The attributions made for a particular event will be the joint function of the situational factors surrounding the event and the attributional style of the individual. Situational cues being equal, people exhibiting this hypothesized depressogenic attributional style would be more likely to become hopeless and in turn to develop motivational, cognitive, emotional and self-esteem symptoms of hopelessness depression. This aspect of hopelessness theory, conceptualized as the diathesis–stress component (Metalsky *et al*. 1982, 1987) implies that a depressogenic attributional style in a particular content domain (for example, for interpersonal events) provides a specific vulnerability to hopelessness depression when an individual is confronted with negative life events in that same content domain (for example, social rejection). This matching of content area, attributional style and life events is reminiscent of Beck's vulnerability theory where latent schemata are reactivated by stressors similar to those which initially formed that schemata.

To date, no research has been carried out to assess the 'proximal sufficient cause' featured in the theory, i.e. hopelessness. Strategies have so far focused on comparisons of the attributional styles of depressed versus non-depressed individuals or future depressed versus future non-depressed individuals (Abramson *et al*. 1988). Given the causal relations specified in the theory, it is argued that it is inappropriate to test validity in this way (Alloy *et al*. 1988) because the differences in depressive attributions will be influenced by a number of factors:

1 base rates of depressogenic attributional style:
2 negative life events;
3 subtypes of depression other than hopelessness depression. (More appropriate strategies of testing this model are discussed on p.76).

Beck's model suggests that those individuals at risk of depression have acquired (as a result of certain types of negative experiences in childhood) dysfunctional cognitive structures, or schemata. When exposed, as adults, to negative events that in some way 'match' the earlier experience on which the schemata were based, these structures will be reactivated. This results in the systematic errors in processing and negative patterns of thinking consistent with these schemata: for example, parental death may sensitize the individual to thoughts of irretrievable loss when separation occurs in later life.

Note the similarity here with the hopelessness model, i.e matching of content domain of life event and attributional styles. Beck's view would suggest that differences should be demonstrable at the level of cognitive schemata between those prone to depression and those not, even at times when the former are not actually depressed. A major methodological problem with the research to test this focuses on how to measure the dysfunctional cognitive structures which characterize those vulnerable to depression. Researchers seem to have accepted that they can be measured by a simple questionnaire – the Dysfunctional Attitudes Scale. But this is questionable. A very consistent finding from the questionnaire studies of thinking and depression in depressed patients has been that during the episode of depression, measures of negative schemata are elevated, but on recovery, scores for depressed patients return to levels not significantly different from controls (see Hamilton and Abramson 1983; Silverman *et al*. 1984; Simons *et al*. 1984). Those studies which have found elevation following recovery (for example, Eaves and Rush 1984) have used remission periods of only two to three weeks. Teasdale (1988) argues that the results are probably more a function of incomplete recovery rather than a true reflection of a recovered cognitive state. Teasdale (1983, 1988) has proposed an alternative approach to the vulnerability to depression – the differential-activation hypothesis. He proposes that it is the differences in patterns of thinking that are activated *in the depressed state* which constitutes the crucial vulnerability factor determining whether a depression is mild and transient or becomes severe and longer lasting. Teasdale (1985) assumes that the normal course of mild depression is one of remission and recovery and so the pertinent factors are those that impede this recovery, leading to clinically significant depression.

The differential-activation hypothesis suggests that depressed mood increases the accessibility of representations in memory of depressing experiences, and the accessibility of negative interpretative categories and constructs. The effects of mood on memory have been most extensively studied and are well established (Blaney 1986; Fennell *et al.* 1987). There is also evidence for effects of depressed mood negatively biasing a range of other cognitive processes, such as interpretations of ambiguous situations, self-efficacy expectations, the evaluation of oneself and estimates of future probability of negative events (Bower 1981, 1983). In this respect, Teasdale's account heavily relies on Bower's associative-network theory. It also overlaps with Beck's idea about accessing negative constructs and representations will increase the likelihood that the individual will interpret their current experiences as highly aversive and uncontrollable. However, Teasdale (1988) points to a central distinction between Beck's view and the differential-activation hypothesis. Beck suggests that negative interpretative constructs become accessible as a result of a precise fit between an environmental event and a cognitive schema. Activation of the schema activates thematically related negative constructs which, presumably, will be in relatively restricted areas close to the content of the schema. By contrast, Teasdale views the increased accessibility of negative constructs and representations as a consequence of the depressed state reactivating the negative constructs that have been most frequently and prototypically associated with previous experience of depression as a whole. It follows that a wider range of constructs would be affected, and most importantly, that these constructs need not bear a particularly close relationship to the event that initially provoked the depression. Teasdale describes a vicious cycle whereby the reciprocal relationship between depressed mood and cognitive processing act in positive feedback fashion to reinforce each other and so to intensify and maintain the depression. He argues that establishing this cycle depends upon a complex interplay between environmental, biological and psychological factors. Environmental adversity and the level of social support can affect the extent to which the experience is seen as aversive and uncontrollable. Biological influences focus on the intensity of the initial depressive response which enhances the effects of mood (Clark and Teasdale 1982). Psychological factors of importance focus on the individual differences in the nature of representations and interpretative constructs that are accessible in the state of mild depression (Teasdale and Dent 1987). However, Martin (1985) suggests that there are persistent individual differences in cognitive processing related to neuroticism which are apparent even in normal mood states, which predispose people towards the development of depression. Interestingly, Teasdale and Dent (1987), showed that these two aspects of vulnerability are not mutually exclusive. In their study women who had previously been depressed were compared with those who had not. The results suggested that a pernicious combination of both negative affectivity (neuroticism) and a tendency for global selfdevaluative concepts which are activated in mild depression may be important in the development of recurrent depression.

TREATMENT

The four models outlined in the first section have developed their own treatment packages for depression. Rehm and Seligman can be subsumed under the broad title 'self-management therapy' and Beck and Ellis under cognitive-restructuring approaches. The two categories reflect the different emphases of the models. Self-management primarily focuses upon the process of cognitive-behavioural control or expectancy of control. Cognitive-restructuring methods focus on the more expansive arena of cognitive structures.

Self-management therapy

These therapies focus on control processes regulating behaviour. They concentrate primarily on covert cognitive processes, and occasionally on cognitive structures.

Clinical methods

Models and techniques have typically focused on problems of self-control behaviour where there is a conflict between delayed and immediate reinforcers. Jogging is a good example, as is dieting. The goal is to obtain important distant rewards. In self-management terms depression is characterized by a generalized low self-efficacy. The two models in the previous section which have given rise to self-management procedures are those of Rehm (1984) and Seligman (1981).

The Seligman model suggests that a depressive attributional style would interact with an aversive major life event to produce a generalized helpless belief and thus depression. The model differentiates between personal helplessness (i.e. the belief that one is individually incapable of producing certain responses) and a universal helplessness (i.e. the belief that desirable consequences are not under anyone's personal control). This corresponds to Bandura's (1977) differentiation between conceptions of efficacy and outcome expectations, but this has not been applied clinically. Seligman (1981) suggested four as yet untested therapeutic strategies:

1 *Environmental enrichment*: where the person is placed in an environment that is relatively undemanding and provides a variety of success and efficacy experiences.
2 *Personal-control training*: where the individual is taught specific skills to give more control in pertinent domains.
3 *Resignation training*: where the individual is helped to accept his or her helplessness in certain domains in ways that would reduce the aversiveness of the helplessness or reduce the desirability of the unobtainable goal.

4 *Attribution training*: where the individual would be taught to attribute failures and successes in a more positive and realistic fashion.

By far the most extensive work in depression comes from Rehm's (1977) model. Fuchs and Rehm (1977) have developed a structured group-therapy programme which has been expanded and revised in a series of therapy outcome studies (Rehm 1984). The programme involves didactic presentation of self-management concepts, discussion of the applicability of these concepts to individual participants and homework assignments where participants practise non-depressive self-management skills. Their programme is summarized in Table 3.2.

Table 3.2   Elements and techniques of the self-management group programme for depression

Elements of self-management	Therapeutic techniques
Self-monitoring	(a) Monitoring positive activities and self-statements. Recording daily moods.
	(b) Focus on monitoring activities with positive delayed outcomes.
Self-evaluation	(a) Goal setting which is positive, realistic and attainable.
	(b) Attributional concepts introduced.
Self-reinforcement	(a) Principles of self-reinforcement. Overt self-reinforcement, i.e. easy and accessible positive activities. Covert self-reinforcement using positive self-statements following increasingly difficult goals.

Outcome studies

Rehm's therapy programme has been evaluated in six outcome studies. The first two involved validation of the programme in contrast to traditional controlled conditions, i.e. non-specific group therapy and waiting-list (Fuchs and Rehm 1977; Rehm *et al*. 1979). Both studies showed superior effects of self-control treatment. At 1 year follow-up they showed that both treatment and control groups retained this improvement but that the self-management subjects reported fewer and less intense episodes of depression and fewer instances of seeking additional therapy than the controls. This finding has been replicated in the four subsequent studies to be described in the next paragraph which suggests that self-management training leads to the acquisition of skills for dealing more effectively with depressive episodes.

The second two studies in the series attempted but failed to identify the major therapeutic components of the therapy programme (Kornblith *et al*. 1983; Rehm *et al*. 1981). No significant differences resulted between the therapy conditions (self-monitoring, self-evaluation and self-reinforcement), all of which reduced depression. Tressler and Tucker (1980) compared self-monitoring and self-evaluation with self-monitoring and self-reinforcement and found that at post-test and at 12 week follow-up, the self-monitoring and self-reinforcement condition proved significantly superior. The last two studies in the series compared treatment targets. Separate self-management programmes were devised targeting behavioural activity and self-statements. Behavioural, cognitive and combined target conditions were compared and no differences were found (Rehm 1988; Rehm et al. 1985). Again all three programmes were effective and, interestingly, equally effective in achieving cognitive and behavioural targets.

The programme has been compared to other approaches: Fleming and Thornton (1980) compared Beck's cognitive therapy with the self-management programme and a non-directive therapy control condition. All conditions improved significantly at post-test and follow-up, with the greatest improvement on several measures occurring in the self-management condition. Roth et al. (1982) compared the self-management therapy alone with tricyclic antidepressant (TCA) drug therapy. While the TCA group responded faster during therapy, at post-test and 3-month follow-up there were no significant differences between the conditions.

The main problem with evaluating the effectiveness of this cognitive approach against others is that self-management strategies form a significant component of the other cognitive therapies.

Cognitive-restructuring approaches

Like self-management therapies these focus on cognitive processes but primarily in order to access cognitive structures. There is much more emphasis on the structural dimension of cognitions compared to the self-management therapies.

Clinical methods

The two most widely used cognitive restructuring methods are rational-emotive therapy (RET) (Ellis 1970) and cognitive therapy (CT) (Beck 1976). The major differences between the former and the latter are, first, that RET aims from the outset to expose the individual's central irrational beliefs whereas CT initially focuses on the automatic thoughts, and only in the latter stages of therapy are the underlying assumptions examined. Second, RET uses semantic and persuasive techniques to a greater extent than CT (Hollon and Beck 1979).

According to Dryden and Ellis (1988), there are three key phases in RET. Initially, the client is helped to identify the links between their irrational beliefs and the dysfunctional emotions and behavioural responses to these. The therapist then helps the individual to gain 'intellectual insights' by challenging these distorted beliefs and encouraging the person to see the self-enhancing value of alternative rational beliefs. The final working-through phase of RET then helps them achieve 'emotional insight', whereby the client is able to internalize these rational ideas – i.e. they are able to act on them, and integrate them into their emotional repertoire. RET uses a combination of behavioural, cognitive and emotive techniques. The behavioural strategies focus on self-reinforcement, anti-procrastination exercises and 'stay in there' activities (where the client is taught to tolerate uncomfortable situations for extended periods). Cognitive techniques help the client challenge their irrational philosophies predominantly through question-ing, hypothesis testing and imagining. Emotive strategies use direct challenges to clients' irrational beliefs through humorous confrontation, therapist self-disclosure and other vigorous disputing methods. Evidence for the efficacy of RET in overcoming depression and suicidal ideas is mainly derived from uncontrolled case-studies (for example, Emmelkamp and Mersch 1982).

Beck's (1976) cognitive therapy (CT) combines cognitive and behavioural methods into a specific therapeutic package that aims to help the individuals to examine and understand the content of their thinking. They are then encouraged to distance themselves from the thought by viewing it as hypothesis to be tested rather than fact, i.e. a possible but not necessarily true proposition. Through careful consideration of their beliefs the individual gradually develops more adaptive thinking patterns. Changing the belief will change the emotional reaction to it.

The most prominent behavioural methods in CT include self-monitoring and scheduling activities. While these methods are at times used to increase activity and to provide experiences of mastery and pleasure, the cognitive change resulting from these methods is the primary focus of therapy. Behavioural assignments will serve either to test a hypothesis that the individual holds, or to provide a setting that will provoke the formation of new hypotheses that can subsequently be tested.

Much of CT centres on the use of the 'Daily Record of Dysfunctional Thoughts Form' (DRDT) (Beck et al. 1979) (see Figure 3.2). This comprises four columns: situation, belief, emotional consequence and the alternative or counter responses (i.e. the more rational or functional belief). The individual is taught to use the DRDT by noting when they experience an unpleasant or puzzling affective state.

First of all the individual is helped to distinguish between thoughts and feel-ings – for example, that they were feeling anxious about coming to therapy and thinking that they might be asked upsetting questions. They then note the situation and the stream of thoughts that immediately preceded or occurred coincidentally with the emotional response (i.e. the automatic thoughts). Intervention begins by helping the individual come up with alternative responses to the automatic thoughts by examining the inferences made when emotionally upset.

The DRDT has several secondary but very useful purposes. Individuals can record the degree of conviction in the automatic thought before and after it is examined. This allows for a check on the questioning. When a strong conviction in an automatic thought remains, this shows that questioning has not resolved the initial concern; either a key issue has been missed or the individual has made an accurate characterization of the situation. In the latter case the therapist can help the individual to examine the significance of the meaning of their characterization. Similarly, the degree of affective response can be recorded both before and after the thinking analysis. Little or no change in affect is evidence that the individual

DATE	SITUATION Describe: 1. Actual event leading to unpleasant emotion, or 2. Stream of thoughts, daydream, or recollection, leading to unpleasant emotion.	EMOTION(S) 1. Specify sad/anxious/angry etc 2. Rate degree of emotion, 1:100	AUTOMATIC THOUGHT(S) 1. Write automatic thought(s) that preceded emotion(s) 2. Rate belief in automatic thought(s) 0:100%	RATIONAL REPSONSE 1. Write rational response to automatic thought(s) 2. Rate belief in rational response, 0:100%	OUTCOME 1. Re-rate belief in automatic thought(s) 0-100% 2. Specify and rate subsequent emotions, 0-100

EXPLANATION: when you experience an unpleasant emotion, note the situation that seemed to stimulate the emotion. (If the emotion occurred while you were thinking, daydreaming, etc., please note this.) Then note the automatic thought associated with the emotion. Record the degree to which you believe this thought: 0%=not at all; 100%=completely. In rating degree of emotion: 1=a trace; 100=the most intense possible.

Figure 3.2 Daily record of dysfunctional thoughts
Source: Aaron T. Beck *et al.* (1979) Guildford Press

still holds relevant beliefs that have not been identified, indicating the need for further investigations. Finally, the degree of conviction in the rational response can be recorded so that whether or not it is convincing to the individual can be picked up. The DRDT can be worked on in the session and can be used independently by the individual in homework assignments outside the therapy session.

CT teaches the individual to ask themselves three specific questions (see DeRubeis and Beck 1988):

1   What is the evidence for and against the belief?
2   What are the alternative interpretations of the event or situation?
3   What are the real implications if the belief is correct?

As DeRubeis and Beck (ibid.) point out, a thought is often reported initially in a form that is not able to be directly challenged in these three ways – for example, 'she has snubbed me because she thinks I am boring'. Here it is important to extract the implications or meanings that are important for the individual, rather than asking questions about how reasonable the inference is. An appropriate question here would be 'and what would it mean if it were true if you were boring?' This is what Beck calls the 'downward arrow' or vertical questioning technique. It also allows the client and therapist to identify underlying schemata.

An alternative and often complementary approach to these three questions involves teaching individuals to recognize when their thinking falls into one of the categories of logical thinking errors discussed previously (see p. 57). By doing this the individual can discount the improbable or illogical inference, reframe it in a less extreme form or analyse the inference using the three questions mentioned above.

Later on in therapy the client and therapist should begin to notice consistencies in the kinds of beliefs that are integral to the feelings of depression. This consistency will not be evident at a surface level but rather at a deeper level of personal meaning: for example, many of the individual's entries may include the belief 'if I am not the best ... I am worthless'. The assumptions are identified and analysed in a similar way to the beliefs. The aim is to alter maladaptive underlying schemata and to reduce the individual's vulnerability to a depressive relapse.

Outcome studies

Although many case-studies support the clinical utility of RET in depression (see Dryden and Ellis 1988), there is a disappointing lack of any larger scale controlled clinical trials. In a detailed review of RET by Haaga and Davison (1989) six studies of its use in depression are quoted, but only two of them used clinical populations (Kelly 1982; McKnight *et al*. 1984). Both studies were on quite small samples and the treatment programmes were brief. RET was found to be equivalent to a behavioural treatment of depression or a supportive treatment in the first study (Kelly 1982) and as effective as social-skills training in the second (McKnight *et al*. 1984).

Beck's CT has been extensively researched over the past 25 years. The first major study of its use in a clinically depressed sample was published by Rush *et al.* (1977). They found that, at 12 weeks, individuals treated with CT experienced greater symptom remission than those treated with imipramine. The methodology of this study has been justifiably criticized but it still represents an important milestone in psychological research as it was the first time that a form of psychotherapy had been found to be more effective than a drug therapy in the treatment of an acute depressive episode. Since that time numerous controlled trials have been published, which, when taken together, answer many of the questions relating to the efficacy of CT. Summarizing these findings we may currently state that:

1 There is no study yet published that shows individual CT to be less effective than pharmacotherapy in unipolar, non-psychotic out-patient depressives when used in the treatment of the *acute* depression episode (Beck *et al.* 1979; Blackburn *et al.* 1981; McLean and Hakstian 1979; Murphy *et al.* 1984; Teasdale *et al.* 1984).
2 CT appears to be superior to other forms of psychological intervention given for equivalent periods of time (McLean and Hakstian 1979) and produces a more rapid improvement than the usual treatment prescribed for depressed clients seen in the primary-care setting (Teasdale *et al.* 1984).
3 There is a trend which reaches significance in some studies for CT to have a lower drop-out rate than other treatments offered (Blackburn *et al.* 1981; Murphy *et al.* 1984; Rush *et al.* 1977).
4 CT does not appear to be contraindicated in those endogenous-type symptoms and those of lower socio-economic class (Blackburn *et al.* 1986), or those of lower intelligence (Williams and Moorey 1989).
5 The use of CT in combination with drug therapy does not appear to have any negative effects but the evidence for any additive effects is less clear cut (Beck *et al.* 1979; Blackburn *et al.* 1981; Murphy *et al.* 1984).

The outcome for group CT for depression is less researched and less impressive. All but one study (Ross and Scott 1985) found that individual therapy was more beneficial than group CT (for example, Rush and Watkins 1981). However, Shaw (1977) found that group CT was more effective than group behaviour therapy or a non-directive group therapy.

In the past few years, four research groups have completed follow-up studies of their original controlled trials of individual CT to examine the potential prophylactic effect of this approach, (1-year follow-up: Beck *et al.* 1985; Kovacs *et al.* 1981; Simons *et al.* 1986; 2-year follow-up: Blackburn *et al.* 1986). The naturalistic design and lack of adequate drug treatment in the follow-up phase mean that the results must be treated with some caution, but all of these studies support the prophylactic role of CT in depression. In addition, differences in outcome between drug-treated and CT-treated groups have always favoured the CT-treated clients, and these differences reached significance at some points during the follow-up period (for example, Blackburn *et al.* 1986). More research is required in this area, but these initial results must be viewed as very promising.

FUTURE DEVELOPMENTS

To bring this chapter to a close, we would like to address the issue of future developments in the cognitive-behavioural theories of depression and the therapies to which they give rise. First, it is important to remember that just because a *therapy* appears to be effective, it does not mean that the underlying *theory* is correct. Cognitive theories do appear to have validity when applied to maintenance models of depression, but there are still many gaps when we examine closely the current aetiological models. In order to test out the hopelessness theory of depression (Alloy *et al.* 1988), researchers will first need to demonstrate that the interaction between hypothesized attributional style and negative life events precipitates a depressive episode. Second, as Alloy *et al.* (ibid.) point out, this interaction should reliably predict the symptom profile shown by the individual (i.e. hopelessness depression should be a recognizable syndrome). Early attempts to do such studies have not yet proved conclusive (for example, Parry and Brewin 1988), but have highlighted once again the heterogeneity of depressive disorders and the inherent difficulties of carrying out this type of research. Ideally, future studies should be prospective and longitudinal (as cross-sectional analysis cannot identify temporal sequencing). Even with this approach the role of underlying cognitive structures (irrational beliefs, attributions, schemata) is likely to remain problematic. With regard to Beck's model, early studies using the DAS (Weissman 1979) showed a significant reduction in the dysfunctional-attitudes scores as the depression became less severe (Simons *et al.* 1984); one interpretation of this was that the underlying assumptions of a depressive might be *state* rather than *trait* markers of the disorder (Williams and Moorey 1989). However, since then it has been shown that remitted depressives compared to controls may continue to have abnormally high DAS scores (Dobson and Shaw 1986), or, even if their scores return into the normal range they show specific dysfunctional attitudes which persist despite receiving pharmacotherapy (Reda *et al.* 1985). Perhaps it is these more specific assumptions that act as trait markers for cognitive vulnerability to depression. Also, it could be postulated that cognitive therapies might have a particular role in tackling these 'drug resistant' cognitions.

Two problems need to be overcome before the role of cognitive structures can be validated. First, we need to develop more subtle assessment tools with less bias towards self-referent material. Hopefully, we will then be in a position to measure what we *need* to measure as opposed to what we *can* measure. Second, we need to consider carefully at what point in a study these assessments are introduced. Teasdale's (1988) work suggests that depressive schemata may lie dormant during remission, so tests on recovered depressives may be uninformative. His hypothesis suggests that these individuals would differ from normals in the amount of affective disturbance needed to produce global negative self-evaluations (Teasdale and Dent

1987). Thus, the optimal time to elicit vulnerability to depression is when there is likely to be some small amount of affective disturbance (Williams and Moorey 1989).

Arguments about the sensitivity of measures of cognitive structures are also pertinent to discussions of the assessment of cognitive processes. The negative bias in a depressive's thinking is well documented (see Lloyd and Lishman 1975), but recently tests of autobiographical memory in depression have revealed a subtle deficit in their recall. Depressives (as opposed to normal controls) are also less *specific* when asked to recall positive and negative events from the past. This deficit is more marked for positive memories (Williams and Scott 1988). Further work is required to evaluate the implications of this finding. Is it a trait marker that persists even in remitted depressives? Might it help to explain the very valuable function of diary-keeping during therapy (where the individual is constantly monitoring specific events rather than being asked for general information)?

Lastly, with regard to cognitive theories it is important to have in mind that depression does not occur in a vacuum. External and internal events will influence the cognition–emotion interface. Scott (1988a) has recently reviewed social and biological influences that may precipitate the cognitively vulnerable individual into depression. She also supported the need to integrate social and biological models with Beck's and Teasdale's cognitive theories. Similarly, Healey and Williams (1988) tried to formulate a model incorporating information on circadian dysrhythmias and their interaction with, and influence upon, cognitive components of the learned helplessness theory of depression. A comprehensive aetiological model of depression presents a tremendous challenge, but we would postulate that the interaction of cognitions and affect will play a central role in any such proposal. Linking social and cognitive models of depression may help explain why individuals respond differently to the same life event. An individual's cognitive interpretation of their experience will determine the contextual threat of a life event and affect its perceived consequences. Alternatively, mood change as a consequence of neuro-endocrine dysfunction may access more negative cognitive processing as suggested in the differential-activation hypothesis.

Developments in cognitive therapies are likely to proceed on two fronts: first, the extension of controlled studies to establish the efficacy of the different types of approach and its adaption to different client groups: this work will also attempt to identify factors predictive of individual treatment response; and second, experiments within therapy sessions or using different cognitive interventions focused on trying to identify the mechanisms of action of these techniques.

The role of Beck's CT for out-patient depressives is now well established on both sides of the Atlantic. However, it would be encouraging if more extensive controlled studies with clinical samples were applied to the other therapies, particularly the cognitive-restructuring approach of RET. The next phase will then be to establish the role of these therapies in preventing relapse. The evidence from the currently available studies of the long-term effects of Beck's CT is encouraging. However, such evidence should only be viewed as preliminary because of the use of 'naturalistic' follow-up techniques. The subjects were not engaged from the start in a long-term study; they all took part in short-term treatment studies of 12–15 weeks; and the researchers then attempted to trace these individuals 1–2 years later and retrospectively assess their progress. Criteria such as retrospective reporting of depressive symptoms or return treatment were used to assess outcome. However, too many factors may influence the reasons that an individual seeks further help. In some cases re-referral will be a function of relapse; others may have no such symptoms or signs. Others still may show evidence of depression but decide not to obtain further therapy. Thus, a carefully designed prospective study of the prophylactic effects of CT versus pharmacotherapy is required that defines from the outset its criteria for relapse and recovery.

Analysis of the original studies of individual 'Beck-style' CT for depression suggests that we can make some predictions about who may respond to this type of approach. The most interesting finding so far is that learned resourcefulness (or self-control) correlates highly with response to CT (Simons *et al*. 1985). High scores on the self-control measure used was the single best predictor of a good response to CT and a poor response to drug therapy. This work should be pursued as it could be postulated that individuals with an internally located locus of control will relate well to a therapy in which they actively work to promote self-change, while those who perceive an external locus will respond more positively to being a recipient of an externally imposed treatment. Not surprisingly, psychological mindedness and clients who identify strongly with cognitive explanation of their depression also seem to respond well to this form of treatment. Dysfunctional attitude scores are also predictive of relapse. If DAS scores remain high at the end of treatment the client is at significantly greater risk of relapse (Simons *et al*. 1986).

A major challenge to the cognitive therapies will be their ability to produce change in the atypical depressives. Can it help the severely depressed in-patient, the psychotically ill client or the individual with a chronic depressive disorder? The answers at present are unclear. Case-studies of CT with individual in-patients (for example, Blackburn 1989) and group approaches (Eidelson 1984) are encouraging. Scott (1988b) has developed a model of CT that can be applied to chronically depressed clients. The results are modest, but show some promise. The therapy also addresses the secondary handicaps developed by the individual during the course of a prolonged illness and incorporated family sessions to address negative cognitions within this network (which may impede the patient's recovery). The use of CT with psychotic patients should still be treated with caution. Some work has shown how moderately severe problems can be approached using cognitive techniques. Beck's original guideline suggested that psychosis was a contra-indication to CT because of the individual's impaired reality testing. Interestingly, one possible use of CT with this client group might be to use cognitive strategies to enhance compliance with medication (Cochrane 1984).

A fertile research area in the next few years will be the studies trying to elicit the 'active ingredients' of these therapies. Obviously, if it were possible to define more clearly the mechanisms of change it might be feasible to develop an even shorter form of this treatment package. Thought-change procedures (as used in cognitive restructuring) have been compared with thought-exploration techniques (more typical of dynamic psychotherapies). Within-session experiments suggest that thought-change procedures produce a greater mood shift than thought-exploration techniques (Teasdale and Fennel 1982). This finding was confirmed by Persons and Burns (1985), who also noted that the more intensely held the original belief, the smaller the mood change. When procedures to reduce the frequency of negative thoughts are used with clients with higher endogenous depression scores, they show a more attenuated mood shift than those at the neurotic end of the spectrum (Fennell *et al.* 1987). Why is this? Bebbington (1985) has suggested that in severe endogenous depressions the negative cognitions become autonomous of mood state. Further studies are required to see if endogenous symptoms render cognitive techniques less effective. The problems of identifying causal mechanisms of change have been clearly outlined by Hollon *et al.* (1987). Their review also provides useful guidelines on the direction future research in this area should take.

This overview must of necessity be selective and the reader should refer to other recent publications to supplement this review (Dobson 1988; Scott 1988a, Williams and Moorey 1989). There are still many important and quite fundamental questions to be answered about cognitive theories and cognitive-behavioural therapies. In attempting to do so, cognitive-behavioural therapies will continue to lead the field in clinical research on the efficacy of psychological approaches to depression because of their emphasis on setting up testable hypotheses. The cognitive revolution is by no means over. It is an exciting time to be a cognitive therapist!

REFERENCES

Abramson, L. J., Alloy, L. B. and Metalsky, G. I. (1988) 'The cognitive diathesis-stress theories of depression: toward an adequate evaluation of the theories' validities', in L. B. Alloy (ed.) *Cognitive Processes in Depression*, New York: Guilford Press.

Abramson, L. J., Seligman, M. E. P. and Teasdale, J. D. (1978) 'Learned helplessness in humans: critique and formulation', *Journal of Abnormal Psychology* 87: 49–74.

Alloy, L. B., Abramson, G. I. and Hartlage, S. (1988) 'The helplessness theory of depression: attributional aspects', *British Journal of Clinical Psychology* 27: 5–21.

Alloy, L. B., Clements, C. and Kolden, G. (1985) 'The cognitive diathesis – stress theories of depression: therapeutic implications', in S. Reiss and R. Bootzin (eds) *Theoretical Issues in Behavior Therapy*, New York: Academic Press.

Arnkoff, D. B. and Glass, C. R. (1982) 'Clinical cognitive constructs: examination, evaluation and elaboration', in P. C. Kendall (ed.) *Advances in Cognitive-Behavioral Research and Therapy*, Vol. 1, New York: Academic Press, pp. 1–34.

Bandura, A. (1977) 'Self-efficacy: towards a unifying theory of behavior change', *Psychological Review* 84: 191–215.

Bebbington, P. (1985) 'Three cognitive theories of depression', *Psychological Medicine* 15: 759–69.

Beck, A. T. (1976) *Cognitive Therapy and the Emotional Disorders*, New York: New American Library.

———, Rush, A. J., Shaw, B. F. and Emery, G. (1979) *Cognitive Therapy of Depression*, New York: Guilford Press.

Beck, A. T., Weissman, A., Lester, D. and Trexler, L. (1974) 'The measurement of pessimism: the hopelessness scale', *Journal of Consulting and Clinical Psychology* 42(6): 861–5.

Beck, A. T., Brown, G., Steer, R. A., Eldelson, J. I. and Riskind, J. H. (1987) 'Differentiating anxiety and depression utilizing the cognition checklist', *Journal of Abnormal Psychology* 96: 179–83.

Beck, A. T., Hollon, S. D., Young, J., Bedrosian, R. C. and Budenz, D. (1985) 'Combined cognitive-pharmacotherapy versus cognitive therapy in the treatment of depressed outpatients', *Archives of General Psychiatry* 42: 142–8.

Beck, A. T., Ward, C. H., Mendelson, M., Mock, J. E. and Erbaugh, J. K. (1961) 'An inventory for measuring depression', *Archives of General Psychiatry* 33: 561–71.

Blackburn, I. M. (1989) 'Severely depressed inpatients', in J. Scott, J. M. G. Williams and A. T. Beck (eds) *Cognitive Therapy in Clinical Practice: An Illustrative Case Book*, London: Routledge.

——— and Bishop, S. (1983) 'Changes in cognition with pharmacotherapy and cognitive therapy', *British Journal of Psychiatry* 143: 609–17.

Blackburn, I. M., Eunson, K. M. and Bishop, S. (1986) 'A two year naturalistic follow-up of depressed patients treated with cognitive therapy, pharmacotherapy and a combination of both', *Journal of Affective Disorders* 10: 67–75.

Blackburn, I. M., Bishop, S., Glen, I. M., Whalley, L. J. and Christie, J. E. (1981) 'The efficacy of cognitive therapy in depression: a treatment trial using cognitive therapy and pharmacotherapy, each alone and in combination', *British Journal of Psychiatry* 139: 181–9.

Blaney, P. H. (1986) 'Affect and memory: a review', *Psychological Bulletin* 99: 229–46.

Bower, G. H. (1981) 'Mood and memory', *American Psychologist* 36: 129–48.

——— (1983) 'Affect and cognition', in D. E. Broadbent (ed.) *Functional Aspects of Human Memory*, London: The Royal Society, pp. 149–64.

Brown, G. W. and Harris, T. (1978) *Social Origins of Depression*, London: Tavistock.

Clark, D. A. (1986) 'Factors influencing the retrieval and control of negative cognitions', *Behaviour Research and Therapy* 24: 151–9.

——— (1988) 'The validity of measures of cognition', *Cognitive Therapy and Research* 12: 1–20.

——— and de Silva, P. (1985) 'The nature of depressive and anxious intrusive thoughts: distinct or uniform phenomena?', *Behaviour Research and Therapy* 23: 383–93.

Clark, D. M. and Teasdale, J. D. (1982) 'Diurnal variation in clinical depression and accessibility of memories of positive and negative experiences', *Journal of Abnormal Psychology* 91: 87–95.

Cochrane, S. D. (1984) 'Preventing medical non-compliance in the outpatient treatment of affective disorders', *Journal of Consulting and Clinical Psychology* 52: 873–8.

Coyne, J. C. and Gotlib, I. H. (1983) 'The role of cognition in depression: a critical appraisal', *Psychological Bulletin* 94: 472–505.

Crandell, C. J. and Chambless, D. L. (1986) 'The validation of an inventory for measuring depressive thoughts: the Crandell Cognitions Inventory', *Behaviour Research and Therapy* 24: 403–11.

Davis, F. W. and Yates, B. T. (1982) 'Self-efficacy expectancies versus outcome expectancies as determinants of performance deficits and depressive affect', *Cognitive Therapy and Research* 6: 23–35.

Depue, R. A. and Monroe, S. M. (1978) 'Learned helplessness in the perspective of the depressive disorders: conceptual and definitional issues', *Journal of Abnormal Psychology* 84: 3–20.

DeRubeis, R. J. and Beck, A. T. (1988) 'Cognitive therapy', in K. S. Dobson (ed.) *Handbook of Cognitive-Behavioral Therapies*, New York: Guilford Press.

Dobson, K. S. (1988) 'The present and future of the cognitive-behavioural therapies', in K. S. Dobson (ed.) *Handbook of Cognitive-Behavioral Therapies*, New York: Guilford Press.

—— and Shaw, B. F. (1986) 'Cognitive assessment with major depressive disorders', *Cognitive Therapy and Research* 10: 13–29.

Dryden, W. and Ellis, A. (1988) 'Rational-emotive therapy', in K. S. Dobson (ed.) *Handbook of Cognitive-Behavioral Therapies*, New York: Guilford Press.

Eaves, G. and Rush, A. J. (1984) 'Cognitive patterns in symptomatic and remitted unipolar major depression', *Journal of Abnormal Psychology* 90: 14–22.

Eidelson, J. (1984) 'Cognitive group therapy for depression', *International Journal of Mental Health* 13: 54–60.

Ellis, A. (1962) *Reason and Emotion in Psychotherapy*, New York: Lyle Stuart.

—— (1970) *The Essence of Rational Psychotherapy: A Comprehensive Approach to Treatment*, New York: Institute of Rational Living.

—— (1988) *How to Stubbornly Refuse to Make Yourself Miserable about Anything – Yes Anything!*, New York: Lyle Stuart.

Emmelkamp, P. M. G. and Mersch, P. P. (1982) 'Cognition and exposure *in vivo* in the treatment of agoraphobia: short-term and delayed effects', *Cognitive Therapy and Research* 6: 77–90.

Fennell, M. J. V., Teasdale, J. D., Jones, S. and Damle, A. (1987) 'Distraction in neurotic and endogenous depression: an investigation of negative thinking in major depressive disorder', *Psychological Medicine* 17: 441–52.

Finkel, C. B., Glass, C. R. and Merluzzi, T. V. (1979) 'Differential discrimination of self-referent statements by depressives and non-depressives', paper presented at the Meeting of the Association for the Advancement of Behavior Therapy, San Francisco, December.

Fleming, B. M. and Thornton, D. W. (1980) 'Coping skills training as a component in the short-term treatment of depression', *Journal of Consulting and Clinical Psychology* 48: 652–5.

Försterling, F. (1985) 'Rational-emotive therapy and attribution theory: an investigation of the cognitive determinants of emotions', *British Journal of Cognitive Psychotherapy* 3(1): 12–25.

Fry, P. S. (1976) 'Success, failure and self-assessment ratings', *Journal of Consulting and Clinical Psychology* 44: 413–19.

Fuchs, C. Z. and Rehm, L. P. (1977) 'A self-control behavior program for depression', *Journal of Consulting and Clinical Psychology* 45: 206–15.

Garber, J. and Hollon, S. D. (1980) 'Universal vs. personal helplessness in depression, belief in uncontrollability or incompetence?', *Journal of Abnormal Psychology* 89: 56–66.

Giles, D. E. and Shaw, B. F. (1987) 'Beck's cognitive theory of depression: convergence of constructs', *Comprehensive Psychiatry* 28(5): 416–27.

Golin, S. and Terrell, F. (1977) 'Motivational and associative aspects of mild depression in skill and chance tasks', *Journal of Abnormal Psychology* 86: 389–401.

Gotlib, I. H. (1979) 'Self-control processes in depressed and non-depressed psychiatric patients: self-evaluation', paper presented at the meeting of the American Psychological Association, New York, September.

Haaga, D. A. and Davison, G. C. (1986) 'Cognitive change methods', in F. H. Kanfer and A. P. Goldstein (eds) *Helping People Change*, New York: Pergamon.

—— (1989) 'Outcome studies of rational-emotive therapy', in M. Bernard and R. Di-Giuseppe (eds) *Inside REI*, San Diego: Academic Press.

Hamilton, E. W. and Abramson, L. J. (1983) 'Cognitive patterns and major depressive disorder: a longitudinal study in a hospital setting', *Journal of Abnormal Psychology* 92: 173–84.

Hamilton, M. (1960) 'A rating scale for depression', *Journal of Neurology, Neurosurgery and Psychiatry* 23: 56–62.

Healey, D. and Williams, J. M. G. (1988) 'Dysrhythmia, dysphoria and depression: the interaction of learnt helplessness and circadian dysrhythmia in the pathogenesis of depression', *Psychological Bulletin* 103: 163–78.

Heiby, E. M. (1982) 'A self reinforcement questionnaire', *Behaviour Research and Therapy* 20: 397–401.

Heimberg, R. G., Vermilyea, J. A., Dodge, C. S., Beckter, R. E. and Barlow, D. H. (1987) 'Attributional style, depression and anxiety: an evaluation of the specificity of depressive attributions', *Cognitive Therapy and Research* 11: 537–50.

Hollon, S. D. and Beck, A. T. (1979) 'Cognitive therapy of depression', in P. E. Kendall and S. D. Hollon (eds) *Cognitive Behavioral Interventions: Theory, Research, Procedures*, New York: Academic Press.

Hollon, S. D. and Kendall, P. C. (1980) 'Cognitive self-statements in depression: development of an automatic thoughts questionnaire', *Cognitive Therapy and Research* 4: 383–95.

Hollon, S. D., DeRubeis, R. J. and Evans, M. D. (1987) 'Causal mechanisms of change in treatment for depression: discriminating between non-specificity and non-causality', *Psychological Bulletin* 102: 139–49.

Jones, R. G. (1968) 'A factored measure of Ellis's irrational belief system, with personality and maladjustment correlates', unpublished doctoral dissertation, Texas Technological College.

Kanfer, F. H. (1970) 'Self-regulation: research, issues, and speculations', in C. Neuringer and J. L. Michael (eds) *Behavior Modification in Clinical Psychology*, New York: Appleton-Century-Crofts.

Kelly, L. M. (1982) 'Rational-emotive therapy versus Lewinsohnian-based approaches to the treatment of depression', unpublished doctoral dissertation, University of Georgia.

Kendall, P. C. and Hollon, S. D. (1981) 'Assessing self-referent speech: methods in the measurement of self-statements', in P. C. Kendall and S. D. Hollon (eds) *Assessment Strategies for Cognitive-Behavioral Interventions*, New York: Academic Press.

Klein, D. C. and Seligman, M. E. P. (1976) 'Reversal of performance deficits and perceptual deficits in learned helplessness and depression', *Journal of Abnormal Psychology* 85: 11–25.

Klein, D. C., Fencil-Morse, E. and Seligman, M. E. P. (1976) 'Learned helplessness, depression and the attribution of failure', *Journal of Personality and Social Psychology* 33: 508–16.

Kornblith, S. J., Rehm, L. P., O'Hara, M. W. and Lamparski, D. M. (1983) 'The contribution of self-reinforcement training and behavioral assignments to the efficacy of self-control therapy for depression', *Cognitive Therapy and Research* 7: 499–527.

Kovacs, M., Rush, A. J., Beck, A. T. and Hollon, S. D. (1981) 'Depressed outpatients treated with cognitive therapy or pharmacotherapy: a one year follow-up', *Archives of General Psychiatry* 38: 33–9.

Kuiper, N. A. (1978) 'Depression and causal attribution for success and failure', *Journal of Personality and Social Psychology* 36: 236–46.

LaPointe, K. and Crandell, C. (1980) 'Relationship of irrational beliefs to self-reported depression', *Cognitive Therapy and Research* 4: 239–50.

Linden, M. and Simons, G. (1983) 'Formal and content thought disorders in depression', unpublished manuscript, Psychiatrische Klinik Der Freien Universität Berlin, Berlin, FRG.

Lloyd, G. G. and Lishman, W. A. (1975) 'Effects of depression on the speed of recall of pleasant and unpleasant experiences', *Psychological Medicine* 5: 173–80.

Lobitz, W. C. and Post, R. D. (1979) 'Parameters of self-reinforcement and depression', *Journal of Abnormal Psychology* 83: 33–41.

McKnight, D. L., Nelson, R. O., Hayes, S. C. and Jarrett, R. B. (1984) 'Importance of treating individually assessed response classes in the amelioration of depression', *Behavior Therapy* 15: 315–35.

McLean, P. D. and Hakstian, A. R. (1979) 'Clinical depression: comparative efficacy of outpatient treatments', *Journal of Consulting and Clinical Psychology* 47: 818–36.

Manly, P. C., McMahan, R. J., Bradley, C. F. and Davidson, P. O. (1982) 'Depressive attributional style and depression following childbirth', *Journal of Abnormal Psychology* 91: 245–54.

Martin, M. (1985) 'Neuroticism as cognitive predisposition towards depression: a cognitive mechanism', *Personality and Individual Differences* 6: 353–65.

Mavissakalian, M., Michelson, L., Greenwald, D., Kornblith, S. and Greenwald, M. (1983) 'Cognitive-behavioral treatment of agoraphobia: paradoxical intention v. self-statement training', *Behaviour Research and Therapy* 21: 75–86.

Metalsky, G. I., Halberstadt, L. J. and Abramson, L. Y. (1987) 'Vulnerability to depressive mood reaction: toward a more powerful test of the diathesis–stress and causal mediation components of the reformulated theory of depression', *Journal of Personality and Social Psychology* 52: 386–93.

Metalsky, G. I., Abramson, L. J., Seligman, M. E. P., Semmel, A. and Peterson, C. (1982) 'Attributional styles and life events in the classroom: vulnerability and invulnerability to depressive mood reactions', *Journal of Personality and Social Psychology* 43: 612–17.

Missel, P. and Sommer, G. (1983) 'Depression and self-verbalisation', *Cognitive Therapy and Research* 7: 141–8.

Murphy, G. E., Simons, K. D., Weizel, R. D. and Lustman, P. J. (1984) 'Cognitive therapy and pharmacotherapy: simply and together in the treatment of depression', *Archives of General Psychiatry* 41: 33–41.

Nelson, R. O. (1977) 'Methodological issues in assessment via self-monitoring', in J. D. Cone and R. P. Hawkins (eds) *Behavioural Assessment: New Directions in Clinical Psychology*, New York: Brunner/Mazel.

Parry, G. and Brewin, C. R. (1988) 'Cognitive style and depression: symptom related, event-related or independent provoking factor?', *British Journal of Clinical Psychology* 27: 23–5.

Perris, C. (1989) 'Cognitive therapy in schizophrenia', in C. Perris and I. M. Blackburn (eds) *Cognitive Psychotherapy: Theory and Practice*, Heidelberg: Springer Verlag.

Persons, J. B. and Burns, D. D. (1985) 'Mechanisms of action of cognitive therapy: the relative contributions of technical and interpersonal interventions', *Cognitive Therapy and Research* 9: 539–51.

Raps, C. P., Peterson, C., Reinhard, K. E., Abramson, L. J. and Seligman, M. E. P. (1982) 'Attributional style among depressed patients', *Journal of Abnormal Psychology* 91: 102–8.

Reda, M. A., Carpiniello, B., Secchiaroli, L. and Blanco, S. (1985) 'Thinking, depression and antidepressants: modified and unmodified depressive beliefs during treatment with amitryptiline', *Cognitive Therapy and Research* 9: 135–44.

Rehm, L. P. (1977) 'A self-control model of depression', *Behavior Therapy* 8: 787–804.

—— (ed.) (1981) *Behavior Therapy for Depression*, New York: Academic Press.

—— (1984) 'Self-management therapy for depression', *Advances in Behaviour Research and Therapy* 6: 83–98.

—— (1988) 'Self-management and cognitive processes in depression', in L. B. Alloy (ed.) *Cognitive Processes in Depression*, New York: Guilford Press.

——, Lamparski, D., Romano, J. M. and O'Hara, M. W. (1985) 'A comparison of behavioral, cognitive, and combined target versions of a self-control therapy program for depression', manuscript (quoted in Rehm 1988).

Rehm, L. P., Fuchs, C. Z., Roth, D. M., Kornblith, S. T. and Romano, J. M. (1979) 'A comparison of self control and assertion skills treatments of depression', *Behavior Therapy* 10: 429–42.

Rehm, L. P., Kornblith, S. J., O'Hara, M. W., Lamparski, D. M., Romano, J. M. and Volkin, J. (1981) 'An evaluation of the major components in a self-control behavior therapy program for depression', *Behavior Modification* 5: 459–90.

Rohsenow, D. J. and Smith, R. E. (1982) 'Irrational beliefs as predictors of negative affective states', *Motivation and Emotion* 2: 299–314.

Rosenbaum, M. (1980) 'Self control schedule', *Behavior Therapy* 11: 109–21.

Ross, S. M. and Scott, M. (1985) 'An evaluation of the effectiveness of individual and group cognitive therapy in the treatment of depressed patients in an inner city health centre', *Journal of the Royal College of General Practitioners* 35: 239–42.

Ross, S. M., Gottfredson, D. K., Christensen, P. and Weaver, R. (1986) 'Cognitive self-statements in depression: findings across clinical populations', *Cognitive Therapy and Research* 10: 159–66.

Roth, D., Bielski, R., Jones, M., Parker, W. and Osborn, G. (1982) 'A comparison of self control therapy and combined self control therapy and antidepressant medication in the treatment of depression, *Behavior Therapy* 13: 133–44.

Rozensky, R. A., Rehm, L. P., Pry, G. and Roth, D. (1977) 'Depression and self-reinforcement behavior in hospital patients', *Journal of Behavior Therapy and Experimental Psychiatry* 8: 35–8.

Rush, A. J. and Watkins, J. T. (1981) 'Group versus individual cognitive therapy: a pilot study', *Cognitive Therapy and Research* 5: 95–103.

Rush, A. J., Beck, A. T., Kovacs, M. and Hollon, S. (1977) 'Comparative efficacy of cognitive therapy and pharmacotherapy in the treatment of depressed outpatients', *Cognitive Therapy and Research* 1: 17–38.

Scott, J. (1988a) 'Psychological models of depression', *Current Opinion in Psychiatry* 1: 719–24.

—— (1988b) 'Cognitive therapy with depressed inpatients', in W. Dryden and P. Trower (eds) *Developments in Cognitive Psychotherapy*, London: Sage.

Segal, Z. V. and Shaw, B. F. (1988) 'Cognitive assessment: issues and methods', in K. S. Dobson (ed.) *Handbook of Cognitive-Behavioral Therapies*, New York: Guilford Press.

Seligman, M. E. P. (1981) 'A learned helplessness point of view', in L. P. Rehm (ed.) *Behavior Therapy for Depression*, New York: Academic Press.

——, Abramson, L. J., Semmel, A. and Von Baeyer, C. (1979) 'Depressive attributional style', *Journal of Abnormal Psychology* 88: 242–7.

Shaw, B. F. (1977) 'Comparisons of cognitive therapy and behavior therapy in the treatment of depression', *Journal of Consulting and Clinical Psychology* 45: 543–51.

Silverman, J. S., Silverman, J. A. and Eardley, D. A. (1984) 'Do maladaptive attitudes cause depression?', *Archives of General Psychiatry* 41: 28–30.

Simons, A. D., Garfield, S. L. and Murphy, G. E. (1984) 'The process of change in cognitive therapy and pharmacotherapy: changes in mood and cognition', *Archives of General Psychiatry* 43: 43–50.

Simons, A. D., Lustman, P. J., Wetzel, R. D. and Murphy, G. E. (1985) 'Predicting response to cognitive therapy of depression: the role of learned resourcefulness', *Cognitive Therapy and Research* 9: 79–90.

Simons, A. D., Murphy, G. E., Levine, J. L. and Wetzel, R. D. (1986) 'Cognitive therapy and pharmacotherapy of depression', *Archives of General Psychiatry* 43: 43–8.

Teasdale, J. D. (1983) 'Negative thinking in depression: cause, effect or reciprocal relationship?', *Advances in Behaviour Research and Therapy* 5: 3–25.

—— (1985) 'Psychological treatments for depression: how do they work?', *Behaviour Research and Therapy* 23: 157–65.

—— (1988) 'Cognitive vulnerability to persistent depression', *Cognition and Emotion* 2: 247–74.

—— and Dent, J. (1987) 'Cognitive vulnerability to depression: an investigation of two hypotheses', *British Journal of Clinical Psychology* 26: 113–26.

Teasdale, J. D. and Fennell, M. J. V. (1982) 'Immediate effects on depression of cognitive therapy interventions', *Cognitive Therapy and Research* 6: 343–52.

——, Hibbert, G. A. and Amies, P. L. (1984) 'Cognitive therapy for major depression in primary care', *British Journal of Psychiatry* 144: 400–6.

Thorpe, G. L., Barnes, G. S., Hunter, J. E. and Hines, D. (1983) 'Thoughts and feelings: correlations in two clinical and two nonclinical samples', *Cognitive Therapy and Research* 7: 565–74.

Tressler, D. P. and Tucker, R. D. (1980) 'The comparative effects of self-evaluation and self-reinforcement training in the treatment of depression', paper presented at the meeting of the Association for the Advancement of Behavior Therapy, New York, November.

Watkins, J. T. and Rush, A. J. (1983) 'Cognitive response test', *Cognitive Therapy and Research* 7(5): 425–36.

Weintraub, M., Segal, R. M. and Beck, A. T. (1974) 'An investigation of cognition and affect in the depressive experiences of normal men', *Journal of Consulting and Clinical Psychology* 42: 911.

Weissman, A. N. (1979) 'The Dysfunctional Attitude Scale: a validation study', *Dissertation Abstracts International* 40: 1389–90B.

Wilkinson, I. M. and Blackburn, I. M. (1981) 'Cognitive style in depressed and recovered depressed patients', *British Journal of Clinical Psychology* 20: 283–92.

Williams, J. M. G. (1984) *The Psychological Treatment of Depression. A Guide to the Theory and Practice of Cognitive-Behaviour Therapy*, London: Croom Helm.

—— and Moorey, S. (1989) 'The wider application of cognitive therapy: the end of the beginning', in J. Scott, J. M. G. Williams and A. T. Beck (eds) *Cognitive Therapy in Clinical Practice: An Illustrative Casebook*, London: Routledge.

Williams, J. M. G. and Scott, J. (1988) 'Autobiographical memory in depression', *Psychological Medicine* 18: 689–95.

Willis, M. and Blaney, P. H. (1978) 'Three tests of the learned helplessness model of depression', *Journal of Abnormal Psychology* 87: 131–6.

Wilson, P. H., Golden, J. C. and Charbonneau-Powis, M. (1983) 'Comparative efficacy of behavioral and cognitive treatments of depression', *Cognitive Therapy and Research* 7: 111–24.

Young, L. D., Moore, S. D. and Nelson, R. E. (1981) 'Effects of depression on acceptance of personality feedback', paper presented at the meeting of the Association for the Advancement of Behavior Therapy, Toronto, Canada, November (quoted in Rehm 1988).

Chapter 4

Anger and violence

Ron Tulloch

INTRODUCTION

To the average citizen at least, there seems little doubt that we live in violent times, worse than any that have gone before. Violence is regarded as a major social problem and its control continues to preoccupy many agencies and individuals. While it may be true that the 'fear of violence' is greater than the likelihood of actually becoming a victim, it remains the case that aggression in its various forms is relatively commonplace and is presented to clinical psychologists in different guises. Marital violence, physical child abuse and violence associated with mental disorder and criminality feature increasingly on clinical case-loads.

There is a long tradition of psychological research into human aggression, mostly stemming from social psychology, personality theory and, recently, social-cognition research, but with an emphasis on explaining aggression as a universal psychological phenomenon. Within this field Bandura's (1973) 'social learning' analysis was a major impetus towards the development of cognitively orientated models. It is only recently, however, that clinical approaches to the problems of violence and aggression have come to the fore (Howells 1982; Howells and Hollin 1989). Here, the focus is on aggressive individuals, particularly those who display habitual violence.

Anger on the other hand, is much less of a public issue and to many is only significant to the extent that it might lead to the acts of aggression that so concern us. Increasingly, however, clinical interest in the problems of dysfunctional anger has begun to redress this balance. More attention is now being paid to the deleterious effects of anger and to its pivotal role in understanding and preventing other clinical and social difficulties, including violence. Novaco's (1975) research was a landmark in counteracting the relative neglect of this topic and in promoting cognitive-behavioural approaches to anger. Novaco's model has continued to develop (Novaco 1979; Novaco and Welsh 1989) and has been extended into a range of clinical problem areas. These include, for example, cardiovascular problems (Chesney and Rosenmann 1985), adolescent difficulties (Feindler and Ecton 1986) and abusive parents (Nomellini and Katz 1983).

Anger and violence present major challenges to clinicians and these are increasingly being met from a cognitive-behavioural perspective. The aims of this chapter are to outline how anger and violence may be understood from this perspective and to look at cognitive-behavioural approaches to treatment. The main focus of the chapter will be on anger. This is because in many of the presenting problems of violence faced by clinicians, anger is often implicated, and it is at the level of anger control that much of the therapeutic effort is directed. Another reason for focusing on anger is to offset the relative neglect of this topic in the clinical literature and to illustrate the broadening view of anger as a significant human emotion, and often a major clinical problem, in its own right.

CONCEPTUALIZATION

The nature of anger and violence: an overview

Defining human aggression and achieving some consensus about that definition has been a surprisingly difficult task for psychologists. At its broadest, aggression has been used to describe events as varied as physical assault, verbal abuse, imposing one's will upon another, refusal to co-operate and making a hostile or cutting remark. Clearly, there is no unitary concept of aggression. A glance at any text on aggression will indicate the extent to which these definitional problems still preoccupy the field (for example, Geen 1990), but for now we can acknowledge that the central issues are as follows: what are the minimal requirements for an adequate definition, and how broad should the definition be – that is, what range of events should be included?

Most psychologists have accepted the definition offered by Buss (1961) as a starting point. Buss suggests that aggression is a response which delivers noxious stimulation to another organism. Many feel that this definition is inadequate, however, as it does not allow us to distinguish accidental from non-accidental harm, and it strips aggression of its context. As Blackburn (1989) has noted, clinical interest is in violent behaviour that is 'malevolently intended and contrary to social norms, and hence tends to exclude passive acts of harm doing or injurious behaviour which is socially legitimised, such as disciplinary punishments or self-defence'.

Thus, some reference to intention and motivation are usually required to provide a minimal definitional set. Geen (1990) suggests that a working definition of aggression needs three components; (a) delivery of noxious stimuli by one organism to another; (b) an intention to harm the victim; and (c) an expectation on the part of the aggressor that the noxious stimuli will have their intended effect. Both intent and expectancy are intervening, inferred variables that cannot be directly observed. Broadly, then, our definition of aggression recognizes the need for both behavioural and cognitive components.

The second main concern is the breadth of the concept that we are working with and it is clear that psychologists do not always agree on what events to consider under the label of aggression or violence. For some the emphasis on physical harm is arbitrary and limiting and an argument has been mounted to suggest that the concept should be widened to include any coercive or punitively motivated behaviour (for example, Tedeschi 1983). This broader notion of 'social coercion', which goes beyond simply physical violence, is certainly more appropriate to the range of problems that present in the clinical setting. It has the virtue of reminding us of the interactional nature of violence and recognizes that the ultimate intention may not always be to cause physical harm but rather to gain power over another or impose our will. Some instances of rape, for example, fit this model.

While there is still much dispute in this area, for our purposes, violence will be taken to be 'social coercion' which may vary in terms of behavioural topography and cognitive content (for example, differing intentions) but is ultimately an act which results in aversive stimulation being delivered to another individual, who is typically motivated to avoid it. This may, or may not, include acts of physical harm doing.

Although problems of definition are not so apparent in the case of anger, it is true to say that how anger is conceptualized will depend ultimately upon the theory of emotion that one holds. Anger is an emotional state that has physiological, cognitive and expressive aspects. Taking Frijda's (1986) model of emotions, it can be regarded as a change in 'action readiness'. In relation to anger this is usually taken to mean an inclination to act in an antagonistic or confrontative manner towards a given source of provocation. For Novaco (1978), anger is a state of heightened physiological arousal which is cognitively labelled as anger, and typically accompanied by antagonistic cognitions. This is a derivative of Schachter and Singer's (1962) two-factor theory of emotion. In this model any emotion is the result of a state of physiological arousal and associated cognitions which are used to label and understand the situation. The theory holds that if an individual experiences a state of arousal and attributes this to some 'provoking' event, then the relevant cognitions are likely to be hostile and antagonistic, thus facilitating the labelling of the emotional state as anger, rather than some other emotion, such as fear.

The Schachter–Singer theory, and original experiments, have been criticized on many grounds (for example, Manstead and Wagner 1981), but the general notion still influences clinical cognitive models. Berkowitz (1983) has also rejected these 'attributional' notions of anger. Using Leventhal's (1980) theory of emotions, Berkowitz suggests that the feeling of anger is not dependent upon cognitive processes. Rather, it is part of an automatic perceptual-motor reaction to an aversive stimulus. Following this, other, similar emotional experiences may be recalled through a cognitive, associational network, which may intensify and elaborate the emotion. While not denying the role of cognitions in emotional experiences like anger, Berkowitz does not see cognitive labelling as necessary. Most currently popular theories of emotion will invoke cognitive processes at some level, but as we can see, not all agree as to the role and place of these.

The relationship between anger and violence is also a contentious issue, it often being assumed that the two go hand in hand. As has been pointed out by Buss (1961), among others, anger is not a necessary precondition for violence. It is common to distinguish different types of aggression according to antecedents and motivation (Geen 1990), particularly 'affective aggression' and 'instrumental aggression'. In the latter case an aggressor may not have any anger towards a victim, or any particular emotional response at all, but the function of the aggression is to obtain some desired reward. An example here would be that of a hired assassin who kills for money rather than malice. Research has shown, however, that anger may make aggression more likely (Rule and Neasdale 1976), and in these instances we refer to affective or angry aggression.

Here it is assumed that the function of the aggressive behaviour is to deal with the provocation experience in such a way as to reduce or eliminate the aversive state of anger. Therefore, on these occasions, anger is legitimately seen as an intervening state between provocation and response.

So, anger and violence do not always go together. Relatively little is known about instrumental aggression, however, and in the clinical field most of the presenting problems of violence are aspects of angry or affective aggression. How anger leads to aggression in these instances is also a subject of great debate. The most common view is that anger, as a particular state of arousal, energizes or activates the most prepotent responses in the situation. Given that the most readily available response to provocation *may* be physical retaliation, then aggressive behaviours may be activated. Notice that this view also allows for non-aggressive behaviours to be preferentially activated if these have been well developed and are available. Zillman (1978) has proposed a model of 'excitation transfer'. This model starts from the recognition that autonomic arousal does not dissipate immediately after an arousing event. Zillman argues that if two arousing events are separated by a short period of time, then some of the arousal caused by the first will transfer and add to the arousal caused by the second. In theory arousal from different sources can combine in this fashion. Thus, if someone is sexually aroused and then some time later made angry, the angry response may be enhanced by residual arousal. There is some experimental evidence to support this view, although it may also be true that if an early source of arousal is very different from the subsequent provoking (angry) event then the effect may not be so noticeable (see Zillman 1983).

From the perspective of excitation transfer, then, some instances of arousal may be enhanced, having an even greater effect on aggressive responses.

It is worth noticing that not all psychologists view anger as having a *causal* role in relation to aggression. Berkowitz (1983) suggests that the feeling of anger accompanies (a parallel process) but does not cause anger-relevant behaviour.

Cognitive models of anger and aggression

There is no single, unified model of either anger or aggression from a cognitive perspective. Here, two models, one of affective aggression and one of anger, will be presented. The merit of the first lies in its simplicity, while the latter also has the added value of being the most influential in the clinical context to date.

Affective aggression

If we take affective aggression as our main consideration here, then we are in a position to explore the process of anger and violence in more detail. Figure 4.1 provides a schematic outline of the processes and variables in affective or angry aggression (from Geen 1990).

Both the person and the situation are thought to contribute to the experience of anger and violence. The process begins with some form of provocation: this may include frustration, various forms of interpersonal provocation (for example, physical attacks, verbal insults, threats to self-esteem) and environmental stressors such as noise and heat. As can be seen, this model holds that the individual is not responding directly to the event, but rather to some cognitive representation. Geen utilizes Lazarus's notion of primary and secondary appraisal to represent the cognitive mediation of the provoking event (Lazarus 1966; Lazarus and Folkman 1984). The individual first makes some judgements and interpretations which broadly determine the relevance of the event for the individual. In relation to aggression, four judgements seem to be important – namely, intentionality, motive, forseeability and violation of norms. Ferguson and Rule (1983) detail these in their attributional perspective on anger and aggression. The basic premiss is that not all provocations will lead to aggression but that those that are seen as intentional, malicious, avoidable and a violation of normative behaviour are most likely to promote an aggressive response. Experiments with children and adults tend to support this view. Epstein and Taylor (1967), for example, demonstrated that experimental subjects who thought that another subject planned to 'attack' them with a highly intense electric shock retaliated more aggressively than when they did not have this information. This was true even when the anticipated shock was not delivered. In their work with children, Dodge *et al*. (1984) suggest that the *perception* of hostile intent tends to determine an aggressive reaction whether or not the aggressor is actually hostile.

Thus, following a provocation experience the individual makes some judgements about the event, typically involving attributions of intent and maliciousness. To the extent that the event is seen in this way then the aversive conditions will promote stress, seen as arousal *and* anger, in the individual. It is at this point that the contribution from the person, within this model, is considered to be relevant. First, if aggression is to be a likely response it must first exist in the individual's repertoire; that is, behavioural responses of an aggressive type must have previously been acquired. This point is clearly made by Bandura (1973, 1986). It is not assumed that some innate repertoire of aggressive behaviours exists in all of us. These behaviours are learned, as any others, through various mechanisms such as imitation and observational learning. To the extent that we may all have 'acquired' some aggressive responses we all have the potential for aggression, but each of us will vary in this given that our learning histories are unique.

According to the model a process of secondary appraisal takes place, whereby the individual evaluates their capacity to cope with this aversive situation. For

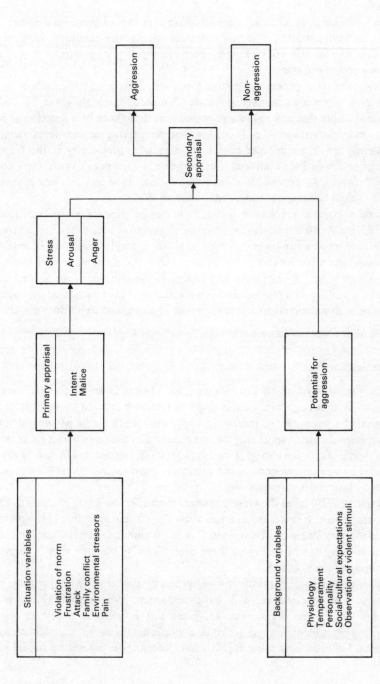

Figure 4.1 **Model of variables and processes in affective aggression**

example, aggression may be only one alternative if other effective coping responses are available to the individual. The response, whatever its form, is an attempt by the person to cope with the problem situation and reduce the aversive state of arousal.

If aggression does occur there are a number of possible effects. First, it may lead to a reduction in arousal, or it may terminate the aversive condition. However, it may also have the effect of making the person feel guilty or anxious, or conversely, increase power and status.

This, then, is a general, cognitively orientated model of affective or angry aggression. There are a number of features that need to be highlighted. First of all we need to note that any aggressive response is thought to be a function of both person and situation variables. From a clinical perspective the situational variables of interest are of an interpersonal type. Similarly, personality is the primary 'background' variable of interest. Here, however, we are not so much interested in trait *labels* such as 'introversion' but rather the cognitive-motivational constructs which *explain* behavioural consistency (Alston 1975).

Another point to emphasize is that there can be great individual variation in aggressivity. At the cognitive (for example, cognitive structures such as schemata, information-processing biases), behavioural (for example, repertoire of available responses) and affective (for example, arousability, labelling tendency) levels, the unique experience, development and history of the individual can influence the process of dealing with provocation. Finally, it should be stressed that provocation or aversive stimulation does not always lead to anger, and anger does not always lead to violence.

Anger

It is only relatively recently that clinicians have begun to devote serious attention to anger. Within cognitive models anger is typically thought to result from the appraisal of a wrong, in the form of an unjustified attack on the personal domain. The emotional state of anger may be accompanied by thoughts which focus on the blameworthiness of the transgressor. Novaco (1975, Novaco and Welsh 1989) has provided the most developed cognitive model of anger to date. Figure 4.2 represents Novaco's model diagrammatically.

Novaco (1979) takes the view that anger is an affective stress reaction to some provoking event. It is a cognitively mediated emotional state that is reciprocally related to cognitions and to behaviour. That is, the emotional arousal and the course of action instigated by that arousal are determined by the individual's cognitive structuring of the situation.

In his early formulation Novaco was primarily concerned with cognitive processes such as appraisal, self-talk and expectations. More recently (Novaco and Welsh 1989) he has argued that too often this is taken to imply an 'event-interpretation tandem proceed' – that is, a simple mediation between stimulus and response. He calls for a more sophisticated information-processing model to be

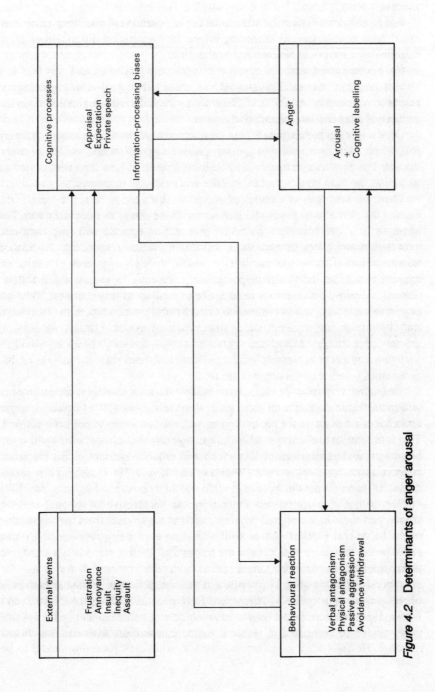

Figure 4.2 Determinants of anger arousal

invoked, one which recognizes that cognitive mediation is an automatic and intrinsic part of the perceptual process. Cognitive 'dispositions' such as schemata and scripts will also be influential. Thus, in addition to the cognitive events and processes already noted, Novaco suggests that five information-processing biases should be considered, namely: attentional cueing, perceptual matching, attribution error, false consensus and anchoring effects (for a detailed discussion of these cognitive processes see Novaco and Welsh 1989).

For Novaco, then, external events are cognitively processed and may lead to a state of emotional arousal. This arousal is regarded as being a general physiological response which may be labelled differently by the individual depending upon the contextual cues and interpretation of events.

Once anger has been aroused there are four main behavioural reactions that may follow: physical or verbal antagonism, passive aggression and avoidance withdrawal. The particular response is liable to be a result of how the event is viewed as well as the individual's past experience and predicted outcomes.

There are a number of features of the model that need to be made clear. First, each of the elements in the model interacts with the others in a complex way. For example, how one handles a particular provocation episode will feed back into expectation and appraisal processes, influencing future responding. Avoidance withdrawal may encourage rumination which, through a process of excitation transfer makes an individual inappropriately sensitive to events which follow. Second, the provocation events need not be immediate to cause arousal. Through cognitive variables such as rumination or core cognitive constructs, the individual may be responding to distal rather than proximal events. Finally, we have to acknowledge that just as with the aggression model, there will be great individual variation in anger proneness. It is the significance of the event to the individual that determines whether or not anger is aroused.

Two other cognitive theorists have made reference to anger, although only within the framework of their more general models. Beck (1976) describes anger as an appraisal of an *attack* on, or *violation* of, one's domain which is unjustified. This is in contrast to events perceived as *endangering* the domain, which will result in anxiety, and perceptions of *loss* which will provoke sadness. Some empirical support exists for Beck's view (Wickless and Kirsch 1988) although it seems difficult to separate out the types of thought and their corresponding emotions. Ellis (1977a, b) has also considered anger from the perspective of rational-emotive theory, and for him, emotional problems such as anger stem from the interaction of the individual's belief system with activating events or experiences. Dryden (1984) notes that anger results from the frustration where a personally valued role is transgressed. In particular, anger results from 'the irrational demands that the other person should not break my rule and that that person is damnable as a result of breaking my rule' (p. 297). Zwemer and Deffenbacher (1984) examined the links between particular irrational beliefs and specific emotional content and noted that anger tended to be related to personal perfection, anxious over-concern, blame proneness and catastrophizing. There was, however, considerable overlap between the beliefs predictive of anger and anxiety.

Anger and violence as clinical problems

For most people anger and violence reflect the less worthy, more destructive aspects of human nature. Often, they are taken to indicate a loss of control, and the abdication of reason to more primitive, instinctual forces. It is worth emphasizing, however, that both have long been part of the human condition and have no automatic status as clinical problems. Anger is a normal human emotion that may well have adaptive functions (Novaco 1983).

Similarly, the extent to which we regard violence as a problem depends very much upon cultural, contextual and individual value judgements (Blackburn 1989). There are clearly occasions, however, when both anger and violence present difficulties to individuals and to those around them. From a clinical perspective these are seen as instances of failed or inappropriate problem solving, or poor coping responses, rather than a failure to check some innate, destructive drive.

Both the model of aggression offered by Geen (1990) and that of anger proposed by Novaco (1975) can be located within a stress paradigm (Lazarus 1966; Lazarus and Folkman 1984). Within this framework stress is seen to result when the demands made upon the individual exceed their capacity to cope or act effectively. The stressors themselves may be social, physical or psychological and usually represent a change from a state of accommodation or adaptation that the individual has achieved. To this extent the experience may be aversive and thereby promote arousal. Thus, both violence and anger are seen as responses invoked as the individual attempts to cope with the demands made upon them. The stress paradigm allows us to consider stress that is both ambient or acute. An individual presenting with an anger problem may be experiencing this in response to some *change* in circumstances, for example. Here the 'stress' is acute. Someone who is chronically angry, however, may be displaying a learned coping response, over a period of time.

Violence tends to present as a clinical problem when it is used habitually, either across a broad spectrum of situations, or as a consistent feature of one problem situation, for example domestic disputes. We will focus, however, on anger since it is less well known as a clinical problem and since it is a primary link in the chain of events leading to violence.

In order to decide whether anger is a problem or not it needs to be evaluated in terms of various response parameters, namely: frequency, intensity, duration and mode of expression. Anger may be a problem for a client if it happens too often, or lasts too long, or is too intense, or is expressed inappropriately. The severity of the anger reactions are gauged by their effects on the client's performance, health and relationships. For one client the major difficulty may be elevated blood pressure, for another, a marital break-up. Thus, the dimensions of the anger reactions are considered in relation to the costs, or consequences.

It is also necessary to separate out the extent to which the individual's anger is adaptive as opposed to maladaptive. Novaco (1983) suggests eight functions of anger, illustrated in Figure 4.3. For any one individual anger may be an issue to the extent that maladaptive functions predominate.

Individuals vary, then, in how anger and violence present as difficulties. It may be a recent problem, reflecting a change in conditions (either in relation to the person or the situation) or a longer-term concern, reflecting a learned response style. The adaptiveness of the response must be considered and its variation along a number of dimensions in relation to the consequences for the individual.

Development and maintenance of anger and violence

When attempting to understand and remediate clinical problems it is necessary to consider two fundamental issues: first, how the problem developed and, also, how it is maintained. As research into anxiety and depression seems to suggest, the mechanisms and processes involved in each of these may be quite different. The importance of these issues for the prevention and amelioration of clinical disorders cannot be overstated.

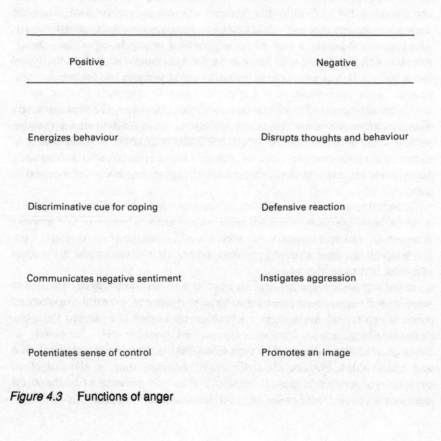

Positive	Negative
Energizes behaviour	Disrupts thoughts and behaviour
Discriminative cue for coping	Defensive reaction
Communicates negative sentiment	Instigates aggression
Potentiates sense of control	Promotes an image

Figure 4.3   Functions of anger

Unfortunately, in relation to anger and violence we are still very much in the dark regarding these concerns. Given that anger has only recently been acknowledged as a significant clinical problem, investigations into associated mechanisms and processes lag substantially behind that of other problem areas. Aggression, outside of the clinical field, does have a more solid empirical base upon which we can draw. However, much of what may be said about development and maintenance remains at the level of speculation.

We need to be clear at the outset that we may be discussing two different types of problem. If we consider anger for the moment, a typical clinical case may involve a middle-aged man who has recently been experiencing hypertensive and social difficulties as a result of frequent episodes of anger arousal. Exploration may reveal a change in the demands of his job, such that his usual capacity to cope is overstretched. This may broadly be seen as a disjunctive change, a departure from the normal state of affairs for the individual. In seeking to explain the development of the problem we could consider the types of demands now being placed on the client, how he interpreted these and what areas of coping response show deficiencies.

This must be contrasted with the case of a middle-aged man who has displayed chronic anger problems more or less all of his life. In this situation a typical case might present with a history of broken relationships, poor work performance and, often, numerous brushes with the law following aggressive behaviour. Here we are not so much seeking the aetiology of the problem in the demands of the environment but rather the dispositions of the individual. These two types of problem present regularly to clinicians, the former being regarded as 'ego-dystonic', the latter as 'ego-syntonic'.

It is broadly assumed that shorter-term, disjunctive anger problems are maintained by the same types of information-processing bias as can be seen in cases of anxiety. Once an individual has labelled a situation as anger arousing then it is highly likely that they will be hypervigilant for similar ones in future, thus predisposing them to interpret situations in this way in future and thus increasing the likelihood of an angry response. We can also see how the behavioural response might be influential in maintaining anger. How an individual copes may reinforce the already existing outcome expectancies and self-efficacy judgements. These will in turn feed back into the appraisal systems. Anger may also be maintained through positive reinforcement, where, for example, a display of anger potentiates a sense of control. Thus, medium-term anger problems are held to be the result of stressful conditions. Dysfunctional anger is maintained over the short term by cognitive-processing mechanisms that influence the interpretation of events as aversive and provocative. Over a longer period cognitive structures, such as schemata, may play a more significant role.

Bandura (1973) has noted that there are four maintaining mechanisms for aggression – that is, external reinforcement, vicarious reinforcement, punishment and self-regulatory mechanisms. Bandura (1976) argues that people are not simply reactors to external influences but that self-generated inducements and self-produced consequences can influence behaviour. Bandura sees this self-system as cognitive structures that provide the standards against which behaviour is judged and also subfunctions for the perception, evaluation and regulation of action. An individual may judge his aggressive behaviour favourably and thus reinforce it. Thus, aggression may be maintained by the various reinforcing mechanisms that we know well, but also by self-regulatory mechanisms.

For clinicians the problems of chronic anger and habitual violence over the long term are a major challenge. Often these clients are considered in terms of personality disorder and clinicians tend to look to early developmental processes to indicate the source of the difficulty. Despite earlier criticisms it has now been demonstrated that aggressive behaviour does show consistency over time.

Olweus (1979, 1980) has shown that the degree of consistency in aggressive behaviour patterns over time is substantially greater than that suggested by proponents of behavioural specificity (for example, Mischel 1968). Further, central determinants of this stability are to be found in personality variables. We need to distinguish here between 'trait labels' which *describe* average behaviour and cognitive-motivational constructs which *explain* behaviour. 'Scripts', 'schemata' and 'networks' are example of the latter.

Thus, there is in some individuals an enduring feature of aggressivity. It is assumed that for these individuals, cognitive structures which predispose them to hostile interpretations of the world maintain a state of anger proneness and likelihood of aggression. Blackburn and Lee-Evans (1985) provide support for this view in their study of psychopaths. The results of a questionnaire study indicate that psychopaths as a group more readily interpret provocation or threats from others as unwarranted attack – that is, an attributional bias to perceiving malevolent intent.

Further support comes from work with aggressive children. Lochman (1987) found that aggressive boys minimized their perceptions of their own aggressiveness and perceived their partners as more aggressive than they themselves were, in comparison with non-aggressive boys. Perry *et al.* (1986) showed that compared to non-aggressive children, aggressive subjects reported that it is easier to perform aggression and more difficult to inhibit aggressive impulses. They were also more confident that aggressive behaviour would bring tangible rewards. Thus, aggressive children had greater self-efficacy for aggressive behaviour and outcome expectancies that such behaviour would produce desired results, when compared with non-aggressive children.

In their studies Dodge and Frame (1982) confirmed the presence of a hostile attributional bias in aggressive boys. On a slightly different tack Asarnow and Callan (1985) showed that boys who were deficient in cognitive problem-solving skills were more inclined to evaluate aggressive responses positively, and had more social-adjustment difficulties.

Thus, we can see that there is evidence to suggest that a stable disposition to aggression exists in some individuals, and this may be detected in childhood as a result of attributional biases, poor problem-solving skills and differences in self-efficacy and outcome-expectancy judgements. Cognitive structures, such as schemata, are thought to maintain this problem disposition over the long term and into adulthood. Although we are far from understanding the precise mechanisms which underlie the development and maintenance of chronic anger and habitual violence, recent research has pointed to some useful avenues.

TREATMENT

The number of studies reporting on the treatment of anger and aggression is small in relation to other clinical problem areas such as depression or anxiety. Over the last 15 years, however, there has been a steady growth in the available literature, with three shifts in emphasis becoming apparent. First, the recognition that anger may play a significant role in aggressive behaviour, intervening between provocation and response, has led to an increased emphasis on anger control as the main therapeutic target for individuals displaying affective aggression problems. Also, since Novaco's (1975) seminal work there has been significant growth in studies using cognitive approaches. Perhaps most noticeable of all is the increase in reports where anger itself is the primary target for intervention.

Bornstein *et al.* (1981) provided an extensive review of treatments for aggression, including : (a) desensitization and its variants, (b) operant treatments, (c) social-skills training and (d) cognitive-behavioural/coping skills interventions. While some studies in each category were able to demonstrate an impact on aggression, a number of substantial problems were noted. The lack of long-term follow-up, or demonstrated generalizability of treatment effects, limit the value of the results. Similarly, most interventions tended to be 'packages' of combined techniques, and without detailed 'parametric' analysis it remains to be seen which therapeutic components were most effective.

It is also clear that we cannot proceed as if aggression were a 'singular concept' if we are to develop effective interventions. There do seem to be differing forms of violence, such as instrumental and affective (angry) violence, and it may be necessary to develop treatment programmes specifically geared to these various forms.

Our main concern here is with cognitive-behavioural treatments for anger, both as a problem in its own right and as a crucial element of affective aggression. This section will provide, first, an outline of the most frequently utilized cognitive-behavioural programmes for anger control; this being followed by a review of treatment applications and their efficacy and, finally, a consideration of the value of the various elements of the treatment systems.

Cognitive approaches to anger control

As readers of this volume will be aware, cognitive-behavioural methods draw upon a range of conceptualizations and intervention techniques (cf. Brewin 1988; Dryden and Golden 1986). Broadly, they share the assumption that faulty 'cognitions' lie at the heart of many psychopathological conditions. Although distinctions between the various therapeutic systems can be identified (Golden and Dryden 1986) the clinical practice within any one system seems to be quite eclectic. One broad distinction referred to separates cognitive restructuring, problem-solving training and coping-skills training.

A salient feature of cognitive-restructuring methods, which would include Beck's (1976) cognitive therapy and Ellis's (1977a) rational-emotive therapy, is the focus on 'core' change – that is, of cognitive 'structures', such as schemata. Problem-solving training (for example, Spivack *et al*. 1976) attempts to teach the client an effective set of *cognitive skills* with which to understand, mediate and resolve problem situations. Coping-skills therapies seek to provide clients with cognitive and behavioural *resources* for dealing with *stressful* situations. Meichenbaum's (1985) Stress Inoculation Training reflects this approach.

Cognitive treatments for anger control have, to date, been combinatorial in format and usually invoke elements of the three broad systems outlined above. Most take their lead from the treatment programme outlined by Novaco (1975, 1983) which, although regarded as a coping-skills package, includes aspects of cognitive restructuring and problem-solving training. The major influences behind Novaco's Anger Control Training are Lazarus's (1966) stress model, Meichenbaum's stress-inoculation intervention (Meichenbaum 1977, 1985) and Ellis's (1962) rational-emotive model, with its emphasis on cognitive mediation and the influence of irrational beliefs upon behaviour.

The treatment is essentially a stress-inoculation approach which sets out to help clients develop coping skills and then exposes them to manageable doses of stressors. The client is also taught to appreciate the relationship between thoughts, emotions and behaviour, and by regulating this relationship, *prevent* anger arousal.

The goals of therapy are comprehensive, namely: to prevent maladaptive anger being aroused, to regulate or manage arousal when it does occur and to develop the performance skills to manage the provocation situation. There are three stages in the treatment programme: cognitive preparation, skill acquisition and application training.

Cognitive preparation

Novaco identifies four objectives for this phase of treatment, which may take up to four sessions, namely to: educate the client about the functions of anger, identify personal anger patterns, provide a shared language system between therapist and client and to introduce the rationale for treatment. By the end of this phase both client and therapist should have a broad appreciation of the particular anger problem being presented and the client (typically by keeping a diary and reading a treatment manual) should understand the emotion–cognition–behaviour links, both in general and in terms specific to them. Finally, both therapist and client should be engaged in a *collaborative* enterprise to tackle the anger problem.

Skill acquisition

During this stage of treatment the task is to teach the client the relevant cognitive, arousal reduction and behavioural skills that suit their particular needs. At the cognitive level this may mean modifying expectations and appraisals. Self-statement modification may also be utilized here. Arousal reduction/management is typically taught through progressive-relaxation training, and counter-conditioning procedures may be used to 'desensitize' the client to difficult provocation events.

The behavioural coping skills focus upon effective communication, assertiveness and problem solving, developed through a fairly standard social-skills training approach.

Application training

Anger management aims to build personal competence and involves developing the client's ability to manage provocative situations progressively. Initially this may be done by presenting the client with a hierarchy of provoking situations in imagination until these can be coped with. Then the client moves on to role-playing the situations and, finally, *in vivo* practice. The aim is to develop and practise the various skills without being overwhelmed. Application training need not be a discrete phase of therapy, but rather a process that spans the various sessions of treatment as appropriate.

It will be obvious that anger-control training draws from a broad range of relevant models and methods within the cognitive-behavioural field. It seeks to promote change at all three levels, cognitive, affective and behavioural. Cognitive-change techniques such as those outlined in Beck *et al.* (1979) – for example, decentering, distancing, reattribution – are invoked, such that previously provoking events may be seen in a different light. In particular, the client is taught to modify the often exaggerated importance attached to events, not to have inordinately high expectations of others, and not to take things too personally. Although there is no evidence to support this view, it is assumed that successful cognitive changes may work through 'schematic' change, or in Bandura's (1986) term, changes in outcome expectancies and estimates of coping self-efficacy.

The treatment also provides the client with the ability to keep arousal under control, which should, in turn, promote a 'task-centred' approach to problem solving, and also minimize the risk of 'energizing' prepotent aggressive or maladaptive behaviours. The behavioural skills training sets out to increase the client's repertoire of effective responses, providing greater flexibility and, possibly, alternative prepotent responses which may be 'energized' or activated in the face of provocation.

This, in summary, then, is the basic treatment model for anger-control difficulties. The aim is to reduce the likelihood of anger causing distress to the client in both the long- and short-term. Clearly, different aspects of the programme will be emphasized depending upon the particular type of presenting problem and where the major dysfunctional elements (i.e. cognitive, behavioural, affective) are thought to lie for that individual. For one client the inability to handle arousal may be central, while for another, the lack of alternative behavioural responses may be a crucial issue. Most of the recently reported studies on cognitive approaches to anger and violence have utilized and acknowledged some variation of this basic programme.

Novaco (1975) conducted a pioneering study on an early version of his therapeutic programme. Thirty-four students, assessed as experiencing chronic anger problems from their responses to the Novaco Provocation Inventory and physiological and self-report responses to simulated provocations, received one of four treatments. These were: relaxation alone; self-instructional training alone; relaxation plus self-instructional training; and an attention control. The subjects were measured before and after treatment on the provocation inventory and measures of anger arousal (including self-ratings and blood pressure) in response to imaginal, role-playing and laboratory-contrived provocations. The results showed that those in the combined group improved most in relation to the control group. Those in the 'self-instructions alone' group also did better than controls but not as well as the combined group. Novaco also concluded that the cognitive method (self-instruction) on its own was more effective than relaxation training alone.

Thus, this initial study showed some promise. It should be noted, however, that the group sizes were small, there was no follow-up and no real estimate of generalizability of treatment effects in the real environment. It is also the case that the cognitive method, self-instructional training, was more limited in comparison to the variety and sophistication of methods currently utilized.

Novaco (1977) subsequently did use an extended version of his programme with a depressed in-patient who was prone to impulsive outbursts of aggression. Following treatment (eleven sessions) the patient's self-reported anger had substantially diminished. This was supported by the diminution in aggressive outbursts and an improvement in constructive coping responses, as estimated by ward-staff behaviour ratings. Further, the improvements were maintained at discharge and extended to the home and work environments. As a case-study, without appropriate experimental controls, however, this cannot be taken as equivalent to a full replication of the earlier study.

To summarize, then, anger-control training as developed by Novaco is a cognitive-behavioural treatment programme relevant to problems of anger and violence. It is broadly a coping-skills therapy, pragmatic and eclectic in content, but also seeking to promote change at the cognitive, affective and behavioural levels. It is a short-term treatment which acknowledges all the accepted principles of cognitive therapy. The Novaco programme itself has modest support as to its efficacy, but more often other investigators have utilized the broad framework, recast to suit their own needs, to tackle a range of problems and provided evidence relating to the efficacy of this approach. It is to these other workers we now turn, to look at applications of anger control and its efficacy.

Treatment application and outcome

As already noted the absolute number of treatment reports on anger control is relatively small. However, the diversity of applications of cognitive methods of anger control is undoubtedly increasing. Examples can be found in relation to offenders, marital violence, adolescents, abusive parents and antisocial behaviour in children.

Turning first to violence, Frederiksen and Rainwater (1981) examined the utility of a comprehensive cognitive and behavioural programme for impulsively aggressive in-patients. These investigators adopted a multifaceted assessment approach to examine the multidimensional deficits of this explosively violent group. This included behavioural interviews, role-play assessments, unobtrusive evaluations of social skills, assessment of maladaptive expectations of others and physiological measures. The treatment programme included social-skills training, relaxation, cognitive restructuring and generalization training. Those patients who completed the programme showed improvement on all the measures and reports indicate that these gains were maintained at six months to four years in the home environment. Although this is encouraging, the study has a number of limiting features, most notably the small number of clients, the possible biasing effect of a 50 per cent drop-out rate and the lack of experimental controls. Nonetheless, for these clients, this comprehensive cognitive behavioural package does seem to have reduced the frequency of violent outbursts.

Bistline and Frieden (1984) report a successful case-study using the stress-inoculation component of Novaco's programme with a long-standing case of chronic anger and aggression in a hospitalized client. Over the course of therapy and at twelve months follow-up there was an increase in the frequency of prosocial acts and a decrease in aggression episodes. The cognitive-change methods used in this case were self-statement modification and cognitive rehearsal.

Two studies have been reported using anger-control training with groups of offenders. Stermac (1987) utilized a six-session programme with offenders remanded to a forensic psychiatric facility for assessment, in Canada. Forty subjects, all male, primarily diagnosed as personality disorders, were divided into two groups, twenty to receive anger-control training and the other twenty a psycho-educational group session, acting as a control group for the study. In this instance the cognitive components of the treatment were more sophisticated and comprehensive. Stermac reports that the sessions included Ellis's ABC of emotional arousal, examination of personal assumptions and expectations, and identification of irrational ideas. Overall, at both cognitive and behavioural levels, this study comes very close to utilizing the full Novaco-type package. The results of the programme were encouraging, with the treatment group showing reduced self-reported anger levels and increased self-reported use of adaptive coping strategies in relation to the control group. However, the lack of behavioural referents and follow-up, once again, means that the results must be treated cautiously.

Another study, carried out in a British Youth Custody Centre (McDougall *et al.*

1987) also utilized Novaco's anger-control treatment. In this instance subjects who had received treatment showed a reduction in the number of 'Governor's Reports' (action taken in the event of antisocial behaviour) compared to a control group. It is inferred from the study that this effect was due to the treatment group controlling their anger more effectively. However, while the evaluation measure (number of reports) has ecological validity, it is impossible to demonstrate a clear link with the treatment programme in this instance. This study, then, provides only weak support for the efficacy of anger-control methods with offenders in a custodial setting.

Another area where anger treatment is pertinent is in the field of spouse abuse or domestic violence. As Averill's (1982) study revealed, 53 per cent of the people who were the *targets* of anger, in a survey of recent episodes, were either loved ones or well known to the angry individual. A recent study by Maiuro *et al*. (1988) indicated that domestically violent men evidenced higher levels of anger and hostility than control subjects, and were, indeed, very similar to generally assaultive men. 'Wife battering' or spouse abuse is clearly a major area where anger control is a relevant treatment target. Margolin (1979) describes a successful case-study for a couple troubled by domestic violence, drawing on cognitive-behavioural principles and practice.

It is, however, in work with children that a number of excellent examples of cognitive-behavioural treatments are to be found. Lochman *et al*. (1981) developed a programme from Novaco's model for aggressive elementary school children. Emphasis was given to teaching the children to inhibit initial aggressive reactions to cognitively related stimuli perceived as threatening and to solve problems by generating alternative coping responses. The results of the treatment were in the direction of improvement as measured by teacher ratings of aggressive and on-task behaviours and a problem-behaviour check-list.

Kazdin *et al*. (1989) noted that between one-third to a half of all children referred to clinics in the USA are referred as a result of aggressive and antisocial behaviour problems. In a well conducted study this group of investigators demonstrated that problem-solving training *with* in vivo *practice* was significantly better than problem-solving training alone, or client-centred relationship therapy in reducing antisocial behaviour and improving prosocial behaviour for children aged between 7 and 13 years, referred for aggressive and antisocial behaviour problems. The treatment effects generalized to the home and school, and were maintained at 1-year follow-up.

Cognitive-behavioural approaches to anger control are clearly being applied to a diverse range of problems as illustrated by the studies reported here. All of those studies suggest some positive outcome for the use of cognitively orientated anger-control techniques in impacting upon the various target problems. However, a number of issues need to be acknowledged. First, the methodological quality of the research is highly variable and in few instances is it sound enough to allow for more than 'encouraging' interpretations. Second, treatment protocols also vary greatly and while two different investigators may refer to Novaco's work, they need not be implementing exactly the same clinical programme. Usually, different elements are emphasized to suit the conditions of the study or the taste of the investigator. Third, from the studies reported it cannot be determined whether the procedures are having the anticipated effects on cognitive processes. These tend to be inferred from changes in the overall problem behaviour rather than reassessed directly. Finally, the studies presented here do not allow us to examine the treatments for their most effective ingredients – that is, what components (for example, relaxation or cognitive restructuring) are having most impact. It is to studies which allow for some 'parametric' analysis that we must now turn.

Component analysis of cognitive-behaviour therapy for anger and violence

Cognitive treatments for anger and violence are typically comprehensive, eclectic packages, recognizing the multifaceted nature of these problems and individual variation in presentation. Programmes tend to include elements of cognitive restructuring, social-skills training, problem-solving training and arousal-management techniques such as relaxation. They also vary in the extent to which they *emphasize* the cognitive, affective and behavioural components of therapy. Finally, even within one component, great variation may be found. For Stermac (1987), for example, cognitive methods involved elements of rational-emotive therapy (Ellis 1962) and Bandura's (1986) self-efficacy and outcome-expectation model. Bistline and Frieden (1984), on the other hand, focus almost exclusively on self-statement modification. With all of these effects compounded, in many of the available studies it is not possible to determine the relative impact of the various treatment components. However, a few studies exist which do address this issue directly.

Novaco's (1975) original study to some extent tackled this issue. His research suggested that a combination of cognitive and relaxation interventions had the most powerful effect. Cognitive intervention alone was almost as effective as the combined treatment while relaxation alone had a limited impact. For Novaco, then, the cognitive component was clearly the most important ingredient in the treatment programme.

It has been suggested, however, that the effects of relaxation may have been underestimated. Deffenbacher *et al.* (1988) suggest that the treatment rationale may have been confusing. For example, the role of relaxation appears to be in counter-conditioning, which is at odds with the general theme of self-control that pervades the treatment. They also suggest that not enough time was devoted to actual training in relaxation techniques. Overall, they feel that relaxation has been too readily discarded as a central component of treatment for anger control.

This group cites three studies which have examined this issue. Using students who scored above the 25th percentile on the Trait Anger Scale (Spielberger *et al.* 1983), Hazaleus and Deffenbacher (1986) compared relaxation with cognitive restructuring and a control group. For the relaxation treatment an adaptation of Suinn's (1977) anxiety-management procedure was used. The investigators state that the reasons for choosing this approach were that anxiety management had a consistent self-control rationale, a well developed procedure for training relaxation coping skills and a demonstrated effectiveness for arousal reduction. The cognitive treatment was based around procedures similar to Novaco's, drawing from stress inoculation (Meichenbaum 1977). The control group received no treatment. Treatment effects were measured on a range of standardized self-report measures, person-specific ratings and physiological responses.

Following treatment both the cognitive and the relaxation groups showed a significant reduction across measures. An initial but slight advantage for the cognitive method disappeared at 4-week follow up. Both maintained their effects at 1 year. Thus, this reopens the question as to the role of relaxation. If relaxation coping skills are appropriately developed in training then there may be no clear advantage of cognitive methods in anger control.

This result was replicated in another study comparing anxiety management with a control group (Deffenbacher *et al*. 1986). These authors stated that 'when sufficient attention was paid to training and applying relaxation coping skills, they too were effective in reducing anger and that Novaco's (1975) conclusions regarding the relative effectiveness of relaxation interventions may have underestimated their potency for anger reduction' (p. 489).

In the most recent study Deffenbacher *et al*. (1988) again reaffirmed this view. It is also noted that while both cognitive and relaxation methods are effective in reducing general anger, when combined in this study there was no synergistic effect as in Novaco (1975) – that is, adding the relaxation component to the cognitive treatment did not produce enhanced effects.

Moon and Eisler (1983) compared social-skills training, problem solving and stress-inoculation treatments with student samples. All had significant effects in reducing the cognitive component of anger but in different ways. As one might expect, subjects in the cognitive stress-inoculation group appeared to reduce their anger-provoking thoughts but did not improve in terms of behavioural competence. Interestingly, the other two treatment groups prompted change on both cognitive and behavioural indices. The authors suggest that stress inoculation alone may help with the cognitive component of anger but may encourage passive behavioural responding. Social-skills and problem-solving subjects are thought to have developed more competence and flexibility in controlling their anger by using a combination of cognitive *and* behavioural strategies.

It would seem, then, that we are still relatively ignorant of the differential efficacy of the various components in anger-control treatments. It seems too early to disregard the role of arousal reduction (relaxation) treatments. Novaco's (1975) pessimism about their value almost certainly stems from a confused use of these methods (i.e. in a counter-conditioning process as opposed to coping skills).

In the final analysis it may be premature to pitch different therapeutic components against each other in this way. The programme is, after all, eclectic and multifaceted in order to meet the demands of the presenting clinical problem. No two clients with anger or violence difficulties will be exactly the same, even though the end state, i.e. chronic anger, appears similar. For one individual the lack of alternative behavioural responses in their repertoire may be a major factor, and another, the tendency to attribute hostile intent too readily. The components of the package will, as Novaco (1983) has said, need to be adapted to the individual. To date, the few parametric or component-analysis studies have been carried out with analogue, student samples, thus disguising the individual differences in presentation found in clinical groups. A more relevant question, then, is which combination of components for which client? This will inevitably be a function of presenting problem and client characteristics.

FUTURE DEVELOPMENTS

Although anger and violence are attracting more interest from clinical psychologists, from both theoretical and therapeutic perspectives, it is regrettably, the case that we still know relatively little about their distribution and prevalence as clinical problems. Both are emotive topics, readily sensationalized and subject to categorical, convenient and stereotypical explanations depending upon the stance of the observer or commentator. The pessimistic view of anger and aggression as unchecked passions, entirely deviant and not amenable to change has inhibited the growth of an equivalent body of knowledge as is to be found in the study of depression, for example. A major concern for future investigators must be to fill in the detail of our currently sketchy drawing.

We need to improve our understanding of anger, particularly, at three levels: the epidemiological, the clinical and the individual.

There have been few comprehensive surveys of the population at large to inform us about anger as an everyday experience. Averill's (1982) study, for example, produced some illuminating results. Some 88 per cent of anger incidents involved another person. Of these, 53 per cent were loved ones or well known to the 'angry' individual. It would seem, then, that anger is largely an interpersonal and 'intimate' phenomenon.

This points to a dilemma for investigators as most laboratory-based studies use strangers in their experiments (Biaggio 1987), thus threatening the external validity of the research. We are, in fact, remarkably ignorant about how anger is perceived in normal circumstances and we know even less about the extent to which it is perceived to be a problem by groups who have not yet used clinical services. Thus, there is a clear need for extensive surveys to study anger as an everyday experience and to try and ascertain the extent to which it is causing problems.

At the clinical level it is necessary that we understand more about the effects of dysfunctional anger, and also how it relates to other clinical conditions. Deffenbacher et al. (1988) suggest that anxiety may be closely related to anger, while Maiuro et al. (1988) are concerned that chronically angry and domestically violent men may be experiencing significant problems of depression. The work of Wickless and Kirsch (1988) and Zwemer and Deffenbacher (1984) also indicates an overlap between anxiety and anger. It seems likely, therefore, that until anger is acknowledged as a significant clinical problem in its own right, the focus of treatment may remain, mistakenly, or at least only partially appropriately, on the more easily recognized conditions. The converse also applies, however. Angry clients do not always engender the same empathic response in clinicians as anxiety or depression, and thus, states of anxiety and so on may not be attributed to them, therefore remaining untreated. Anger should, therefore, be included in the multi-dimensional assessment and conceptualization of other human emotional disorders.

Up until recently cognitive conceptualization of anger problems at the individual level have been rather simplistic. Novaco's (1975) starting point provoked a good deal of interest but it is only very recently that we have begun to see the more comprehensive and sophisticated cognitive models applied to anger. The recent 'updating' of Novaco's model in information-processing terms (Novaco and Welsh 1989) is a step in the right direction. A significant gap in the work to date has been attempts to examine anger in relation to 'core' cognitive processes (Safran *et al*. 1986). Issues such as schemata, self-systems and core beliefs need to be elaborated in relation to anger, as indeed they are in respect of other clinical concerns. Similarly, those interested in anger need to be cognizant of the developments in the field of emotional theories, particularly with regard to the role of preconscious processing and affective responding (for example, Berkowitz, 1983; Izard *et al*. 1984; Leventhal, 1980) It would be tempting to stick with the rather tidy, linear model as offered by Novaco but we must go beyond this to consider the role of the so-called 'feed-forward' cognitive processes as well as the cognitive structures that provide stability.

This is also crucial from a treatment focus. Current cognitive-behavioural methods of anger control may be thought to work at the 'peripheral' level. In relation to issues such as chronic anger and habitual violence, then, it is changes in 'central' or core structures/processes that we need to promote. Methods to produce 'schematic' change need to be developed and tested with angry and violent individuals.

A number of disparate strands do seem to be coming together in such a way as to enhance our ability to understand and remediate the problems presented by the chronically angry and habitually violent. Themes from personality theory, structural cognitive therapy (Guidano and Liotti 1983) and Bowlby's (1973, 1985) attachment theory would seem to present an opportunity for profitable interweaving.

After many years in the wilderness, personality theory is undergoing something of a 'renaissance'. It is now acknowledged that there can be stability and consistency in behaviour and that the *explanation* of this is to be found in cognitive-motivational constructs (for example, schemata) as opposed to trait labels (for example, extraversion) which merely *describe* (Blackburn 1989) average behaviour. Our task, then, is to understand these core structures and processes in relation to provoking events, and how those of chronically angry and violent people differ from others. We also need to appreciate their development and organization. Personality researchers are increasingly developing novel ways to assess and understand the relationship between personality constructs and criterion behaviours and the methodological sophistication in this field could well benefit clinical cognitive investigators (Ickes 1984).

Guidano and Liotti (1983) tackle this issue squarely:

> from the standpoint of cognitive-structural psychology, premorbid personality is a concept that can be reduced to that of cognitive organisation. Personality 'traits' are conceivable as epiphenonema of enduring belief systems or 'basic assumptions'. Undesirable personality traits should be considered as expressions of specific irrational beliefs. The bridge between early experiences and actual symptoms is no longer the vaguely defined premorbid personality, but the ordered and structured ensemble of beliefs and theories that the individual has developed on the basis of those experiences and that prevent him or her assimilating the new ones, represented by the precipitating factors of the 'illness'.
>
> (ibid.: 315, 316)

A personality trait is a constellation of cognitive phenomena which is general, distinctive and enduring (Scott *et al.* 1979). By viewing the problems of habitual violence and anger proneness as aspects of cognition/personality, we may begin to examine the nature of the continuities and consistencies, which are often more apparent than the dysfunctions in the presenting problem, allowing us to consider the 'ego-syntonic' presentations as well as the 'ego-dystonic'.

The constructivist view proposed by Guidano and Liotti (1984) indicates how the 'attachment' style between parents and child promotes the development of self-knowledge in the child. 'Self-schemata' are central to this model as with others (for example, Goldfried and Robins 1983).

Numerous studies have implicated threats to the self as a major component in the genesis of anger and aggression (for example, Feshbach 1970; Toch 1969). One way forward in our dealings with anger and violence, then, is to understand the nature of self-schemata and develop methods to change them. At a theoretical level it is appreciated that change at this core level may be quite difficult (Guidano and Liotti 1984), while at the practical, clinical level, the issue of resistance is attracting increasing attention (Dryden and Trower 1989).

In essence, then, models of anger and violence have to move from essentially pragmatic, clinical models towards unified cognitive models of personality if we are appropriately to understand both the sudden, disjunctive onset of a clinical problem, and the enduring, continuous problem that we may also face.

Cognitive theories and therapies present golden opportunities for the study and remediation of anger and violence. Theoreticians and clinicians need to grasp these opportunities and promote the understanding of these two, central human phenomena, to their rightful place.

REFERENCES

Alston, W. P. (1975) 'Traits, consistency and conceptual alternatives for personality therapy', *Journal of the Theory of Social Behavior* 5: 17–48.

Asarnow, J. R. and Callan, J. W. (1985) 'Boys with peer adjustment problems: social cognitive processes', *Journal of Consulting and Clinical Psychology* 53.

Averill, J. R. (1982) *Anger and Aggression: an Essay on Emotion*, New York. Springer-Verlag.

Bandura, A. (1973) *Aggression: A Social Learning Analysis*, Englewood Cliffs, NJ: Prentice-Hall.

—— (1976) 'Self-reinforcement: theoretical and methodological considerations, *Behaviorism* 4: 135–55.

—— (1986) *Social Foundations of Thought and Action*, Englewood Cliffs, NJ: Prentice-Hall.

Beck, A. T. (1976) *Cognitive Therapy and the Emotional Disorders*, New York: International Universities Press.

——, Rush, A. J., Shaw, B. F. and Emery, C. (1979) *Cognitive Therapy of Depression*, New York: Guilford Press.

Berkowitz, L. (1983) 'Aversively stimulated aggression: some parallels and differences in research with animals and humans', *American Psychologist* 38(11): 1135–44.

Biaggio, M. K. (1987) 'Therapeutic management of anger', *Clinical Psychology Review* 7: 663–75.

Bistline, J. L. and Frieden, F. P. (1984) 'Anger control: a case study of a stress inoculation treatment for a chronic aggressive patient', *Cognitive Therapy and Research* 8: 551–6.

Blackburn, R. (1989) 'Cognitive-behavioural approaches to understanding and treating aggression', in C. Hollin and K. Howells (eds) *Clinical Approaches to Criminal Behaviour*, Chichester: Wiley.

—— and Lee-Evans, J. M. (1985) 'Reactions of primary and secondary psychopaths to anger-evoking situations', *British Journal of Clinical Psychology* 24: 93–100.

Bornstein, P. H., Hamilton, S. B. and McFall, M. E. (1981) 'Modification of adult aggression: a critical review of theory, research and practice', in M. Hersen, R. M. Eisler and P. M. Miller (eds) *Progress in Behaviour Modification*, Vol. 12, New York: Academic Press.

Bowlby, J. A. (1973) *Attachment and Loss, Vol. 2: Separation: Anxiety and Anger*, London: Hogarth Press.

—— (1985) 'The role of childhood experience in cognitive disturbance', in M. J. Mahoney and A. Freeman (eds) *Cognition and Psychotherapy*, New York: Plenum.

Brewin, C. (1988) *Cognitive Foundations of Clinical Psychology*, London: Lawrence Erlbaum.

Buss, A. H. (1961) *The Psychology of Aggression*, New York: Wiley.

Chesney, M. A. and Rosenmann, R. (1985) *Anger and Hostility in Cardiovascular and Behavioral Disorders*, New York: Hampshire.

Deffenbacher, J. L., Demm, P. M. and Brandon, A. D. (1986) 'High general anger: correlates and treatment', *Behaviour Research and Therapy* 24: 481–9.

Deffenbacher, J. L., Story, D. A., Brandon, A. D., Hogg, J. A. and Hazaleus, S. L. (1988) 'Cognitive and cognitive-relaxation treatments of anger', *Cognitive Therapy and Research* 12(2): 167–84.

Dodge, K. A. and Frame, C. L. (1982) 'Social cognitive biases and deficits in aggressive boys', *Child Development* 53: 620–35.

Dodge, K. A., Murphy, P. R. and Buchsbaum, K. (1984) 'The assessment of intention – cue detection skills in children: implications for developmental psychopathology', *Child Development* 55: 163–73.

Dryden, W. (1984) 'Social skills assessment from a rational-emotive perspective', in P. Trower (ed.) *Radical Approaches to Social Skills Training*, London: Croom Helm.

—— and Golden, W. (eds) (1986) *Cognitive-Behavioural Approaches to Psychotherapy*, London: Harper and Row.

Dryden, W. and Trower, P. (eds) (1989) *Cognitive Psychotherapy: Stasis and Change*, London: Cassell.

Ellis, A. (1962) *Reason and Emotion in Psychotherapy*, Secaucus, NJ: Citadel Press.

—— (1977a) 'The basic clinical theory of rational-emotive therapy', in A. Ellis and R. Grieger (eds) *Handbook of Rational-Emotive Therapy*, New York: Springer.

—— (1977b) *How to Live with – and without – Anger*, New York: Reader's Digest Press.

Epstein, S. and Taylor, S. P. (1967) 'Instigation to aggression as a function of degree of defeat and perceived aggressive intent of the opponent', *Journal of Personality* 35: 265–89.

Feindler, E. L. and Ecton, R. B. (1986) *Adolescent Anger Control: Cognitive-Behavioural Techniques*, New York: Pergamon.

Ferguson, T. J. and Rule, B. G. (1983) 'An attributional perspective on anger and aggression', in R. G. Geen and E. Donnerstein (eds) *Aggression: Theoretical and Empirical Reviews, Vol. 1: Theoretical and Methodological Issues*, New York: Academic Press.

Feshbach, S. (1970) 'Aggression', in P. H. Mussen (ed.) *Carmichael's Manual of Child Psychology, Vol. 2*, New York: Wiley.

Frederiksen, L. W. and Rainwater, N. (1981) 'Explosive behavior: a skill development approach to treatment', in R. B. Stuart (ed.) *Violent Behaviour: Social Learning Approaches to Prediction, Management and Treatment*, New York: Brunner/Mazel.

Frijda, N. H. (1986) *The Emotions*, Cambridge: Cambridge University Press.

Geen, R. G. (1990) *Human Aggression*, Milton Keynes: Open University Press.

Golden, W. L. and Dryden, W. (1986) 'Cognitive-behavioral therapies: commonalities, divergencies and future development', in W. Dryden and W. Golden (eds) *Cognitive-Behavioral Approaches to Psychotherapy*, London: Harper and Row.

Goldfried, M. R. and Robins, C. (1983) 'Self-schema, cognitive bias, and the processing of therapeutic experiences', in P. C. Kendall (eds) *Advances in Cognitive Behavior Research and Therapy, Vol. 2*, London: Academic Press.

Guidano, V. F. and Liotti, G. (1983) *Cognitive Processes and Emotional Disorders*, New York, Guilford Press.

—— (1984) 'A constructivist foundation for cognitive therapy', in M. J. Mahoney and A. Freeman (eds) *Cognition and Psychotherapy*, New York: Plenum.

Hazaleus, S. L. and Deffenbacher, J. L. (1986) 'Relaxation and cognitive treatments of anger', *Journal of Consulting and Clinical Psychology* 54(2): 22–6.

Howells, K. (1982) 'Aggression: clinical approaches to treatment', in D. R. Black (ed.) *Symposium: Broadmoor Psychology Department's 21st Birthday*, Leicester: British Psychological Society.

—— and Hollin, C. (eds) (1989) *Clinical Approaches to Violence*, Chichester: John Wiley.

Ickes, W. (1984) 'Personality', in A. S. Bellack and M. Hersen (eds) *Research Methods in Clinical Psychology*, New York: Pergamon.

Izard, C., Kagan, J. and Zajono, R. B. (1984) *Emotions, Cognitions and Behaviour*, Cambridge: Cambridge University Press.

Kazdin, A. E., Bass, D., Siegel, T. and Thomas, C. (1989) 'Cognitive-behavioral therapy and relationship therapy in the treatment of children referred for antisocial behavior', *Journal of Consulting and Clinical Psychology* 57(4): 522–35.

Kendall, P. C. and Bemis, K. M. (1983) 'Thought and action in psychotherapy: the cognitive-behavioral approaches', in M. Hersen, A. E. Kazdin and A. S. Bellack (eds) *The Clinical Psychology Handbook*, New York: Pergamon.

Lazarus, R. S. (1966) *Psychological Stress and the Coping Process*, New York: McGraw-Hill.

—— and Folkman, S. (1984) *Stress Appraisal and Coping* New York: Springer.

Leventhal, H. (1980) 'Towards a comprehensive theory of emotion', in C. Berkowitz (ed.) *Advances in Experimental Social Psychology, Vol. 13*, New York: Academic Press.

Lochman, J. E. (1987) 'Self and peer perceptions and attributional biases of aggressive and non-aggressive boys in dyadic interactions', *Journal of Consulting and Clinical Psychology* 55(3): 404–10.

——, Nelson, W. M. and Sims, J. P. (1981) 'A cognitive behavioral program for use with aggressive children', *Journal of Clinical Child Psychology* Autumn: 146–8.

McDougall, C., Barnett, R. M., Ashurst, B. and Willis, B. (1987) 'Cognitive control of anger', in B. J. McGurk, D. Thornton and M. Williams (eds) *Applying Psychology to Imprisonment*, HMSO: London.

Maiuro, R. D., Cahn, T. S., Vitaliano, P. P., Wagner, D. C. and Zegree, J. B. (1988) 'Anger, hostility and depression in domestically violent versus generally assaultive men and non-violent control subjects', *Journal of Consulting and Clinical Psychology* 56 (1): 17–23.

Manstead, A. S. R. and Wagner, H. L. (1981) 'Arousal, cognition and emotion: an appraisal of two-factor theory', *Current Psychological Reviews* 1: 35–54.

Margolin, G. (1979) 'Conjoint marital therapy to enhance anger management and reduce spouse abuse', *American Journal of Family Therapy* 20: 17–23.

Meichenbaum, D. (1977) *Cognitive Behavior Modification*, New York: Plenum.

—— (1985) *Stress Inoculation Training*, New York: Pergamon.

Mischel, W. (1968) *Personality and Assessment*, New York: Wiley.

Moon, J. R. and Eisler, R. M. (1983) 'Anger control: an experimental comparison of three behavioral treatments', *Behavior Therapy* 14: 493–505.

Nomellini, S. and Katz, R. C. (1983) 'Effects of anger control training on abusive parents', *Cognitive Therapy and Research* 7: 57–68.

Novaco, R. W. (1975) *Anger Control*, Lexington, Mass.: Heath.

—— (1977) 'Stress inoculation: a cognitive therapy for anger and its application to a case of depression', *Journal of Consulting and Clinical Psychology* 45: 600–8.

—— (1978) 'Anger and coping with stress', in J. P. Foreyt and D. P. Rathjon (eds) *Cognitive Behavior Therapy*, New York: Plenum.

—— (1979) 'The cognitive regulation of anger and stress', in P. C. Kendall and S. D. Hollon (eds) *Cognitive-Behavioral Interventions: Theory, Research and Procedures*, New York: Academic Press.

—— (1983) 'Stress inoculation therapy for anger control: a manual for therapists', unpublished manuscript, University of California, Irvine.

—— and Welsh, W. N. (1989) 'Anger disturbances: cognitive mediation and clinical prescriptions', in K. Howells and C. Hollin (eds) *Clinical Approaches to Violence*, Chichester: Wiley.

Olweus, D. (1979) 'Stability of aggressive reaction patterns in males: a review', *Psychological Bulletin* 86(4): 852–75.

—— (1980) 'The consistency issue in personality psychology revisited – with special reference to aggression', *British Journal of Social and Clinical Psychology* 19: 377–90.

Perry, D. G., Perry, L. C. and Rasmussen, P. (1986) 'Cognitive social learning mediators of aggression', *Child Development* 57: 700–11.

Rule, B. G. and Neasdale, A. R. (1976) 'Emotional arousal and aggressive behaviour', *Psychological Bulletin* 83: 851–63.

Safran, J. D., Vallis, T. M., Segal, Z. U. and Shaw, B. F. (1986) 'Assessment of core cognitive processes in cognitive therapy', *Cognitive Therapy and Research* 10(5): 500–26.

Schachter, S. and Singer, J. (1962) 'Cognitive social and physiological determinants of emotional state', *Psychological Review* 69: 379–99.

Scott, W. A., Osgood, D. W. and Peterson, C. (1979) *Cognitive Structure, Theory and Measurement of Individual Differences*, New York: Wiley.

Spielberger, C. D., Jacobs, G. A., Russell, S. and Crane, R. J. (1983) 'Assessment of anger: the state–trait anger scale', in J. N. Butcher and C. D. Spielberger (eds) *Advances in Personality Assessment, Vol. 1*, Hillsdale, NJ: Lawrence Erlbaum.

Spivack, G., Platt, J. J. and Shure, M. D. (1976) *The Problem Solving Approach to Adjustment*, San Francisco: Jossey-Bass.

Stermac, L. E. (1987) 'Anger control treatment for forensic patients', *Journal of Interpersonal Violence* 1(4): 446–57.

Suinn, R. M. (1977) *Manual-Anxiety Management Training*, Fort Collins, Colorado: Rocky Mountains Behavioral Sciences Institute.

Tedeschi, J. T. (1983) 'Social influence theory and aggression', in R. G. Geen and E. Donnerstein (eds) *Aggression: Theoretical and Empirical Reviews, Vol. 1: Theoretical and Methodological Issues*, New York: Academic Press.

Toch, H. (1969) *Violent Men*, Harmondsworth: Penguin.

Wickless, C. and Kirsch, I. (1988) 'Cognitive correlates of anger, anxiety and sadness', *Cognitive Therapy and Research* 12(4): 367–77.

Zillman, D. (1978) 'Attribution and misattribution of excitatory reactions', in J. H. Harvey, W. J. Ickes and R. F. Kidd (eds) *New Directions in Attribution Research, Vol. 2*, Hillsdale, NJ: Lawrence Erlbaum.

—— (1983) 'Arousal and Aggression', in R. G. Geen and E. Donnerstein (eds) *Aggression: Theoretical and Empirical Reviews: Vol. 1: Theoretical and Methodological Issues* New York: Academic Press.

Zwemer, W. A. and Deffenbacher, J. L. (1984) 'Irrational beliefs, anger, and anxiety', *Journal of Consulting and Clinical Psychology* 31(3): 391–3.

Chapter 5

Eating disorders

Celia McCrea

INTRODUCTION

Concern about obesity and the pursuit of slenderness is not new. The privileged classes have been preoccupied through the ages with the question of how to stay slim in the face of abundance. The ancient Greeks are supposed to have envied their cultural predecessors, the Cretans, for having known of a drug that permitted them to stay slim while eating as much as they wanted. Both the old Spartans and Athenians frowned upon obesity, and Roman ladies were literally starved to make them slim, their efforts being helped by the invention of the vomitorium (Bruch 1957: 35–59).

Over the last two decades the incidence of eating disorders has risen dramatically (Shisslak *et al.* 1987), with some investigators concluding that epidemic proportions have been reached, at least in western society (Maloney and Klykylo 1983). Certainly it is generally accepted that eating disorders represent a major health problem (Beutler 1987; Mitchell and Eckert 1987), and against this background it is hardly surprising to find that research efforts have markedly increased in recent years. Issues relating to obesity, self-starvation and self-induced purging have been highlighted for investigation. However, because these disorders appear to result from a number of factors, including biological variables, personality traits and cultural attitudes, investigators from a wide range of backgrounds are needed.

Brownell and Foreyt (1986) have emphasized the need to involve many disciplines in the study and treatment of the eating disorders. For example, the importance of nutrition and exercise should not be underestimated. Just as some foods may trigger physiological reactions which induce hunger and satiety, thus precipitating binge eating or weight gain, similarly, exercise is important because of its influence in energy balance and weight regulation. Nevertheless, the role of these factors has not been thoroughly investigated. Although some attempt has been made to investigate the relationship between weight and exercise (Stern and Lowney 1986), further research is needed.

This chapter is primarily concerned with the cognitive-behavioural approach, which argues that, rather than being simply symptomatic, dysfunctional beliefs and values appear to be of primary importance in the maintenance of eating disorders, and that therefore their change is a prerequisite for recovery. However, it must be recognized that an integrated approach is necessary for the best understanding and treatment of eating disorders. Cognitive-behavioural interventions should not be considered in isolation. Instead they must be viewed as part of an interdisciplinary approach to disorders which appear to result from, and be maintained by, a combination of factors.

DIAGNOSTIC CRITERIA

Anorexia nervosa

Diagnostic thinking about anorexia nervosa has passed through several phases (see Strober 1986). It has been considered entirely somatic and entirely psychological at different times and by different investigators. Gull (1874) and Laseque (1873) described anorexia nervosa as a psychological disorder with physical manifestations, but Simmonds's (1914) subsequent description of a patient with anterior pituitary damage and weight loss resulted in a long period of diagnostic confusion between anorexia nervosa and primary endocrine illness.

Today, most clinicians recognize a core syndrome of primary anorexia nervosa that is distinct from other disorders (Bruch 1970, 1973; Crisp 1965; Garfinkel *et al*. 1980; and Russell 1970). Preoccupation with body size and intense efforts to reduce weight at the expense of other areas of life are seen as being specific to the disorder, in contrast to its secondary form, where weight loss occurs not because of the pursuit of thinness *per se*, but rather due to associated problems such as schizophrenia, depressive illness and so on.

The diagnostic criteria for anorexia nervosa are now generally agreed, (see Table 5.1), although prior to the publication of Russell's criteria, (Russell 1970), many still used the term anorexia nervosa in a non-specific manner to refer to various psychological disorders in which there was significant weight loss. By highlighting an essential feature of anorexia nervosa, namely 'morbid fear of becoming fat', Russell's diagnostic criteria narrowed the identified patient group.

Table 5.1   Russell's diagnostic criteria for anorexia nervosa (Russell 1970)

(1)	The patient's behaviour leads to a marked loss of body weight.
(2)	There is an endocrine disorder which manifests itself clinically by cessation of menstruation in females. (In males the equivalent symptom is loss of sexual appetite.)
(3)	There is psychopathology characterized by a morbid fear of becoming fat.

Recognition of the importance of extreme concerns about weight and shape have stemmed from a number of different theoretical orientations (Bruch 1973; Crisp 1967; Wilson *et al*. 1983), and in the latest diagnostic system (DSM-III-R – APA

Table 5.2   DSM-III-R diagnostic criteria for anorexia nervosa*

(A)   Refusal to maintain body weight over a minimal normal weight for age and
      height, e.g. weight loss leading to maintenance of body weight 15 per cent
      below that expected; or failure to make expected weight gain during period
      of growth, leading to body weight 15 per cent below that expected.
(B)   Intense fear of gaining weight or becoming fat, even though underweight.
(C)   Disturbance in the way in which one's body weight, size, or shape is
      experienced, e.g. the person claims to 'feel fat' even when emaciated,
      believes that one area of the body is 'too fat' even when obviously
      underweight.
(D)   In females, absence of at least three consecutive menstrual cycles when
      otherwise expected to occur (primary or secondary amenorrhea). (A
      woman is considered to have amenorrhea if her periods occur only
      following hormone (e.g. oestrogen) administration.)

* Reprinted with permission from *Diagnostic and Statistical Manual of Mental Disorders*,
  Third Edition, Revised, p. 67. Copyright 1987. American Psychiatric Association.

1987), the presence of such attitudes is necessary for a diagnosis of anorexia
nervosa (see Table 5.2).

However, some argue that these new diagnostic criteria are still problematic.
Fairburn and Garner (1988) challenge the usefulness of amenorrhea (or loss of
sexual appetite in males) as a diagnostic criterion, on the grounds that there is no
evidence to suggest that it is likely to demarcate a group with a distinctive natural
history or response to treatment. Also, debate exists concerning how much weight
should be lost. Some diagnostic schemes required that a certain percentage (generally 15–25 per cent) of premorbid weight be lost, whereas others require weight to
fall below a percentage (usually 75–85 per cent) of the population norm for the
person's age, height and sex with no account being taken of their premorbid weight.
However, the 'set point' theory (Keesey 1986) is concerned with how ingested
energy is utilized and expended. It examines adjustments in energy expenditure
which may aid in stabilizing an organism's body weight at a physiologically
regulated level or 'set point', thus suggesting that individuals may each have a
'natural' weight, which may differ from the population average for that person's
age, height and sex.

Bulimia nervosa

In contrast to anorexia nervosa, general agreement does not exist regarding the
clinical features necessary for a diagnosis of bulimia. It is commonly accepted that
the central feature of this disorder is a loss of control over eating but debate abounds
as to which other clinical features should be regarded as necessary (Fairburn and
Garner 1988).

This disorder has been variously labelled as 'bulimarexia' (Boskind-Lodahl
1976), 'the dieting chaos syndrome' (Palmer 1979), 'bulimia nervosa' (Russell

1979) and 'bulimia' (American Psychiatric Association 1980), the latter two being most frequently used in the literature.

Fairburn and Garner (1988) propose that three elements constitute the core of the disorder, namely: (1) the subjective loss of control over eating and the associated bulimic episodes (in which there is rapid consumption of large amounts of food in a discrete period of time, usually less than 2 hours); (2) behaviour designed to control body weight; and (3) characteristic extreme concerns about shape and weight. However, although Russell's (1979) original set of criteria encompasses these three core elements of the syndrome, the diagnostic criteria for DSM-III bulimia (American Psychiatric Association 1980) did not. The DSM-III classification was over-inclusive, in that it focused primarily on overeating, without specifying the other two core clinical features to be present (behaviour designed to control body weight and extreme concerns about shape and weight), a large heterogeneous population therefore being eligible for inclusion. Proposed revisions to the DSM-III criteria were therefore published (American Psychiatric Association 1985), offering a more succinct and satisfactory definition of binge eating, and including behaviour designed to control body weight as an essential diagnostic feature. However, Fairburn and Garner (1986) highlighted continuing problems. Rather than bulimia nervosa, the term 'bulimic disorder' had been suggested for inclusion in DSM-III, and this meant that confusion over the meaning of the word bulimia was likely to continue (i.e. ambiguity resulting from using the word bulimia to refer both to the overeating associated with the disorder and the full clinical syndrome itself). In addition, because the diagnosis could still be made in the absence of any characteristic concerns about shape and weight, a heterogeneous patient population was still eligible for inclusion. The subsequent revision, DSM-III-R (American Psychiatric Association 1987), addressed both of these criticisms. The disorder is now name 'bulimia nervosa', and the characteristic attitudes to shape and weight are a necessary diagnostic feature (see Table 5.3).

Table 5.3   DSM-III-R diagnostic criteria for bulimia nervosa*

(A)	Recurrent episodes of binge eating (rapid consumption of a large amount of food in a discrete period of time).
(B)	A feeling of lack of control over eating behaviour during the eating binges.
(C)	The person regularly engages in either self-induced vomiting, use of laxatives or diuretics, strict dieting or fasting, or vigorous exercise in order to prevent weight gain.
(D)	A minimum average of two binge eating episodes for at least three months.
(E)	Persistent over-concern with body shape and weight.

* Reprinted with permission from *Diagnostic and Statistical Manual of Mental Disorders, Third Edition, Revised,* pp. 68–9. Copyright 1987. American Psychiatric Association.

Obesity

When there is an increase in body weight above some arbitrary standard (usually defined in relation to height), an individual is classified as 'overweight'. In contrast, 'obesity' refers to the presence of an abnormally high percentage of body fat (adiposity). To differentiate between individuals who are obese, and those who are overweight because of an increase in lean body mass (as often seen with athletes), techniques and standards are needed for quantifying body fatness.

The most accurate method for measuring total body fat is underwater weighing, but this is a cumbersome operation, not readily available to the majority. Measures of skin-fold thickness provide a useful indication of adiposity at various body sites, but they are not technically easy to obtain, causing the error of measurement to be relatively large. Thus, the most widely used indices for overweight are based on body weight in relation to height, and of these the body mass index (BMI) has the best correlation with body fat (Bray 1978). This index is the weight divided by height squared $[Wt/(Ht)^2]$. It provides an easily obtained, relatively error-free measure, which, while correlating well with the more complex measures of adiposity such as underwater weighing and skin-fold thickness, provides a useful clinical indicator of adiposity and degree of overweight.

Some argue that whereas anorexia nervosa and bulimia nervosa are psychiatric disorders involving disturbances of behaviour and mental state, obesity refers to a purely physical condition of excess body fat, and therefore should not be regarded as a 'true' eating disorder. In their review of eating disorders, Cooper and Cooper (1988) conclude:

> evidence that obesity is a disorder with a significant psychological component is weak. The condition presents as an essentially physical disorder of body weight and the role of disturbed eating in its aetiology and maintenance is, at best, unproven. It is therefore not reasonable to regard obesity as an eating disorder in the sense that anorexia nervosa and bulimia nervosa are clearly such disorders.
>
> (ibid.: 269)

Investigation of the importance of genetic factors would seem to support this conclusion. In an adoption study carried out by Stunkard et al. (1986), a strong relationship was found between adoptees' weights and the BMIs of their biological parents. However, a similar relation was not found when the adoptees' weight was compared with the BMIs of the adopted parents, thus supporting the importance of genetic factors in the aetiology of obesity.

Nevertheless, Brownell and Foreyt (1986) argue that, although obesity is likely to include crucial physiological factors in its aetiology, it also has important cultural and psychological causes and consequences. These authorities in the field suggest that while obesity may not be an eating disorder per se, and potential disadvantages are associated with this label, the interactions such an approach might facilitate between the clinical and research information available for anorexia nervosa, bulimia nervosa and obesity may be a more important consideration. The most compelling reason for including obesity when considering the eating disorders is the likelihood that research and clinical work in each area will benefit all three.

CONCEPTUALIZATION

Anorexia nervosa

Anorexia nervosa has been conceptualized from a range of theoretical perspectives. Emphasis has been placed on early development, faulty interactional patterns, fears of psychosexual maturity, specific personality traits, behavioural contingencies, biological determinants and the social context (Garfinkel and Garner 1982; Garner and Garfinkel 1985). It seems likely that each may be relevant to a particular subset of patients, and Garfinkel and Garner (1982) thus propose that anorexia nervosa is probably best understood as a final common pathway that may be entered through the interaction of various psychological, familial and social predisposing factors. Some investigators argue that anorexia nervosa reflects an attempt to cope with maturational problems through the mechanism of avoidance of biological maturity (Crisp 1984). By placing emphasis on weight, anorexics may derive relief from the challenges of growth (such as the establishment of autonomy, separation from the family, the formation of peer relationships, acceptance of the self and coping with sexual feelings). Because weight has the promising quality of being potentially controllable it seems that the anorexic seeks to manipulate it, as a means of exerting control. Szmukler (1985) notes that weight loss may thus become rewarding, if the individual values the feeling of being in control. However, if the underlying core problems remain unaltered, as they are likely to, then the anorexic may intensify her efforts for weight loss in the vain hope that this will help. (Because eating disorders are characterized by a preponderance of females, the convention of using female pronouns when referring to patients has been adopted in this chapter.) A vicious circle can develop whereby the effort to lose weight becomes so important to the anorexic that it assumes even greater importance.

However, as hunger increases, so the fear of losing control develops, the anorexic believing that any weight gain would destroy her 'special achievement'. When this fear is recognized, the anorexic's strategy of redoubling her slimming effort to provide a 'safety-margin' is understandable. Meanwhile, as more and more energy is directed towards weight control, so alternative sources of satisfaction are likely to decline, while the problems associated with maturation develop.

A cognitive-behavioural approach to the understanding of anorexia nervosa emphasizes how the symptom pattern logically derives from the patient's faulty assumptions, attitudes towards shape and weight being of central importance. Bruch (1962, 1973) was the first to recognize the importance of maladaptive thinking in the development of anorexia nervosa, and since her early observations, distorted attitudes about food, weight and the body have been increasingly recognized as characteristic of anorexia nervosa. These observations have led to the development of cognitive-behavioural management principles aimed at the range of misconceptions that appear to maintain the disorder. Garner and Bemis (1982) see distorted thinking patterns as important in the maintenance of anorexia nervosa, and they suggest that a modified version of the cognitive model described by Beck and his co-workers (Beck 1976; Beck *et al*. 1979) may be helpful in attempts to understand the thinking patterns of anorexic patients. Typical cognitive distortions which may be relevant to the development and maintenance of anorexia nervosa are shown in Table 5.4. (Empirical confirmation will be needed to verify the prominence and specificity of these and other erroneous thinking styles in anorexia nervosa.)

Table 5.4   Cognitive distortions characteristic of anorexia nervosa

Cognitive distortion	Example
Dichotomous reasoning (thinking in extreme and absolutistic terms).	If I am not in complete control, I will lose all control.
Selective abstraction (selecting out small parts of a situation and ignoring others).	If only I weighed less then I would feel better (weight being seen as the only frame of reference necessary for self-evaluation).
Arbitrary inference (where a conclusion is inferred from irrelevant evidence).	Everyone stared at me because my stomach was so bloated.
Overgeneralization (where it is concluded from one negative event that another negative event is thereby likely).	I wasn't successful at that, and now everything is probably going to fall apart.
Catastrophizing (thinking the very worst of a situation).	I've gained a pound – now I'm bound to become obese.
Excessive reliance on the words 'should' and 'must'.	I should avoid fattening foods. I must do these exercises every day.

Logical errors such as these may result in the faulty thinking so typical of the anorexic, and it is possible that, as many of the assumptions are values the anorexic patient holds, these may provide support for her relentless dieting and its associated fear of weight gain and food. Garner and Bemis (1985) argue that such distorted assumptions, expectations and beliefs are not only symptomatic of anorexia nervosa, but are also of primary importance in its maintenance, extreme dieting being maintained by the cognitive self-reinforcement which stems from the sense of mastery, virtue and self-control that this denial provides to the anorexic patient.

Bulimia nervosa

Ever since bulimia nervosa was first recognized there has been a great deal of speculation as to how it can best be construed. The cognitive-behavioural conceptualization highlights the importance of patients' dysfunctional beliefs and values concerning their shape and weight, concerns which, because of their prominence and intensity, have been commented upon by many investigators (Bruch 1973; Crisp 1967; Russell 1979). Fairburn (1986) argues that illogical thinking is of fundamental importance in bulimia nervosa, and that given its presence, most aspects of the condition can be understood. Extreme measures directed at weight control (such as dieting, vomiting and laxative abuse), together with preoccupations concerning food, eating and changes in shape and weight, can all be comprehended. Even apparently paradoxical behaviours such as binge eating can be understood in cognitive terms, as they may represent a secondary response to extreme dietary restraint where an individual is consciously limiting her intake in an attempt to lose weight (Polivy *et al*. 1984).

A relationship appears to exist between bingeing and dietary restraint (Clarke and Palmer 1983; Wardle 1980). Evidence suggests that even in non-clinical situations the breakdown of restraint may lead to an increase in consumption. In a laboratory study Herman and Mack (1975) classified subjects according to whether or not they were habitual restrained eaters. Both groups were given an experimental 'taste test', in which the amount of ice-cream they consumed was measured in relation to whether or not they had been given a dietary preload (in the form of a milk shake). Non-restrained subjects ate less ice-cream after one milk shake and still less after two, whereas the habitually restrained subjects ate substantially more ice-cream once they had consumed a preload of milk shake. Although physiological mechanisms might underlie such over-consumption in the face of previous deprivation, evidence supporting the role of cognitive factors stems from the finding that it is the subject's belief about the calorie content of the preload rather than its actual substance that determines subsequent eating behaviour (Polivy 1976; Spencer and Fremouw 1979). Furthermore, other factors found to produce counter-regulation (the tendency towards rebound overeating in the face of dietary restraint), in dieters are dysphoric mood state and the consumption of alcohol (Polivy *et al*. 1984; Wardle and Beinhart 1981).

To reconcile schools of thought emphasizing the biological control of eating with others which highlight the importance of psychological and social influences, Herman and Polivy (1984) have proposed a 'boundary model' for the regulation of eating. The crucial notion associated with this model is that normally, food consumption is controlled within the boundaries of hunger and satiety, and that within this range non-physiological factors manifest their influence. Thus, if an individual is neither hungry nor satiated, there is little biological pressure to eat, but as a consequence, social, cognitive and other psychological influences may operate to affect the amount of food that is eaten (for example, attractive food, and congenial company, may tempt a person to eat, even if she is not particularly hungry).

Herman and Polivy suggest that dieters, as opposed to non-dieters, are characterized by a reduced level of physiological control governing their eating. Dieting is seen as an attempt to replace normal physiological controls with cognitive ones, and to this end it is proposed that dieters possess an additional 'diet' boundary (representing the individual's self-imposed quota for consumption, which, for weight loss to occur, must by definition fall short of the satiety boundary). As a result of attempting to respond to such a cognitive 'diet' boundary, instead of natural bodily demands, it is likely that the dieter becomes less sensitive to the physiological pressures which might otherwise help her to regulate her consumption, and this may account for the fact that dieters are characterized by lower hunger and higher satiety boundaries.

The cognitive 'diet' boundary may account for the counter-regulation manifested by restrained eaters in the Herman and Mack study. As the preload (milk shake) may have in itself caused the dieter to think that she had transgressed her diet boundary, then it is understandable that the 'what-the-hell' effect may occur, whereby, because there seems to be no point in restraining further consumption, the dieter eats in an uninhibited manner, until satiety pressures begin to operate. However, although under these circumstances most dieters limit their consumption because of the pressures of satiety, it seems that binge eaters are less constrained by these aversive sensations. At the behavioural level what is most notable about bingers is their apparent willingness to tolerate the discomfort of the upper aversive zone in their quest for the satisfaction which eating provides for them, although of course vomiting is often resorted to as a means of obtaining relief from the aversive sensations caused by overeating. (It should be noted too that at the other end of the scale the anorexic is characterized by her willingness to tolerate the discomforts associated with starvation, because for her it is not the satiety boundary which is irrelevant, but rather the hunger boundary.)

Indirect support exists to suggest that dietary restraint (or rigid dieting) is implicated in the development of bulimic episodes as they occur in bulimia nervosa. Among these patients, for the majority the onset of bulimic episodes coincided with a period of dietary restriction (Fairburn and Cooper 1984; Mitchell *et al.* 1985), and it has been noted that it is rare to find bulimic episodes in the absence of attempts at dietary restriction (Polivy and Herman 1985). It has also been reported that greater degrees of restraint are associated with more severe bulimic episodes (Hawkins and Clement 1980).

Cooper and Cooper (1988) suggest that systematic longitudinal studies should be carried out to determine whether at least some people who restrict their food intake subsequently lose control of their eating. These investigators have also highlighted some of the methodological difficulties inherent in any attempts to examine the role of dietary restraint in bulimia nervosa. For example, they note that the Restraint Scale used by Herman and Mack (1975) has been shown to confound dietary restriction *per se* with fluctuations in body weight, and they draw attention to the fact that within a cognitive-behavioural model, it is still necessary to consider why some individuals respond to the dilemmas of restrained eating by developing bulimia nervosa and others do not.

Obesity

The role of psychological variables in the aetiology and maintenance of obesity has been the subject of considerable research interest (for a review see Striegel-Moore and Rodin 1986). Psychodynamic explanations have been offered and an extensive literature established on the personality traits and psychological functioning believed to characterize obese people. However, more recent models view obesity as multiply determined, and it is now generally acknowledged that obese and normal weight individuals do *not* differ on global measures of personality traits or psychological adjustment.

Behaviour therapists have also examined eating patterns, seeing these as potentially significant in the aetiology of obesity. However, methodological problems intrinsic to both laboratory and field studies have complicated this work, and no consistent differences in eating style or amount eaten have emerged between overweight and normal weight subjects.

The possibility that people at different weights use different cues to stimulate eating has been investigated (Nisbett 1968; Schachter and Rodin 1974), and in this context 'locus of control' (Rotter 1966) has been of interest because of its postulated link with dependency and self-regulation skills. Individuals with external locus of control are more dependent and less effective in their use of self-reinforcement than individuals with internal locus of control, and thus it has been suggested that while the eating pattern of normal-weight individuals may be influenced by internal signals (such as gastric motility and other peripheral and central physiological cues signalling hunger and satiety), the eating pattern of an obese person may be influenced largely by external cues (for example, time, the taste and sight of food, and the number of highly palatable food cues present). Numerous studies have investigated this proposal, but findings indicate that although individuals do vary with respect to external responsiveness and eating behaviour, overweight individuals as a group are no more 'external' than their normal-weight counterparts.

Today the role of psychological variables in the aetiology of obesity remains unclear. The fact that obesity is not a homogeneous disorder has been noted by Striegel-Moore and Rodin (1986) as an important factor which may contribute to this confusion. These investigators suggest that a better understanding of aetiological factors might be gained by prospective studies, and by a closer examination of the psychological and behavioural factors that relate to exercise.

Another aspect of obesity which warrants further investigation is the role of body-image disturbance in its aetiology. Body-image distortion is perhaps one of the most powerful examples showing how distorted cognitions can influence the cause and course of an eating disorder, and in a cognitive-behavioural conceptualization of obesity, excessive concern over matters of body weight and shape is a common thread which links this disorder with anorexia nervosa and bulimia nervosa. Many obese individuals are characterized by their extreme concern about body image and weight loss, regarding their body as a 'battleground'. Because the majority view themselves negatively they are more likely to attempt to restrict their eating, the cognitive 'diet' boundary then influencing eating patterns in a manner similar to that already described with anorexic and bulimic patients.

Bruch (1973) has emphasized that ideally there should be no discrepancy between body image, body structure and social acceptance. However, for the obese this is not the case, as today fat is stigmatized (Allon 1979). Although contempt for fat has not always existed (see Bennet and Gurin 1982), public opinion currently favours the slender linear figure, the late Duchess of Windsor encapsulating the general mood in her famous quotation, 'no woman can be too rich, or too thin'. It seems that an association has been developed between thinness, self-control and success, with dieting being promoted by the media as an overt sign of self-control and discipline (Brownmiller 1982; Orbach 1978), with parallel associations condemning the fat individual, curvaceousness being linked with incompetence (Silverstein et al. 1986).

Against such a background, it is hardly surprising to find that the obese condition is characterized by body-image distortion. Employing an anamorphic-lens technique, Glucksman and Hirsch (1969) observed obese subjects to overestimate their body size both during and following weight loss. Schonbuch and Schell (1967) asked subjects to estimate their body appearance by selecting from a graded series of pictured physiques, and their findings demonstrated a tendency for the obese subjects, compared with normal-weight controls, to overestimate their body size and shape. Results from studies employing distorting mirrors (Shipman and Sohlkhah 1967), distorting photograph techniques and visual size estimation apparatus (Garner et al. 1976) also support the suggestion that the obese see themselves larger than they actually are.

Investigators studying body-image phenomena believe that an individual's attitude towards the body may influence responses in the same way as do other significant attitudes (Fisher 1972). The manner in which an individual responds to various situations is likely to be influenced by the judgements they make concerning their own body. For example, the choices made between wearing skin-tight trousers or a loose-fitting frock; attempting to run to catch the bus or being resigned to missing it; participating in a healthy life style or an unhealthy one – these are just some of the everyday decisions which may be affected by the individual's perception of herself as being slim and attractive, or fat and unattractive.

Obese individuals tend to evaluate their bodies negatively and they are extremely self-denigratory. It has been suggested that a circular relationship may develop between body-image disturbance, which predisposes to esteem-lowering experiences and depressive moods, which in turn reinforce the disturbed body image (Stunkard and Mendelson 1967). This approach to obesity suggests that the achievement of a realistic body image is therapeutically important for successful weight loss, an issue which will be discussed below under Future Developments.

TREATMENT

Anorexia nervosa

Numerous management plans have been proposed for the treatment of anorexia nervosa. Largely based on the theoretical orientation of the physician and the mechanisms presumed to be responsible for the disorder, these have ranged from nurturance and somatic treatments including pharmacotherapies and surgery, to psychological treatments encompassing psychoanalytic, family-therapy and behaviour-therapy approaches (for an overview see Strober 1986).

More recently there has been considerable interest in the generation of cognitive-behavioural treatments for anorexia nervosa (Garner 1986; Garner and Bemis 1985). Based on cognitive-behavioural principles delineated by Beck and his colleagues for the treatment of depressive and phobic disorders (Beck 1967, 1976; Beck *et al*. 1979; Hollon and Beck 1979), Garner and Bemis (1982) have described how these principles can be adapted specifically for the anorexic patient, so that she learns to identify, evaluate and change faulty thinking patterns and erroneous beliefs. In this context it should be cautioned that over-emphasis on the importance of cognition could lead to the same thing happening as with traditional behavioural interventions, namely that too much attention will be paid to just one aspect of human functioning (Hollin and Lewis 1988). It should be noted that the interdependence between cognitive and behavioural change is so fundamental that it is somewhat misleading to consider them separately. The incorporation of specific graded behavioural exercises with cognitive methods is a fundamental part of cognitive-behavioural therapy. For example, predictions may be tested by means of behavioural experiments. Thus, if the anorexic believes that the slightest reduction in her exercise regime will cause her immediately to gain a vast amount of weight, then a ban on exercise can provide the opportunity for this hypothesis to be tested, and the conclusions used to disprove irrational fears.

However, to date there have been no reports of the systematic application of cognitive-behavioural treatment to anorexic patients. Treatment programmes have been developed on clinical experience and they tend to be multi-component in nature, with the contributions of each component of the therapeutic outcome being uncertain. Agras and Kramer (1984) point out that, for anorexia nervosa, this unsatisfactory state of affairs is contributed to by the relative rarity and chronic nature of the disorder, which makes long-term controlled outcome studies of convincing size difficult if not impossible to carry out. For reasons such as these the effects of different treatment approaches on long-term outcome have not been studied with anorexic patients.

Follow-up research has also suffered from methodological flaws, a major obstacle being that descriptions of the conduct of out-patient psychotherapy typically have not been detailed enough to allow for replication. Garner and Bemis (1985) caution that the cognitive-behavioural techniques they describe have been applied unsystematically in clinical settings, and that no vigorous tests have yet been conducted to support or refute optimism for their efficacy. Although these investigators are not alone in regarding attitude change as a prerequisite for complete recovery from anorexia nervosa, and considering cognitive-behavioural treatment as a valuable method for achieving this end, in the absence of any controlled studies, no particular treatment can be regarded as definitive. Only as more outcome data become available can the comparative effectiveness of different therapies be meaningfully evaluated.

Bulimia nervosa

First reports of bulimia nervosa did not appear until the 1970s, and although since then a number of studies have been carried out, little is still known about the relative effectiveness of various treatments for the disorder. Nevertheless, based on his extensive work with bulimic patients, Fairburn (1986) has concluded that: 'on balance some form of cognitive-behavioural therapy is probably the treatment of choice for bulimia nervosa' (p. 30).

The first series of cases treated with the cognitive-behavioural approach was reported by Fairburn (1981). In an uncontrolled trial eleven patients suffering from bulimia nervosa were given individual treatment, with nine subsequently reducing the frequency of their bouts of overeating and vomiting, this improvement being maintained by the seven who were followed up at approximately 9 months. Although body weight did not change, Fairburn reports that anxiety and depression levels were decreased, and dysfunctional attitudes concerning body shape and weight were modified. In a more recent report, Fairburn (1984) concludes that subsequent experience with over fifty patients confirms that the majority of patients benefit from a cognitive-behavioural approach, with most remaining well and requiring no further treatment.

The cognitive-behavioural techniques used in Fairburn's programme are based on those used by Beck and colleagues in the treatment of depression, (Beck *et al*. 1979), emphasis being placed on the modification of patients' extreme concerns about food, eating, shape and weight. This programme has been the most extensively studied of the cognitive-behavioural treatments, and a standard 'package' has been specified in considerable detail (Fairburn 1985). The treatment is conducted on an out-patient basis, over a period of approximately 5 months, three stages being distinguished. The first stage lasts for approximately 4 weeks, and appointments are twice weekly. Emphasis is placed on establishing control over eating, and the techniques used are largely behavioural. Self-monitoring, the prescription of a pattern of regular eating, the instruction to weigh weekly and stimulus-control measures similar to those used in the behavioural treatment of obesity are some of the techniques used, together with education regarding the consequences of self-induced vomiting and purgative abuse.

In the second stage more attention is given to cognitions, with dysfunctional thoughts, beliefs and values being identified and modified. At weekly appointments over a period of approximately 8 weeks extreme concerns about food, eating, shape and weight are identified and patients are taught to question their validity. In the final stage, issues involved in the maintenance of change are addressed, with guidelines similar to Marlatt's Relapse Prevention Model (Marlatt and Gordon 1985) being proposed to help patients learn to cope more effectively with adverse events and moods without resorting to overeating and dieting. A plan is constructed for use at such times, based on what has been found to be helpful during treatment.

There have been numerous systematic case reports, uncontrolled and controlled trials attesting to the efficacy of cognitive-behaviour treatment for bulimia nervosa. The first controlled treatment study was reported by Lacey (1983). A modification of cognitive-behaviour therapy combined with 'insight' therapy was compared with a waiting-list control group. No improvement was noted in those in the waiting-list control group. However, for those receiving treatment there was a 96 per cent reduction in binge eating and purging by the end of 10 weeks, and twenty-four of the thirty patients had stopped binge eating and vomiting completely by the end of treatment. Little evidence of relapse was found during the 2 years of follow-up. No patients dropped out during the initial period of treatment, and only 7 per cent dropped out during follow-up. In contrast to other studies, depression scores were found to increase during the course of treatment, despite successful reductions in bulimic symptoms.

In another study comparing treatment with no-treatment (Lee and Rush 1986) thirty subjects meeting DSM-III criteria for bulimia nervosa were allocated at random to either a waiting-list condition or to twelve sessions of treatment over a 6-week period. In treatment, patients were given relaxation training (as an alternative to binge eating), and assisted in the identification and challenging of dysfunctional cognitions. It was found that whereas the treatment reduced their binge eating and vomiting by about 70 per cent, the waiting-list control group showed no improvement in terms of binge eating or vomiting.

Although studies such as those described tend to lend support to cognitive-behaviour therapy for bulimia nervosa, the absence of an active control condition offering an alternative form of treatment means that it cannot be concluded that the specific therapeutic procedures used were responsible for improvement. This shortcoming in the research has been addressed by a number of investigators who have attempted to compare cognitive-behaviour therapy with active control conditions. Kirkley et al. (1985) carried out a study involving comparison of group cognitive-behaviour therapy (as described by Fairburn 1981) with a form of non-directive group psychotherapy. At the end of treatment the cognitive-behavioural treatment approach was found to have had a greater effect on eating habits than the comparison approach, but this difference was no longer present at 3 months follow-up. The treatments were no different with regard to their effect on other measures of psychological adjustment. In a second study an exclusively verbal cognitive treatment was compared with treatment in which behavioural (exposure with response prevention of vomiting) and cognitive procedures were combined (Wilson et al. 1986). The combined treatment was found to be markedly superior to the purely verbal treatment (a lowering of self-induced vomiting of 94 per cent as opposed to 71 per cent).

Many investigators in the field, in reviewing the treatment of bulimia nervosa, conclude that a promising basis exists for the use of cognitive-behavioural treatments (Agras 1987; Fairburn 1986). However, Wilson (1986) has highlighted the 'litany of methodological shortcomings in studies' (p. 466) emphasizing the need for future studies to employ superior methodological controls. An example given is the basic outcome measure for bulimia nervosa. This is taken to be the frequency of binge/purge episodes, and typically this information is obtained by self-monitoring, or from the responses to the therapist's enquiry about these behaviours. However, evidence exists to suggest that, perhaps because of the reactive effect of self-monitoring, this method yields lower frequencies than responses at intake to assessors' enquiries about such behaviour (Wilson et al. 1986). In similar vein, Fairburn (1981) has shown how different definitions of bulimia nervosa, sampling procedures and the method and scope of assessment have resulted in conflicting findings, and Garner (1986) has cautioned that differences in patient populations may be a major factor accounting for conflicting opinions about treatment course and duration. In addition, it has not been shown that cognitive-behavioural treatments produce more cognitive change than non-cognitive ones, nor has it been established that a change in the characteristic beliefs and values is a prerequisite for an enduring change in patients' eating habits. Recently Cooper et al. (1989) have carried out an investigation of behavioural treatment for bulimia nervosa. In their study eight patients with bulimia nervosa were treated using purely behavioural techniques in the absence of specific cognitive procedures. The behavioural treatment was derived from the cognitive therapy manual described by Fairburn (1985), patients receiving a protracted version of the first phase of that treatment. Patients monitored their food intake and were advised to eat regular meals, used stimulus-control procedures to regulate their eating and were encouraged to eat a wide variety of foods in a wide range of situations. All were systematically assessed before and after treatment, seven being reassessed at 1-year follow-up. As a group, a substantial improvement in terms of eating habits, a global index of specific psychopathology and mental state was found. The changes were comparable to those which had previously been obtained in an Oxford sample of patients using a cognitive-behavioural treatment (Fairburn et al. 1986). The findings are seen to raise the question as to whether cognitive procedures are necessary to produce change in patients with bulimia nervosa.

Obesity

The risk to health of extra weight increases with rise in body weight (Bray 1986), and all possible treatments should therefore be evaluated in terms of the degree of obesity and its attendant risk. For the massively obese, high-risk treatments such as starvation, very low-calorie protein diets, jaw wiring, intestinal bypass or gastric bypass may be deemed necessary. However, for the majority of patients, low-risk treatments are more suitable. Approaches including drug therapy, exercise, diet and nutrition are part of the vast selection of treatments available, but it has been psychological interventions which have been most widely used.

Stuart (1967) first reported the systematic application of behaviour modification to the treatment of obesity. The programme he used formed the basis for an increasingly sophisticated 'package' of behavioural techniques and sparked off unprecedented activity in the psychological treatment of obesity. Ten years after the publication of 'Behavioural control of overeating' the topic had acquired a huge popularity, with numerous well-controlled clinical trials and reviews.

Today, behavioural procedures have become the backbone of obesity treatment. More than a hundred controlled studies have been conducted, and many comprehensive reviews are available (for a review see Brownell and Wadden 1986). There is general agreement that behaviour-therapy interventions lead to an initial weight loss of approximately 11 pounds, and that this reduction is fairly well maintained for at least a year. Very few patients continue to lose weight after treatment, and there is great interindividual variability in weight loss, but the treatment improves psychological functioning and reduces the rate of attrition.

Initial enthusiasm for behavioural treatments of obesity was unrealistically high. Prior to its introduction the outlook for obese patients had been dismal, and in 1958 Stunkard wrote: 'Most obese persons will not remain in treatment, most will not lose weight, and of those who do lose weight, most will regain it' (p. 79). This pessimistic view is still largely true today. Based on current treatment outcome studies, Brownell (1987) has concluded that 'if "cure" from obesity is defined as reduction to ideal weight and maintenance of that weight for five years, a person is more likely to recover from most forms of cancer than from obesity' (p. 214).

Nevertheless, attempts to improve the efficacy of treatments continue. Cognitive restructuring has been incorporated into many treatments, and the emphasis on exercise has been increased. However, more systematic evaluation of treatment outcome is needed. The importance of exercise for weight loss can be supported by the literature (Brownell and Stunkard 1980; Thompson et al. 1982), but although cognitive restructuring seems to be important clinically, there is only preliminary evidence to show that it boosts programme effectiveness.

Brownell and Wadden (1986) describe an expanded version of the cognitive-restructuring programme developed by Mahoney and Mahoney (1976). In it goal setting, coping with mistakes and motivation are examined, and attempts are made to encourage attitude change so that positive attitudes facilitate adherence to the life style, exercise, relationship and nutrition parts of the programme.

Although efforts are being made to improve the treatment available for obese patients, there is some question whether or not obesity should be treated at all (Wooley and Wooley 1984). Arguing that occasional reports of unusual success should not obscure the fact that techniques based on insight, education, and behaviour modification, have a very modest success rate, Wooley and Wooley draw attention to the negative effects of unsuccessful treatment and the general impact such efforts may have on an already weight obsessed society. Except for the massively obese or others for whom health is genuinely endangered, these investigators suggest that rather than concentrating on weight loss as the major goal of treatment, excess fat should be seen in the context of other problems such as poor self- and body-image, and the adverse consequences of dieting (such as distorted eating patterns, depression, inadequate nutrition, or distorted life styles).

FUTURE DEVELOPMENTS

Assessment

Although the cognitive-behavioural approach has emphasized the importance of concerns about body shape and weight in each of the eating disorders, very little research has been carried out to determine the best method for assessing attitudes towards shape and weight. So far self-report methods have been employed (Cooper *et al*. 1987; Garner and Garfinkel 1979; Garner *et al*. 1983), but, recognizing that these are unlikely to evaluate all aspects of such complex beliefs and values, Cooper and Fairburn (1987) have developed the eating-disorder examination. This is a semi-structured interview designed to measure behaviour, attitude to own shape and weight and the personal importance attached to shape and weight. Because semi-structured interviews require subtle judgements to be made by the interviewer, Fairburn and Garner (1988) have suggested that a more objective measure for assessing beliefs and values is needed. They propose that the Stroop colour-naming task may provide a more objective measure of personal concern about shape and weight. In the original experiment, subjects were asked to name the colour of the ink in which words were written. ignoring the actual content of the words. It was found that colour naming was significantly slowed when the words were the names of colours, and when there was a clash between the colour of the ink in which the words were written and the words themselves (Jensen and Rohwer 1966). Subsequent experiments revealed that words with personal salience also retarded colour naming (Watts *et al*. 1986). Preliminary findings suggest that this effect may also be true for patients with bulimia nervosa as it has been found that these patients took longer than age-matched female control subjects to colour-name words relevant to the characteristic concerns about shape, weight and eating (Fairburn and Garner 1988).

Hopefully the introduction of objective measures of personal concern about shape and weight, such as the Stroop colour-naming task, will improve the assessment of these concerns and help in the understanding of their significance.

Treatment

In recent years there has been a growing body of research drawing attention to the importance of body image in the eating disorders (for review, see Garfinkel and Garner 1982; Garner and Garfinkel 1981; Garner *et al*. 1978). Most investigators adopt Schilder's (1935) definition of body image – 'the picture of our own body which we form in our mind, that is to say the way in which the body appears to ourselves' (p. 11) – but to date methodological problems inherent in attempts to measure body-image disturbances have hindered progress (Garner and Garfinkel 1981). In reviewing evidence from current studies Garfinkel and Garner (1982) conclude that a clear understanding of the role of body-image disturbance is not yet possible. Nevertheless, most investigators regard body-image disturbances as being clinically significant in the eating disorders. Bruch (1973) considers correction of body-image misperception to be a 'pre-condition to recovery' (p. 90) for anorexic patients, and in her extensive work with the obese the importance of body image is again highlighted. However, only a minority of investigators have attempted to assist patients in attaining a realistic awareness of their body image.

Gottheil *et al.* (1969) were among the first to draw attention to the fact that if self-image confrontation is a useful therapeutic tool in combating denial, it should be effective in a condition such as anorexia nervosa where, in addition to disturbances in body concept, visible changes in body structure are clearly evident. In this single case-study, the female patient was confronted with an image of her body on the monitor. This was inconsistent with her own body image, so she had three options: to deny the screen image; to change her self-image; to become disorganized. Initially, she tenaciously denied the evidence on the screen, just as she had previously denied mirror evidence, and resisted information from her family and physicians. Finally, after repeated self-confrontation, it became more difficult for her to maintain this denial, and a change in her body image occurred so that thinness became ugly rather than comforting. However, apart from this report, there has been very little attempt to assist patients with eating disorders in attaining a realistic awareness of their body image. Stunkard and Mendelson (1967) have noted that because of the relatively intractable nature of the disturbance in body image, long-term psychotherapy may be required to ameliorate it, but very few alternative suggestions have been offered as to how the body-image disturbance might be corrected.

The self-viewing experience (by means of video feedback) has attained wide popularity in certain specialities (for example, skills training), and in relation to the study of body image, videotape recordings are liable to be a great asset. However, as yet few investigators have harnessed the full potential of this technique. In a recent treatment study (McCrea and Summerfield 1988), a group of obese subjects successfully lost weight, and appeared to improve the accuracy of their body-image estimates when subjected to regular video feedback over a period of approximately 4 months. Another group of obese subjects who underwent a behaviour-modification programme over the same period also lost weight and showed a lessening of body-image distortion at the end of this intervention, but the changes observed between assessment were much greater for the video group. As concerns about the body are generally regarded to be important in the development and maintenance of eating disorders, further investigation into methods for the systematic alteration of body image would seem to be justified. Video feedback may be useful in this context, and additional studies are needed to evaluate its therapeutic potential.

CONCLUSION

The intensity of patients' beliefs about their weight and shape is one of the most striking characteristics of the eating disorders, and it is argued that rather than merely being symptomatic, such beliefs may maintain the aberrant behaviours associated with these disorders.

Generally there is enthusiasm for the efficacy of cognitive-behavioural approaches in the treatment of eating disorders, with these therapies being applied widely. Nevertheless, just as this chapter began with a reminder that the treatment of eating disorders must, by definition, be multidisciplinary, in concluding, the words of Garner and Garfinkel (1985: 5) should be borne in mind:

> Perhaps more impressive is the trend on the part of those from traditionally opposite ideological poles to describe similar phenomena and offer congruent advice, perhaps using slightly different terminology. Psychodynamic theorists appreciate the importance of focusing directly on issues of food, weight, and renutrition. Cognitive-behavioural approaches have begun to address self-concept deficits and the therapeutic relationship. Therapists from different schools emphasize the recognition and expression of affect; the value of exploring family interactional patterns; and the relevance of such developmental issues as separation, autonomy, sexual fears, and identity formation. These accommodations are reassuring, since they imply that we are attending to what our patients are telling us and are adapting our procedures to address these recurring themes. This parallels a more general move toward integration among clinicians and psychotherapy researches. The systematic application of several strategies may be preferable to operating from a unitary theoretical model.

REFERENCES

Agras, W. S. (1987) *Eating Disorders: Management of Obesity, Bulimia, and Anorexia Nervosa*, New York: Pergamon Press.
—— and Kramer, H. C. (1984) 'The treatment of anorexia nervosa: do different treatments have different outcomes?', in A. J. Stunkard and E. Stellar (eds) *Eating and Its Disorders*, New York: Raven Press.
Allon, N. (1979) 'Self-perceptions of the stigma of overweight in relationship to weight-losing patterns', *American Journal of Clinical Nutrition* 32: 470–80.
American Psychiatric Association (1980) *Diagnostic and Statistical Manual of Mental Disorders*, Third Edition, Washington, DC: APA.
—— (1985) *DSM-III-R in Development* (10-5.85), Washington, DC: APA.
—— (1987) *Diagnostic and Statistical Manual of Mental Disorders*, Third Revised Edition, Washington, DC: APA.
Beck, A. T. (1967) *Depression: Clinical, Experimental and Theoretical Aspects*, New York: Harper and Row.

—— (1976) *Cognitive Therapy and the Emotional Disorders*, New York: International Universities Press.

——, Rush, A. J., Shaw, B. F. and Emery, G. (1979) *Cognitive Therapy of Depression*, New York: Guilford Press.

Bennet, W. and Gurin, J. (1982) *The Dieter's Dilemma: Eating Less and Weighing More*, New York: Basic Books.

Beutler, L. E. (1987) 'Introduction to the special series', *Journal of Consulting and Clinical Psychology* 55: 627.

Boskind-Lodahl, M. (1976) 'Cinderella's stepsisters: a feminist perspective on anorexia nervosa and bulimia', *Signs: Journal of Women in Culture and Society* 2: 342–56.

Bray, G. A. (1978) 'Definitions, measurements and classification of the syndromes of obesity', *International Journal of Obesity* 2: 99–112.

—— (1986) 'Effects of obesity on health and happiness', in K. D. Brownell and J. P. Foreyt (eds) *Handbook of Eating Disorders: Physiology, Psychology and Treatment of Obesity, Anorexia and Bulimia*, New York: Basic Books.

Brownell, K. D. (1987) 'Obesity: understanding and treating a serious, prevalent and refractory disorder', in T. D. Nirenberg and S. A. Maisto (eds) *Developments in the Assessment and Treatment of Addictive Behaviors*, Norwood, NJ: Ablex Publishing Company.

—— and Foreyt, J. P. (1986) *Handbook of Eating Disorders. Physiology, Psychology and Treatment of Obesity, Anorexia and Bulimia*, New York: Basic Books.

Brownell, K. D. and Stunkard, A. J. (1980) 'Exercise in the development and control of obesity', in A. J. Stunkard (ed) *Obesity*, Philadelphia: W. B. Saunders.

Brownell, K. D. and Wadden, T. A. (1986) 'Behavior therapy for obesity: modern approaches and better results', in K. D. Brownell and J. P. Foreyt (eds) *Handbook of Eating Disorders: Physiology, Psychology and Treatment of Obesity, Anorexia and Bulimia*, New York: Basic Books.

Brownmiller, S. (1982) *Femininity*, London: Hamish Hamilton.

Bruch, H. (1957) *The Importance of Overweight*, New York: W. W. Norton.

—— (1962) 'Falsification of bodily needs and body concept in schizophrenia', *Archives of General Psychiatry* 6: 18–24.

—— (1970) 'Instinct and interpersonal experience', *Comparative Psychiatry* 11: 495–506.

—— (1973) *Eating Disorders*, New York: Basic Books.

Clarke, M. G. and Palmer, R. L. (1983) 'Eating attitudes and symptoms in university students', *British Journal of Psychiatry* 142: 299–304.

Cooper, P. J. and Cooper, Z. (1988) 'Eating disorders', in E. Miller and P. J. Cooper (eds) *Adult Abnormal Psychology*, Edinburgh: Churchill Livingstone.

—— and Hill, C. (1989) 'Behavioural treatment of bulimia nervosa', *International Journal of Eating Disorders* 8(1): 87–92.

Cooper, P. J., Taylor, M. J., Cooper, Z. and Fairburn, C. G. (1987) 'The development and validation of the body shape questionnaire', *International Journal of Eating Disorders* 6: 485–94.

Cooper, Z. and Fairburn, C. G. (1987) 'The eating disorder examination: a semistructured interview for the assessment of the specific psychopathology of eating disorders', *International Journal of Eating Disorders* 6: 1–8.

Crisp, A. H. (1965) 'Clinical and therapeutic aspects of anorexia nervosa: study of 30 cases', *Journal of Psychosomatic Research* 9: 67–78.

—— (1967) 'The possible significance of some behavioural correlates of weight and carbohydrate intake', *Journal of Psychosomatic Research* 11: 117–31.

—— (1984) 'The psychopathology of anorexia nervosa: getting the "heat" out of the system', in A. J. Stunkard and E. Stellar (eds) *Eating and Its Disorders*, New York: Raven Press.

Fairburn, C. G. (1981) 'A cognitive-behavioural approach to the management of bulimia', *Psychological Medicine* 11: 707–11.

—— (1984) 'A cognitive-behavioural treatment of bulimia', in D. M. Garner and P. E. Garfinkel (eds) *Handbook of Psychotherapy for Anorexia Nervosa and Bulimia*, New York: Guilford Press.

—— (1985) 'Cognitive behavioural treatment for bulimia', in D. M. Garner and P. E. Garfinkel (eds) *Handbook of Psychotherapy for Anorexia Nervosa and Bulimia*, New York: Guilford Press.

—— (1986) 'Cognitive behaviour therapy for bulimia nervosa', in L. J. Downey and J. C. Malin (eds) *Current Approaches: Bulimia Nervosa*, Southampton: Duphar Laboratories Limited.

—— and Cooper, P. J. (1984) 'The clinical features of bulimia nervosa', *British Journal of Psychiatry* 144: 238–46.

Fairburn, C. G. and Garner, D. M. (1986) 'The diagnosis of bulimia nervosa', *International Journal of Eating Disorders* 5: 403–19.

—— (1988) 'Diagnostic criteria for anorexia nervosa: the importance of attitudes to shape and weight', in D. M. Garner and P. E. Garfinkel (eds) *Diagnostic Issues in Anorexia Nervosa and Bulimia Nervosa*, New York: Brunner/Mazel.

Fairburn, C. G. Kirk, J., O'Connor, M. and Cooper, P. J. (1986) 'A comparison of two psychological treatments of bulimia nervosa', *Behaviour Research and Therapy* 24: 629–43.

Fisher, S. (1972) *Body Experience in Fantasy and Behavior*, New York: Appleton-Century-Crofts.

Garfinkel, P. E. and Garner, D. M. (1982) *Anorexia Nervosa: A Multidimensional Perspective*, New York: Brunner/Mazel.

Garfinkel, P. E., Moldofsky, H. and Garner, D. M. (1980) 'The heterogeneity of anorexia nervosa: bulimia as a distinct subgroup', *Archives of General Psychiatry* 37: 1036–40.

Garner, D. M. (1986) 'Cognitive therapy for anorexia nervosa', in K. D. Brownell and J. P. Foreyt (eds) *Handbook of Eating Disorders: Physiology, Psychology and Treatment of Obesity, Anorexia and Bulimia*, New York: Basic Books.

—— and Bemis, K. M. (1982) 'A cognitive-behavioral approach to anorexia nervosa', *Cognitive Therapy and Research* 6: 123–50.

—— (1985) 'Cognitive therapy for anorexia nervosa', in D. M. Garner and P. E. Garfinkel (eds) *Handbook of Psychotherapy for Anorexia Nervosa and Bulimia*, New York: Guilford Press.

Garner, D. M. and Garfinkel, P. E. (1979) 'The eating attitudes test: an index of the symptoms of anorexia nervosa', *Psychological Medicine* 9: 273–9.

—— (1981) 'Body image in anorexia nervosa: measurement, theory and clinical implications', *International Journal of Psychiatry in Medicine* 11(3): 263–84.

—— (eds) (1985) *Handbook of Psychotherapy for Anorexia Nervosa and Bulimia*, New York: Guilford Press.

—— and Moldofsky, H. (1978) 'Perceptual experiences in anorexia nervosa and obesity', *Canadian Psychiatric Association Journal* 23: 249–63.

Garner, D. M., Olmsted, M. P. and Polivy, J. (1983) 'Development and validation of a multi-dimensional eating disorder inventory for anorexia nervosa and bulimia', *International Journal of Eating Disorders* 2: 15–34.

Garner, D. M., Garfinkel, P. E., Stancer, H. C. and Moldofsky, H. (1976) 'Body image disturbances in anorexia nervosa and obesity', *Psychosomatic Medicine* 38: 227–336.

Glucksman, M. L. and Hirsch, J. (1969) 'The response of obese patients to weight reduction', *Psychosomatic Medicine* 31: 1–7.

Gottheil, E., Backup, C. E. and Cornelison, F. S. (1969) 'Denial and self-image confrontation in a case of anorexia nervosa', *Journal of Nervous and Mental Disease* 148: 238–50.

Gull, W. W. (1874) 'Anorexia nervosa (apepsia hysterica, anorexia hysterical)', *Transactions of the Clinical Society of London* 7: 22–8.

Hawkins, R. C. and Clement, P. F. (1980) 'Development and construct validation of a self-report measure of binge-eating tendencies', *Addictive Behaviors* 5: 219–26.

Herman, C. P. and Mack, D. (1975) 'Restrained and unrestrained eating', *Journal of Personality* 43: 647–60.

Herman, C. P. and Polivy, J. (1984) 'A boundary model for the regulation of eating', in A. J. Stunkard and E. Stellar (eds) *Eating and Its Disorders*, New York: Raven Press.

Hollin, C. and Lewis, V. (1988) 'Cognitive-behavioural approaches to anorexia and bulimia', in D. Scott (ed.) *Anorexia and Bulimia Nervosa: Practical Approaches*, London: Chapman and Hall.

Hollon, S. D. and Beck, A. T. (1979) 'Cognitive therapy for depression', in P. C. Kendall and S. D. Hollon (eds) *Cognitive-Behavioral Interventions: Theory, Research and Procedures*, New York: Academic Press.

Jensen, A. R. and Rohwer, W. D. (1966) 'The Stroop color-word test: a review', *Acta Psychologica 25: 36–93.*

Keesey, R. E. (1986) 'A set-point theory of obesity', in K. D. Brownell and J. P. Foreyt (eds) *Handbook of Eating Disorders*, New York: Basic Books.

Kirkley, B. G., Schneider, J. A., Agras, W. S. and Bachman, J. A. (1985) 'A comparison of two group treatments for bulimia', *Journal of Consulting and Clinical Psychology* 53: 43–8.

Lacey, J. H. (1983) 'Bulimia nervosa, binge eating and psychogenic vomiting: a controlled treatment study and longterm outcome', *British Medical Journal* 286: 1609–13.

Laseque, C. (1873) 'On hysterical anorexia', *Medical Times Gazette* 2: 265–6.

Lee, N. L. and Rush, A. J. (1986) 'Cognitive-behavioural group therapy for bulimia', *International Journal of Eating Disorders* 5: 599–615.

McCrea, C. W. and Summerfield, A. B. (1988) 'A pilot study of the therapeutic usefulness of videofeedback for weight loss and improvement of body image in the treatment of obesity', *Behavioural Psychotherapy* 16: 269–84.

Mahoney, M. J. and Mahoney, B. K. (1976) *Permanent Weight Control: A Total Solution to the Dieter's Dilemma*, New York: W. W. Norton.

Maloney, M. J. and Klykylo, W. M. (1983) 'An overview of anorexia nervosa, bulimia, and obesity in children and adolescents', *Journal of the American Academy of Child Psychiatry* 22: 99–107.

Marlatt, G. A. and Gordon, J. (1985) *Relapse Prevention*, New York: Guilford Press.

Mitchell, J. E. and Eckert, E. D. (1987) 'Scope and significance of eating disorders', *Journal of Consulting and Clinical Psychology* 55(5): 628–34.

Mitchell, J. E., Hatsukami, D., Eckert, E. D. and Pyle, R. L. (1985) 'Characteristics of 275 patients with bulimia', *American Journal of Psychiatry* 142: 482–5.

Nisbett, R. E. (1968) 'Taste, deprivation and weight determinants of eating behaviour', *Journal of Personality and Social Psychology* 10: 107–16.

Orbach, S. (1978) *Fat is a Feminist Issue*, London: Paddington Press.

—— (1982) *Fat is a Feminist Issue II*, Feltham, Middlesex: Hamlyn Paperbacks.

Palmer, R. L. (1979) 'The dietary chaos syndrome: a useful new term?', *British Journal of Medical Psychology* 52: 187–90.

Polivy, J. (1976) 'Perception of calories and regulation of intake in restrained and unrestrained subjects', *Addictive Behaviors* 1: 237–43.

—— and Herman, C. P. (1985) 'Dieting and bingeing: a causal analysis', *American Psychologist* 40: 193–201.

——, Olmsted, M. P. and Jazwinski, C. (1984) 'Restraint and binge eating', in R. C. Hawkins, W. Fremouw and P. F. Clement (eds) *Binge-Eating: Theory, Research and Treatment*, New York: Springer.

Rotter, J. B. (1966) 'Generalized expectancies for internal versus external control of reinforcement', *Psychological Monographs* 80: 1–28.

Russell, G. F. M. (1970) 'Anorexia nervosa: its identity as an illness and its treatment', in J. H. Price (ed.) *Modern Trends in Psychological Medicine*, London: Butterworth.

—— (1979) 'Bulimia nervosa: an ominous variant of anorexia nervosa', *Psychological Medicine* 9: 429–48.

Schachter, S. and Rodin, J. (1974) *Obese Humans and Rats*, Washington, DC: Erlbaum/Halsted.

Schilder, P. (1935) *The Image and Appearance of the Human Body*, London: Kegan Paul, Trench and Trubner.

Schonbuch, S. S. and Schell, R. E. (1967) 'Judgements of body appearance by fat and skinny male college students', *Perceptual and Motor Skills* 24: 999–1002.

Shipman, W. and Sohlkhah, N. (1967) 'Body distortion in obese women', *Psychosomatic Medicine* 19: 540.

Shisslak, C., Crago, M., Neal, M. E. and Swain, B. (1987) 'Primary prevention of eating disorders', *Journal of Consulting and Clinical Psychology* 55(5): 660–7.

Silverstein, B., Peterson, B. and Perone, L. (1986) 'Some correlates of the thin standard of bodily attractiveness for women', *International Journal of Eating Disorders* 5(5): 895–905.

Simmonds, M. (1914) 'Uber embolische prozesse in der hypophysis', *Archives of Pathology and Anatomy* 217: 226–39.

Spencer, J. A. and Fremouw, W. J. (1979) 'Binge-eating as a function of restraint and weight classification', *Journal of Abnormal Psychology* 88: 262–7.

Stern, J. S. and Lowney, P. (1986) 'Obesity: the role of physical activity', in K. D. Brownell and J. P. Foreyt (eds) *Handbook of Eating Disorders*, New York: Basic Books.

Striegel-Moore, R. H. and Rodin, J. (1986) 'The influence of psychological variables in obesity', in K. D. Brownell and J. P. Foreyt (eds) *Handbook of Eating Disorders: Physiology, Psychology, and the Treatment of Obesity, Anorexia and Bulimia*, New York: Basic Books.

Strober, M. (1986) 'Anorexia nervosa: history and psychological concepts', in K. D. Brownell and J. P. Foreyt (eds) *Handbook of Eating Disorders*, New York: Basic Books.

Stuart, R. B. (1967) 'Behavioural control of overeating', *Behaviour Research and Therapy* 5: 357–65.

Stunkard, A. J. (1958) 'The management of obesity', *New York Journal of Medicine* 58: 79–87.

—— and Mendelson, M. (1967) 'Obesity and the body image: I. Characteristics of disturbances in the body image of some obese persons', *American Journal of Psychiatry* 123: 1296–300.

Stunkard, A. J. and Stellar, E. (eds) (1984) *Eating and Its Disorders*, New York: Raven Press.

Stunkard, A. J., Sorenson, T. I. A., Hanic, C., Teasdale, T. W., Chakraborty, R., Schull, W. J. and Schulsinger, F. (1986) 'An adoption study of human obesity', *New England Journal of Medicine* 314: 193–8.

Szmukler, G. I. (1985) 'The epidemiology of anorexia nervosa and bulimia', *Journal of Psychiatric Research* 19: 143–53.

Thompson, J. K., Jarvey, G. J., Lahey, B. B. and Cureton, K. J. (1982) 'Exercise and obesity: etiology, physiology, and intervention', *Psychological Bulletin* 91: 55–79.

Wardle, J. (1980) 'Restraint and binge eating', *Behaviour Analysis and Modification* 4: 201–9.

—— and Beinhart, H. (1981) 'Binge eating: a theoretical review', *British Journal of Clinical Psychology* 20: 97–109.

Watts, F. N., McKenna, F. P., Sharrock, R. and Trezise, L. (1986) 'Colour-naming of phobia-related words', *British Journal of Psychology* 77: 97–108.

Wilson, C. P., Hogan, C. C. and Mintz, I. L. (1983) *Fear of Being Fat*, New York: Jason Aronson.

Wilson, G. T. (1986) 'Cognitive-behavioral and pharmacological therapies for bulimia', in K. D. Brownell and J. P. Foreyt (eds) *Handbook of Eating Disorders: Physiology, Psychology, and Treatment of Obesity, Anorexia and Bulimia*, New York: Basic Books.

——, Rossiter, E., Kleifield, E. and Lindholm, L. (1986) 'Cognitive-behavioural treatment of bulimia nervosa: a controlled evaluation', *Behaviour Research and Therapy* 24: 277–88.

Wooley, S. C. and Wooley, O. W. (1984) 'Should obesity be treated at all?', in A. J. Stunkard and E. Stellar (eds) *Eating and Its Disorders*, New York: Raven Press.

Chapter 6

Alcohol and drug problems

Richard Velleman

Twenty-five years ago, almost everyone involved in working with alcohol and drug problems conceptualized them from within a psychiatric disease model, using the terms 'alcoholism' and 'drug addiction' to signify that these problems each had a unified aetiology, disease course and prognosis. Since then, a quite radical shift has occurred: the weight of empirical and theoretical work has suggested that this 'disease' model has outlived its usefulness (Miller 1980; Pattison *et al*. 1977; Thorley 1983), and alternative approaches have been examined. A leading approach, especially with alcohol problems, was the behavioural one; and in this area in common with most others, researchers increasingly found that a simple behavioural model which does not include cognitive elements was insufficient. Hence, cognitive-behavioural approaches are beginning to come to the fore.

There are, however, two provisos to this statement. The first is that this increase in cognitive-behavioural research and theorizing is far more apparent in the alcohol field (Heather and Robertson 1985; Rollnick 1989) than it is in the case of drugs. For this reason, the bulk of the studies cited within this chapter will come from the alcohol rather than the drugs field.

The second proviso is that writers are increasingly discussing addictive behaviours generally (i.e. a field which also includes smoking, overeating, gambling and sexual behaviour) rather than writing solely about either drugs or alcohol (Miller 1980; Orford 1985; Sutton 1987; Wilson 1987).

CONCEPTUALIZATION

The cognitive-behavioural view portrays man as an active and essentially self-controlling organism: people process information and make decisions about their lives and their behaviour on the basis of that information. This conceptualization stands in stark contrast to many other important perspectives: for example, the psychiatric view, and the view put forward by both psychoanalytic and radical-behavioural psychology, which all see people generally as passive, as being driven (by disease or addictive processes, or instinctual forces, or external reinforcers).

This active and cognitive perspective is underpinned by the view that three factors determine a person's behaviour: the expectations that the person has about the outcomes of their behaviour, the value that the person places on those outcome and the nature of the situation in which the person is behaving (Bandura 1977; Phares 1976; Rotter *et al.* 1972). These three factors of expectations, values and situations are linked by a person's 'schemata' or cognitive generalizations. The schemata will guide their expectations, and influence the value that they place on various outcomes.

All cognitive-behavioural approaches to alcohol and drug problems also focus on expectations, values and situations; but they utilize four additional assumptions concerning alcohol and drug problems. The first assumption is that these behaviours, and others such as smoking, eating and gambling, can all be usefully conceptualized as behaviours which are normative but which can for some people become excessive and lead to the development of problems. Hence, all these behaviours can be viewed along a continuum of use, from no (or little) use, through whatever might be considered as 'normal' use by the society in which the individual lives, through to excessive use. This firmly places alcohol or drug use as being a social phenomenon, where individuals' use of a substance occurs in relation to the socially approved 'norms' of use for that substance. By introducing the concept of a continuum, it also breaks with the simple dichotomous concept of alcoholics or addicts versus 'the rest'. That is, this view does not hold that there is a 'diseased' population which develops problems and a 'normal' one which does not, but instead sees one population lying along a continuum.

A second assumption is that individuals can move along this continuum. It is not the case that individuals have a determined place on the continuum, but rather, that people can move towards the 'excessive' end, and can also move more towards the 'limited use' end. This view has important implications for both prevention (how can we prevent people moving too far along towards the problematic end of the continuum?) and intervention (can we move people back along the continuum away from the problematic end?). This again is in marked contrast to the disease view which has few preventive implications (because one does not know who is going to become an alcoholic or an addict until they become one), and a very simple intervention aim of total cessation of use, once problems are experienced.

A third assumption is that individuals learn how to behave with respect to alcohol, drugs, gambling, eating and so on, and as such this learning can be analysed and modified. The importance of learning in this perspective will be underlined in the next two sections on the development of alcohol and drug problems, and on interventions based on this model.

The fourth assumption is that if people still continue to use alcohol or drugs even though they have developed problems with this use, there must be good reasons for this, even if the individual concerned is not aware of what these reasons are.

These assumptions, and the three factors of expectations, values and situations mentioned above, lead those who follow a cognitive-behavioural approach to be interested in studying a number of elements: first, the *determinants* of the problematic behaviour, which includes such things as the situation and environment, the individual's beliefs and expectations, the individual's prior experiences with the

extent to which the problematic use of alcohol or drugs is acting
anism, a way of reducing current perceived stress by a method
ve short-term consequences at a time when the individual can
ive long-term consequences; and second, the *consequences* of these
or the individual, and for their social and interpersonal life.

Spec ures which a cognitive-behavioural approach needs to address

Compulsion and expectations

Many individuals – lay people, people with problems and professional helpers alike
– view addiction as a physical problem: as a kind of physical urge to which an
addicted person has to respond. As has already been described, however, a
cognitive-behavioural view argues that individuals must be seen as self-controlling,
active decision makers. This creates an anomalous situation – clients (and some
helpers) seeing themselves as out of control, and without the power to alter their
behaviour, and therapists with a cognitive-behavioural orientation seeing them as
able to control their lives. Clearly, an important issue for the cognitive-behavioural
approach is the explanation put forward to account for clients' perception of the
compulsive element in their problems.

Cognitive-behavioural therapists see compulsion as being based on *expectations*
and *learning*. They accept that people with alcohol or drug problems will often *feel*
out of control. Clearly, people who *feel* out of control *act as if they are* out of
control; and this introduces one of the most important cognitive concepts which
this paradigm has introduced to the alcohol and drug field – that of expectations.

The power of expectations in determining the effects of alcohol or drugs has
been shown very well in an experimental setting, using a 2x2 balanced placebo
group design (see, for example, Briddell *et al*. 1978; Marlatt *et al*. 1973; Vuchinich
et al. 1979. In this experimental design, all subjects drink a beverage. All the
beverages look and taste the same, although some of the beverages contain alcohol
and others do not (for example, pure tonic versus vodka and tonic). The experiment
involves manipulating both whether or not the subjects have *actually* drunk alcohol
and whether or not the subjects *think* they have actually drunk alcohol.

Early research using this paradigm investigated the effect of expectancy on the
amount drunk, finding that *being told one had received alcohol* led to more alcohol
being consumed (for example, Marlatt *et al*. 1973). Yet expectations affect much
more than consumption. Considerable research has investigated the relationship
between alcohol and aggressive behaviour. Much of this research was inadequately
controlled but Lang *et al*. (1975) studied this area using the balanced placebo
design, and found that the belief that the person had consumed alcohol was again
the primary factor in determining an aggressive response to alcohol, at least in
heavy-drinking males. Similarly, Abrams and Wilson (1983) found, using the same
balanced placebo design, that a belief that one had drunk alcohol significantly
increased sexual arousal in males, although similar findings have not been

forthcoming with females. In summary, expectations have been shown to affect a whole range of behaviours concerned with the effects of alcohol, including the amount consumed, aggressiveness and sexual arousal.

A second example of the importance of cognitive factors comes from the anthropological literature. MacAndrew and Edgerton (1970) examined a wide range of anthropological material, collected from many cultures around the world, on how people behaved when they had consumed alcohol. They found that, after drinking very similar amounts in very similar contexts, different cultures had different normative ways of reacting to this. Furthermore, they found that these ways were transmissible – that some cultures changed their way of reacting once they had learnt another culture's behaviour. As Heather and Robertson (1989) note, these findings demonstrate 'not only that drinking habits can be transmitted by modelling, but that the kind of behaviour exhibited when drunk can be learnt in this way' (p. 241). Further, this demonstrates again how behaviour when intoxicated is to a large measure determined by the person's expectations of how he or she should behave, rather than being determined by the pharmacological effects of the alcohol.

These and other studies show that individuals' drinking and drug-taking behaviour is determined at least in part by the cognitive expectation of the effect of alcohol and drugs, and the social rules which govern individual and group reactions to alcohol and drugs; and that this is a more important determinant than the physical demand of something which we might call 'craving' for the drug. The anthropological evidence also shows quite convincingly that these expectations are learnt. Hence, a cognitive-behavioural approach utilizes a psychological explanation couched in terms of cognition and learning rather than one couched in terms of physical addiction and physical craving.

Of course, discounting a physiological model of addiction does not mean that the notion of physiological *effects* of alcohol or drug use are discounted. Clearly alcohol and drugs have physiological effects, and these effects may include physiological changes which might lead to an altered physical response to a given amount of alcohol or drug – that is, tolerance may occur, and withdrawal effects may be experienced once drinking or drug use reduces or ceases. But a cognitive-behavioural approach again postulates that use of alcohol or drugs in a withdrawal situation may well be due to an *expectation* that use will reduce the actual or expected withdrawal symptoms, rather than because the person is involuntarily responding to the physical demands of the craving phenomenon. Even in the cases of clients with very high levels of physical dependency, who Stockwell *et al.* (1982) showed can experience a higher level of physiologically induced craving, cognition is the most important mediator of the effects of alcohol or drugs.

Having argued for the importance of expectations and other cognitive factors, it is important that their effects are kept in perspective. Although there are many areas in which expectations play an important role, the balanced placebo design has shown that there are a number of areas in which the main effect is not for expectancy, but for alcohol consumption (or sometimes an interaction between the two). Examples of this are work on cognitive performance, on motor skills and on mood.

Addiction and responsibility

The view expressed thus far describes individuals with problems as behaving as they do for reasons, and according to cognitive factors such as expectations, rather than because they are under the control of a physiological addiction. Yet this does not mean that the individual need accept conscious personal responsibility for all elements of their current condition. People are not responsible for all their past learning experiences, their parenting, the ways that they have been taught to cope with the problems of life. What people are responsible for is actively participating in the process of change. A person is not necessarily responsible for his or her past; but he or she is responsible for attempting to take charge of the future.

Paradoxically, however, this active participation can be difficult to engender when working with individuals with alcohol or drug problems. This is due to the pervasive influence of the disease notion of addiction: as described above, often both client and therapist will share a common view of addiction which concep- tualizes it as a disease process where a client has to use their will-power to alter their use.

Assessment

In assessing a client's alcohol or drug problems a therapist would examine a number of factors. These would include the client's alcohol and drug *use*, their drinking or drug-taking *behaviour*, the *effects* of the alcohol or drug use, their *cognitions* concerning their substance use (expectations, values, definition of the problem, understanding of its cause) and the *context* (family, employment, social) within which the client was consuming the substances.

A number of techniques might be employed:

1 *Standardised questionnaires*: There is growing use being made within the alcohol field of questionnaires which measure clients' level of dependence (Davidson 1987), as well as their alcohol use and symptom levels (Miller 1976). The most widely used of the alcohol-use and symptom-levels questionnaires is the Michigan Alcohol Screening Test or MAST (Selzer 1971), and the most widely used and validated of the dependency measures is the Severity of Alcohol Dependence Questionnaire (Stockwell *et al.* 1979, 1983) or SADQ, a twenty-item self-report questionnaire with each item rated on a four-point, Likert-type frequency scale, thus giving a range of 0 to 60.

2 *Monitoring consumption*: In order to clarify the issue of quantity, frequency and circumstances of consumption, clients might monitor their own behaviour (this will be discussed in more detail in a later section), or a detailed record of use over the last week (or even the last year: see Sobell *et al.* 1980) might be created.

3 *Contextual interviews*: Interviews with other family members might be conducted in order to assess the effects on them of the drug or alcohol use, and which would in turn provide richer data concerning the problem activity.

4 *Physiological measures*: Some cognitive-behavioural therapists commonly use physiological measures as part of their assessment procedures. Examples of these are:

(a) measuring blood-alcohol levels (BALs) via breath tests (Hay 1982). This, however, simply gives information about very recent drinking and is of less use in assessing clients' long-term use of alcohol or their immediate cognitive and physiological response to the ingestion of alcohol;

(b) liver-function tests, with blood samples being assayed for levels of SGOT (serum glutamic-oxaloacetic transaminase) and GGTP (gamma glutamyl transpeptidase), two common indices of liver function (Reyes and Miller 1980), which examines the effects of long-term alcohol use;

(c) testing acute tolerance to the subjective effects of alcohol, which examines immediate responses to alcohol ingestion. Vogler (1982) argues that this is a good test of whether a client might be able to learn how to control their drinking.

5 *Functional analysis*: In almost all cases where a client is assessed within a cognitive-behavioural framework, a functional assessment will be undertaken. This consists of a number of elements. First, identifying in a number of areas – these areas include settings, social-interpersonal situations, thoughts and expectations, and emotions. Second, identifying the immediate and delayed positive and negative consequences of the drinking pattern. In addition to this, further information is often also collected to help with the functional analysis – Noel *et al*. (1982) list nine further types of information which they commonly collect, including the specific quantities of alcohol consumed on a regular basis, usual and unusual drinking patterns, where and with whom drinking occurred, predominant mood states and circumstances before/after the drinking, indicators of tolerance and dependence such as the highest ever recorded blood-alcohol concentration or the largest amount of alcohol ever consumed within a 24-hour period, the history of alcohol withdrawal symptoms, past or present indications of acute or chronic liver dysfunction, possible difficulties clients might encounter in initially refraining from drinking while in treatment, and the risks that the client's present environment might pose for problem drinking such as occupational or social temptations.

Developments of problems

There is a huge literature on the taking up of psychoactive drugs – alcohol, smoking and drugs; this chapter, however, will only examine the development of *problematic* use. Our concern here is with answering the question of how can individuals' non-problematic use of substances lead to a situation in which people can feel powerless to cease or reduce their consumption, and in which concepts of addiction can grow?

The cognitive-behavioural paradigm has contributed a wide range of ideas and concepts to account for the shift between normal and problematic use. This paradigm sees the development and maintenance of problems as a process within which there is constant change, and one in which (due to changes in expectations, values and situations) a person may move more towards developing an alcohol or drug problem, or may move away from such a development. This conceptualization is again in contrast to the disease model of alcohol and drug addiction which portrays the addict or alcoholic in a static way, in all probability born into an addictive fate.

There are a large number of ideas relating to the development of excessive alcohol and drug use, and it is worth examining some of them in more detail.

Modelling

Modelling is of particular importance in the initiation of drinking (and, to a lesser extent, drug taking). Modelling can work at three levels. First, children learn, and can acquire a style of drinking and drug taking, from important others via a process of modelling. They observe their parents, relatives and older siblings, and learn normative patterns from them. These will often be patterns of quantity or timing in the day; but there may also be more complicated patterns: a child may learn about the use of alcohol or drugs when reacting to life problems or adversity, or when dealing with anxiety or depression, or when celebrating. Second, children also learn from the culture as a whole – from television, observation in the street, discussions at home, shared information at school. The work described above by MacAndrew and Edgerton (1970) on the ways that people learn their cultural norms relating to drunken behaviour is primarily about learning through modelling. And third, modelling is not a learning process confined to childhood: adults are also influenced by the models they see. For example, new recruits to journalism or the armed forces will soon discover the prevailing 'drinking culture', where at the least there exists passive modelling of heavy drinking and where in many cases there will be active pressure to conform to the established heavy-drinking norms. Much of the research into the effects of modelling on adult drinking behaviour shows that an individual's consumption will vary to match that of a drinking partner, especially if that partner is male, and especially if the person being observed is or has been a heavy drinker (Sobell and Sobell 1978).

Expectations

Adesso (1985) has described the relationship between expectations and experience in the development of responses to alcohol. He takes as his starting point Bandura's distinction between generalized and specific expectancies, where the former 'are elicited by situations that the individual perceives as having similar stimulus properties'; and the latter 'are based on prior experience with a particular situation' (p. 180). He goes on to show, using the work of Christiansen (Christiansen and Goldman 1983; Christiansen *et al*. 1982), how the two processes of social learning and experience with a drug contribute to the development of expectancies about the effects of a drug. Christiansen's two studies examined the expectations about the effects of alcohol of over 3,000 adolescents. These studies showed that, even before they started to drink alcohol, adolescents had quite well-developed expectancies about its effects; but that as they grew older and accrued more experience of drinking, their expectancies grew more specific. They similarly found that lower frequency drinkers had more global expectations about the effects of alcohol, and higher frequency drinkers had more specific ones. Adesso summarizes thus: 'This is precisely what social learning theory would predict: with increased experience one develops more specific expectancies from the generalized expectancies acquired through social learning processes' (p. 183).

People, then, have knowledge and expectations about the effects of alcohol and drugs long before they commence using them; and as they start to use them, so their knowledge and expectations become more focused, more clear and more specific. How, though, do some people go on to develop problems with this use? And how are these problems maintained – why do people not simply stop usage if they see themselves developing problems?

Tension-reduction theory

One of the most common theories as to why some individuals go on to develop problems with their alcohol or drug use is the tension-reduction theory. This theory simply posits (a) that some individuals are more tense or can cope less well with tension; (b) that alcohol and many drugs act to reduce tension; and (c) that tense people drink or take drugs to achieve this outcome. This is a view which many individuals with alcohol problems hold (Edwards 1972), as do many therapists (Cappell 1975) yet the theory has drawn considerable criticism. Much of this criticism has been directed at older versions of this theory, which held that anxiety was a conditioned physiological drive; more modern versions, however, see the effects of alcohol in reducing tension as being largely determined by the drinker's expectations. Anxiety, in a more cognitively driven theory, is primarily cognitively mediated: it is generated either by one's thoughts about distressing events, or activated on the basis of learned expectations.

Bandura's distinction between action-outcome expectancies – a belief that a given behaviour will lead to a given outcome – and personal-efficacy expectancies – a belief that a person is capable of successfully executing the behaviour required in a given situation to produce a desired outcome – is useful when considering the tension-reduction theory. First, with regard to alcohol and *personal-efficacy expectations,* alcohol can interact with individuals' expectations about themselves and hence reduce tension in two ways. One is by making an individual believe that he or she is more capable of successfully executing a behaviour than the person believed before. For example, there exists a considerable body of evidence to suggest that alcohol serves to enhance an individual's sense of energy and power (Marlatt 1976). The other is by reducing a person's negative self-evaluation. Consuming alcohol enables an individual to attribute any socially disapproved-of behaviour to the effect of alcohol rather than to any personal responsibility.

With reference to alcohol and *action-outcome expectations*, alcohol can also serve to reduce tension by making an individual believe that an action is more likely to be successful than they believed before drinking. For example, Wilson and Abrams (1977) showed, using the balanced placebo design, that for males, the belief that they had consumed alcohol was the determining factor in serving to reduce social anxiety. These writers also showed that the reverse was true for females – women who believe that they have drunk alcohol show increased social anxiety (Abrams and Wilson 1979). Wilson (1987: 345–6) argues that

> consistent with their learned expectations, men are likely to approach more readily when intoxicated (or when they think they are intoxicated)....Women, as a result of a social learning history in which men often act unpredictably and aggressively when intoxicated, and when their own culturally acquired outcome expectations suggest that alcohol will disinhibit their self-control, feel threatened and come to be more defensive in heterosexual situations featuring drinking.

A problem with the evidence reviewed above is that there is a large difference between showing that alcohol has certain *effects* on a person's self-efficacy or action-outcome expectations, and suggesting that the person drinks *because* he or she predicts that such an effect will occur.

There are other forms of the tension-reduction theory which, while still being primarily cognitive, do not rest on self-efficacy or action-outcome expectations. Hull (1981), for example, suggests that alcohol serves to reduce tension by reducing an individual's level of self-awareness; and Steele and Josephs (1988) posit that alcohol impairs the individual's information-processing capacity, restricting attention to immediate events. Hence, if these are pleasurable, there is low anxiety; if these are not, high anxiety occurs. Intoxication with concurrent pleasurable activity reduces anxiety by blocking out of awareness distress-eliciting thoughts.

All of these, however, confuse the issue of the effect of the alcohol with the reason for drinking: do people drink in order to reduce self-awareness or to impair their information-processing capacity (or because they expect these effects), or are these simply effects of the drinking which is done for quite different reasons? A further confusion occurs due to the research which shows that alcohol does not in fact serve to reduce tension at all among heavy drinkers; considerable research exists (for example, Davis 1971) which shows that prolonged drinking leads to an *increase* in negative emotional states. Yet the issue here, of course, is not whether or not alcohol does serve to reduce tension, but whether or not individuals expect or believe that it will, and here the evidence is that individuals, especially if they are heavy or problematic drinkers, do hold these expectations. As Bandura (1977) has argued, it is expected consequences rather than actual ones that govern behaviour.

Drug history

Although expectations, modelling and tension or stress are all important influences on drug and alcohol use, a further major influence is actual experience with the drug or with alcohol; the amount of experience with the drug will affect the individual's expectations concerning the drug effects.

Heavier-drinking individuals appear to hold different expectations concerning the effects of alcohol. Rohsenow (1983), for example, found that moderate and heavy drinkers tended to expect alcohol to enhance social and sexual pleasure and to reduce tension more than light drinkers did. She also found that, whereas all categories of drinker expected similar levels of negative consequences (such as impairment of functioning in some way), heavier drinkers also expected more positive effects than did light drinkers.

It should be stressed that these expected positive effects do not in fact occur; most of these expectations are unrealistic (for example, in 1966 McGuire *et al*. showed that excessive drinkers had highly unrealistic anticipations both that drinking would be associated with relaxation and sociability, and that drinking would be linked with sexual prowess and freedom from family surveillance). What is important in terms of understanding how problems arise is that the drug users *think* that these positive effects will occur.

It can be seen, then, that there is a wide range of factors which influence a person's alcohol- or drug-using activities, including modelling, expectations, a desire to reduce tension and the amount of experience with the drug or alcohol that the individual has accrued. None of these, however, are sufficient on their own to explain the development of problematic use.

Balance of forces

One idea which has increasingly emerged in the addiction field over the last 20 years is that of a balance of forces pulling an individual in different ways (Janis and Mann 1968, 1977; Orford 1985). This idea is quite simple; with all activities which have a potential to become excessive, there is a range of forces which serve either to deter a person from becoming more excessive, or to promote that person's excessive behaviour. For example, forces which act as a deterrent (or a 'restraint' in Orford's (1985) terms) include fear of the effects, religious views, friends' views (if one's peer group is against excessive use) and the lack of availability of opportunities for indulgence in the activity. Examples of forces which act to promote excess again include friends' views (if the peer group are pro-excessive use), availability (both of the substance and the opportunities for indulgence) and parental modelling (i.e. if parents are excessive users of a substance themselves).

This idea of a balance of competing forces, some pushing a person towards excess and others pulling the person away, raises the issue of conflict. Of course, a simplistic view of the 'balance sheet' approach can be held without a notion of conflict. For example, one could imagine a computer program which dispassionately weighs up the possible consequences – some positive, some negative – of a given activity, with a simple solution emerging at the other end of this process of either engaging in the activity or not. The reality, however, is more complex than this, with conflict occurring for two reasons. First, the decision as to whether to indulge or not may often be a highly difficult one. Accounts of problem drinkers and drug takers (and overeaters as well) often describe an approach–avoidance conflict, where strong desire or temptation wars with equally strong restraints. Second, this conflict is not static; instead it increases in intensity: as the positive and negative consequences of engaging in the activity each become more powerful – the escape from tension, or reduction in withdrawal symptoms on the one hand; the difficulties at work or with family on the other – so the conflict becomes more difficult. The issue of conflict or ambivalence will occupy us again when we consider interventions with alcohol and drug problems.

It is the case, then, that alcohol or drug use is influenced by a variety of factors. It is also true that this use can serve a number of different functions, both for different individuals, and within the same person, with some of these functions being to: alter one's mood, allow one to express oneself in a different way, reduce one's tension, enjoy the sensual pleasure of the experience, and so on. Furthermore, the functions that alcohol or drug use can serve may and do change as a person moves through different stages of his or her life.

Exposure vs. adaptation

To say, however, that activity is influenced by a variety of factors, and serves numerous functions, still does not explain how and why alcohol and drug use becomes problematic for some people. Alexander and Hadaway (1982), in reviewing the literature on opiate addiction, argue that all the theories of addiction which are in use can be reduced to two major approaches; and further, that these approaches represent 'two fundamentally different and incompatible views' (p. 367). Their thesis (which is concerned with opiate problems but is applicable across the range of drugs) is that there is an 'exposure' approach, and an 'adaptation' approach. The exposure orientation holds that addiction is a consequence of exposure to the drug or alcohol; whereas the adaptation view holds that drug or alcohol use is a response to some stress, which might be related to personality, life events, family problems and so on – that is, the drugs are used to help the person cope. Yet again, this adaptation view makes expectations central – the issue is not whether or not the drug use actually enables the person to cope better, but whether or not the individual expects that they will be able to cope better.

Of course, as with any attempt to present a difficult issue in terms of a simple dichotomy, the story is far more complex than this. Evidence exists to support both views. For example, there exists considerable data in opposition to any simple exposure notion. Increasingly, evidence is emerging that casual heroin users exist who are not addicted despite their exposure (for example, Zinberg and Jacobson 1976); and the research of Robins on heroin use of US servicemen during Vietnam and on their return to the United States shows convincingly that many people who use and who are therefore highly exposed do not remain addicted (Robins *et al.* 1975). Furthermore, once one starts to examine other behaviours such as drinking alcohol, eating and sexual behaviour, it becomes apparent that exposure alone is insufficient to explain problem use. Finally, the evidence from problem users is that they feel that their use is caused by factors other than just exposure – for example, as mentioned above, many individuals with alcohol problems understand their alcohol use as an attempt to cope with tension.

On the other hand, there also exists considerable evidence to suggest that problem alcohol and drug use is often progressive, and there is evidence, outlined above, to suggest that expectations about the effects of alcohol are influenced by exposure. Furthermore, a large amount of data exists which shows that the number of people with alcohol or drug problems in a population is directly proportional to the availability of the alcohol or drug (Grant *et al.* 1983). If the problems stemmed from an adaptive function, the availability (and hence exposure to the activity) would not significantly alter the number of people with the problem. It seems, then, that for a variety of reasons, neither a simple 'adaptation to stress' approach nor a simple 'exposure to the activity or substance' approach will suffice.

What does seem clear is that certain cognitive processes mediate between the initial taking up of an activity and the development of a problem. Expectations occupy a high place on the list of cognitive mediators, but Orford's idea of the balance struck between the restraints and the incentives (which is a shifting balance over a lifetime) is another important cognitive process. Orford further argues that the research on expectations shows that appetative activities may become over-valued (as we have seen above, the expectations may outstrip reality) and that a process of affective-behavioural-cognitive consistency comes into play to reinforce behaviour at increased levels.

Maintenance of problems

The foregoing section has argued that, due to a complex array of expectations, fantasies, tensions, stresses and the like, it is possible to see why some people allow the conflicting balance between the forces of restraint and excess to be swayed towards over-indulgence in alcohol or drugs. Yet the question immediately arises as to *why people carry on*, once they can see that they are developing problems. After all, a cognitive view would suggest that these individuals will be reflecting upon their behaviour and will therefore be able to detect that their expectations and so on are not being fulfilled – further, that the negative consequences of the behaviour are outstripping the positive ones. We have seen that the disease approach simply uses the concept of uncontrollable addiction to explain the continued use, but this is not a cognitive-behavioural explanation. How, then, is the maintenance of excess understood from within this perspective?

Four main arguments are put forward. First, someone who is developing a problem with their use of alcohol or drugs continues for the same reasons that they started to develop the problem in the first place. That is, if a person started to over-use alcohol or drugs in order to help him or her cope with social encounters, or to be more exact because he or she had an expectation that alcohol or drugs would so help, then this motivation will still be there. As argued above, it matters not whether or not the outcome of the behaviour in fact eases the social encounter, only that the individual believes both that it will and that it has done so.

A second reason for the maintenance of use once problems start to emerge is that the affective-behavioural-cognitive consistency rule is still obeyed; individuals do not at first accept or even notice that the negatives are starting to overtake the positives. What many writers describe as a process of denial (which a more cognitively orientated researcher would see as a process of attribution) occurs, where individuals find reasons for the negative events which occur which lie outside of their own actions: other people act unreasonably, chance events occur, the system is wrong – in other words, people start to attribute negative occurrences to chance events or to powerful others.

A third reason is that, as discussed in the first section of this chapter, it must be accepted that physiological effects of alcohol or drug use will occur – that continued use of alcohol or drugs will have a result of altering the individual's biological response to that substance; and that one effect of this altered biological response will be that the individual will experience discomfort if they cease to take the alcohol or drug. This is commonly known as a withdrawal effect. Once again the role of expectations is crucial here, because individuals will soon learn that more of the same activity will reduce these unpleasant effects, and hence continued use occurs due to the expectation that this will lead to withdrawal relief.

A fourth reason is due to the process of generalization. Orford (1985) cites numerous studies which show in a variety of excessive behaviours how individuals find that an increasingly wide range of stimuli act as triggers for the behaviour. Some of these triggers will be external – a party, a decision which needs to be made, a celebration for getting a new job or a consolation for failing to get one – all will act as reasonable reasons for indulging in the activity. As Reinert (1968) puts it: 'Alcoholics drink for the same reasons as anyone else does but they gradually come either to use a greater variety of reasons or establish particularly strong connections between alcohol and a few of the reasons' (p. 41). While some of the reasons will be external, others will be internal:

a most significant part of this generalization process may be the increasing misattribution of meaning to internal psychophysiological states. Thus, internal cues that might otherwise be interpreted as fatigue, tension, or confusion, or else not labelled at all, may be interpreted as indicating a need to go and [follow the excessive activity].... It may reasonably be argued that the stronger attachment becomes, the more salient or 'pre-potent' relevant acts become...and hence the more likely it becomes that emotional arousal will be interpreted in terms of need, desire, or craving for that substance or activity.

(Orford 1985: 190–1)

The process that is being observed here, then, is one in which an individual is becoming increasingly preoccupied with the activity, with an ever increasing set of stimuli acting as cues for that activity, such that the behaviour starts to appear increasingly automatic and generalized. Orford suggests that this increasing pre-occupation with excessive use could be seen as being similar to an increasing 'commitment' to the activities concerned, which then allows a body of experimental social-psychological research to become relevant, with much of this work suggesting that commitment alters motivation, with greater voluntary commitment to some negative activity being associated with considerably greater motivation to continue it, and with less physiological and psychological signs of discomfort as a consequence of the activity.

This chapter has so far shown that there is a wide range of cognitively based theories and processes which are relevant to alcohol and drug problems. Interestingly, with the exception of Orford (ibid.) – and his model covers more than purely cognitive-behavioural approaches – there has been little attempt to link these various ideas together into an overall cognitive-behavioural model of all aspects of the taking up of potentially excessive activities, the development and maintenance of problems, and intervention with these problems. It is on the intervention side that cognitive-behavioural theorists have made their most sustained mark.

INTERVENTION

Cognitive-behavioural ideas or methods have been utilized in a number of areas in the alcohol and drug field: addressing clients' expectations and dealing with their ambivalence with respect to giving up or reducing their substance use; giving clients information; focusing on clients' goals; helping clients restructure their cognitions about their use of substances; teaching clients new skills to deal with old problems; providing a range of strategies to overcome anticipated problems; and thinking ahead and anticipating problems and their solutions.

Each of the above has particular cognitive-behavioural techniques and interventions associated with them, and they will be examined shortly; but there are also common approaches, and three of these are the emphases on performance, on practice, and on homework:

1 *Performance:* What is meant here is that, although the cognitive element ensures that clients' attitudes, ideas, wishes and so on are addressed, talking on its own is unlikely to provide all the necessary help – there must be a behavioural (performance) component to the intervention as well: people must *do* something different about their problematic behaviour as well as simply talking about it.
2 *Practice or rehearsal:* The issue of practice arises because the behavioural

intervention will almost certainly involve the development of new skills, and as with any new skills, these must be practised.

3 *Homework:* Some of the practice will occur in the therapeutic sessions, but much of it will occur outside of the sessions – in the client's outside life and relating to the client's behaviour, relationships, social networks and community within which their alcohol or drug problems are enacted. A cognitive-behaviourally orientated therapist will usually negotiate with the client some task(s) which the client will carry out during the time between the sessions, and this will usually involve the client practising some of the skills or strategies discussed in the session.

Addressing clients' expectations and dealing with their ambivalence about giving up or reducing their substance use

When people approach agencies for help they are likely to have ambivalent feelings and expectations concerning both the extent to which they actually want to give up or reduce their substance use, and the extent to which they will be able actually to achieve this goal.

Unsure whether they want to change

Traditionally, a client's uncertainty about whether or not they wish to alter their substance use has been interpreted as a 'lack of motivation' and a concommitant resistance to treatment. A cognitive-behavioural approach would see this ambivalence as a realistic appraisal: a major shift in life style (which a serious alteration in drinking or drug-taking habits would imply) would have both positive and negative consequences – positive in terms of improved health, for example, but negative in terms, for example, of reduced or altered social contact with the substance-using group with which the user has associated – which might include spouse, workmates and close friends. Hence a cognitive-behavioural approach would see that a precursor to working therapeutically with a drug or alcohol user would be to clarify the different advantages and disadvantages of continuing versus curtailing the substance use.

This idea of clarifying both sides of the argument is similar, of course, to the 'balance sheet' idea discussed previously; but here it is being utilized, not in the sense of a theoretical construct which can help us better make sense of people's behaviour, but in an overt therapeutic way as suggested by Janis and Mann, who originated the idea in their 1968 work on 'addictive' smoking. They suggested that a 'balance sheet' be constructed of the pluses and minuses associated with each of several ways of resolving the dilemma connected with their smoking; and this idea – variously termed a 'decision matrix' or a 'pay-off matrix' – has been utilized in the alcohol field (Orford 1971) and in the addiction field generally (Marlatt and Parks 1982). The balance sheet is, of course, only one method of addressing this issue. Another has been written about by Miller (1983) under the title 'motivational interviewing' in which again the issues of the positive and negative aspects of excessive drinking, reduced drinking and abstinence are addressed without recourse to terminology such as lack of motivation, denial or resistance to treatment.

The important point here is that the therapist accepts that ambivalence about change is normal, and hence works with it from the outset as opposed to ignoring it until a client 'fails' in treatment and then utilizing a 'lack of will-power' explanation for this failure.

Clearly, not everyone is equally ambivalent, and this relates to the research of Prochaska and DiClemente (1983). Based on their work with tobacco smokers, they suggested that people with dependency problems might be at different stages within a cycle of change. They conceptualized this change cycle as being made up of four stages: 'contemplation', 'action', 'maintenance' and 'lapse or relapse', with a fifth 'pre-contemplation' stage through which people passed before joining the cycle. The 'pre-contemplative' stage is one in which people do not really think about the problematic side of their drug use, or think about it in an unworried fashion. Contemplation occurs when someone starts to think about their inappropriate use and begins to ask themselves 'why?'; action occurs when a client makes a decision to change and puts the process in motion; maintenance occurs when the person has changed and now has to face up to the constant difficulties which can beset someone once they have changed their behaviour; and lapse or relapse occurs when the person succumbs to these pressures to resume the problematic activity.

Three points stand out from this model. The first is that it is not a linear one – people can re-enter the cycle at any point following a lapse. The second is that the skills and techniques used at one stage need not be the ones used at another. For example, Prochaska and DiClemente write about the individuals who stopped smoking in the short term, employing a variety of cognitive strategies such as positive self-talk (telling oneself that stopping was possible); while those who had stopped smoking for a longer period used more behavioural methods such as engaging in alternative behaviours or altering their environments to remove those cues associated with the excessive behaviour. The third point to emerge from this model is that, again, motivation is not seen as a static concept, but one which will clearly alter as individuals move from one position in the cycle to another. Hence, individuals in the pre-contemplative stage certainly do not think that altering their behaviour is a worthwhile task, and both their ambivalence and their motivation will be at a low level; while those in later stages will be far more ambivalent, and the balance between changing and remaining where they are will be a far more unstable one.

Unsure whether they can change

The other area of ambivalence which clients will have is over whether or not they feel they will be able to achieve whatever goal is decided upon. Again, it is not surprising that clients feel ambivalent about this. Most clients will have attempted to alter their behaviour on many occasions without success before seeking professional help; and furthermore, as members of society they will share many of the socially agreed stereotypes about 'alcoholics' and 'drug addicts' as being unable to stop or cut down, being addicted, lacking in will-power and so on. Hence, a major focus of cognitive-behavioural approaches to this issue is on altering this negative expectation, and much of the rest of this section relates to methods of achieving this.

Giving clients information

One of the important cornerstones of a cognitive approach is to give individuals accurate information so that they can make their own decisions. This approach of providing people with information stems from a variety of sources. First, it has been suggested that many people start using substances excessively because they do not know how much is too much. They also do not know about a range of other things: the different strengths of different beverages or drugs, for instance, or the different effects on men and on women. Accordingly, the focus of much health promotional work in recent years has been on providing people with the necessary information to make informed decisions about how much, when and where to drink alcohol, and who with (see, for example, the Health Education Authority's booklet *That's The Limit* (HEA 1989)).

A second reason for the growth in the importance of information stems from the work of Orford and Edwards (1977), who found in the 1970s that simply giving clients a small amount of information and advice as to how to cut down or give up (and why they should do this) led to as much change in behaviour as did a full range of alcoholism treatment services; and this was especially the case with problem drinkers who were less severely physiologically dependent.

A third line of evidence links the two previous ones, and concerns the provision of written information and advice concerning alcohol and drugs to those with developing problems. This is a method first attempted in the United States with the publication in 1976 of Miller and Munoz's book *How to Control Your Drinking*, and subsequently evaluated in a number of studies (for example, Miller 1982); and it has been continued in the UK by Heather and Robertson (1989; Heather *et al*. 1987; Robertson and Heather 1986). These latter authors advertised in the national and local press in Scotland, inviting readers who thought that they were drinking too much to write in for free advice. Respondents were given a structured self-help manual which first gave information about alcohol and its effects, and advised readers on how to decide whether or not they had an alcohol problem, and then went on to show them how to analyse their reasons for drinking, the cues which were associated with their heavy drinking, and suitable and individually relevant alternatives to drinking alcohol to fulfil the same functions as the alcohol. All these methods revolve around enabling individuals to assess and understand their behaviour more successfully.

A final way of using the provision of information as a method of helping individuals with alcohol or drug problems is to inform individuals about high-risk situations and the danger of relapse. This is an issue which will be considered in more detail in a later section.

Focusing on clients' goals

Many writers (for example, Heather and Robertson 1989) underline the importance of focusing on the client's goals. There are two issues here. First, there is the general issue of goal setting. Behavioural methods of intervention have for many years argued strongly for the importance of setting manageable, realistic and achievable goals against which both clients' and therapists can measure progress, and this is equally important in the alcohol and drug field. By the time that someone has sought help he or she will usually have developed problems in a number of areas of life functioning – relationships, employment, finance, health, police and so on – as well as having difficulty in controlling the use of alcohol or drugs. Hence, the goals that are set must address some or all of these issues. Yet for many clients, the enormity of the range and number of problems will seem insurmountable; a good strategy is to help set intermediate, short-term goals which are (and seem to the client) to be achievable in the short term. Furthermore, by being short term, these goals will be realized relatively quickly, which will lead to cognitive (a sense of satisfaction and increased self-efficacy) and tangible (better financial stability, for example, or better employment or family relationships) rewards accruing, which in turn will help to improve the sense of commitment to change, and keep the balance on the reduction-of-use side of the balance sheet.

The second area of importance is that the goals set should be the client's goals, not those of the therapist. This is for a number of reasons. The foremost of these is the evidence that if goals are not the client's, then he or she does not achieve them. For example, Orford and Keddie (1986) and Sanchez-Craig *et al.* (1984), in an attempt to further examine issues concerning controlled drinking versus abstinence, both randomly assigned problem drinkers to either a goal of abstinence or one of controlled drinking. Among other results, both studies reported that very few of the 'abstinence' clients abstained (although most severely moderated their drinking); and that this might be related to the fact that most of the individuals assigned to 'abstinence' rejected this goal from the outset. This finding is part of a general one: when problem drinkers are allowed a choice about the kind of help that they receive (as opposed to simply being given a standard treatment regime which is the same for all clients), the success rates of treatment tend to improve (Parker *et al.* 1979).

Helping clients restructure their cognitions about their use of substances

A number of methods have been devised in order to help clients who want to give up or cut down on their use, but who feel that they cannot. These include getting the problem drinker or drug taker to become more aware of the situational determinants of the drinking or drug taking; and then using more active cognitive-restructuring techniques.

Raising awareness

Increasing awareness involves the collection of good quality data. Many clients come with only a very generalized knowledge concerning their drinking or drug-taking behaviour, and this knowledge is heavily biased by their current negative belief in themselves; hence they selectively perceive negative events about themselves, and examples of their loss of control about their behaviour. A first step in challenging this set of beliefs is getting the clients to monitor their behaviour in a systematic fashion, collecting information about how much is consumed, and when, where and with whom it is consumed. Self-monitoring serves a number of functions. First, it makes the client begin to take control of his or her own behaviour. Instead of having an outside therapist assess the client, the therapist asks the client to collect his or her own data. Second, it enables a client to get a better knowledge of how much drink or drugs he or she is consuming. Third, it makes a client aware of the circumstances in which the activity occurs – what actually triggers off a drinking bout? – and it may serve to clarify the restraining forces which still keep the behaviour in check at some points or with some people. Fourth, it enables precise goals to be set on the basis of a more detailed knowledge of the present behaviour. Fifth, it provides a baseline against which any subsequent progress may be compared.

Furthermore, self-monitoring as described above requires a client to *do* something in between the sessions, and this in itself is a useful thing. Providing a task for the client in the inter-session intervals aids the continuation of any positive changes, and reinforces the idea of the process of change being the client's responsibility as well as the therapist's; and it is often the case that simply getting a client to focus on his or her drug or alcohol use is an effective therapeutic technique, with clients reporting a reduction in their intake as they realize its extent.

It is possible, however (albeit with less accuracy), to collect this data on the range and circumstances of the excessive behaviour in retrospect, by a careful questioning of the client about the previous week's activities and concommitant drink/drug activity. This is best approached as a joint reconstructive exercise, with the client and counsellor together working backwards from 'yesterday', elaborating the activities which a client performed yesterday, clarifying all the possible times when alcohol or drugs could have been consumed, and clarifying exactly how much and the circumstances under which this was consumed.

A further set of awareness techniques is described by Wallace (1985), including: 'practising the opposite', which focuses awareness on habitual ways of approaching and responding to typical situations; 'following the drunk through', which involves getting the client to imagine vividly the entire drinking episode, concentrating on the more delayed negative consequences as well as the initial positive ones; and 'cognitive-behavioural sharpening', in which the client in a group setting has a conversation with himself, alternating between two chairs, with one person being his sober and one his drunk self, in order to 'sharpen and clarify the inner conflict commonly encountered' (p. 114).

Cognitive restructuring

These awareness techniques provide a basis upon which cognitive restructuring can build. Whelan and Prince (1982) argue that, although cognitive restructuring is important, direct cognitive confrontation will serve to increase anxiety, which will therefore precipitate avoidance responses: 'Withdrawal, denial, or placating responses could be elicited that would tend to reinforce rigid patterns of thought and behaviour, thereby increasing resistance to change' (p. 881). Increased anxiety might also increase the chances of a problem drinker or drug user returning to their maladaptive use. Whelan and Prince, therefore, suggest the use of indirect techniques which focus on the inconsistencies within what the client reports. For example, a client might define themselves as someone who cannot stop drinking, but tell the therapist about a time in the past when they had stopped for a period; or come to the clinic that day without having drank.

Whelan and Prince suggest that there are a number of techniques which a therapist might use in order to challenge these inconsistencies without raising anxiety too much. Some of these techniques (see Table 6.1) are: 'juxtapositioning', 'perceptual chipping', 'cognitive double binds', 'analogy' and 'exaggeration', with, for example, perceptual chipping involving indirectly challenging without unduly threatening the client about their present interpretation of an experience, by carefully examining inconsistencies in recall, attribution of success and denial of responsibility concerning drinking, via detailed questioning.

Oei and Jackson (1982) report a study in which they investigated the use of social-skills training with problem drinkers where this was combined with a specific attempt to restructure cognitions. They believed that clients' irrational beliefs and attitudes would have a large effect on their ability to change, and hence attempted to examine these beliefs and help clients alter their perceptions and behaviours accordingly. Although their findings are marred by methodological problems in the study – for example, the follow-up was not blind – they found that all three groups (social skills alone, cognitive restructuring alone and the two combined) were significantly superior to a 'traditional, supportive group' control group, and that the combined group fared best of all.

Prochaska and DiClemente (1983) also delineated a number of cognitive strategies which clients use to restructure their cognitions, including what they term 'consciousness raising' and 'self-re-evaluation'. What all these techniques described above have in common is their attempt to get people to introspect, to increase their awareness of their behaviour and motivations, to think about themselves in relation to their behaviour, and to question and re-evaluate this behaviour in the light of who they want to be and feel that they can become.

Teaching clients new skills to deal with old problems; and providing a range of strategies to overcome anticipated problems

This section so far has discussed expectations and ambivalence, providing clients

Table 6.1   Techniques suggested by Whelan and Prince (1982) for challenging cognitive inconsistencies in alcohol abusers

Perceptual chipping
Indirectly challenging without unduly threatening the client about his or her present interpretation of an experience, by carefully examining inconsistencies in recall, attribution of success and denial of responsibility concerning drinking, via detailed questioning.

Juxtapositioning
For use when inconsistencies become apparent. Juxtapositioning involves comparing the reality of contrasting thoughts, and hence creating cognitive dissonance. For example, if a client says 'I can't seem to stop drinking' the therapist might juxtapose the double message of the client's presence at the therapy session (showing a willingness to stop) with the verbal comment (implying that his or her view is that such stopping is impossible).

Cognitive double binds
The creating in the client of the realization that he or she is capable of responding both like an 'alcoholic' and like someone in control of drinking. For example, contrasting with the present uncontrolled drinking a past period where the client was drinking in a controlled fashion, and asking 'What was different in your life then?'.

Analogy
'The purposeful self-disclosure (analogy) by the therapist concerning specific problems of the patient encourages a more free exploration of ideas. The "I–thou" personalisation of disclosure functions to allow the alcoholic to accept responsibility for harm, thereby mitigating the "normal" cognitive response of avoiding responsibility for harm' (p. 883).

Exaggeration
'The therapist over-emphasises positive aspects of self-aggrandizement, thereby producing a state of cognitive dissonance in which the alcoholic is placed in the position of minimising self-enhancement to portray a realistic self-image' (p. 883).

with information, helping clients set goals and restructuring clients' cognitions – all highly cognitive activities. Yet as Rollnick (1985) argues, 'once the client has moved some way through the process of examining the feasibility of the treatment goal and the need for a change in lifestyle, the whole question of implementing desired behaviour change comes to the fore' (p. 140). A major cornerstone of the cognitive-behavioural approach is that performance-based interventions are better at enabling both behaviour and attitude change than are purely verbal ones.

The rationale for concentrating on performance is simple: if clients have been dealing with a situation over a period of many years by drinking or taking drugs, then they will of necessity lack the skills (or the ability to utilize the skills in context) to enable them successfully to negotiate the situation in the future without drinking or drug taking, certainly for any extended period of time. What is clearly needed is to train the individuals to identify and practise new strategies and skills so that the alcohol or drugs are not required.

Two sorts of skills have been examined in the literature. The first consists of avoidance strategies, of teaching individuals how to recognize problem situations and not get involved with them; the second involves problem-solving strategies which teach individuals about how to cope with the problem situation once the individual is in it. Unfortunately, most research confuses these two issues and teaches both sets of skills. This is particularly unfortunate, as the work which has been carried out where these two sets of skills are separated (for example, Billings and Moos 1983) shows that, as Saunders and Allsop (1987) comment, 'it was the gradual development of problem solving rather than avoidance skills that were characteristic of good outcome' (p. 422).

Teaching problem-solving skills

Chaney *et al.* (1978) designed a treatment package for helping problem drinkers to deal with common situations which had shown themselves to be dangerous in the past. Forty in-patient 'alcoholics' undergoing the conventional hospital treatment regime were divided into three groups – a skills-training one, a discussion one and a no-additional-treatment control group. In the skills-training group, clients were presented with problem situations by the therapist and were then trained to use a problem-solving strategy to deal with it. The therapist first selected a non-drinking response, discussed this response with the group and then modelled it. Each group member then had to decide on their own way of coping with the problem, to rehearse this way in front of the group and to receive feedback from the other group members. At the end of each exercise, the methods and strategies used were summarized by one of the group members. There were only eight 1½-hour sessions, and all role-play was conducted within the confines of the group sessions – there was no real-life practice. Yet at 1-year follow-up the participants in this group had had shorter and less severe relapses than the participants in the other two groups.

Another skills-based approach to help problem drinkers to cope is in the teaching of controlled drinking skills. Many problem drinkers (and drug takers) have attempted to control their intake in the past and have failed, but a number of studies have shown that controlled drinking can be a legitimate and possible goal (especially as so many clients aim for this anyway) if the skills are taught effectively. Teaching controlled drinking does not mean simply telling clients to control their drinking; it means analysing the times, places and cues which are responsible for the drinking going out of control, and teaching a range of alternative strategies, behaviours and skills for dealing with these cues. Sobell and Sobell (1973, 1978, 1984), for example, had clients participate in seventeen sessions of intensive broad-spectrum behavioural treatment including learning about appropriate drinking (drinking in sips rather than gulps, putting the glass down between sips, drinking more diluted drinks and so on), problem solving, assertiveness training, education, rehearsal of coping responses and watching videotapes of the person's own drunken behaviour. Some of the clients were aiming for controlled drinking, and others were aiming for abstinence, and both groups had no-extra-treatment controls (all clients were undergoing traditional in-patient alcoholism therapy at the same time). The results showed that at 6, 12, 18 and 24 months both experimental groups were functioning at better levels than the control groups, as measured by their drinking outcome, and the controlled drinking experimental group had fewer drunken days and fewer days in hospital or jail, and more days abstinent and controlled drinking, than did the experimental abstinent group.

Neither the Chaney *et al*. study nor that of the Sobells involved practice in the 'real world', and it is interesting to examine other research which was more extensively integrated into the general environment. As part of a far more extensive 'social engineering' study (which in fact conceptualized alcohol problems from an operant-conditioning and contingency-management viewpoint), in which clients were assisted in finding jobs, accommodation and friends, as well as being helped to purchase a telephone and a television, Azrin (Azrin 1976; Hunt and Azrin 1973) approached clients' problems from a skills perspective. The highly successful treatment package which they developed included teaching clients interviewee and job-finding skills, marital and family-interaction skills, and the skills involved in the development of new friendships. In both of Azrin's studies, the intervention group had far better success rates than did the control groups. One problem with the Azrin studies is that it is difficult to disentangle the different strands of the research and hence to assess the effectiveness of different elements.

An important problem-solving skill involves the development of alternative constructive behaviour. Blakey and Baker (1980) used an exposure method where the client was exposed to situations which he had identified as previously being a trigger to the drinking of alcohol, but where instead he performed some alternative (and non-avoidance) behaviour, sometimes suggested by the client, sometimes by the therapist. Working with single cases (and hence with very small numbers overall) and with each client generating a hierarchal range of trigger situations, these authors report that five out of six clients attained abstinence from drinking by the end of therapy, this abstinence being maintained over follow-ups of up to 9 months, and being accompanied by an absence of a desire to drink by the end of therapy.

Other researchers have also examined the issue of exposure to the stimuli associated with drinking in situations where the drinking response was prevented. Hodgson and Rankin (1982) and Rankin (1982) discuss this in terms of 'cure exposure'. They liken the compulsion felt by many problem drinkers to that felt by other sorts of client who complain of compulsions – compulsive handwashers, checkers, obsessional ruminators. Arguing that 'cue exposure' – exposing the client to the anxiety-provoking situation and getting them successfully to resist the urge to indulge in their checking behaviour – has been shown to be a powerful method of breaking up compulsive behaviour in general, Hodgson and Rankin put forward the hypothesis that the compulsion felt by many problem drinkers, which is heightened by having one or a few drinks, might be 'in part learned phenomena which can be unlearned through repeated cue exposure' (p. 222). The case-studies they present suggest that cue-exposure techniques have the effect of breaking the link between cues to drink and the compulsion to do so to excess. Again, these are techniques which do not allow avoidance – clients have to learn new strategies such as reality testing.

The research outlined above, and the division between avoidance and problem-solving alternatives, highlights the importance of coping strategies in a cognitive-behavioural analysis of alcohol or drug therapy. Saunders and Allsop (1987) argue that a number of studies show that it is those clients who can transfer from positive self-talk, or from simple avoidance strategies, to engaging in altern-ative behaviours, or a coping style of response to problems, who appear to do well in the long term. This raises the question as to whether therapists should attempt to teach clients a *general* coping strategy such as that outlined by D'Zurilla and Goldfried (1971), which clients can then use in specific situations as and when they arise, as opposed to teaching specific coping responses to individual problems.

D'Zurilla and Goldfried isolated six processes of problem solving which Heather and Robertson (1989) have utilized in their analysis of problem drinking. These processes are: mental set, problem definition, generation of potential solu-tions, decision making, verification and feedback. 'Mental set' includes individuals' overall approach to the solving of their problems, and to problems in general. A healthy mental set would be one in which individuals see problems as a normal feature of everyday life which require a flexible approach to enable solutions to be found. Unfortunately, some people act as if there is only one possible way of reacting to any given problem, rather than realizing that there are always a range of alternative solutions and reactions. Others create for themselves highly pressurized belief systems which irrationally propel them into inescapable situ-ations. It is important, therefore, as a first step in problem-solving skills to learn to understand that problems can affect anyone and that the skills to overcome problems are learnable and achievable by anyone.

A number of writers have commented on this counter-productive mental set. Beck was one of the first authors to discuss the logical flaws which pervade the thinking of those with a range of emotional and behavioural dysfunctions. He isolated a number of these logical flaws and grouped them into various categories – for example, overgeneralization (where, for example, the taking of one drink is seen as signifying total loss of control); catastrophization (where, for example, one bad event or decision is taken to signify that everything about the person is lacking and that nothing will ever be able to help); and jumping to conclusions (where one out of a range of possible explanations for a question or event is selected, which shows oneself in a bad light or leads negative consequences). Marlatt (1985) suggested that some problem drinkers are so heavily directed towards the fulfilment of a variety of 'shoulds' about the world that they can only escape from this pressurized situation by heavy drinking. What links these different ideas is the view of clients' lack of detachment, their inability to see clearly beyond the immediate confines of the problem in such a way that the range of solutions is apparent.

D'Zurilla and Goldfried's second stage in problem solving is problem definition. This relates to the previous stage, in that many people see their problems in
inexact and global terms rather than in precise ones; and yet it is only when the
problem is delineated in precise terms that its boundaries are clear and potential
solutions become apparent. Their third stage of generation of potential solutions
involves the 'brainstorming' of solutions, the opening up of a range of possibilities
of new responses which might not previously have been considered. Their fourth
stage of decision making involves the selection from the range of potential solutions
generated by the brainstorming of a small number which might be feasible and
achievable, and from that to select one to try out. The fifth stage of verification
involves testing out this chosen solution – by talking it through with others, trying
it out in imagination, role-playing it or actually attempting it in real life. The final
stage of feedback involves assessing (with the help of others) the effectiveness of
this preferred strategy, and re-evaluating the usefulness of this chosen solution.
These processes are similar to those described by Egan (1986) in his five-stage
model of counselling.

This section has concentrated on the teaching of new or alternative approaches
to old problems. Yet once someone with a long-standing alcohol or drug problem
begins to deal with this problem, a host of new situations and problems, some
completely new and others which the person has not had to deal with for many
years, will start to emerge. A cognitive-behavioural approach recognizes that
effective therapy needs to anticipate and deal with these problems as well. Part of
the method of dealing with this will be the utilization of the range of problem-
solving skills which have been described above; part of it will be the employment
of a particular set of skills which go under the title of 'relapse management', which
will be considered in the next section .

Thinking ahead and anticipating problems and their solutions

The ideas grouped together under the term 'relapse prevention' are primarily the
work of Alan Marlatt and his colleagues, although other writers (for example,
Litman) have contributed to the research into the relapse phenomenon. Marlatt sees
relapse as comprising two stages: (a) the triggering of a resumption of drinking or
drug taking; and (b) continued excessive substance use.

Marlatt (1985) conceptualizes the first stage as being precipitated by a high-risk
situation in which the individual is unable to cope; whereas the second stage is
precipitated by something he terms the abstinence violation effect (or AVE), which
is caused by a sense of failure or hopelessness on the part of the individual who
sees their failure to keep to their plan as a signal that there is something fundamentally lacking in them. This sense of hopelessness which turns a slip into a
full-blown relapse is of course a familiar one to people who have attempted to diet,
where one slip is seen to have ruined months of dieting to the extent that a person
eating one biscuit feels that they might as well eat the whole packet. Wardle and
Beinart (1981) have recently suggested that an eating binge following eating of a

'forbidden' food was understandable as a response to a belief that the decision to diet had already been broken, and they suggest that this response is analogous to that of an excessive drinker who takes one drink while attempting abstinence, and then goes on a binge. The relationship between substance abuse and binge eating has recently been further elaborated by Filstead *et al.* (1988), who examine the similarity between high-risk situations as triggers for these two different forms of excessive activity.

The importance of Marlatt's work, however, is that not only has he provided a theoretical explanation for the commonly observed phenomenon of relapse, but he has also provided a method of attempting to prevent it. Marlatt believes that clients must be prepared for relapse and taught how to deal with potential relapse situations as part of their therapy. This teaching has two parts: first, recognizing and dealing with at-risk situations; and second, dealing with a lapse situation such that it does not turn into a full-blown relapse.

Recognising and dealing with at-risk situations

Relapse is common with individuals with alcohol and drug problems. A central feature of the relapse-management approach is that this fact is not hidden from clients due to the fear that it might reduce their motivation, but rather that it is openly discussed so that clients have the maximum opportunity to prepare for potential relapse-provoking situations. Marlatt advises that individuals and groups should describe in a highly detailed fashion possible at-risk situations, which should then be analysed so that the specific alternative skills needed can be delineated and practised. Again, Marlatt suggests that these skills are more likely to generalize and become long lasting if they are practised in real-life situations – hence clients should physically place themselves in increasingly difficult situations and practise these new coping strategies until they are confident that they can use these techniques in post-therapy contexts.

Dealing with a lapse situation

Marlatt suggests a number of strategies to prevent a slip turning into a full-scale relapse. He suggests that clients are given a set of 'reminder cards' which are sealed and only opened after a slip has occurred, which rehearse the self-talk about not catastrophizing a slip into a relapse; he suggests cognitive-restructuring techniques to persuade clients not to view a slip as a personal failure which must inevitably lead to a full relapse. He also suggests a 'controlled' or 'programmed relapse' which involves the client 'lapsing' under the supervision of the therapist, with the client rehearsing possible 'controlling' strategies (see, for example, the 'slip cards' described by Goldman and Klisz 1982). Some of the advice Marlatt gives his clients concerning the prevention of a slip becoming a relapse is to

look on the slip as a learning experience. What were the elements of the high-risk situation which led to the slip? What coping response could you have used to get around the situation?... Look upon the slip as a single, independent event, something which can be avoided in the future by the use of an appropriate coping response.

(Marlatt, quoted by Heather and Robertson 1989; 265)

It is also important to recognize the centrality of elements other than skills in this relapse model. Heather *et al.* (1983), for example, found that beliefs about the probability of loss of control over drinking after an initial drink were significantly related to relapse, whereas a measure of physical dependency was not. This finding further underlines the central importance of cognitive factors – expectations, beliefs and so on – in this conceptualization of alcohol and drug problems.

FUTURE DEVELOPMENTS

A coherent theory

As mentioned previously, although there has been considerable work on all aspects of alcohol and drug problems from a cognitive-behavioural viewpoint, there has so far been no coherent account put forward which covers all elements. The nearest to this to date is the excellent book by Orford (1985) which is, however, an eclectic offering covering far more than a cognitive-behavioural view. Nevertheless, it may safely be predicted that this situation will be remedied within the next few years: the number of authors writing from a cognitive-behavioural perspective is growing rapidly, and ever-more comprehensive models are being produced (for example, the wide-ranging work on relapse by Marlatt and his colleagues, and by Saunders and Allsop 1987; and the work by Wilson (1987) on general cognitive processes in addiction).

So little on drugs

As outlined in the introduction to this chapter, far less has been written concerning drug problems from a cognitive-behavioural viewpoint than has been written about alcohol problems. This mirrors a more general phenomenon: although theoretically there is much in common between alcohol and drug problems, services for these two areas have tended to develop in isolation from each other, and different techniques have been developed. Hence, drug services have tended to concentrate on the physical-addiction side, with, as Thorley (1983) remarks, 'treatment (centring) too much on the transaction of the legal opiate prescription to the detriment of other treatment techniques' (p. 105), or alternatively have centred on the issue of abstinence within a drug-free environment, usually provided within a drug rehabilitative therapeutic community. Research on different theoretical orientations to intervention, and on different techniques, has been sadly lacking within this context. Furthermore, there is also a tendency for the drugs field to mimic the alcohol one, with a number of issues emerging within the drugs field being ones which have been extant within the alcohol field for some time – the issue of controlled use, for example; or that of harm minimization; or that of the efficacy of centralized drug clinics versus localized street-level agencies. It is to be hoped that this mimicking process will also incorporate the development of a cognitive-behavioural perspective within the drugs as well as the alcohol field.

The importance of physical dependency

The cognitive-behavioural approach lays great emphasis on non-physical elements in this field; but it is important to be aware of the evidence which does exist which implies that there is an interaction between the physical and non-physical components. The work by Stockwell and colleagues (for example, Stockwell *et al*. 1982) shows that there is a relationship between degree of dependence (as measured by the SADQ) and the effect of an initial drink (or a few drinks) on drinking speed, subjectively reported craving and physiological measures such as heart rate. These studies (using a balanced placebo design) appear to show that for *moderately dependent clients,* the important factor was the clients' expectations about whether or not they had consumed alcohol, whereas for *highly dependent clients* the determining factor was whether or not they had drunk alcohol. Although these results are not accepted wholeheartedly – for example, Heather and Robertson (1983) argue that the difference between highly and moderately dependent clients might be due to different learning histories – they do show that more sophisticated concepts of such traditional ideas as craving and loss of control need to be, and are being, developed and incorporated within a cognitive-behavioural approach.

Heather and Robertson's nine ingredients for effective counselling

Heather and Robertson (1989) conclude their review of cognitive-behavioural approaches to problem drinking with 'a list of nine ingredients in a recipe for effective counselling' (p. 281–2). These nine are (a) understanding and treating drinking in context; (b) problem solving; (c) more action, less words; (d) family, friend and community involvement; (e) make change worthwhile for clients; (f) mastering the cues; (g) self-management and target setting; (h) counsellors who are trained to be competent in cognitive-behavioural methods; and (i) client choice. Together these make an impressive package for intervention with drug and alcohol problems, being based as they are on both empirical evidence and on a cognitive-behavioural theoretical grounding. Nevertheless, an important future direction is the continuation of the careful evaluations which the cognitive-behavioural paradigm has supported in this field, and hence the continued evaluation of the effectiveness of each of these nine ingredients is important.

This last point deserves underlining. Saunders and Allsop (1985) describe a number of reviews of the effectiveness of alcohol and drug interventions, and conclude that all of them are equally unequivocal about the lack of particular success of any one technique or set of techniques over any other. This however is not surprising. The cognitive-behavioural viewpoint espoused within this chapter demands an individual approach to clients, and as such no one technique would be expected to be superior to any other; rather, what would be expected is that different techniques will work better with different clients, depending on their reasons for developing the problem, their reasons for maintaining it, the impact of other factors within their lives and so on. What is important is that the evaluation of cognitive-behavioural approaches should not be confined to large-scale studies which, by grouping subjects, will tend to obscure any individual effects, but instead should be designed to study small-scale groups and individual cases in an attempt to delineate which interventions work for which people under which sets of circumstances. Researchers should cease to attempt to discover 'an efficient, safe, effective treatment' (McFall 1978: 712) – a panacea for all variants of drug or alcohol problems.

Learning from natural history

It is possible to conclude from a chapter that describes in detail one theoretical and therapeutic paradigm that 'treatment', 'therapy' or 'formal intervention' is a necessary prerequisite for someone to solve their alcohol or drug problem. An examination of the natural history of alcohol and drug users, however, shows that relatively large numbers of people with drug or alcohol problems do manage to overcome these problems without outside formal help. Thorley (1981), for example, has reviewed long-term longitudinal studies of what amounted to spontaneous remission in physically dependent opiate drug users and concluded that at least 10 per cent are drug free after 1 year, 25 per cent are drug free after 5 years and 40 per cent are drug free after 10 years, with 2–3 per cent of any sample dying from drug-related causes in each year. Similarly, from their review of the literature on the spontaneous remission of those with drinking problems, Roizen *et al.* (1978) concluded that 'remission in the sense of 6 months of abstinence can be expected in 15 per cent of the cases, and remission in the sense of some improvements in about 40 per cent' (p. 201). A clear need for future research is the investigation of these naturally occurring ways in which people give up their addictions. Such investigations might enable us, by learning from those who do it without formal help, to develop yet further methods of intervention which could be incorporated within a cognitive-behavioural paradigm.

REFERENCES

Abrams, D. and Wilson, G. (1979) 'Effects of alcohol on social anxiety in women: cognitive versus physiological processes', *Journal of Abnormal Psychology* 88: 161–73.
—— (1983) 'Alcohol, sexual arousal and self-control', *Journal of Personality and Social Psychology* 45: 188–98.
Adesso, V. (1985) 'Cognitive factors in alcohol and drug abuse', in M. Galizio and S. Maisto (eds) *Determinants of Substance Abuse*, New York: Plenum.

Alexander, B. and Hadaway, P. (1982) 'Opiate addiction: the case for an adaptive orientation', *Psychological Bulletin* 92: 367–81.

Azrin, N. (1976) 'Improvement in the community reinforcement approach to alcoholism', *Behaviour Research and Therapy* 14: 339–48.

Bandura, A. (1977) 'Self-efficacy: towards a unifying theory of behavioral change', *Psychological Review* 84: 191–215.

Billings, A. and Moos, R. (1983) 'Psychosocial processes of recovery among alcoholics and their families: implications for clinicians and programme evaluators', *Addictive Behaviors* 8: 205–18.

Blakey, R. and Baker, R. (1980) 'An exposure approach to alcohol abuse', *Behaviour Research and Therapy* 18: 319–25.

Briddell, D., Rimm, D., Caddy, G., Krawitz, G., Sholis, D. and Wunderlin, R. (1978) 'Effects of alcohol and cognitive set on sexual arousal to deviant stimuli', *Journal of Abnormal Psychology* 87: 418–30.

Cappell, H. (1975) 'An evaluation of tension models of alcohol consumption', in R. Gibbons, Y. Israel, H. Kalant, R. Popham, W. Schmidt and R. Smart (eds) *Research Advances in Alcohol and Drug Problems, Vol. 2*, New York: Wiley.

Chaney, E., O'Leary, M. and Marlatt, G. A. (1978) 'Skill training with alcoholics', *Journal of Consulting and Clinical Psychology* 46: 1092–104.

Christiansen, B. and Goldman, M. (1983) 'Alcohol-related expectancies versus demographic/background variables in the prediction of adolescent drinking', *Journal of Consulting and Clinical Psychology* 51: 249–57.

—— and Inn, A. (1982) 'Development of alcohol-related expectancies in adolescents: separating phamacological from social learning influences', *Journal of Consulting and Clinical Psychology* 50: 336–44.

Davidson, R. (1987) 'Assessment of the alcohol dependence syndrome: a review of self-report screening questionnaires', *British Journal of Clinical Psychology* 26: 243–55.

Davis, D. (1971) 'Mood changes in alcoholic subjects with programmed and free-choice experimental drinking', in N. Mello and J. Mendelson (eds) *Recent Advances in Studies of Alcoholism: an Interdisciplinary Symposium*, Washington: US Government Printing Office.

D'Zurilla, T. and Goldfreid, M. (1971) 'Problem solving and behavior modification', *Journal of Abnormal Psychology* 78: 107–26.

Edwards, G. (1972) 'Motivation for drinking among men: survey of a London suburb', *Psychological Medicine* 2: 260–71.

Egan, G. (1986) *The Skilled Helper*, 3rd edn, Monterey, Calif.: Brooks/Cole.

Filstead, W., Parrella, D. and Ebbitt, J. (1988) 'High-risk situations for engaging in substance abuse and binge-eating behaviors', *Journal of Studies on Alcohol* 49: 136–41.

Goldman, M. and Klisz, D. (1982) 'Behavioral treatment of alcoholism: the unvarnished story', in W. Hay and P. Nathan (eds) *Clinical Case Studies in the Behavioral Treatment of Alcoholism*, New York: Plenum.

Grant, M., Plant, M. and Williams, A. (eds) (1983) *Economics and Alcohol: Consumption and Controls*, London: Croom Helm.

Hay, W. (1982) 'The behavioral assessment and treatment of an alcoholic marriage: the case of Mr. and Mrs. L.', in W. Hay and P. Nathan (eds) *Clinical Case Studies in the Behavioral Treatment of Alcoholism*, New York: Plenum.

HEA (1983) *That's The Limit*, London: Health Education Authority.

Heather, N. and Robertson, I. (1983) *Controlled Drinking, 2nd Edition*, London: Methuen.

—— (1989) *Problem Drinking* 2nd edn. Oxford: Oxford University Press.

Heather, N., Rollnick, S. and Winton, M. (1983) 'A comparison of objective and subjective measures of alcohol dependence as predictors of relapse following treatment', *British Journal of Clinical Psychology* 22: 11–17.

Heather, N., Robertson, I., MacPherson, B., Allsop, S. and Fulton, A. (1987) 'Evaluation of a controlled drinking self-help manual – one year follow-up results', *British Journal of Clinical Psychology* 26: 279–87.

Hodgson, R. and Rankin, H. (1982) 'Cue exposure and relapse prevention, in W. Hay, and P. Nathan (eds) *Clinical Case Studies in the Behavioral Treatment of Alcoholism*, New York: Plenum.

Hull, J. (1981) 'A self-awareness model of the causes and effects of alcohol consumption', *Journal of Abnormal Psychology* 90: 586–600.

Hunt, G., and Azrin, N. (1973) 'A community-reinforcement approach to alcoholism', *Behaviour Research and Therapy* 11: 91–104.

Janis, I. and Mann, L. (1968) 'A conflict theory approach to attitude change and decision making' in A. Greenwald, T. Brock and T. Ostrom (eds) *Psychological Foundations of Attitudes*, New York: Academic Press.

—— (1977) *Decision-Making: a Psychological Analysis of Conflict, Choice, and Commitment*, New York: Free Press.

Lang, A., Goeckner, D., Adesso, V. and Marlatt, G. A. (1975) 'Effects of alcohol on aggression in male social drinkers', *Journal of Abnormal Psychology* 84: 508–18.

MacAndrew, C. and Edgerton, R. (1970) *Drunken Comportment: A Social Explanation*, London: Nelson.

McFall, R. (1978) 'Smoking-cessation research', *Journal of Consulting and Clinical Psychology* 46: 703–12.

McGuire, M., Mendelson, J. and Stein, S. (1966) 'Comparative psychosocial studies of alcoholic and non-alcoholic subjects undergoing experimentally induced ethanol intoxication', *Psychosomatic Medicine* 28: 13–26.

Marlatt, G. A. (1976) 'Alcohol, stress and cognitive control', in I. Sarason and C. Spielberger (eds) *Stress and Anxiety*, Washington: Hemisphere.

—— (1985) 'Cognitive factors in the relapse process', in G. A. Marlatt and J. Gordon (eds) *Relapse Prevention*, New York: Guilford Press.

—— and Parks, G. (1982) 'Self-management of addictive disorders', in P. Karoly and F. Kanfer (eds) *Self-Management and Behavior Change*, New York: Pergamon.

Marlatt, G. A., Demming, B. and Reid, J. (1973) 'Loss of control drinking in alcoholics: an experimental analogue', *Journal of Abnormal Psychology* 81: 233–41.

Miller, W. (1976) 'Alcoholism scales and objective assessment methods: a review', *Psychological Bulletin* 83: 649–74.

—— (ed.) (1980) *The Addictive Behaviors*, New York: Pergamon.

—— (1982) 'When is a book a treatment? Bibliotherapy for problem drinkers', in W. Hay and P. Nathan (eds) *Clinical Case Studies in the Behavioral Treatment of Alcoholism*, New York: Plenum.

—— (1983) 'Motivational interviewing with problem drinkers', *Behavioural Psychotherapy* 11: 147–72.

—— and Munoz, R. (1976) *How to Control Your Drinking*, Englewood Cliffs, NJ: Prentice-Hall.

Noel, N., Sobell, L., Cellucci, T., Nirenberg, T. and Sobell, M. (1982) 'Behavioral treatment of outpatient problem drinkers: five clinical case studies', in W. Hay and P. Nathan (eds) *Clinical Case Studies in the Behavioral Treatment of Alcoholism*, New York: Plenum.

Oei, T. and Jackson, P. (1982) 'Long-term effects of group and individual social skills training with alcoholics', *Addictive Behaviors* 5: 129–36.

Orford, J. (1971) 'Aspects of the relationship between alcohol and drug abuse', in L. Kiloh and D. Bell (eds) *Proceedings of the 29th International Congress, Sydney, Australia*, North Ryde, Australia: Butterworth.

—— (1985) *Excessive Appetites: A Psychological View of Addictions*, Chichester: Wiley.

—— and Edwards, G. (1977) *Alcoholism: A Comparison of Treatment and Advice, with a Study of the Influence of Marriage*, Oxford: Oxford University Press.

—— and Keddie, A. (1986) 'Abstinence or controlled drinking in clinical practice', *British Journal of Addiction* 81: 495–504.

Parker, M., Winstead, D., Willi, F. and Fisher, P. (1979) 'Patient autonomy in alcohol rehabilitation: II program evaluation', *International Journal of the Addictions* 14: 1177–84.

Pattison, E., Sobell, M. and Sobell, L. (1977) *Emerging Concepts of Alcohol Dependency*, New York: Springer.

Phares, E. (1976) *Locus of Control in Personality*, New Jersey: General Learning Press.

Prochaska, J. and DiClemente, C. (1983) 'Stages and processes of self-change of smoking: toward an integrative model of change', *Journal of Consulting and Clinical Psychology* 51: 390–5.

Rankin, H. (1982) 'Cue exposure and response prevention in South London', in W. Hay and P. Nathan (eds) *Clinical Case Studies in the Behavioral Treatment of Alcoholism*, New York: Plenum

Reinert, R. (1968) 'The concept of alcoholism as a bad habit', *Bulletin of the Menninger Clinic* 32: 35–46.

Reyes, E. and Miller, W. (1980) 'Serum gamma-glutamyl transpeptidase as a diagnostic aid in problem drinkers', *Addictive Behaviors* 5: 59–65.

Roberston, I. and Heather, N. (1986) *Let's Drink to Your Health: A Self-help Guide to Sensible Drinking*, Leicester: British Psychological Society.

Robins, L., Helzer, J. and Davis, D. (1975) 'Narcotic use in Southeast Asia and afterwards', *Archives of General Psychiatry* 32: 955–61.

Rohsenow, D. (1983) 'Drinking habits and expectancies about alcohol's effects for self versus others', *Journal of Consulting and Clinical Psychology* 51: 752–6.

Roizen, R., Cahalan, D. and Shanks, P. (1978) 'Spontaneous remission among untreated problem drinkers', in D. Kandel (ed.) *Longitudinal Research on Drug Use: Empirical Findings and Methodological Issues*, Washington: Hemisphere.

Rollnick, S. (1985) 'The value of a cognitive-behavioural approach to the treatment of problem drinkers', in N. Heather, I. Robertson and P. Davies (eds) *The Misuse of Alcohol*, London: Croom Helm.

Rotter, J., Chance, J. and Phares, E. (eds) (1972) *Applications of a Social Learning Theory of Personality*, New York: Holt, Rinehart & Winston.

Sanchez-Craig, M., Annis, H., Bornet, A. and McDonald, K. (1984) 'Random assignment to abstinence and controlled drinking: evaluation of a cognitive-behavioral program for problem drinkers', *Journal of Consulting and Clinical Psychology* 52: 390–403.

Saunders, W. and Allsop, S. (1985) 'Giving up addictions', in F. Watts (ed.) *New Developments in Clinical Psychology*, Chichester: BPS and Wiley.

—— (1987) 'Relapse: a psychological perspective', *British Journal of Addiction* 82: 417–29.

Selzer, M. (1971) 'The Michigan alcoholism screening test: the quest for a new diagnostic instrument', *American Journal of Psychiatry* 127: 1653–8.

Sobell, M. and Sobell, L. (1973) 'Individualised behavior therapy for alcoholics', *Behavior Therapy* 4: 49–72.

—— (1978) *Behavioral Treatment of Alcohol Problems: Individualised Therapy and Controlled Drinking*, New York: Plenum.

—— (1984) 'The aftermath of heresy: a response to Pendery *et al.*'s (1982) critique of "individualised behaviour therapy for alcoholics"', *Behaviour Research and Therapy* 22: 413–40.

Sobell, M., Maisto, S., Sobell, L., Cooper, A., Cooper, T. and Sanders, B. (1980) 'Developing a prototype for evaluating alcohol treatment effectiveness', in L. Sobell, M. Sobell and

E. Ward (eds) *Evaluating Alcohol and Drug Abuse Treatment Effectiveness: Recent Advances*, New York: Pergamon.

Steele, C. and Josephs, R. (1988) 'Drinking your troubles away, II: an attention-allocation model of alcohol's effect on psychological stress', *Journal of Abnormal Psychology* 97: 196–205.

Stockwell, T., Hodgson, R., Edwards, G., Taylor, C. and Rankin, K. (1979) 'The development of a questionnaire to measure severity of alcohol dependence', *British Journal of Addiction* 77: 287–96.

Stockwell, T., Hodgson, R., Rankin, H. and Taylor, C. (1982) 'Alcohol dependence, beliefs and the priming effect', *Behaviour Research and Therapy* 20: 513–22.

Stockwell, T., Murphy, D. and Hodgson, R. (1983) 'The severity of alcohol dependence questionnaire: its use, reliability and validity', *British Journal of Addiction* 78: 145–55.

Sutton, S. (1987) 'Social-psychological approaches to understanding addictive behaviours: attitude–behaviour and decision-making models', *British Journal of Addiction* 82: 355–70.

Thorley, A. (1981) 'Longitudinal studies of drug dependence', in G. Edwards and C. Busch (eds) *Drug Problems in Britain: A Review of Ten Years*, London: Academic Press.

—— (1983) 'Problem drinkers and drug takers' in F. Watts and D. Bennett (eds) *Theory and Practice of Psychiatric Rehabilitation*, Chichester: Wiley.

Vogler, R. (1982) 'Successful moderation in a chronic alcohol abuser: the case of Bob S', in W. Hay and P. Nathan (eds) *Clinical Case Studies in the Behavioral Treatment of Alcoholism*, New York: Plenum.

Vuchinich, R., Tucker, J. and Sobell, M. (1979) 'Alcohol, expectancy, cognitive labelling and mirth', *Journal of Abnormal Psychology* 88: 641–51.

Wallace, J., (1985) 'Behavioral modification methods as adjuncts to psychotherapy, in S. Zimberg, J. Wallace and S. Blume (1985) *Practical Approaches to Alcoholism Psychotherapy*, 2nd edn., New York: Plenum.

Wardle, J. and Beinart, H. (1981) 'Binge eating: a theoretical review', *British Journal of Clinical Psychology* 20: 97–109.

Whelan, M. and Prince, M. (1982) 'Towards indirect cognitive confrontation with alcohol abusers', *International Journal of the Addictions* 17: 879–86.

Wilson, G. (1987) 'Cognitive processes in addiction', *British Journal of Addiction* 82: 343–53.

—— and Abrams, D. (1977) 'Effects of alcohol and social anxiety and physiological arousal: cognitive versus pharmacological processes', *Cognitive Therapy and Research* 1: 195–210.

Zinberg, N. and Jacobson, R. (1976) 'The natural history of "chipping"', *American Journal of Psychiatry* 133: 37–40.

Chapter 7

Schizophrenia

Max Birchwood and Martin Preston

INTRODUCTION

In 1986, Alan Bellack, one of the most distinguished figures in cognitive-behaviour therapy, published an article entitled 'Schizophrenia: behaviour therapy's forgotten child', in which he reflected on the declining interest shown by cognitive-behaviour therapists in the problems of schizophrenia. He argued that responsibility for this lay with four misconceptions:

1 that schizophrenia does not exist;
2 as schizophrenia is a biological disorder, behaviour therapy can play no part;
3 that schizophrenia is adequately handled by medication;
4 that schizophrenia is too severe for behaviour therapy.

One could perhaps add a fifth reason why cognitive-behaviour therapy has turned its attention away from schizophrenia: namely, the limitations and inadequacies of previous attempts to explain and manage the symptoms of schizophrenia *wholly* within a cognitive-behavioural framework (Marzillier and Birchwood 1981). These early attempts drew heavily upon the conditioning paradigms and Albert Bandura's social-learning model. As we shall see below, the problems of schizophrenia are primarily *experiential*, in particular auditory hallucinations, delusional beliefs and disorders of thinking, and these are not readily explained by reference to social or environmental circumstances. Furthermore, the symptoms erupt and subside over time in an episodic pattern and it is stretching credulity to argue that such undulations are the result of purely social determinants. Thus, in this chapter, the conceptualization we shall outline is rather different from many others in this book in that it draws on some concepts and language which lie outside the cognitive-behavioural framework (however, the intervention strategies they inform are predominantly cognitive-behavioural and throughout the chapter we shall endeavour to highlight these and those derived from other psychosocial formulations). Cognitive-behavioural approaches have, however, recently found new strengths as the limitations of a purely *biological* model have become apparent. Exciting developments in cognitive-behavioural treatments are emerging which are predicated upon a new conceptualization which models the maintenance (but not the genesis) of the disorder as an *interaction* of biological and psychosocial influences. In this chapter we shall outline the nature of this interactionist frame-work, which has become known as the 'transactional' model (Birchwood *et al*. 1988). A number of very promising cognitive-behavioural intervention strategies have recently emerged – whose origins lie in this model – which hold out the prospect of ameliorating the symptoms and disabilities of schizophrenia to a highly significant degree and to which we devote most of our attention.

CONCEPTUALIZATION

What is schizophrenia?

The existence and utility of the concept of schizophrenia has been the subject of much controversy in the past (Szasz 1979) and also more recently (Bentall *et al*. 1988). The veracity and definition of any concept is clearly fundamental to any attempt at conceptualization: does schizophrenia exist, and if it does, what is it?

The concept of schizophrenia was born out of a very practical need of clinicians, who at the turn of the century were faced with the problem of helping those individuals then collectively described as 'the insane'. Their chosen approach was to attempt to classify this population into meaningful homogeneous categories following the example set by medicine and many of the sciences: thus the concept of schizophrenia emerged. How it is defined and the precise demarcation between this and other disorders is at the present time largely a matter of consensus and convention (Kendall 1975). Many operational definitions have been proposed which show substantial areas of overlap between one another (Berner 1986) but which differ in the emphasis they place on different kinds of symptoms or their duration. The majority of definitions include the following symptoms: *auditory hallucinations* (including voices heard arguing or commenting on thoughts or actions); *experiences of control* (volitional acts experienced as the work of others); *delusions* (persecutory, grandiose and so on); *disorders of thinking* (thoughts experienced as broadcast, inserted or withdrawn from the mind); *emotional and volitional changes* ('flat' emotions, loss of initiative or energy); *formal thought disorder* (illogical thinking, word association, neologisms). The definition pre-ferred in the UK is based on that of Kurt Schneider's (1959) 'first-rank' symptoms, which are essentially those described above under hallucinations, delusions of control and disorders of thinking.

We would argue that the concept of schizophrenia should be regarded as a *hypothesis* whose validity should be evaluated in terms of its *utility*; thus, the concept acquires validity to the degree that it enables prediction, explanation and intervention. We have argued elsewhere (Birchwood *et al*. 1988) that in these terms the concept has been a productive and useful one; however, the advances which the syndrome concept has offered should not deter attempts to search for useful subdivisions or alternate approaches based on, for example, dimensions of psycho-pathology or analyses focusing on single symptoms (Bentall *et al*. 1988).

Primary and secondary impairment

Development of a conceptual framework requires clarity about the nature of the impairments which schizophrenia can bring. This is particularly important since the extent of the disabilities associated with schizophrenia is so great: it has been estimated for example that less than one-third of affected individuals return to an 'average' level of functioning (WHO 1980). The British social psychiatrist John Wing (1978) draws an important distinction between impairments which are *intrinsic* to this order and those which are secondary. The core experiences (delusions, hallucinations and so on) are the *impairments*: the individual's ability to function in everyday social roles (for example, ability to work, to participate in social networks, to live an independent life) are the *disabilities: handicaps* represent the social impact of disabilities (for example, loss of social status, restricted access to jobs, housing and so on). Disabilities and handicaps are of course not specific to schizophrenia but represent the impinging of the primary impairments on the psychosocial and cultural environment (see Table 7.1).

Table 7.1   Impairments, disabilities and handicaps in schizophrenia

Intrinsic impairments
Core experiences: auditory hallucinations, delusions, thought disorders (Sartorius et al. 1986)
Vulnerability to emotional blunting, loss of volition, social withdrawal (Crow et al. 1986)
Vulnerability to relapse (Crow et al. 1986)
Cognitive impairments: attention, memory, problem solving (Williams et al. 1985).

Disabilities
Social/community survival skills impaired (Wallace 1984)
Low self-image; depression; higher risk of suicide (Drake and Cotton 1986)
Distress due to difficulties with residual symptoms (Falloon and Talbot 1981; Tarrier 1987).

Handicaps
High rate (60–70 per cent) of unemployment; downward social drift (Floyd 1984).
Diminished social networks (Sokolovsky et al. 1978)
Family discord/rejection (Leff and Vaughn 1985)
Institutionalization (Mann and Cree 1975)

Assessment

Table 7.2 presents a range of assessments and measurement instruments or procedures which are most frequently used with schizophrenic and related populations.

There are many scales of comparable quality which are available and in routine use; those in Table 7.2 are selected for breadth of coverage and because each has undergone rigorous validation procedures. Two issues are worth highlighting here. The assessment of core symptoms such as hallucinations and delusions by

Table 7.2 Assessment procedures for schizophrenic and related populations

Assessment area	Title	Function	Authors
PHENOMENOLOGY	Present State Examination	Identification of (psychotic) symptoms	Wing et al. 1974; Tress et al. 1987
	Psychiatric Assessment Scale	Global ratings of (psychotic) symptoms	Krawiecka et al. 1977
SOCIAL DISABILITY	Disability Assessment Schedule	Global ratings of social/role dysfunction	Jablensky et al. 1980
	Social Behaviour Assessment Schedule	Global ratings of social-role performance	Platt et al. 1980
GENERAL NEEDS ASSESSMENT	MRC Needs for Care Assessment	Identification of symptoms and behaviour problems, personal/social skills and specification of appropriate interventions	Brewin et al. 1987
RELAPSE RISK	Camberwell Family	Identification of high relapse risk (high expressed emotion) family environments	Leff and Vaughn 1985
MEDICATION COMPLIANCE		Prediction of compliance with neuroleptic medication regimes	Hogan et al. 1983
REHABILITATION	REHAB	Standardized assessment of social functioning and behavioural problems for rehabilitation planning	Baker and Hall 1983
COPING BEHAVIOUR	Video Coping Interview	Assessment of families' ability to cope with behavioural challenges	Birchwood and Cochrane 1990
		Assessment of individuals' strategies for coping with residual symptoms	Tarrier 1987

interview procedures (for example, the Present State Examination) is subject to considerable error. Individuals may choose to conceal symptoms or may be unresponsive or unclear during questioning, or there may be real fluctuations in phenomenology over time. Although the PSE shows high interrater reliability, its retest reliability is considerably lower (Brockington and Meltzer 1982).

Assessments of social functioning and deficits are necessarily descriptive: identification of *needs* requires not only descriptive data but value judgements based upon what the individual expresses, upon the judgement of professionals and by comparison with other individuals or reference groups. Brewin *et al.* (1987) have taken this a stage further by incorporating recommendations for *action* in their definition of need: that is to say, a need is defined on the basis of (a) an observed deficit or problem *and* (b) a value judgement about its significance for the individual *and* (c) the availability of an intervention that might remedy the situation. This move towards action-based needs assessments, while requiring consensus about the appropriateness and efficacy of the prescribed intervention (often the subject of controversy), bridges an important gap between the identification of disability in this population and the organization of services to respond effectively.

MAINTENANCE FACTORS

Once schizophrenia has emerged its subsequent unfolding is not a homogeneous affair: in some, the first episode is followed by a permanent recovery and in others, signs of a long-term decline are already apparent (Crow *et al.* 1986). For the majority, their lives are punctuated by episodes of relapse of the symptoms followed by complete or partial recovery. It follows that any cognitive-behavioural and broader psychosocial influence must have an enduring quality over the course of the individual's lifetime; thus, attention has focused on factors such as the cultural milieu, psychosocial stressors, aspects of family life and the individual's psychological response to schizophrenia and its symptoms.

Socio-cultural factors

It is known that the *form* of schizophrenic symptomatology is largely culture-independent (Jablensky *et al.* 1986) whereas the precise way in which symptoms are expressed varies from culture to culture and, indeed, from individual to individual (Leff 1989). Thus, a delusion of control is a universal symptom yet it may be elaborated in western cultures in terms of physical forces (X-ray, radio waves and the like) and in other cultures in terms of, for example, witchcraft, telepathy and so on. These elaborations may therefore represent an attempt by the individual to achieve some psychological consistency between the 'reality' afforded by their 'schizophrenic' experiences and that of the individual's socio-cultural milieu. Of greater significance is the evidence for differences in prognosis between cultures. Early studies suggestive of a better prognosis in non-industrialized societies (Kulhara and Wig 1978; Murphy and Rahman 1971) were strengthened by results of cross-cultural studies by the World Health Organization (Jablensky *et al.* 1986; WHO 1979). The *International Pilot Study of Schizophrenia* (WHO 1979), a unique cross-cultural study of over a thousand patients from nine countries, employing standardized methodology, found that over a 2-year follow-up period over 40 per cent of patients in non-industrialized countries had *no* further episodes compared to 17 per cent from the industrialized nations. This was paralleled by marked differences in social functioning in favour of the non-industrialized countries. The prognostic differences are so marked that a socio-cultural effect is strongly suggested (Kleinman 1987). Carstairs (1985) contrasts the socio-cultural response to schizophrenia in industrialized and developing countries. He notes the greater familial tolerance to schizophrenia and the greater opportunity for social reintegration, particularly in the rural agricultural-based economics of the developing countries. Studies of these factors *within* cultures have supported these speculations – to which we now turn.

Psychosocial stress: life events

The notion that acute forms of stress might trigger an episode of schizophrenia arose from early observations that overzealous rehabilitation regimes could prompt the appearance of florid symptoms in otherwise stable individuals. Intensive research activity in the 1970s and early 1980s produced evidence that day-to-day stressful life events might *trigger* episodes of disorder in vulnerable individuals: this line of research has however declined as the inherent methodological problems of this work became apparent (Day 1981). Brown and Birley (1968) reported that nearly 50 per cent of their sample of relapsing schizophrenics experienced life events within the week prior to relapse which represented a significant increase over the preceding 4 weeks. By comparison, a large community sample reported a low and unchanging level of life events throughout a parallel time frame. Leff *et al.* (1973) found that recent (within 5 weeks) life events were associated with relapse in medicated patients only, which is consistent with subsequent data (Leff and Vaughn 1980) that life events were associated with relapse only in those who were otherwise at low risk for relapse. In other words, relapse risk is high in 'unprotected' individuals: those protected by medication or other factors might still relapse if they experience a major life event. Evidence from centres in the USA has not proved so consistent. Jacob and Myers (1976) found a similar association which held only for events which were 'dependent' (i.e. the result of illness) and Schwartz and Myers (1977) found a high level of events in *non-relapsed* schizophrenics compared to controls. A recent study (Chung *et al.* 1986) utilized a more refined measure of life events involving 'contextual threat' (a measure of the personal significance of life changes for the individual). They found an excess of threatening events in the 6 months prior to relapse versus controls in those with briefer periods of psychosis rather than those of longer duration (true schizophrenia).

While the early work does seem to suggest that stress can prompt relapse, subsequent research indicates that life events are neither necessary nor sufficient for three reasons: first, 'independent' events occur only in a minority of patients; second, non-relapsing patients in the community report higher levels of events compared to normal controls; and finally, most important of all, no *prospective* study has yet attempted to predict relapse on the basis of the experience of a stressful life event. Thus, while stressful life events probably have the capacity to trigger an episode of schizophrenia, the sensitivity and specificity of an individual's response to a life event is as yet unknown.

Psychosocial stress: the family environment

The stress and tensions which family life can bring may represent a continuing source of instability which, for those with a known vulnerability to schizophrenia, may conceivably trigger a relapse. Evidence gathered slowly and painstakingly over three decades provides strong support for this possibility. Research by Brown *et al.* (1972) has identified families characterized by high levels of expressed emotion (EE) assessed upon an individual's admission to hospital. These families will tend to express high levels of criticism, emotional over-involvement or signs of hostility directed towards the affected individual when interviewed about the circumstances leading up to the admission of an individual to hospital (Leff and Vaughn 1985). The presence of an individual with schizophrenia in such a 'high EE' family raises by a factor of four the probability of a subsequent relapse within 9 months of discharge (Falloon 1988). Those in greater face-to-face contact with their family, or who do not take regular neuroleptic medication, are at even greater risk of relapse (see Figure 7.1).

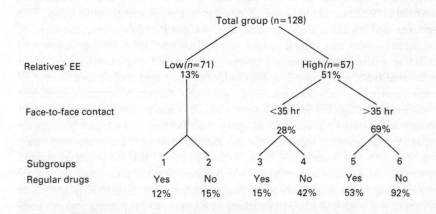

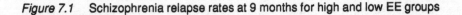

Figure 7.1 Schizophrenia relapse rates at 9 months for high and low EE groups

The predictive efficacy of high EE has been replicated in the USA (Vaughn *et al*. 1984), Germany (Dulz and Hand 1986) and India (Leff *et al*. 1987), and has been the entry point for a number of successful intervention programmes (see below). There have, however, been two failures to replicate, in the UK and Australia (MacMillan *et al*. 1986; Parker *et al*. 1988).

There is, then, overwhelming evidence that certain types of family environment can trigger a relapse of florid symptoms within months of in-patient treatment, particularly if the individual is not receiving neuroleptic medication. There are, however, many aspects of these studies which should caution against unbridled generalization. The follow-up period of these studies has for pragmatic reasons been short – 9 months, and in some instances 2 years. It is not known whether the level of prediction will remain stable over longer periods or whether other factors will begin to exert their influence. In a 1-year follow-up of their 1976 cohort, Leff and Vaughn (1981) report a significant level of prediction over 2 years yet this is entirely accounted for by the relapses observed *within the first 9 months*. This and other studies reveal that people from low EE homes do relapse with the passage of time and, contrary to the expectations of Figure 7.1, medication is helpful to individuals from these families (ibid.; MacMillan *et al*. 1986). This explains the apparent paradox that the paucity of relapse associated with low EE does not seem to impair the recruitment of large samples of these individuals into studies following their acute re-admission. Conversely, because families are classified during acute admission we are unaware of the number of high EE cases who 'escape' re-admission. Studies of first admission are unbiased in this respect and reveal a very much weaker level of prediction (Birchwood and Smith 1987; Leff and Brown 1977; MacMillan *et al*. 1986). The true, long-term risk of residing in a high EE family has yet to be clearly established.

Reducing the levels of the EE from high to low in the context of a continued neuroleptic treatment is the clear therapeutic implication of these findings. This assumes that high/low EE is a stable trait-like quality of families which can be taught or in some way passed on to other families; thus, the pathology is assumed to reside in the family in such a manner, for example, that 'cross-fostering' an individual from a high to a low EE family might be regarded as an effective (if unlikely) strategy to control relapse. There is little evidence in support of a trait-like construction of high EE. Follow-up studies have revealed that EE does not always remain stable (Brown *et al*. 1972; Hogarty *et al*. 1986) and that high EE is closely related to high levels of behavioural disturbance in the individual cross-sectionally and prospectively (Brown *et al*. 1972). A 'transactional' model has been suggested to accommodate these observations which argues that the emergence of schizophrenia triggers an ongoing dynamic interaction between the individual and his or her family in which the latter is seeking to comprehend and cope with an individual's change in behaviour and circumstances. Under this model, high EE is construed as an indicator of stress in this relationship (Birchwood 1983; Birchwood and Smith 1987). High or low EE may not, then, be a family trait, but rather a 'thermometer' of stress in a *particular* relationship at a *particular* point or period of time. Thus, the origin of high EE probably resides in complex interactions between an individual and his family, the implication of this being that the family which shows low EE responses to one individual would not necessarily do so to another.

The individual and his illness

In an empirical study of the prospects for self-regulation of the symptoms of psychosis, Breier and Strauss (1983) note: 'the rarity of reports focusing on self-control in psychotic disorders implies that persons... do not have an intact 'self' or psyche... a prerequisite to effective self control'. Indeed, the stereotype of the 'schizophrenic patient' is one who is the hapless victim of illness, a passive recipient of treatment where the philosophy of management is one of containment rather than exploration of potential. The antithesis is one of individuals who play an active part in their illness, who seek to comprehend their illness, to assimilate their abnormal experiences into their prior construction of reality and to cope with and ameliorate the symptoms and associated disabilities.

Success and failure in this interaction between the individual and his illness is readily apparent. For example, as we have already discussed, an individual's expression of a delusion represents an interaction of the 'reality' afforded by the basic symptom and the 'reality' afforded by the socio-cultural milieu (p. 175). The high rate of suicide in schizophrenia provides a further example that this is not always an 'insane' act but frequently occurs in the context of an insightful individual beginning to comprehend the limitations which the disorder can impose upon his life (Drake and Cotton 1986).

A number of levels of interaction between the individual and his illness have been studied which might profit from further investigation in order to inform the development of new intervention approaches and to permit some individuals to profit from the success of others.

Coping with residual psychotic symptoms

Falloon and Talbot (1981) were the first to examine the naturalistic coping strategies of patients with residual symptoms, in this case auditory hallucinations. In their sample of forty subjects they found three broad categories of strategy. The first involved *behavioural* changes such as initiating leisure/work activities or social contact. The second involved manipulation of *sensory input* such as relaxing or sleeping, putting hands over ears or listening to loud music. The third involved *cognitive* strategies, including reduction in attention to 'voices' (for example, generating distracting thoughts or verbalizations). Falloon and Talbot observed that the subgroup with a more favourable community adjustment were more likely to use strategies involving social contact or sensory control, to use them more consistently and to be more aware of stimuli which apparently triggered their voices. Tarrier (1987), using a similar procedure applied to a sample of twenty-five patients in respect of both hallucinations and delusions, found a very similar range of strategies, but also found that: (a) one half of the sample could identify external triggers for symptoms and (b) the patients using more than one strategy reported a favourable level of self-control. Breier and Strauss (1983) reported a similar investigation with a range of diagnoses and persisting symptoms. Subjects reported three kinds of strategy:

1 *self-instruction:* subjects would talk to themselves in a positive way to combat delusions (for example, 'how could a perfect stranger know what I am thinking?');
2 *reduced activity:* subjects who felt that anxiety might lead to depressive delusions would try to relax or rest themselves;
3 *increased activity:* subjects with hallucinations would talk to other people, and try to keep busy.

These preliminary studies show that some individuals feel they play an active role in the regulation of their symptoms. They suggest three possibilities: (1) that stress-reduction tactics may be used in those cases where there are stressful antecedent symptoms; (2) increases in verbal and intellectual activity may be used to combat auditory hallucinations; and (3) challenging self-statements are often used to combat delusional thinking. Whether these strategies are in fact successful can only be judged from experimental manipulation (see section on Treatment and Interventions). There may however be other factors which interact to determine their utility and need to be considered when formulating an intervention programme. Insight may be a prerequisite for people to challenge their delusional experiences and those taking part in the above studies were generally insightful; and thus to what extent their strategies would apply to those lacking in insight is unknown. It is also mistaken to assume that an individual's symptoms are independent of one another. Some symptoms derive from other more primary experiences, for example delusions frequently arise from hallucinations or passivity experiences. There may also be theoretical reasons why some strategies could prove unhelpful, the work of Hemsley and Garrety (1986) and Brett-Jones *et al.* (1987), for example, suggesting that 'normal' psychological processes may be involved in the maintenance of delusional beliefs and therefore in their eradication.

Finally, it is now known that people with schizophrenia and their families can learn to recognize changes in their mental life which herald a forthcoming relapse (Birchwood *et al.* 1989; Herz and Melville 1980). Breier and Strauss describe eight individuals who identified affective symptoms (for example, depression, fatigue, anxiety) which they believed preceded psychosis, control of which they felt influenced the subsequent appearance of psychosis.

Self-esteem

The psychological health of people with schizophrenia has received relatively little attention. This is surprising since suicide can be expected in up to 20 per cent of cases. Studies of depression and suicide in schizophrenia (for example, Drake and Cotton 1986) have tended to be descriptive and have not sought to determine their origins. The study of Roy *et al*. (1983) provides some clues. Those who are depressed tend to be isolated with low self-esteem, to have limited support and to have had a greater number of re-admissions to hospital (factors identified by Drake and Cotton (1986) to be risk factors for suicide). Such individuals become privately despairing of the illness and lose hope. Whether this psychological dimension can be influenced in a positive direction has yet to be established, although recent evidence (Goldman and Quinn 1988; Greenberg *et al*. 1988) suggests that through the medium of giving education about the disorder, improvements in confidence and self-esteem can be achieved.

Maintenance factors: a transactional model

The evidence from cross-cultural and family studies suggests that the probable biological basis of the disorder does not lead inexorably to the continued expression of symptoms once the disorder has emerged. Rather, the underlying pathology may be viewed as conferring a *vulnerability* which depends on psychosocial factors for its continued expression and development; in contrast a pure biological model would construe remission of symptoms as temporary respites of mental health in the course of a continuing disorder (Zubin *et al*. 1983). The transactional model (Birchwood *et al*. 1988) speculates that episodes of schizophrenia are prompted by acute or enduring psychosocial stress: the likelihood of an episode depending on the level of vulnerability and stress: the higher the level of stress, the lower the level of vulnerability required to trigger an episode and vice versa. Three categories of psychosocial influence are posited. The first are independent life events which tax the individual's coping resources and lead to subjective stress; the ability of the individual to cope effectively varies as a function of the level of social support and the quality of the individual's coping resources. The second category consists of those psychosocial influences which may occur as a secondary response to the emergence of schizophrenia (Table 7.1). The stress-prone life styles of schizophrenics in developed, urbanized countries (due to geographical mobility, alienation, social segregation and stressful circumstances which their lives create) may directly influence the appearance of symptoms. The accumulation of secondary handicap in the form of social isolation and impairments of social/life skills might increase the impact of stressing experiences as they reflect, in part, the individual's resources to cope with the vicissitudes of life. We also model the influence of the family environment as a secondary handicap as the evidence points towards the conclusion that the chronic, stressful qualities of these environments are emergent ones resulting from the difficulties of coping with the burden of schizophrenia. Finally, it is suggested that the individual's response to his or her own disorder (for example, fear, loss of self-esteem, loss of confidence) will influence the disabilities associated with the disorder; a more direct impact on symptoms may derive from the individual's response to his or her hallucinations or delusions or to early symptoms suggestive of an impending relapse.

The repeated appearance of symptoms and the emergence of chronicity is modelled as a reciprocal, developmental interaction between psychosocial and vulnerability factors: (a) secondary psychosocial handicaps influence the appearance and duration of symptoms, which in turn exacerbate the disabilities and so on; (b) since each relapse increases the possibility of further relapse and persisting symptoms, it is suggested that these cumulative interactions raise the individual's *intrinsic* vulnerability to a point where the symptoms are unremitting. In sum, the model suggests that a synergistic relationship exists between psychosocial factors, intrinsic vulnerability and symptomatic status which can represent a potent force 'driving' an individual towards chronicity and social disablement (for a fuller account, see Birchwood *et al.* 1988).

Some elements of the foregoing model include cognitive-behavioural elements in addition to broader influences such as the psychosocial, familial and cultural factors. The purely cognitive-behavioural elements include: the individual's response to 'illness' and symptoms; acquisition and loss of interpersonal and social and community survival skills and the coping skills appropriate to deal with stress within and beyond the individual's family.

TREATMENT AND INTERVENTION

Cognitive-behavioural approaches to residual symptoms

Auditory hallucinations

A substantial number of schizophrenics experience persistent auditory hallucinations despite neuroleptic medication. Since 'voices' may occasion the individual distress, underpin delusion formation, prompt bizarre behaviour, impair treatment compliance and disrupt social adjustment, the development of strategies for their management is clearly a matter of some importance. Psychological approaches to the problem have been extremely varied, procedures thus far explored including differential social reinforcement (for example, Ayllon and Kandel 1976); verbal conditioning with assertiveness training (Nydegger 1972); punishment via the delivery of aversive stimuli such as electric shock (Turner *et al.* 1977), white noise (Fonagy and Slade 1982) and enforced exercise (Belcher 1988); punishment via the removal of privileges (Richardson *et al.* 1972); time out (Davis *et al.* 1976); covert sensitization (Moser 1974); massed practice or satiation (Liberman *et al.* 1974); imaginal and *in vivo* desensitization (for example, Siegal 1975; Slade 1973); cognitive restructuring (Alford *et al.* 1982);belief modification with distraction (Fowler and Morley 1989); attentional training (Spaulding *et al.* 1986); distraction via listening to a radio (Feder 1982), portable cassette (Morley 1987) or watching television (Magen 1983); diversion by typing (Allen *et al.* 1985) or preferred recreational activity (Wong *et al.* 1987); thought-stopping alone (Lamontagne *et al.* 1983), with flooding and reciprocal reinforcement (Samaan 1975), with thought substitution (Allen *et al.* 1985), and with covert assertion and diversional activity (Errickson *et al.* 1978); the generation of incompatible vocal activity such as humming, singing or talking (Erickson and Gustafson 1968; Field and Ruelke 1973); the use of a 'stop and name' procedure in which the patient verbally describes objects in the external environment (Green and O'Callaghan 1980; James 1983; Birchwood 1986); and the unilateral occlusion of auditory input using an ear-plug (Birchwood 1986; Done *et al.* 1986; Morley 1987).

The findings of such studies are in the main encouraging, most indicating at least some reduction in hallucinatory frequency, duration or intensity as judged from verbal reports or other overt hallucinatory behaviour. The degree of change across studies is however variable, some reporting improvement which is significant, durable, generalized and associated with general improvement in mental state and social adjustment, but others noting outcomes which are more modest, short lived or restricted to the treatment setting. Evaluation of the utility of different techniques is unfortunately confounded by the predominance of single case designs and subject variability, while the frequent use of multiple interventions, or the failure to provide adequate controls or details of procedures used, limits the possibilities of identifying critical treatment components even when significant improvement has been noted. Moreover it is often far from certain whether interventions have influenced hallucinatory experiences themselves, or merely the patients' verbal reports of their occurrence. Such uncertainty is particularly evident in respect of operant procedures where there is a clear incentive to change verbal reports to gain access to reinforcers or avoid aversive stimuli, and is strengthened by the lack of conviction that can be attached to purely operant models of hallucinatory acquisition and development (Birchwood et al. 1988: 213).

Notwithstanding the above, tentative recommendations concerning those procedures meriting further investigation may be made by considering the nature of hallucinations and the factors influencing their occurrence. Birchwood *et al.* (ibid.) have thus proposed a model which suggests:

1 The hallucinatory experience is generated by the individual's own subvocal speech – what is heard as a 'voice' is the person talking to themselves. Evidence for this proposition comes from measures of electromyogram (EMG) and subvocal correlates of hallucinatory occurrence (Gould 1950; Green and Preston 1981; Inouye and Shimizo 1970), demonstrations of 'voice' blocking by gross mouth movements, gargling and vocal activity incompatible with subvocalization (Bick and Kinsbourne 1987; Erickson and Gustafson 1968; Green and Preston 1981), and incidental observations in several clinical and experimental studies of voice suppression during periods of overt speech and conversation (for example, Margo *et al.* 1981; Cooklin *et al.* 1983).

2 Conditions making voices more likely may variously include stress and anxiety, hyperarousal, the content of other people's conversations, being in situations previously associated with voices, lack of structured and meaningful environ-

mental stimulation and reduced levels of ongoing behaviour that demand attention to and interaction with the external environment.

3 Reinforcers for voices may include the person's own responses to their occurrence, such as talking back, looking for their source, laughing at their content, doing what they say, and so on. Such post-voice responses may be considered analogous to the conditions of reciprocal control exerted in normal two-way conversation, or as elements of a complex behavioural chain maintained by a remote or intermittent reinforcer. In some cases voices may also be reinforced by the positive mood they promote.

4 A precondition to the experience of voices is a predisposing abnormality of a cognitive or, more probably, neuropsychological type.

The adoption of such a model would therefore recommend as the most promising strategies those which seek to prevent voice occurrence by, for example, stress and arousal reduction or the promotion of activity involving attention to and engagement with the external environment: and those which seek to reduce voices which do occur by encouraging the use of voice interruption (for example, thought stopping), the immediate redirection of attention to external stimuli which are structured, meaningful, carry response requirements and necessitate engagement, and particularly the production of overt speech which is incompatible with hallucinatory production (via, for example, describing objects in the environment or conversing). To the extent that interaction with the external environment and overt speech disrupt the patient's own responses to the voices, such tactics would moreover be predicted to promote extinction. It is interesting to note that the use of an ear-plug was also originally predicated on the above model in terms of a hypothesized neuropsychological predisposition. While its theoretical rationale and mechanism of effect remains obscure, its potential benefits with even some clients also clearly warrants further investigation.

The use of such strategies is moreover supported by their similarity to methods spontaneously employed by some schizophrenics in natural settings – Falloon and Talbot (1981) and Breier and Strauss (1983) noting the common use of tactics such as changes in activity, manipulation of sensory input or arousal, reducing attention to the voices, and self-instruction; and McGuffin (1979) reporting on cases of the spontaneous use of ear-plugs. However, their generalized utility is clearly as yet unestablished. Given variability in the factors which appear to promote voices in different individuals, it is in fact evident that no single technique will prove effective in all cases, and that treatment choice will require analysis of the factors relevant to each particular case. Moreover, self-control techniques clearly demand substantial co-operation on the part of the patient, and the limits of their applicability in the face of cognitive and motivational deficits remain to be seen. In some instances their use may depend upon the prior remediation of cognitive impairments (for example, by attentional training), or the use of cognitive restructuring, education or incentive systems to enhance motivation. Many of the techniques may in fact find their most useful application with acute cases who retain a degree of insight. The possibilities of developing voice-control programmes tailored to the circumstances of each case, and drawing upon relevant preventive and self-control strategies, however, clearly merit further investigation.

Delusions

Like hallucinations, delusions of influence, persecution and identity often survive pharmacological intervention and continue to interfere with social adjustment. Cognitive-behavioural approaches to their management have again been varied, techniques thus far examined including extinction and the use of social reinforcement, tokens, privileges or feedback differentially to reinforce non-deluded talk (for example, Wincze et al. 1972); verbal conditioning and assertiveness training (Nydegger 1972); the use of a cue, pause and point training procedure to replace delusional speech by stimulus-appropriate social responses (Foxx et al. 1988); satiation (Wolff 1971); time out (Davis et al. 1976); coping-skill training, time out and differential reinforcement of other behaviour (Burgio et al. 1985); thought stopping (Lamontagne et al. 1983); the use of a graded and non-confrontational cognitive restructuring procedure in which subjects are encouraged to evaluate the evidence for their beliefs and generate their own alternative explanations (Milton et al. 1978); cognitive restructuring in conjunction with other cognitive-behavioural techniques (Hartman and Cashman 1983); and encouragement to re-attribute experiences previously interpreted in a delusional manner (Johnson et al. 1973; Adams et al. 1981).

Most of the above studies have reported positive results as judged by reductions in the overt verbal expressions of delusional beliefs, and in some instances by changes in measures of belief strength. As with 'voices', however, the degree of improvement across studies is variable, with evaluation of the relative merits or critical components of different procedures being again constrained by the prevalence of single-case designs, subject variability and the use in some instances of multiple treatments. On the face of it the most impressive changes have been afforded by use of contingency management procedures, but serious doubts must remain concerning the validity of operant models of delusion formation and maintenance, the operational equation of delusions with their verbal expression, and accordingly the extent to which contingency procedures have actually modified delusional beliefs as opposed to delusional speech. While in some cases a reduction in delusional talk may of course be a significant clinical achievement in its own right, cognitive-restructuring procedures would accordingly appear to have more face validity and to have achieved more definite, if modest, demonstrations of belief modification. The generalized utility of cognitive techniques themselves, however, must remain uncertain in the absence of further evidence concerning the possibilities of significant, durable and generalized change, the extent to which belief modification facilitates social function, the minimum level of cognitive capacity necessary if patients are to co-operate with treatment requirements, and so on. Similarly, insufficient evidence is currently available to judge the potential utility of self-control procedures, although extrapolating some of the findings with cases of 'voices' might suggest the merits of techniques promoting distraction and externally directed attention and engagement. That this line of enquiry is worthy of further pursuit is perhaps also suggested by observations that some schizophrenics in natural settings use a variety of self-management procedures to control irrational ideation (Breier and Strauss 1983; Marzillier and Birchwood 1981).

Cognitive deficits

Prominent among the intrinsic impairments of schizophrenia are deficits in such cognitive functions as attention, memory, information processing, thought organization, language and problem solving. Such deficits inevitably interfere with the efficiency of day-to-day functioning, but moreover represent important obstacles to the use of treatment programmes demanding reasonable levels of cognitive competence. Attention has therefore recently been paid to the clinical utility of cognitive-behavioural strategies designed to train directly skills of attention, self-monitoring and cognitive self-regulation, problem solving, reality testing and so on.

A number of workers have, for example, sought to enhance attentional function by requiring patients to practise task engagement under conditions of distraction, improvements following such training being reported in terms of thought disorder and social effectiveness (Adams *et al*. 1981), inattention-related mistakes (Spaulding *et al*. 1986) and the acquisition of social skills in a group setting (Stuart 1985). The promotion of attentional skills was also an element of Meichenbaum and Cameron's (1973) attempt to teach schizophrenics self-instructions through which they might regulate their own thinking and cognitive processes. Using instruction, modelling, shaping, rehearsal and reinforcement, patients were initially trained to monitor and evaluate their performance on sensory-motor tasks by self-questioning and self-instruction to attend and behave in a task-relevant manner, and later were taught to extract information from the expression and behaviour of others, and to respond to cues that they were emitting inappropriate speech by using self-instructions such as 'be relevant and coherent, make myself understood'. Results of the study suggested clear improvements on measures of thought disorder and distractability, and Meyers *et al*. (1976) subsequently described the successful use of self-instructional training with a chronic schizophrenic whose gains were maintained 6 months after discharge. Although some other studies reported negative results (Gresen 1974; Margolis and Shemberg 1976), Meichenbaum and Camerons's original findings have recently been confirmed by Bentall *et al*.'s (1987) clear demonstration of self-instructional training effects across a variety of memory, intellectual, matching and sorting tasks. However, the clinical utility of such training must at this stage remain uncertain, Bentall *et al*. noting that training was in practice difficult and time consuming, that treatment effects were specific to the tasks for which training was provided and did not generalize to those demanding different strategies, and that procedures to facilitate generalization must be explored if the approach is to be of practical significance (for example, by conducting training in a variety of settings with a variety of trainers, teaching general or 'metacognitive' self-instructional skills and so on).

Other cognitive skill-training procedures that have received preliminary invest-igation include reality testing or monitoring through which patients are taught to discriminate between the real and unreal (Johnson and Raye 1981; Shemberg and Leventhal 1972), and problem-solving training, the elements of which typically follow D'Zurilla and Goldfried's (1971) model and address problem identification, definition and analysis, the generation of alternative solutions, decision making and outcome evaluation. Bentall *et al.* (1987) have for example noted that general problem-solving training improved the performance of chronic schizophrenics on intellectual tasks, although as with self-instructional training the effects were task specific and did not generalize. Social-skill training programmes which are en-hanced by a problem-solving approach have been described by Liberman *et al.* (1986) and Wallace and Liberman (1985), and the use of problem solving with chronic patients has also been reported by Spivack *et al.* (1976) and Bedell and Michael (1985). In the absence of further work clarifying the extent to which problem-solving deficits reflect limited cognitive skills or the disorganization of available skills due to cognitive dysfunction (for example, distractability, slowed thinking, inefficient assimilation of meaning), and in particular in lieu of evidence demonstrating clinically significant, durable and generalized improvement, the utility of attempts to improve cognitive processing must remain an open question. While clinical outcomes are to date rather modest, the potential benefits of improved cognitive function are clearly nonetheless such as to recommend further exploration of these novel techniques.

Interpersonal and social functioning

Since the majority of schizophrenics display pervasive social deficits, considerable attention has been paid to the use of cognitive-behavioural procedures in promoting interpersonal communication and social function. Most research in the area has examined the use of variously elaborate social-skill training programmes (SST), a spate of controlled within-subject and between-group studies over the last 15 years clearly demonstrating that psychotic patients can be trained in such basic verbal and non-verbal skills as eye contact, smiling, posture, gesture, speech duration and response latency on an individual and group basis (see Birchwood *et al.* 1988; Shepherd 1986; Wallace *et al.* 1980).

Conclusions about the therapeutic utility of SST nonetheless remain constrained by variability in subject characteristics across studies, individual variability in response to treatment procedures and the limited evidence for generalization to 'real life' situations. Rather more encouraging findings have recently been reported by Liberman and colleagues in two studies with medicated schizophrenics at risk of relapse (Liberman *et al.* 1984, 1986), one programme following a problem-sol-ving model involving training in receiving, processing and sending skill, and the other using an elaborate personal-effectiveness approach involving the training of skills relevant to hospital, family and community settings. Attempts were made in both programmes to facilitate generalization (by, for example, practice with novel partners, homework assignments and so on), and the results of both were positive in terms of improvements in social functioning, and reductions in psychopathology and time hospitalized (the problem-solving programme being additionally superior to a comparison holistic health-treatment programme).

While the latter results are clearly promising, a priority for further research remains the demonstration that SST can effect durable and meaningfully generalized improvements in the effectiveness of social performance and quality and satisfaction or interpersonal interaction, and that it can equip patients to make and retain friends, use leisure, recreational and informational facilities, and handle novel and demanding interpersonal situations in a confident and efficient manner. If such a demonstration is to be achieved, a number of refinements in the SST approach are likely to be required (Birchwood *et al.* 1988: 264). In the first instance, attentional, memory or other cognitive deficits (which constrain the perception or processing of interpersonal information, or the ability to comply with treatment requirements) will in some cases require definition and remediation as a prerequisite to the emergence of higher order social skills. Second, increasing emphasis must be placed on building in generalization enhancement procedures, such as varying treatment times, settings and trainers, undertaking training and providing homework in natural settings, and teaching self-control skills as targets (for example, self-reinforcement, self-instruction), as well as providing long-term support arrangements through which others in the patient's environment prompt and reinforce effective social function. Finally, increasing emphasis must be placed on the design of highly tailored programmes whose targets are relevant and important to each individual client and whose format involves training in natural rather than artificial settings.

Family interventions

The exciting results of the expressed-emotion research (see pp. 177–9) have led to a proliferation of studies whose principal goal has been the control of relapse through reductions in intrafamilial stress. Hitherto, seven controlled studies have appeared (Table 7.3) with many still in progress. With the exception of the Goldstein and Kopeikin (1981) study all have concentrated on high EE families. Although all the interventions have as their goal the reduction of high EE, the means by which this is achieved varies from study to study, which is perhaps not surprising as our understanding of high and low EE family environments remains at the level of stereotype.

The Goldstein and Kopeikin intervention was structured as a sequence of four steps. The first included information about schizophrenia, concentrating particularly on the role of stress. This led to a second step in which the therapist attempted to identify two or three stressful situations within the family and strategies to

Table 7.3   Family-intervention studies: relapse rates[1]

Study	N	9 or 12 months	24 months
Goldstein and Kopeikin (1981)[2]			
Family intervention	25	0	–
Routine treatment	28	16	–
Leff et al. (1982)			
Family intervention	12	8	20
Routine treatment	12	50	78
Kottgen et al. (1984)			
Family intervention	15	33	–
Control (high EE)	14	43	–
Control (low EE)	20	20	–
Falloon et al. (1985)			
Family intervention	18	6	17
Individual intervention	18	44	83
Hogarty et al. (1986)			
Family intervention	21	19	–
Social-skill training	20	20	–
Combined intervention	20	0	–
Control	17	41	–
Tarrier et al. (1988a)			
Family intervention	25	12	33
Education only	14	43	57
Routine treatment	15	53	60

Notes
1   All subjects in these studies were in receipt of neuroleptic medication.
2   The follow-up period for the Goldstein and Kopeikin (1981) study was 6 months.

manage or avoid these situations. Finally, future difficulties were anticipated and planned for. An example of such a stressful situation might be the friction created where the individual appears apathetic or lazy as the result of negative symptoms or drug side-effects. The Leff intervention consisted of three components. The first was an educational package in which relatives were informed about the nature, course and treatment of schizophrenia. The second was a 'relatives group' in which high and low EE families met together and therapists facilitated interaction between them. The third comprised individual sessions using 'dynamic interpretations or behavioural interventions'. Subsequent interventions have become more structured in their approach and their methods are predominantly cognitive-behavioural. This is exemplified by the study of Hogarty et al. (1986) which is undoubtedly the most sophisticated study in design and execution to date. They identify four goals in their intervention:

1 *Increasing the understanding of the illness by the family:* where the therapist is
   particularly concerned that the family should construe the behaviour of the

individual, where appropriate, in 'illness' rather than 'personality' terms to reduce criticism and improve empathy;

2 *Reducing family stress:* where they are concerned to reduce stressful interactions by providing families with concrete suggestions for coping with the behaviour of the individual and to improve clarity of communication;

3 *Enhancing social networks:* this is a further stress-reduction measure where the individual and family are encouraged to develop personal, social, recreational or work contacts outside the family;

4 *Reducing intrafamilial conflict:* arising out of long-standing relationship problems are addressed by traditional family-therapy techniques.

The outcome of these interventions has been uniformly positive (Table 7.3). Typically relapse is reduced from the expected figure of approximately 50 per cent over 9 months for those receiving medication only, to less than 10 per cent with the addition of family intervention. Those that have reported 2-year follow-ups of their samples showed that these group differences are sustained, but reveal a gradual accumulation of relapse in the family-intervention groups. The Falloon group has reported on the social functioning and well-being of the individual and his or her family and has shown clear advantage for family intervention (Falloon and Pederson 1985).

The interaction between drug and family interventions has yet to be determined. The results of the correlational studies suggest that family interventions alone cannot control relapse for other than a very limited period (Birchwood *et al.* 1988). The Falloon team reports that its family-intervention group could be successfully stabilized on a much lower dose of neuroleptic medication than the control group, suggesting that there is an inverse relationship between family stress and medication dosage. Goldstein and Kopeikin (1981) varied drug dose ('moderate' vs. 'low') across both experimental and control groups. The high rate of relapse in the low-dose group (48 per cent) was halved with the addition of family intervention (21 per cent) but did not match the group receiving family therapy and the moderate dose (0 per cent). In view of the potential side-effects of neuroleptics, the interaction of drug dose and psychosocial intervention is an important area for further study.

It is important to recognize that these interventions, while representing a very significant advance for theory as well as practice, are not preventing relapse but delaying it. Table 7.3 shows the gradual accumulation in relapse over 2 years. Whereas the statistical results are impressive, the clinical outcome is somewhat variable: for example in the Leff study (Leff *et al.* 1982) some patients in the experimental group relapsed due to drug non-compliance and in two further instances, suicide was reported. Thus, it remains an open question whether these interventions can alter the course of schizophrenia with or without continued family intervention. The service implications of these advances are limited by the fact that only a minority of people with schizophrenia live with a high EE family (McCreadie and Robinson 1987).

Broadening the focus of family interventions to embrace the quality of life and well-being of the individual and his or her family would enlarge their therapeutic scope, particularly if this was to include the needs of 'low EE' families.

Community-focused interventions

There have been a number of complementary studies which have attempted to improve the adaption of the individual with schizophrenia to life in the community following a period of hospitalization. Many of the methods used here have been cognitive-behavioural in approach.

Hogarty and colleagues (1974) studied the impact of 'sociotherapy' on the community survival of young people with schizophrenia. Sociotherapy consisted of a 'problem solving method designed to respond to interpersonal, social and rehabilitative needs of patients' (p. 104). In one instance, for example, this included support in the management of a difficult family relationship, practical instruction in budgeting, cooking and helping to secure stable employment/accommodation, all of which helped her to cope with the 'day-to-day realities of life'. This programme was evaluated in interaction with neuroleptic medication (active vs. placebo). As anticipated, by 24 months, 80 per cent of placebo patients relapsed compared to 48 per cent of those receiving medication only. For those who survive in the community beyond the seventh month (60 per cent of the placebo group and 80 per cent of the drug group) there was a significant benefit of sociotherapy for relapse in combination with medication: 53 per cent of the drug-only group had relapsed compared to 37 per cent of those receiving the social and drug treatment. This study is however weakened by the presence of selective attrition in the treatment groups.

A number of studies have compared the treatment of 'serious mental illness' (mainly schizophrenia) in the community as an alternative to standard in-patient care. A study by Stein and Test (1980) is generally regarded as the best because of the quality of their community programme and research design. They compared two groups of sixty-five individuals, one receiving in-patient care plus aftercare, the other receiving 'training in community living'. This included: ensuring the availability of material resources (food, shelter and so on); training in basic community survival skills; developing social-support networks; reducing dependency on family or institutions by promoting autonomy and involvement in wider community life; support and education of community members who were involved with the individual (for example, hostel workers, families and so on). The results of the programme were highly impressive: during the first 12 months of the study twelve out of sixty-five experimental subjects were re-admitted compared to fifty-eight of sixty-five controls with equally favourable outcome in terms of social functioning and residual symptoms; however, when the programme ceased, the gains were steadily lost. Those in the community programme were not 'cured': many continued to experience symptoms and were functioning at a socially marginal level. Marks et al. (1988) suggested that the reduced need for re-admission came about as a result of the 'availability to supporters and carers of a 24 hour emergency service which even though little used, the knowledge that it could be...prevented re-admission (p. 22). Similar results have been reported in parallel investigations in Australia (Hoult *et al*. 1988) and the USA (Fenton *et al*. 1982) with encouraging early results from an attempted British replication (Marks *et al*. 1988). The success of the two family and community models of management suggest a clear pathway for future developments which we shall address in the concluding section .

FUTURE DEVELOPMENTS

We have emphasized in this chapter the significant advances which have come from a broad-spectrum cognitive-behavioural approach to schizophrenia. It is our firm view however, that the full impact of these advances will not be felt by the individual (or appreciated by service managers and powerful vested-interest groups unless they are integrated in a coherent way and evaluated within a service context. This view derives logically from the transactional model which argues that the development of the disorder, with its impairments, disabilities and handicaps, represents a cumulative interaction of cognitive, psychological and environmental factors; retarding this process requires a multilevel, ongoing intervention. A clinical evaluation study will be required to develop a model of care and management which can successfully integrate cognitive-behavioural and medical interventions and to examine the impact of this upon the evolution of the impairments and disabilities of schizophrenia. Directing this kind of intervention to those with recent experience of schizophrenia is likely to have greater impact as the disabilities will be more remediable. However, the task is not likely to be an easy one: recent studies of people at the first episode of schizophrenia reveal that the seeds of long-term decline are already sown and in many cases well advanced (Crow *et al*. 1986; Sartorius *et al*. 1986).

Much remains to be done before we can reach the point at which all of these interventions can be confidently applied and successfully married. Below we describe the central components of such an integrated model of management and indicate how these interventions might operate or where further work is required.

Community monitoring and maintenance

Community-focused interventions such as those of Stein and Test (1980) and Hoult (1986) are of proven effectiveness in controlling re-admission to hospital. One of their crucial components is the ability to respond rapidly to crises. This reactive strategy would be enhanced by an ability to anticipate crises, particularly relapse. Crisis intervention consumes considerable man-hours in these studies and in a conventional service setting this might be prohibitive. On a different note, attempts to incorporate low-dose maintenance medication strategies into clinical practice (see below) will also require a means of controlling the increased risk of relapse which they incur.

A system of monitoring which can predict relapse and which is clinically feasible, would be of considerable benefit. Studies in the USA (Herz and Melville 1980) and the UK (Birchwood *et al*. 1989) have shown that relapse is preceded by 'early-warning signs', often subtle changes in behaviour and mental processes. Such behavioural monitoring systems are presently under development. Birchwood *et al*. (ibid.) have reported on such a system which involves the close co-operation of patients and 'significant others'. This system (see Figure 7.2) has considerable predictive power and is currently undergoing further development to integrate it within a community maintenance programme. Further research is required to study different methods of early intervention, in particular the extent to which cognitive-behavioural strategies can arrest the process of relapse.

Family interventions

Future development in cognitive-behavioural family interventions should centre around three main issues. The first concerns the scope of these interventions which have hitherto concentrated exclusively on a subsample of (high-EE) families. The needs of other (low-EE) families have yet to be addressed and as we have indicated, there is every reason to suppose that cognitive-behavioural interventions may be of significant benefit with these families too. However, in order for this to be recognized, the goals of family intervention would have to be wider than that of relapse: social functioning, family well-being and improved affective ties between the individual and his or her family should legitimately fall within their purview. This will require considerable attention to the content of the interventions which have generally been of a stress-management variety. Ultimately, research should be able to answer the question, 'What kind of intervention is appropriate for what kind of family and for what kind of outcome?'

The second area for further work concerns the mode of action of family intervention in reducing relapse. Psychophysiological data suggests that the effect on the individual may be mediated autonomically (Tarrier *et al*. 1988a). However, what remains unclear is the nature of the intrafamilial changes which are crucial to achieve change: until models of the family interior are available to inform research and clinical practice, further empiricism alone will not provide the necessary illumination. The third area concerns the implementation of family interventions in clinical practice (it is puzzling how these advances have made little impact upon service provision). Attempts to implement these interventions in clinical practice meet with resistance due to conflicting attitudes and conflicting conceptual approaches to families which derive from the disparate training and background of the various health professionals. Implementation will require considerable organizational change concerned with training, resources, priorities and so on. In our view cognitive-behavioural approaches to organizational change will be required if we are to translate theory into practice (Smith and Birchwood 1990).

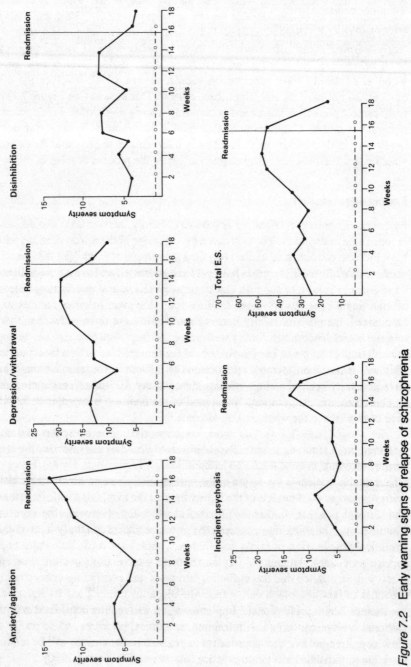

Figure 7.2 Early warning signs of relapse of schizophrenia

Drug–behaviour interactions

Neuroleptics are of proven efficacy in controlling the positive symptoms and preventing relapse. Clearly no serious intervention programme should ignore this. Indeed, cognitive-behavioural interventions should seek to maximize their effectiveness. For example, drug non-compliance is a continual problem and a major cause of relapse. Studies (for example, Smith and Birchwood 1987) have revealed a low level of understanding among patients and their relatives about medication which education programmes might improve (Smith and Birchwood 1990).

Further work is needed here. It is possible to predict non-compliance by questionnaire (Hogan *et al*. 1983) and an educational intervention targeted at those 'at-risk' individuals could be useful.

Neuroleptics do give rise to some significant side-effects (for example, problems of gait and balance) and in their third decade of use, disquiet is now also being expressed about what their long-term effects are likely to be. In addition, the drugs exacerbate the negative/cognitive impairments and impair social functioning. Reducing exposure to neuroleptics without impairing their effectiveness is clearly a crucial area for further investigation. We would accordingly suggest the following clinical and research strategies:

1 There is evidence from correlational studies that psychosocial, particularly family interventions, could act in partial substitution for drug therapy (Birchwood and Smith 1987). Future studies of psychosocial interventions should therefore study this interaction experimentally by manipulating drug dose – for example, placebo, low dose and conventional dose.

2 Two kinds of drug non-responders are often identified: those who remain well without drugs and those who remain unwell in spite of drugs (Carpenter and Heinrichs 1981). Predicting non-response in the *individual* case cannot be undertaken clinically without manipulating the medication regime itself. Further research is required to assess *intrinsic* vulnerability, for example, by psychophysiological and cognitive measures (for example, Dawson and Neuchterlein 1984) as an independent means of isolating *who* the non-responders are likely to be.

3 High doses of medication are frequently used with little empirical reason to do so (Hogarty *et al*. 1976); low-dose regimes should be explored with higher doses given only when an impending relapse is apparent. This would require the development of a behavioural monitoring system to predict relapse such as that described above.

Cognitive-behavioural approaches to symptoms and deficits

This chapter has reviewed some very promising strategies which could help to ameliorate symptoms such as hallucinations and delusions and the deficits of attention and cognition. The latter are of particular importance as any beneficial change they may yield will facilitate responsivity to skill-based training. The time is now well overdue when these approaches, which are predominantly based on single-case methodology, should be carefully evaluated in large-scale studies. Strategies for controlling drug-resistant symptoms such as hallucinations and delusions are also based on single-case methodology and could equally benefit from more rigorous evaluation. Such studies must not, however, assume a uniformity of deficit across individuals, as this will lead to an oversimplified 'cook-book' approach; effort must be directed towards *individually* based strategies if they are to have any long-term benefit.

REFERENCES

Adams, S. H., Brantley, P., Malatesta, V. and Turkat, I. (1981) 'Modification of cognitive processes: a case study of schizophrenia', *Journal of Consulting and Clinical Psychology* 49: 460–4.

Alford, G. S., Fleece, L. L. and Rothblum, E. (1982) 'Hallucinatory–delusional verbalizations: modification in a chronic schizophrenic by self-control and cognitive restructuring', *Behavior Modification* 6: 412–35.

Allen, H. A., Halperin, J. and Friend, R. (1985) 'Removal and diversion tactics and the control of auditory hallucinations', *Behaviour Research and Therapy* 23: 601–5.

Ayllon, T. and Kandel, H. (1976) 'I hear voices but there's no one there' (A functional analysis of auditory hallucinations), in H. J. Eysenck (ed.) *Case Studies in Behaviour Therapy*, London: Routledge & Kegan Paul.

Baker, R. and Hall, J. N. (1983) *Rehabilitation Evaluation of Hall and Baker*, Scotland: Vine Publishing.

Bedell, J. P. and Michael, D. D. (1985) 'Teaching problem-solving skills to chronic psychiatric patients', in D. Upper and S. M. Ross (eds) *Handbook of Behavioral Group Therapy*, New York: Plenum Press.

Belcher, T. L. (1988) 'Behavioral reduction of overt hallucinatory behavior in a chronic schizophrenic', *Journal of Behavior Therapy and Experimental Psychiatry* 19: 69–71.

Bellack, A. (1986) 'Schizophrenia: behavior therapy's forgotten child', *Behavior Therapy* 17(3): 192–213.

Bentall, R. P., Higson, P. J. and Lowe, C. F. (1987) 'Teaching self-instructions to chronic schizophrenic patients: efficacy and generalization', *Behavioural Psychotherapy* 15: 58–76.

Bentall, R. P., Jackson, H. F. and Pilgrim, D. (1988) 'Abandoning the concept of schizophrenia: some implications of validity arguments for psychological research into psychotic phenomena', *British Journal of Clinical Psychology* 27: 303–24.

Berner, P. (1986) 'Approaches to the assessment of schizophrenia in Europe', *Pharmacopsychiatria* 19: 33–6.

Bick, P. A. and Kinsbourne, M. (1987) 'Auditory hallucinations and subvocal speech in schizophrenic patients', *American Journal of Psychiatry* 144: 222–5.

Birchwood, M. J. and Cochrane (1990) 'Families coping with schizophrenia: coping styles, their origins and correlates', *Psychological Medicine* 20: 857–65.

—— (1986) 'The control of auditory hallucinations through the occlusion of monaural auditory input', *British Journal of Psychiatry* 149: 104–7.

—— and Smith, J. (1987) 'Expressed emotion and the first episodes of schizophrenia', *British Journal of Psychiatry* 152: 859–60.

Birchwood, M. J., Hallet, S. and Preston, M. C. (1988) *Schizophrenia: An Integrated Approach to Research and Treatment*, London: Longman.

Birchwood, M. J., Smith, J., MacMillan, J. F., Hogg, B., Prasad, R., Harvey. C. and Bering, S.

(1989) 'Predicting relapse in schizophrenia: the development and implementation of an early signs monitoring system using relatives and patients as observers', *Psychological Medicine* 19, 649–656.

Breier, A. and Strauss, J. S. (1983) 'Self control in psychotic disorders', *Archives of General Psychiatry* 40: 1141–5.

Brett-Jones, J., Garety, P. and Hemsley, D. (1987) 'Measuring delusional experiences: a method and its application', *British Journal of Clinical Psychology* 26: 257–65.

Brewin, C. R., Wing, J. K., Mangen, S. P., Brugha, T. S. and MacCarthy, B. (1987) 'The MRC "needs for care" assessment', *Psychological Medicine* 17: 971–82.

Brockington, I. F. and Meltzer, H. Y. (1982) 'Documenting an episode of psychiatric illness', *Schizophrenia Bulletin* 8: 485–92.

Brown, G. and Birley, J. L. T. (1968) 'Crises and life changes and onset of schizophrenia', *Journal of Health and Social Behaviour* 9: 203–14.

—— and Wing, J. K. (1972) 'Influence of family life on the course of schizophrenic disorders: a replication', *British Journal of Psychiatry* 121: 241–58.

Burgio, L., Brown, K. and Tice, L. (1985) 'Behavioral covariation in the treatment of delusional verbalisation with contingency management', *Journal of Behavior Therapy and Experimental Psychiatry* 16: 173–82.

Carpenter, N. T. and Heinrichs, D. N. (1981) 'Treatment of relevant subtypes of schizophrenia', *Journal of Nervous and Mental Disease* 169: 113–19.

Carstairs, J. M. (1985) 'Mental health and the environment in developing countries', in H. Freeman (ed.) *Mental Health and the Environment* London: Methuen.

Chung, R. K., Langeluddecke, P. and Tennant, C. (1986) 'Threatening life events in the onset of schizophrenia, schizophreniform psychosis and hypomania', *British Journal of Psychiatry* 148: 680–8.

Cooklin, R., Sturgeon, D. and Leff, J. (1983) 'The relationship between auditory hallucinations and spontaneous fluctuations of skin conductance in schizophrenia', *British Journal of Psychiatry* 142: 47–52.

Crow, T., Johnston, T. J., Johnson, A. L. and MacMillan, J. F. (1986) 'A randomised controlled trial of prophylactic neuroleptic treatment', *British Journal of Psychiatry* 148: 120–7.

Davis, J. R., Wallace, C. J., Liberman, R. P. and Finch, B. F. (1976) 'The use of brief isolation to suppress delusions and hallucinatory speech', *Journal of Behavior Therapy and Experimental Psychiatry* 7: 269–75.

Dawson, M. E. and Neuchterlein, K. H. (1984) 'Psychophysiological dysfunctions in the developmental course of schizophrenic disorders', *Schizophrenia Bulletin* 10: 204–32.

Day, R. A. (1981) 'Life events and schizophrenia: the "triggering" hypothesis', *Acta Psychiatrica Scandinavica* 64: 97–122.

Done, D. J., Frith, C. D. and Owens, D. C. (1986) 'Reducing persistent auditory hallucinations by wearing an earplug', *British Journal of Clinical Psychology* 25: 151–2.

Drake, T. and Cotton, T. (1986) 'Suicide among schizophrenics: a comparison of attempted and completed suicides', *British Journal of Psychiatry* 149: 784–7.

Dulz, B. and Hand, I. (1986) 'Short term relapse in young schizophrenics: can it be predicted and affected by family, patient and treatment? An experimental study', in M. Goldstein, I. Hand, and K. Halweg *Treatment of Schizophrenia: Family Assessment and Intervention*, Berlin: Springer.

D'Zurilla, T. J. and Goldfried, M. R. (1971) 'Problem-solving and behavior modification', *Journal of Abnormal Psychology* 78: 1067–126.

Erickson, G. and Gustafson, G. (1968) 'Controlling auditory hallucinations', *Hospital and Community Psychiatry* 19: 327–9.

Errickson, E., Darnell, M. H. and Labeck, L. (1978) 'Brief treatment of hallucinatory behavior with behavioral techniques', *Behavior Therapy* 9: 663–5.

Falloon, I. R. H. (1988) 'Expressed emotion: current status', *Psychological Medicine* 18: 269–74.

—— and Pederson, J. (1985) 'Family management in the prevention of morbidity of schizophrenics. The adjustment of the family unit', *British Journal of Psychiatry* 147: 156–63.

Falloon, I. R. H. and Talbot, R. F. (1981) 'Persistent auditory hallucinations: coping mechanisms and implications for management', *Psychological Medicine* 11: 329–39.

Falloon, I. R. H., Boyde, J. L., McGill, C. W., Williamson, M., Razani, J., Moss, H. B., Gliderman, A. M. and Simpson, G. M. (1985) 'Family management in the prevention of morbidity of schizophrenia: clinical outcome of a 2 year longitudinal study', *Archives of General Psychiatry* 42: 887–96.

Feder, R. (1982) 'Auditory hallucinations treated by radio headphones', *American Journal of Psychiatry* 139: 1188–90.

Fenton, F. R., Teisser, L., Struening, E. L., Smith, F. A. and Beniot, C. (1982) *Home and Hospital Psychiatric Treatment*, London: Croom Helm.

Field, W. and Reulke, W. (1973) 'Hallucinations and how to deal with them', *American Journal of Nursing* 4: 638–40.

Floyd, M. (1984) 'The employment problems of people disabled by schizophrenia', *Journal of Social and Occupational Medicine* 34: 93–5.

Fonagy, P. and Slade, P. (1982) 'Punishment as negative reinforcement in the aversive conditioning of auditory hallucinations', *Behaviour Research and Therapy* 20: 483–92.

Fowler, D. and Morley, S. (1989) 'The cognitive-behavioural treatment of hallucinations and delusions: a preliminary study', *Behavioural Psychotherapy* 17: 267–82.

Foxx, R. M., McMorrow, M. J., Davis, L. A. and Bittle, R. G. (1988) 'Replacing a chronic schizophrenic man's delusional speech with stimulus appropriate responses', *Journal of Behavior Therapy and Experimental Psychiatry* 11: 43–50.

Goldman, C. R. and Quinn, F. L. (1988) 'Effects of a patient education program in the treatment of schizophrenia', *Hospital and Community Psychiatry* 39: 282–6.

Goldstein, M. F. and Kopeikin, H. S. (1981) 'Short and long term effects of combining drug and family therapy', in M. J. Goldstein, (ed.) *New Directions for Mental Health Services: 12 New Developments in Interventions with Families of Schizophrenics*, San Francisco: Jossey-Bass.

Gould, L. N. (1950) 'Verbal hallucinations as automatic speech. Reactivation of dormant speech habit', *American Journal of Psychiatry* 107: 110–19.

Green, W. P. and O'Callaghan, M. J. (1980) 'Incompatible vocalisation as a means of reducing auditory hallucinations', unpublished manuscript, Department of Psychology, All Saints Hospital, Birmingham, England.

Green, W. P. and Preston, M. (1981) 'Reinforcement of vocal correlates of auditory hallucinations by auditory feedback: A case study', *British Journal of Psychiatry* 139: 204–8.

Greenberg, L., Fine, S. B., Cohen, C., Larson, K., Michaelson-Baily, A., Robinton, P. and Glick, I. R. (1988) 'An interdisciplinary psychoeducation program for schizophrenic patients and their families in an acute care setting', *Hospital and Community Psychiatry* 39: 277–82.

Gresen, R. (1974) 'The effects of instruction and reinforcement on a multifaceted self-control procedure in the modification and generalization of behavior in schizophrenics', unpublished Ph.D. dissertation, Bowling Green State University.

Hartman, L. M. and Cashman, F. E. (1983) 'Cognitive-behavioural and psychopharmacological treatment of delusional symptoms: a preliminary report', *Behavioural Psychotherapy* 11: 50–61.

Hemsley, D. and Garrety, P. A. (1986) 'The formation and maintenance of delusions: a Bayesian analysis', *British Journal of Psychiatry* 149: 51–6.

Herz, M. and Melville, C. (1980) 'Relapse in schizophrenia', *American Journal of Psychiatry* 137: 801–12.

Hogan, T. P., Awad, A. G. and Eastwood, R. (1983) 'A self-report predictive of drug compliance in schizophrenics: reliability and discriminative validity', *Psychological Medicine* 13: 177–83.

Hogarty, G. E., Anderson, C. M. and Reiss, D. J. (1986) 'Family psychoeducation, social skills training and maintenance chemotherapy in the aftercare treatment of schizophrenia: one year effects of controlled study on relapse and expressed emotion', *Archives of General Psychiatry* 43: 633–42.

Hogarty, G. E., Goldberg, S. C. and Schooler, N. R. (1974) 'Drug and sociotherapy in the aftercare of schizophrenic patients II: two-year relapse rates', *Archives of General Psychiatry* 31: 703–28.

Hogarty, G. E., Ulrich, R. F., Mussare, F. and Aristigutz, N. (1976) 'Drug discontinuation among long term successfully motivated schizophrenic outpatients', *Disease of the Nervous Systems* 37: 494–500.

Hoult, J. (1986) 'Community care of the acute mentally ill', *British Journal of Psychiatry* 149: 137–44.

Inouye, T. and Shimizo, A. (1970) 'The electromographic study of verbal hallucinations', *Journal of Nervous and Mental Disease* 151: 415–22.

Jablensky, A., Sartorius, N. and Lorten, G. (1986) 'Early manifestations and first contact incidence of schizophrenia in different cultures', *Psychological Medicine* 16: 900–28.

Jablensky, A., Schwartz, R. and Tomor, T. (1980) 'WHO collaborative study on impairments and disabilities associated with schizophrenic disorders', *Acta Psychiatrica Scandinavica* 62 (Supplement 285): 152–63.

Jacob, S. and Myers, J. (1976) 'Recent life-events and acute schizophrenic psychosis', *Journal of Nervous and Mental Disease* 162: 75–87.

James, D. A. E. (1983) 'The experimental treatment of two cases of auditory hallucinations', *British Journal of Psychiatry* 143: 515–16.

Johnson, M. and Raye, C. (1981) 'Reality monitoring', *Psychological Review* 88: 67–85.

Johnson, W., Ross, J. and Mastria, M. (1973) 'Delusional behavior: an attributional analysis of development and modification', *Journal of Abnormal Psychology* 86: 421–6.

Kendall, R. E. (1975) *The Role of Diagnosis in Psychiatry*, London: Blackwell.

Kleinman, A. (1987) 'Anthropology and psychiatry: the role of culture in cross-cultural research on illness', *British Journal of Psychiatry* 151: 447–54.

Kottgen, C., Sonnichsen, I., Mollenhauer, K. and Jurth, R. (1984) 'Group therapy with families of schizophrenic patients: results of the Hamburg Camberwell family interview study III', *International Journal of Family Psychiatry* 5: 83–94.

Krawiecka, M., Goldberg, D. and Vaughan, M. (1977) 'Standardised psychiatric assessment scale for chronic psychotic patients', *Acta Psychiatrica Scandinavica* 36: 25–31.

Kulhara, P. and Wig, N. N. (1978) 'The chronicity of schizophrenia in North West India', *British Journal of Psychiatry* 132: 186–90.

Lamontagne, Y., Audet, N., and Elie, R. (1983) 'Thought-stopping for delusions and hallucinations: a pilot study', *Behavioural Psychotherapy* 11: 177–84.

Leff, J. (1989) *Psychiatry around the Globe*, New York: Marcel-Dekker.

—— and Brown, G. (1977) 'Family and social factors in the course of schizophrenia', *British Journal of Psychiatry* 130: 417–20.

Leff, J. and Vaughn, C. (1980) 'The interaction of life events and relatives' expressed emotion in schizophrenia and depressive neurosis', *British Journal of Psychiatry* 136: 146–53.

—— (1981) 'The role of maintenance therapy and relatives' expressed emotion in relapse in schizophrenia: a two-year follow up', *British Journal of Psychiatry* 139: 102–4.

—— (1985) *Expressed Emotion in Families*, New York: Guilford Press.

Leff, J., Hirsch, S. R. and Stevens, B. C. (1973) 'Life events and maintenance therapy in schizophrenic relapse', *British Journal of Psychiatry* 123: 659–60.

Leff, J., Wig, N. and Ghosh, A. (1987) 'Expressed emotion and schizophrenia in North India 3. Influence of relatives' EE on the course of schizophrenia in Chandigarh', *British Journal of Psychiatry* 151: 166–73.

Leff, J., Kuipers, L., Berkowitz, R., Eberlein-Veries, R. and Sturgeon, D. (1982) 'A controlled trial of social intervention in the families of schizophrenic patients', *British Journal of Psychiatry* 141: 121–34.

Liberman, R. P., Mueser, K. T. and Wallace, C. J. (1986) 'Social skills training for schizophrenic individuals at risk for relapse', *American Journal of Psychiatry* 143: 523–6.

Liberman, R. P., Wallace, C. J., Teigen, J. and Davis, J. (1974) 'Interventions with psychotic behaviours', in K. S. Calhoun, H. F. Adams and K. M. Mitchell (eds) *Innovative Treatment Methods in Psychopathology*, New York: Wiley.

Liberman, R. P., Lillie, F., Falloon, I. R. H., Harpin, R. E., Hutchinson, W. and Stoute, B. (1984) 'Social skills training with relapsing schizophrenics: an experimental analysis', *Behavior Modification* 8: 155–79.

McCreadie, R. G. and Robinson, A. (1987) 'The Nithsdale Schizophrenia Survey VI Relatives' expressed emotion: prevalence patterns and clinical assessment', *British Journal of Psychiatry* 150: 640–4.

McGuffin, P. (1979) 'Schizophrenics who wear ear-plugs', *British Journal of Psychiatry* 134: 651.

MacMillan, J. F., Gold, A., Crow, T. J., Johnson, A. L. and Johnston, E. C. (1986) 'The Northwick Park study of first episodes of schizophrenia. 4: Expressed emotion and relapse', *British Journal of Psychiatry* 148: 135–43.

Magen, J. (1983) 'Increasing external stimuli to ameliorate hallucinations', *American Journal of Psychiatry* 140: 269–70.

Mann, S. A. and Cree, N. (1975) '"New" long stay patients. A sample of fifteen mental hospitals in England and Wales, 1972–3', *Psychological Medicine* 6: 603–16.

Margo, A., Hemsley, D. R. and Slade, P. D. (1981) 'The effects of varying auditory input on schizophrenic hallucinations', *British Journal of Psychiatry* 139: 122–7.

Margolis, R. B. and Shemberg, K. M. (1976) 'Cognitive self-instructions in process and reactive schizophrenics: a failure to replicate', *Behavior Therapy* 7: 668–71.

Marks, I., Connolly, J. M. and Muijen, M. (1988) 'The Maudsley daily living programme', *Bulletin of the Royal College of Psychiatrists* 12: 22–4.

Marzillier, J. S. and Birchwood, M. J. (1981) 'Behavioral treatment of cognitive disorders', in L. Michelson, M. Hersen and S. M. Turner (eds) *Future Perspectives in Behavior Therapy*, New York: Plenum.

Meichenbaum, D. H. and Cameron, R. (1973) 'Training schizophrenics to talk to themselves: a means of developing attentional control', *Behavior Therapy* 4: 515–34.

Meyers, A., Mercatoris, M. and Sirota, A. (1976) 'Use of covert self-instruction for the elimination of psychotic speech', *Journal of Consulting and Clinical Psychology* 44: 480–3.

Milton, F., Patwa, V. K. and Hafner, R. J. (1978) 'Confrontation vs. belief modification in persistently deluded patients', *British Journal of Medical Psychology* 51: 127–30.

Morley, S. (1987) 'Modification of auditory hallucinations: experimental studies of head-phones and earplugs', *Behavioural Psychotherapy* 15: 240–51.

Moser, A. J. (1974) 'Covert punishment of hallucinatory behavior in a psychotic male', *Journal of Behavior Therapy and Experimental Psychiatry* 5: 297–9.

Murphy, H. B. M. and Rahman, A. C. (1971) 'The chronicity of schizophrenia in indigenous tropical people', *British Journal of Psychiatry* 118: 489.

Nydegger, R. V. (1972) 'The elimination of hallucinatory and delusional behavior by verbal conditioning and assertive training: a case study', *Journal of Behavior Therapy and Experimental Psychiatry* 3: 225–7.

Parker, G., Johnston, P. and Hayward, L. (1988) 'Parental "expressed emotion" as a predictor of schizophrenic relapse', *Archives of General Psychiatry* 45: 806–13.

Paul, G. L. and Lentz, R. J. (1977) *Psychosocial Treatment of Chronic Mental Patients*, Cambridge, Mass.: Harvard University Press.

Platt, S., Weyman, A., Hirson, S. and Hewett, S. (1980) 'The Social Behavior Assessment Schedule (SBAS)', *Social Psychiatry* 15: 43–55.

Richardson, R., Karkalas, Y. and Lal, H. (1972) 'Application of operant procedures in treatment of hallucinations in chronic psychotics', in R. D. Rubin, H. Fensterheim, J. D. Henderson and L. P. Ullmann (eds) *Advances in Behavior Therapy*, 11, New York: Academic Press.

Roy, A., Thompson, R. and Kennedy, S. (1983) 'Depression in chronic schizophrenia', *British Journal of Psychiatry* 143: 465–70.

Samaan, N. (1975) 'Thought-stopping and flooding in a case of hallucinations, obsessions and homicidal-suicidal behavior', *Journal of Behavior Therapy and Experimental Psychiatry* 6: 65–7.

Sartorius, N., Jablensky, A., Lorten, G. and others (1986) 'Early manifestations and first contact incidence of schizophrenia in different cultures', *Psychological Medicine* 16: 909–28.

Schneider, K. (1959) *Clinical Psychopathology*, New York: Grune and Stratton.

Schwartz, C. C. and Myers, J. K. (1977) 'Life events and schizophrenia: I-comparison of schizophrenics with a community sample', *Archives of General Psychiatry* 34: 1238–41.

Shemberg, K. and Leventhal, D. (1972) 'Outpatient treatment of schizophrenic students in a university clinic', *Bulletin of the Menninger Clinic* 36: 617–40.

Shepherd, G. (1986) *Rehabilitation*, London: Longman.

Shuart, W. (1985) 'Effects of self instructional training on performance in a social skills training group', unpublished doctoral dissertation, University of Nebraska.

Siegal, J. M. (1975) 'Successful systematic desensitization of a chronic schizophrenic patient', *Journal of Behavior Therapy and Experimental Psychiatry* 6: 345–6.

Slade, P. D. (1973) 'The psychological investigation and treatment of auditory hallucinations: a second case report', *British Journal of Medical Psychology* 46: 293–6.

Smith, J. V. E. and Birchwood, M. J. (1987) 'Specific and non-specific effects of an educational programme for families living with a schizophrenic relative', *British Journal of Psychiatry* 150: 645–52.

—— (1988) 'Families and schizophrenia: from theory to practice', in N. Eisenberg and D. Glasgow (eds) *Current Issues in Clinical Psychology*, Aldershot: Gower Press.

—— (1990) 'Relatives and patients as partners in management of schizophrenia: the development of a service model', *British Journal of Psychiatry*, 156: 654–60.

Sokolovsky, J., Cohen, C., Berger, D. and Geiger, J. (1978) 'Personal networks of ex-mental patients in a Manhattan SRO hotel', *Human Organisation* 37: 5–15.

Spaulding, W. D., Storms, L., Goodrich, V. and Sullivan, M. (1986) 'Applications of experimental psychopathology in psychiatric rehabilitation', *Schizophrenia Bulletin* 12: 560–77.

Spivack, G., Platt, J. J. and Shure, M. B. (1976) *The Problem Solving Approach to Adjustment*, San Francisco: Jossey-Bass.

Stein, L. I. and Test, M. (1980) 'Alternative to mental hospital treatment. 1. Conceptual model, treatment program and clinical evaluation', *Archives of General Psychiatry* 37: 392–7.

Sturgeon, D., Turpin, G., Kuiper, L., Berkowitz, R. and Leff, J. (1984) 'Psychophysiological responses of schizophrenic patients to high and low expressed emotional relatives: a follow up study', *British Journal of Psychiatry* 145: 62–9.

Szasz, T. D. (1979) *Schizophrenia: The Sacred Symbol of Psychiatry*, London: Oxford University Press.

Tarrier, N. (1987) 'An investigation of residual psychotic symptoms in discharged schizophrenic patients', *British Journal of Clinical Psychology* 26: 141–3.

——, Barrowclough, C., Porceddo, K. and Watts, S. (1988a) 'The assessment of psychophysiological reactivity to the expressed emotion of the relatives of schizophrenic patients', *British Journal of Psychiatry* 152: 618–24.

——, Barrowclough, C., Vaughn, C., Bamrah, J. S., Porceddu, K., Watts, S. and Freeman, H. L. (1988b) 'The community management of schizophrenia: a controlled trial of a behavioural intervention with families to reduce relapse', *British Journal of Psychiatry* 153: 532–42.

Tress, K. H., Bellenis, L., Brownlow, J. M., Livingston, G. and Leff, J. P. (1987), 'The present state examination change rating scale', *British Journal of Psychiatry*, 150: 201–7.

Turner, S. M., Hersen, M. and Bellack, A. S. (1977) 'Effects of social disruptions, stimulus interference and aversive conditioning on auditory hallucinations', *Behavior Modification* 1: 249–58.

Vaughn, C., Synder, K. S., Jones, S., Freeman, W. B. and Falloon, I. R. H. (1984) 'Family factors in schizophrenic relapse', *Archives of General Psychiatry* 41: 1169–77.

Wallace, C. J. (1984) 'Community and interpersonal functioning in the course of schizophrenic disorders', *Schizophrenia Bulletin* 10: 233–57.

—— and Liberman, R. P. (1985) 'Social skills training for patients with schizophrenia: a controlled clinical trial', *Psychiatry Research* 15: 239–47.

Wallace, C. J., Nelson, C., Liberman, R. P., Lukoff, D., Aitchison, R. A. and Ferris, C. (1980) 'A review and critique of social skills training with chronic schizophrenics', *Schizophrenia Bulletin* 6: 42–64.

Weinman, B., Gelbeart, P., Wallace, M. and Post, M. (1972) 'Inducing assertive behavior in chronic schizophrenics: a comparison of social environmental desensitization and relaxation therapies', *Journal of Consulting and Clinical Psychology* 39: 246–52.

Williams, A. D., Reverley, T., Kolakowska, T., Arden, M. and Mandelbrote, B. M. (1985) 'Schizophrenia with good and poor diagnosis II: Cerebral ventricular size and clinical significance', *British Journal of Psychiatry* 146: 237–44.

Wincze, J. P., Leitenberg, H. and Agras, W. S. (1972) 'The effects of token reinforcement and feedback on the delusional verbal behaviour of chronic paranoid schizophrenics', *Journal of Applied Behavior Analysis* 5: 247–62.

Wing, J. K. (1978) *Reasoning about Madness*, London: Wiley.

——, Cooper, J. and Sartorius, N. (1974) *The Measure and Classification of Psychiatric Symptoms: An Instruction Manual for the PSE and CATEGO systems*, Cambridge: Cambridge University Press.

Wolff, R. (1971) 'The systematic application of the satiation procedure to delusional verbiage', *Psychological Record* 21: 459–63.

Wong, S., Terranova, M. D., Bowen, L., Zarate, R., Massel, H. K. and Liberman, R. P. (1987) 'Providing independent recreational activities to reduce stereotypic vocalizations in chronic schizophrenics', *Journal of Applied Behavior Analysis* 20: 77–81.

World Health Organization (1979) *An International Pilot Study of Schizophrenia*, Chichester: Wiley.

—— (1980) *International Classification of Impairment Disabilities and Handicaps*, Geneva: WHO.

Zubin, J., Magaziner, J. and Steinhauer, S. R. (1983) 'The metamorphosis of schizophrenia: from chronicity to vulnerability', *Psychological Medicine* 13: 551–71.

Chapter 8

Problems of elderly people

Nicola Bradbury

CONCEPTUALIZATION

Introduction

Arguably, one of the greatest achievements of the western industrial world in the twentieth century has been the increase in life expectancy. There has been a dramatic rise in the number of people surviving beyond the age of 75 over the last 50 years. The emphasis in health services for elderly people is changing from keeping alive to ensuring that quality of life is maintained into old age. Over the past decade, the profession of clinical psychology has started to recognize the value of its potential contribution in this area.

At one time it was assumed by investigators and theorists in the area of cognitive development that there were no major changes in cognition beyond adolescence. More recent research indicates that this is not the case (Schaie 1978; Schaie and Strother 1968). A number of misconceptions in the understanding of age-related changes can be attributed to previous developmental research strategies. In the past, most studies employed a cross-sectional design. Samples of people of different ages were gathered at the same point in time and given questionnaires, tests or interviews. The results of the different age groups were then compared. Most cross-sectional studies found an increase in performance up until the early adult years, and then a decline.

However, more recently there has been increasing awareness that these studies measured age differences, not age changes. A cohort (a group of people born at about the same time) moves through the life-span together and therefore experiences similar historical and cultural influences. The shared experiences of a cohort affect the attitudes, values and world view of the individuals living through them. Changes in levels of education, nutrition, health care, expectations and technology will all contribute to the ways in which an individual functions. Each cohort of people carries its own experience of history through its life-span. Cross-sectional studies, by sampling individuals from different cohorts, do not separate differences in functioning due to cultural-historical factors from those due to age (Kimmel 1980).

Longitudinal studies, on the other hand, follow a group of individuals over a series of assessments. Thus, the performance of an individual or group can be compared at different ages. Longitudinal studies have tended to find far greater stability in many areas of performance (Savage *et al.* 1973).

Even with longitudinal designs there are difficulties. Rapid cultural changes may still affect the population studied and practical problems can arise, such as difficulties with finance, or the measures used seeming to be inappropriate to investigators in later years (Britton 1983). Inevitably some subjects will not be available to be reassessed due to loss of contact or changes in health and motivation. It is also questionable to what extent the results obtained from a study of one cohort will generalize to other cohorts. With increasing longevity, two generations of the same family can fall into the category described as 'old'. Data obtained from a longitudinal study of elderly children may not hold true for their even older parents. Various alternative models have been suggested which combine features of cross-sectional and longitudinal methodology (Baltes 1968; Schaie and Labouvie-Vief 1974; Schaie and Strother 1968), but even these have failed to provide all the solutions or satisfy all the critics (Woods and Britton 1985).

As with any study of general populations, average results tell us little about individuals. Individual differences in patterns of change are large, and different abilities may change at different rates. Results from a methodologically sophisticated study by Siegler and Botwinick (1979) provided further evidence of lack of overall decline in intellect. They found a sizeable proportion of old people who declined very little as old age advanced or declined not at all, except perhaps in extreme old age. From other studies too, a group of older people emerges who are exceptionally well preserved in physical health and adjustment, performing significantly higher than their peers on tests of intellectual functioning, showing less evidence of intellectual deterioration and surviving longer than would have been expected (Gaber 1983; Neugarten *et al.* 1968; Savage *et al.* 1973). It does seem that there is a relationship between intellectual performance and survival. Rather than implying that brighter people live longer, this reflects the connection between physical and intellectual factors. Increased physical illness is related to a reduction in scores on a number of intellectual measures (Bergmann *et al.* 1981).

Allowing for methodological difficulties, it seems that the extent of cognitive decline with age has been overestimated. An expectation of significant decline as a matter of course in all old people is not justified by the evidence.

Cattell's model of 'fluid' and 'crystallized' intelligence has been applied for many years to age-related intellectual changes (Cattell 1963). Fluid ability, the immediate adaptive ability to perceive relationships between objects and events, to reason and to abstract, is more dependent on the physiological integrity of the individual and will be more prone to change. Crystallized abilities, reflecting the aggregate experience of the individual, the acquired familiarity with materials and relationships, may well go on developing into extreme old age (Woods and Britton 1985). This model has stood the test of time quite well. It helps us to see the overall cognitive consequences of ageing as a process of change, not necessarily as an inevitable decline.

Age is generally accompanied by decreased ability to analyse and synthesize abstract material, difficulty in focusing attention for long periods of time, relatively small memory changes and greater distractability. Older adults take longer to organize their thoughts before they speak and may have difficulty retaining information from week to week. The common effect of all ageing is to reduce the body's spare capacity for dealing with change. Church (1986) illustrates this by considering a young person who may have 95 per cent of his spare capacity in reserve as compared to an elderly person having 5 per cent or less. If both undergo an experience which calls upon the use of 10 per cent of spare capacity, this will be barely noticed by the younger individual but will mean acute distress to the older person. The direct consequence of this reduction in spare capacity is to increase dependence on the environment in its broader sense.

Church (1983, 1986) has identified a number of factors which seem to enhance the effectiveness of therapeutic activity with older people:

1 Changes in language ability and abstract thinking suggest that a less interpretative approach is more appropriate, with the therapist taking an active rather than a passive role.
2 It is important that the therapist is free of any prejudice against older people and is able to appreciate what goals might be important for someone who has only 5 or 10 years of life left to them.
3 Therapy with elderly people should be time limited, with a degree of flexibility in both the location, and the length, of sessions.
4 The therapist needs to be aware of possible drug effects in elderly people and any physical factors which may exacerbate so called 'psychological' problems.

It is perhaps important to mention that a number of therapists disagree with Church's views concerning the appropriateness of more abstract techniques with older people. Increasingly, dynamic psychotherapeutic approaches are being offered to elderly clients in order to allow them to explore the difficulties encountered in later life (Hildebrand 1986; Stern *et al.* 1984).

Common problems encountered by clinicians working with elderly people

Problems presented by elderly people can be divided into four broad and not mutually exclusive categories:

1 Elderly people are subject to all the psychological problems experienced by adults of any age. These may be of recent origin or have developed prior to or during early adulthood. They might have problems related to eating disorders, anxiety states, drug dependence, family, marital or sexual difficulties.
2 Problems related to loss and bereavement, although not unique to older people, do occur more frequently in later life, for example depression, abnormal grief, role-performance dysfunction.
3 Similarly the challenge of coping with chronic health problems is more likely

to face those in later life, for example cardiovascular dysfunction, severe arthritis, sensory loss.

4 Chronic Organic Brain Syndrome, although only affecting an estimated 5–6 per cent of the total older population, rises to approximately 20 per cent in people over 80 years of age (Gurland and Cross 1982; Kay and Bergman 1980; Kay *et al.* 1970). Problems associated with the senile dementias include language disorders, memory loss and challenging behaviours.

When presented with adult mental-health problems, provided the factors identified by Church are taken into account, there is good reason to assume that therapeutic approaches found to be effective with younger adults will be equally relevant to this age group. Unfortunately, this assumption has not been tested in many of these areas in spite of the frequency with which some psychological problems occur in older people. For example, survey data from the US suggests that anxiety symptoms are more common in elderly people than in any other age group, occurring at more than twice the rate in this population than in young adults (Sallis and Lichstein 1982). However, little work has been done on evaluating the effectiveness of teaching anxiety-management techniques to older adults. The aim of this chapter is to concentrate on those problems where therapeutic approaches have been modified and evaluated in terms of their effectiveness in addressing the particular needs of elderly people.

Loss is very much a part of growing old. Increasing age tends to bring with it loss of job, reduced social roles and status, reduced income, failing health, loss of independence and the death of family and friends. While the majority of older people adjust well to the changes of later life, a few require help in coming to terms with the boredom and reduced social contact which tends to follow retirement, and the loneliness and depression of bereavement. It is sometimes assumed by young people – incorrectly – that fear of death is predominant in old age. Many older people talk openly about dying and it often seems, particularly for those in institutional care, that rather than fearing death, they await it with eager anticipation. Nevertheless, for some elderly individuals, the approach of the end of their lives is a source of considerable anxiety. It is also a time for others to review the past in an attempt to make sense of their experiences and to come to terms with their successes and failures. An understanding of the process of grieving as well as personal comfort with the concept of death would seem to be vital prerequisites of working with older people.

Considering the frequency and range of losses in old age, it is perhaps not surprising that depression is the most common mental-health problem in elderly people (Gurland 1976; Gurland *et al.* 1983; Kay *et al.* 1964). This may explain why it is an area which has received so much attention in the published literature. Although the exact prevalence of depression in elderly people is hard to establish, using strict psychiatric criteria, Murphy (1982), in a British study, found 29 per cent of a sample of elderly people living at home to be either seriously depressed or 'borderline', i.e. having a definite cluster of psychiatric symptoms not severe enough to warrant a definite diagnosis. It has been suggested by other studies that up to 50 per cent of elderly people living at home might have some degree of depression (Hanley and Baikie 1984). As might be expected, suicide rates are particularly high among older people. Suicide attempts are much more common than suicides among younger people, but suicide attempts among older persons almost always reflect an intent to die. Men over 65 are estimated to be four times more likely to take their own life than men under 25, the next highest peak period (Chaisson-Stewart 1985). Suicide rates for women may not show such a marked increase in old age but suicide occurs more frequently in later years than in the first three decades of life.

Illness and resulting physical handicap is an issue at any age but one of the major consequences of growing old is the growing susceptibility to chronic disease. While many people retain good health into old age, many more show the symptoms of one or more chronic impairments and may be disabled to some degree. Even where there is little apparent evidence of disability, decreased hearing, impaired vision or the pain and reduced mobility resulting from arthritis can serve to isolate the elderly person from social and psychological stimulation. Ageing is often thought to bring about a wide range of changes that, in fact, probably result more from disease and its consequences than from ageing *per se*.

Additional challenges to the ones described above are presented by elderly people with cognitive impairments. Due to the progressive and incurable nature of the senile dementias the role of the clinician is often one of attempting to identify the abilities that the person still retains and to find ways of maintaining and building on these. Some elderly sufferers of senile dementia show patterns of behaviour which cause considerable problems for their carers. The intervention here might be to help with advice on management and, by providing support to the carers, attempt to increase their ability to cope with their extremely stressful task.

Elderly people with psychological problems will be encountered in community and residential settings. In practice, much of the literature on behavioural treatment approaches concentrates on institutionalized groups. This raises the concern that behaviours seen as problems by people other than the elderly person may be selected for intervention (for example, incontinence, attention-seeking or manipulative behaviour), rather than those identified by older individuals themselves (for example, depression, boredom or social isolation). The tendency to address needs of the service (or service providers) rather than those of the service users is beginning to be challenged in services for people with learning difficulties through the application of the Life Planning approach (Chamberlain 1985). This is a process which involves working with the client, or their advocate, in order to identity individual clients' needs from their perspective. The wider application of this approach with elderly people will increase the likelihood that, for individuals, their whole range of human needs will be addressed (Goodall 1988; Sutton 1988).

For elderly people living at home, the increased time spent together by a couple following retirement can put pressure on an existing relationship, and chronic ill-health in one spouse will put further stress on a marriage. The way in which a husband or wife copes with a partner's disability can result in further dependency and loss of skills. An elderly person living with (or living alone and supported by) younger family members may be seen as the cause of family disharmony or conflict, leading to scapegoating or, in extreme cases, physical or emotional abuse. Often, problems in old age encountered by clinicians are best approached by viewing the elderly person as part of a social network rather than as an isolated individual (Herr and Weakland 1979).

Conceptualization of problems from a cognitive-behavioural perspective

Many of the factors in an elderly person's life which may result in detrimental changes in behaviour or cognitions are both unchangeable and continually present. A large number of older people have access to fewer options, opportunities and pleasures than they had at almost any time in their lives. Loss of family and friends and restricted social roles reduce an older person's opportunities for rewarding relationships. Increasing physical frailty and losses in sensation, memory and attention make an elderly person's environment progressively less manageable and functional behaviour is discouraged.

Murphy (1982) found an association between severe life events, major social difficulties, poor physical health and the onset of depression. She also suggests that many kinds of loss in elderly people appear to be irretrievably hopeless in a way that is rare for younger people. The older we are, the less we can expect to reverse the circumstances which are the outcome of severe events – for example, when an only child emigrates to Australia, the chances of meeting them again are reduced with age. Murphy's proposal is backed up by Davis *et al*. (1987) who investigated differences in perceived threat for a variety of life events. They found that older adults judged the long-term impact of events as more severe than younger people. These results indicate the danger of younger professionals underestimating the long-term threat of life events to older adults.

Although circumstances in old age may not be easily changed, it is possible to be more hopeful about changing a person's perception of them (Sherman 1981). According to Yost *et al*. (1986), in a publication looking specifically at the application of cognitive approaches with older adults, cognitive distortions for this age group tend to be clustered in three areas: unrealistic expectations of themselves and old age, exaggerated meanings given to daily events, and the values held by many older adults.

If retirement is seen as a time for relaxation and enjoyment, free from the stresses of work and a growing family, the unexpected problems of ageing can come as a shock. If older adults have developed unrealistically high expectations of their own ability to adjust to new and distressing situations, the impact may be intensified by the smallest failure to cope adequately. This may lead to perceptions of personal inadequacy ('I'm not good for anything now') or the making of unrealistic comparisons ('when I was 20 I could have done this in a tenth of the time').

Unfortunately, many of the cognitions concerning old age itself (for example, 'It's just going to get worse – there's no point in trying') contain an element of truth.

The values held by many older adults can be another source of negative cognitions. Elderly people may consider that they have become outdated, by changes in social ideas and standards as much as by modern technology. They may worry about their own physical security and that of their adolescent grandchildren. Such beliefs as 'You are only of value to society if you've got a job' may have served them well during their working years but can be a considerable impediment to the acceptance of retirement.

Although, increasingly, clinicians in this specialty have been applying cognitive approaches in their work, support for a cognitive theory of depression in elderly people has not been universal. In their chapter 'Understanding and Treating Depression in the Elderly', Hanley and Baikie (1984) question the validity of cognitive theory in explaining the development of most depressions in elderly people. By placing greater emphasis on depressogenic cognitions, cognitive theory relegates behavioural and affect changes to second-order 'symptoms'. Although many older individuals do show clear evidence of cognitive distortion and reduced self-esteem, they often present as apathetic, inert and somatically preoccupied. On the other hand the two authors point out that cognitive therapy (Beck *et al.* 1979), although derived from the theory, is more problem orientated and behavioural. In view of its effectiveness with younger depressives, they suggest that the merits of cognitive therapy may bear little relationship to the adequacy of the underlying theory.

From a behavioural perspective, the essential characteristic of a depressed person is their reduced frequency of positively reinforced behaviours. In particular, two aspects of depressed behaviour appear particularly relevant to older individuals, i.e. depressed elderly people tend to be restricted in their range of social interactions and they become, through lack of power and status in society, the passive recipients of the care offered to them. In health-care settings, negative stereotyping can lead staff to reinforce inappropriate behaviour while failing to respond to more appropriate non-depressed behaviour (Solomon 1982). An elderly depressed person's social network may be seen as providing sympathy, interest and concern which strengthens and maintains depressive behaviours. As these become aversive, however, other people eventually come to avoid the depressed person, which further reduces the amount of positive reinforcement available to them (Hanley and Baikie 1984).

Seligman's (1975) model of learned helplessness may have particular relevance to elderly people as, due to the ageing process itself and the individual's changing position in society, previously appropriate responses are no longer reinforced by the environment.

Assessment

The past few years have seen increasing interest in the construction of psychological tests appropriate for older people which draw on vastly increased knowledge in such areas as information processing and neuropsychology (Britton 1983). Two popular assessments in clinical practice, both developed in the UK, are the Clifton Assessment Procedure for the Elderly (Pattie and Gilleard 1979) and the Kendrick Battery for the detection of dementia (Gibson and Kendrick 1979). The extensively researched Clifton Assessment Procedure (CAPE) contains tests of orientation and concentration as well as a behavioural rating scale. These tests have usually been found to have satisfactory reliability (Holden and Woods 1982: 109–11) and their validity is well established (Pattie and Gilleard 1979).

The Kendrick Battery for the detection of dementia was developed for the differential diagnosis of depression and dementia in people aged 55 to 75 and over. A lack of initiative, loss of interest and difficulties in memory are often found in individuals with either diagnosis. Diagnostic confusion also occurs when individuals with mild cognitive decline are depressed as well. Although near perfect discrimination of clear-cut acute cases has been demonstrated (Kendrick et al. 1979), Gibson et al. (1980) report that nearly half of a sample of long-stay psychiatric patients was misclassified.

Two more recently published assessment tools have been designed to offer a more detailed examination of the range of cognitive functions in older people. The Cambridge Mental Disorders of the Elderly Examination (CAMDEX) is a new interview schedule for the diagnosis and measurement of dementia in elderly people. It includes a structured clinical interview with the patient, a structured interview with a relative or other informant and a mini-neuropsychological battery (Roth et al. 1988). The Middlesex Elderly Assessment of Mental State (MEAMS) has been designed to differentiate between functional illnesses and organically based cognitive impairments (Golding 1989). MEAMS systematically surveys the major area of cognitive performance using a range of subtests.

Of the functional problems, depression in elderly people has been the area where most work has been done on assessment. A great many scales measuring morale, life satisfaction and well-being have been developed. Many of the items have been drawn from the same pool and there is considerable overlap (Woods and Britton 1985). Woods and Britton recommend two measures as being particularly useful in monitoring depression in elderly people. These are Bigot's Life Satisfaction Index (Bigot 1974) and a depression scale (Schwab et al. 1973). Gilleard et al. (1981) document the validity of these scales within an elderly population.

Reliability estimates of the Beck Depression Inventory (BDI) with people over 60 years of age have been found to be sufficient to indicate that the BDI is a potentially useful clinical screening instrument with this population (Gallagher and Thompson 1982). However, it has been suggested that the response gradations in the BDI (for example, never, sometimes, usually, always) are confusing to many older patients. Some clinicians prefer to use the shorter Geriatric Depression Scale (Brink et al. 1982). This thirty-item scale, requiring a 'Yes/No' response, has been found to distinguish between depressed aged and control groups and correlates highly with other better known scales.

It has been suggested that the pattern of responses to self-report measures with elderly people can be distorted by the overlap between depressive symptomatology and changes associated with the ageing process, for example alterations in sleep, appetite, physical health and vigour (Gilleard *et al*. 1981). It has been argued that older people produce a differential pattern of response to depression questionnaires, with preferential responses to somatic, physiological symptoms (Zemore and Eames 1979). The Hamilton Rating Scale is especially thorough in assessing somatic aspects of depression (Williams 1984), and might therefore lead to an overrating of the level of depression in an elderly individual.

Development and maintenance of problems

As we have already seen, the transition from the middle years to old age, generally marked by retirement from full-time occupation, brings many changes. In general, retired people seem to adapt to the changes in role and to tolerate the negative aspects that may be associated with the retired status in our society in much the same way as they probably adapted to previous life changes. After all, retired people are 'survivors' in an important sense – they have survived all sorts of social changes, milestones and crisis points earlier in their lives (Kimmel 1980).

Research shows that the majority of elderly people adjust satisfactorily to old age (Woods and Britton 1985). Having adapted to the new life style and routines, the ageing person can reasonably expect a period of relatively active and productive life. Changes in the locomotor, cardiovascular and respiratory systems may begin to impose restrictions on activity, but unless these occur simultaneously, a reasonable level of functioning can be maintained (Britton 1983).

However, limited by economic, social and health problems, some elderly people may find themselves leading a relatively passive and sterile existence, which is a fertile ground for cognitive distortions. They are likely to have greatly increased leisure time but fewer social contacts and perhaps reduced energy for activities which might stimulate or distract them. Elderly people review past events and reflect on present ones more than younger people. When, on the whole, these thoughts and memories are pleasant they make a valuable contribution to an older person's life. However, if the thoughts are predominantly negative, their frequency increases the older person's vulnerability to depression (Yost *et al*. 1986). The approach of death and the need to review and reorder their lives provides older adults with the opportunity to brood over past mistakes in addition to present difficulties or stresses and future events.

Anxiety and depression, as well as increasing in frequency with age, seem to take a different form in older people. There is evidence that, with both disorders, elderly people experience more somatic, physiological symptoms than emotional or 'psychological' ones In their work on anxiety and elderly people, Sallis and Lichstein (1982) suggest that older individuals have diminished capacity to withstand stress and engage in more body monitoring than those in younger age groups. This 'heightened vigilance' leads to greater awareness of physical symptoms which results in psychological distress and a reaction which can be viewed as a symptom phobia. Although somatic manifestations of anxiety may become more pronounced with age, cognitive symptoms are more stable across the age range. The close association between life events and stress has repeatedly been documented. In view of Sallis and Lichstein's findings and Church's suggestion that elderly people have a reduced capacity for dealing with change, it is hardly surprising that anxiety is a common problem.

Depression in elderly patients is one of the health problems most frequently missed by general practitioners (Kline 1976; Williamson *et al.* 1964). In older people the typical depressive symptomatology overlaps with changes associated with the normal ageing process, for example, alterations in sleep, appetite and physical health. It can be tempting mistakenly to accept such symptoms as an avoidable part of ageing. It is well known that elderly people may visit their GP complaining of non-specific physical symptoms such as weight loss and lack of energy which mask an underlying depression. Some elderly patients may have a well defined physical symptom, most commonly pain, and deny, sometimes aggressively, any symptoms of depression (Evans 1986). It is likely that depression in many elderly people goes unrecognized and therefore untreated.

This unusual presentation of affective disorders in elderly people may be at least partially accounted for by the particular cohort attitudes towards emotional well-being and mental health that often characterize those whose ideas were formed five, six or seven decades ago. While society has become more psychologically minded, contemporary elderly people may continue to hold some suspicions or doubts regarding the value of psychological concepts. They may be reluctant to interpret their problems in a psychological way or seek help from mental-health specialists. They may also be uncomfortable with, or insensitive to, discussions about causal relationships between emotional well-being and physical status (Yost *et al.* 1986).

Those brought up in Britain during and between the world wars were subjected to considerable social pressure to maintain a 'stiff upper lip', which is likely to make them wary of people who express strong emotions and reluctant to express their own. Grief in particular can be seen as a weakness accompanied by the fear that a failure to maintain rigid self-control will lead to a 'breakdown' (Parkes 1985).

As well as tending not to interpret their difficulties in a psychological way, older people may be reluctant to accept the offer of therapy, particularly in a group setting. In general they have been brought up to be independent, to solve their own problems without outside help and to avoid 'washing dirty linen in public'. Beliefs such as 'I should be able to sort out my own problems. It's weak to ask for help' and 'I've never talked about my feelings. I can't do it' may make the admission of their difficulties almost impossible (Yost *et al.* 1986). Elderly people are certainly not immune to society's myths and stereotypes about old age. The chances of establishing an atmosphere of therapeutic optimism in therapy is not likely to be increased by sayings, often upheld by elderly people themselves, like 'you can't teach an old dog new tricks', leading perhaps to the destructive cognition 'I'm too old to change'.

TREATMENT/INTERVENTION

Introduction

If there is a paucity of published literature on theoretical considerations in the application of cognitive-behavioural approaches with elderly people, this is even more true of empirical studies of treatment interventions. Consequently, this section will largely concentrate on the special considerations of using these approaches with older people, highlighting where interventions with this client group differ from those with younger adults.

Behaviour-therapy techniques that have been found useful with younger populations seem effective with elderly people, at least in those areas in which applications have been reported. Unfortunately, many of these studies are poorly designed and research results can confound 'the elderly' with 'the chronically institutionalized patient' (Richards and Thorpe 1978). The majority of applications seem to have been inspired by the model of loss, debility and decline in later life, rather than by an optimistic viewpoint which would generate attempts to foster growth and development.

One of the obvious differences between working with older people and younger client groups is the likely age gap, sometimes that of grandparent and grandchild, between client and therapist. As well as influencing the therapeutic relationship, this gap can also make it more difficult to determine appropriate therapeutic goals. It is certainly not easy for a younger therapist (with 50 or more years of life yet to come) always to appreciate what goals might be important for someone who has perhaps 5 or 10 years of life left to them (Church 1983). Herr and Weakland (1979) recommend that when working with elderly people and their families the therapist must be willing to limit his or her goals appropriately so that the intervention can be effective and helpful. Therapeutic efforts need to be directed at helping clients deal more effectively with the problems which confront them rather than towards long-term personality change. Doing so may make the consequences of any pathology that exists less troublesome. The temptation to attempt to change a client's personality or values instead of helping him or her change the situation should be resisted.

Some situations in human existence have no really satisfactory solution. These situations are more likely to occur in an older person's life, for example death, divorce, pain, disease and irreversible material and social loss. The therapist's role with elders and their families may have the limited goal of helping a family avoid making an unhappy, painful situation worse, or helping them to choose the least unsatisfactory of a number of unsatisfactory options (Herr and Weakland ibid.).

It can be tempting for those who have little contact with older people to view them as a homogeneous client group. This is certainly a mistake. Steuer and Hammen (1983) note that elderly people differ more from another than do other age groups. They suggest that in a typical psychotherapy group with members of mixed ages, individual differences in health, memory, capacity for abstract reasoning and educational level are commonly expected to be fairly small but this may not be true for groups of elderly people. Steuer and Hammen see cognitive-behavioural approaches as having particular advantages in working with older people in that they (a) focus on current concerns and on skill building, (b) counter inactivity, social withdrawal and apathy and (c) challenge negative beliefs about ageing.

Chaisson-Stewart (1985) comments on a number of characteristics of cognitive-behavioural approaches which would suggest that they are particularly relevant for older people. They are generally:

- accepting and non-stigmatizing;
- structured;
- time limited;
- goal orientated;
- suitable and effective as a group approach;
- can be taught to non-mental-health specialists and to the client;
- have demonstrated effectiveness.

There is, however, some evidence that, in spite of their advantages, these approaches may need to be modified when used with elderly people. Church and Bennett (1982) ran into difficulties when using cognitive-behaviour therapy with a group of elderly people attending a day hospital. They found a problem in applying some of the more abstract techniques such as dysfunctional thought sheets (Beck *et al.* 1979). The focus had to be on practical, concrete events brought into the session and discussed. It seemed to the therapists that their elderly clients found it difficult to understand how using the sheets to record dysfunctional thoughts could benefit them. Through discussion of real events, clients were better able to appreciate the arbitrary nature of their interpretations, develop more realistic ones and begin to make changes in behaviour outside the sessions.

Behavioural techniques used with older adults have included modelling and shaping of behaviour, various reinforcement and extinction schedules and desensitization and relaxation programmes (Cautela and Mansfield 1977; Stern *et al.* 1984; Storandt 1983). A number of studies have demonstrated how minor environmental changes in institutions, such as altering seating arrangements, providing recreational materials and reorganizing ward routines, can have quite profound effects on behaviour, for example increasing levels of communication and purposeful activity in elderly patients (Jenkins *et al.* 1977; Melin and Gotestam 1981). Behavioural interventions have also been found to be successful in increasing mobility, reinstating self-feeding, promoting continence and treating chronic pain (Richards and Thorpe 1978).

It seems that when planning behavioural interventions, there are also particular considerations to be taken into account when working with older adults. Storandt (1983) points out that many behavioural techniques are based on research with younger people and more work is necessary to determine whether or not there are significant learning differences between older and younger people which might affect their use. For example, in classical conditioning it has been established that more pairings of the unconditioned and conditioned stimuli are needed to produce conditioned responses in older adults. Cautela and Mansfield (1977) report that more sessions per item may be necessary in the desensitization hierarchy and modifications may be required either with increasing reliance on *in vivo* desensitization or with imagined scenes being broken down into smaller parts. The acquisition of operant responses also appears to be slower in older adults, but more difficult to extinguish (Storandt 1983). However, Schonfield (1980) points out that older adults as a group show great variability in their learning rates. Some appear to be very difficult to condition while others differ very little from younger adults.

There have been attempts by behaviour therapists to counteract the previously identified tendency to work to a model of debility and decline in old age. Flemming *et al.* (1983) describe the application of an approach to changing behaviour of elderly people which concentrates on the adaptive behaviours in the patient's repertoire, in contrast to the usual tendency to look only at the problems or deficiencies. This 'constructional' approach places great emphasis on increasing the client's behaviour or range of behaviours. The underlying assumption is that the behaviour identified as a problem can be developed and used to help the individual reach a specified objective. For example, in the case of an elderly person described as a 'wanderer', the goal of treatment using the constructional approach would not be to ensure that the individual spent more time in one place. Rather, his or her mobility and energy would be directed towards more purposeful activity, such as helping carers with domestic tasks or going on an accompanied walk.

Another recent positive development in work with elderly people has been the application of individual programme planning with this client group (Barrowclough and Flemming 1985). Work with other disabled people has drawn attention to the value of identifying needs, not only in terms of skill deficits but also in terms of opportunities or provisions required to improve quality of life. At the same time, clients' strengths are highlighted and are used as the basis from which to develop new skills or compensate for losses.

Loss and grieving

We have already seen how central the issues of loss and grieving are in the lives of many older people. Friends and relatives die; diminishing mobility can make it difficult to maintain contact with those who remain; jobs and the colleagues associated with them are lost; sight, hearing and other physical functions diminish. Indeed, it is remarkable that many older people do seem to maintain a contented existence despite such major changes in their lives.

The loss which has received most attention in therapeutic interventions with any age group is the psychological reaction to bereavement following the death of a significant other. These approaches, however, apply equally to other losses (Parkes 1972, 1980, 1985). For elderly people it seems that there are additional difficulties when faced with a bereavement.

William Worden (1982) has presented a task-orientated approach to understanding the process of adapting to loss. This framework can help the cognitive-behavioural therapist identify the most appropriate intervention when treating a client with an abnormal reaction to bereavement.

Task 1: To accept the reality of the loss Completion of this first task is particularly difficult for elderly people with severe memory defects who may not be able to remember that their loved one has indeed died. This impedes their ability to move on to tackle later tasks.

Task 2: To experience the pain of grief It is recognized that some western societies are uncomfortable with the mourner's feelings and may communicate the subtle message 'You don't need to grieve'. This may be compounded in elderly people by an upbringing which emphasized the need to 'maintain a stiff upper lip' in the face of loss. If grief is seen as a weakness it is likely to inhibit the experience of pain.

Task 3: To adjust to an environment in which the deceased is missing Following the loss of a partner, the bereaved person is likely to have to come to terms with living alone, making decisions without support and learning to relate socially as a single person. As well as losing the emotional and social roles played by a partner, many survivors have to develop new practical skills and to take on new roles themselves. Adapting to new roles and responsibilities presupposes that new roles and responsibilities are in fact available. To many elderly bereaved people this must seem doubtful. No longer an employee, children and grand-children living at a distance and a diminishing number of friends, most of an elderly person's significant roles involved a partner who is no longer there.

Task 4: To withdraw emotional energy and reinvest it in another relationship For elderly people, establishing a new relationship can be particularly difficult. Their opportunities for social contact, already reduced by retirement from work and perhaps restricted physical mobility and limited income, will be likely to be further hampered following the loss of a social companion. For widows in particular, the chances of re-establishing an emotional or sexual relationship with a member of the opposite sex is reduced simply by the much larger proportion of women in the older age group.

The majority of bereaved people work through the process of grieving, often supported by family and friends, without recourse to professional help. Mourning generally takes much longer than anyone expects. It may be 2 years or more before the bereaved person is able to think about the one who has died without pain, (although there may always be a sense of sadness), and reinvest his or her emotions back into life and into the living.

In their cognitive-behavioural analysis of grief, Gauthier and Marshall (1977) speculate that two factors could be involved in unreasonably protracted or excessive grief. First, the social reinforcement of grief behaviours by family and friends in the form of solicitousness and sympathy; and second, the conspiracy of silence, in which the bereaved is carefully protected from all reminders of the person who has died. This second factor could result in the 'cognitive incubation' of grief responses. Although not specifically directed at grief reactions in older adults these two factors would seem to have particular relevance for elderly people.

For those who experience abnormal grief reactions, a number of behavioural and cognitive techniques have been found to be useful. Certain thoughts are common in the early stages of grieving but usually disappear over time. Sometimes, however, these thoughts persist and trigger feelings that can lead to depression or anxiety. For example, most guilt experienced by a bereaved person is irrational and leads to statements such as 'I didn't do enough'. Reality testing may help the bereaved person to see that their reaction is based on interpretation rather than facts. The aim of this technique is to seek, with the client's help, evidence for and against the negative thoughts and assumptions (Williams 1984; Worden 1982).

Gauthier and Marshall (1977) taught the close companions of their patients to restructure their responses to the person's grieving behaviour, being relatively non-sympathetic to grief-related depression and giving attention to other behaviours. The patients also received flooding sessions in which they were asked to confront, as vividly as possible, imagery relating to the deceased. The authors reported marked success in only half a dozen treatment sessions.

A question which arises in grief therapy with older adults is whether it is ever inappropriate to set out to encourage someone to face the tasks of grieving? Many elderly people have many years of life to look forward to. If their way of coping with a bereavement is only prolonging their misery and the misery of those around them then it is clearly beneficial to help them undertake the tasks of grieving which have been avoided. But some forgetful old people live out their lives in, apparently, blissful ignorance that their partner has died. Some succeed in avoiding reminders of their lost spouse and Parkes (1985) suggests that to confront them with an album of photographs would be an act of cruelty. An example from my own clinical practice will help to illustrate this point. Mrs S, a very elderly widow, was a permanent resident on a geriatric continuing-care ward. She had been diagnosed as having Alzheimer's disease and had substantial memory problems. When talking to me about her husband she mentioned that he was with her every night when she went to bed. She went on to add that she no longer spoke to the nursing staff about this as they couldn't see him, and would insist on telling her that he was dead! The principle of colluding with the confused reality of elderly people has long been discredited (Holden and Woods 1982) but it seems that Parkes (1985) has a point when he suggests that we have no right to interfere with ways of coping that are helping elderly individuals get through a chapter of their lives that might otherwise be miserable. Through discussions with the ward staff it was agreed that we would respect Mrs S's way of coping with her loss. From then on, rather than correcting her when she spoke about seeing her husband, staff would talk to her in general terms about her past and her family. She died about 5 months later.

Interventions with depressed elderly people

Most published work looking at psychotherapeutic approaches with older clients has addressed the needs of depressed older people. In younger age groups the prognosis of affective disorders is relatively good. However, in old age, depressive illness is often characterized by frequent and prolonged relapses. Murphy (1983), in her study of 124 elderly people suffering a first episode of depression, found that only just over a third had made a good recovery at 1-year follow-up. Treatments employed included anti-depressant medication, electro-convulsive therapy (ECT) and social support via day hospital and out-patient facilities. An earlier study by Post (1972) found that of ninety-two elderly in-patients followed up 3 years later, only 26 per cent had made a sustained recovery. Although it can be argued that outcome studies of in-patient populations may tend to over-select the more severe cases, with mild depressions being effectively treated by GPs, the results are still not encouraging. They must reflect, in part at least, the degree to which traditional treatments are effective (Hanley and Baikie 1984).

In a more recent study, ninety-one elderly people with a major depressive disorder were treated for between sixteen and twenty sessions with behavioural, cognitive or brief psychodynamic psychotherapy (Thompson *et al.* 1987). Prior to treatment twenty subjects were assigned to a 6-week delayed treatment control condition. Overall, 70 per cent of the patients responded well to psychotherapy in that they either achieved remission of their depression (52 per cent) or improved substantially (18 per cent) by the end of treatment. There were no significant differences by treatment modality. These results compare favourably with improvement and failure rates reported with other forms of therapy used with both young and elderly patients. Results from the delayed-treatment controls indicated very little evidence of spontaneous remission. Although the delay was only 6 weeks, treated patients improved significantly over time on all measures used, while the delayed-treatment patients did not. A 1-year follow-up found no significant differences in rates of relapse between the treatment groups (Thompson *et al.* 1988).

Although it is encouraging to see research looking specifically at therapeutic interventions with older clients, one of the criteria for acceptance into this study was being 60 years of age at intake, making the mean age of subjects 67.07 years. It is unclear whether these findings would be replicated with 'older' elderly people. The lack of difference between types of treatment agrees with the non-specific improvements effects in depression found with younger patients (Zeiss *et al.* 1979).

Many elderly people who come into contact with health services have lost some measure of control over their lives. Hanley and Baikie (1984) see a cognitive-behavioural approach to depression as encouraging the elderly patient to exercise control, take over responsibility for action and develop more realistic interpretations of events. With the emphasis on action, helplessness is challenged, and, through the discussion of events, attribution patterns and negative cognitive set may be changed.

Any attempt to evaluate the effectiveness of psychological interventions with elderly depressed people is hampered by the shortage of substantial trials comparing the outcomes of different treatment approaches. In younger depressed patients a combined medical and psychological approach (cognitive therapy) has been found superior to either one alone (Blackburn et al. 1981). It may well be that the either/or dichotomy will turn out to be no more appropriate for elderly people. In many cases a psychological component will form part of a multilevel approach to therapy, incorporating physical treatments and social support (Hanley 1988).

Group interventions

Chaisson-Stewart (1985) suggests that using cognitive-behavioural therapy in a group setting with elderly people has the added benefit of counteracting loneliness and social isolation, building confidence, showing that others of the same age also have problems and providing the opportunity to give to others. Garland (1982) used a problem-solving approach with small groups of elderly people attending a psychogeriatric day hospital. He took into account what Emery (1981) describes as 'treatment socialization', bearing in mind that this client group may have little experience of, and a lot of misconceptions about, 'therapy'. Garland used an educational model of therapy as a systematic way to teach more effective strategies for coping with ageing. A high percentage of problems raised in the group were eventually solved and group members were able to develop some skills as problem solvers. Individual homework was an integral part of this intervention .

Goodall and Moffat (1988) have recently reported on the evolution of a group intervention using cognitive-behavioural techniques. Membership was offered to any older person, regardless of diagnosis, who was able to work at their problem by working with their thoughts. The groups included individuals described as depressed, anxious, bereaved or having personality problems. They met twice a week for a total of sixteen 2-hour sessions. They found that it was difficult for some people to understand the relationship between action, thought and feeling, and it was necessary to use several examples to help group members with this. On this point, Yost et al. (1986) suggest the use of a three-stage procedure, namely:

1 give an age-appropriate example;
2 give a partially completed second example and encourage the group to complete it;
3 encourage the group to give examples.

Goodall and Moffat made regular use of behavioural tasks, particularly in encouraging individuals to test out assumptions resulting from errors in thinking and in putting into practice more helpful thoughts. Following the more intensive sixteen sessions, the groups continued to meet on a monthly basis for 6 months. Using the Geriatric Depression Scale (Brink et al. 1982) and the State–Trait Anxiety Inventory (Spielberger 1983) they found some evidence for the effectiveness of the group in reducing depression, but less support in its effectiveness in helping to reduce anxiety. Without a comparison group and with considerable amounts of incomplete data, they admit that any conclusions must be tentative.

The experience of Goodall and Moffat support the findings of Gallagher and Thompson (1982) that, in general, the people who benefited most from a cognitive-behavioural approach were well educated and verbally competent.

Reminiscence

Another essentially cognitive approach is life review or reminiscence. Reminiscing is an experience distinguishable from the memory of less personal information by the fact that it involves the process of reliving the past rather than the factual recall of historical events (Norris 1986). At one time thinking about the past was regarded as positively unhealthy for elderly people but over the past 20 years this view has changed and reminiscence has become increasingly popular as a general therapeutic approach with older adults. Coleman (1986) distinguishes between 'life review' reminiscence as described by Butler (1963) and 'informative' or 'teaching' reminiscence which is used to transmit the culture's stories and traditions.

It does seem that there are considerable individual differences in attitudes towards reminiscence and its value in their lives by older people themselves. Some elderly people regard their memories as their most treasured possession while, for others, the past is unimportant. Anyone considering using reminiscence as a means of therapy should therefore try to understand from the elderly person's perspective his or her life history and circumstances (Coleman 1986).

Norris (1986) cites a number of ways in which reminiscing can help an elderly person adapt to or come to terms with growing older:

1 It can serve as a means of highlighting the assets of older people rather than their disabilities. As past events are generally the best remembered by those who may have short-term-memory difficulties, reminiscing can help to maintain self-esteem by focusing on something which they are still able to do.
2 It can enhance feelings of self-worth by providing an opportunity for older people to share the wisdom and experience they have accumulated through their lives with others.
3 It can help the elderly person retain a sense of individual identity and aid in conveying this to others.
4 It can aid the life-review process.
5 It can be an enjoyable and stimulating experience both for older persons themselves and for the 'youngsters' who have the opportunity to listen.

Although most of the evidence on the effectiveness of Reminiscence Therapy is anecdotal rather than quantitative, (Norris and Abul El Eileh 1982), it is consistently positive. Hanley and Baikie (1984) suggest that it could be of benefit to elderly people suffering from depression. In this regard it has been proposed that the projection of negative thinking into the past can be countered by simply changing the focus of attention and seeing that there were positive things as well as negative. Coleman, however, holds that it would be naive to think that all problems arising from unhappy memories of a past life could be solved through cognitive-therapy techniques such as 'disattribution' or the rational disputation of thoughts. For instance, a person's sense of guilt may be well founded and the wrong has to be accepted, not disputed.

Interventions with elderly people suffering from dementia

The term 'dementia' has been used in many different ways by many different people. Hanley (1988) offers the following as a rough definition: 'the term applied to a diffuse deterioration in the mental functions resulting in most cases from an organic disease of the brain and manifesting itself primarily in thought and memory and secondarily in feeling and conduct' (p. 2). From a psychological perspective, the fundamental change in a dementia sufferer is in learning ability. The person no longer finds it easy to retain new information which leads to difficulty with later recall. Although the dementia sufferer may present with a memory problem, in fact it is faulty learning which is primarily responsible. The progressive nature of these diseases and the learning impairments which are associated with them limit the range of interventions thought to be appropriate with this client group.

Reality Orientation (RO) is an approach to the management of people with dementia which originated in the United States in the 1960s (Holden and Woods 1982). It seeks to create an environment, both physical and social, which enables an elderly person with memory problems to function in all spheres to the limits of his or her abilities. RO has attracted a great deal of criticism, much of it well founded (Powell-Procter and Miller 1982), and its poor theoretical foundations have limited the development of the technique. However, RO has had some positive outcomes in an area of work which was previously beset by therapeutic nihilism. For instance, it has now been established that some people with dementia show significant relearning in verbal orientation following structured retraining (for example, Citrin and Dixon 1977; Harris and Ivory 1976; Woods 1979). Hanley (1981) demonstrated that the use of memory aids (pictoral and lettered signs) in the physical environment can improve spatial orientation if elderly residents are trained to make use of them. He also found that following the end of training, ward orientation was maintained.

Much of the criticism directed at the approach has centred on the relevance and appropriateness of RO to the individual needs of elderly people with dementia. Hanley's recent work on individualized RO shows clearly that if targets for change are carefully selected, then RO methods can make a valuable clinical contribution to an individual's quality of life (Hanley 1988b).

The mechanisms by which RO produces significant behaviour change, over and above the general improvements produced through increased stimulation and attention, are not well understood. However, from a behavioural perspective it has been suggested that:

1 Repeated exposure to success begins to combat the learned helplessness of elderly people with dementia and assists them to function at a level more in keeping with their full potential.
2 Modifications to the physical and social environment increase the frequency of orientated behaviour which is then socially reinforced by staff members.

Interventions with carers

Although this chapter is concerned with the application of cognitive-behavioural approaches with elderly people themselves, it is worth at least touching on the contribution these approaches can make to the well-being of unpaid carers. Family and friends play a central role in supporting frail elderly people at home and their mental health will have a considerable impact on those for whom they care.

The responsibility for caring for an elderly dependent person usually falls to the nearest female relative (Equal Opportunities Commission 1980) and often begins as a short-term solution to a particular problem – bereavement, illness or convalescence. That temporary solution may then become permanent, at a time when other responsibilities (for example, child care) are diminishing and the female carer is anticipating relative independence. Caring that was undertaken willingly at a time of crisis can become a seemingly unending response to demands which become greater over the years.

In spite of the amount of information available about the high levels of stress this caring role engenders there are few evaluated studies of cognitive-behavioural interventions with informal carers. Although the burden of caring can be eased by the provision of practical support such as day-care, regular breaks for 'holiday relief' and, for the lucky few, an occasional night sitter (Sanford 1975), many of the carer's circumstances may not be easily changed. However, it has been suggested that the way in which the carers think about, and respond to, their situation may contribute to their experience of stress or depression (Collins 1983).

As part of an experimental support service for carers of confused elderly people in their own homes, Collins (ibid.), produced a set of training materials aimed at teaching carers behavioural techniques. Two of the eight training topics related to carers' own emotions. The first, entitled 'Talk sense to yourself', was based on the ABC exercise of identifying the situation (A), thought (B) and resulting feeling (C). The aim was to train carers in positive rather than negative self-instruction by which they could regain control of their own emotions. The second was a short course of three, linked, relaxation exercises. In a questionnaire assessing the value of the material to the carers, these two modules were rated more highly than the information on managing an elderly person's behaviour.

Since the well-being of the informal carer has such an impact on their dependent elderly person, another valuable area of investigation is the extent to which therapeutic intervention with elderly people affects those who support them. A study by Greene et al. (1983) found an improvement in the mood of relatives at home following the elderly person's inclusion in RO sessions at a day hospital.

Therapist cognitions

As we have seen, loss, degeneration and death are issues of particular relevance to elderly people. Particularly when working with depressed individuals, treatment sessions are likely to focus on unhappy events and upsetting emotions. In the course of a group intervention, a member may receive diagnosis of a terminal illness, be admitted to hospital on a permanent basis or even die. Therapists may find that they experience negative cognitions concerning the relevance of psychotherapy when clients' medical problems are so overwhelming. They may also find themselves thinking that some day they too could be in the same position; old, sick, poor and depressed.

Yost *et al.* (1986) highlight the need for therapists to monitor their own cognitions about their clients and about ageing more generally. Once recognized, they can then be challenged and substituted with more rational alternatives, as in Table 8.1.

Table 8.1   Therapist cognitions of ageing

A Situation	B Belief	C Feeling
Medical problems in client.	You have to be young and healthy to enjoy life. Therapy won't help her.	Frightened, useless.

Disputes:
1 Are there no exceptions to this belief? I know quite a few older people in poor health who are still happy.
2 Being young and healthy certainly isn't a guarantee that I'll enjoy life.
3 Psychotherapy won't make her medical problems go away but if it makes them easier to bear then it is certainly worthwhile.

Various writers have recommended that therapists should not work full time with depressed elderly people and should consult regularly with colleagues or supervisors, whose objectivity allows them to recognize therapist burnout and evaluate client progress.

FUTURE DEVELOPMENTS

Perhaps the first question to ask is – should working with elderly people be seen as a speciality? Does this encourage us to continue viewing older people as in some way different from younger adults, therefore maintaining an element of ageism?

In an ideal world it would seem sensible that all adults, whatever their age, intellectual or physical disabilities, would have equal access to the same expertise and services. Therapists working in the field of adult mental health would acquire the background knowledge and be trained in the relevant skills to work with elderly people. Certainly, in some areas this may be the case. More commonly, however, those working with adult populations can seem reluctant to take on older clients and they are often excluded on the basis of age from general mental-health facilities. Unless people are assessed according to need rather than chronological age this practice is unlikely to change. In reality, where consumers compete for limited services and where it is still frequently believed that therapeutic optimism is misplaced, older people lose out in terms of easy access to trained and skilled staff.

Garland (1988) argues that there are a number of distinctive features about the specialty of working with elderly people and their carers:

- the practioner's need for a grounding in gerontology;
- the universality of ageing;
- predominance of concern with death and preparation for death;
- selectivity in age-related settings and in liaison with age-specialized colleagues and organizations;
- characteristic aspects of family dynamics.

Garland warns that to stress differences is to weaken our contact with the mainstream of psychology and to increase the morale-sapping feelings of professional isolation. It seems, however, that in the immediate future at least, there will be a continual need to provide specialist services for elderly people, not only to develop and implement appropriate approaches but also to fight for their rights in the battle for scarce resources.

In part, the development of cognitive-behavioural approaches to elderly people will follow on from progress made in the understanding of psychological problems in younger adults. Empirical research about the role cognitions play in the development and maintenance of psychological difficulties and how interventions based on the findings can be applied therapeutically will gradually be disseminated. One aspect of the role of the clinician working with elderly people is to combine these research findings with their knowledge and understanding of gerontology and devise approaches which are acceptable to, and effective with, older clients. Setting out to write a chapter of this sort has highlighted how much of the available literature on psychotherapeutic approaches with elderly people is anecdotal in nature. What is needed then is the publication of more controlled, empirical studies demonstrating the effectiveness of these techniques to an older age group. The inclusion in the literature of more single case-studies would also serve to illustrate the variety of problems and range of approaches which psychologists use in their work with older clients.

Many of the future developments discussed elsewhere in this book are likely to be equally relevant to work with older people. There are, however, a number of issues which do seem to be of particular importance when looking at psychological approaches with this client group.

A problem, for the researcher as much as the clinician, is the effect of cohort factors. As we have already seen, the fast rate of change in all areas of life, not least in terms of expectations, raises the question of applicability of research findings to subsequent generations of elderly people. With signs of increasing longevity this problem is likely to become more pronounced in the future.

Over the last few years there has been a gradual but significant change in the role of many of the caring professions working with elderly people. This change has involved a move away from custodial care towards a more interventionist approach. In spite of the change in emphasis 'from keeping people alive to ensuring that the quality of life is maintained into old age' (Britton 1983: 171), it is of some concern that so many of the published studies, particularly those describing behavioural interventions, are directed at meeting the needs of the service providers rather than those of elderly people themselves. Clearly these types of interventions are unlikely to be directed primarily at improving the quality of life of service users. It seems that, all too often, services for elderly people fail to use assessment procedures which identify what the clients (or their advocates) need from the service. Then the real challenge comes in attempting to develop services which have the flexibility and resources to meet the identified needs of individuals.

Older patients do not always gain access to the services which are available. We live in an ageist society where elderly people are at risk of being seen as less valuable than younger adults. Not only are they generally no longer economically productive, they are also likely to be seen as having less influence as consumers due to reduced income or largely satisfied material needs. As we have seen, many elderly people are likely to have little understanding or experience of therapy. They are less likely than younger adults to view their difficulties from an emotional or psychological perspective. In addition, some older adults may have stereotypical beliefs about what can, and cannot, be accomplished in old age. This suggests, then, that elderly people are less inclined to see their problems as being psychologically based and therefore to seek help themselves from mental-health services. Even if help is sought from a General Practitioner, his or her response may well be affected by society's commonly held beliefs concerning the effects of ageing, which, combined with an awareness of limited resources, may reduce the chance of a referral to a psychotherapist.

With the increasing awareness in western industrial societies of the psychological factors influencing human behaviour, it can be predicted that future generations of elderly people will be more psychologically orientated than our present ones. We need to ensure that the general public, as well as the helping professions, receive accurate information about the reality of ageing.

Assuming that an elderly person's GP does think that a referral to the mental-health services is appropriate, this does not always guarantee that specialist help will be available. Many studies point to antipathy towards elderly people by professional groups (Geiger 1978; Liddell and Boyle 1980). It seems that therapeutically skilled individuals, from whatever professional background, are reluctant to specialize in working with elderly people. This means older adults could lose out in the competition with younger people for scarce psychotherapeutic resources. Traditional specialist day provisions for elderly people are more likely to provide social stimulation and recreational activities than the opportunity for individual or group psychotherapy. Future generations of elderly people may well prove to be more demanding consumers of health care than their predecessors have been. Expanding the use of citizen advocates, as is being done in services for people with learning difficulties, could help to provide a voice for those elderly people who are no longer able to speak out for themselves (Sang and O'Brien 1984).

Like many professions in the mental-health field, clinical psychology has been slow to apply its expertise to the needs of elderly people. The 1970s saw a move into the application to elderly people of a wide variety of psychological treatment techniques which have been found to be as relevant to this age group as to many others (Britton 1983). However, in spite of the greater lack of acceptance of the common myth of inevitable deterioration, the prospect of working with elderly people does not seem at all appealing to many new members of the profession (Liddell and Boyle 1980). This may go some way to explaining why relatively little work has been carried out in the UK on the effectiveness of therapeutic approaches with elderly people.

Clearly, one of the first places to tackle a shortage of clinical psychologists working with older people is during training. This means being able to provide high calibre supervisors who are able to demonstrate to trainees the scope and challenge of work in this area. The argument then becomes a circular one – to employ more psychologists to work with elderly people it is necessary to offer good experiences during training. In order to offer good experiences during training it is necessary to employ more psychologists! Slow but steady progress is being made in this area.

However, even if all health districts were able to provide the recommended minimum level of psychology service for elderly people (Bradbury 1989; Twinning 1986), in view of the time-consuming nature of individual therapy and the growing numbers of potential clients, it is unlikely that demand could ever be satisfied. Jeffrey and Saxby (1984) suggest that the ultimate challenge for psychologists is to develop 'a clearly defined systematic approach to the care of the elderly which concerns itself with organisation, teams, social systems, communities and the effective use of resources' (p. 261). It is almost certain, however, that some elderly people and their families will always need to be seen as individuals and offered skilled assessment and treatment. Having seen the appropriateness of cognitive-behavioural approaches with elderly people, it may be that the most effective way forward for the clinical psychologist is initially to demonstrate the effectiveness of this treatment approach. The next task may be to disseminate skills and knowledge as widely as possible to other care givers. Due to the complexity of many problems presented by older clients, there is often a tradition of multiprofessional co-operation. Goodall and Moffat (1988) worked as co-therapists with social workers in their study. Nursing and residential care staff are the primary agents in the use of Reality Orientation and Reminiscence Therapy and trained and supported voluntary counsellors already work extensively with bereaved older people.

In conclusion, a number of psychological approaches based on cognitive-behavioural theory and techniques are being made available to elderly people. Increasingly, evaluations of these approaches are appearing in the literature. Provided certain factors relating to cognitive changes in older adults and elderly persons' position in their life cycle are taken into account, there is no reason to believe that cognitive-behaviour therapy is not a suitable approach for use with older clients. In fact certain characteristics of this therapy suggest that it is particularly suitable for elderly people. The results so far are generally encouraging.

REFERENCES

Baltes, P. B. (1968) 'Longitudinal and cross-sectional sequences in the study of age and generational effects', *Human Development* 11: 145–71.

Barrowclough, C., and Flemming, I. (1985) *Goal Planning with Elderly People*, Manchester: Manchester University Press.

Beck, A. T., Rush, A. J., Shaw, B. F. and Emery, G. (1979) *Cognitive Therapy of Depression*, New York: Guilford Press.

Bergmann, K., Britton, P. G., Hall, E. H. and Blessed, G. (1981) 'The relationship of ageing, physical health, brain damage and affective disorder', in W. M. Beattie (ed.) *Ageing: A Challenge to Science and Society 2*, Oxford: Oxford University Press.

Bigot, A. (1974) 'The relevance of American Life Satisfaction Indices for research on British subjects before and after retirement', *Age and Ageing* 3: 113–21.

Blackburn, I. M., Bishop, S., Glen, A. J. M., Whalley, L. J. and Christie, J. E. (1981) 'The efficacy of cognitive therapy in depression', *British Journal of Psychiatry* 139: 181–9.

Bradbury, N. M. (1989) 'Guidelines for clinical psychology services', *Clinical Psychology Forum* 21: 17–18.

Brink, T. L., Yesavage, J. A., Lum, O., Heersem, P. H., Adey, M. and Rose, T. L. (1982) 'Screening tests for geriatric depression', *Clinical Gerontologist* 1: 37–43.

Britton, P. G. (1983) 'Psychological services for the elderly', in A. Liddell (ed.) *The Practice of Clinical Psychology in Great Britain*, Chichester: John Wiley.

Butler, R. N. (1963) 'The life review: an interpretation of reminiscence in the aged', *Psychiatry* 26: 65–76.

Cattell, R. B. (1963) 'The theory of fluid and crystalline intelligence', *Journal of Educational Psychology* 54: 1–22.

Cautela, J. R. and Mansfield, L. (1977) 'A behavioral approach to geriatrics', in W. D. Gentry (ed.) *Geropsychology: A Model of Training and Clinical Service*, Cambridge, Mass.: Ballinger.

Chaisson-Stewart, G. M. (1985) 'Depression incidence past, present and future', in G. M. Chaisson-Stewart (ed.) *Depression in the Elderly: An Interdisciplinary Approach*, New York: John Wiley.

Chamberlain, P. (1985) *Life Planning Manual*, BABP, P.O. Box 52, Southsea, Hants.

Church, M. (1983) 'Psychological therapy with elderly people', *Bulletin of the British Psychological Society* 36: 110–12.

—— (1986) 'Issues in psychological therapy with elderly people', in I. Hanley and M. Gilhooly (eds) *Psychological Therapies with the Elderly*, London: Croom Helm.

—— and Bennett, A. (1982) 'Group cognitive therapy with elderly patients recovering from depression', paper presented at the Annual Conference of the British Society of Gerontology, Exeter.

Citrin, R. and Dixon, D. (1977) 'Reality Orientation', *Gerontologist* 17: 39–43.

Coleman, P. (1986) 'Issues in the therapeutic use of reminiscence with elderly people', in

I. Hanley and M. Gilhooly (eds) *Psychological Therapies for the Elderly*, London: Croom Helm.

Collins, P. (1983) 'Caring for confused elderly: an experimental support service', unpublished Ph.D. thesis, University of Birmingham.

Davis, A. P. M., Saunders, C. and Newton, T. J. (1987) 'Age differences in the rating of life-stress events: does contextual detail make a difference?', *British Journal of Clinical Psychology* 26: 199–205.

Emery, G. (1981) 'Cognitive therapy with the elderly', in G. Emery, S. D. Hollon and R. C. Bedrosian (eds) *New Directions in Cognitive Therapy*, New York: Guilford Press.

Equal Opportunities Commission (1980) *The Experience of Caring for Elderly and Handicapped Dependents: Survey Report*, Overseas House, Quay Street, Manchester M3 3HN.

Evans, J. Grimley (1986) 'The interaction between physical and psychiatric disease in the elderly', *Update* 15 Feb.: 265–72.

Flemming, I., Barrowclough, C. and Whitmore, B. (1983) 'The constructional approach', *Nursing Mirror* 156(23): 21–3.

Gaber, L. (1983) 'Activity/disengagement revisited: personality types in the aged', *British Journal of Psychiatry* 143: 490–7.

Gallagher, D. and Thompson, L. W. (1982) 'Treatment of major depressive disorder in older adult outpatients with brief psychotherapies', *Psychotherapy: Theory, Research and Practice* 19: 482–90.

Garland, J. (1982) 'The problem-solving group in a psychiatric day centre', *PSIGE Newsletter* 6.

—— (1988) 'That is not all: some distinguishing features of psychological practice with older people', *PSIGE Newsletter* 27: 3–7.

Gauthier, J. and Marshall, W. L. (1977) 'Grief: a cognitive-behavioral analysis', *Cognitive Therapy and Research* 1: 39–44.

Geiger, D. L. (1978) 'How future professionals view the elderly: an analysis of social work, law and medical students perceptions', *Gerontologist* 18: 591.

Gibson, J. A. and Kendrick, D. C. (1979) *The Kendrick Battery for the Detection of Dementia in the Elderly*, Windsor: NFER Publishing Company.

Gibson, J. A., Moyes, I. C. A. and Kendrick, D. C. (1980) 'Cognitive assessment of the elderly long-stay patient', *British Journal of Psychiatry* 137: 551–7.

Gilleard, C. J., Willmott, M. and Vaddadi, K. S. (1981) 'Self-report measures of mood and morale in elderly depressives', *British Journal of Psychiatry* 138: 230–5.

Golding, E. (1989) *The Middlesex Elderly Assessment of Mental State*, Fareham: Thames Valley Test Company.

Goodall, A. (1988) 'Life planning', *PSIGE Newsletter* 28: 25–9.

—— and Moffat, N., (1988) 'Running a cognitive therapy group for older adults', East Dorset: unpublished manuscript.

Greene, J. G., Timbury, G. C., Smith, R. and Gardiner, M. (1983) 'Reality Orientation with elderly patients in the community: an empirical evaluation', *Age and Ageing* 12: 38–43.

Gurland, B. J. (1976) 'The comparative frequency of depression in various adult age groups', *Journal of Gerontology* 31: 283.

—— and Cross, P. S. (1982) 'Epidemiology of psychopathology in old age: some implications for clinical services', *The Psychiatric Clinics of North America* 5(1): 11–26.

Gurland, B. J., Copeland, J., Kuriansky, J., Kelleher, M., Sharpe, L. and Dean, L. L. (1983) *The Mind and Mood of Ageing*, London: Croom Helm.

Hanley, I. (1981) 'The use of signposts and active training to modify ward disorientation in elderly patients', *Journal of Behavior Therapy and Experimental Psychiatry* 12: 241–7.

—— (1988) 'Psychological treatment of emotional disorders in the elderly', in F. N. Watts (ed.) *New Developments in Clinical Psychology*, Volume Two, Chichester: John Wiley.

—— and Baikie, E. (1984) 'Understanding and treating depression in the elderly', in

I. Hanley and J. Hodge (eds) *Psychological Approaches to the Care of the Elderly*, London: Croom Helm.

Harris, C. and Ivory, P. (1976) 'An outcome evaluation of Reality Orientation therapy with geriatric patients in a state mental hospital', *Gerontologist* 16: 496–503.

Herr, J. J. and Weakland, J. H. (1979) *Counselling Elders and Their Families*, Springer Series on Adulthood and Ageing, Vol. II, New York: Springer Publishing Company.

Hildebrand, P. (1986) 'Dynamic psychotherapy with the elderly', in I. Hanley and M. Gilhooly (eds) *Psychological Therapies for the Elderly*, London: Croom Helm.

Holden, U. P. and Woods, R. T. (1982) *Reality Orientation*, Edinburgh: Churchill Livingstone.

Jeffrey, D. and Saxby, P. (1984) 'Effective psychological care for the elderly', in I. Hanley and J. Hodge (eds) *Psychological Approaches to the Care of the Elderly*, London: Croom Helm.

Jenkins, J., Felce, D., Barry, L. and Powell, L. (1977) 'Increasing engagement in activity in Old People's Homes by providing recreational material', *Behaviour Research and Therapy* 15: 429–34.

Kay, D. W. K. and Bergman, K. (1980) 'Epidemiology of mental disorders among the aged in the community', in J. E. Birren and R. B. Sloane (eds) *Handbook of Mental Health and Ageing*, Englewood Cliffs, NJ: Prentice-Hall.

Kay, D. W. K., Beamish, P. and Roth, M. (1964) 'Old Age Disorders in Newcastle-Upon-Tyne', *British Journal of Psychiatry* 110: 146–58.

Kay, D. W. K., Bergman, K., Foster, E. M., McKechnie, A. A. and Roth, M. (1970) 'Mental illness and hospital usage in the elderly: random sample followed up', *Comprehensive Psychiatry* 110: 668–82.

Kendrick, D. C., Gibson, A. J. and Moyes, I. C. A. (1979) 'The revised Kendrick Battery: clinical studies', *British Journal of Social and Clinical Psychology* 18: 329–40.

Kimmel, C. D. (1980) *Adulthood and Aging*, 2nd Edn, New York: John Wiley.

Kline, N. (1976) 'Incidence, prevalence and recognition of depressive illness', *Diseases of the Nervous System* 37(3): 10–14.

Liddell, A. and Boyle, M. (1980) 'Characteristics of applicants to the M.Sc. in Clinical Psychology at NELP', *DCP Newsletter* 30: 20–5.

Melin, L. and Gotestam, K. G. (1981) 'The effects of rearranging ward routines on communication and eating behaviors of psychogeriatric patients', *Journal of Applied Behavior Analysis* 14: 47–51.

Murphy, E. (1982) 'Social origins of depression in old age', *British Journal of Psychiatry* 141: 135–42.

—— (1983) 'The prognosis of depression in old age', *British Journal of Psychiatry* 142: 111–19.

Neugarten, B. L., Havighurst, R. J. and Tobin, S. S. (1968) 'Personality and patterns of ageing', in B. L. Neugarten (ed.) *Middle Age and Ageing*, Chicago: Chicago University Press.

Norris, A. (1986) *Reminiscence with Elderly People*, London: Winslow Press.

—— and Abu El Eileh, M. T. (1982) 'Reminiscence groups', *Nursing Times* 78: 1368–9.

Parkes, C. Murray (1972) *Bereavement: Studies of Grief in Adult Life*, New York: International Universities Press.

—— (1980) 'Bereavement counselling: does it work?', *British Medical Journal* 281: 3–6.

—— (1985) 'Bereavement in the elderly', *Geriatric Medicine Today* 4: 5.

Pattie, A. H. and Gilleard, C. J. (1979) *Manual of the Clifton Assessment Procedures for the Elderly (CAPE)*, Sevenoaks: Hodder and Stoughton Educational.

Post, F. (1972) 'The management and nature of depressive illness in late life: a follow-through study', *British Journal of Psychiatry* 121: 393–404.

Powell-Procter, L., and Miller, E. (1982) 'Reality Orientation: a critical appraisal', *British Journal of Psychiatry* 140: 457–63.

Richards, W. S. and Thorpe, G. L. (1978) 'Behavioral approaches to the problems of later life', in M. Storandt, I. C. Seigler and M. F. Elias (eds) *The Clinical Psychology of Ageing*, New York: Plenum Press.

Roth, M., Huppert, F. A., Tym, E. and Mountjoy, C. Q. (1988) *CAMDEX, The Cambridge Examination for Mental Disorders of the Elderly*, Cambridge: Cambridge University Press.

Sallis, J. F. and Lichstein, K. L. (1982) 'Analysis and management of geriatric anxiety', *International Journal of Ageing and Human Development* 15(3): 197–211.

Sanford, J. R. A. (1975) 'Tolerance of debility in elderly dependents by supporters at home: its significance for hospital practice', *British Medical Journal* 3: 471–3.

Sang, R. and O'Brien, J. (1984) *Advocacy*, London: King Edward's Hospital Fund.

Savage, R. D., Britton, P. G., Bolton, N. and Hall, E. H. (1973) *Intellectual Functioning in the Aged*, London: Methuen.

Savage, R. D., Gaber, L. B., Britton, P. G., Bolton, N. and Cooper, A. (1977) *Personality and Adjustment in the Aged*, London: Academic Press.

Schaie, K. W. (1978) 'Towards a stage theory of adult cognitive development', *Journal of Ageing and Human Development* 8: 129–38.

—— and Labouvie-Vief, G. (1974) 'Generational versus ontogenetic components of change in adult cognitive behavior: a fourteen year cross-sequential study', *Developmental Psychology* 10: 305–20.

Schaie, K. W. and Strother, C. R. (1968) 'A cross-sequential study of age changes in cognitive behavior', *Psychological Bulletin* 70: 671–80.

Schonfield, A. (1980) 'Learning and memory', in J. Birren and R. Sloane (eds) *The Handbook of Mental Health and Aging*, New York: Van Nostrand Reinhold.

Schwab, J. J., Holzer, C. E. and Warheit, G. J. (1973) 'Depressive symptomatology and age', *Psychosomatics* 14: 135–41.

Seligman, M. E. P. (1975) *Helplessness: On Depression, Development and Death*, San Francisco: Freeman.

Sherman, E. (1981) *Counseling the Aging: An Integrative Approach*, New York: Free Press.

Siegler, K. and Botwinick, J. (1979) 'A long-term study of intellectual abilities of older adults – the matter of selective attrition', *Journal of Gerontology* 34: 242–7.

Solomon, K. (1982) 'Social antecedents of learned helplessness in the health care setting', *Gerontologist* 33: 282–7.

Spielberger, C. D. (1983) *Manual for the State–Trait Anxiety Inventory*, Palo Alto, Calif.: Consulting Psychologists Press.

Stern, H., Weiss, D. and Perkins, S. (1984) 'A conceptual approach to counseling elders and their families', *Counseling Psychologist* (Special edn.: Counseling Psychology and Ageing) 12(2): 55–61.

Steuer, J. L. and Hammen, C. L. (1983) 'Cognitive-behavioral group therapy for the depressed elderly: issues and adaptations', *Cognitive Therapy and Research* 7: 285–96.

Storandt, M. (1983) *Counseling and Therapy with Older Adults*, Boston: Little, Brown and Co.

Sutton, L. (1989) 'Case illustration of Life Planning', *PSIGE Newsletter* 28: 18–21.

Thompson, L. W., Gallagher, D. and Breckenridge, J. S. (1987) 'Comparative effectiveness of psychotherapies with depressed elders', *Journal of Consulting and Clinical Psychology* 55: 385–90.

Thompson, L. W., Gallagher, D. and Zeiss, A. (1988) 'Effective treatments of depression in the elderly', paper presented at the Behaviour Therapy World Congress, Edinburgh.

Twinning, C. (1986) 'How many clinical psychologists for the elderly?', *Clinical Psychology Forum* 3: 4–7.

Williams, J. M. G. (1984) *The Psychological Treatment of Depression*, London: Croom Helm.

Williamson, J., Stokoe, I. H., Gray, S., Fisher, M., Smith, A., McGhee, A. and Stephenson, E. (1964) 'Old people at home: their unreported needs', *Lancet* 1: 1117–20.

Woods, R. T. (1979) 'Reality Orientation and staff attention: a controlled study', *British Journal of Psychiatry* 134: 502–7.

—— and Britton, P. G. (1985) *Clinical Psychology with the Elderly*, London: Croom Helm.

Worden, W. (1982) *Grief Counselling and Grief Therapy*, London: Tavistock Publications.

Yost, E. B., Beutler, L. E., Corbishley, M. A. and Allender, J. R. (1986) *Group Cognitive Therapy. A Treatment Approach for Depressed Older Adults*, New York: Pergamon Press.

Zeiss, A. M., Lewinsohn, P. M. and Munoz, R. F. (1979) 'Non-specific improvement effects in depression using interpersonal skills training, pleasant activity schedules, or cognitive training', *Journal of Consulting and Clinical Psychology* 47: 427–39.

Zemore, R. and Eames, N. (1979) 'Psychic and somatic symptoms of depression among young adults, institutionalised aged and non-institutionalised aged', *Journal of Gerontology* 34: 716–22.

Chapter 9

Mental handicap

Alastair Ager

CONCEPTUALIZATION

Definition

Mental handicap is a social construct. Despite their numerous forms, formal definitions of mental handicap (see Clarke and Clarke 1974) always share a requirement for an individual to exhibit social incompetence in addition to demonstrable intellectual impairment. This is no less true for terms often presumed to carry less social stigma, such as developmental disability or learning difficulty.

Mild mental handicap has been defined with respect to IQ scores in the range 70 to 50, with severe mental handicap being associated with IQs below 50 (Reddy 1987). Relying on IQ data alone, however, would predict a prevalence rate for mental handicap far in excess of that actually encountered. This is particularly the case with regards to the former group, who predominantly constitute those simply falling at the lower end of the normal distribution of IQ scores (Hagberg and Hagberg 1984). (It is only with the latter group that there is commonly any evidence of any genuine impairment associated with neural damage or malformation.) It is generally accepted, therefore, that the term 'mental handicap' should only be used with respect to those individuals whose intellectual difficulties are accompanied by a judged lack of social competence.

With a judgement of social competence at the core of its definition, it is clear to see the extent to which mental handicap is socially constructed. As the moral and cultural norms of society change, so does its definition of mental handicap. The social changes within Britain within the last century, for example, have considerably altered our expectations of competence. Whereas minor acts of theft were in the 1920s sufficient to establish that a person lacked appropriate moral competence and therefore warranted consideration as a mentally handicapped (or, as it then was, subnormal) individual (Ryan 1987), it is unthinkable that such a judgement would be made on these grounds today. With the present preoccupation with individualism, it is now more likely to be a lack in the ability to function independently of support that would lead to such a ruling.

Social context

With societal judgement at the heart of the definition of mental handicap, it is perhaps not surprising that what can be termed the secondary consequences of the condition have such a major impact on the quality of life enjoyed by an individual. Primary consequences are those resulting directly from impairment, such as an individual's learning difficulties. These may be seen to constitute the individual's *disability*. Secondary consequences then comprise the social effects of this disability, which in formal terms actually constitute the individual's *handicap*.

The manner in which secondary consequences develop the handicapped role of an individual is vividly illustrated by the 'devaluation spiral' (Figure 9.1), commonly used as an explanatory device in the teaching of the principle of normalization (O'Brien and Tyne 1981). As this figure shows, once learning difficulties have attracted the label of mental handicap, the expectations of individuals are lowered. The lowering of expectations in turn leads to a reduction in the range of opportunities afforded such individuals. With reduced opportunities, individuals are restricted in their life experiences and in their acquisition of new skills. Such deficits in skill and experience may then act to confirm lowered expectations, and a 'vicious circle' (Chamberlain *et al.* 1984) is formed. The mechanism described acts to devalue the social role of the individual, which spirals down through a repeated cycle of lowered expectations, reduced opportunities and increasingly devaluing experiences. While having little empirical support (Baldwin 1985), the 'devaluation spiral' is nonetheless commonly seen as a useful clinical tool for understanding the social processes at work in the lives of people with a mental handicap.

Social devaluation of a client has been seen to be such a powerful process that services have been encouraged to see the establishment of a valued social role for people with a mental handicap as a central part of their task (King's Fund 1980). Increased opportunities, more valued experiences and more meaningful personal relationships all play an important part in establishing such a role, and have appropriately received increased attention. However, skills acquisition – historically the first targeted area on the move away from custodial models of care (Kiernan 1978) – still has an important part to play in work in this area.

The importance of skill acquisition is related not only to its role in reversing the path of the devaluation cycle, that is by providing evidence for higher expectations of individuals with a mental handicap. Even if the devaluation process were fully reversed – and all secondary consequences were thus removed – the primary consequences of impairment remain. The learning difficulties of people with a mental handicap constitute the factor which sets the spiral turning in the first place, and a comprehensive service must therefore address them. Few services take this challenge seriously, however, not least as a consequence of clinical psychologists' frequent disinclination to invest resources into a rigorous psychological analysis of the nature of learning difficulty. To be complete, a psychological analysis of mental handicap must, however, have at its core an understanding of the *nature* of

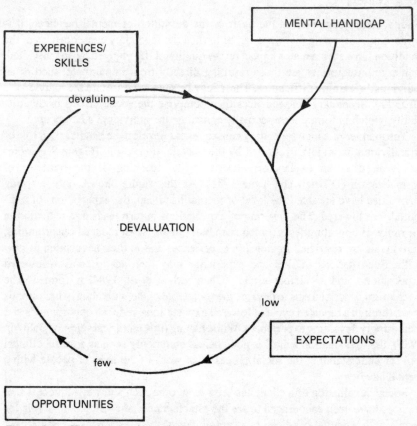

Figure 9.1   The devaluation spiral

the learning difficulties of people with a mental handicap and of the *means* that may be used to ameliorate such difficulties. Failure to appreciate this point can all too easily lead to services which appropriately address secondary consequences of handicap, but pay no attention at all to the original difficulties experienced by such individuals.

Analysis of learning difficulties

The general lack of interest shown by clinical practitioners in the analysis of learning difficulties of people with mental handicaps is, in part, no doubt related to the conceptual problems of conceiving how one could draw any useful general conclusions from the study of learning in such individuals when the physiological origins of impairment are accepted as being so heterogeneous (Alberman 1984). In other words, if individuals vary so much in the neurological impairment that

they have sustained, is it not reasonable to assume that the psychological consequences of impairment are equally varied?

This argument is persuasive but, in reality, fallacious. With regard to brain
pathology, it is quite reasonable to conceive of different kinds of structural damage
having similar functional consequences (Luria 1980). This important principle is
perhaps best explained by analogy. Imagine that a telephone network is identified
as a target by a terrorist group that co-ordinates the simultaneous detonation of a
small grenade in a large number of identical exchanges. Further, suppose that the
structural damage sustained by each exchange is unique. If the *functional* damage
of each exchange is then assessed, the following outcome is likely. Some exchanges
will essentially still be functioning normally, damage having been sustained in
redundant parts of the system. At the other extreme, some other exchanges will be
totally inoperative, with damage having been sustained at critical points of influence. Between these two poles there will be exchanges with faults groupable
according to the functional system affected (for example, some will take incoming
calls but not outgoing calls, others will have lost operator services, and so on). Each
of these exchanges will have experienced unique structural damage, but they will
share similar functional problems with those exchanges where damage has disturbed the same functional system. Likewise, individuals with quite dissimilar
structural impairment can display similar functional deficits if it is the same
cognitive system that has been disrupted (Luria 1980).

Having established that it is theoretically appropriate to seek commonalities in
the functional learning difficulties of people with mental handicaps, it must be
conceded that the sterile formulations of researchers in the field have produced a
further disincentive for psychological practitioners to consider such work of
clinical relevance. Much of the work conducted in the 1950s and 1960s, for
instance, can be 'written off' to the extent that it asked unproductive questions
essentially of the form 'do poor learners learn poorly?' (Haywood 1976). Clarke
and Clarke (1980) suggest that in the work of this period mentally handicapped
people were seen by many researchers as 'little more than a captive population,
available for trivial experimental work' (p. 2).

There were, naturally, a few exceptions to this general rule. In the 1950s, the
work of Tizard and his colleagues (for example, Tizard 1953) bore eloquent
testimony to the fact that relatively subtle adjustments to the learning environment
could significantly assist mentally handicapped learners in the acquisition of new
skills. In the 1960s it was the three theoretical formulations of learning difficulty
offered in Ellis's (1963) volume *Handbook of Mental Deficiency* that stood out by
way of constructive development. The theories of Zeaman and House, Ellis and
Luria located the primary focus of learning difficulties in the mentally handicapped
in directing attention to the relevant aspects of a problem, in retaining a representation of a stimulus in short-term memory and in the association of speech and
motor systems respectively. Although these different formulations have been taken
to demonstrate the generality of the learning difficulties of people with a mental
handicap, it is possible to view these theories as essentially summarizing similar

data. In essence, they each implicate difficulties in the organization of incoming information, and they accordingly suggest certain means by which such difficulties may be ameliorated.

Historically, however, work in mental handicap was soon hit by the tide of behavioural interventions which came to dominate both theory and practice in the field. Encouraged by the development of behavioural technologies demonstrably capable of nurturing and strengthening adaptive behaviour in clients, theorists and clinicians alike commonly eschewed consideration of 'cognitive deficits' and focused instead on the 'lawfulness' of behaviour. The resulting 'cognitive-behavioural divide' – which generally persists today – has been of major disservice to people with a mental handicap to the extent that it has restricted the cross-fertil-ization of ideas between work of the two traditions.

In recent years there have been a number of studies of learning difficulty which, while of a cognitive orientation, have potential implications for behavioural inter-ventions. The work of O'Connor and Hermelin (1972, 1978), for example, has suggested that individuals with severe learning difficulties may display a prefer-ence for coding complex stimuli in visuo-spatial rather than auditory-sequential terms. This is the reverse of the coding bias displayed by non-handicapped individuals. Such a finding is of major relevance to the debate on the use of sign and symbol systems by people with a mental handicap (Ager 1985; Kiernan 1977). It indicates a clear value in making visually based modes of communication available to such individuals. These studies also further implicate problems with the organization of incoming information as a key factor underlying many indi-viduals' learning difficulties.

One implication of such work is that the individual with a mental handicap may have many intact cognitive capacities (such as basic association) which are never-theless not truly capitalized upon because of failure and/or difficulty in other discrete – but critical – functions (such as organization of input). This line of reasoning is most vividly illustrated with respect to the work of Belmont and his associates (Belmont 1978; Belmont and Butterfield 1971; Butterfield et al. 1973).

Figure 9.2 depicts the performance of 'normal' and 'retarded' groups over a three-part short-term memory task. In parts 1 and 3 subjects were free to adopt whatever strategy they wished. For part 2, however, some subjects were instructed in the use of an (adaptive) rehearsal strategy, and others were instructed in the use of a (maladaptive) scanning strategy. Scores during part 2 indicated that 'retarded' individuals instructed in using an adaptive strategy outperformed 'normal' indi-viduals using a maladaptive approach, but failed both to equal the performance of 'normals' using rehearsal and to retain this more productive strategy in part 3 of the task. From this one might conclude that training in an appropriate strategy had been of encouraging benefit, but that its impact had been constrained by the functional inability of individuals with a mental handicap to deploy the appropriate strategy (a) with total reliability and (b) without external prompting.

Figure 9.3 comprises a re-examination of data from the 'retarded' group, which serves to suggest a quite different conclusion. It proved possible to divide the

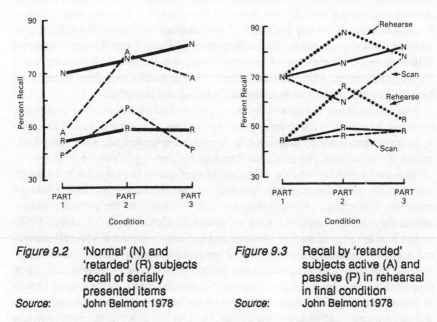

Figure 9.2   'Normal' (N) and
              'retarded' (R) subjects
              recall of serially
              presented items
Source: John Belmont 1978

Figure 9.3   Recall by 'retarded'
              subjects active (A) and
              passive (P) in rehearsal
              in final condition
Source: John Belmont 1978

'retarded' group who had been instructed to rehearse into two subgroups – those who had remained active in its adoption in part 3, and those who became passive. Plotting data separately for these two subgroups against the performance of 'normal' and 'retarded' groups who had remained 'self-programmed' through each part of the task reveals an interesting effect. Those remaining active in the use of the strategy had, in fact, outperformed the 'normal' group during part 2, and had retained its use with reasonable benefit. Those who had become passive in its use are seen to compose a subgroup for whom rehearsal had been ineffective at that time. For the active group it may now be concluded that, with appropriate instruction, individuals were not only capable of adopting a complex learning strategy but displayed sufficiently intact general cognitive processing for the strategy to prove fully effective. In addition, such individuals appeared to recognize the value of the strategy and persevere in its use. This clearly encourages further the view that it is possible to identify specific cognitive difficulties, remediation of which need not be inevitably obstructed by generalized intellectual deficit. Indeed, a further study (Butterfield *et al*. 1973) established that the difficulties of the passive group could be overcome with appropriate training, and should not therefore be attributed to basic cognitive functions not being intact.

These studies have been described at length because they demonstrate an important principle at variance with many assumptions commonly made about the learning performance of individuals with mental handicaps. Generalized learning difficulty need not imply generalized cognitive deficit. It is quite plausible that, even for the individual with pervasive problems in the acquisition of new skills, cognitive processes are fundamentally (or embryonically) intact, and 'retarded' performance results from deficits in one or two discrete – but obviously crucial – functions. There is clearly a danger of overstating this case, and implying that learning difficulty is *always* the consequence of limited and discrete cognitive failure. Rather it is a question of being unwilling to make a premature defection to the 'organic' camp, where failure to learn is over-readily explained in terms of hypothetical judgements of an individual's functional potential.

It should be noted in the course of this argument that a mechanism of organizing incoming information (here the generation of an appropriate mnemonic strategy) is, in the studies reported above, again implicated as underlying presenting difficulties. There is, then, this recurrent theme of the learning difficulties of mentally handicapped individuals being (principally) attributable to problems in the handling of input, with other cognitive processes being fundamentally intact. While for many this will remain a highly speculative abstraction from the literature, neurological data broadly supports such a contention. Goldstein and Oakley (1985) review a wide range of studies – animal and human – concerned with behavioural and cognitive capacity following diffuse cortical damage, and argue that expectations of function following such damage have been unduly pessimistic. They suggest that 'the achievements of a grossly damaged brain may far exceed expectations derived from the traditional view of the relationship between brain mass and the possibility of adaptive behaviour' (p. 13), but that this requires 'training procedures which are appropriate to its particular capacities for information gain and storage' (p. 14). Their review thus supports not only the notion that mentally handicapped individuals may have unexpectedly intact cognitive capabilities, but also the principle that to capitalize upon these it is necessary to identify means of circumventing definable deficits.

Goldstein and Oakley's review (ibid.) prompts a schematic representation of function along the lines shown in Figure 9.4. Within this structure three classes of neural/cognitive activity may be defined. Class I comprises those fundamental processes such as the control of physiological systems, which are essentially out of consciousness. Class III comprises patterns of activity associated with the planning and implementation of complex behaviours, which are largely within consciousness. Class II then comprises a large range of processes somewhere in between classes I and III in the extent to which they are unconscious/routinized or conscious/reflective. This class involves a number of patterns which were established through the activity of higher cognitive processes, but which are now maintained at a somewhat 'lower' level (these might include quite complex activities such as driving, which have become largely routinized).

Individuals sustaining structural damage in areas supporting class I and class II patterns (particularly the former) will clearly have very restricted life expectancy due to an inability to sustain vital functions. Although some mentally handicapped individuals may fall into this category, their numbers will inevitably be severely limited. Goldstein and Oakley (1985) contend, however, that individuals with

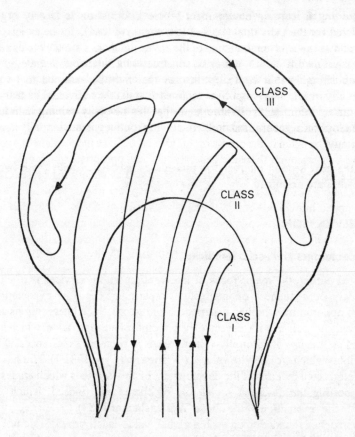

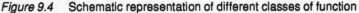

Figure 9.4   Schematic representation of different classes of function

damage in areas sustaining class III activity will, despite restricted higher cognitive abilities, still have considerable functional capacity as a result of intact structures in other areas. The surviving mentally handicapped are most likely to fall into this category.

The obvious implication of this conceptualization is as follows. If individuals are impaired in their ability to *initiate* (class III) complex activities, but not in their ability to *sustain* (class II) such activity once established, can intervention procedures be devised which circumvent deficits and access latent capabilities? This model has coherence if we identify the organizing of incoming information as one of the key higher processes likely to be disrupted by a wide variety of forms of cortical damage.

Such an analysis of learning difficulty suggests two main directions for intervention:

1 providing a learning environment where information is largely organized/
ordered for the individual (i.e. has low cognitive load). To the extent that this
directs us towards manipulation of the environment as a strategy to compensate
for learning difficulties, it may be construed as a *behavioural* strategy.
2 establishing, within cortical structures that may be assumed to be at least
partially intact, 'metacognitive' routines to assist the individual in dealing with
incoming information. To the extent that this involves training individuals in
the adoption of generalized problem-solving routines, it is essentially a *cognitive*
strategy.

In the next section intervention procedures associated with these two broad
approaches are examined.

INTERVENTION

Service changes and social handicap

As noted earlier, the major focus of intervention within services is often on the
secondary consequences of intellectual impairment (i.e. low expectations, restricted opportunities, limited experiences and so on). Such interventions are most
commonly conceived with respect to the principle of normalization, which has been
defined as 'the use of culturally valued means to promote experiences, skills and
behaviours which are likewise valued' (O'Brien and Tyne 1981:1). This has usually
been interpreted in terms of the development of new services which are less prone
to supporting the devalued social role of clients and, indeed, which actively
promote the revaluation of the client (Wolfensberger 1983).

Approaches founded upon such a global, value-laden principle do not readily
lend themselves to scientific evaluation. In recent years, however, there have been
an increasing number of attempts to identify which aspects of service change appear
to contribute most to any increases in the quality of life enjoyed by clients (Emerson
1985; Flynn and Nitsch 1980). It has been demonstrated, for example, that deployment of staff with small numbers of clients and with a clear understanding of their
role (Jones *et al*. 1987) leads to substantive increases in the engagement of clients
in appropriate activities. Research has also shown that while community placement
clearly can have a major impact on the quality of life enjoyed by an individual
(Evans *et al*. 1987), physical presence alone is not sufficient to guarantee either
community participation (Humphreys *et al*. 1983; Landesman-Dwyer and Berkson
1984) or a substantial increase in life experiences (Ager 1988a). Community
service developments based upon the principle of normalization generally appear
to have been rather more successful in prompting positive changes for people with
a mental handicap in areas such as living environments and leisure opportunities,
than they have with regard to the relationships and freedoms they enjoy (ibid.).

Learning difficulties

As far as the primary consequences of intellectual impairment (i.e. learning difficulties) are concerned, as discussed earlier, it is possible to conceive of relevant interventions fitting into one of two broad categories. One category includes all those interventions focused at the level of environmental manipulation, which effectively seek to minimize the effects of an individual's difficulties in processing information. The other includes those procedures which attempt directly to improve the cognitive repertoires available to mentally handicapped learners.

Behavioural interventions

A vast amount has now been written on the former strategy which, because of its emphasis on environmental manipulation, may be seen essentially to comprise behavioural interventions. Detailed reviews are provided by Kiernan (1978) and Clements (1987). It is possible to conceive of behavioural work at two main levels: first, that involving setting conditions conducive to learning; second, that involving discrete teaching interventions.

Much of the impact of behavioural interventions in the field of mental handicap has been purely with regard to the first level. Behavioural theory has provided the context for the development of a range of teaching packages and schemes acknowledged to be of wide utility in work with mentally handicapped individuals (for example, Goal Planning (Houts and Scott 1975), the Bereweeke Skill Teaching System (Jenkins *et al.* 1983) and Education of the Developmentally Young (McBrien and Foxen 1987)). The common features of such schemes include: the use of distraction-free, precision-teaching environments, the explicit and intense use of reinforcement contingencies to shape and maintain appropriate behaviour, the setting of clear behavioural targets for teaching interventions and an emphasis on rigorous evaluation of the progress of learning (Ager 1989).

Such a foundation may frequently be sufficient to enable a student with a mental handicap to learn a new skill. In terms of the conceptualization of learning difficulty constructed earlier, by organizing presented material in a clear manner, such schemes sufficiently lower the demand on (impaired) higher cognitive functions for learning to take place. In many circumstances, however, the individual may require further simplification of incoming information, which then calls for the adoption of an explicit teaching intervention.

The most commonly adopted teaching intervention is probably *task analysis*. This involves the breaking down of a task into discrete topographical components, and the teaching of each component in turn. If we represent learning by the task of travelling from A to B (Figure 9.5), then task analysis involves the identification of component parts of this learning task and their being addressed individually (Figure 9.6).

With regard to the conceptualization of learning difficulty in terms of difficulties in organizing incoming information, this teaching procedure again has clear face

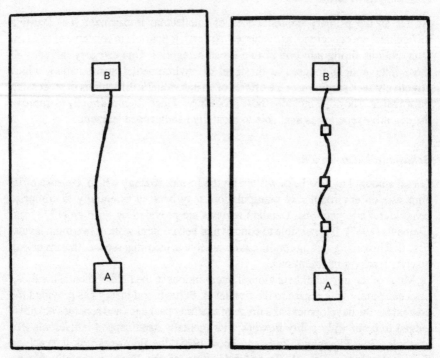

Figure 9.5   The learning of a new skill   *Figure 9.6*   Task analysis

validity. Notwithstanding the problems that some tasks present in terms of being broken down in this manner, and the controversies regarding the sequence in which components should be taught, task analysis is acknowledged to be practically most effective (Kiernan 1978). Nevertheless, this strategy may with some individuals again insufficiently lessen the cognitive demand of a learning situation, and teaching must therefore involve the ordering of input still more.

There are two distinct ways in which such further ordering can take place. The first involves the addition of further information and/or assistance in order to facilitate correct responding. This is usually referred to as a *prompting* strategy (see Figure 9.7). Additional prompting stimuli – in the form of verbal or gestural cues or physical guidance – are added until the individual performs the required skill. Once correct responding is firmly established, attempts are made gradually to fade out these additional cues such that independent responding is achieved. Thus, in teaching an individual to feed themselves with a spoon, one might begin by prompting the required motor movements by physically guiding the individual's hand through the required sequence. Subsequently this dominant physical prompt might be gradually faded by guiding the client at the point of their wrist, then forearm and then elbow, before finally withdrawing guidance altogether. Such

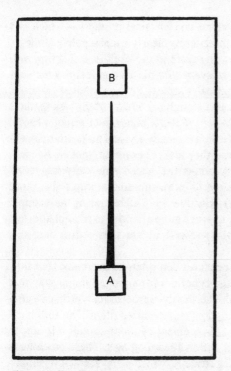

Figure 9.7   Prompting

procedures are widely adopted in work with people with mental handicaps, encouraged by the use of assessment materials which frequently assess function with respect to the level of prompting an individual requires in order to perform a task (Chamberlain *et al*. 1984; Perkins *et al*. 1980).

Prompting procedures are not without their problems, however. These problems are, in fact, readily predictable in terms of the previously presented conceptualization of the functional nature of learning difficulties of people with severe mental handicaps. If individuals have difficulty in organizing incoming information – lacking a suitable breadth of attention (Zeaman and House 1963) to process the large number of stimuli impinging on their senses – the addition of still *further* stimuli will clearly (in some circumstances at least) exacerbate rather than ameliorate learning difficulties. Individuals may attend solely to these additional stimuli such that they learn nothing of the task at hand. At the point where prompts are completely faded out, a sudden decrease in the level of performance is then inevitable (Tennant *et al*. 1981). This is likely to be the case particularly when a large 'cocktail' of prompting stimuli are added, all of which bear no relation to the stimulus features of the task to which the individual must ultimately attend if they are to respond independently.

The use of simultaneous verbal, gestural and physical prompts – which is a widespread practice in the field – is in these terms clearly a maladaptive strategy. Prompting stimuli need to be selected with regard to the likelihood that they will encourage attention to be paid to task-relevant stimuli. Two guidelines are suggested here, both of which have empirical support. First, whenever possible, prompts should be chosen to be of the same stimulus modality as the task features to which the individual needs to attend (Ager 1983; O'Connor and Hermelin 1963). Thus, in teaching letter discrimination (which is clearly a visual task) prompts will be more effective if they are visual than if they are, for example, spoken. Second, what may be termed within-stimulus prompts (i.e. those physically integrated within task materials) should be preferred to extra-stimulus prompts (i.e. those physically removed from task materials) (Rincover 1978). Thus, using the example of letter discrimination again, it is likely to prove more effective to prompt a correct response through a visual cue integrated within the letter shapes than one, say, vertically above them.

Such difficulties with prompting procedures can often be overcome, but they do encourage active consideration of the benefits of the second major way that further ordering of input can be achieved. This involves procedures which, pursuing a little further the logic of the above discussion, require the addition of no additional stimuli, but rather an exaggeration or enhancement of those stimuli relevant to correct performance which are inherent within a learning task. These procedures may be considered to constitute a *shaping* strategy, which is represented schematically in Figure 9.8.

In theoretical terms, at least, one might conceive of any task being simplified and/or its key features exaggerated to the point where organizing the information (planning an appropriate strategy) relevant to that task is relatively undemanding. Once task performance is established with the task parameters so adjusted, a stepwise transformation of the task back to 'standard' parameters can take place in the hope that (by not demanding switches in attention) successful independent performance will be retained. Again, this approach has a clear coherence with the conceptualization of learning difficulty offered earlier. It first ensures that minimal demand is made on the organising/planning role of higher cognitive processes (as this has largely been done for the individual by the exaggeration of key task features). It, then, assumes that basic cognitive functions will be sufficiently intact to maintain performance once it has been successfully established.

To illustrate this strategy, consider the teaching of a skill such as coat buttoning reported by Ager (1989). An adapted coat was prepared which allowed the interchange of four discrete sets of buttons. Set I comprised standard-sized buttons (2 cm. in diameter) mounted on a standard length 'stalk' (1 cm. in length). Dimensions were increased through sets II and III to set IV, which consisted of 4 cm.-diameter buttons on 'stalks' in excess of 10 cm. in length. Button 'holes' on the coat could correspondingly be adapted through the release of 'velcro' fasten-

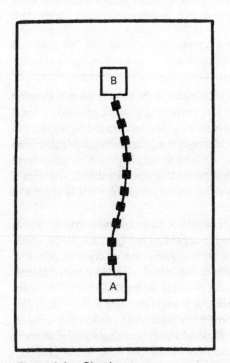

Figure 9.8   Shaping

ings. Mentally handicapped students, who had previously been the focus of unsuccessful attempts to teach coat buttoning through prompting procedures, not only swiftly established independent buttoning when they were presented with set IV buttons, but maintained their level of performance in the stepwise transformation of the task (through set III and set II) to the standard conditions of set I buttons. The speed of acquisition – and encouraging generalization of learning – reported in this study, and others following a shaping approach (for example, Strand and Morris 1988), suggest that such interventions are worthy of far wider application than is presently the case.

To conclude this review of behavioural interventions in relation to the learning difficulties of people with a mental handicap, it is clear that their effectiveness may be readily attributable to the extent that they involve the structuring of the environment in a manner which reduces the disabling effects of impaired higher cognitive processes. The broadest impact of such work has undoubtedly been at the level of simply encouraging a teaching approach where (a) task goals are made clear, (b) swift and reliable feedback is provided for students and (c) progress is effectively monitored. As has been shown, behavioural interventions can, however, be considerably more sophisticated than this. If the greatest gains are to be made with mentally handicapped people it is imperative that clinicians become more aware of some of these sophisticated approaches, and integrate them within their current practice.

Cognitive interventions

The literature on cognitive interventions with regard to the amelioration of learning difficulties is considerably smaller than that pertaining to work of a behavioural orientation. Cognitive work is, however, receiving increased attention, not least as a result of the generally disappointing evidence of the generalization of gains from behavioural interventions (Ager 1987). An assumption here is that gains from cognitive training should prove relatively portable across situations, although it will become apparent from what follows that firm evidence for this is at present lacking (Gow 1986).

It is important to conceive of the aim of cognitive interventions correctly, which may be illustrated with respect to the scheme suggested in Figure 9.4. Behavioural interventions may be seen to attempt the prior organization of material such that the demand on class III cognitive functions is minimized. Cognitive interventions, on the other hand, attempt to exploit as far as possible the residual class III capacity of an individual. Attempts are made to establish general problem-solving strategies (metacognitive skills) which are functional notwithstanding cortical impairment, and which may be deployed by the individual when approaching novel situations. In distinction from the essentially compensatory nature of behavioural interventions (i.e. providing compensatory resources to assist an individual), cognitive interventions attempt to be genuinely educative (i.e. educating an individual in the effective deployment of their existing resources).

Although, as was shown earlier, there has been a long tradition of cognitive research into learning difficulty, work with clear implications for intervention has a somewhat shorter history. A good deal of this work stems from the research of Ann Brown in the 1970s (Brown et al. 1973). In the light of evidence that students with a mental handicap frequently deploy inappropriate learning strategies, it is logical to investigate the benefits of such students receiving explicit teaching regarding the adoption of strategies appropriate to a given kind of task. Brown and Barclay (1976) trained mentally handicapped students in the adoption of a self-testing routine appropriate to a particular verbal task. In results analogous to the studies of Belmont reviewed earlier, all students successfully learned the strategy and gained from its use, although only the more able deployed it spontaneously. Those deploying the strategy spontaneously were also found to make appropriate use of the strategy in a novel task (Brown et al. 1979).

This latter result suggests the possibility of teaching general strategies which may be suitably adopted by individuals across a range of tasks. Explicit attempts to teach such strategies have usually followed a format suggested by the work of Meichenbaum (1977), involving extensive use of self-instructional training. Gow

(1986), for example, has evaluated the use of a self-instructional teaching package in the learning of complex assembly-type tasks. Students are prompted in the use of self-questioning and self-statements as they learn to manipulate task materials (for example, 'now, where does this go?', 'I'm doing fine' and so on). Evidence suggests that the self-monitoring encouraged by such an approach not only facilitates learning of a skill, but may also assist the acquisition of related skills. Generalization of such strategies remains unreliable, however, to more unrelated tasks (ibid.).

Another strand of work in this area proceeds with rather more of an explicit emphasis on the development of the higher-order (metacognitive) skills assumed to maintain learning in non-handicapped individuals. Feuerstein (1979), for example, has suggested that intensive, programmed exposure to what he terms 'mediated learning experiences' can lead to the development of key information ordering skills in handicapped learners. Such 'mediated learning experiences' involve an instructor rehearsing with students the abstract or conceptual relationships between items of information. Intensive matching and discrimination exercises are used, for example, with the aim of establishing a conceptual understanding which will ultimately 'mediate' the individual's interaction with a complex environment.

In a similar vein the work of Waldon (1980) emphasizes the importance of the individual gaining fundamental cognitive skills for interaction with the environment on which to base subsequent learning. Behaviours acquired through instrumental learning will always be restricted in their generalizability, if this foundation of information handling skills has not been laid. Waldon (1980) thus commends a programmed sequence of information handling tasks – analagous to those tackled spontaneously by the normally developing child – to encourage their establishment. There are clear difficulties in evaluating the impact of interventions upon hypothetical cognitive structures. Not only do effects have to be deduced from observable behaviour, but changes may justifiably only be expected in the long term. The theoretical coherence of such approaches with the conceptualization of learning difficulty presented earlier, however, should encourage serious examination of the potential for integrating such ideas within intervention programmes for individuals with mental handicaps.

It would be wrong, in concluding this review of intervention strategies, to convey too absolute a distinction between cognitive and behavioural interventions. Work in the developing area of 'self-control', for example, bears close allegiance to both cognitive and behavioural traditions within the study of mental handicap, as well as to cognate cognitive-behavioural analyses outside the field altogether (Clements 1987). The work of Woods and Lowe (1986) on verbal self-regulation training is developed within a clear behavioural scheme, but addresses traditionally 'cognitive' concerns. Nonetheless, these are exceptions rather than the norm. Interventions with respect to the learning difficulties of people with a mental handicap are typically either clearly behavioural or clearly cognitive in conception and, at present, are by a long measure most commonly the former.

FUTURE DEVELOPMENTS

It is often suggested that the major problems now faced by workers in the field of mental handicap concern the implementation of that which is already known, rather than the development of further knowledge (Sartorius 1984). When one considers the present quality of services for people with a mental handicap across the world, such an argument appears persuasive. This is particularly so when one considers evidence such as that regarding the implementation of vaccination programmes. Notwithstanding the fact that the introduction of comprehensive world-wide vaccination for conditions such as rubella and whooping cough would curb the incidence of intellectual impairment dramatically, such programmes remain a relative rarity (King 1987).

Even if one constructs priorities against this backdrop of deficient services and common lack of political will, however, there are still areas where further knowledge and analysis is self-evidently required. These may, in fact, profitably include the broad-based study of factors influencing the allocation of resource priorities within nations and the whole topic of efficient service delivery (Ager 1990). Advances are needed within the study of mental handicap itself, however, and in areas concerned with both conceptualization and intervention.

Required developments in conceptualization

Analysis of social behaviour and social cognition

Given the importance of social factors in influencing the quality of life enjoyed by people with a mental handicap, it is vital that analysis of the factors influencing social behaviour and social cognition with respect to such individuals is furthered. The existing literature in this field (McGill and Emerson 1987) is promising to the extent that it illuminates certain mechanisms associated with the social devaluation of people with a mental handicap, but it remains focused primarily on the parochial concerns of service personnel. Analysis of broader social trends and attitudes is required if a fully comprehensive analysis of the social context of mental handicap is to be achieved. Such analysis would include consideration of the factors which establish and/or maintain negative attitudes towards mentally handicapped people in the general population, as well as investigating the manner in which the needs of persons with a mental handicap are commonly accorded low social priority (King 1987).

Integration of cognitive and behavioural analyses

The conceptualization of learning difficulty offered earlier clearly provides a framework for the integration of cognitive and behavioural analyses of such problems. Such integration is, however, at present fragmentary. Further work is necessary which explicitly seeks to integrate findings from the established databases of cognitive and behavioural research. That such integration is *possible* is readily demonstrated by the work of Sidman, who has explored the 'cognitive' processes associated with the development of a skill such as reading using an approach entirely consistent with behavioural analysis (Sidman and Cresson 1973). That such integration is *desirable* should be clear given the continued naivety of behavioural teaching programmes with respect to the subtle information-processing difficulties of many individuals with a mental handicap and the continued sterility of many cognitive accounts of learning deficit in terms of plausible intervention (Ager 1983).

Required developments in intervention

Social intervention based upon social analysis

The need for a more comprehensive and empirically founded analysis of the social factors associated with mental handicap was noted above. There follows a need for explicit interventions to be framed with respect to this analysis. Social interventions – at the level of neighbourhood, community, district or nation – need to be devised, which will allow clear evaluation of their impact on the social roles assumed by persons with a mental handicap. Development of educative and attitudinal interventions are vital if mentally handicapped people are to be enabled to lead more fulfilled lives. It is crucially important, however, that such interventions are based upon a clear understanding of the manner in which social roles are created.

Generalizable behavioural interventions

While behavioural interventions have proved valuable in assisting people with a mental handicap to learn new skills, the clear weakness of such an approach remains the commonly poor generalization of gains to new settings and tasks. While, as noted earlier, some have concluded that this is an inherent limitation of the behavioural approach, there do seem to be certain clear means of improving the durability and generalizability of change created by such interventions (Ager 1987). The central principle here appears to be a sensitivity – *prior* to intervention – to the factors that will need to sustain change *subsequent* to intervention. This applies at a wide variety of levels. In teaching discriminations, it appears wise to establish responding by manipulating inherent features of the task that will, in consequence, be in a position to maintain responding once teaching has ceased (Strand and Morris 1988). In establishing new services, the participation of staff and consumers in the planning of developments is a valuable means of fostering the 'ownership' – and consequent durability – of change (Ager 1990; Partridge 1984). This principle remains insufficiently worked through in a good deal of clinical practice. Overall, there is a clear need for more emphasis on addressing generalization issues *prior* – rather than *subsequent* – to intervention (Horner *et al.* 1988).

Development of cognitive interventions

Cognitive interventions in the field of mental handicap remain primarily associated with research programmes, having exerted little influence on the mainstream of clinical practice. The one area where they appear to be having a significant impact is with respect to the use of self-control procedures with individuals with impulsive, aggressive or socially unacceptable behaviour (Clements 1987). Cognitive procedures here offer a means of influencing the behaviour of a client across settings, where consistent behavioural management of a client would likely prove impracticable. The use of self-control procedures will hopefully encourage a wider experimentation with cognitive interventions in general. Such a move is clearly necessary if we are to test the genuine potential of such approaches to provide portable and generalizable strategies which assist mentally handicapped people in making sense of their world.

Such work is also of importance in the manner in which it may focus rather more attention on the emotional and affective experience of individuals with a mental handicap – a hitherto neglected area. One of the few studies conducted in this area by Kushlick *et al.* (1986) reported positive outcomes following sessions of 'cognitive-behavioural' counselling of both handicapped clients and care givers. Further work is clearly necessary to develop our understanding of this area and extend therapeutic competence.

Intellectual prostheses

Most speculatively, advances are needed in relation to the development of intellectual prostheses for individuals with learning difficulties. Within the general population, devices to supplement or supplant cognitive functions are widespread. Digital watches, calculators, personal computers, word processors and so on, can all be construed as devices which lessen cognitive demands on the user. Advances in microtechnology promise the possibility that if a human cognitive process can be specified it may plausibly be emulated. This suggests the possibility of developing aids – intellectual prostheses – which assist a mentally handicapped individual in the discrete cognitive operations with which they have difficulty (Ager 1988b). The technology may well be close to hand, but our understanding of the subtleties of cognitive difficulties is still embryonic. For people with a mental handicap genuinely to gain from the new technology, considerable advances in our understanding of the precise prosthetic interventions required are necessary.

REFERENCES

Ager, A. K. (1983) 'An analysis of learning and attentional processes in mentally handicapped individuals', unpublished doctoral dissertation, University of Wales.
—— (1985) 'Alternatives to speech for the mentally handicapped', in F. N. Watts (ed.) *New Developments in Clinical Psychology*, Leicester/London: British Psychological Society/Wiley.

—— (1987) 'Minimal intervention: a strategy for generalised behaviour change with mentally handicapped individuals', *Behavioural Psychotherapy* 15: 16–30.

—— (1988a) 'Studies of "quality of life" using the Life Experiences Checklist', Mental Handicap Research Group Research Report 1, Department of Psychology, University of Leicester.

—— (1988b) 'Applications of microcomputer technology in the field of mental retardation', in J. A. Mulick and R. F. Antonak (eds) *Transitions in Mental Retardation: Applications and Implications of Technology*, New Jersey: Ablex.

—— (1989) 'Behavioural teaching strategies: a re-examination', Mental Handicap 17: 56–9.

—— (1990) 'Planning sustainable services: principles for effective targeting of resources in developed and developing nations', in W. Fraser (ed.) *Key Issues in Mental Retardation Research*, London: Routledge.

Alberman, E. (1984) 'Epidemiological aspects of severe mental retardation', in J. Dobbing (ed.) *Scientific Studies in Mental Retardation*, London: Royal Society of Medicine/Macmillan.

Baldwin, S. (1985) 'Sheep in wolf's clothing: impact of normalisation teaching on human services and service providers', *International Journal of Rehabilitation Research* 8: 131–42.

Belmont, J. M. (1978) 'Individual differences in memory: the cases of normal and retarded development', in M. M. Gruneberg and P. Morris (eds) *Aspects of Memory*, London: Methuen.

—— and Butterfield, E. C. (1971) 'Learning strategies as determinants of memory deficiencies', *Cognitive Psychology* 2: 411–20.

Brown, A. L. and Barclay, L. R. (1976) 'The effects of training specific mnemonics on the metamnemonic efficiency of retarded children', *Cognitive Development* 47: 70–80.

Brown, A. L., Campione, J. C. and Barclay, L. R. (1979) 'Training self-checking routines for estimating test readiness: generalisation from list learning to prose recall', *Child Development* 50: 501–12.

Brown, A. L., Campione, J. C., Bray, N. W. and Wilcox, B. L. (1973) 'Keeping track of changing variables: effects of rehearsal training and rehearsal prevention in normal and retarded adolescents', *Journal of Experimental Psychology* 101: 123–31.

Butterfield, E. C., Wambold, C. and Belmont, J. M. (1973) 'On the theory and practice of improving short-term memory', *American Journal of Mental Deficiency* 77: 654–9.

Chamberlain, P., Eysenck, A., Hill, P. and Wallis, J. (1984) *STEP – Staff Training Package*, Rossendale, Lancashire: British Association for Behavioural Psychotherapy.

Clarke, A. M. and Clarke, A. D. B. (1974) *Mental Deficiency: The Changing Outlook*, 3rd edn, London: Methuen.

—— (1980) 'Jack Tizard 1919–1979', *Journal of Child Psychology and Psychiatry* 21(1): 1–4.

Clements, J. (1987) *Severe Learning Disability and Psychological Handicap*, Chichester: Wiley.

Ellis, N. R. (1963) *Handbook of Mental Deficiency*, New York: McGraw-Hill.

Emerson, E. B. (1985) 'Evaluating the impact of deinstitutionalisation on the lives of mentally retarded people', *American Journal of Mental Deficiency* 90: 277–88.

Evans, G., Todd, S., Blunden, R., Porterfield, J. and Ager, A. (1987) 'Evaluating the impact of a move to ordinary housing', *British Journal of Mental Subnormality* 33: 10–18.

Feuerstein, R. (1979) *Instrumental Enrichment: Redevelopment of Cognitive Functions of Retarded Performers*, Baltimore: University Park Press.

Flynn, R. J. and Nitsch, K. E. (1980) *Normalisation: Integration and Community Settings*, Baltimore: University Park Press.

Goldstein, L. H. and Oakley, D. A. (1985) 'Expected and actual behavioural capacity after diffuse reduction in cerebral cortex: a review and suggestions for rehabilitative techniques with the mentally handicapped and head injured', *British Journal of Clinical Psychology* 24: 13–24.

Gow, L. (1986) 'Improving the efficiency of instruction of adults with an intellectual disability by enhancing the far generalisation of verbal self-instruction', in J. M. Berg (ed.) *Science and Service in Mental Retardation: Proceedings of the 7th World Congress of the ISSMD*, London: Methuen.

Hagberg, B. and Hagberg, G. (1984) 'Aspects of prevention of pre-, peri- and post-natal brain pathology in severe and mild mental retardation', in J. Dobbing (ed.) *Scientific Studies in Mental Retardation*, London: Royal Society of Medicine/Macmillan.

Haywood, C. (1976) 'The ethics of doing research and of not doing it', *American Journal of Mental Deficiency* 81: 311–17.

Horner, R. H., Dunlap, G. and Koegel, R. L. (1988) *Generalization and Maintenance: Life-style Changes in Applied Settings*, Baltimore: Paul Brookes.

Houts, P. S. and Scott, R. A. (1975) *Goal Planning with Developmentally Disabled Persons: Procedures for Developing an Individualised Client Plan*, Pennsylvania: Department of Behavioral Science, Pennsylvania State University College of Medicine.

Humphreys, S., Lowe, K. and Blunden, R. (1983) *Long Term Evaluation of Services for Mentally Handicapped People in Cardiff: Annual Report for 1982*, Cardiff: Mental Handicap in Wales Applied Research Unit.

Jenkins, J., Felce, D. and Mansell, J. (1983) *The Bereweeke Skill Teaching System*, Windsor: NFER/Nelson.

Jones, A. A., Blunden, R., Coles, E., Evans, G. and Porterfield, J. (1987) 'Evaluating the impact of training, supervisor feedback, self-monitoring and collaborative goal-setting on staff and client behaviour', in J. Hogg and P. Mittler (eds) *Staff Training in Mental Handicap*, London: Croom Helm.

Kiernan, C. C. (1977) 'Alternatives to speech: a review of research on manual and other forms of communication with mentally handicapped and other non-communicating populations', *British Journal of Mental Subnormality* 23: 6–28.

—— (1978) 'Behaviour modification', in A. M. Clarke and A. D. B. Clarke (eds) *Readings from Mental Deficiency: The Changing Outlook*, London: Methuen.

King, M. (1987) 'Health services and the prevention of mental handicap in the developing world', in G. Hosking and G. Murphy (eds) *Prevention of Mental Handicap: A World View*, London: Royal Society of Medicine.

King's Fund (1980) *An Ordinary Life: Comprehensive Locally-Based Residential Services for Mentally Handicapped People*, London: King's Fund Centre.

Kushlick, A., Hubert, J. and Smith, J. (1986) 'An intervention package to teach parents, residential care staff and teachers of children and adults with severe learning difficulties and serious self-defeating behaviours', *Educational and Child Psychology* 3: 87–91.

Landesman-Dwyer, S. and Berkson, G. (1984) 'Friendships and social behaviour', in J. Wortis (ed.) *Mental Retardation and Developmental Disabilities: An Annual Review, Volume 13*, New York: Plenum Press.

Luria, A. R. (1980) *Higher Cortical Functions in Man*, New York: Basic Books.

McBrien, J. A. and Foxen, T. H. (1987) 'A pyramid model of staff training in behavioural methods: the E. D. Y. project', in J. Hogg and P. Mittler (eds) *Staff Training in Mental Handicap*, London: Croom Helm.

McGill, P. and Emerson, E. (1987) 'The social psychology of community services', paper presented at the conference Contemporary Issues in Mental Handicap, Welsh DCP Special Interest Group, Abergavenny.

Meichenbaum, D. (1977) *Cognitive Behavior Modification*, New York: Plenum.

O'Brien, J. and Tyne, A. (1981) *The Principle of Normalisation: A Foundation for Effective Services*, London: Campaign for Mentally Handicapped People.

O'Connor, N. and Hermelin, B. (1963) *Speech and Thought in Severe Subnormality*, Oxford: Pergamon Press.

—— (1972) 'Seeing and hearing and space and time', *Perception and Psychophysics* 11(1A): 46.

—— (1978) *Seeing and Hearing and Space and Time*, London: Academic Press.

Partridge, K. (1984) *Changing Institutions? Quality of Care and Innovations in Hospitals for People with a Mental Handicap*, Birmingham: University of Birmingham.

Perkins, E. A., Taylor, P. D. and Capie, A. C. M. (1980) *Helping the Retarded – A Systematic Behavioural Approach*. Kidderminster: British Institute of Mental Handicap.

Reddy, G. N. N. (1987) 'Prevention of mental handicap – a world view', in G. Hosking and G. Murphy (eds) *Prevention of Mental Handicap: A World View*, London: Royal Society of Medicine.

Rincover, A. (1978) 'Variables affecting stimulus fading and discriminative responding in psychotic children', *Journal of Abnormal Psychology* 87: 541–3.

Ryan, J. (1987) *The Politics of Mental Handicap*, 2nd edn, Harmondsworth: Penguin.

Sartorius, N. (1984) 'Mental retardation – a world view', in J. Dobbing (ed.) *Scientific Studies in Mental Retardation*, London: Royal Society of Medicine/Macmillan.

Sidman, M. and Cresson, O. (1973) 'Reading and crossmodal transfer of stimulus equivalences in severe retardation', *American Journal of Mental Deficiency* 77: 515–23.

Strand, S. C. and Morris, R. C. (1988) 'Criterion-related versus non-criterion-related prompt training with severely mentally handicapped children', *Journal of Mental Deficiency Research* 32: 137–51.

Tennant, L., Cullen, C. and Hattersley, J. (1981) 'Applied behavioural analysis: intervention with retarded people', in G. C. L. Davey (ed.) *Applications of Conditioning Theory*, London: Methuen.

Tizard, J. (1953) 'The effects of different types of supervision on the behaviour of mental defectives in a sheltered workshop', *American Journal of Mental Deficiency* 58: 143–51.

Waldon, G. (1980) *Learning How to Learn How to Understand*, Didsbury, Manchester: Centre for Learning to Learn More Effectively.

Wolfensberger, W. (1983) 'Social role valorization: a proposed new term for the principle of normalisation', *Mental Retardation* 21: 234–9.

Woods, P. and Lowe, F. (1986) 'Verbal self-regulation of inappropriate social behaviour with mentally handicapped adults', in J. M. Berg (ed.) *Science and Service in Mental Retardation: Proceedings of the 7th World Congress of the IASSMD*, London: Methuen.

Zeaman, D. and House, B. (1963) 'The role of attention in retardate discrimination learning', in N. R. Ellis (ed.) *Handbook of Mental Deficiency*, New York: McGraw-Hill.

Chapter 10

Interpersonal problems

Peter Trower and Windy Dryden

CONCEPTUALIZATION AND ASSESSMENT

There is now abundant scientific support for the idea that humans are an inherently *social* species (Chance 1988; Gilbert 1989) and that failure in interpersonal relationships is a survival-threatening problem in that those with poor relationships are more unhappy, have worse physical and mental health and die earlier than those with good relationships (Argyle 1987; Argyle and Henderson 1985). It is not surprising that, unlike other topic areas in this book, interpersonal problems do not simply constitute another problem area but rather pervade practically all clinical problems (Hollin and Trower 1986). For this reason we will be referring to interpersonal difficulties across a range of clinical problems.

The range of interpersonal problems can be described from a number of viewpoints. We can look at them in terms of stages in the life-span, taking in childhood, adolescence, young and middle-age adulthood and old age, each of which is characterized by a type of interpersonal task which can create difficulty, such as establishing new relationships in the earlier years, marital and other longer-term relationships in the middle years, and loss of important relationships in late life. Or we can look at interpersonal problems in terms of a mild–severe continuum, with at one end such common experiences as loneliness, shyness or relationship breakdown, and at the other end, problems associated with psychiatric disorders. Indeed, psychiatric disorders themselves can be ranked on a severity continuum, ranging from specific social phobias such as fear of public speaking where other relating abilities are intact, through to chronic schizophrenia where there may be an almost complete loss of ability to relate to others.

Recent research shows that difficulty in forming relationships is surprisingly widespread. World-wide surveys reveal that at least 30 per cent of young people everywhere consider themselves too shy, and more than 70 per cent say that at some time in their lives shyness has hampered them socially (Jones *et al*. 1986). Loneliness – one of the consequences of excessive shyness – is also widespread (25 per cent of US subjects reported recent loneliness) and lonely people are more likely than non-lonely people to be psychiatric casualties, to be problem drinkers, to have psychosomatic disorders, to be prone to suicide, to have self-deprecatory beliefs and to be unhappy and pessimistic (Peplau and Perlman 1982). Lack of satisfactory long-term relationships is also associated with more physical illness in general and with higher mortality (Argyle and Henderson 1985).

There is a wealth of research which shows these and other deleterious effects of poor relationships on psychosocial adjustment, especially when they come early in life. A major predictor of poor prognosis in a number of psychiatric disorders such as schizophrenia is an early history of social isolation and few or poor relationships. A good deal of work has gone into understanding the attachment system, and the disruption that disturbances in attachment can later bring (for example, Bowlby 1980; Reite and Field 1985). The same processes that occur in attachment – care and safety – continue in a modified form in all good relationships in the form of emotional and practical support. Conversely failure in attachment has equally bad effects in that it makes it difficult either to give or receive such support throughout the life-span.

Cognitive-behavioural theories of interpersonal problems

Humans are endowed with potentialities for establishing and maintaining different types of social relationships (Gardner 1988), such as co-operating, competing, care giving and care eliciting (Gilbert 1989). However, individuals must have relevant cognitive-social learning experiences before they can turn these potentialities into social skills which they can utilize in social interaction. The term 'social skills' has become a widely used term to refer to the skills people need for social interaction, but it originated in a theory, known as the social-skill model, first developed by Argyle and Kendon (1967), to explain the acquisition of social behaviour and to explore how failure may come about in such acquisition. A number of theories have subsequently been developed, extending or providing more comprehensive alternatives to the original model (for example, Bandura 1977; Carver 1979; Trower and Turland 1984).

Perhaps the best way of describing social-skills theory is to make a distinction between social *skills* – the behavioural components or repertoire of actions – and social *skill* – the process of generating skilled behaviour (Trower 1980, 1982).

Social *skills* (i.e. components) are the actual normative behaviours – single elements (looks, nods, lexical clauses and so on) or identifiable sequences of elements (greetings, partings, segments of discourse) – that a person may use in a given subculture and that conform to social rules. Such components are learned by experience or observation, retained in memory in symbolic form and subsequently run off automatically as complete behavioural units without conscious monitoring of the constituent parts (for example, Bandura 1977). They thus provide the substance of the individual's skills repertoire.

On the other hand social *skill* (i.e. the process) is the individual's ability to generate skilled behaviour according to rules and goals and in response to social feedback. The social-skill model of Argyle and Kendon (1967) is in this sense a process model, and similar models have been developed by others such as Bandura (1977) Carver (1979) and McFall (1982) and Wallace (1982) and all bear a family resemblance to the TOTE function (test-operate-test-exit) first developed by Miller *et al.* (1960).

According to the Argyle and Kendon model, the component social skills are acquired much like serial motor skills in that the individual goes through a *process* of monitoring the immediate situation and continually adjusting his or her behaviour in the light of feedback. There are three stages. The first is the existence of some goal to be achieved. The second stage includes the perception of cues from the environment, the (cognitive) translation of these into plans for action, and the motor response which entails performing the chosen action. The third stage is the consequent change in the environment (or goal state). A feedback loop connects this with the perceptual level of the second stage. Because so much social behaviour is predictable, repeating sequences can be run off as a 'skilled' sequence. The other models elaborate on this concept of central cognitive processing. McFall (1982), for example, describes three sets of processing skill: decoding skill (reception, perception and interpretation), decision-making skill (response search, response test, response selection, repertoire search and utility evaluation) and encoding skill (execution, self-monitoring).

Failure in social behaviour can be described in terms of component skills deficits and/or process skill deficits. There is a good deal of evidence that a wide range of psychiatric patients exhibit patterns of deficiency in component skills, and these will be described below for a number of clinical problems. There is less research on processing skill, but the research that has been done clearly indicates that this is a major problem area. The main problems so far investigated lie in two main areas. The first, already alluded to, is in the area of decoding, decision making and response selection (McFall 1982) or similarly receiving, processing and sending in Wallace's (1982) terminology, the treatment of which draws on the problem-solving tradition (D'Zurilla and Goldfried 1971; Spivack *et al.* 1976). The second area is concerned with cognitive distortions such that people misinterpret incoming information at the decoding level, leading them to select dysfunctional actions or no actions, leading in turn to the execution and thereby the learning of dysfunctional skills or no skills, and the inevitable failure to achieve goals. Indeed, cognitive distortions may give rise to dysfunctional goals in the first place. The treatment of this area draws on the cognitive therapies. In this chapter we shall focus on the cognitive distortions and their assessment and treatment by cognitive-behavioural methods.

Cognitive distortions

It is useful to make a distinction between two types of thoughts which can lead to deficits in processing skill (Dryden 1984a, b, 1987). The first type are called inferences, which are interpretations about the meaning of events, and may be true or false. Beck (1976) has been in the forefront of work in the assessment and modification of faulty inferences, and has identified many of those commonly expressed by clients. An example is an arbitrary inference, which means drawing a conclusion among a range of possible conclusions that has no more justification than a random guess. A person may see the other smile, but infer that the other is laughing at him, rather than, say, sending a friendly greeting.

The second type of thoughts are called evaluations. The role of irrational evaluative beliefs is a core element in rational-emotive therapy, and the concept was developed by Ellis (1962). Evaluations are judgements that the event, as inferred, is good or bad. Not only do people have mistaken evaluations – characteristically judging events to be bad when they are in fact good or neutral, but tend to jump to extremes, seeing events as catastrophically bad, or 'terrible' or 'awful'.

Strongly held beliefs – inferences or evaluations – influence what the person attends to and cause selective filtering and interpretation of information to fit the construct, a process which Snyder (1981) calls 'cognitive bolstering'. The more belief based a person is, the less able he or she is to monitor the situation for feedback, and the less able to respond in an appropriate, skilful way. Furthermore, actions chosen will tend to follow from what the belief dictates, resulting in behavioural confirmation. The two processes tend to operate together, such that cognitive bolstering leads to behavioural confirmation and vice versa. We can see that here the normally 'virtuous' cycle of adaptive skill learning becomes a 'vicious' cycle of maladaptive learning, and simply exacerbates psychopathological patterns of thought, emotion and action (Trower 1981).

A crucial feature of the skill-learning process is the reduction of the discrepancy between a desired and an actual social goal or subgoal – a point brought out much more clearly in Carver's (1979) cybernetic model. The acquisition of social skill is, after all, about achieving greater and greater approximations to desired social goals. People *care* about the discrepancy – if they fail to reduce it they are in danger, not only of failing to achieve a goal, but more importantly of experiencing learned helplessness. Such a failure may be perceived as an example of social-skill deficiency. Social-skill deficiency may, in turn, be magnified through the 'lens' of cognitive distortion to mean that the failure is a failure within me as a person due to me rather than the situation (attributional inference to self); is likely always to occur in the future and in all situations (generalization inferences); and is 'awful' (exaggerated evaluation). These types of cognitive distortions have been well documented in the reformulated theory of learned helplessness (Abramson *et al.* 1978). Research in recent years has shown that the variety of cognitive distortions is truly enormous. There are now some excellent reviews of this literature (for example, Brewin 1988; Williams *et al.* 1988).

DEVELOPMENT AND MAINTENANCE

It has been known for some time that level of premorbid social competence is the best predictor of post-hospital adjustment in a wide range of psychiatric disorders, irrespective of the patient's diagnostic label (i.e. schizophrenia, alcoholism, depression) and regardless of the treatment carried out (Hersen 1979).

Many of these problems would undoubtedly have manifested initially in early shyness, and research on shyness reveals a variety of social-developmental as well as genetic factors (Daniels and Plomin 1985). In brief the body of this research seems to indicate the following:

1 *Parental style*   Either a rejecting or an overprotective parental style led to high needs for approval, preoccupation with others' evaluative remarks and a fear of negative evaluation (Allaman *et al*. 1972). Buss (1986) suggests that such fears also arise out of excessive parental emphasis on proper grooming, dress, manners and other aspects of social decorum. Finally, parents that avoid and discourage social interaction with others are more likely to be shy and have shy children (Daniels and Plomin 1985).
2 *Developmental variables*   Research indicates that shy children have more physical illness (stomach ailments, sleep disturbances, headaches and allergies) (Briggs and Cheadle 1986), are more likely to be single or first born (Zimbardo 1977) and are more likely to be *neglected* rather than either rejected by or unpopular with other children (for example, Coie and Dodge 1983) – a characteristic that lasts into adulthood (Gilmartin 1987).

Another important antecedent of shyness is acute self-consciousness in early adolescence. This is believed to be due to three developmental processes: onset of puberty, entering a new school situation and the onset of formal operations thinking in which the child is able to distinguish between the perspectives of others and one's self view (Cheek *et al*. 1986).

Many of the above variables are known to play a role in a variety of psychological disorders. Bruch *et al*. (1988) showed, for example, that a majority of these precursors were associated with social phobia. And it is now well established that a hostile family atmosphere is the most important trigger of relapse in schizophrenia (for example, Vaughn and Leff 1976), suggesting that a rejecting parental style is important in the development of the disorder.

Many of the above variables are also related to core irrational and dysfunctional beliefs identified by Ellis (1962) and Beck and Emery (1985), and are the focus of cognitive psychotherapy. Examples of such beliefs are 'I must be approved of by virtually everyone or else I am worthless' and 'I must do everything perfectly or I am no good'. Such beliefs are often learnt in childhood from parent figures and then sustained into adulthood in the form of constantly repeated cognitive rules for living. Such beliefs are self-maintaining, and give rise to and maintain dysfunctional patterns of social behaviour. Such belief–behaviour cycles operate as self-maintaining principally because they function as self-fulfilling prophecies, as we outlined earlier. For example, someone who believes that he or she is unworthy and will always be rejected by others, will (a) selectively attend to and interpret the behaviour of others in accordance with the beliefs (cognitive bolstering) and (b) behave in ways guided by the beliefs which tend to elicit responses from others which confirm the beliefs (behavioural confirmation) (Trower 1981).

Cognitive-behavioural assessment of interpersonal problems

We commented above that most psychological disorders exhibit a component concerned with interpersonal problems, and asserted that these difficulties may be either a cause or an effect of the psychological disorder itself. The task of researchers has been, first, to establish valid ways of assessing interpersonal problems and, second, to provide descriptive and explanatory accounts of the patterns of difficulties found.

One way of evaluating interpersonal problems is to assess the social skills (and deficiencies in such skills) and closely associated phenomena in the domains of emotion, cognition and personality, of individuals within clinical problem areas. Before considering the specific applications, we shall briefly review and evaluate the most popular assessment methods.

Bellack (1979, 1983) reviewed a number of strategies employed in assessing social skills, including the clinical interview, self-report and self-monitoring, behavioural observation, peer rating and physiological monitoring. Of these the most commonly employed techniques, in the research literature at least, are self-report and self-monitoring, and behavioural observation.

The self-report measures – of which there are many dozens in the SST literature – include questionnaires, check-lists, rating scales and self-monitoring devices. These measures are designed to assess a variety of variables, including general personality dispositions, specific behaviours, cognitive and emotional reactions to stimuli and situations, performance of skills at global and specific levels, and monitoring of these reactions over time and situations. These measures vary greatly in their degree of psychometric acceptability, with more recent research showing an improvement over earlier ones. A popular and useful self-report measure of social skills is the Social Performance Survey Schedule (Lowe and Cautela 1978) which has a reasonable level of predictive validity (Miller and Funabiki 1984).

Assessment of social-skills components is the most advanced area. Most authors have favoured observational assessment as less biased, more objective and more sensitive to treatment effects, though this has been contested by Jacobson (1985). While naturalistic observation is the most preferred, in practice this has been difficult to achieve, and two main alternatives have been used. The first is a staged 'naturalistic' interaction, for example observing a social-skills trainee's behaviour in a waiting-room situation, while the trainee is unaware that assessment is taking place (Gutride *et al.* 1973). More commonly, however, a structured role-play is used, where the trainee acts out a response to a set scene. There are at least four different types of role-play test, some of which have been heavily criticized as lacking in 'ecological' (real-life) validity, to such an extent that Bellack (1983) has urged that the use of single-prompt role-play and taped role-play tests should be abandoned. Other types have more promise and have been endorsed by several authors (for example, Kern *et al.* 1983). Merluzzi and Biever (1987) found that structured and unstructured role-plays had some validity when social skills were rated on molar scales. Pettit *et al.* (1987) also found greater ecological validity for molar ratings but not for molecular ratings in a laboratory simulation of social interactions among children.

One of our criticisms of most behavioural measures is that the basic assumptions about the nature of social interaction are too simplistic, and do not take account of the context, interaction or linguistic structure of discourse (Trower 1982). However, recent developments are encouraging – for example, the application of discourse analysis from the field of linguistics (Gervasio 1987) and the growth of more appropriate experimental and statistical procedures for analysing sequences of social interaction (for example, Bakeman and Gottman 1986; Faraone and Hurtig 1985).

Assessment of process variables, including social perception, cognition and emotion, is still in its relative infancy. Assessment of cognitions is acknowledged as a particularly difficult area. However, there is some progress in this area. Heimberg *et al.* (1987b), for example, found considerable support for the validity of the thought-listing technique. A number of suggestions as to the kinds of assessments which should be developed or adapted from existing ones are made in Shepherd (1984) and Hollin and Trower (1986), including: objective tests of the perception of social cues; standard questionnaires on such phenomena as attributional style, self-monitoring and irrational beliefs; repertory grids and semantic differential scales; thought listing and thought and emotion record forms. Schlundt and McFall (1985) offer a useful model for conceptualizing the assessment of social competence and social skills. A number of measures have been developed for specific problems, as we shall see below.

We shall now review progress on the conceptualization and assessment of a selected range of clinical problems from the interpersonal perspective.

Social anxiety/social phobia

Social anxiety has a long history of interest among social psychologists and specifically social-skills researchers, both from a theoretical and a practical point of view. This has not been the case in the clinical literature, however (Barlow and Wolfe 1981; Liebowitz *et al.* 1985), and it is only recently that this neglected problem has been fully recognized (APA 1980; Heimberg 1989).

The main findings of a clear relationship between levels of social skill and social anxiety have remained fairly robust across a substantial number of studies, and are reviewed in Trower (1986). These can be summarized as follows. At the behavioural level, there are general findings that socially anxious people (clients and non-clients) are seen as less skilled than low-anxiety people at the level of general impressions (for example, Halford and Foddy 1982), but the picture with regard to specific behavioural differences is mixed, with some studies showing differences in, for example, amount of speaking, response latency, amount of looking and general avoidant behaviour, but other studies not showing differences. At the cognitive level, socially anxious subjects have various negative beliefs which disrupt the performance of social skills (for example, Alden and Cappe 1981); for example, they see themselves as less skilful than others see them, endorse perfectionistic standards, attribute failure to themselves and successes to situational causes, and endorse other irrational beliefs. In a well designed study, Beidel *et al.* (1985) not only confirmed these findings across several social-evaluative situations, but found higher physiological arousal, in particular higher blood pressure and heart-rate readings, in subjects with clinical levels of social anxiety compared to non-anxious controls.

There is a wealth of assessment devices for social anxiety. Self-report measures alone can be subdivided into questionnaires on social anxiety *per se*, shyness, specific situations, assertiveness, social skills, cognitions and questionnaires which attempt to combine two or more of these variables. Again, validity of various kinds is a problem with many measures, and even such established instruments as the Fear of Negative Evaluation Scale has come under scrutiny with regard to content validity. Second, with regard to behavioural measures, these are usually based on some form of role-play tests with associated rating scales. Types of role-play vary greatly, and some have decidedly better ecological validity (that is, where valid simulations of natural social interactions take place) than others. There are various problems with most rating scales too – many of them are so constructed that they miss critical features of social performance, by segmenting behavioural interactions into artificial chunks and failing to measure the sequential nature of social interaction.

Depression

Depression is another problem area where social-skills deficits exist but in a more subtle form than originally thought. Early studies found that depressives gave less verbal output, fewer initiations and a lower rate of positive reinforcing behaviour (for example, Libet and Lewinsohn 1973). Gotlib and Robinson (1982) found that they made fewer statements of direct support, a greater number of negative content statements, had more monotonous speech, smiled less frequently, engaged in gestures not related to their speech and had less positive facial expressions. In drawing together the results of several studies (for example, Gotlib and Meltzer 1987), it appears that such behaviour does not lead conversation partners to judge the depressed person as less socially skilled but rather to judge *themselves* as less socially skilled than they would normally. This effect on others now seems fairly robust, and supports Coyne's (1976) original finding that ordinary subjects who had telephone conversations with depressives, felt more depressed, anxious and hostile, and rejected opportunities for future contact. There was evidence from this and two other studies (Hammen and Peters 1978; Howes and Hokanson 1979) that it is the content of what is said, i.e. intensely personal and negative self-disclosure, that creates such impressions and reactions, leading to a negative spiral of rejection and further depression. In other words, depressives do exhibit social-skills 'deficits' but in a way and at a level which is not revealed by simple behavioural measures. Depression has been one of the most studied problems from a cognitive-therapy perspective (Beck *et al*. 1979) and characteristic cognitions of depressed people well documented (Teasdale 1983), but there has as yet been little work connecting the pattern of depressive cognitions with the interpersonal style of depressed people. The likelihood is that the two (cognitions and behavioural style) combine to produce a self-fulfilling prophecy (beliefs affect social actions which affect beliefs).

Williams (1986) gives a useful framework and review of social-skills assessment measures in depression. These include self-ratings of difficulty with interpersonal situations, structured interviews of interpersonal adjustment, self-monitoring of positive and negative reactions, observer ratings of positive and negative actions and reactions, and finally observer ratings of the elements of social behaviour. Williams claims that it is an open question whether these measures are valid as measures sensitive to social-skill deficiency. In addition, we do not know of any studies that have attempted specifically to link measures of social perception or thinking style with social-skills deficits.

Mental handicap

Part of the accepted definition of mental handicap includes deficits in adaptive behaviour, particularly social behaviour (Wetherby and Baumeister 1981). Clearly, people with mental handicaps may show deficiencies in almost any of the huge range of social-skills components and processes. Social-skills deficits are particularly pronounced in this group, which makes people with such handicaps extremely vulnerable to stigmatization. Deficits that have been focused upon by various researchers include gestures, facial mannerisms, eye contact, number of words spoken, voice intonation, verbal content and overall social skills (for example, Senator *et al*. 1982), subject changes, discussion of past problems, using words appropriately and duration of speech (Stephens *et al*. 1981). As can be seen, the emphasis has been strongly on components rather than processes.

Two instruments used for assessing types of skills are the NOSIE – a general scale for assessing social functioning adapted for people with mental handicaps (Matson *et al*. 1983) and the SPSS, which assesses more specific components (Lowe and Cautela 1978; adapted by Matson *et al*. 1983). Matson *et al*. claim that both have reported good 'validity and reliability data'. However, Castles and Glass (1986) have broken new ground recently in developing three measures for people with mild and moderate mental handicaps which are directly related to Argyle and Kendon's social-skills model. These are (to use the authors' terms) attitudinal-expectancy variables (Interpersonal Self Efficacy Scale), cognitive abilities (Social Problem-Solving Test) and motoric/performance skills (Behavioural Social Skills Assessment). The measures have sufficient reliability and discriminant validity and – exceptionally – high content validity. There are a number of other existing scales which could also be adapted for this population, such as the Vineland Social Maturity Scalke (Doll 1953, 1965).

Despite these developments, few authors have attempted to develop a cognitive-behavioural perspective in the mental handicap field. Lindsay and Kasprowicz (1987) note that few therapists readily consider a cognitive-behaviour-therapy approach to be relevant to this population, yet staff who work with people with mental handicaps recognize that problems in self-image, self-confidence and negative self-statements are of crucial importance. Lindsay *et al.* (1985) found significant problems with lack of confidence when introducing adults to new skills and experiences in the community. Due to the lack of available measures, Lindsay and Kasprowicz (1987) developed a 'confidence' schedule, consisting of five sections on social and community and living skills, each section having between four and seven questions, asked in colloquial language and requiring simple 'yes' or 'no' answers. The final score is obtained by adding together the questions answered positively – the higher the score, the greater the individual's degree of confidence. No psychometric properties are reported.

Schizophrenia

Long-stay institutionalized schizophrenic patients are among the most skills-deficient of all psychiatric groups (Sylph *et al.* 1978) and it has been long established that level of social competence plays a major role in the aetiology and prognosis of the disorder (for example, Zigler and Phillips 1961). It is clear that the characteristics of schizophrenia – both positive (such as disorders of thought and perception, mannerisms and posturing, and inappropriate or incongrous affect) and negative (such as lack of energy and motivation and social withdrawal) – create extreme difficulty in initiating and maintaining social interactions. In common with work in most of the clinical problem areas, researchers have tended to focus on social-skills component deficits in schizophrenia. Lindsay (1984), for example, found that, compared to non-schizophrenic controls, schizophrenic subjects performed worse on such components as speech volume, tone and clarity, amount spoken, facial expression, eye contact and posture. Others, however, have not found such consistent differences. There has been a lack of work on more interactive skills and on skill processing. Reflecting this pattern, assessment measures have also focused on measuring components, either quantitatively or on rating scales, in either role-play simulations or *in vivo* (Bellack 1983). Again, the assessment of feelings and various types of cognitions has been neglected. Shepherd (1984) and Mulhall (1976) have developed the Personal Questionnaire in this direction. This questionnaire method has the advantage that it provides an internally consistent yet individual-centred approach where the item content is selected by the client. Another area of development is the assessment of the social networks of schizophrenics (Shepherd 1986). This is an important development since it is well established that the extent and quality of social networks is a major indicator of prognosis in these clients (and as we have emphasized, many other clients).

Substance abuse

An early finding of a relationship between poor social competence and alcoholism (Sugerman *et al*. 1965) has been viewed with some scepticism for a number of years, but recent research has supported and refined the earlier findings. One area of research has focused on the psychosocial development of alcoholism. Asher and Renshaw (1984), for example, found that children and adolescents who are at risk for alcohol abuse are likely to have poor social skills. Similar results have been found in drug addicts (Van Hasselt *et al*. 1978). A number of studies have been conducted to examine the comparative differences between problem drinkers and other groups, as well as the specific skill deficits shown, and specific situations that trigger skills failure. Hamilton and Maisto (1979) found that problem drinkers exhibited more discomfort in assertion-requiring situations than non-problem drinkers. Miller and Eisler (1977) found a significant correlation between deficiency in negative assertion and alcohol consumption. Indeed, a number of studies indicate that a lack of assertiveness in some problem drinkers may lead to excessive drinking as a alternative to coping behaviour (Monti *et al*. 1986).

Recent emphasis has been aimed at tackling the high relapse rate in ex-problem drinkers – some 70–80 per cent within 6 months (Marlatt and Gordon 1980). Marlatt and Gordon found two situations preceded relapse in 39 per cent of cases – interpersonal conflict and social pressure to drink. It was just such situations that non-relapsers were found to handle in a more assertive and drink-refusing manner (Rosenberg 1983). A number of studies have produced findings regarding interpersonal difficulties in alcohol and drug abusers.

Monti *et al*. (1986) reviewed social-skills assessment methods for substance abuse in four areas: questionnaire self-report, *in vivo* observation, naturalistic interaction and role-play tests. In addition, they subdivided measures into general skills and specific skills (measures tailored to social situations of special importance to a particular client group). However, the authors reported that there has been 'little evidence for the validity of the measures reported in the literature' and not enough attempt to integrate measures across behavioural, cognitive and physiological modes of response. They offer a triple-response-mode approach to fill this gap. This approach simultaneously assesses across all three modes.

There are many other problem areas in which interpersonal difficulties play an important role (for example, in childhood, old age, forensic groups and so on), and the reader is referred to Hollin and Trower (1986) for further discussion.

COGNITIVE-BEHAVIOURAL INTERVENTIONS

The focus of our review of cognitive-behavioural interventions will be on those studies which have tried to look at the comparative effectiveness of social-skills training alone, cognitive-behaviour therapy alone, and/or an intervention which combines the two. We will also look at some other approaches which may complement these.

Our review makes it immediately apparent that little work has been carried out in the area of interpersonal problems using interventions from the cognitive-behavioural perspective. The most advanced area is social anxiety, where difficulties in interactions both from a social skills and from a cognitive point of view have proceeded hand in hand. This imbalance will be reflected in our review of interventions for some of the psychological disorders referred to above.

Social anxiety/social phobia

Social anxiety is a problem *par excellence* where a combination of social-skills training (SST) and cognitive psychotherapy would theoretically be more effective than either treatment alone. This is because social anxiety is simultaneously a social problem and one where a belief-based fear of negative evaluation is a defining characteristic. SST acts as an appropriate form of exposure as well as helping with new skills, while cognitive psychotherapy is designed to change dysfunctional self-evaluative beliefs which would otherwise be expected to block the acquisition of skills or undermine the benefit of exposure. As Butler (1989) reports, for example, the fear of being negatively evaluated, criticized or rejected appears not to decrease after exposure alone, and points up the need for cognitive strategies to facilitate realistic appraisals and thereby help patients find out whether or not their expectations were erroneous.

Most of the earlier outcome studies on SST did not include a cognitive-psychotherapy component, nor did they include evaluations of whether cognitive changes were taking place as well as behavioural ones. There are a number of reviews of these studies, including Arkowitz 1977; Curran 1977; Marzillier 1978; and Twentyman and Zimering 1979. Another more recent set of reviews included some evaluations of cognitive psychotherapy, and more studies based on clinical cases (including Curran *et al.* 1985; Emmelkamp 1982; Heimberg and Barlow 1988; Shepherd 1983; Stravynski and Shahar 1983).

A considerable proportion of the studies in this first set of reviews were judged to be flawed methodologically and it was difficult to draw any conclusions from them. However, conclusions that *were* drawn included: (1) SST could produce behavioural change in the short term, compared to no-treatment control groups, and *some* evidence that it was superior to viable alternative treatments; (2) there was little convincing evidence that changes were durable or generalized to real-life settings. Twentyman and Zimering (1979) found that both SST and systematic desensitization produced equally effective results with socially anxious clients.

Some of the findings from the second set of reviews were: (1) a majority view that SST and cognitive restructuring together produce the most promising results for socially anxious clients (Emmelkamp 1982; Heimberg and Barlow 1988; but not Stravynski and Shahar 1983); (2) SST is superior to no-treatment controls and a number of viable treatment alternatives including short-term psychotherapy, group discussion, sensitivity training and bibliotherapy (Stravynski and Shahar 1983); (3) *some* evidence that effects are maintained but evidence on generalization remains weak; (4) the full package of SST components works better than any single component. The authors also noted that there were still far too many methodological weaknesses in studies.

Two studies found cognitive interventions added nothing to SST or exposure. Stravynski *et al.* (1982) found that SST alone and SST combined with cognitive modification based on rational-emotive therapy were equally effective in increasing social interaction with reduced anxiety, reduced depression and reduced irrational beliefs, but cognitive modification did not enhance the effectiveness of SST. A study by Biran *et al.* (1981) found that cognitive restructuring added nothing to exposure in therapeutic change in patients whose main problem was 'scriptophobia' (fear of writing in the presence of others). However, Heimberg and Barlow (1988) argue that these studies may have administered cognitive procedures in a way that would not be deemed acceptable by cognitive therapists, and did not take account of recent developments in knowledge of the cognitive processes involved in social phobia.

Cognitive interventions have been found effective in several studies both as independent treatments (Emmelkamp *et al.* 1985; Jerremalm *et al.* 1986; Kanter and Goldfried 1979) or in combination with exposure or SST (Butler *et al.* 1984; Heimberg *et al.* 1987a; Mattick and Peters 1988).

In the most recent review of cognitive-behavioural interventions for social phobia, Heimberg (1989) calls for greater differentiation between diagnostic subtypes, more investigation of specific responses to specific treatments or combinations of treatments, and more study of the mechanisms of change.

Intervention procedures

Research centres vary in the cognitive-behavioural therapeutic procedures they develop for socially anxious clients, but there seems to be a common core to recent approaches, which combine cognitive restructuring with exposure to feared social situations, but does not include an explicit SST component. We will give two examples of these approaches.

The first example comes from Heimberg *et al.* (1987a). This group has a programme which is administered by two co-therapists to five or six patients with social phobia in twelve weekly sessions and is comprised of several components:

1 developing a cognitive-behavioural explanation of social phobia;
2 training patients in the skills of identification, analysis and disputation of problematic cognitions through the use of structured exercises;
3 exposing patients to simulations of anxiety-provoking situations in the context of the treatment group;
4 using cognitive-restructuring procedures, such as those mentioned in step 2, to teach patients to control their maladaptive thinking before and during the 'exposure simulations' described in step 3;
5 using similar procedures to teach patients to engage in rational self-analysis

rather than negative self-evaluation after the conclusion of an exposure simulation;

6 assigning homework in which patients would expose themselves to real anxiety-provoking events after they have confronted these events in exposure simulations;

7 teaching patients a self-administered cognitive-restructuring routine so that they may engage in cognitive preparation for homework assignments and in rational self-analysis after their completion.

In one study evaluating this multi-component approach, Heimberg *et al.* (1988) found that there were significant gains on the main measures, both immediately and at 6 months follow-up, compared to a credible placebo control group.

Mattick *et al.* (1988) developed a package that was similar in many respects to the above. They also emphasized the importance that both avoidance behaviour and maladaptive irrational thoughts and attitudes have in initiating and maintaining social phobia. Subjects were told that it was essential to address these factors together by entering phobic situations and in these situations identifying and altering their aberrant thought patterns. It was emphasized that the feared situations were not in themselves anxiety provoking, but rather the anxiety experienced was due to maladaptive and irrational thoughts and attitudes. It was suggested that concern about the opinions of others, the feeling that others were watching and the belief that others could see signs of anxiety were largely unfounded and were responsible for the anxiety experienced in phobic situations. Once the approach was understood, great importance was placed on systematically identifying these irrational thoughts, re-evaluating them objectively, and changing the thoughts to be more realistic and rational. By way of practice the subjects were required within each session to analyse at least two phobic situations for two sources of irrationality: (a) how likely it was that the interpretation of the situation was in fact realistic; (b) what the ultimate implications were for the subject of the way he or she had labelled the situation. Initially the therapists played a very active role in this process but as the method was understood, active direction was gradually withdrawn. However, therapists continued closely to supervise and monitor subjects' practice. Subjects were encouraged to practise on their own, being told that emotional reactions in social settings would now serve as a 'cue' to start rational re-evaluations. These techniques were practised in each session. At the first session, subjects were given a booklet (Young 1974) explaining the rational-emotive approach, which was discussed at the following session. At the third session selected irrational assumptions from Ellis (1962) were incorporated into the practise sessions. Subjects were given six homework assignment sheets each week and asked to enter phobic situations (graded in order of increasing difficulty) and to write about those phobic episodes. The sheets provided for recordings of: (a) a description of the situation; (b) anxiety experienced upon initially encountering the situation (0–100); (c) irrational thoughts that occurred; (d) rational reappraisal of the situation; (e) subsequent anxiety level (0–100). They also recorded the number of minutes spent in the situation.

In two evaluation studies (Mattick and Peters 1988; Mattick *et al.* 1988) the treatment that combined exposure and cognitive restructuring was superior on the main measures to all other treatment groups (exposure alone, cognitive restructuring alone and waiting-list control) – a difference that tended to increase at follow-up.

Neither of the above approaches included SST explicitly, except in so far as clients are 'exposed' to simulated and real social situations. A package that does integrate both components, namely rational-emotive therapy and SST, has been developed by Dryden (1984b), though the procedure has not yet been empirically evaluated. The programme is in two parts – assessment and training. We will give a summary of the training procedure, though it should be emphasized that the assessment phase is essential (for a full description of this assessment phase see Dryden 1984a).

Dryden subdivides training into two major treatment strategies for dealing with distorted inferences and irrational evaluations. These strategies are designed to be used in conjunction with skills-training assignments, and are intended to help clients overcome blocks to carrying out skills assignments, and to interpret and evaluate more realistically and constructively those assignments that they do carry out.

Major Strategy 1 is for helping clients make accurate *inferences* (automatic thoughts about what external events mean). Figure 10.1 describes ten major inferential distortions and corresponding treatment strategies. Illustrative examples are shown in Figure 10.2. For example, the first category of inferential distortion is all-or-nothing thinking, where the client views his or her performances or personal qualities in extremist black-or-white categories. The treatment strategy is to help the client view his or her social performance or personal quality along a continuum of 'more or less'. To illustrate, imagine Paul faltered in speech twice in 30 minutes while talking to a class-mate at lunch. His all-or-nothing distortion is 'I ruined the whole conversation.' Using a continuum he can make a factually more accurate response of 'I faltered twice in 30 minutes, but for the vast majority of time I spoke reasonably fluently.'

Major Strategy 2 is for helping clients make rational *evaluations* (beliefs about how good or bad those events are for themselves or significant others). Figure 10.3 outlines major strategies to help clients give up irrational 'demands' and replace them with realistic 'preferences'. The demands may come in the form of a premiss ('I *must* do well at all times') or a conclusion which follows from it ('I'm no good if I don't do what I must'). Adopting a preference ('I'd really like to do well at all times') leads to a different conclusion ('I'm disappointed if I don't do what I'd like'). Changes in such beliefs are designed to help clients become less fearful of making 'mistakes' when they attempt new skills. Illustrative examples are given in Figure 10.4.

Category of inferential distortion	Description	Treatment strategy
(1) All-or-nothing thinking	Client views performances or personal qualities in extremist black-or-white categories.	Help client view performances or personal qualities along a continuum. Introduce 'grey' area into human experience.
(2) Overgeneralization	Client concludes that a single negative event will keep recurring.	Help client to conclude that a single negative event *may* recur but is not bound to do so.
(3) Disqualifying the positive	Client discounts data which conflict with negative self-attitude and pessimistic outlook.	Help client to accept data which conflict with negative self-attitude and pessimistic outlook, thus introducing dissonance which serves as base to effect changes in underlying attitude and outlook.
(4) Personalization	Client relates event – usually negative – to him- or herself when there is no basis for doing so.	Help client to think in a less egocentric fashion – to view the event as outside his or her personal domain.
(5) Negative prediction	Client imagines that something bad is about to happen and takes prediction as fact although this may be unrealistic.	Help client to view prediction as a hypothesis and not fact. Helping him or her to gather data prior to hypothesis testing.
(6) Emotional reasoning	Client takes emotions as evidence for the way things really are.	Help client understand that emotions are not a guide to reality but stem from inferences and evaluations of reality.
(7) Mind reading	Client makes assumption that others are looking down on him or her without validating the assumption.	Help client view assumption as a hypothesis and collect further data prior to testing the hypothesis.
(8) Magnification	Client exaggerates situation or mistakes beyond realistic bounds.	Help client view situation or mistakes realistically and to view event in wider context by including all relevant facts.
(9) Selective negative focus	Client picks out and dwells exclusively on negative details, concluding that whole situation is negative.	Help client collect and focus on *all* relevant data and to view negative details in context of the Gestalt.
(10) Minimization	Client views positive situations, talents or efforts as less important than they really are.	Help client view positive events in context by helping to collect *all* relevant data and background material.

Figure 10.1 Major Strategy 1 – helping clients make accurate inferences (general principles)

	Inferential Distortion	Context	Example of distortion	Empirical response
(1)	All-or-nothing-thinking	Paul faltered in speech twice in 30 minutes while talking to a classmate at lunch.	'I ruined the whole conversation.'	'I faltered twice in 30 minutes but for the vast majority of time I spoke clearly. Also, the other person is equally responsible for the conversation.'
(2)	Over-generalization	Richard asked a girl for a date but she declined.	'I'm never going to get a date. Girls will always turn me down.'	'Just because this girl turned me down doesn't mean I'll never get a date. Since she was only the second girl I've asked, I can't conclude anything about how often girls will turn me down.'
(3)	Disqualifying the positive	Ruth went to a discotheque where several men asked her to dance and showed interest in her.	'They only asked me to dance because they felt sorry for me.'	'I have no evidence they were pitying me. It is more likely they were simply interested in me.'
(4)	Personalization	David saw a colleague talking to their mutual boss. He became angry and uncommunicative.	'He's telling the boss about me. He's trying to make trouble for me.'	'He could be talking about anything. I don't know what he was talking about. I'll check it out with the boss at our next routine meeting.'
(5)	Negative prediction	Annie became anxious in case her tutor asked her opinion in class.	'If he asks me everyone will laugh no matter what I say.'	'I have no evidence that people will laugh no matter what I say. They might like what I say, or not react at all.'
(6)	Emotional reasoning	Roy became depressed after spending the evening on his own afraid to go out dating.	'I feel nothing will ever change. I'll never lose my fear of women in dating situations.'	'*Feeling* nothing will change doesn't mean things won't change. Feelings don't predict the future. I can overcome my fear of dating.'
(7)	Mind reading	Bill felt hurt after seeing his lecturer in the street.	'He ignored me because he doesn't like me. He thinks I'm stupid as I never speak in class.'	'I don't know if he likes me or not. I don't even know if he saw me. He was with someone and they were talking. I'll ask him about the incident next time.'
(8)	Magnification	Jane met an acquaintance in the street and asked about his father's health, only to learn he died a few days earlier.	'He'll think I'm awful. That was the stupidest thing I've ever asked.'	'It might have been a slight *faux pas* but nothing more since I didn't know about his father's death.'
(9)	Selective negative focus	Sue overheard some of her fellow students criticizing her friend's clothes.	'That's what people are like — hurtful and insensitive.'	'People can be hurtful and insensitive but they are often not. I might equally have heard them saying nice things.'
(10)	Minimization	Stan got praise all round from fellow therapy group members for asking a girl for a date and being accepted. Stan hadn't asked a girl for a date in 4 years.	'It's no big deal really.'	'Of course it's a big deal! It took a lot of courage to ask her out and it's the first time for ages.'

Figure 10.2   Major Strategy 1 – helping clients make accurate inferences (specific examples)

Irrational evaluation	Reasons why the irrational evalution is untenable	Rational evaluation
Premiss: I must do well in social conversations.	'Must' implies that there is a law of the universe that states that I must do well. Clearly no such law exists except in my head and I can change that.	I really want to do well in social conversations but I don't have to.
Conclusion 1: I'm less worthwhile if I don't do well in social conversations.	This implies that I equate myself with my performance. It is clearly an over-generalization to say that I'm more worthwhile if I do well and less worthwhile if I do poorly. 'I', as a human, am too complex to be given a global rating 'less worthwhile' implies. 'I' am an ongoing ever-changing process and as such can't be given a global rating which implies that 'I' am static. 'I am less worthwhile' implies everything about me is less worthwhile since 'I am' is a statement about my total identity. This is clearly incorrect. If I have 'worth' as a human this is invariant and thus does not vary with my performances. I can take the position that I am worthwhile no matter what I do since someone could argue that I am worthless no matter what I do. I would do better to adopt the position 'I exist as an unrateable fallible human being and can choose to accept myself as such'. Rating myself will hinder rather than help me achieve my goals.	I'm neither less nor more worthwhile if I perform poorly or well. I'm a fallible human being who can't be given a global rating. I can choose to accept myself as a fallible human and still not like the fact that I don't do well (sometimes) in conversation.
Conclusion 2: I can't stand not doing well in social conversations.	I obviously have 'stood' not doing well in social conversations many times before. I have stood it as I'm still here. If I really could not stand it I would perish or disintegrate. This hasn't happened. Telling myself that I can't stand something is not the same as not actually standing it. I am, in fact, standing it although I could benefit from tolerating it better. I can stand it until I disintegrate then it won't matter. So I'd better more accurately remind myself that I can stand it.	I can stand not doing well in social conversations although I'll never like it. I can stand what I don't like.
Conclusion 3: It's awful.	'Awful' means first that my performance is totally 100 per cent bad which is incorrect since it could have been worse. 'Awful' further means that my behaviour is more than 100 per cent bad i.e. 101 per cent or even greater. Since nothing exists that is 101 per cent anything, my performance is not awful. 'Awful' further means that there is no behaviour in the universe worse than my performance. Hardly likely!	If I don't do well in social conversations that's bad but hardly 'awful'.

Figure 10.3   Major Strategy 2 – helping clients make rational evaluations (general principles)

Assuming the inference is correct	Irrational evaluation	Rational evaluation
(1) 'I ruined the conversation.'	'I'm a failure' (evaluative conclusion derived from premiss: I must ensure that conversations go well).	'I failed in this conversation but that doesn't make me a failure' (evaluative conclusion derived from premiss: I would like to ensure conversations go well).
(2) 'I'm never going to get a date. Girls will always turn me down.'	'This is awful' (evaluative conclusion derived from premiss: I must get a date with a girl to be happy).	'This is very bad, but hardly awful. I could gain satisfaction in other social and non-social activities' (evaluative conclusion derived from premiss: I would like to get a date although I don't have to have this for my happiness).
(3) 'They only asked me to dance as they felt sorry for me.'	'I can't stand being pitied. That makes me a pitiful creature' (evaluative conclusion derived from premiss: other people must take me seriously and not feel sorry for me).	'I can stand being pitied although I'll never like it. I'm a (fallible) human being with social anxieties' (evaluative conclusion derived from premiss: I'd prefer people to take me seriously and not feel sorry for me).
(4) 'He's telling the boss about me. He's trying to make trouble for me.'	'How dare he make trouble for me. He's rotten' (evaluative conclusion derived from premiss: other people must act fairly towards me).	'There's no law against people behaving unfairly towards me, although I strongly dislike this. They are rotten, just human beings acting in a rotten fashion' (evaluative conclusion derived from premiss: I would prefer it if people would act fairly towards me).
(5) 'If he asks me, everyone will laugh no matter what I say.'	'That would be unbearable. I will have made a fool of myself' (evaluative conclusion derived from premisses: (a) I need other people's approval; (b) I must not act foolishly).	I cannot make a fool of myself. I can accept myself as a fallible human who acts foolishly and I can bear it when I do' (evaluative conclusion derived from premisses: (a) I want other people's approval; (b) I don't like acting foolishly).
(6) 'I feel nothing will ever change. I'll never lose my fear of women in dating situations.'	'That would be awful' (evaluative conclusion derived from premiss: I must overcome my fear of women in dating situations).	'If I never lost my fear of women in dating situations that would be bad but hardly awful. I can still approach women even though I am anxious' (evaluative conclusion derived from premiss: I would like to (rather than must) overcome my fear of women in dating situations).
(7) 'He ignored me because he doesn't like me. He thinks I'm stupid as I never speak up in class.'	'I'm not worthy if people don't like me' (evaluative conclusion derived from premiss: I need other people to show they like me).	'If people don't like me that's sad but doesn't prove I'm unworthy. I can accept myself as a complex human whether others like me or not' (evaluative conclusion derived from premiss: I want other people to show they like me but don't need them to).
(8) 'He'll think I'm terrible. That was the stupidest thing I've ever said.'	'What a stupid idiot I am' (evaluative conclusion derived from premiss: I must not ask people stupid questions).	'I'm not a stupid idiot for asking a stupid question. A stupid idiot can always and only do stupid things. I don't qualify for that label!' (conclusion derived from premiss: I would greatly prefer it if I don't ask people stupid questions).

Figure 10.4   Major Strategy 2–helping clients make rational evaluations (specific examples)

Depression

We will first look at some of the conclusions that have been drawn in reviews of the outcome literature (for example, Williams 1986) on the comparative effects of SST, cognitive-behavioural therapy and other therapies. First, controlled studies consistently show that SST alleviates depression, and maintains and even enhances such improvements at follow-up (for example, Sanchez *et al.* 1980). A form of SST which included cognitive-behavioural components was equal in effectiveness to amitriptyline and psychodynamic psychotherapy but no more so (Bellack *et al.* 1983). Second, SST combined with cognitive-behavioural therapy does have a specific effect, in changing interpersonal skills as opposed to other aspects of depression. Hersen *et al.* (1984), for example, found a variety of significant differences and trends on behavioural skills (such as speech duration, voice tone, gaze and assertiveness) favouring cognitive-behavioural SST compared with drugs and psychotherapy, such differences being maintained at 6-month follow-up. However, Williams (1986) argues that such changes in skills are also produced by other therapies which are not specifically geared to change skills *per se*, such as cognitive therapy alone, pleasant-events scheduling (Zeiss *et al.* 1979) and self-control training (Fuchs and Rehm 1977), and raises the question whether social-skill improvements may be no more than a correlate of increased general motivation and increased motor activity which comes about as a result of any effective treatment. General conclusions about the effect of SST alone or SST plus cognitive-behavioural therapy on depression (and indeed other disorders) are limited because not enough research has been done to indicate which subtypes and symptoms of depression do best with which treatment. Research of the recommended kind includes the study of McKnight *et al.* (1984), who compared the effects of SST and cognitive therapy in reducing depression. They found that the effectiveness of treatment is greatly enhanced when the treatment is related to the findings of the initial assessment. They found, for example, that social-skills deficits improved with SST, cognitive deficits with cognitive therapy. A problem with interpreting the literature is that it is not always entirely clear whether SST procedures included cognitive-therapy components.

Despite the limitations in findings, it is encouraging that cognitive-behavioural SST has been shown to be effective in alleviating depression, and has the benefit (a) of having a much lower drop-out rate than, for example, drugs (Bellack *et al.* 1983), (b) of having no known 'side-effects', (c) of working with clients who do not respond to drugs and (d) of being reasonably cost effective. It is noteworthy that this tradition of research has not drawn on the literature referred to in the assessment section earlier on the connection between depressive cognitions and the interpersonal style of depressed people. In a recent review of this literature Gotlib (1990) points in the direction of systems theory and family therapy (for example, Minuchin and Fisman 1981) rather than cognitive-behavioural social-skills training as a promising treatment model, and develops a treatment procedure based on such a model (Gotlib and Colby 1987). Below we give brief examples drawing from each of these approaches. We note here that there is ample scope for a fruitful integration of the two.

One well established method of cognitive-behavioural SST has been developed by Bellack and Hersen and his colleagues (Becker and Heimberg 1985; Bellack *et al*. 1981; Hersen *et al*. 1982). The first stage (following assessment) is direct behavioural training. This focuses on a specific situation, and the clinician instructs the client both in the specifics of behavioural performance and in the reasons why the target behaviour is important. Several role-play rehearsals of the problem situations are conducted. The second stage is practice and generalization, in which homework assignments are set so that newly acquired skills may be put into practice in everyday life. The third stage is social-perception training, which focuses on the wheres and whens of adaptive responding rather than the hows. Attention is paid to the context in which a response occurs, such as appropriate times, places and reasons for a response, the historical context, the impact of recent interactions. Again, role-play is a major aid to learning. The fourth stage is self-evaluation and self-reinforcement training. This tackles negative beliefs which may block the acquisition and implementation of better social skills. For example, clients are helped to modify perfectionistic standards (by which they judge their performances as 'failures') by such questions as (a) what could make the response acceptable?; (b) is this modification realistically attainable?; (c) what standard might be more adaptive? The effectiveness of this approach is reviewed above.

The 'interpersonal systems approach' to the treatment of depression (Gotlib 1990; Gotlib and Colby 1987) combines systems theory with components of cognitive-behaviour therapy. The systems-theory part of this approach clearly involves the marital partner or the whole family, and begins with joining, which is communicating to the family that they are important, and that they can work with the therapist. Other techniques include reframing the depression in such a way that the family members relinquish their previous entrenched conceptualizations of the problem; restructuring, which allows the family to alter dysfunctional patterns of interaction; altering boundaries, which is designed to help break down subgroup barriers that separate family members. The cognitive-behavioural component has the two goals of (a) helping the individual understand the effect of the depression on those around him or her and (b) to attenuate the depressed person's increased accessibility to negative stimuli. Techniques for the latter task include monitoring thoughts and perceptions more accurately by use of a daily thought record, especially at the time of critical incidents; the recording of positive events, and the behaviours and reactions of others, both positive and negative; increasing the number of pleasurable activities and incorporating these into a daily activities schedule. Gotlib (1990) reports that a number of studies using the above approach have shown promising results, but more empirical work is required.

Mental handicap

Cognitive-behavioural interventions for interpersonal difficulties in people with mental handicaps is, as we show below, in its infancy. Research on SST for this group is better established and we shall briefly review this literature first.

Experimental studies of the effectiveness of SST with people with mental handicaps began in earnest in the early 1970s. In their comprehensive review, Robertson *et al.* (1984) identified twenty-two single-case experimental design studies and sixteen group-comparison studies up to 1982. They concluded that a wide variety of verbal and non-verbal social behaviours – up to thirty listed – were significantly improved with SST. Andrasik and Matson (1985) reviewed studies in a number of different settings: long-term residential care (eleven studies), short-term residential care (five studies), community-based programmes, including group homes (two studies), sheltered workshops (three studies), special education programmes (one study) and out-patient clinics (three studies). They reported significant behaviour change, and generalization and maintenance in several studies. Finally, Matson and DiLorenzo (1986) reviewed a number of studies under the headings of simple contingencies, social-skills packages, social-skills games and social-skill curriculum, with findings similar to those above.

Despite the significant findings, a number of serious shortcomings in most of these studies have been identified by all the reviewers. Robertson *et al.* (1984) observe that the goals of such studies are overwhelmingly behavioural, and only four studies deal with cognitive components. There was insufficient attempt to measure generalization, durability or change in the natural environment. There was little attempt to relate outcome to different training methods, duration of training or characteristics of clients or environments. There was a lack of convincing evidence to show that change in specific behaviours was related to more independent living. Andrasik and Matson (1985) and Matson and DiLorenzo (1986) criticize the bulk of the studies for relying on unidimensional rather than multimodal assessment, for neglecting basic psychometric principles in developing assessment instruments, for neglecting social-validation procedures and not controlling for variables such as motivation and mood induction which may account for pre–post changes in role-play tests.

Some recent studies have, however, made headway on some of these issues. Matson and his colleagues have developed reliable and valid measures across a broader spectrum, including direct observation measures for use in naturalistic settings, rating scales and check-lists, as well as indirect measures (Matson and DiLorenzo 1986). This group has also developed, promoted and utilized social-validation procedures, in particular social comparison and subjective evaluation (Kazdin and Matson 1981).

A number of recent studies have specifically addressed generalization issues. Matson and Earnhart (1981) found that consistent implementation of two procedures – self-monitoring and prompting of target behaviour *in vivo* – led to successful training and generalization. Matson and Andrasik (1982) found that social skills with self-monitoring and self-reinforcement was better than SST alone in obtaining generalization. Reese *et al.* (1984) found that self-recording was the critical component in maintaining behaviour change in a group home setting. In other studies, Matson has successfully used other patients as assistants or 'buddies'. Hecimovic *et al.* (1985) used a potential generalization programming tactic – the provision of socially competent peers with whom the subjects could interact. This did not prove effective, probably because of other naturally occurring factors which could have inhibited transfer. However, Shafer *et al.* (1984) used retarded children as peer-trainers to prompt responses from autistic children, and obtained generalization across settings, but no maintenance without additional training.

A number of studies have looked at the differential effectiveness of different forms of SST for different client groups, and at more valid training goals, such as independent living, rather than simply increased performance skills (Matson and DiLorenzo 1986).

Compared to behavioural approaches, cognitive-behavioural approaches have been notably absent from the literature, but are undoubtedly promising. In an exploratory study Lindsay and Kasprowicz (1987) used a form of cognitive-behaviour therapy based upon Meichenbaum's work (1977), and found that four out of five clients improved their 'confidence' scores on a measure reported above. The authors provide useful extracts to illustrate their work. The following illustrates three negative self-statements: 'I can't do this'; 'Oh this is terrible' and 'I feel bad'.

Margaret: I can't do this.
Therapist: Why can't you do it?
Margaret: Oh this is terrible.
Therapist: Why is it terrible?
Margaret: I don't know, it's just terrible, it's terrible.
Therapist: Think why it's terrible.
Margaret: I don't know. I feel bad.

In the next segment the therapist is trying to challenge Margaret's self-statements of feeling terrible.

Therapist: What do you think will happen to you?
Margaret: I don't know.
Therapist: Will anything happen?
Margaret: I don't know.
Therapist: Will you fall down?
Margaret: No.
Therapist: Will somebody scare you away?
Margaret: No. (*Laughs*)
Therapist: Will somebody hit you when you talk to them?
Margaret: No. (*Still laughing*)
Therapist: Will you sit on a seat and it will break?
Margaret: No, don't be silly. (*Laughing*)
Therapist: Well, what will happen?
Margaret: I don't know. (*Laughing*)
Therapist: Will anything happen?

Margaret: No.

Therapist: So nothing is going to happen?

Margaret: No.

Therapist: So why do you feel terrible if nothing is going to happen?

Margaret: I don't know.

Therapist: What could you say instead of 'I feel terrible'?

Margaret: I don't know. I can't do it.

Therapist: (To the group) What could Margaret say instead of 'I can't do it?'

Therapist: ...We think you could say to yourself something like: 'Just relax and it will be all right.' What do you think?

Margaret: I don't know.

Therapist: Well try it, say 'Just relax and it will be all right.'

Margaret: What?

Therapist: Say it to me. 'Just relax and it will be all right.'

Margaret: Just relax and I'll be all right.

Therapist: Great! Now try that again. (*The therapist asked Margaret to repeat this statement three times*).

Therapist: Great! Now say to yourself, 'Take a deep breath.'

Schizophrenia

Cognitive-behavioural approaches to interpersonal problems in schizophrenia constitute another neglected topic area. Again, most work has been done on SST and this will be reviewed first.

Many studies, both single-case design and control-group design, were carried out, mainly in the 1970s, and there are a number of reviews of these studies (Hersen 1979; Marzillier and Winter 1978; Shepherd 1981; Wallace *et al.* 1980). The general consensus of the reviews was similar to that of SST in other areas – that SST could produce behavioural change in the short term, but equivocal evidence that such changes were maintained or generalized, and a questioning of the relevance of some of the target behaviours as well as inappropriate training goals and procedures.

More recently, several large-scale clinical trials have documented that schizophrenics can acquire and maintain new skills, and that social-skills training can have a significant effect on relapse (Bellack *et al.* 1984; Hogarty *et al.* 1986; Wallace and Liberman 1985). As a result of this accumulating body of research, SST is now regarded as one of the most important psychosocial components of a comprehensive treatment programme for schizophrenia.

There has more recently been a marked shift in emphasis in SST research with schizophrenia, with more attention paid to understanding the causes and effects of poor social skills on symptoms and relapse, and a more functional and person-centred approach to implementing training programmes (Shepherd 1986).

One such shift has been to integrate SST better into ongoing rehabilitation programmes, such as partial hospitalization. Bellack, Turner, Hersen and Luber

(1984), for example, treated twenty chronic schizophrenic patients in a 12-week day hospital programme and forty-four equivalent patients in the same programme supplemented by SST. While both groups showed improvement immediately following treatment, the SST group continued to improve or maintained their gains on most measures during a 6-month follow-up, compared to the non-SST group which either maintained gains or lost them. However, half the patients in both groups were hospitalized again in the year following treatment, and the authors argue that SST needs to be embedded in a yet more comprehensive rehabilitation programme than the one they used.

Another area of recent focus has been the use of SST to reduce the factors that lead to relapse in schizophrenia – a considerable problem, with 50–60 per cent of discharged schizophrenics readmitted within 2 years (Brown 1982). Liberman and his colleagues (Liberman *et al*. 1982) based their approach on a two-way model of relapse, namely relapse is a function of too much stress and too few social coping skills. This led to the development of two applications of SST. First, families high in expressed emotion (high EE, which refers to over-emotional, usually hostile forms of interaction), which is a major trigger of relapse (Hooley 1985), were taught better communication skills (Falloon *et al*. 1984). Second, patients were given highly task- and situation-relevant SST (Liberman *et al*. 1984). Results in both areas have been promising. Falloon *et al*. (1984), for example, found less symptomatology and less relapse following family training. Liberman *et al*. (1984) found significant increases in skilled behaviour across situations – hospital, family and community and evidence of spontaneous generalization.

A further development concerns the design of the 'community' into which patients are discharged. Shepherd (1986) criticizes the notion of SST as a prescribed therapy irrespective of the environment, and the associated outcome studies based on this approach. The design of environments means attempting to ensure that patients have opportunities to function in as normal a social context as possible, where normal social behaviour is indeed the norm. Then, instead of starting with the skills and hoping they will generalize, we should start with the role setting and work out which skills are necessary. 'This is like turning the social skills model upside down. By trying to start from the place where we hope to end up, we might achieve more significant improvements in "real" social adaption' (ibid.: 31).

Cognitive therapy has played little part in this largely behavioural SST approach, although other cognitive processes, such as training in social perception and problem solving, have now been fairly widely developed and integrated with SST for this population (for example, Liberman *et al*. 1986). More purely cognitive-orientated approaches include Meichenbaum's self-instructional training (Bentall *et al*. 1987; Meichenbaum and Cameron 1973) and cognitive restructuring (Watts *et al*. 1973). These developments have not, for the most part been concerned with schizophrenics' social functioning, but to improve performance on matching, sorting and other intellectual tasks.

Bellack *et al*. (1988) question the utility of problem-solving training in schizophrenia and suggest that more fundamental deficits, including sensitivity to negative affect and disordered communication, and other information-processing dysfunctions, may mean schizophrenics are unable to engage in problem-solving thinking. This question also needs to be asked of cognitive therapy approaches. It may mean that the underlying dysfunctions have to be addressed first, before traditional cognitive psychotherapy methods can be used. We believe that the investigation of these underlying dysfunctions is one of a number of developments that should be pursued in the future – a topic to which we now turn.

FUTURE DEVELOPMENTS

We have argued in this chapter that interpersonal problems form a major, if not central component of most psychological disorders, and that a cognitive-behavioural approach may be a fruitful and so far somewhat neglected approach to such problems. We have emphasized a particular form of the cognitive-behavioural approach, namely cognitive-behavioural social-skills training, on the hypothesis that dysfunctional beliefs are one of the major blocks to the learning and implementation of social skills, which in turn is one of the most promising 'behavioural' approaches to improving interpersonal relations. We have looked at the application of this approach to a number of major disorders, and have noted strengths and weaknesses in the literature in each area in the attempts to assess and treat interpersonal aspects of that problem, and have evaluated the probability of cognitive-behavioural social-skills training, with or without other approaches, being a treatment of choice.

Perhaps the most crucial single issue as to whether a cognitive-behavioural treatment approach to interpersonal problems is relevant for a particular disorder is the degree of psychological (or indeed neurological 'damage' to the individual. This issue is most clearly spelt out by Bellack *et al.* (1988) who observe that the recent literature on SST has placed an increasing emphasis on the role of cognitive factors in social failure. The point they make can be turned into a general one – that some disorders or dysfunctional states are so severe that affective and information-processing capabilities at a very basic level are deficient and unable to support the level of cognitive processing that would be required to carry out traditional cognitive therapy. This may well be the case, for example in some kinds of schizophrenia and mental handicap, but much less likely in social anxiety and unipolar depression. This would imply that therapy should adopt a kind of 'bottom-up' approach, tackling the fundamentals first, such as (in mental handicap) enabling individuals to establish simple levels of communication with others – not only the behavioural skills but also the underlying conceptual understanding and information-processing capability – where previously they may be entirely asocial at all these levels. Such a hierarchical approach may be useful in assessment, and in helping to decide a sequence with which to introduce therapeutic procedures. In this regard a psychobiological model of the individual such as that put forward by Gilbert (1989) may be helpful. According to this model, based on substantial ethological evidence, individuals are endowed by evolutionary development with a repertoire of psychobiological competencies. These range from those that are phylogenetically most recent and are designed for co-operative social group living down to those that are phylogenetically oldest and most primitive and are designed for responding to threat from predators and physical dangers, and are entirely asocial. Psychiatric disorders, ranked from the least to most severe, may be mapped against such an evolutionary scale, such that the greater the severity, the more likely it is that more primitive response systems will be triggered. Since cognitive therapy deals with comparatively recent competencies from a phylogenetically developmental point of view, severely disordered individuals may not find such approaches accessible. Though this theory is speculative in its application to psychological disorders, there is nonetheless a growing body of research that supports the model theoretically and empirically (Bailey 1987; Chance 1988; Marks 1987) and demonstrates explanatory power with a number of disorders such as social anxiety (Gilbert and Trower 1990; Trower and Gilbert 1989). The implications of this model have yet to be worked out, but may entail more traditional behavioural treatments based on operant and classical conditioning for severe disabilities, with more cognitive approaches being appropriate for those functioning at later developmental stages.

REFERENCES

Abramson, L. Y., Seligman, M. E. P. and Teasdale, J. D. (1978) 'Learned helplessness in humans: critique and reformulation', *Journal of Abnormal Psychology* 87: 49–74.

Alden, L. and Cappe, R. (1981) 'Nonassertiveness: skill deficit or selective self-evaluation?', *Behavior Therapy* 12: 107–14.

Allaman, J. D., Joyce, C. S. and Crandell, V. C. (1972) 'The antecedents of social desirability response tendencies of children and young adults', *Child Development* 43: 1135–60.

American Psychiatric Association (1980) *Diagnostic and Statistical Manual of Mental Disorders*, 3rd edn, Washington, DC: MA.

Andrasik, F. and Matson, J. L. (1985) 'Social skills training for the mentally retarded', in L. L'Abate and M. A. Milan (eds) *Handbook of Social Skills Training and Research*, New York: Wiley.

Argyle, M. (1987) *The Psychology of Happiness*, London: Methuen.

—— and Henderson, M. (1985) 'The rules of friendship', *Journal of Social and Personal Relationships* 1: 211–37.

Argyle, M. and Kendon, A. (1967) 'The experimental analysis of social performance', in L. Berkowitz (ed.) *Advances in Experimental Social Psychology*, Vol. 3, New York: Academic Press.

Arkowitz, H. (1977) 'Measurement and modification of minimal dating behavior', in M. Hersen, R. Eisler and P. M. Miller (eds) *Progress in Behavior Modification*, New York: Academic Press.

Asher, S. and Renshaw, P. D. (1984) 'Children without friends: social knowledge and social skills training', in S. Asher and J. Gottman (eds) *The Development of Children's Friendships*, New York: Cambridge University Press.

Bailey, K. (1987) *Human Paleopsychology: applications to Aggression and Pathological Processes*, Hillsdale, NJ: Lawrence Erlbaum.

Bakeman, R. and Gottman, J. (1986) *Observing Interaction*, New York: Cambridge University Press.

Bandura, A. (1977) *Social Learning Theory*, Englewood Cliffs, NJ: Prentice-Hall.

Barlow, D. H. and Wolfe, B. E. (1981) 'Behavioral approaches to anxiety disorders: a report on the NIMH-SUNY Albany Research Conference', *Journal of Consulting and Clinical Psychology* 49: 448–54.

Beck, A. T. (1976) *Cognitive Therapy and the Emotional Disorders*, New York: International Universities Press.

—— and Emery, G., with Greenberg, R. (1985) *Anxiety Disorders and Phobias: A Cognitive Perspective*, New York: Basic Books.

Beck, A. T., Rush, A. J., Shaw, B. F. and Emery, G. (1979) *Cognitive Therapy of Depression*, New York: Guilford Press.

Becker, R. E. and Heimberg, R. G. (1985) 'Social skills training approaches', in M. Hersen and A. S. Bellack (eds) *Handbook of Clinical Behavior Therapy with Adults*, New York: Plenum, pp. 201–26.

—— and Bellack, A. S. (1985) *Social Skills Training Treatment for Depression*, New York: Pergamon.

Beidel, D. C., Turner, S. M. and Dancu, C. V. (1985) 'Physiological, cognitive and behavioral aspects of social anxiety', *Behavior Research and Therapy* 23: 109–17.

Bellack, A. S. (1979) 'A critical appraisal of strategies for assessing social skill', *Behavioral Assessment* 1: 157–76.

—— (1983) 'Recurrent problems in the behavioral assessment of social skill', *Behavior Research and Therapy* 21: 29–42.

—— Hersen, M. and Himmelhoch, J. M. (1981) 'Social skills training compared with pharmacotherapy and psychotherapy in the treatment of unipolar depression', *American Journal of Psychiatry* 138: 1562–7.

—— (1983) 'A comparison of social skills training, pharmacotherapy and psychotherapy for depression', *Behavior Research and Therapy* 21: 101–7.

Bellack, A. S., Morrison, R. L. and Mueser, K. T. (1988) 'Social problem solving in schizophrenia', manuscript submitted for publication, Medical College of Pennsylvania, Philadelphia.

Bellack, A. S., Turner, S. M., Hersen, M. and Luber, R. F. (1984) 'An examination of the efficacy of social skills training for chronic schizophrenic patients', *Hospital and Community Psychiatry* 35: 1023–8.

Bentall, R. P., Higson, P. J. and Lowe, C. F. (1987) 'Teaching self-instructions to chronic schizophrenic patients: efficacy and generalization', *Behavioural Psychotherapy* 15: 58–76.

Biran, M., Augusto, F., and Wilson, G. T. (1981) 'In vivo exposure vs. cognitive restructuring in the treatment of scriptophobia', *Behavior Research and Therapy* 19: 525–32.

Bowlby, J. (1980) *Loss, Sadness and Depression: Attachment and Loss, Vol. 3*, London: Hogarth Press.

Brewin, C. R. (1988) *Cognitive Foundations of Clinical Psychology*, Hove and London: Lawrence Erlbaum Associates.

Briggs, S. R. and Cheadle, L. M. (1986) 'Retrospective accounts of the development of shyness', paper presented at the Southwestern Psychological Association, Fort Worth, TX.

Brown, M. (1982) 'Maintenance and generalization issues in skills training with chronic schizophrenics', in J. P. Curran and P. M. Monti (eds) *Social Skills Training: A Practical Handbook for Assessment and Treatment*, New York: Guilford Press.

Bruch, M. A., Heimberg, R. G., Berger, P. and Collins, T. M. (1988) 'Social phobia and perceptions of early parental and personal characteristics', manuscript submitted for publication.

Buss, A. (1986) *Social Behavior and Personality*, Hillsdale, NJ: Lawrence Erlbaum Associates.

Butler, G. (1989) 'Issues in the application of cognitive and behavioral strategies to the treatment of social phobia', *Clinical Psychology Review* 9: 91–106.

——, Cullington, A., Munby, M., Amies, P. and Gelder, M. (1984) 'Exposure and anxiety management in the treatment of social phobia', *Journal of Consulting and Clinical Psychology* 52: 642–50.

Carver, C. S. (1979) 'A cybernetic model of self-attention processes', *Journal of Personality and Social Psychology* 37: 1251–81.

Castles, E. E. and Glass, C. R. (1986) 'Empirical generation of measures of social competence for mentally retarded adults', *Behavioral Assessment* 8: 319–30.

Chance, M. R. A. (ed.) (1988) *Social Fabrics of the Mind*, Hove and New York: Lawrence Erlbaum Associates.

Cheek, J. M., Carpentieri, A. M., Smith, T. G., Rierdan, J. and Koff, E. (1986) 'Adolescent shyness', in W. H. Jones, J. M. Cheek and S. R. Briggs (eds) *Shyness: Perspectives on Research and Treatment*, New York: Plenum, pp. 105–15.

Coie, J. D. and Dodge, K. A. (1983) 'Continuities and changes in children's social status: a five-year longitudinal study', *Merrill-Palmer Quarterly* 29: 261–82.

Coyne, J. C. (1976) 'Depression and the response of others', *Journal of Abnormal Psychology* 85: 186–93.

Curran, J. P. (1977) 'Skills training as an approach to the treatment of heterosexual-social anxiety: a review', *Psychological Bulletin* 84: 140–57.

——, Wallander, J. L. and Farrell, A. D. (1985) 'Heterosocial skills training', in L. L'Abate and M. A. Milan (eds) *Handbook of Social Skills Training and Research*, New York: Wiley.

Daniels, D. and Plomin, R. (1985) 'Origins of individual differences in infant shyness', *Developmental Psychology* 21: 118–21.

Doll, E. A. (1952) *Measurement of Social Competence: A Manual for the Vineland Social Maturity Scale*, Minneapolis: Educational Publishers.

—— (1965) *Social Maturity Scale*, Circle Pines, Minnesota: American Guidance Service.

Dryden, W. (1984a) 'Social skills assessment from a rational-emotive perspective', in P. Trower (ed.) *Radical Approaches to Social Skills Training*, London: Croom Helm.

—— (1984b) 'Social skills training from a rational-emotive perspective', in P. Trower (ed.) *Radical Approaches to Social Skills Training*, London: Croom Helm.

—— (1987) *Counselling Individuals: The Rational-Emotive Approach*, London: Taylor & Francis.

D'Zurilla, T. J. and Goldfried, M. R. (1971) 'Problem solving and behavior modification', *Journal of Abnormal Psychology* 78: 107–26.

Ellis, A. (1962) *Reason and Emotion in Psychotherapy*, New York: Lyle Stuart.

Emmelkamp, P. M. G. (1982) *Obsessions and Phobias*, New York: Plenum.

——, Mersch, P. P., Vissia, E. and van der Helm, M. (1985) 'Social phobia: a comparative evaluation of cognitive and behavioral interventions', *Behaviour Research and Therapy* 23: 365–9.

Falloon, I. R. H., Boyd, J. L. and McGill, C. W. (1984) *Family Care of Schizophrenia*, New York: Guilford Press.

Faraone, S. V. and Hurtig, R. R. (1985) 'An examination of social skill, verbal productivity, and Gottman's model of interaction using observational methods and sequential analyses', *Behavioral Assessment* 7: 349–66.

Fuchs, C. Z. and Rehm, L. P. (1977) 'A self-control behavior therapy program for depression', *Journal of Consulting and Clinical Psychology* 45: 206–15.

Gardner, R. (1988) 'Psychiatric syndromes of infrastructures for intraspecific communication', in M. R. A. Chance (ed.) *Social Fabrics of the Mind*, London: Lawrence Erlbaum Associates.

Gervasio, A. H. (1987) 'Assertiveness techniques as speech acts', *Clinical Psychology Review* 7: 105–19.

Gilbert, P. (1989) *Human Nature and Suffering*, London: Lawrence Erlbaum Associates.

—— and Trower, P. (1990) 'Social anxiety: its evolution and manifestation', in R. Crozier (ed.) *Shyness and Embarrassment*, New York: Cambridge University Press.

Gilmartin, B. G. (1987) 'Peer group antecedents of severe love-shyness in males', *Journal of Personality* 55: 467–89.

Gotlib, I. H. (1990) 'An interpersonal systems approach to the conceptualization and treatment of depression', in R. E. Ingram (ed.) *Contemporary Approaches to the Study of Depression*, New York: Plenum.

—— and Colby, C. A. (1987) *Treatment of Depression: An Interpersonal Systems Approach*, New York: Pergamon.

Gotlib, I. H. and Meltzer, S. J. (1987) 'Depression and the perception of social skill in dyadic interaction', *Cognitive Therapy and Research* 11: 41–54.

Gotlib, I. H. and Robinson, L. A. (1982) 'Responses to depressed individuals: discrepancies between self-report and observer-rated behavior', *Journal of Abnormal Psychology* 91: 231–40.

Gutride, M. E., Goldstein, A. P. and Hunter, G. F. (1973) 'The use of modeling and role-playing to increase social interaction among asocial psychiatric patients', *Journal of Consulting and Clinical Psychology* 40: 408–15.

Halford, K. and Foddy, M. (1982) 'Cognitive and social skills correlates of social anxiety', *British Journal of Clinical Psychology* 21: 17–18.

Hamilton, F. and Maisto, S. (1979) 'Assertive behavior and perceived discomfort of alcoholics in assertion-required situations', *Journal of Consulting and Clinical Psychology* 47: 196–7.

Hammen, C. L. and Peters, S. D. (1978) 'Interpersonal consequences of depression: responses to men and women enacting a depressed role', *Journal of Abnormal Psychology* 87: 322–32.

Hecimovic, A., Fox, J. J., Shores, R. E. and Strain, P. S. (1985) 'An analysis of developmentally integrated and segregated free play settings and the generalization of newly acquired social behaviors of socially withdrawn preschoolers', *Behavioral Assessment* 7: 367–88.

Heimberg, R. G. (1989) 'Social phobia: no longer neglected?', *Clinical Psychology Review* (Special Issue: Social Phobia) 9: 1–2.

Heimberg, R. G. and Barlow, D. H. (1988) 'Psychosocial treatments for social phobia', *Psychosomatics* 29: 27–37.

Heimberg, R. G., Nyman, D. and O'Brien, G. T. (1987b) 'Assessing variations of the thought-listing technique: effects of instructions, stimulus intensity, stimulus modality and scoring procedures', *Cognitive Therapy and Research* 11: 13–24.

Heimberg, R. G., Dodge, C. S., Hope, D., Kennedy, C. R., Zollo, L. and Becket, R. E. (1988) 'Cognitive-behavioural treatment of social phobia in a group setting: comparison to a credible placebo control', manuscript submitted for publication.

Hersen, M. (1979) 'Modification of skill deficits in psychiatric patients', in A. S. Bellack and M. Hersen (eds) *Research and Practice in Social Skills Training*, New York: Plenum.

—— Bellack, A. S. and Himmelhoch, J. M. (1982) 'Skills training with unipolar depressed women', in J. P. Curran and P. M. Monti (eds) *Social Skills Training: A Practical Handbook for Assessment and Treatment*, New York: Guilford Press.

—— and Thase, M. E. (1984) 'Effects of social skills training, amitriptyline, and psychotherapy in unipolar depressed women', *Behavior Therapy* 15: 21–40.

Hogarty, G. E., Anderson, C. M., Reiss, D. J., Kornblith, S. J., Greenwald, D. P., Javna, C. D. and Madonia, M. J. (1986) 'Family psycho-education social skills training and maintenance chemotherapy: I. One year effects of a controlled study on relapse and expressed emotion', *Archives of General Psychiatry* 43: 633–42.

Hollin, C. R. and Trower, P. (eds) (1986) *Handbook of Social Skills Training* (Vols 1 and 2), Oxford: Pergamon.

Hooley, J. M. (1985) 'Expressed emotion: a review of the critical literature', *Clinical Psychology Review* 5: 119–39.

Howes, M. J. and Hokanson, J. E. (1979) 'Conversational and social responses to depressive interpersonal behaviour', *Journal of Abnormal Psychology* 88: 625–34.

Jacobson, N. S. (1985) 'The role of observational measures in behavior therapy outcome research', *Behavioral Assessment* 7: 297–308.

Jerremalm, A., Jansson, L. and Öst, L. G. (1986) 'Cognitive and physiological reactivity and the effects of different behavioral methods in the treatment of social phobia', *Behaviour, Research and Therapy* 24: 171–80.

Jones, W. H., Cheek, J. M. and Briggs, S. R. (eds) (1986) *Shyness: Perspectives on Research and Treatment*, New York: Plenum.

Kanter, N. J. and Goldfried, M. R. (1979) 'Relative effectiveness of rational restructuring and self-control desensitization in the reduction of interpersonal anxiety', *Behavior Therapy* 10: 472–90.

Kazdin, A. E. and Matson, J. L. (1981) 'Social validation in mental retardation', *Applied Research in Mental Retardation* 2: 39–54.

Kern, J. M., Miller, C. and Eggers, J. (1983) 'Enhancing the validity of role-play tests: a comparison of three role-play methodologies', *Behavior Therapy* 14: 482–92.

Liberman, R. P., Neuchterlein, K. H. and Wallace, C. J. (1982) 'Social skills training and the nature of schizophrenia', in J. P. Curran and P. M. Monti (eds) *Social Skills Training: A Practical Handbook of Assessment and Treatment*, New York: Guilford Press.

Liberman, R. P., Lillie, F., Falloon, I. R. H., Harpin, R. E., Hutchinson, W. and Stoute, B. (1984) 'Social skills training with relapsing schizophrenics', *Behavior Modification* 8: 155–79.

Liberman, R. P., Mueser, K. T., Wallace, C. J., Jacobs, H. E., Ekman, T. and Massel, K. (1986) 'Training skills in the psychiatrically disabled: learning coping and competence', *Schizophrenia Bulletin* 12: 631–47.

Libet, J. and Lewinsohn, P. M. (1973) 'The concept of social skill with special reference to the behaviour of depressed persons', *Journal of Consulting and Clinical Psychology* 40: 304–12.

Liebowitz, M. R., Gorman, J. M., Fyer, A. J. and Klein, D. F. (1985) 'Social phobia', *Archives of General Psychiatry* 42: 729–36.

Lindsay, W. R. (1984) 'A comparison between schizophrenic patients and non-patient matched controls on several aspects of social skill under three conditions of labelling', *American Journal of Psychiatry* 142: 1233–5.

—— and Kasprowicz, M. (1987) 'Challenging negative cognitions: developing confidence in adults by means of cognitive behaviour therapy', *Mental Handicap* 15: 159–62.

—— and Smith, A. W. H. (1985) 'The evaluation of a comprehensive package of training social and community living skills to mentally handicapped adults', unpublished manuscript, Strathmartine Hospital, Dundee.

Lowe, M. R., and Cautela, J. R. (1978) 'A self-report measure of social skill', *Behavior Therapy* 9: 535–44.

McFall, R. M. (1982) 'A review and reformulation of the concept of social skills', *Behavioral Assessment* 4: 1–33.

McKnight, D. L., Nelson, R. O., Hayes, S. C. and Jarrett, R. B. (1984) 'Importance of treating individually assessed responses classes in the amelioration of depression', *Behavior Therapy* 15: 315–35.

Marks, I. M. (1987) *Fears, Phobias and Rituals*, New York: Oxford University Press.

Marlatt, G. A. and Gordon, J. R. (1980) 'Determinants of relapse: implications for the maintenance of behavior change', in P. E. Nathan, G. A. Marlatt and T. Loberg (eds) *Alcoholism: New Directions in Behavioral Research and Treatment*, New York: Plenum.

Marzillier, J. S. (1978) 'Outcome studies of skill training: a review', in P. Trower, B. M. Bryant and M. Argyle (eds) *Social Skills and Mental Health*, London: Methuen.

—— and Winter, K. (1978) 'Success and failure in social skills training: individual differences', *Behaviour Research and Therapy* 16: 67–84.

Matson, J. L. and Andrasik, F. (1982) 'Training leisure-time social-interaction skills to mentally retarded adults', *American Journal of Mental Deficiency* 86: 533–42.

Matson, J. L. and DiLorenzo, T. D. (1986) 'Mental handicap and organic impairment', in C. R. Hollin and P. Trower (eds) *Handbook of Social Skills Training*, Oxford: Pergamon.

Matson, J. L. and Earnhart, T. (1981) 'Programming treatment effects to the natural environment: a procedure for training institutionalized retarded adults', *Behavior Modification* 5: 27–37.

Matson, J. L., Helsel, W. J., Bellack, A. S. and Senatore, V. (1983) 'Development of a rating scale to assess social skill deficits in mentally retarded adults', *Applied Research in Mental Retardation* 4: 399–407.

Mattick, R. P. and Peters, L. (1988) 'Treatment of severe social phobia: effects of guided exposure with and without cognitive restructuring', *Journal of Consulting and Clinical Psychology* 56: 251–60.

—— and Clarke, J. C. (1988) 'Exposure and cognitive restructuring for severe social phobia: a controlled study', *Behaviour Therapy*, 20: 3–8.

Meichenbaum, D. H. (1977) *Cognitive-Behavior Modification*, New York: Plenum.

—— and Cameron, R. (1973) 'Training schizophrenics to talk to themselves: a means of developing attentional control', *Behavior Therapy* 4: 515–34.

Merluzzi, T. V. and Biever, J. (1987) 'Role-playing procedures for the behavioral assessment of social skill: a validity study', *Behavioral Assessment* 9: 361–78.

Miller, G. A., Galanter, E. and Pribram, K. (1960) *Plans and the Structure of Behavior*, New York: Holt.

Miller, L. S. and Funabiki, D. (1984) 'Predictive validity of the social performance survey schedule for component interpersonal behaviors', *Behavioral Assessment* 6: 33–45.

Miller, P. M. and Eisler, R. M. (1977) 'Assertive behavior in alcoholics: a descriptive analysis', *Behavior Therapy* 8: 146–9.

Minuchin, S. and Fisman, C. (1981) *Family Therapy Techniques*, Cambridge, Mass.: Harvard University Press.

Monti, P. M., Abrams, D. B., Binkoff, J. A. and Zwick, W. R. (1986) 'Social skills training and substance abuse', in C. R. Hollin and P. Trower (eds) *Handbook of Social Skills Training: Clinical Applications and New Directions*, Vol. 2, Oxford: Pergamon.

Mulhall, D. J. (1976) 'Systematic self-assessment by PQRST (Personal Questionnaire Rapid Scaling Technique)', *Psychological Medicine* 6: 591–7.

Peplau, L. A. and Perlman, D. (eds) (1982) *Loneliness: A Sourcebook of Current Theory, Research and Therapy*, Wiley: New York.

Pettit, G. S., McClaskey, C. L., Brown, M. M. and Dodge, K. A. (1987) 'The generalizability of laboratory assessments of children's socially competent behavior in specific situations', *Behavioural Assessment* 9: 81–96.

Reese, R. M., Sherman, J. A. and Sheldon, J. (1984) 'Reducing agitated-disruptive behavior of mentally retarded residents of community group homes: the role of self-recording and peer-prompted self-recording', *Analysis and Intervention in Developmental Disabilities* 4: 91–107.

Reite, M. and Field, T. (eds) (1985) *The Psychobiology of Attachment and Separation*, New York: Academic Press.

Robertson, I., Richardson, A. M. and Youngson, S. C. (1984) 'Social skills training with mentally handicapped people: a review', *British Journal of Clinical Psychology* 23: 241–64.

Rosenberg, H. (1983) 'Relapsed versus non-relapsed alcohol abusers: coping skills, life events and social support', *Addictive Behaviors* 8: 183–6.

Sanchez, V., Lewinsohn, P. M. and Larson, D. W. (1980) 'Assertion training: effectiveness in the treatment of depression', *Journal of Clinical Psychology* 36: 526–9.

Schlundt, D. G. and McFall, R. M. (1985) 'New directions in the assessment of social competence and social skills', in L. L'Abate and M. A. Milan (eds) *Handbook of Social Skills Training and Research*, New York: Wiley.

Senator, V., Matson, J. L. and Kazdin, A. E. (1982) 'A comparison of behavioral methods to train social skills to mentally retarded adults', *Behavior Therapy* 13: 313–24.

Shafer, M. S., Egel, A. L. and Neef, N. A. (1984) 'Training mildly handicapped peers to facilitate changes in the social interaction skills of autistic children', *Journal of Applied Behavior Analysis* 17: 461–76.

Shepherd, G. (1981) 'A review of social skills training with psychiatric patients, 1970–1980', Department of Psychology, Institute of Psychiatry, University of London (unpublished).

—— (1983) 'Social skills training with adults', in S. Spence and G. Shepherd (eds) *Developments in Social Skills Training*, London: Academic Press.

—— (1984) 'Assessment of cognitions in social skills training', in P. Trower (ed.) *Radical Approaches to Social Skills Training*, London: Croom Helm.

—— (1986) 'Social skills training and schizophrenia', in C. R. Hollin and P. Trower (eds) *Handbook of Social Skills Training*, Oxford: Pergamon.

Snyder, M. (1981) 'On the self-perpetuating nature of social stereotypes', in D. L. Hamilton (ed.) *Cognitive Processes in Stereotyping and Inter-group Behavior*, Hillsdale, NJ: Lawrence Erlbaum Associates.

Spivack, G., Platt, J. J. and Shure, M. B. (1976) *The Problem-Solving Approach to Adjustment*, San Francisco: Jossey-Bass.

Stephens, R. M., Matson, J. L., Westmoreland, T. and Kulpa, J. (1981) 'Modification of psychotic speech with mentally retarded patients', *Journal of Mental Deficiency Research* 25: 187–91.

Stravynski, A. and Shahar, A. (1983) 'The treatment of social dysfunction in non-psychotic psychiatric outpatients: a review', *Journal of Nervous and Mental Diseases* 171: 712–8.

Stravynski, A., Marks, I. and Yule, W. (1982) 'Social skills problems in neurotic outpatients: social skills training with and without cognitive modification', *Archives of General Psychiatry* 39: 1378–85.

Sugarman, A. A., Reilly, D. and Albahar, R. S. (1965) 'Social competence and essential-reactive distinction in alcoholism', *Archives of General Psychiatry* 12: 552–6.

Sylph, J. A., Ross, H. E. and Kedward, H. B. (1978) 'Social disability in chronic psychiatric patients', *American Journal of Psychiatry* 134: 1391–4.

Teasdale, J. D. (1983) 'Negative thinking in depression: cause, effect or reciprocal relationship?', *Advances in Behaviour Research and Therapy* 5: 3–25.

Trower, P. (1980) 'Situational analysis of the components and processes of behavior of socially skilled and unskilled patients', *Journal of Consulting and Clinical Psychology* 30: 526–37.

—— (1981) 'Social skill disorder: mechanisms of failure', in R. Gilmour and S. Duck (eds) *Personal Relationships in Disorder*, London: Academic Press.

—— (1982) 'Towards a generative model of social skills: a critique and synthesis', in J. P. Curran and P. M. Monti (eds) *Social Skills Training: A Practical Handbook for Assessment and Treatment*, New York: Guilford Press.

—— (1986) 'Social skills training and social anxiety', in C. R. Hollin and P. Trower (eds) *Handbook of Social Skills Training*, Oxford: Pergamon.

—— and Gilbert, P. (1989) 'New theoretical conceptions of social anxiety and social phobia', *Clinical Psychology Review* 9: 19–35.

Trower, P. and Turland, D. (1984) 'Social phobia', in S. M. Turner (ed.) *Behavioral Theories and Treatment of Anxiety*, New York: Plenum.

Twentyman, C. T. and Zimering, R. T. (1979) 'Behavioral training of social skills: a critical review', in M. Hersen, R. M. Eisler and P. M. Miller (eds) *Progress in Behavior Modification* Vol. 7, New York: Academic Press.

Van Hasselt, V. B., Hersen, M. and Milliones, J. (1978) 'Social skills training for alcoholics and drug addicts: a review', *Addictive Behaviors* 3: 221–3.

Vaughn, C. and Leff, J. (1976) 'The influence of family and social factors on the course of psychiatric patients', *British Journal of Psychiatry* 129: 125–37.

Wallace, C. J. (1982) 'The social skills training project of the mental health clinical research center for the study of schizophrenia', in J. P. Curran and P. M. Monti (eds) *Social Skills Training: A Practical Handbook*, New York: Guilford Press.

—— and Liberman, R. P. (1985) 'Social skills training for patients with schizophrenia: a controlled clinical trial', *Psychiatry Research* 14: 239–47.

Wallace, C. J., Nelson, C. J., Liberman, R. P., Aitchison, R. A., Lukoff, D., Elder, J. P. and Ferris, C. (1980) 'A review and critique of social skills training with schizophrenic patients', *Schizophrenia Bulletin* 6: 42–63.

Watts, F., Powell, G. E. and Austin, S. V. (1973) 'The modification of abnormal beliefs', *British Journal of Medical Psychology* 46: 359–63.

Wetherby, B. and Baumeister, A. A. (1981) 'Mental retardation', in S. M. Turner, K. S. Calhoun and H. E. Adams (eds) *Handbook of Clinical Behavior Therapy*, New York: Wiley.

Williams, J. M. G. (1986) 'Social skills and depression', in C. R. Hollin and P. Trower (eds) *Handbook of Social Skills Training*, Oxford: Pergamon.

——, Watts, F. N., McLeod, C. and Mathews, A. (1988) *Cognitive Psychology and Emotional Disorders*, Chichester: Wiley.

Young, H. S. (1974) *A Rational Counselling Primer*, New York: Institute for Rational Living.

Zeiss, A. M., Lewinsohn, P. M. and Munoz, R. F. (1979) 'Nonspecific improvement effects in depression using interpersonal skills training, pleasant events schedules, or cognitive training', *Journal of Consulting and Clinical Psychology* 45: 543–51.

Zigler, E. and Phillips, L. (1961) 'Social competence and outcome in psychiatric patients', *Journal of Abnormal and Social Psychology* 63: 264–71.

Zimbardo, P. G. (1977) *Shyness: What It Is and What To Do About It*, New York: Jove.

Chapter 11

Marital and family problems

Norman Epstein and Stephen E. Schlesinger

Marital and family therapists treat many of the problems covered in other chapters of this book (for example, depression, alcohol and drug dependence), but they focus on the interpersonal interactions among family members that influence such difficulties in the lives of individual family members. This focus on the dynamics of family interactions commonly involves attention to problems such as (1) family members' deficits in communication skills, (2) inappropriate or inadequate ways of expressing positive and negative emotions, (3) conflicts among family members' values and preferences (such as those concerning friends and career choices), (4) role conflicts and role ambiguity (for example, a child operating in an adult role), (5) power struggles, (6) money problems, (7) ineffective or abusive child rearing and discipline, (8) sexual conflicts and dysfunctions, (9) conflicts concerning in-laws and other extended family, (10) ineffective family decision making and problem solving, and (11) boundary issues such as ambiguity or conflict about the degree of privacy that is appropriate for individual family members. Although couples and families commonly present their problems in terms of undesirable behaviour on the part of one member, this initial explanation may not necessarily be the basis of their distress. Marital and family therapists strive to identify and modify the interpersonal factors that either elicit or maintain problematic behaviour in individual family members.

This chapter describes a cognitive-behavioural approach to the assessment and treatment of marital and family problems. It focuses on both the intrapersonal cognitions and the interpersonal behaviours that contribute to family difficulties, noting how it is often the combination of cognitions and behaviours of two or more members that results in relationship problems. The chapter begins with a review of theory and research concerning cognitive and behavioural factors in marital and family dysfunction, and it proceeds to a description of cognitive-behavioural assessment and treatment approaches.

A COGNITIVE-BEHAVIOURAL MODEL OF MARITAL AND FAMILY INTERACTION

Among the foundations of cognitive-behavioural approaches to marital and family problems are cognitive mediation models of individual functioning (for example, Beck 1976; Ellis 1962), which describe how an individual's idiosyncratic interpretations of life events influence his or her emotional and behavioural reactions to those events. Increasingly, marital and family therapists (for example, Baucom and Epstein 1990; Dryden 1985; Ellis 1976, 1986; Epstein 1982; Epstein *et al*. 1988; Jacobson 1984; Schlesinger and Epstein 1986) have focused on how family members constantly interpret each others' behaviours, and how various cognitive processes serve as 'filters' through which each individual draws conclusions about causes and meanings of those actions, evaluates the behaviours (for example, as acceptable or not), and makes predictions about the other members' future behaviours.

A cognitive-behavioural model of marital and family relationships takes into account ways in which cognitions, behaviours and emotions exert *mutual* influences upon one another. A cognition (for example, viewing one's spouse as intentionally trying to hurt one's feelings) can elicit emotional responses (for example, anger) and behaviours (for example, criticizing the spouse). On the other hand, an individual's emotional state (for example, anger) can influence his or her cognitions (for example, noticing only the unpleasant actions by the spouse and overlooking the spouse's positive gestures) and behaviours (for example, yelling rather than expressing one's thoughts and emotions in a direct but calm manner). Furthermore, a behaviour (for example, withdrawing from the spouse by leaving the house in the middle of an argument) can affect one's emotions (for example, decreased feelings of intimacy) and cognitions (for example, drawing the conclusion, 'This relationship must be dying, because I can't even stand staying in the same room with him [her] any more').

Cognitive-behavioural marital and family therapists draw on a systems model of family dynamics (for example, Watzlawick *et al*. 1967) in their assumption that members of a family simultaneously influence each other. Thus, one member's behaviour elicits cognitions, emotions and behaviours in other members, and in return the other members' responses elicit cognitions, behaviours and emotions in the former individual. In such a cycle among family members, a dysfunctional cognition, behaviour or emotion at any point can lead to a spiral of negative exchanges. For example, if a parent misinterprets a child's misbehaviour as due to malicious intentions and therefore punishes the child, the child may in turn think, 'I don't deserve this', become angry and slam the door of his or her room. Subsequently, the parent might interpret that behaviour as a sign that the child lacks respect for parents and might escalate the punishment. Both parent and child respond to their cognitions about the other individual as if those views reflect the reality of the situation, and once the conflict based on their misperceptions escalates, it may be very difficult for either individual to identify the manner in which his or her cognitions and behaviours transformed a fairly benign interaction into an argument.

The greater the number of family members involved in a particular interaction, the more complex are the behavioural events that each member observes, and the more complex are the cognitions that may result. Among the events that each family member may observe are (1) the individual's own cognitions, behaviours and emotions regarding family interaction, (2) the actions of other individual members towards him or her, (3) the combination of reactions that two or more other members have towards him or her and (4) the characteristics of the relationships among other family members. The following is a description of several types of cognitions that family members may experience concerning these four types of events in family interactions.

TYPES OF POTENTIALLY PROBLEMATIC COGNITIONS

Five major types of cognitions have been implicated in marital and family dysfunction (Baucom and Epstein 1990; Epstein and Baucom 1989). These include (1) selective *perceptions* about what events have occurred during family interactions, (2) biased *attributions* about the causes of particular family events, (3) inaccurate *expectancies* (predictions) about the probabilities that certain events will occur in the future, (d) unrealistic *assumptions* about the characteristics of family members and their relationships and (e) extreme *standards* about the characteristics that family members and their relationships 'should' have. The following is a summary of research findings concerning the roles that these five types of cognitions can play in family problems.

Perceptions

Cognitive theorists, therapists and researchers have noted that individuals cannot possibly notice and assimilate all of the complex information available in situations where they are interacting with other people. Consequently, an individual selectively notices some of the available stimuli and overlooks other aspects of the situation (cf. Nisbett and Ross 1980). *Perceptions* are those subsets of the available information that each individual notices in a situation. For example, Beck and his associates (Beck *et al.* 1979) have described a process of 'selective abstraction' whereby depressed individuals are prone to focus their attention on negative events in their daily lives and overlook positive events. Similarly, behaviourally orientated marital and family therapists (for example, Jacobson and Margolin 1979; Patterson and Reid 1984) have described how distressed family members 'track' negative behaviours by other family members and overlook positive ones. Furthermore, a number of research studies (for example, Christensen *et al.* 1983; Elwood and Jacobson 1982; Floyd and Markman 1983) have indicated that spouses engage in selective perception when they observe their marital interactions. When investigators have asked spouses to keep written logs of specific behaviours occurring in their interactions, the rates of agreement between spouses concerning which behaviours occurred are very low (often less than 50 per cent), as are the rates of agreement between spouses and outside observers who code couples' behavioural interactions in specific situations. Causes for such perceptual biases may include factors such as the perceiver's emotional state (for example, one may pay more attention to others' negative behaviours when one is angry), fatigue and values (for example, one may be especially sensitive to events that violate personal values) (Beck *et al.* 1979; Wessler and Wessler 1980). Also, Kelly (1955) noted how the basic concepts that an individual has learned to use for categorizing people and events influence what aspects of the stimuli one notices in daily events. For example, an individual who grew up in a family where achievement was emphasized may be especially likely to notice characteristics of other people that might reflect their records of achievement or failure.

Cognitive-behavioural approaches to identifying and modifying family members' perceptual biases are described later in this chapter. It is also important to note that there is a need for much more empirical research to increase our understanding of the nature of perceptual distortions, as well as factors that produce them. Such knowledge will aid in the development of effective therapeutic interventions.

Attributions

The large majority of empirical investigations of cognition in marital and family problems has been focused on the inferences that family members make about the causes of the events in their interactions (see reviews by Baucom 1987; Baucom *et al.* 1989; Thompson and Snyder 1986). Making such attributions can serve a variety of functions in a close relationship, such as giving an individual a sense of understanding another family member and his or her actions, and a sense of control over the relationship due to that understanding (Baucom 1987). Also, attributing stable negative traits to a family member (for example, 'I don't expect her to comply with my request, because she is a domineering person') makes the person seem predictable.

Many of the studies of marital attributions have examined attributional dimensions based on Abramson *et al.*'s (1978) reformulated learned helplessness model of depression. This model proposes that an individual will experience more depression if he or she attributes uncontrollable negative life experiences to global, stable and internal causes (for example, concluding that one's poor performance at work is due to a broad, enduring characteristic such as low intelligence). Marital and family theorists (for example, Doherty 1981a) have hypothesized that family members will be more distressed about problems in their relationships when they see the problems as due to global and stable causes that are likely to affect many aspects of a relationship and are likely to continue indefinitely. Doherty has argued that such trait-like attributions elicit distress among family members because they suggest little hope that the problems can improve.

Whereas in the attributional model of depression the individual attributes life problems to causes within the self, the attributional model of relationship distress proposes that family members attribute problems to *other* members (external to oneself, although not to the relationship). Studies that have differentiated between attributing marital problems to oneself or to one's partner have tended to find that distressed spouses blame their partners (Baucom and Epstein 1990; Notarius and Vanzetti 1983). However, Baucom (1987) reports that among couples which include a depressed spouse, it is common for *both* spouses to blame the depressed individual for their marital problems. Doherty (1981a) proposes that individuals who attribute problems to their family members are also likely to engage in blaming *behaviour* rather than making collaborative efforts to resolve conflicts.

Most studies of family attributions have focused on attributions between marital partners (cf. Baucom 1987). Although not all of the studies assessed all three of the global–specific, stable–unstable and internal–external attributional dimensions, the most common pattern of results has been that distressed spouses tend to rate causes of their partners' negative behaviours as more stable and global than do non-distressed spouses. In contrast, non-distressed spouses tend to attribute positive partner behaviours to stable, global causes more than distressed spouses do. Thus, distressed spouses are more likely than non-distressed spouses to view their partners' negative behaviours as due to broad traits that are unlikely to change. Furthermore, to compound the problem, distressed spouses tend to discount their partners' positive behaviours as transitory. Research studies have not identified whether or not spouses' trait attributions concerning their partners may be at least somewhat accurate. Nevertheless, the pessimistic views of one's partner that are reflected in trait attributions are likely to discourage spouses from collaborating with their partners to change distressing behaviours and improve their marriages. Consequently, as described later in this chapter, cognitive-behavioural marital and family therapists attempt to focus their clients on specific distressing behaviours that can be modified rather than on their inferences about global characteristics of other family members.

A few studies have examined attributions that spouses make about the motives, intentions and emotions underlying a partner's behaviour. These studies (for example, Epstein *et al.* 1987; Fincham, *et al.* 1987) have found that the more distressed spouses are, the more they attribute marital problems to malicious intentions, a lack of love and selfish motivation of their partners. Whether or not future research indicates that some of these negative attributions are accurate (as clinical experience suggests they sometimes are), clinicians must still help spouses counteract negative cognitive sets that impede their ability to recognize any positive efforts that their partners might make to improve their marriages.

In terms of methods for assessing attributions, a number of questionnaires have been developed to tap the attributional dimensions derived from learned helplessness theory. For example, Baucom *et al.*'s (1987) Dyadic Attributional Inventory (DAI) consists of twenty-four items, each describing a hypothetical marital event (twelve positive and twelve negative). The respondent is instructed to imagine that each event has occurred in his or her own marriage and to write down one major cause of the partner's behaviour in each situation. The respondent is then asked to rate the cause of the partner's behaviour in each situation on attributional dimensions concerning: (a) the degree to which it was due to the self,

(b) the degree to which it was due to the partner, (c) the degree to which it was due to circumstances outside the relationship, (d) how stable versus unstable it is and (e) how global versus specific it is. The individual is also asked to rate how important each event would be if it actually occurred (i.e. its relevance and how good or bad he or she would feel if it occurred). Fourteen subscale scores are derived, based on the seven attributional ratings for positive events and the seven ratings for the negative events. The internal consistencies of the DAI subscales are moderate (alpha coefficients ranging from .88 to .71), indicating that spouses have some general attributional styles, but also that their attributions about marital problems to some extent vary across situations. The DAI has also exhibited evidence of validity, in that its subscales correlate with marital adjustment in a manner similar to findings from other studies of marital attributions (for example, distress is associated with blaming the partner and viewing the causes of negative behaviour as global and stable). Among the other attribution scales available, Fincham and O'Leary's (1983) instrument assesses attributions similar to those included in the DAI and has a similar format. Baucom *et al.*'s (1984) Partner Observational/Attributional Questionnaire (POAC) asks spouses to make attributional ratings on the same dimensions as those of the DAI, but for *actual* positive, neutral and negative partner behaviours selected from logs that each person keeps over a 24-hour period.

In contrast to the attribution scales that tap attributional dimensions derived from learned helplessness theory, Pretzer *et al.*'s (1985) Marital Attitude Survey (MAS) assesses the content of marital attributions. The MAS subscales include attributions to one's own personality, own behaviour, partner's personality, partner's behaviour, partner's lack of love and partner's malicious intent. For example, the subscale assessing attributions to malicious intent includes items such as 'My partner intentionally does things to irritate me'. The MAS subscales vary in their internal consistency, with coefficient Alphas ranging from .93 for attributions to the partner's malicious intent to .58 for attributions to one's own behaviour. Correlational data have demonstrated that MAS subscale scores reflecting attributions to the partner's behaviour, personality, lack of love and malicious intent are associated with indices of lower marital adjustment, as well as with scores on scales measuring depression and communication problems. A positive correlation between attributing marital problems to one's own personality (but not one's own behaviour) and both lower marital adjustment and poorer marital communication suggests that spouses may blame themselves as well as their partners for marital problems if they focus on consistent personality characteristics rather than their specific behaviours (Pretzer *et al.* 1985).

The few existing studies of attributions made by family members other than the marital partners have produced findings that tend to be consistent with the findings from the marital studies. Larrance and Twentyman (1983), for example, asked a group of physically abusive mothers, a group of neglectful mothers and a comparison group of mothers with no known history of abuse or neglect to rate the causes of their own children's positive and negative behaviours. The abusive mothers rated the causes of their children's negative behaviours as more internal and stable (i.e. due to traits) than did the comparison group, whereas they rated the causes of their children's positive behaviours as more external and unstable than did the comparison group mothers. The ratings by neglectful mothers had a more complex pattern but tended to fall between those of the abusive and comparison groups. As is the case with the marital studies described earlier, Larrance and Twentyman note that their correlational results do not indicate whether the negative attributions of the abusive mothers represent cognitive distortions or accurate descriptions of their children. However, even if a parent is reacting to actual difficult behaviour on the part of a child, the parent may develop a global negative cognitive set about the child. If this occurs, the parent's view of the child may lead him or her to discount any positive behaviour changes that the child may make, or to reinforce the child's negative behaviour by responding to it more consistently. In Azar's (1986) study, the more that abusive parents attributed their children's misbehaviour to negative traits, the more they behaved negatively and the less they behaved positively towards the children. Consequently, family therapists need to help parents alter any inaccurate attributions about their children's behaviour, and they also need to help the parents be aware of (and reward) their children's positive behaviours and decreases in negative behaviours.

Kurdek and Berg (1987) found that the degrees to which children blamed parental conflict and divorce on their fathers, their mothers or themselves tended to be associated with anxiety on the children's part, as well as with more negative self-concepts concerning their relationships with their parents. Considerably more research is needed to investigate the attributions that family members make for a variety of other family problems, such as conflicts over power, decision making and expression of affection. It will be important for future studies to examine the degree to which family members' attributions cause (or result from) particular emotions and behaviours towards other family members. Fincham and Bradbury's (1987) study is an example of the type of research design that is needed. Fincham and Bradbury assessed both the attributions and the marital satisfaction of spouses over an interval of a year. They found that wives' attributions about factors influencing their husbands' behaviours were significantly correlated with the wives' levels of marital satisfaction a year later, but that initial satisfaction was not predictive of attributions a year later. In contrast, husbands' attributions and satisfaction did not predict each other over the course of the year. Fincham and Bradbury note that the lack of statistically significant results for husbands is consistent with previous findings suggesting that women are more sensitive to the functioning of their marriage than are men.

Expectancies

Social-learning theorists such as Rotter (1954) and Bandura (1977) have described how individuals develop expectancies or predictions about the probabilities that certain events will occur in the future under particular circumstances. These expectancies develop from a wide range of the individual's life experiences, including direct experience of others' reactions to his or her own behaviour, observations of the outcomes of other people's behaviours, and 'lessons' that others teach him or her verbally (for example, mother says, 'If you don't share with your friends, they won't like you'). According to social learning theory, an individual continuously makes decisions to act or not act in certain ways, based on the outcomes anticipated from each action. Rotter (1954) has noted that expectancies can be situation specific (for example, 'If I ask Johnny to help with chores when he is sitting in front of the television, he will ignore me') or more generalized (for example, 'If I try to initiate anything, she will battle me for control'). Another way of categorizing expectancies has been proposed by Bandura (1977), who differentiated between *outcome expectancies* (predictions about the probability that a particular action will lead to a particular outcome in a certain situation) and *efficacy expectancies* (estimates about the likelihood that one will be able successfully to perform the actions which would lead to a particular outcome). An individual tends to make choices about which behaviours to exhibit towards other people based on (a) predictions about the outcomes of alternative behaviours, (b) predictions about his or her efficacy in performing the required behaviours *and* (c) the degree to which he or she finds each outcome pleasant or unpleasant.

As is the case with the other types of cognitions described in this chapter, expectancies are normal and common phenomena that increase the efficiency with which an individual learns from life experiences. However, although many of an individual's expectancies (including those pertaining to family interactions) are accurate, sometimes they are distorted. When an individual's behaviour towards other family members is a result of inaccurate expectancies, that behaviour can be detrimental to the relationship, because it may initiate negative behavioural spirals and block conflict resolution between the parties (Doherty 1981b). For example, if an individual expects that the only behaviour likely to attract other family members' attention is yelling, he or she may use that means of expression more than any other. Unfortunately, the yelling may elicit either retaliatory aggression or withdrawal from the other family members, which in turn may lead the initiator to yell more.

A family member who holds an inaccurate expectancy may also experience inappropriate emotional responses. In the situation above, for example, the individual who expects that only yelling will draw others' attention may experience anger and depression due to a view that 'no one in the family cares enough about me to listen'.

Pretzer *et al.* (1985) found that the more that spouses reported an expectancy of improving their relationships, the higher was their marital satisfaction and the more they attributed marital problems to their own behaviour. In addition, the more that spouses expected improvement in their marriages, the lower were their levels of depression, and the less likely they were to attribute marital problems to their partner's behaviour, personality traits, malicious intent and lack of love. In Kurdek and Berg's (1987) study, children of divorced parents reported more anxiety when they held an expectancy that their custodial parent might abandon them. These preliminary correlational results are consistent with the idea that individuals' expectancies can influence family relationships, but much more research is needed in order to clarify any causal roles that expectancies may have in determining family members' emotions and behaviours towards one another.

Assumptions and standards

Cognitive theorists and researchers have used terms such as 'cognitive structures', 'knowledge structures' and 'schemata' (Nisbett and Ross 1980; Seiler 1984; Turk and Speers 1983) to describe basic concepts that an individual develops about the characteristics of objects (including other people and the self) as a result of experiences that begin very early in life. These cognitions serve as 'templates' by which the individual understands and categorizes objects and situations in the future.

One useful way to categorize cognitive structures is to distinguish between *assumptions* concerning characteristics of objects and events that an individual believes *do* exist and *standards* that a person holds about the characteristics that objects and events *should* have (Baucom and Epstein 1990). The following are descriptions of theoretical concepts and empirical findings about the impacts that assumptions and standards can have on family relationships.

Assumptions

An assumption is a basic conception than an individual holds about the characteristics of things and events. For the purposes of this chapter, we focus on assumptions about people and relationships, as well as beliefs about the degrees to which those characteristics are intercorrelated. For example, an individual may hold an assumption that a 'child' is a young person who tends to be impulsive, eager to learn about the world, fun-loving and lacking in good judgement. This individual may also assume that these characteristics are highly intercorrelated. Consequently, when this person meets a child who exhibits a high degree of fun-loving behaviour, he or she will be likely to make inferences about the degrees to which the child is impulsive, eager to learn and lacking in judgement. Such inferences to unseen characteristics may not be accurate for the particular child who was observed.

In contrast to assumptions about the characteristics of objects, 'scripts' are assumptions about typical sequences of events that occur in particular situations. For example, members of a couple each commonly develop scripts concerning the sequence of behaviours that they assume typically to occur when two people have a sexual encounter (i.e. who does what, when and in what order). Baucom and Epstein (1990) have proposed that both scripts and assumptions about the characteristics of people and relationships form the bases for the attributions and expectancies that family members make about their interactions. Studies have revealed correlations between assumptions and attributions (for example, Epstein *et al.* 1987; Fincham and Bradbury 1987), but such correlational findings have not identified the causal direction between these two types of cognitions.

Standards

Geiss and O'Leary (1981) conducted a survey of 250 members of the American Association of Marriage and Family Therapists and found that the area ranked by therapists as the second most damaging to marital relationships (following communication) was unrealistic expectations of marriage or one's spouse. Practitioners of rational-emotive therapy (RET) (for example, Dryden 1985; Ellis 1977, 1986) have paid considerable attention to standards that adversely affect the quality of marital and family relationships. According to the RET model, family members experience distress when (1) events in their relationships do not meet their unrealistic, extreme standards ('irrational beliefs') and (2) they evaluate the failure of their relationships to meet those standards very negatively (for example, as 'awful'). Beck's cognitive model (cf. Beck *et al.* 1979) also identifies the role of extreme standards in producing distress in individuals' lives, but it gives heavier weight than RET to distortions in perceptions and inferential processes such as attributions.

Sometimes individuals develop standards concerning family life based on a desire to re-create the best characteristics that they have previously observed in family relationships (their own or those of others). On the other hand, individuals also commonly create some standards in order to attempt to avoid unpleasant relationships that they observed or experienced in the past. For example, an individual whose parents fought frequently may have developed a standard that 'good' relationships should not include any overt conflict. Mass media (for example, popular songs, novels, movies) offer enticing standards about family relationships, but unfortunately these media representations often involve unrealistic, idealized notions of intimate relationships.

It is important to note that standards are not dysfunctional *per se*. In fact, they help provide a sense of order for people in the complex experiences of their lives, and one must distinguish between unrealistic standards and more reasonable standards that may guide people's ethical behaviour with others (for example, the widely held standard that parents should not abuse their children physically or psychologically). However, both standards that are dysfunctional and those that facilitate individual and family functioning can provide a sense of order and a belief that one is 'doing the right thing'. Consequently, cognitive-behavioural marital and family therapists help family members conduct careful examinations of the consequences of living according to their standards.

Epstein and Eidelson (1981) found that spouses' reports of their levels of marital distress, their preference for individual rather than marital therapy and their pessimism about improving their marriages were positively correlated with their scores on a questionnaire measuring unrealistic assumptions and standards about intimate relationships. The Relationship Belief Inventory (RBI; Eidelson and Epstein 1982) assesses three assumptions (disagreement is destructive to a relationship, partners cannot change themselves or their relationship, and the two sexes cannot understand each other because of innate differences in thinking and personality) and two standards (partners should be able to read each other's minds and one should be a perfect sexual partner). The RBI has demonstrated validity in terms of its correlations with measures of marital distress, communication problems and dysfunctional attributions (for example, Epstein *et al*. 1987; Fincham and Bradbury 1987), and it has been a sensitive measure of cognitive change in studies investigating the effects of cognitive-behavioural therapy with distressed couples (for example, Baucom and Lester 1986; Huber and Milstein 1985). Because the RBI was not designed to be a comprehensive measure of problematic assumptions and standards, there is a need for additional measures of such cognitive structures. In addition, future research should investigate the relationships of assumptions and standards to attributions, expectancies and perceptions.

The Family Beliefs Inventory (FBI; Roehling and Robin 1986) is intended to assess unrealistic beliefs held by parents and adolescents. The FBI includes six subscales for parents and four for adolescents. It appears that some of the subscales assess assumptions, whereas others assess standards. For example, the parental *ruination* subscale (teenagers given too much freedom will ruin their futures) and *self-blame* subscale (parents are at fault when their adolescents misbehave) seem to tap assumptions, and the parental *obedience* subscale (parents deserve absolute respect and obedience) reflects a basic standard. Similarly, the adolescent *ruination* subscale (parents' rules and restrictions will ruin one's life as a teenager) assesses an assumption, whereas the *autonomy* subscale (parents should give adolescents complete freedom to make decisions) addresses a standard. Roehling and Robin (ibid.) report moderate internal consistency for the FBI subscales (except for parental and adolescent subscales regarding approval). Unrealistic belief scores on the FBI subscales (except for those assessing beliefs about approval and self-blame) were higher for distressed than for non-distressed fathers and adolescents, but the FBI did not differentiate between distressed and non-distressed mothers. Current findings with the FBI demonstrate that family members' assumptions and standards are associated with relationship distress, but it appears that further research is needed to test the limits of the instrument's validity. Also, both the FBI and the Relationship Belief Inventory (Eidelson and Epstein 1982) assess a limited number of the possible assumptions and standards that may be held by family members, so marital and family therapists need to supplement such questionnaires with careful clinical interviews in order to identify other unrealistic cognitive structures not assessed by these scales.

Azar and her colleagues (for example, Azar and Rohrbeck 1986) developed a Parent Opinion Questionnaire (POQ) to compare the standards concerning children's behaviour that are held by physically abusive and non-abusive parents. The POQ includes subscales assessing expectations about self-care, family responsibility and care of siblings, help and affection to parents, leaving children alone, behaviour and feelings, and punishment. A sample item from the scale assessing family responsibility and care of siblings is, 'A 5 year old can be expected to help by feeding, dressing and changing diapers for an infant.' The research indicated that abusive mothers had significantly higher levels of unrealistic standards than non-abusive mothers.

Visher and Visher (1979, 1988) have described several myths about the characteristics of life in stepfamilies, and they argue that these myths (which are prevalent in society) often operate as standards about the ways that stepfamily relationships 'should be'. For example, members of stepfamilies often believe that, because stepfamilies look like traditional nuclear families on the surface, close bonds of affection and respect should develop instantly among members who were previously not related. Visher and Visher use many case examples to illustrate the negative impact that these standards have on stepfamily relationships, but there is a need for empirical research to test how and to what degree stepfamily members' adherence to unrealistic standards affects their behavioural interactions and relationship satisfaction.

The roles that unrealistic standards can play in a variety of other family problems have also been noted. For example, Schlesinger (1988) describes how the unrealistic standards that family members of substance abusers and addicts hold about the manner in which they should be able to handle their stresses commonly lead to frustration and pessimism when their attempts to cope fall short of the standards. DiGiuseppe (1988) stresses that parents who have children with conduct disorders and who hold unrealistic standards about good parenting (for example, 'One should never cause one's child undue distress') often have considerable difficulty setting behavioural limits with their children. Qualls (1988) describes how unrealistic standards held by adult children concerning the qualities of a 'good child' (for example, 'A good child does not disobey the wishes of a parent') can elicit guilt in the adult children concerning decisions about placing seriously ill or disabled parents in settings such as nursing homes. It is often necessary to alter unrealistic standards regarding all of the above family problems before family members will be willing to take constructive actions.

BEHAVIOURAL COMPONENTS OF MARITAL AND FAMILY DYSFUNCTION

In a cognitive-behavioural approach to marital and family therapy, the major behavioural foci of the assessment and treatment process are (1) excesses of negative behaviours and deficits in pleasing behaviours exchanged by family members, (2) expressive and listening skills used in communication, (3) problem-solving skills and (4) negotiation and behaviour-change skills. These are the traditional foci of behaviourally orientated marital and family therapy (for example, Falloon *et al.* 1984; Jacobson and Margolin 1979).The theoretical models underlying behavioural approaches to marital and family therapy, social learning theory and social exchange theory include an assumption that family members exert mutual influences over each other's behaviour. Social learning theory (for example, Bandura 1977; Rotter 1954) emphasizes that interpersonal behaviour is learned through past experiences (particularly through observing and imitating other people's actions) and is controlled by its consequences (reinforcement, punishment). As described earlier, social learning theorists such as Bandura and Rotter also note how people's behaviours towards one another are influenced by cognitions such as expectancies regarding consequences of alternative actions.

Social exchange theory (Thibaut and Kelley 1959) views social relationships such as marriages as economic exchanges of 'goods', in which each party's satisfaction is a function of the ratio of his or her benefits to costs in the exchange. The goods that are exchanged in an intimate relationship include a wide variety of affectional behaviours (for example, companionship) and instrumental behaviours (for example, doing household chores). Behavioural marital therapists devote a considerable amount of attention to identifying deficits of positive behaviours and excesses of negative behaviours being exchanged by distressed spouses, and to assisting spouses in developing more satisfying exchange ratios. Efforts to reduce negative exchanges also take into account the social exchange theory concept of reciprocity, which proposes that people tend to reciprocate the ratios of negative and positive behaviours they receive from another individual.

Both social learning theory and social exchange theory have shaped research and clinical practice with marital and family relationships. The following descriptions of problematic behaviours that are foci of cognitive-behavioural assessment and treatment reflect the influences of these two theories.

Pleasing and displeasing behavior exchanges

In a number of research studies (for example, Barnett and Nietzel 1979; Birchler *et al.* 1975; Jacobson *et al.* 1982), spouses have been asked to record on a daily basis the frequencies with which they exchange a variety of specific pleasing and displeasing behaviours. Consistent with social exchange theory, spouses who score in the distressed range on marital satisfaction scales report that they receive significantly more displeasing and fewer pleasing behaviours from their partners than non-distressed spouses. Also, spouses' reports of frequencies of pleasing and displeasing partner behaviours have been found to be significantly correlated with their reported *daily* levels of marital satisfaction (for example, Christensen and Nies 1980; Jacobson *et al.* 1982; Margolin 1981; Wills *et al.* 1974). Furthermore, studies have found evidence to support the social exchange concept that exchanges in a relationship tend to be reciprocal; that is, each party tends to give what he or she receives from the other person (for example, Gottman *et al.* 1977; Margolin and Wampold 1981; Revenstorf *et al.* 1984; Schaap 1984). Patterson's research on families with aggressive children (cf. Patterson 1982) has also identified reciprocal exchanges of aversive behaviour between parents and children. One of the goals of the behavioural interventions described later in this chapter is to reduce cycles of reciprocal negative exchanges between family members and to foster positive reciprocity.

Behavioural marital therapists (for example, Jacobson and Margolin 1979; O'Leary and Turkewitz 1978) have increasingly described how, whether a partner intends an action to be positive or negative, it is the recipient's interpretation of the behaviour that determines whether it is pleasurable or not. Thus, as long as a spouse *perceives* the exchange in his or her relationship as inadequate or inequitable, he or she will react accordingly, and the result is likely to be marital distress. This integration of social exchange and cognitive mediation principles has been applied to other family relationships as well, and the intervention procedures described in this chapter take into account both the actual behaviours that family members exchange and the ways in which the members interpret those behaviours.

Communication problems

When family members complain that 'We can't communicate', this sometimes refers to instances in which messages that one person intends to send are received inaccurately by other individuals. These misinterpretations can result from faulty expression of messages (for example, vague or incomplete descriptions of thoughts and emotions) or from ineffective listening (for example, giving advice to the other person rather than attending carefully to what he or she is saying). Family members may also complain that they cannot communicate when in fact they receive each other's messages clearly but find them unacceptable. In fact, Birchler *et al.* (1975) demonstrated that distressed spouses who communicated in negative ways with their partners exhibited positive communication in conversations with strangers. Consequently, it is crucial to determine whether family members have real skill deficits that could be remedied with communication skills training, or basic conflicts in values and preferences that call for interventions focused on conflict resolution. In the latter case, it is likely that therapy should include attention to cognitive factors (for example, negative attributions about others' intentions) that interfere with family members' use of their communication skills.

In spite of the emphasis that marital and family therapists commonly place on clear communication, there has been some controversy about the benefits and costs of *unlimited* self-disclosure in family relationships. For example, whereas Alberti and Emmons (1986) argue that the more that spouses are honest and open with each other about all aspects of their marriages, the more successful the relationships will be, there is evidence that uncensored communication is more characteristic of distressed than it is of non-distressed relationships (Bornstein and Bornstein 1986). Stuart (1980) suggests that spouses make judgements about when and how much they will disclose when discussing issues that could hurt or alienate their spouses.

The importance of constructive communication for the long-term quality of close relationships is underscored by Markman's (1979, 1981, 1984) findings that premarital couples' ratings of the positive or negative impacts of their partners' communication significantly predicted marital satisfaction both $2\frac{1}{2}$ and $5\frac{1}{2}$ years later. Consequently, in a cognitive-behavioural approach to marital and family problems, the clinician conducts a careful assessment of communication, in order to identify any excesses of negative behaviours and deficits in positive behaviours that should be modified in therapy. The following are descriptions of the targets of such a behavioural assessment.

Deficits in expressive and listening skills

Marital and family therapists (for example, Falloon *et al*. 1984; Gottman *et al*. 1976) have described how members of couples and families frequently send vague and confusing messages to each other which do not provide other family members with adequate information about each other's preferences. Among the communication deficits that can contribute to unclear messages are lack of specific descriptions of thoughts and emotions, frequent topic shifts, lack of fluent speech, overgeneralized statements, illogical statements and inconsistencies between verbal and non-verbal components of messages (Bornstein and Bornstein 1986; Falloon *et al*. 1984; Stuart 1980; Thomas 1977). Noller (1984) found more frequent inaccuracies in the communication of distressed couples than among non-distressed couples, due more to encoding errors (unclear messages by the sender) than to decoding errors (the receiver fails to recognize the message's cues). The greater numbers of encoding and decoding errors in distressed couples were primarily due to husbands.

Guerney (1977) has described a number of factors that can impede effective listening to another person's messages. He notes that it is difficult to listen well when one is thinking about one's own opinions, judgements or advice. Weiss (1980) has used the term 'sentiment override' to describe the process by which spouses' perceptions of each other's current behaviour are coloured by their general positive or negative sentiments towards each other. Consistent with this idea, Weiss *et al*. (1981) found that up to 50 per cent of spouses' positive or negative ratings of their partners' communication during a specific conversation were due to the spouses' own levels of marital satisfaction.

Constructive and destructive communication

Studies using behavioural coding systems such as the Family Interaction Coding system (FICS; Patterson *et al*. 1969), the Marital Interaction Coding System (MICS; Hops *et al*. 1972; Weiss and Summers 1983) and the Couples Interaction Scoring System (CISS; Gottman 1979) have indicated that distressed couples and families exhibit higher rates of negative communication behaviours and lower rates of positive communication behaviours than those who are non-distressed (Baucom and Adams 1987; Patterson 1982). The coding systems, which include a variety of verbal and non-verbal behaviours, differentiate distressed from non-distressed relationships better when researchers create summary scores for sets of positive behaviours (for example, approve, positive physical contact) and negative beha-

behaviours (for example, criticize, negative non-verbal), rather than examining each code separately. A number of studies (for example, Gottman 1979; Margolin and Wampold 1981; Patterson 1982; Revenstorf *et al*. 1984) have identified problematic behavioural *sequences* between spouses and between parents and children, particularly escalating aversive exchanges. Such findings emphasize the mutual influence process in negative family communication.

Although behavioural coding systems have been very valuable in interaction research studies, they are too cumbersome, time consuming and expensive for use in clinical practice. However, marital and family therapists can still be guided by the coding systems when they observe their clients' interactions in a much more informal manner during therapy sessions. An alternative approach to the assessment of communication is the use of self-report questionnaires designed to assess communication in couples and families, such as the communication and affective responsiveness subscales of the McMaster Family Assessment Device (Epstein *et al*. 1983), the Marital Communication Inventory (Bienvenu 1970), the Primary Communication Inventory (Navran 1967), the self-report version of the Verbal Problems Checklist (Chavez *et al*. 1981) and the problem-solving communication and affective communication subscales of the Marital Satisfaction Inventory (Snyder 1981). Baucom and Adams (1987) provide a review of the reliability and validity of such self-report scales. Because the scales tend to be highly correlated with measures of overall relationship satisfaction and other aspects of clients' general cognitive sets about their relationships, they can be limited in their ability to provide an accurate picture of actual communication patterns (Baucom and Epstein 1990; Epstein *et al*. 1987).

Problem-solving skill deficits

Couples and families commonly face a variety of problems, ranging from the relatively trivial (for example, how to decide on tonight's dinner) to the relatively significant (for example, how to cope with sudden unemployment of one of the parents) that require them to devise and implement solutions. Research studies have identified difficulties in problem-solving behaviour among members of dysfunctional family relationships such as distressed couples (Schaap 1984), abusive parents (Azar *et al*. 1984) and families of schizophrenics (Falloon *et al*. 1984). For example, members of distressed relationships commonly attempt to resolve conflicts and problems by using coercion (for example, threats, punishment) to influence each other (Patterson 1982; Schaap 1984).

Effective problem solving is a cognitive-behavioural process that involves a sequence of skills for (1) clearly defining the nature of a problem, (2) generating alternative solutions, (3) evaluating the relative costs and benefits of the alternative solutions, (4) reaching family consensus on a solution, (5) implementing the solution (with each family member fulfilling his or her specific role) and (6) evaluating the effectiveness of the solution and revising it if necessary (Baucom and Epstein, 1990; Bornstein and Bornstein 1986; Jacobson and Margolin 1979;

Stuart 1980). Consequently, a cognitive-behavioural assessment of marital and family problems typically includes an evaluation of possible problem-solving skill deficits that may need remediation.

Behaviour-change skill deficits

Behavioural marital therapists (for example, Jacobson and Margolin 1979) have noted how distressed spouses commonly attempt to induce each other to change undesirable behaviour by means of aversive strategies such as coercive threats and criticism. These behaviour-change strategies tend to be characterized by a 'win–lose' orientation in which one acts in a manner that is likely to maximize one's own benefit/cost ratio in relation to the other person; i.e. it is a 'zero-sum game' in which one person's gain is another's loss. Stuart (1980) stresses the importance of avoiding an adversarial 'win–lose' orientation when striving to reach agreements with one's intimates about the behavioural changes that each person will make in order to implement a solution to a specific problem. Behavioural marital and family therapists have devised forms of behavioural 'contracts' that can be used to structure *mutual* behaviour changes. Because all parties in the contract make changes desired by the others, it is a 'win–win' solution to a problem. For example, in highly structured *quid pro quo* contracts, each member of a relationship agrees to behave in certain ways in exchange for particular behaviour changes by other members. In contrast, in *holistic* contracts (ibid.), each individual agrees to behave in some ways that he or she selects from a list of requests by other family members, with no reinforcements contingent on doing so. As is the case with the assessment of communication, researchers (for example, Koren *et al*. 1980) have devised systems for coding specific constructive and destructive problem-solving behaviour, but such coding systems are cumbersome outside of research laboratories, and the clinician must rely on careful observation of families' problem-solving and behaviour-change efforts during treatment sessions.

Summary of cognitive and behavioural factors in marital and family problems

In evaluating and treating marital and family problems, cognitive-behavioural therapists focus on both the inappropriate and distorted cognitions (for example, selective perceptions, unrealistic standards) and the ineffective or destructive behaviours (for example, vague messages, coercive threats) that contribute to relationship conflict and distress. Because cognitive-behavioural therapists recognize that family members' behaviours can shape their cognitions, and vice versa, they consider it essential to conduct a careful assessment of both, and to select treatments that will address the particular cognitions and behaviours contributing to problems in each family. The next section of this chapter describes the major cognitive and behavioural interventions used with couples and families, as well as research bearing on their efficacy.

TREATMENT INTERVENTIONS

Although in practice therapists tend to combine cognitive and behavioural interventions, in this section we describe these two types of interventions separately for clarity of presentation. As yet, no research studies have investigated whether certain sequences of cognitive and behavioural interventions produce optimal results.

Cognitive interventions

People generally do not question the validity of their own thinking. Consequently, therapists strive to increase each family member's abilities to (a) observe his or her own cognitions and (b) collect data for evaluating the appropriateness and validity of those cognitions.

Building cognitive self-monitoring skills

Cognitive-behavioural therapists commonly begin treatment by teaching family members about the ways in which cognitions can influence emotions and behaviours. Therapists typically describe a cognitive mediation model and concrete examples of how individuals' responses to life events are influenced by their interpretations of those events. Family members often relate best to illustrations of cognitive mediation from their own personal life experiences.

Helping family members to become more aware of their ongoing cognitions includes introducing the concept that many cognitions are 'automatic' (Beck *et al*.1979); that is, they occur spontaneously, are fleeting, may not be fully conscious, and seem highly plausible to the individual when they occur. Therapists can teach family members to ask themselves questions such as 'What thoughts popped into my mind when I was getting upset about her actions?' Commonly, clients are asked to keep written records of their thoughts, associated emotions and behaviours, using logs such as Beck *et al*.'s (ibid.) Daily Record of Dysfunctional Thoughts (DRDT). In order to sensitize clients to circular causality in their interactions with other family members, therapists also instruct the clients to record *sequences* of interactions between the self and other individuals.

Procedures for altering selective perceptions

Family members can be sensitized to selective perceptions through the examination of (a) the logs that they keep concerning family interactions, and (b) reviews of audiotapes or videotapes of interactions that occur in the therapist's office. The therapist and clients examine actual data to test how accurate an individual is when he or she has any automatic thought that may be a misrepresentation of another person's actions, such as, 'He/she *always*....' or 'He/she *never* ....'

Modification of inaccurate attributions

As is done in individual cognitive therapy, a therapist can use a Socratic line of questioning in order to guide family members in a *logical analysis* of the attributions that they make about each other's behaviour. Clients are assisted in examining whether or not it makes logical sense that events were due to the particular causes that they have inferred. In addition, family members can be coached in thinking of *alternative explanations* (attributions) for an event. On the one hand, the therapist acknowledges that each individual's attributions may be accurate, but on the other hand he or she stresses that it is important to consider other possible explanations in order to avoid making inferential errors. Family members can assist each other in 'brainstorming' alternative causes of an event, and then they can help the individual to gather evidence concerning the validity of each alternative explanation. Evidence to test the degree to which an attribution is valid or reasonable can be derived from sources such as *memories of past experiences, logs of current daily family interactions* and in vivo *family interactions during therapy sessions*.

Modification of inaccurate expectancies

Interventions for altering problematic expectancies are similar to those used to modify inaccurate attributions. For example, logical analysis of an expectancy involves examining whether it makes sense that other family members will react in predicted ways to one's particular behaviours. Furthermore, memories of past outcomes and logs of current outcomes in similar situations can provide evidence about the probability that a certain behaviour would lead to a particular outcome. *In vivo* experiments with the behaviour during therapy sessions and at home may provide compelling evidence that an anticipated outcome will not occur.

Modification of unrealistic or inappropriate assumptions and standards

A variety of the standard cognitive restructuring methods used with other types of cognitions can be applied with assumptions and standards: logical analysis, examinations of alternative assumptions and standards that seem more logical, review of past and current experiences that are or are not consistent with the assumptions and standards, and behavioural experiments to identify under what conditions an assumption is accurate. In addition, family members can be coached in generating lists of the advantages and disadvantages of adhering to a particular assumption or standard, deciding whether the disadvantages outweigh the advantages, substituting a more realistic or appropriate assumption or standard, and experimenting with living according to the new belief. Procedures for coaching family members in examining the utility of their assumptions and standards are described elsewhere (for example, Baucom and Epstein 1990 Epstein *et al.* 1988).

Behavioural interventions

The following are interventions that cognitive-behavioural marital and family therapists commonly use to address each of the four major types of behavioural problems previously described. For more detailed descriptions of specific behavioural interventions, the reader can consult the references cited.

Methods for altering behavioural exchanges

Some clients are able to increase their exchanges of positive affectional and instrumental behaviours when a therapist merely stresses to them how much daily exchanges affect the quality of close relationships and then instructs them in the use of 'love days' or 'caring days' in which the spouses are to take turns doing nice things for each other on alternate days (cf. Weiss *et al.* 1973; Stuart 1980). Each spouse is also instructed to look for such caring acts by the partner and to express his or her appreciation. However, this procedure may have limited utility with highly distressed couples who have little goodwill towards each other. In Stuart's (1980) holistic contracts, each spouse agrees to engage in a specified number of behaviours during the next week which were listed by the partner as pleasurable, without indicating which behaviours will occur, or when. Holistic contracts are designed to maximize the chance that both the giver and receiver will perceive that positive behaviours are enacted by choice.

Deficits in positive exchanges can result when family members spend little time together in shared activities. When this appears to be the case, therapists can help family members brainstorm lists of activities that they can share and can assist them in forming agreements that they will engage in certain activities from the list between therapy sessions.

Communication skill training

The most common form of communication training used with couples and families involves teaching expressive and listening skills. This skill training has been applied with problems ranging in severity from well functioning families seeking enrichment experiences (for example, Guerney *et al.* 1985) to families who are having major difficulties coping with a schizophrenic member (for example, Falloon *et al.* 1984). The therapist takes on the role of educator, giving family members specific instructions about problematic and constructive forms of communication, modelling good communication and coaching the family as they rehearse the skills during therapy sessions. Guerney's (1977) widely used Relationship Enhancement programme provides specific guidelines for expressive skills (for example, be brief and specific) and empathic listening skills (for example, strive to understand the expresser's thoughts and emotions, and convey that understanding by paraphrasing the message back to him or her).

Therapists also design communication training based on an individualized assessment of excesses and deficits in a particular family's communication. When problems such as deficits in eye contact, confusing body posture and gestures, poverty of content in verbal messages, vagueness, mixed messages, overgeneralized statements, interruptions and hostile threats are identified, a therapist uses feedback and coaching to shape more constructive communication behaviour (cf. Falloon *et al*. 1984).

Problem-solving skill training

As described earlier, problem solving is a specialized form of communication that involves defining a problem, devising possible solutions, evaluating the costs and benefits of solutions, and selecting a solution that will be implemented and evaluated. In order to teach family members these problem-solving skills, therapists use the same components of skill training (instruction, modelling and coaching in behavioural rehearsal) that are used in the training of expressive and listening skills. It is crucial for the family to become proficient with each step of the problem-solving process before attempting the next step. For example, if the family is unable to define a problem in terms of specific situations and behaviours (for example, 'When Mom tells Tommy that he cannot do something, he goes to Dad to ask permission to do it'), they will not be able to generate adequate solutions. There are a number of detailed descriptions of problem-solving training with couples (for example, Baucom and Epstein 1990; Bornstein and Bornstein 1986; Jacobson and Margolin 1979; Schlesinger and Epstein 1986) and with families (for example, Epstein *et al*. 1988; Falloon *et al*. 1984).

Training in behaviour-change skills

Stuart's early (1969) work on contingency contracting with distressed couples and Patterson's use of behavioural contracts with families involving child-behaviour problems (for a summary see Patterson 1982) provided a major impetus to the development of behaviour therapy with couples and families. In recent years, training in communication and problem-solving skills has become a more prominent component of behavioural approaches (Falloon *et. al*. 1984), but contracting is still widely used with couples and families who have difficulty following through on agreements to change their behaviours without some imposed structure.

What the various forms of contracts (for example, *quid pro quo, holistic*) have in common is that they force family members to specify concrete examples of each other's pleasing and displeasing behaviours that they would like increased or decreased. They also require explicit agreements among family members to collaborate in their efforts to solve problems, an orientation that is inconsistent with the 'win–lose' approach that many members of dysfunctional families have used in their previous unsuccessful problem-solving attempts.

Research on the effectiveness of therapy

Behavioural and cognitive approaches to the treatment of marital and family problems have developed fairly recently, with the initial reports of behavioural contracting appearing in the late 1960s, and the first publications describing cognitive interventions appearing in the late 1970s. Consequently, as yet only a limited number of controlled outcome studies has been conducted. The following is a summary of the findings from the existing studies.

The outcome studies of behavioural interventions have demonstrated the effectiveness of behavioural treatments with families that include delinquent adolescents (Alexander and Parsons 1973), schizophrenics (Falloon *et al*. 1984) and children with a variety of behaviour problems (Karoly and Rosenthal 1977; Patterson 1982). However, Gurman and Kniskern (1981) note that parents who have serious marital problems may have difficulty carrying out the tasks involved in behavioural approaches that are intended to improve behaviour problems exhibited by their children.

Recent reviews of the outcome of behavioural marital therapy (Baucom and Epstein 1990; Baucom and Hoffman 1986; Beach and O'Leary 1985) indicate that communication training, problem-solving training and contingency contracting all have favourable impacts on negative communication, reported problem areas, requests for change and self-reported marital adjustment. However, the studies have produced inconsistent results concerning increases in couples' positive communication behaviours. Baucom and Hoffman (1986) note that it is apparently easier to teach distressed couples to stop their negative behaviours than it is to induce them to increase positive behaviour.

The few studies that have compared the relative effectiveness of different components of behavioural marital therapy (for example, communication training, contracting) have not found consistent differences (Baucom and Hoffman 1986; Beach and O'Leary 1985). However, in these studies couples have not been assigned to particular treatments based on their individual types of behavioural excesses and deficits. In order to determine whether all behavioural interventions will be of equivalent value to a particular couple, future studies must match treatments with couples' special needs (Baucom and Epstein 1990; Baucom and Hoffman 1986).

Bennun (1985a, b) found that behavioural marital therapy did not help with problems of jealousy, psychopathology of one spouse, and care and non-sexual affection. It will be important for future therapy-outcome studies to examine whether treatments that focus more directly on cognitions and emotions may be more likely to assist couples with such problems.

Jacobson *et al*. (1984) found that only 35–40 per cent of treated couples in the published behavioural marital therapy outcome studies had post-therapy marital adjustments scale scores in the non-distressed range. Thus, although treated couples consistently exhibit significant improvement, for many of them improvement is a matter of becoming less distressed, rather than happy. It remains for future studies to determine whether greater improvement would occur with treatments longer than the typically brief interventions (between ten and fourteen sessions) used in outcome studies, and whether alternative treatments might be more effective for couples whose response to behavioural marital therapy is limited. Also, the outcome studies have not addressed the possibility that successful marital therapy may lead some highly alienated couples to decide to end their relationships.

Of the few existing controlled studies investigating cognitive-behavioural treatment of couples, three have examined the effects of using only cognitive interventions (Emmelkamp *et al*. 1988; Epstein *et al*. 1982; Huber and Milstein 1985), and two have tested whether cognitive restructuring adds to the effectiveness of behavioural marital therapy (Baucom 1985; Baucom and Lester 1986). For the most part these studies used short-term, highly structured interventions that focused primarily on attributions and standards.

When the existing outcome studies were conducted, the only available measure of cognitions was Eidelson and Epstein's (1982) Relationship Belief Inventory (a measure of unrealistic assumptions and standards). The overall results of the studies were that (a) cognitive interventions, alone or in combination with behavioural interventions, reduced negative cognitions and increased marital adjustment, but (b) cognitive and behavioural interventions produced similar improvement in marital adjustment. Future studies should investigate whether cognitive and behavioural interventions are also equivalent when measures of other types of cognitions (for example, attributions) are used to assess cognitive changes, and when treatments are assigned to clients based on the clients' cognitive and behavioural problems.

Little research has been conducted to evaluate cognitive interventions with families. Azar and Twentyman (1984) compared three treatments for abusive and neglectful mothers: (1) cognitive-behavioural group treatment, (2) cognitive-behavioural group treatment plus further treatment during home visits and (3) insight oriented group treatment. The components of the cognitive-behavioural treatment included training in child-management skills and problem-solving skills, education about behaviours that parents can realistically expect of children of various ages, training in anger control and monitoring of unrealistic cognitions about children. Although the three interventions had equally positive effects at the end of treatment and at a 2-month follow-up, at a 1-year follow-up the recidivism rates for the three treatments (in the order listed above) were 21 per cent, zero and 38 per cent. Because the cognitive-behavioural intervention consisted of a 'package' treatment with both cognitive and behavioural components, this study's results do not indicate how much the cognitive-restructuring components contributed to positive outcomes.

In summary, research studies have provided encouraging evidence that both cognitive and behavioural interventions with couples and families have beneficial effects. However, research in this area is in its early stages, and a number of issues, such as matching of treatments to clients' problems, need to be addressed in future studies. The final section of this chapter presents suggestions for the future development of cognitive-behavioural theory, practice and research with couples and families.

DIRECTIONS FOR FUTURE DEVELOPMENT

Further development of cognitive-behavioural marital and family therapy will require attention to (a) theory development, (b) development of assessment instruments and (c) refinement of treatment methods and outcome research. The following are suggestions for future work in these areas.

Theory development

There is a need for basic theoretical models describing interrelationships among cognitions, behaviours and emotions in intimate relationships. Models proposed by Bradbury and Fincham (1987), Fincham and Bradbury (1987), and Doherty (1981a, b) have begun to provide a conceptual structure for the field, but no model has yet been developed that accounts for the complex mutual influences among cognitions, behaviours and emotions. Furthermore, Baucom *et al.* (1989) have noted that most theoretical and research work on marital and family cognitions has been focused on attributions. Models of marital and family functioning should include roles for perceptual processes, expectancies, attributions, assumptions and standards, and it remains for research to determine whether any of those types of cognitions have more significant impacts on relationships than others.

Some initial therapy outcome studies (for example, Emmelkamp *et al.* 1988) have indicated that behavioural interventions can be as effective as cognitive interventions in changing cognitions. Consequently, additional research is needed to clarify the mechanisms of change in therapy and the direction of causality between cognitions and behaviours. For example, longitudinal studies could investigate whether assumptions and standards that individuals hold as they enter a new relationship influence the attributions, expectancies, behaviours and emotions that they exhibit as the relationship develops.

Development of assessment instruments

The measures that have been developed in recent years to assess marital and family cognitions have focused primarily on attributions, assumptions and standards. Consequently, there is a need for new instruments that will measure expectancies and perceptions. Also, the existing instruments assess a limited range of the types of cognitions that they were designed to measure. For example, the Relationship Belief Inventory (Eidelson and Epstein 1982) assesses only three assumptions and two standards, whereas there are many other schemata that may influence relationships. Researchers will need more comprehensive cognitive measures in order to conduct adequate tests of cognitive-behavioural models of marital and family functioning.

Refinement of treatment methods and outcome research

As noted earlier, the cognitive and behavioural interventions used in most outcome studies included multiple components intended to modify a number of problematic cognitions and behaviours. Consequently, it will be important to investigate the relative effectiveness of different treatment components, and to refine treatments accordingly to focus on the effective components. Matching treatments to the specific needs of client couples and families will also help refine interventions. It will also be important to investigate whether Bennun's (1985a, b) finding that behavioural marital therapy was effective for some types of presenting problems but not for others may apply to cognitive interventions as well.

An issue rarely addressed in written descriptions of cognitive interventions concerns the characteristics of what different individuals label 'cognitive restructuring'. Readers of clinical and research literature need to exercise care in identifying the nature of potentially highly variable forms of treatment that are given the same label. Such an evaluation is also important when one compares the results of various outcome studies, particularly when they produce conflicting results. Thus, clinical writers and researchers should provide detailed descriptions of the cognitive variables that they intend to modify and the specific interventions that they use (Epstein and Baucom 1988).

REFERENCES

Abramson, L. Y., Seligman, M. E. P. and Teasdale, J. (1978) 'Learned helplessness in humans: critique and reformulation', *Journal of Abnormal Psychology* 87: 49–94.

Alberti, R. E. and Emmons, M. L. (1986) *The Professional Edition of Your Perfect Right: A Manual for Assertiveness Trainers*, San Luis Obispo, Calif.: Impact.

Alexander, J. F. and Parsons, B. V. (1973) 'Short-term behavioral intervention with delinquent families: impact on family process and recidivism', *Journal of Abnormal Psychology* 81: 219–25.

Azar, S. T. (1986) 'Identifying at-risk populations: a research strategy for developing more specific risk indicators and screening devices', paper presented at the annual meeting of the Association for Advancement of Behavior Therapy, Chicago, November.

—— and Rohrbeck, C. A. (1986) 'Child abuse and unrealistic expectations: further validation of the Parent Opinion Questionnaire', *Journal of Consulting and Clinical Psychology* 54: 867–8.

Azar, S. T. and Twentyman, C. T. (1984) 'An evaluation of the effectiveness of behaviorally versus insight oriented group treatments with maltreating mothers', paper presented at the annual meeting of the Association for Advancement of Behavior Therapy, Philadelphia, November.

Azar, S. T., Robinson, D., Hekimian, E. and Twentyman, C. T. (1984) 'Unrealistic expectations and problem solving ability in maltreating and comparison mothers', *Journal of Consulting and Clinical Psychology* 52: 687–91.

Bandura, A. (1977) *Social Learning Theory*, Englewood Cliffs, NJ: Prentice-Hall.

Barnett, L. R. and Nietzel, M. T. (1979) 'Relationship of instrumental and affectional behaviors and self-esteem to marital satisfaction in distressed and nondistressed couples', *Journal of Consulting and Clinical Psychology* 47: 946–57.

Baucom, D. H. (1985) 'Enhancing behavioral marital therapy with cognitive restructuring and emotional expressiveness training', paper presented at the annual meeting of the Association for Advancement of Behavior Therapy, Houston, TX, November.

——— (1987) 'Attributions in distressed relations: how can we explain them?', in S. Duck and D. Perlman (eds) *Heterosexual Relations, Marriage and Divorce*, London: Sage, pp. 177–206.

——— and Adams, A. (1987) 'Assessing communication in marital interaction', in K. D. O'Leary (ed.) *Assessment of Marital Discord*, Hillsdale, NJ: Erlbaum, pp. 139–82.

Baucom, D. H. and Epstein, N. (1990) *Cognitive-Behavioral Marital Therapy*, New York: Brunner/Mazel.

Baucom, D. H. and Hoffman, J. A. (1986) 'The effectiveness of marital therapy: current status and application to the clinical setting', in N. S. Jacobson and A. S. Gurman (eds) *Clinical Handbook of Marital Therapy*, New York: Guilford Press.

Baucom, D. H. and Lester, G. W. (1986) 'The usefulness of cognitive restructuring as an adjunct to behavioral marital therapy', *Behavior Therapy* 17: 385–403.

Baucom, D. H., Sayers, S. L. and Duhe, A. (1987) 'Attributional style and attributional patterns among married couples', unpublished manuscript, University of North Carolina at Chapel Hill.

Baucom, D. H., Wheeler, C. M. and Bell, G. (1984) 'Assessing the role of attributions in marital distress', paper presented at the annual meeting of the Association for Advancement of Behavior Therapy, Philadelphia, November.

Baucom, D. H., Epstein, N., Sayers, S. and Sher, T. G. (1989) 'The role of cognitions in marital relationships: definitional, methodological, and conceptual issues', *Journal of Consulting and Clinical Psychology* 57: 31–8.

Beach, S. R. H. and O'Leary, K. D. (1985) 'Current status of outcome research in marital therapy', in L. L'Abate (ed.) *The Handbook of Family Psychology and Therapy*, Vol. II, Homewood, Ill.: Dorsey, pp. 1035–72.

Beck, A. T. (1976) *Cognitive Therapy and the Emotional Disorders*, New York: International Universities Press.

———, Rush, A. J., Shaw, B. F. and Emery, G. (1979) *Cognitive Therapy of Depression*, New York: Guilford Press.

Bennun, I. (1985a) 'Behavioral marital therapy: an outcome evaluation of conjoint, group and one spouse treatment', *Scandinavian Journal of Behavior Therapy* 14: 157–68.

——— (1985b) 'Prediction and responsiveness in behavioral marital therapy', *Behavioral Psychotherapy* 13: 186–201.

Bienvenu, M. J. (1970) 'Measurement of marital communication', *The Family Coordinator* 19: 26–31.

Birchler, G. R., Weiss, R. L. and Vincent, J. P. (1975) 'Multimethod analysis of social reinforcement exchange between maritally distressed and nondistressed spouse and stranger dyads', *Journal of Personality and Social Psychology* 31: 349–60.

Bornstein, P. H. and Bornstein, M. T. (1986) *Marital Therapy: A Behavioral-Communications Approach*, New York: Pergamon.

Bradbury, T. N. and Fincham, F. D. (1987) 'Affect and cognition in close relationships: towards an integrative model', *Cognition and Emotion* 1: 59–87.

Chavez, R. E., Samuel, V. and Haynes, S. N. (1981) 'Validity of the Verbal Problems Checklist', paper presented at the annual meeting of the Association for Advancement of Behavior Therapy, Toronto, November.

Christensen, A. and Nies, D. C. (1980) 'The Spouse Observation Checklist: empirical analysis and critique', *American Journal of Family Therapy* 8: 69–79.

Christensen, A., Sullaway, M. and King, C. (1983) 'Systematic error in behavioral reports of dyadic interaction: egocentric bias and content effects', *Behavioral Assessment* 5: 131–42.

DiGiuseppe, R. (1988) 'A cognitive-behavioral approach to the treatment of conduct disorder children and adolescents', in N. Epstein, S. E. Schlesinger and W. Dryden (eds) *Cognitive-Behavioral Therapy with Families*, New York: Brunner/Mazel, pp. 183–214.

Doherty, W. J. (1981a) 'Cognitive processes in intimate conflict: I. Extending attribution theory', *American Journal of Family Therapy* 9(1): 5–13.

—— (1981b) 'Cognitive processes in intimate conflict: II. Efficacy and learned helplessness', *American Journal of Family Therapy* 9(2): 35–44.

Dryden, W. (1985) 'Marital therapy: the rational-emotive approach', in W. Dryden (ed.) *Marital Therapy in Britain*, Vol. 1, London: Harper and Row, pp. 195–221.

Eidelson, R. J. and Epstein, N. (1982) 'Cognition and relationship maladjustment: development of a measure of dysfunctional relationship beliefs', *Journal of Consulting and Clinical Psychology* 50: 715–20.

Ellis, A. (1962) *Reason and Emotion in Psychotherapy*, New York: Lyle Stuart.

—— (1976) 'Techniques of handling anger in marriage', *Journal of Marriage and Family Counseling* 2: 305–16.

—— (1977) 'The nature of disturbed marital interactions', in A. Ellis and R. Grieger (eds) *Handbook of Rational-Emotive Therapy*, New York: Springer, pp. 170–6.

—— (1986) 'Rational-emotive therapy applied to relationship therapy', *Journal of Rational-Emotive Therapy* 4: 4–21.

Elwood, R. W. and Jacobson, N. S. (1982) 'Spouses' agreement in reporting their behavioral interactions: a clinical replication', *Journal of Consulting and Clinical Psychology* 50: 783–4.

Emmelkamp, P. M. G., van Linden van den Heuvell, C., Ruphan, M., Sanderman, R., Scholing, A. and Stroink, F. (1988) 'Cognitive and behavioral interventions with distressed couples', *Journal of Family Psychology* 1: 365–77.

Epstein, N. (1982) 'Cognitive therapy with couples', *American Journal of Family Therapy* 10(1): 5–16.

—— and Baucom, D. H. (1988) 'Outcome research on cognitive-behavioral marital therapy: conceptual and methodological issues', *Journal of Family Psychology* 1: 378–84.

—— (1989) 'Cognitive-behavioral marital therapy', in A. Freeman, K. M. Simon, L. Beutler and H. Arkowitz (eds) *Comprehensive Handbook of Cognitive Therapy*, New York: Plenum.

Epstein, N. and Eidelson, R. J. (1981) 'Unrealistic beliefs of clinical couples: their relationship to expectations, goals and satisfaction', *American Journal of Family Therapy* 9(4): 13–22.

Epstein, N., Pretzer, J. L. and Fleming, B. (1982) 'Cognitive therapy and communication training: comparisons of effects with distressed couples', paper presented at the annual meeting of the Association for Advancement of Behavior Therapy, Los Angeles, November.

—— (1987) 'The role of cognitive appraisal in self-reports of marital communication', *Behavior Therapy* 18: 51–69.

Epstein, N., Schlesinger, S. E. and Dryden, W. (eds) (1988) *Cognitive-Behavioral Therapy with Families*, New York: Brunner/Mazel.

Epstein, N. B., Baldwin, L. and Bishop, S. (1983) 'The McMaster Family Assessment Device', *Journal of Marital and Family Therapy* 9: 171–80.

Falloon, I. R. H., Boyd, J. L. and McGill, C. W. (1984) *Family Care of Schizophrenia*, New York: Guilford Press.

Fincham, F. D. and Bradbury, T. N. (1987) 'The impact of attributions in marriage: a longitudinal analysis', *Journal of Personality and Social Psychology* 53: 510–17.

—— (1987) 'Cognitive processes in close relationships: an attribution-efficacy model', *Journal of Personality and Social Psychology* 53: 1106–18.

Fincham, F. D. and O'Leary, K. D. (1983) 'Causal inferences for spouse behavior in maritally distressed and nondistressed couples', *Journal of Social and Clinical Psychology* 1: 42–57.

Fincham, F. D., Beach, S. R. H. and Nelson, G. (1987) 'Attribution processes in distressed and nondistressed couples: 3. Causal and responsibility attributions for spouse behavior', *Cognitive Therapy and Research* 11: 71–86.

Floyd, F. and Markman, H. (1983) 'Observational biases in spouse interaction: toward a cognitive/behavioral model of marriage', *Journal of Consulting and Clinical Psychology* 51: 450–7.

Geiss, S. K. and O'Leary, K. D. (1981) 'Therapist ratings of frequency of marital problems: implications for research', *Journal of Marital and Family Therapy* 7: 515–20.

Gottman, J. M. (1979) *Marital Interaction: Empirical Investigations*, New York: Academic Press.

——Markman, H. and Notarius, C. (1977) 'The topography of marital conflict: a sequential analysis of verbal and nonverbal behavior', *Journal of Marriage and the Family* 39: 461–77.

Gottman, J. M., Notarius, C., Gonso, J. and Markman, H. (1976) *A Couple's Guide to Communication*, Champaign, Ill.: Research Press.

Guerney, B. G., Jr. (1977) *Relationship Enhancement*, San Francisco: Jossey-Bass.

——, Guerney, L. and Cooney, T. (1985) 'Marital and family problem prevention and enrichment', in L. L'Abate (ed.) *The Handbook of Family Psychology and Therapy*, Homewood, Ill.: Dorsey, pp. 1179–217.

Gurman, A. S. and Kniskern, D. P. (1981) 'Family therapy outcome research: knowns and unknowns', in A. S. Gurman and D. P. Kniskern (eds) *Handbook of Family Therapy*, New York: Brunner/Mazel, pp. 742–75.

Hops, H., Wills, T. A., Patterson, G. R. and Weiss, R. L. (1972) *Marital Interaction Coding System*, Eugene, Oreg.: University of Oregon and Oregon Research Institute.

Huber, C. H. and Milstein, B. (1985) 'Cognitive restructuring and a collaborative set in couples' work', *American Journal of Family Therapy* 13(2): 17–27.

Jacobson, N. S. (1984) 'The modification of cognitive processes in behavioral marital therapy: integrating cognitive and behavioral intervention strategies', in K. Hahlweg and N. S. Jacobson (eds) *Marital Interaction: Analysis and Modification*, New York: Guilford Press, pp. 285–308.

—— and Margolin, G. (1979) *Marital Therapy: Strategies Based on Social Learning and Behavior Exchange Principles*, New York: Brunner/Mazel

Jacobson, N. S., Follette, W. C. and McDonald, D. W. (1982) 'Reactivity to positive and negative behavior in distressed and nondistressed married couples', *Journal of Consulting and Clinical Psychology* 50: 706–14.

Jacobson, N. S., Follette, W. C., Revenstorf, D., Baucom, D. H., Hahlweg, K. and Margolin, G. (1984) 'Variability in outcome and clinical significance of behavioral marital therapy: a reanalysis of outcome data', *Journal of Consulting and Clinical Psychology* 52: 497–504.

Karoly, P. and Rosenthal, M. (1977) 'Training parents in behavior modification: effects on perceptions of family interactions and deviant child behaviors', *Behavior Therapy* 8: 406–10.

Kelly, G. A. (1955) *The Psychology of Personal Constructs*, New York: W. W. Norton.

Koren, P., Carlton, K. and Shaw, D. (1980) 'Marital conflict: relations among behaviors, outcomes, and distress', *Journal of Consulting and Clinical Psychology* 48: 460–8.

Kurdek, L. A. and Berg, B. (1987) 'Children's beliefs about parental divorce scale: psychometric characteristics and concurrent validity', *Journal of Consulting and Clinical Psychology* 55: 712–18.

Larrance, D. T. and Twentyman, C. T. (1983) 'Maternal attributions and child abuse', *Journal of Abnormal Psychology* 92: 449–57.

Margolin, G. (1981) 'Behavior exchange in happy and unhappy marriages: a family cycle perspective', *Behavior Therapy* 12: 329–43.
—— and Wampold, B. E. (1981) 'Sequential analysis of conflict and accord in distressed and nondistressed marital partners', *Journal of Consulting and Clinical Psychology* 49: 554–67.
Markman, H. J. (1979) 'The application of a behavioral model of marriage in predicting relationship satisfaction of couples planning marriage', *Journal of Consulting and Clinical Psychology* 47: 743–9.
—— (1981) 'Prediction of marital distress: a 5-year follow-up', *Journal of Consulting and Clinical Psychology* 49: 760–2.
—— (1984) 'The longitudinal study of couples' interactions: implications for understanding and predicting the development of marital distress', in K. Hahlweg and N. S. Jacobson (eds) *Marital Interaction: Analysis and Modification* New York: Guilford Press, pp. 253–81.
Navran, L. (1967) 'Communication and adjustment in marriage', *Family Process* 6: 173–84.
Nisbett, R. and Ross, L. (1980) *Human Inference: Strategies and Shortcomings of Social Judgement*, Englewood Cliffs, NJ: Prentice-Hall.
Noller, P. (1984) *Nonverbal Communication and Marital Interaction*, New York: Pergamon Press.
Notarius, C. I. and Vanzetti, N. A. (1983) 'The Marital Agendas Protocol', in E. E. Filsinger (ed.) *Marriage and Family Assessment: A Sourcebook for Family Therapy*, Beverly Hills, Calif.: Sage, pp. 209–27.
O'Leary, K. D. and Turkewitz, H. (1978) 'Marital therapy from a behavioral perspective', in T. J. Paolino and B. S. McCrady (eds) *Marriage and Marital Therapy: Psychoanalytic, Behavioral and Systems Theory Perspectives*, New York: Brunner/Mazel, pp. 240–97.
Patterson, G. R. (1982) *Coercive Family Process*, Eugene, Oreg.: Castalia.
—— and Reid, J. B. (1984) 'Social interaction processes within the family: the study of moment-by-moment family transaction in which human social development is embedded', *Journal of Applied Developmental Psychology* 5: 237–62.
Patterson, G. R., Ray, R. S., Shaw, D. A. and Cobb, J. A. (1969) *Manual for Coding of Family Interactions*, New York: Microfiche Publications.
Pretzer, J. L., Epstein, N. and Fleming, B. (1985) 'The Marital Attitude Survey: a measure of dysfunctional attributions and expectancies', unpublished manuscript.
Qualls, S. H. (1988) 'Problems in families of older adults', in N. Epstein, S. E. Schlesinger and W. Dryden (eds) *Cognitive-Behavioral Therapy with Families*, New York: Brunner/Mazel, pp. 215–53.
Revenstorf, D., Hahlweg, K., Schindler, L. and Vogel, B. (1984) 'Interaction analysis of marital conflict', in K. Hahlweg and N. S. Jacobson (eds) *Marital Interaction: Analysis and Modification*, New York: Guilford Press, pp. 159–81.
Roehling, P. V. and Robin, A. L. (1986) 'Development and validation of the Family Beliefs Inventory: a measure of unrealistic beliefs among parents and adolescents', *Journal of Consulting and Clinical Psychology* 54: 693–7.
Rotter, J. B. (1954) *Social Learning and Clinical Psychology*, Englewood Cliffs, NJ: Prentice-Hall.
Schaap, C. (1984) 'A comparison of the interaction of distressed and nondistressed married couples in a laboratory situation: literature survey, methodological issues, and an empirical investigation', in K. Hahlweg and N. S. Jacobson (eds) *Marital Interaction: Analysis and Modification*, New York: Guilford Press, pp. 133–58.
Schlesinger, S. E. (1988) 'Cognitive-behavioral approaches to family treatment of addictions', in N. Epstein, S. E. Schlesinger and W. Dryden (eds) *Cognitive-Behavioral Therapy with Families*, New York: Brunner/Mazel, pp. 254–91.
—— and Epstein, N. (1986) 'Cognitive-behavioral techniques in marital therapy', in P. A.

Keller and L. G. Ritt (eds) *Innovations in Clinical Practice: A Source Book*, Vol. 5, Sarasota, Fla.: Professional Resource Exchange.

Seiler, T. B. (1984) 'Development of cognitive theory, personality, and therapy', in N. Hoffman (ed.) *Foundations of Cognitive Therapy: Theoretical Methods and Practical Applications*, New York: Plenum, pp. 11–49.

Snyder, D. K. (1981) *Manual for the Marital Satisfaction Inventory*, Los Angeles: Western Psychological Services.

Stuart, R. B. (1969) 'Operant-interpersonal treatment for marital discord', *Journal of Consulting and Clinical Psychology* 33: 675–82.

—— (1980) *Helping Couples Change: A Social Learning Approach to Marital Therapy*, New York: Guilford Press.

Thibaut, J. W. and Kelley, H. H. (1959) *The Social Psychology of Groups*, New York: Wiley.

Thomas, E. J. (1977) *Marital Communication and Decision-Making*, New York: Free Press.

Thompson, J. S. and Snyder, D. K. (1986) 'Attribution theory in intimate relationships: a methodological review', *American Journal of Family Therapy* 14: 123–38.

Turk, D. C. and Speers, M. A. (1983) 'Cognitive schemata and cognitive processes in cognitive-behavioral interventions: going beyond the information given', in P. C. Kendall (ed.) *Advances in Cognitive-Behavioral Research and Therapy*, Vol. 2, New York: Academic Press, pp. 1–31.

Visher, E. B. and Visher, J. S. (1979) *Stepfamilies: A Guide to Working with Stepparents and Stepchildren*, New York: Brunner/Mazel.

—— (1988) *Old Loyalties, New Ties: Therapeutic Strategies with Stepfamilies*, New York: Brunner/Mazel.

Watzlawick, P., Beavin, J. H. and Jackson, D. D. (1967) *Pragmatics of Human Communication*, New York: W. W. Norton.

Weiss, R. L. (1980) 'Strategic behavioral marital therapy: toward a model for assessment and intervention', in J. P. Vincent (ed.) *Advances in Family Intervention, Assessment and Theory*, Vol. 1, Greenwich, Conn.: JAI Press.

—— and Summers, K. J. (1983) 'Marital Interaction Coding System – III', in E. E. Filsinger (ed.) *Marriage and Family Assessment: A Sourcebook for Family Therapy*, Beverly Hills, Calif.: Sage, pp. 85–115.

Weiss, R. L., Hops, H. and Patterson, G. R. (1973) 'A framework for conceptualizing marital conflict, a technology for altering it, some data for evaluating it', in L. A. Hamerlynk, L. C. Handy and E. J. Mash (eds) *Behavior Change: Methodology, Concepts and Practice*, Champaign, Ill.: Research Press.

Weiss, R. L., Wasserman, D. A., Wieder, G. R. and Summers, K. (1981) 'Subjective and objective evaluation of marital conflict: couples versus the establishment', paper presented at the annual meeting of the Association for Advancement of Behavior Therapy, Toronto, November.

Wessler, R. A. and Wessler, R. L. (1980) *The Principles and Practice of Rational-Emotive Therapy*, San Francisco: Jossey-Bass.

Wills, T. A., Weiss, R. L. and Patterson, G. R. (1974) 'A behavioral analysis of the determinants of marital satisfaction', *Journal of Consulting and Clinical Psychology* 42: 802–11.

Chapter 12

Sexual problems

Martin Cole and Windy Dryden

CONCEPTUALIZATION

Introduction

Until the 1960s most individuals with sexual problems were offered therapies largely grounded in the psychoanalytical mode. If, as it was then believed, these problems were a consequence of deep-seated emotional stress and were symptoms of underlying conflicts acquired in childhood, resolution of these conflicts should have led to normal functioning. However, apart from the obvious disadvantages that analysis was both very expensive and time consuming, it was also, reportedly, rarely ever successful in changing the problem behaviour (Allgeier and Allgeier 1984; Cooper 1978; Ellis 1980).

In the 1960s and 1970s Masters and Johnson (1966, 1970) and Kaplan (1974, 1979) led a scientific renaissance from which were born the New Sex Therapies. These were based upon the largely empirical approach to sexual function and behaviour initiated some 20 years earlier by Kinsey (Kinsey *et al.* 1948, 1953). For example, Masters and Johnson (1966) described four stages in their sex-response cycle: excitement, plateau, orgasm and resolution. This was later to be reformulated by Kaplan (1974), initially as a biphasic response where she recognized an initial vasocongestive phase (arousal), followed by a reflexive muscular reaction (orgasm). Finally, she added to this the desire/drive phase, resulting in her triphasic model which is generally accepted today.

From this theoretical base, which was supported by a wealth of concurrent research into the physiology of sexual behaviour, came the birth of the New Sex Therapies, characterized by a directive interventionist approach which relied heavily upon behavioural and psychoeducational elements. In addition, but to a lesser extent, the more intangible humanistic psychotherapies still played an important part in sex therapy in their role of encouraging attitudinal change, permission giving and self-acceptance. This amalgam of therapies, psychodynamic, behavioural and humanistic, persists to this day in sex therapy.

The psychodynamic component of modern sex therapy remains partly as a result of the work of Kaplan (1974), who appeared to achieve a seemingly remarkable marriage between the psychodynamic and the behavioural approaches. So well did she succeed that a 'quasi-eclectic modified Masters and Johnson x Kaplan hybrid programme' appears to be the chosen method of sex therapists, at least in the UK (Cole 1985: 341; Cooper 1988). Evidence of the existence of this kind of eclecticism is further illustrated in Crown and d'Ardenne (1982) when they state that 'we embed our behavioural approaches firmly in a psychodynamic attitude' (p. 72). Eclecticism notwithstanding, there was now taking place a subtle shift in emphasis away from the psychodynamic and humanistic and towards the behavioural therapies (Hawton 1985; Jehu 1979; Leiblum and Pervin 1980; LoPiccolo and LoPiccolo 1978): a shift which prepared the way for the arrival of a cognitive-behavioural approach to sex therapy.

Although the increasing reliance upon behavioural therapies in sex therapy had earlier led to Masters and Johnson's rapid treatment programme and the use of home assignments, these new directive therapies did not produce the results that was hoped of them. In the first place it was soon obvious that the rapid treatment residential programmes, that were so much a feature of the Masters and Johnson approach, could not be adopted by others for purely practical reasons. Instead, other sex therapists had to rely upon the more conventional weekly or fortnightly consultations. As a result, some therapy programmes lasted months rather than weeks, with the inevitable consequence of drop-outs. Second, the outcomes of the new sex therapies were often very disappointing by any standards and certainly did not match those achieved earlier by Masters and Johnson (Cole 1985) (and see p. 345). Whatever the reasons for this, and they have been widely debated (Cole 1985; Kolodny 1981; Zilbergeld and Evans 1980), the way was now open for any approach which might break new ground, and the arrival of the cognitive-behavioural therapies fulfilled that need. Here was an opportunity to try the modern and empirically based methods of behaviour modification, which at the same time could prove to be labour- and cost-effective (for example, Bishay 1988).

Ellis (1976) played an important part in the introduction of cognitive-behavioural methods in sex therapy when he made the distinction between sex dysfunctions and sex disturbances. As he saw it the *sex dysfunctions* were an occasional and inevitable part of many individuals' sex lives but these hiccups in sexual response did not usually create too much distress. He argued that situational loss of erection and quick ejaculation in men and occasional difficulties in achieving orgasm in women, for example, are usually accepted for what they are and do not lead to an escalation of anxiety nor long-term difficulties – nor do they usually disrupt relationships. What does often require therapeutic intervention, however, is when sex dysfunctions lead to emotional stress which in turn precipitates further problems. These *sexual disturbances,* according to Ellis, are a consequence of disturbed thinking, are more profound in their effect and may require the attention of the cognitive therapist.

The underlying principles behind cognitive-behaviour therapy therefore assert that adult sexual functioning has been, and is being, shaped by three main factors: biological events, environmental conditioning and negative emotions such as anger, anxiety and depression. Most importantly these latter feeling states are, to the cognitive therapist, sustained by maladaptive and distorted thoughts, attitudes and beliefs which have often been acquired in early life (Walen and Perlmutter 1988). For treatment to be effective and sexual function restored, these irrational beliefs need to be challenged.

Ellis's Rational-Emotive Therapy provides a relatively simple way of conceptualizing the role of cognitions in influencing behaviours and mood. Using his *ABCD* paradigm (see p. 338) in the treatment of, for example, psychogenic erectile dysfunction, *A* (the activating experience or event) represents the opportunity to have sex and *C* (the emotional or behavioural consequence) would be the patient's performance anxiety and failure to get an erection. *A* does not cause *C* directly but instead is brought about by *B* (*A* → *B* →*C*), *B* being the patient's belief system or, more precisely, his evaluation of *A*. ('There is nothing good nor bad but thinking makes it so'.)

An instance to support this view was provided by Hoch *et al.* (1981), in their study of 120 sexually dysfunctional and 60 normal couples. They found that a traditional, religious upbringing, sexual ignorance, sexual prejudices and communication problems were much more common in the dysfunctional group and that these attitudes and beliefs had resulted in rigid, stereotyped sexual behaviours for both partners, behaviours which in turn potentiated the sex dysfunction.

The sex dysfunctions

For many people intercourse, for various reasons, is either not possible or is insufficiently rewarding that it is rarely practised. In many cases specific problems can be identified and a generally agreed classification of these so-called sex dysfunctions is presented in Table 12.1.

Although it is important to be able to arrive at an accurate diagnosis before one begins to help those with sexual problems, it is equally important to try to avoid labelling patients with their condition. Effective 'treatment' and 'cures' are not always available and sometimes it is necessary instead to help the individual or couple to see the problem in a different perspective so that they can avoid unrealistic expectations of either themselves or their partners (Cole 1985).

Table 12.1   A classification of the sex dysfunctions

Dysfunction	In men	In women
Desire or drive	Impaired sexual desire	Impaired sexual desire
Arousal	Erectile dysfunction	Impaired sexual arousal
Orgasm	Premature ejaculation	Orgasmic
	Delayed ejaculation	dysfunction
Other	Dyspareunia	Vaginismus
	Sexual phobias	Dyspareunia
		Sexual phobias

Impaired sexual desire

This is a complex and heterogeneous group of behaviours, sometimes known as frequency dissatisfaction when one, but not both, of the partners is affected. It may result from a low sex drive, from sexual habituation with one's partner, though more often it is a consequence of the negative effects of childhood experiences which have resulted in a denial of sexual feelings. Not infrequently, impaired sexual desire is manifest not as an indifference to sex but as a positive aversion to the prospect of any sexual intimacy.

Erectile dysfunction

Erectile inadequacy refers to those circumstances where a man discovers that his penis is not stiff enough to penetrate and remain erect in the vagina during intercourse. It is probably the commonest sex disorder in the western world. Probably as many as one half of all those who suffer from erectile disorders have their condition caused by physical or organic factors (Melman *et al.* 1984), though a distinction between organogenic and psychogenic aetiologies is not always either clear or valid.

Impaired sexual arousal in women

Blocks in arousal in women are less easily recognized than in men. One specific sign is the lack of vaginal lubrication. In addition, the absence of the expected constellation of responses normally associated with sexual arousal such as the flushing of the face, an increase in spontaneous body movements, vocalization and of course a parallel increase in heart and respiratory rates, also indicate blocks in arousal.

Premature ejaculation

This is the condition where a man reaches orgasm and ejaculates so rapidly that normally neither he nor his partner are satisfied. Quick ejaculation is not easy to define objectively and though commonly met it is often better tolerated than erectile dysfunction unless, for example, ejaculation takes place before penetration.

Delayed ejaculation

This is a relatively rare problem where a man finds it difficult, if not impossible, to reach orgasm and ejaculate. The condition may be *absolute* when ejaculation has never been possible in either masturbation or in intercourse, or it may be *partial* when ejaculation can only be achieved in self- or partner-masturbation.

Orgasmic dysfunction

This describes the condition where a woman finds it difficult or impossible to achieve a climax. Between one third and one half of all sexually active women never or rarely achieve an orgasm in intercourse without some form of additional stimulation (Cole 1988a) and this fact has led some sex therapists to conclude that the absence of an 'unassisted coital orgasm' cannot be regarded as a sex disorder because it is so frequent. Be that as it may, the fact remains that the great difficulty that many women experience in achieving a climax in intercourse does cause considerable distress to them and their partners, distress that often leads them to seek help.

Vaginismus and dyspareunia

Normally during sexual arousal the vagina relaxes and dilates spontaneously to allow the penis to enter. However, in some women the muscles surrounding the lower third of the vagina constrict reflexively when attempts at penetration take place and intercourse becomes either impossible, or at least extremely painful and distressing. This phobic response is known as *vaginismus*. Associated with, and sometimes indistinguishable from, vaginismus is an allied condition called *dyspareunia*, which describes the pain experienced within the vagina once penetration has been achieved. Dyspareunia may also occur in the male during intercourse and may be caused, for example, by an infection, by a tight foreskin or, rarely psychogenically.

Sexual phobias

Men and women sometimes seek treatment for specific sexual phobias. For example, a woman may find it difficult or impossible to touch her partner's penis, or more rarely, have a fear of having her vulva stimulated by his hand. More common is an aversion to semen. Sexual phobias in men are less common – a fear of the foreskin being retracted is one good example.

The causation, development and maintenance of sexual problems

The causation of sexual problems is complex: they can be identified as those causes which have a physical or 'medical' base (the organogenic or biogenic), those which have a psychological origin (the psychogenic) and those which are the interactive product of both the organogenic and psychogenic. For example, a man who has diabetes may develop erectile difficulties, either as a result of an organogenic factor (neuropathy or arteriopathy), a psychogenic factor (anxiety arising from having heard that erectile loss may sometimes be a complication of diabetes) or as a consequence of the synergistic effect of both physical and psychological causes but where neither on their own would have been sufficient to trigger the dysfunction. The aetiology of the sexual disorders is further complicated by the fact that sex normally involves another person. Attempts to understand the complexities of a relationship often reach imponderable levels which then defy simple analysis and therapeutic intervention.

The physical and medical (organogenic) causes influencing sexual responses are many and varied and beyond the scope of this chapter. The reader is referred to Bancroft (1989) for an excellent review. In her discussion of those psychological factors involved in the aetiology of the sex disorders, Kaplan (1974) distinguished between those experiences which she described as *remote* (acting in childhood) and those which are *immediate* (acting in the here and now) (see p. 334). An application of her approach to the aetiology of the male sex disorders is discussed by Cole (1985) and is illustrated in Figure 12.1.

Once they appear, sexual disorders may, or may not, persist. Many people have sexual problems which are quite short lived: a temporary loss of erection due to stress or fatigue, transient vaginismus or quick ejaculation at the beginning of a relationship or a period when orgasm in women is elusive in coitus as a result of, for example, depression or a relationship problem. Most sexual difficulties of this kind get better without recourse to treatment.

Some sexual problems may, however, be more persistent and not remit nor respond to treatment, and this probability has to be accepted by both the therapist and the patient – indeed, outcome studies (see p. 345) bear this out. If there are resistant physical or 'medical' factors in the aetiology that do not and will not respond to treatment and the clinicians involved are confident that these are insurmountable problems, it is almost certainly better to make this information available to the patient so that he or she can be helped to use their cognitive resources to accept and then deal with the situation.

Sexual problems with a psychological origin can also be self-perpetuating. Notable is the role played by performance anxiety, which can easily enter a self-maintaining cycle of fear, blocking all sexual responses (Masters and Johnson 1970). Such a shut-down often confuses patients because they believe that such a dramatic loss of response can only be explained by a physical cause. Even more confusing are blocks in sexual function which follow bereavement or divorce. The associated sense of loss and grief may have a long-term and devastating effect upon the patient, and unless opportunities arise so that a new supportive relationship can be entered into within a year or so, sometimes an irrevocable shut-down in sexual function may follow. Whether this occurs or not obviously depends upon the personality of patients, their age, the strength of their sex drive and whether, for example, they can enjoy regular self-masturbation during this period of grief.

The cognitive model

Liberation from the use of the classical S–R model in therapy began with the recognition and understanding of the importance of the role of covert stimuli, responses and reinforcers in behavioural change. To summarize, 'private events

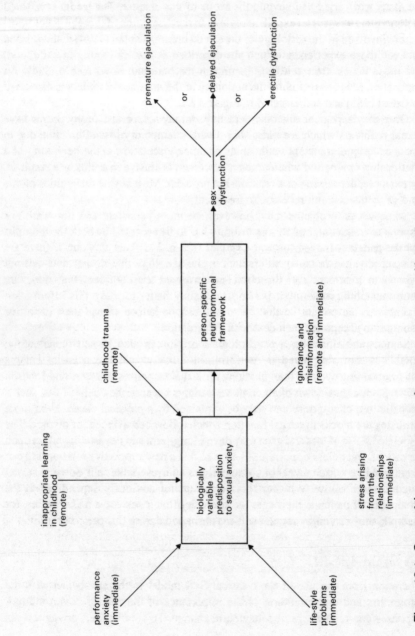

Figure 12.1 Some of the consequences of sex stress, remote and immediate in the male

The diagram shows the following elements flowing into a central box labelled **biologically variable predisposition to sexual anxiety**:

- performance anxiety (immediate)
- inappropriate learning in childhood (remote)
- childhood trauma (remote)
- stress arising from the relationships (immediate)
- life-style problems (immediate)
- ignorance and misinformation (remote and immediate)

This leads to a **person-specific neurohormonal framework**, which leads to **sex dysfunction**, producing:

- premature ejaculation
- or
- delayed ejaculation
- or
- erectile dysfunction

were viewed as obeying the same laws of learning as were applicable to publicly observed behaviours' (Walen and Roth 1987: 225). However, this assumption that covert experiences could easily fit into the model of classical behaviourism was not universally accepted (Mahoney 1974) if only on the grounds that it was over-simplistic. For example, how could it be assumed that we always feel what we think when it is self-evident to some that we also think what we feel and that it is common parlance to say 'I'll see how I feel at the time' or 'I feel it's not right'.

Phylogenetically speaking, affect evolved long before the capacity for thinking, and while it is clear that in the evolutionary process cognitions are steadily gaining ground at the expense of affect in their role in decision making and the control of behaviour, this process is far from complete. Moreover, the 'balance of power' between cognition and affect varies dramatically from person to person, and this inescapable biological diversity will have an obvious effect on the outcome of therapy. Thus, we have a biologically mediated continuum from the 'thinkers' on the one hand, where their brains run their bodies, to the 'feelers' on the other, where their bodies run their brains. Oversimplified as this idea may appear, it nevertheless raises a number of important questions. For example, which group, the 'thinkers' or the 'feelers', is more likely to benefit from cognitive-behaviour therapy? Are some sexual problems more likely to be found in one group than in the other? Are sexual and emotional problems more likely in those where brain and body bio-chemistry are not in synchrony? (see p. 331). And why is it that there appears to be no precise psychometry with which to identify what appears to be an important dimension of personality? Research studies are required to attempt to elicit some answers to these questions.

Figure 12.2 presents the authors' view of this cognitive–affect framework. Four assumptions are made in this model: first, that the 'balance of power' between cognitions and affect varies from person to person; second, that there is two-way traffic between cognition and the affect; third, that events may act directly upon the cognitive–affect framework bypassing conscious evaluations; and fourth, that unconscious, goal-directed or 'irrational' drives may play a significant part in determining sexual behaviour in particular.

Perceptions and evaluations in sexual response

Cognitions can be divided into perceptions and evaluations. *Perceptions* in turn can be divided into three entities: detection, labelling and attribution (Walen 1980). *Detection* refers to the process of recording the presence of a stimulus and discriminating it from others: *labelling* refers to the step by which the individual categorizes or classifies the stimulus, while *attribution* is the attempt of the individual to find an explanation of the event. Clearly there are many opportunities for cognitive errors of perception to take place (Beck 1976).

Evaluations, though not always totally distinct from perceptions, focus on the *value* of a cognition – that is, when the stimulus is judged or ranked on a continuum

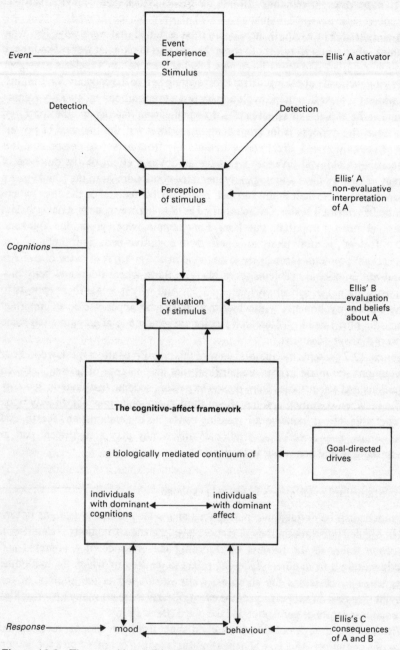

Figure 12.2   The cognitive–affect framework

from 'good' to 'bad'. In Ellis's *ABC* framework, for example, evaluations are represented by *B*, his belief system.

To illustrate the often subtle differences between these various types of cognitions, imagine an event (stimulus) where a woman has made a particularly insulting comment about the size of a man's penis as they were about to attempt intercourse. Her comments would be heard (detected) and interpreted as applying to him (there was no one else present) (labelling). Opportunities for cognitive errors appear with attribution. Why should she say this? Is it really true? How does she know – or is she simply saying this to hurt me? Finally, he is left to evaluate these perceptions. He may experience a wide variety of evaluative cognitions or beliefs, some rational, some irrational, ranging from amusement, indifference to devastation. He might think 'I know my penis is OK so go to hell' or 'I've always wondered about its size; perhaps she is right – what can I do about it?' or 'I will never be able to face another woman again, I feel so humiliated, I am not a real man, this is the end of my sex life.'

The behavioural model

Conceptually, the behavioural model is well understood. Over the years a number of specific techniques have been developed and applied to a wide range of presenting problems requiring behaviour modifications. While it is now recognized that some of those behavioural approaches were over-simplistic, their initial popularity reflected a reaction against what had appeared to be the earlier unscientific methods of the analytical and holistic therapies. Simplistic or not, behavioural psychotherapy, even in its strictest sense, still plays a major role in the New Sex Therapies. Well known strategies such as relaxation techniques, systematic desensitization, flooding, aversion therapy, stimulus fading and the covert methods used, for example, in masturbation and fantasy training are widely practised (see p. 332).

Such behavioural methods do, however, have their limitations. For example, there are often problems of motivating patients to follow assignments conscientiously, there are difficulties integrating what appears to be an 'over-clinical' approach to therapy into the therapeutic relationship module, and certainly the poor therapeutic outcomes (see p. 345) often achieved do not foster as much enthusiasm as they should in those who work in this field.

Clearly there is no simple way to predict the relative effectiveness of the behavioural *versus* the cognitive therapies, particularly since they are so often used conjointly. Nevertheless, the ways by which they each catalyse behavioural change are quite different. Cognitive therapy accesses the higher cognitive centres of the brain, whereas behaviour therapy accesses the more primitive emotional centres. It would therefore be surprising if individuals did not respond quite differently to these two types of therapy.

The role of anxiety in the mediation of sex dysfunction

Because it has always been assumed that anxiety plays an important part in the genesis of most sex dysfunctions it is not surprising that, as a result, methods of anxiety reduction are well represented in the armamentarium of most sex therapists, whatever school they represent. Thus, these methods are found, for example, in the analytic (Fenichel 1945); the behavioural (Wolpe 1958); the eclectic (Kaplan 1974; Masters and Johnson 1970) and the cognitive therapies (Ellis 1962, 1975). However, this belief that raised anxiety levels are always an important aetiological factor in most individuals, in most sex dysfunctions, persuasive as it appears at first sight, turns out to be based largely upon clinical impressions and subjective judgements and has very little empirical evidence to support it (Schiavi 1976).

In the late 1970s and early 1980s a number of studies began to appear which showed that anxiety was either independent of, or even had a potentiating effect upon sex arousal. However, in spite of this research momentum these results were, and still remain, largely disregarded by those in the mainstream of therapy. Moreover, the important distinction between the role of generalized anxiety and performance anxiety in its effect upon sex arousal, which also emerged from these studies, was also ignored, as was the fact that different people respond in different ways to this kind of 'sex stress' (Barlow 1986).

As early as 1943 Ramsey (later to be corroborated by Bancroft 1970) reported non-erotic erections in adolescent boys where fear or excitement such as near accidents or being chased by the police acted as the stimulus. Sarrel and Masters (1982) also described men who were able to achieve intercourse when molested by women, in spite of the fact that these men were threatened by knives if they failed. In their review of the role of anxiety in sex dysfunction, Norton and Jehu (1984), also supported the view that consciously experienced anxiety is so commonly a feature of good sex that it would not be sensible to adopt the view that anxiety is always a liability. Further evidence that anxiety plays a positive role in sex arousal comes from the widely observed fact that men who engage in the paraphilias (for example voyeurs, paedophiles and exhibitionists) are often aroused as much by the fear of the forbidden and the risk of being caught as they are by the practice itself (Stoller 1976). Chambless and Liftschitz (1984) also reported that sex arousal and anxiety were uncorrelated, concluding that there was no obvious relationship between self-reported levels of anxiety and sexual arousal.

Laboratory experiments also support this view. Hoon et al. (1977) and Wolchik et al. (1980) describe how an initial exposure of women and men to an anxiety-evoking film led to an increase in sex arousal when the subjects were later exposed to an erotic film. Such an increase in arousal was not observed when the subjects had instead viewed a neutral film before the erotic film. The idea that anxiety may in some situations potentiate as well as block sexual responses in some individuals is clearly of considerable importance if only because it draws attention to the fact that the global and unrestricted use of anxiety-reduction methods cannot be relied upon in all circumstances (Cole 1985).

Fortunately, some evidence is beginning to emerge about the way in which different individuals respond to sex stressors and anxiety. For example, it appears that subjects who have a sex dysfunction are much more likely to be inhibited by anxiety than those who function well sexually, who in contrast may actually be aroused by anxiety-provoking experiences (Barlow 1986). Not all workers felt they could accept this discovery uncritically. For example, Wolpe (1978) took the view that increases in sexual arousal following an anxiety-provoking event such as a film could be the result of what he described as 'anxiety relief' rather than anxiety playing a direct facilitive role. To address this issue Barlow *et al.* (1983) examined the effects of anxiety triggered by the threat of a shock during a sexually explicit film on a group of sexually functional men. In one situation the subjects were told that there was a 60 per cent chance of shock if they did not achieve adequate arousal (*contingent threat*). In the second treatment the subjects were told that the risk of shock was unrelated to their arousal (*non-contingent threat*). These two forms of threat were used to differentiate between performance anxiety (contingent threat) and generalized anxiety (non-contingent threat). These two treatments were compared with a control, no-shock, condition. The results indicated that compared with the no-shock condition, *both* the contingent and non-contingent threats increased sexual arousal. Surprisingly these results failed to distinguish between the effects of performance and generalized anxiety but did confirm the overall potentiating effect of anxiety on sex arousal. Beck *et al.* (1984) repeated this experiment but used matched samples of sexually dysfunctional and functional men. They found that the non-contingent threat (generalized anxiety) raised arousal over the control non-shock conditions, but unlike the previous report a contingent threat (performance anxiety) did not, though they say that this difference might have resulted from the older mean age of this group compared with the others (38 years compared with 26 years). However, the most important finding was that unlike the sexually functional subjects, the dysfunctional subjects produced significantly less sexual arousal during both types of shock-threat condition. Thus, 'anxiety operationalized as shock threat increased sexual arousal in sexually functional subjects and decreased sexual arousal in sexually dysfunctional subjects' (Barlow 1986: 142).

The role of cognitions in sexual arousal

The importance of the influence of cognitions on the process of sexual arousal is now well recognized (Rook and Hammen 1977; Wolfe and Walen 1982). Generally speaking, expectations of sex performance have been regarded as a self-fulfilling prophecy. Briddell *et al.* (1978) showed that in sexually functional subjects the expectation of achieving a good sex response was never in doubt. Conversely, Laws and Rubin (1969) and Henson and Rubin (1971) demonstrated that sexually functional subjects could suppress their erections while watching erotic films if instructed to do so. This suppression was usually achieved by self-distraction. This kind of cognitive interference (or distraction) was recognized by both Masters and Johnson (1970) and Kaplan (1974) when they referred to these competing cognitions as 'spectatoring', 'performance demand characteristic' and 'failure self-statements'.

A further powerful role that cognitions play in mediating sexual responses is seen in the process known as scripting (Gagnon and Simon 1973). They point out that a system of naming often needs to exist before an event can either occur or take on any significance. For example, before female orgasm was named and talked about, arguably it did not exist. Of course such cognitions can also play a negative role, and when the medical model uses diagnostic categories such as 'premature ejaculation' and 'orgasmic dysfunction', they can, by taking on a life of their own, distort reality.

In his examination of this interface between sexual arousal and cognitive function, Barlow (1986) identifies a number of factors which appear to discriminate between those men who fail sexually and those who do not (see also Beck and Barlow 1984). Apart from his observation (referred to above) that anxiety may have an opposite effect upon sex functional and sex dysfunctional men, Barlow also established that sexually dysfunctional males, in contrast to functional males, respond with negative affect in sexual situations and that they also underreport their levels of sex arousal.

These (and other) observations led Barlow to propose a new working model for psychogenic sexual dysfunction. He suggests that negative and distracting cognitions (cognitive interference) interact with autonomic arousal (the physiological aspects of anxiety and sexual response) to block sexual performance. Thus, if these physiological arousal mechanisms (sex and anxiety) are not synchronized with the psychological cognitive response systems but are instead competing with each other, sexual responses may be blocked. Thus, anxiety can be seen to be acting either as a potentiator or an inhibitor of sexual arousal, depending upon the associated cognitions. In the sexually dysfunctional man, negative cognitions set up a negative-feedback loop which in turn reinforces the negative cognitions. Conversely, in the sexually functional man, positive cognitions lead to a positive-feedback loop. Barlow suggests that the development and maintenance of these competing task-irrelevant thoughts in those who are dysfunctional seem to stem from early experiences (negative reinforcers) though why some men become dysfunctional and others, with the same learning history, do not is unclear.

TREATMENT/INTERVENTION

Introduction

The success of any therapeutic programme – and sex therapy is no exception – depends upon two main factors. First, there is the need for therapists to have a good academic base and be aware of recent developments in research relating to their therapeutic specialty. Second, they should be able to integrate these ideas, wherever appropriate, into treatment programmes using those core skills generally recognized as being essential for the development of a good therapeutic alliance, viz. acceptance, empathy, genuineness and communication (Truax and Carkhuff 1967).

The fact that, since Masters and Johnson, there has been little dramatic change in the armamentarium of sex therapists would at first sight appear to support the view that many sex therapists do not keep themselves up to date with recent advances in their subject (Morrow-Bradley and Elliot 1986). However, it is probably more true to say that apart from a few significant developments in pharmacotherapy (for example, the now widely accepted use of papaverine in the treatment of some erectile problems – Virag 1985), the only really significant advance in sex therapy has been the increasing recognition of the importance and hence use of cognitive methods.

However, it cannot be denied that the acceptance of cognitive therapy in some quarters has been, and continues to be, slow and this may be for a number of reasons, not least of which is the shortage of therapists with the particular skills and experience required to use these cognitive methods effectively.

The behavioural treatment of sexual problems

Before Masters and Johnson, behavioural techniques were only rarely used in the treatment of the sex dysfunctions – indeed, sexual disorders were largely ignored by behaviour therapists, reliance instead being placed upon therapists which depended more upon providing insight and the interpretation of unconscious conflicts. Only in the treatment of so-called deviant sexual behaviours was systematic desensitization and aversion therapy widely used (Feldman and MacCullough 1971; Wolpe 1958). Very occasionally, however, 'behavioural' therapies were applied to the treatment of sexual problems. For example, the now well established techniques of relaxation and desensitization (Friedman 1968), masturbation techniques (Hastings 1963), and more importantly a ban on intercourse (Schultz 1951), later to be adopted as a major component by the Masters and Johnson therapies, were all introduced some time before the publication of Masters and Johnson's (1970) work.

Masters and Johnson

Masters and Johnson's work still profoundly influences mainstream sex therapy throughout the world. It has never proved easy to provide a distillate of their work, nor to identify clearly some of the psychological methods implicit in their approach. This is because their programmes were presented in a somewhat doctrinaire manner, providing as they did a unique type of therapy which was both eclectic and yet also singularly theirs. There is no doubt that both the behavioural and cognitive strands of therapy are strongly represented, but in addition there are other important yet often intangible elements to their programmes. For example, a powerful therapeutic alliance between patient and therapist developed in their

2-week intensive programmes at St Louis where any number of other ill-defined psychotherapeutic processes became involved.

Masters and Johnson focused primarily on the couple (the relationship is the patient); they always used two therapists, one male, one female (cotherapy), and they developed their own special rapid-treatment residential programme lasting about 2 weeks, which was followed by home assignments. In particular, they laid great emphasis upon encouraging a positive and accepting view of sex using psychoeducational methods to provide factual information and dispel those sexual myths which so often bedevilled a relationship. Unlike their predecessors, Masters and Johnson argued that most sexual problems normally resulted from high levels of anxiety and were not normally a consequence of any pre-existing psychopathology.

Probably the most significant factor that contributed to the popularity of their methods was the way in which they formulated a series of treatment packages specifically designed for each presenting problem. These mini-programmes could be readily understood not only by the patients but also by their therapists! Since they relied heavily upon methods of anxiety reduction (and in particular the reduction of performance anxiety), they proposed that most, if not all, these 'mini-programmes' should begin with pleasuring exercises known as sensate focus. This normally involves each partner pleasuring the other *in turn* using a gentle massage or 'by fondling' various parts of their partner's body; thus, in a relaxed state the passive partner could (perhaps for the first time) begin to enjoy the other's touch knowing that he or she need not respond in any particular way. At this stage in sensate focus there is a ban on intercourse and also on genital stimulation. Verbal communication or guiding the other's hand is obviously desirable as long as it does not interfere with the need for the 'receiver' to be relaxed. Sensate focus is a simple relaxation technique which, if successful as Masters and Johnson point out, enables the sexual reflexes to operate naturally. Finally, by gradually incorporating a more varied repertoire of sexual stimulation into the sensate-focus programme, effective sexual responses are achieved by a process of systematic desensitization.

The more specific techniques popularized by Masters and Johnson are also largely 'behavioural' in nature. For example, the use of a graded series of vaginal dilators (or trainers) in the treatment of vaginismus (earlier proposed by Shaw 1954) helps to eliminate the reflexive contraction of the vaginal musculature either by systematic desensitization or by flooding to extinction. There is still some mystery about how the squeeze technique works in the treatment of premature ejaculation, but the general consensus is that it may play an aversive role in helping to delay ejaculation. There is, of course, the possibility that it plays no behavioural role at all, at least for some patients, but is only valuable because of its ritual element. The stop–start method (Semans 1956) would appear to have a more rational basis – working by 'crowding the threshold' so as to raise it to a more acceptable level, possibly by habituation.

Stimulus-fading is used now both in the treatment of women who have difficulty achieving orgasm in intercourse and in men who in intercourse experience delayed ejaculation, though Masters and Johnson described it only for the latter. Orgasm is initially obtained by self-stimulation in the absence of a partner, and once this goal has been achieved satisfactorily, the partner slowly begins to become involved. Self-stimulation is 'faded out' and partner stimulation gradually 'faded in' – the so-called 'bridge manoeuvre' (Kaplan 1975).

One of the benefits of these so-called directive therapies was that since it was possible to define a fairly precise therapeutic contract, treatment outcome could be quantified with some degree of accuracy. It is well known that the results that Masters and Johnson achieved at St Louis were almost unbelievably good, results which have not been achieved since by others. It is assumed that Masters and Johnson's success was largely the result of using a pre-selected sample of patients and particularly those who were intelligent, articulate and extremely well motivated – a luxury that most therapists rarely experience – together with the fact that they were also able to use their intense 2-week therapeutic programme. This fact should not, however, detract from the importance of Masters and Johnson's work.

Helen Kaplan

The contribution that Helen Kaplan made to sex therapy (Kaplan 1974, 1979, 1983) is often underestimated. Although she had the benefits of the Masters and Johnson publications, she was able to reflect upon their work, sift out the very best elements and incorporate their ideas into a much less rigid, more comprehensive, indeed more authentically eclectic programme.

She was one of the first sex therapists to propose that the choice of therapy, indeed the school of therapy, might be dictated by the aetiology of the problem. Thus, she divided the causes of the sex disorder into those which were *remote* and those which were *immediate*. She lists as examples of the remote causes a repressive, traditional and sexually negative home background, trauma such as rape or molestation and maladaptive relationships with parents in childhood, as indeed would any early aversive experience and long-standing neurotic conflict. Immediate causes, on the other hand, might include ignorance, inappropriate attitudes to sex, a poor relationship, anxiety about sexual feelings and in particular performance fears.

Kaplan then proposed that the initial focus of attack should be on those presenting problems whose causes were thought to be immediate in origin using behavioural methods (McCarthy 1977). If no progress was made then attention should be directed to the remote causes, should they be found to exist, using a psychodynamically orientated programme. Kaplan therefore attempted to consummate a marriage between the psychodynamic and behavioural methodologies introducing a flexible strategy which had considerable strength.

Keith Hawton

Hawton (1985) adopts a largely pragmatic approach to sex therapy. His methods incorporate much of Masters and Johnson, together with the behavioural elements of Kaplan. However, he places a much greater emphasis on the educational and cognitive aspects of sex therapy, for example by focusing on the need for patients to have access to, and an awareness of, up-to-date information on sex. He also stresses that the therapist should look for any negative thoughts or attitudes held by the patient which may interfere with the progress of therapy – so that these can be identified and changed.

Overall there appears to be little doubt that this directive approach to the treatment of sexual problems is more effective than the less tangible forms of psychotherapeutic intervention, and many, many reports in the literature attest to this. For example, in the treatment of orgasmic problems in women, Wilcox and Hager (1980) showed that instructing women about direct clitoral stimulation was more effective in helping them to achieve appropriate cognitive and attitudinal changes than the alternative strategy of psychoeducation. Anderson (1981) similarly demonstrated that directed masturbation was the preferred method (when compared with systematic desensitization) for the treatment of primary anorgasmia.

The role of cognitive factors in sex therapy

Walen and Roth (1987) argue that most, if not all, sex dysfunctions share certain features. For example, they identify sexual underarousal as being a characteristic of those who suffer from both quick ejaculation and retarded ejaculation. Such a view is supported by Kaplan (1974), Zilbergeld (1978) and Apfelbaum (1980). That this underarousal is a common occurrence in those with sex disorders is probably not in dispute since underarousal would be expected in those who experience high levels of performance anxiety, which in turn blocks their responses.

Walen and Roth (1987) suggest that this performance anxiety is generated largely by cognitive errors of perception and evaluation – the high-risk individual being one who 'approaches the job of sex (rather than the joy of sex) as a way to prove himself (rather than enjoy himself)' (p. 357).

The importance of cognitions in mediating an adequate and appropriate sexual response is evident in those sexually active individuals who experience situational sex dysfunctions. Quick ejaculation, erectile difficulties and delayed ejaculation in men, and arousal and orgasmic dysfunction in women, are often contingent upon specific situations which in turn have created negative cognitions and hence emotional distress. In support of this view is the frequently observed self-limiting nature of these dysfunctions, which ameliorate or disappear as attitudinal change takes place. Sometimes, however, couples either do not allow sufficient time for these adaptive changes to take place spontaneously or they fail to seek advice and the relationship is either terminated or the pattern of failure becomes firmly entrenched. For example, a promising relationship may end abruptly and prematurely with 'first-night impotence' where a man personalizes and magnifies his failure, believing he will *never* be able to respond with his partner.

In order for cognitive (or any) sex therapy to be effective, the presence of a stable, motivated, involved and empathetic relationship will improve the chances of a successful outcome. However, sometimes there is no meaningful relationship with which to work, and this explains why sex therapy (of any kind) often fails. If this is the case then therapeutic attention may have to be directed towards the individual so that as a first step he or she can resolve their own problems before couple therapy can be tried again (or a partner found).

Whether one is working with a couple or an individual, a cognitively based programme might include the following elements:

1 *Psychoeducation*   This serves to provide accurate and up-to-date information about the anatomy and physiology of sexual function while at the same time disposing of any sexual myths (Zilbergeld 1980).

2 *Fantasy*   The use of erotic fantasies before and during love-making should be encouraged. It should, of course, also be recognized that some people find it almost impossible to fantasize and those who cannot should not be made to feel inadequate or different in any way.

3 *Sex aids*   The use of so-called sex aids or sex toys such as vibrators should be encouraged. Apart from enhancing arousal this may produce a desirable change in attitudes by injecting some humour into love-making. However, some people do not enjoy using them and once again no pressure should be brought to bear to change their views.

4 *Dealing with selective abstraction*   Occasionally a partner's perception of his or her own arousal may be distorted. They may fail to identify or acknowledge some of the psychological signals which accompany or herald arousal. By providing patients with information about these signals it may encourage them to perceive these feelings more accurately, which in turn will help potentiate the arousal process.

5 *Encouraging positive evaluation*   Concomitant with the actual perception of these psychological signals is also the need for their positive evaluation. For example, vaginal lubrication needs to be recognized as being an indication of sexual arousal and also evaluated as being good and not messy.

6 *Sensate focus*   This provides an ideal way of modifying ritualized and unrewarding patterns of love-making. Couples can learn how to relax and share in a totally unstructured manner their sexual experience, thus hopefully reducing the need for a goal-orientated response. Using sensate focus, the pressures of *having* to please and *having* to perform are removed, releasing the couple from what can be the burden in ritualized love-making. At the same time negative and distracting cognitions are contained, disinhibiting sexual responses.

7 *Assertiveness training*   An often different but essential part of therapy is to enable the couple to establish open, effective and honest means of communication. There is a natural reticence, modesty and shyness in many intimate relationships which may persist for a lifetime. Love-making becomes ritualized, largely dependent upon non-verbal communication and much is lost in terms of

potential experimentation, growth and fulfilment. To overcome these blocks assertion training may be needed to foster communication if bad habits are to be changed.

8 *Coping strategies*   Finally, couples should be taught cognitive coping strategies to deal with any difficulties that may arise. For example, they should be reminded that any set-backs they experience in their sex lives are not disasters, that they should not personalize them but instead are instructed to adopt alternative strategies to ensure that they do not enter a self-maintaining cycle of sexual frustration. A good yet brief account of the use of cognitive therapy in the treatment of sexual problems is provided by Kowalski (1985).

McCarthy (1984) reports on the outcome of his use of a cognitive-behavioural model for treating inhibited sexual desire (ISD) in couples and single males. He concludes that (1) there is better progress if the ISD presents alone, uncomplicated by other problems, (2) women have a better outcome than men, (3) it is crucial to break the self-defeating cycle of negative evaluations, aversive experience and avoidance and (4) therapy should focus on the quality of the relationship rather than on performance orientated behaviours. Follow-ups indicated the effectiveness of his approach. Southern (1985), successfully using a cognitive approach in the treatment of male hypoactive sexual desire, suggests that in this case the problem originated from the patient's failure to discriminate cues that signal erotic situations and sexual arousal, a failure which in turn probably derived from earlier maladaptive learning. Bass (1985) also discusses the use of a cognitive approach to the treatment of low sexual desire.

Cognitive restructuring

Bishay (1988) provides a good example of how patients can be treated by cognitive restructuring where they were thought to be either untreatable by more traditional methods of sex therapy or were not motivated to try these methods. He treated two patients presenting with vaginismus, one with vaginitis leading to the avoidance of intercourse, and one with delayed ejaculation.

In the first case, a 20-year-old woman, the vaginismus was related to an earlier traumatic experience of what amounted to rape at the age of 16. She had not had intercourse since, but at an earlier examination for a cervical smear it had taken the doctor half an hour to introduce the speculum. Her own cognitions about intercourse were that it would harm her (cause tissue damage). These thoughts were replaced by cognitive restructuring with the belief that 'it is fear that makes the muscles contract and cause the pain: the penis [flesh and blood] cannot possibly hurt if the speculum [made of metal] did not'. She was asked to repeat this statement four to five times a day and before intercourse. Two months later her husband confirmed that normal intercourse was taking place two to three times a week. The improvement was maintained for a year at follow-up.

The case of delayed ejaculation occurred in a 20-year-old man where he was unable to ejaculate in intercourse, though he could do so in masturbation. Convinced that ejaculation in the vagina was dirty, a belief that arose from his strict Baptist background, cognitive restructuring enabled him to re-examine his beliefs: he was told to repeat, several times a day and during love-making, 'in this marriage sex and ejaculation are Holy'. Within 4 weeks he was able to ejaculate every time he had intercourse, which was two or three times a week. Bishay stressed that all these cases responded using very little of the therapist's time.

Rathus (1978) likewise used covert assertions in his treatment of a 25-year-old nurse who rarely experienced orgasms. She perceived herself as being unworthy and unattractive and the resulting anxiety blocked her arousal and prevented orgasm. In therapy she was instructed to prepare a number of positive statements about herself such as 'I am attractive'; 'I can enjoy sex as much as a man'; 'He is lucky to be with me.' Initially these statements were rehearsed orally with the therapist. At follow-ups of 3 and 6 months she reported orgasms on 50 per cent of sexual encounters. Four other patients also benefited from this form of cognitive restructuring. Good as these results appear there is clearly an urgent need for controlled trials to establish the validity, or otherwise, of these methods.

Rational-emotive therapy and psychoeducation

Rational-emotive therapy

The ideas implicit in Ellis's Rational-Emotive Therapy (RET; see Dryden 1990) provide a distillate of the cognitive approach. Like Masters and Johnson, Ellis is seen by some as being somewhat doctrinaire in the manner in which he presents his ideas: however, such an approach has certain advantages – in particular it has the effect of simplifying what might otherwise be regarded as quite a complex treatment scenario. For example, if one wished to explain the basis of cognitive therapy to a lay person, Ellis's *ABCD* scheme provides, in a few words, the best way of achieving this.

Fundamental to RET is the idea that since thinking (cognitions) and feelings (emoting) are causally and reciprocally related, they can be regarded as essentially the same thing. Thus, private thoughts and self-talk and the feelings and moods that accompany them, are inseparable – the one influences, even determines, the other. Thus, in line with other cognitive methods, Ellis argues that in therapy, emphasis should be focused on changing thoughts as a way of changing feelings (and thus behaviours) because it is believed that thoughts are more accessible to change than affect.

Bass and Walen (1986) crystallize the role of the RET therapist in the treatment of sex dysfunction when they stress his commitment to the view that it is not the unfortunate life event (the sex problem) but rather the individual's perception and evaluation of the event that causes distress.

Using his *ABCD* paradigm (see p. 321) Ellis thus encourages the patient to focus on *B*, his belief system, to dispute his irrational beliefs (*iB*'s) and replace them with rational beliefs (*rB*'s). Where a man presents with a psychogenic erectile problem his irrational belief about *A* might be 'If I don't get an erection, as I *must*, this will prove that I am inadequate as a person', 'It will be a disaster if I cannot please her. 'If I fail with her I will always fail from now on', 'My sex life is at an end', and so on. However, he should dispute these (*iB*'s), replacing them with some new rational beliefs (*rB*'s) such as 'I would like to get an erection, it will be a pity if I don't and I will be disappointed but it certainly won't be a disaster.' 'My partner may be put out but this does not prove that I am inadequate', and so on. If he argues with himself in this way, substituting *iB*'s with new *rB*'s, he may still be disappointed but he will not be so anxious. Moreover, this reduction in anxiety may well enable him to get an erection.

Ellis's ideas are not new but incorporated into his *ABCD* framework provide a very convenient working model which is usually readily understood by most patients without too much difficulty.

Ellis identified a number of evaluative cognitions which he regarded as irrational:

1 *Mastabatory* (absolutist ideas or 'should' statements which reflect a belief that there are universal rules or 'musts') – for example, *I must perform well sexually. You, my partner, must do the things I want you to do. I must succeed sexually and be approved by my partner*.
2 *Awfulising* (adopting a belief that there are terrible catastrophes likely to occur) – for example, *If I cannot get an erection with you it would be awful and I won't be able to get one ever again*.
3 *Human worth statements* (reflecting the belief that people can be categorized and rated instead of their actions being judged).

Other similar irrational cognitions which Beck *et al*. (1979) found in his depressed patients were:

1 *magnification:* exaggerating the consequences of a single event;
2 *minimization:* not fully acknowledging personal achievements;
3 *arbitrary inference:* interpreting an event negatively without considering the alternatives (jumping to conclusions);
4 *selective abstraction:* focusing on one event out of context and failing to put it into perspective;
5 *over-generalization:* making unjustifiable generalizations from one incident;
6 *personalization:* unjustly blaming oneself, where there is no clear evidence – taking things too personally;
7 *dichotomous thinking:* seeing things in black and white, for example, as either success or failure instead of regarding most experiences as a point on a continuum;
8 *emotional reasoning:* using one's feelings to justify an evaluation or perception rather than the other way around.

These additional cognitive errors are not always distinct from each other but they do serve to add emphasis to the kinds of common cognitive errors that cause and maintain problem sexual behaviours.

RET is not exclusively cognitive (Ellis 1980) but also focuses on emotions and behaviours directly. For example, in Rational-Emotive Imagery (Maultsby 1975) the patient is required to fantasize the worst consequences of him failing to get an erection – for example, deep humiliation or feelings of depression and worthlessness. He is then told to focus on these feelings while at the same time arguing with himself that instead he is only disappointed and sorry but not devastated that this has happened.

Whether rationality and the capacity for sexual arousal are always related may be open to question. Thyer and Papsdorf (1981) showed that sexual arousability and the presence of rational beliefs were only weakly associated and they question the appropriateness of RET in the treatment of sexual dysfunctions in women. On the other hand, Bishay (1988) used cognitive restructuring, which is one element of RET, very effectively when treating vaginismus (see p. 337).

By and large, outcome research suggests that RET can be used effectively in the treatment of sex dysfunctions. Munjack et al. (1984) report that there was a significant improvement in men with erectile dysfunction using RET over a control group assigned to a waiting-list, and though this improvement was not fully maintained at follow-up significant progress was nevertheless achieved in comparison to pre-treatment levels of performance. Similarly, Everaerd and Dekker (1985) showed that RET led to an improvement in both sexual functioning and satisfaction with the relationship.

Psychoeducation

Closely allied to and overlapping with these cognitive methods is the psychoeducational approach of Ellis (1983) and others, the purpose of which is to provide *information* and *instruction* so that new life-style strategies can be adopted by the patient. Zilbergeld (1980) had earlier recognized that an important part of this process was to help the patient dispose of any false ideas and expectations that he had of himself and the opposite sex. Challenges to some of these commonly held sexual myths are listed in Cole (1988b) for example:

1 Men don't always want sex nor are they always ready for it – they are not sex machines. Indeed, it is not essential that all physical contact should lead to sex, or should it do so then sex does not necessarily mean intercourse. For example, Bass (1986) using RET, focuses on trying to de-emphasize erection as a prerequisite of sexual satisfaction.
2 Men remain sexually responsive throughout their lives and though advancing age may slow down their responses there is no particular cut-off point at which a man's capacity to respond sexually disappears altogether.
3 As men age they require more direct and prolonged physical stimulation to the penis. It is important that they communicate this need to their partner verbally

or non-verbally instead of hoping that the partner will discover this fact by telepathy or intuition.

4 It is often thought that by not masturbating a man can save himself and ensure a stronger and more long-lasting erection when the opportunity for intercourse arises. If anything the reverse is true since the neurohormonal mechanisms are then unprepared if there has been a long interval between ejaculations.

5 Quantity is not quality. It is not the length of intercourse (nor the size of his penis) that matters but the quality of the total experience. A man's attention should be drawn to the more subtle physical and emotional reward afforded by extending precoital sex play. Most men, once they have penetrated, last only three or four minutes; indeed, some women will complain that men go on too long.

6 A large number of women, perhaps as many as one in two, do not achieve an orgasm in intercourse without some manual assistance. This is a fact of life and it does not reflect badly either on him or her. Communication between them later can help solve any difficulty that may arise, though he must be reminded that both he and she can have good sex without her being orgasmic.

Pietropinto (1986) reports on some of the ways by which the stereotyped male sexual behaviours appear to sabotage not only men's own love-making techniques but also those of their partners. Whereas women were more likely to read books to improve their sex lives, men obtained much of their sex education from pornography which tended to depersonalize women. Clearly here is a role for the intervention of a more appropriate psychoeducational approach.

Sex therapy for individuals

Those heterosexual men and women who display a fear of the opposite sex and who have difficulties in marshalling effective courtship skills may be unable to form lasting relationships. They are described as heterophobic (Cole 1986, 1988b). Similar behavioural deficits of course occur in homosexuals (homophobia).

The individual without a partner is in the classical 'catch 22' situation of having a problem which may prevent him or her from forming a relationship, but at the same time needing a relationship in order to confront and resolve the problem. However, the area of social- and sexual-skills training required to help these often lonely and isolated individuals (who, incidentally, lose out both ways, having neither sex nor a relationship) does provide a unique interface for the psycho-educational, behavioural and cognitive therapies.

For example, Reynolds et al. (1981) used teaching, role-play and homework assignments to help dispose of sexual myths and establish behaviours which would be more likely to lead to effective sexual function. Zilbergeld and Ellison (1979) also argue that social-skills training in either group or individual format plays an essential part in sex therapy for individuals without partners, and Bancroft (1989) also devotes considerable attention to the needs of patients without partners, suggesting the use of methods such as individual sensate focus, masturbation and fantasy training and other covert methods of desensitization. Stravynski (1986) specifically reports on the successful treatment of a patient with erectile failure and premature ejaculation in a man without a partner. His treatment involved social-skills training by a regime of behavioural interventions.

Heterosocial-skills training is difficult to organize. In the best of all possible worlds it works well (Altman *et al.* 1985), but it is unlikely to become a standard procedure, at least in the UK, until there is a vast increase in resources.

Script theory

Script theory sees human social behaviour as a series of everyday dramas where individuals play out one or more sequences of roles, normally of a relatively brief duration (McCormick 1987). In other words, adult social behaviour is not usually inventive, innovatory or unpredictable, nor does it respond uniquely to each new situation; instead, it is expressed in pre-prepared behavioural packages which approximate to demands of particular situations.

Role-play of this kind is clearly adaptive because each role will have been tested in the past and shaped to suit the individual's personality and the types of environment he or she is likely to meet. Most psychologists, at least, argue that behaviour of this kind is largely cognitively based and is therefore capable of modification and reshaping to suit changing situations. Alternatively, new scripts can be written and adopted where there are obvious deficiencies in an existing behavioural repertoire.

The most useful scripts will be those that produce scenarios in which the self is cast as a hero. A script which incorporates appropriate and effective social skills at a party to enable a person to meet and relate to someone of the opposite sex is a good example. Such a script will have had to have been shaped by previous learning, trial and error, imitative behaviour and so on, but eventually, tested and tried, it will evolve into a set piece which works more often than not.

Clearly, some will be able to perfect effective heterosexual skill scripts with little difficulty, others only after much practice, and a minority may never be able to achieve this without outside help. In therapy, the idea is to present patients with a script and allow them to modify it according to their own idiosyncratic needs, stressing throughout that the idea is not in this case to achieve specific short-term goals, such as forming a relationship, but to teach them instead how to acquire the actual skills necessary and to be prepared for failure and rejection. *It is the language, process and progress of the script that is important at this stage, not the outcome.*

The great strength of script theory is that an acceptance and belief in the approach, together with the recognition of the role of theatre in life, can be powerfully liberating and act as a catalyst in behavioural change. Emphasis is then directed away from the psychopathology of the individual and towards a recognition that social forces are largely responsible for maintaining inappropriate behaviours (McCormick 1987). The disposal of sexual myths (Zilbergeld 1980) (see p. 340) clearly plays a large part in this process of rewriting sexual scripts. By rescripting existing stereotypic sexual behaviours, as a result new behaviours can be developed and the therapeutic benefits will be substantial.

Whereas scripts are a universal part of our behavioural repertoire and have obvious social advantages – for example, they provide an easy way of recognizing and predicting the behaviour of others and hence enable us to know how to respond ourselves – if these scripts become too rigid they can be difficult to change. For example, most sexual behaviours are highly ritualized and may eventually become self-sabotaging or unfulfilling and need therefore to be challenged. For example, negotiations between couples for different positions of coitus usually take place without speaking (Gagnon and Simon 1973) and this lack of communication and dependence upon non-verbal cues may lead to the retention of totally inappropriate scripts. Couples may not be able to change the situation without outside help but in therapy they can be encouraged to alter habits of a lifetime.

Script theory, therefore, operates at two levels: first, a recognition of the concepts is in itself valuable because it provides a liberating influence and catalyses changes because change appears to be possible; and second, it is powerful in its didactic role since it provides an opportunity to rewrite, or at least modify, a script in whatever way circumstances dictate.

The paraphilias

Those who engage in unusual sexual behaviours, the so-called paraphilias, show a remarkably high resistance to behavioural change, so much so that very often a serious commitment to treatment by therapists is not entered into because of the difficulties involved and the likelihood of a poor outcome.

The clinical impressions of many authors would support the general view that those who enjoy at least some forms of unusual sex share at least two features. They will have had an upbringing which is often authoritarian and sexually repressive, and they also appear, in many cases, to have an almost obsessive interest in sex, either because they have a high sex drive or perhaps because they are deeply inhibited (or both). Whatever particular experiental (and genetic) factors may have led an individual to select a target for his or her paraphilia, it is clear that whatever its nature, the behaviour is very powerfully motivated. Moreover, because the subjective experience is usually both sexually arousing and anxiety provoking, the combination of both pleasure and guilt produces an almost unstoppable behaviour, akin, for example, to those behaviours observed in the obsessive-compulsive patient. Perhaps the apocryphal Aly Sloper's comment 'a dirty mind is a perpetual feast' goes some way to describe how many paraphiliacs feel. Because the appetitive and consummatory nature of these behaviours is so well developed, they will normally be powerfully self-reinforcing, leading to the maintenance of the behaviour over long periods of time, and even when 'punished' or 'treated' often reoccurring in a recidivistic manner.

Cognitive-behavioural methods of treatment of the paraphilias divide into the strictly *cognitive* (changing perceptions and evaluations), the *cognitive-behavioural* (covert sensitization and orgasmic reconditioning) and the *behavioural* (flooding). Walen and Roth (1987) and Ellis (1975) argue that the first thing to do is to try to deal with the patient's distress about his or her life style in general and the paraphilia in particular. Until patients can begin first to understand themselves and then to accept themselves, at least in part, their motivation to change will be minimal. One way of achieving this necessary level of self-acceptance is by teaching them to separate their 'self' from their 'behaviour', trying to point out that there cannot be such a thing as a 'bad' person, only 'unacceptable' acts. A considerable amount of time may have to be spent initially to produce this attitudinal change, but it needs to be tackled positively and returned to throughout the treatment programme if necessary. There is an additional cognitive change which some therapists may wish to achieve with their patients and that is the approach which attempts to foster an unconditional acceptance of the fantasy (and even the behaviour) in question. The idea behind this approach is that by normalizing the paraphilia the patient's anxieties (and hence arousal and reinforcement) will be reduced. This process of permission giving may only be appropriate for the more benign paraphilias but it is a powerful tool to assist in the process of self-acceptance and the reduction of obsessionality. Naturally there is an urgent need for research into the outcome of these differing approaches.

Covert sensitization is the therapeutic process where the therapist instructs the patient to pair aversive images with his 'deviant' fantasy. For example, a man who engages in paedophilia would be told to associate his paedophilic fantasies with the image of vomiting over himself, then to imagine the response of his young sexual partner to his condition. Covert sensitization has been reported by many therapists as being an effective way of treating incest (Harbert *et al.* 1974), transvestism (Gersham 1970), exhibitionism (Hughes 1977) and paedophilia (Barlow *et al.* 1969). Discouraging the patient from using his 'deviant' fantasies in this way does not, however, necessarily lead him to substitute and enjoy more appropriate fantasies. New target fantasies need to be incorporated into his fantasy repertoire and for this to be possible he needs to learn how to become aroused by these new fantasies. This can sometimes be achieved by *orgasmic reconditioning* (Marquis 1970). The patient is told to masturbate using his 'deviant' fantasies to achieve arousal until he approaches orgasm. At the point of orgasm and ejaculation he is instructed to substitute a more acceptable target fantasy. As he slowly begins to enjoy these alternative fantasies he is then encouraged to use them more extensively at an earlier and earlier stage in masturbation until he can eliminate the deviant fantasies altogether. Once he has achieved this then clearly he is in a much better position to detach himself from his unacceptable behaviours.

Finally, the more specifically behavioural approach of flooding to extinction has been used with exhibitionists in order to produce a change in their behaviours. These patients have been encouraged to expose themselves repeatedly in front of volunteer females who have been instructed to respond with either derision or indifference.

It should be apparent that there is clearly a conflict between some of the therapeutic strategies outlined above. The idea of unqualified self-acceptance together with the process of giving permission to use and enjoy a 'deviant' fantasy is clearly at variance with the principles implicit in 'masturbation training' using either covert sensitization or orgasmic reconditioning and there does not appear to be any obvious way by which they may be reconciled. What may determine the relative emphasis placed upon these alternative strategies may rest either upon the value judgements of the therapists or alternatively upon the severity of the paraphilia.

The role of hidden and overt judgements in therapy should of course never be overlooked. A good example of the way in which values have influenced therapy is demonstrated by the changing attitudes that most professionals now have to the counselling of homosexuals. A few years ago all the methods outlined above (and others) might have been attempted to try to bring about a change in the behaviour of gay men. Nowadays such a strategy would not normally be considered. Perhaps it also ought to be mentioned, sobering as it sounds, that the difficulties that therapists are experiencing nowadays in their attempts to modify the behaviour of paraphiliacs may prove to be as great as those encountered by their predecessors in their earlier attempts to change homosexuals into heterosexuals.

Treatment outcomes

The inherent and often insurmountable difficulties in trying to make an accurate assessment of the outcome of treatment are well known (Bancroft 1981). At the outset it is important to be able to *define* the presenting problem objectively, to feel certain that the patient's *report* of his or her condition is reliable and that an adequately sized and relatively unbiased *sample* of these patients is available. Moreover, not all sexual problems can be easily conceptualized as arbitrarily defined dysfunctions; many instead simply result from a subjective feeling that 'something is wrong'. However, because problems of this kind are not easily categorized they should not be overlooked and it is clearly important in research studies that this distinction be recognized (Begg *et al*. 1976).

Added to those difficulties are the often uncontrolled (and uncontrollable) variables of the relationships under treatment. There are imponderables associated with the intervention of the personality of the therapist and above all many difficulties are met in attempting to measure to what extent changes have taken place as a result of treatment and whether these changes are maintained in follow-up. As a result, published work on therapeutic outcome is often highly suspect (Kuriansky and Sharpe 1976). Unfortunately, some of these problems may never be overcome because of the inevitable conflict of interest between research and therapy, though Milne and Cordle (1984), in a brief but excellent review of evaluation criteria, take a more optimistic position.

The need for an objective evaluation of the outcome of therapy has at last received some attention. Until quite recently the literature was flush with almost meaningless and sometimes contradictory phrases such as 'total improvement', 'worthwhile improvement' or 'problem largely resolved'. Fortunately, a number of standardized questionnaires designed to assess sexual and marital satisfaction objectively are now available and provide an objective way of assessing behavioural change. They include, for example, the earlier sexual interaction inventory (LoPiccolo and Steger 1974) and the sexual arousal inventory (Hoon *et al*. 1976), now little used. The more recent Golombok–Rust Inventory of Sexual Satisfaction (GRISS) (Rust and Golombok 1985) and the Golombok–Rust Inventory of Marital State (GRIMS) (Rust *et al*. 1986) provide good methods of assessment. The reliability of these latter measures is discussed in Golombok and Rust (1988).

A summary of outcomes of the various types of treatment interventions are provided in Table 12.2. Most of these references refer to behaviourally orientated programmes and it can be seen that there is a wide variation in the published data. For example, in an exhaustive survey of outcomes up to 1976, Wright *et al*. (1977) concluded that claims for the overall effectiveness of the directive sex therapies could not be justified. A survey of outcomes by Hawton (1983) was equally cautious, referring to 'more or less consistent although undramatic evidence for the short-term superiority of the Masters and Johnson approach over other methods of treatment or no treatment'. There were, however, 'considerable doubts about the long-term efficacy of sex therapy especially because of couples lost to follow-up'. Equally diffident were Watson and Brockman (1982) whose main conclusion was that only a minority of couples attending a hospital clinic, whose primary aim was to provide sex therapy, completed such courses or benefited from them. They made the important point that sex therapy is often only a final attempt to avert an inevitable marital breakdown.

Zilbergeld and Evans (1980) attacked Masters and Johnson's sex-therapy research, saying that it 'is so flawed by methodological errors and slipshod reporting that it fails to meet customary standards and their own for evaluation'. Tullman *et al*. (1981), on the other hand, had reported a beneficial change in sexual and related behaviours in couples undergoing treatment at the Masters and Johnson Institute, as did Whitehead and Matthews (1986) using a modified Masters and Johnson programme in the UK. By and large the data presented here are somewhat confusing and, certainly, nothing approaching the successes of Masters and Johnson have been achieved elsewhere.

FUTURE DEVELOPMENTS

Speculation about the future of sex therapy is beset with more than its fair share of difficulties. The discipline is relatively young and for that reason alone its future is unpredictable. However, above all is the importance of those secular changes which continue to erode the hitherto stabilizing role of the monogamous nuclear family, changes which in turn are leading to a new overt pluralism of relationships and sexual behaviours.

Other changes, such as the normalization of behaviours previously regarded as problem behaviours (for example, female coital orgasmic dysfunction, homosexual behaviour and some forms of inhibited sexual desire), together with the increasing recognition of the importance of biogenic factors in the aetiology of sex disorders in turn leading to a greater use of pharmacotherapy in treatment, will also add to the changing face of sex therapy.

Further understanding of the psychophysiology of brain function, a recognition of the importance of both the role of goal-directed behaviour and the status of unconscious drives, together with a growth in empiricism in the psychotherapies, will all have their uncertain impact. Moreover, increasing attention will no doubt be paid to executing accurate outcome research which one day may be able to distinguish between the tangible and intangible rewards of therapy.

Whatever turns out to be the final outcome of these changes, there will, we are sure, always remain a need for a healthy eclecticism where the psychodynamic, humanistic, behavioural and cognitive therapies (together with 'biomedical' intervention) will be represented either sequentially or in combination. It has to be said, however, that those therapies which prove to be cost-, time- and labour-effective may flourish at the expense of those which are not, and it is in this respect that some of the cognitive-behavioural approaches may well benefit (as has pharmacotherapy in psychiatry).

However, ultimately an eclecticism of sorts must prevail if only because of the diversity of practitioners who need to express their differing interpretations of the human condition, the existence of an equally diverse population of patients and problems and the overriding recognition that no one philosophy can please all the people all the time. Indeed, despite a professed slavish and doctrinaire adherence to one or other of the therapies, in practice most therapists serve up some form of eclecticism (Cooper 1986).

Much of the strength of the cognitive and psychoeducational approach, however, stems from the fact that they provide more than simple therapy. Instead, they offer a philosophy of life by providing guidelines to help individuals reappraise, take responsibility and then learn to manage their lives more effectively. Such an approach contrasts with the more passive role of the humanistic and psychodynamic philosophies.

Since it is unlikely that all therapies will be equally effective with all patients and all problems, it is particularly important to try to establish a kind of consumers' guide to therapy to ensure that the maximum benefit may be derived for anyone about to enter therapy so that an informed and rational choice can be made, either by themselves or by their therapist. Though one might surmise that those individuals of low affect would respond more readily to the cognitive therapies and those with high affect to the behavioural, humanist or the psychodynamic, the answer to this important question is not readily available. *In vivo* flooding in the treatment of pathological jealousy, for example, may be very effective for one patient, whereas cognitive or psychodynamic methods may be more effective for another. In addition, it is known that there are important ethnic differences in the way patients choose and respond to therapy. Asians, for example, often prefer a logical, rational, cognitive approach rather than an instructional, reflective approach (Atkinson *et al.* 1978; Sue 1981). Such differences are, of course, also found between individual Caucasian patients. For example, the strictly cognitive approach of Bishay (1988) would clearly not be acceptable to every patient with vaginismus, others preferring behavioural therapy or even a psychodynamic programme (Valins 1988).

More specifically, there does appear to be an urgent need to investigate the relative effectiveness of the cognitive and behavioural methods in the treatment of sexual problems. The purpose of this would be to compare therapeutic outcomes in patients who occupy different points on the cognitive–affect continuum (see Figure 12.2). Barlow (1986) has already shown that different individuals respond differently to the same sex-stressors, depending upon the way in which they are, or are not, able to synchronize their cognitive and physiological responses, and this capacity may, in some way, depend upon the relative dominance of the affective and cognitive processes in any one individual.

It must be said, in conclusion, that however tempting it is to cling to the empirically based cognitive-behavioural approach because these therapies are both modern and accountable, the importance of the role that humanistic therapies play should not be overlooked. If a meeting point for *all* therapies exists, it is in the paradigm: *know yourself, accept yourself, change yourself* – each therapy differing only in the emphasis it places upon each step. Once patients cease to catastrophize and are able to put their problems in perspective, the way is open for them to address any remaining difficulties in a sensible and rational manner. After all, therapy is not always to do with solving problems; often, it is more concerned to help people accept themselves as fallible human beings whether or not they overcome their sexual problems.

Table 12.2 Outcome of treatment for sexual problems

Author	Sample	Sex disorder	Treatment programme	Outcome after treatment	Outcome at follow-up
Masters and Johnson (1970)	US couples	PE (n=186) RE (n=17) 1° ED (n=32) 2° ED (n=213) 1° ED (n=193) 2° OD (n=149) V (n=29)	Masters and Johnson	Initial failure rates PE 2.2% RE 17.6% 1° ED 40.6% 2° ED 26.2% 1° OD 16.6% 2° OD 22.8% V 0.0%	At 5 years (overall failure rate) PE 2.7% RE 17.6% 1° ED 40.6% 2° ED 30.9% 1° OD 17.6% 2° OD 24.8%
Kockott et al. (1975)	Three groups of eight males – mean age 31 (n=24)	Primary and secondary ED	Comparison of: systematic desensitization, medication and advice and waiting-list	SD 25% 'cured' M+A 25% 'cured' WL no 'cure' 'cure' = maintenance of E for one minute after penetration with ejaculation before loss of E	Planned but no data
Ansari (1976)	Men with sex problems	ED	Comparison of: modified M/J chemotherapy and no treatment	No difference between two treatments and controls	No data
Bancroft and Coles (1976)	Men and women consecutive patients at sex-problem clinic mean age 38 years (n=78)	PE RE V OD LL	Modified Masters and Johnson programmes	'successful outcome' 37% 'worthwhile improvement' 31% 'no change' 13% 'dropped out' 19%	No data
Levine and Agle (1978)	US couples age 25–9 wide cross-section (n=16)	Secondary psychogenic ED	M/J and Kaplan programme	'potent' 38% 'improved' 25% 'no change' 37%	Only 6% (one patient) maintained full function after one year
Mears (1978)	(n=1,373)	OD V ED	The Balint approach 'brief interpretive psychotherapy'	Successful outcome: OD 26% V 45% ED 30%	No data

Author	Sample	Sex disorder	Treatment programme	Outcome after treatment	Outcome at follow-up
Mears (1978) (continued)		PE RE		PE 30% RE 28%	
Kaplan (1979)	Wide spectrum (n=ca. 1,000)	All problems	Kaplan's methods	'cured' 63% 'improved' 7% 'failed or drop-out' 30%	No data
Crowe et al. (1981)	Couples with sexual problems (n=48 couples)	ED OD LL	Comparison of Masters and Johnson (one and two therapists) and marital therapy based on 'discussion'	Statistically significant improvement using validated scales – no difference between programmes	Improvement persistent for one year at least – no difference between programmes
Crown and d'Ardenne (1982)	UK couples (n=51)	ED PE RE V OD LL	Modified Masters and Johnson programmes	♀ positive change 59% some improvement 23% ♂ positive change 38% some improvement 26%	No data
Hawton (1982)	UK couples (n=100) 70 completed treatment	ED PE RE V OD LL	Modified Masters and Johnson programmes	Problem largely resolved 63% ♀ 70% ♂	After 3 months 52% ♀ 63% ♂
Watson and Brockman (1982)	UK couples (n=116)		Comparison of various treatment formats		53% follow-up (n=61) 42% (n=26) of whom maintained improvement
Heisler (1983)	NMGC clients (n=684)	All problems	Modified Masters and Johnson programmes	♂ ♀ 'some improvement' 6% 23% 'sufficient improvement' 5% 8% 'total improvement' 31% 26%	(n=460) 36% response improvement 20% no change 42% deterioration 38%

For a review of outcome in 18 independent studies up to and including 1976 see Wright *et al.* (1977) and text.
Key: PE: premature ejaculation; RE: retarded ejaculation; ED: erectile dysfunction; OD: orgasmic dysfunction; LL: loss of libido; V: vaginismus;
NMGC: National Marriage Guidance Council.
Note: 1 Reproduced with permission from Cole, M. (1985) 'Sex Therapy – a critical appraisal', *British Journal of Psychiatry* 147: 345–6.

REFERENCES

Allgeier, E. R. and Allgeier, A. R. (1984) *Sexual Interactions*, Lexington: D. C. Heath & Co.

Altman, I., Gahan, P. and Jehu, D. (1985) 'Psychoeducational treatment of impotence', *British Journal of Sexual Medicine* 12: 55–7.

Anderson, B. L. (1981) 'A comparison of systematic desensitisation and directed masturbation in the treatment of primary orgasmic dysfunction in females', *Journal of Consulting and Clinical Psychology* 49(4): 568–70.

Ansari, J. M. A. (1976) 'Impotence: prognosis (a controlled study), *British Journal of Psychiatry* 128: 194–8.

Apfelbaum, B. (1980) 'The diagnosis and treatment of retarded ejaculation'. in S. Leiblum and L. Pervin (eds) *Principles and Practice of Sex Therapy*, London: Tavistock Publications.

Atkinson, D. R., Marruyama, M. and Natsui, S. (1978) 'The effects of counselor race and counselor approach to Asian Americans' perceptions of counselor credibility and utility', *Journal of Counseling Psychology* 25: 76–83.

Bancroft, J. (1970) 'Disorders of sexual potency', in O. Hill (ed.) *Modern Trends in Psychosomatic Medicine*, New York: Appleton-Century-Crofts.

—— (1981) 'Some methodological aspects of treatment outcome research', in *Proceedings of the VII World Congress of Sexology*, Israel, June.

—— (1989) *Human Sexuality and its Problems*, 2nd edition, London: Churchill Livingstone.

—— and Coles, L. (1976) 'Three years' experience in a sexual problems clinic', *British Medical Journal* 1: 1575–7.

Barlow, D. H. (1986) 'Causes of sexual dysfunction: the role of anxiety and cognitive interference', *Journal of Consulting and Clinical Psychology* 54: 140–8.

——, Leitenberg, H. and Agras, W. S. (1969) 'Experimental control of sexual deviation through manipulation of noxious scenes in covert sensitization', *Journal of Abnormal Psychology* 74: 596–601.

Barlow, D. H., Sakheim, D. K. and Beck, J. G. (1983) 'Anxiety increases sexual arousal', *Journal of Abnormal Psychology* 92(1): 49–54.

Bass, B. A. (1985) 'The myth of low sexual desire: a cognitive-behavioural approach to treatment. Special issue: sex education past, present and future', *Journal of Sex Education and Therapy* 11(2): 61–4.

—— (1986) 'The elegant solution to the problem of impotence', *Journal of Rational-Emotive Therapy* 4(2): 113–18.

—— and Walen, S. R. (1986) 'Rational-emotive treatment for the sexual problems of couples. Special Issue: Rational-emotive couples therapy', *Journal of Rational-Emotive Therapy* 4(1): 82–94.

Beck, A. T. (1976) *Cognitive Therapy and the Emotional Disorders*, New York: International Universities Press.

——, Rush, A. J., Shaw, B. F. and Emery, G. (1979) *Cognitive Therapy of Depression*, New York: Guilford Press.

Beck, J. G. and Barlow, D. H. (1984) 'Current conceptualizations of sexual dysfunction: a review and an alternative perspective', *Clinical Psychology Review* 4: 363–78.

——, Sakheim, D. K. and Abrahamson, D. J. (1984) 'Sexual responding during anxiety: clinical versus non-clinical patterns', paper presented at the 18th Annual Convention of the Association for the Advancement of Behavior Therapy, Philadelphia.

Begg, A., Dickerson, M. and Loudon, N. B. (1976) 'Frequency of self-reporting sexual problems in a family planning clinic', *Journal of Family Planning Doctors* 2: 41–8.

Bishay, N. R. (1988) 'Cognitive therapy in psychosexual dysfunctions: a preliminary report', *Sexual and Marital Therapy* 3(1): 83–90.

Briddell, D. W., Rimm, D. C., Caddy, G. R., Krawitz, G., Sholis, D. and Wunderlin, R. J.

(1978) 'The effects of alcohol and cognitive set on sexual arousal to deviant stimuli', *Journal of Abnormal Psychology* 87: 418–30.

Chambless, D. L. and Liftshitz, J. L. (1984) 'Self-reported sexual anxiety and arousal: the expanded arousability inventory', *Journal of Sex Research* 20: 241–54.

Cole, M. J. (1985) 'Sex therapy – a critical appraisal', *British Journal of Psychiatry* 147: 337–51.

—— (1986) 'Socio-sexual characteristics of men with sexual problems', *Sexual and Marital Therapy* 1(1): 89–108.

—— (1988a) 'Normal and dysfunctional sexual behaviour: frequencies and incidences', in M. Cole and W. Dryden (eds) *Sex Therapy in Britain*, Milton Keynes: Open University Press.

—— (1988b) 'Sex therapy for individuals', in M. Cole and W. Dryden (eds) *Sex Therapy in Britain*, Milton Keynes: Open University Press.

Cooper, A. J. (1978) 'Treatment of male potency: the present status', in J. LoPiccolo and L. LoPiccolo (eds) *Handbook of Sex Therapy*, New York: Plenum Press.

Cooper, G. F. (1986) *Survey of Sex Therapists in Britain*, Birmingham: Training and Consultancy Services.

—— (1988) 'The psychological methods of sex therapy', in M. Cole and W. Dryden (eds) *Sex Therapy in Britain*, Milton Keynes: Open University Press.

Crowe, M. J., Gillan, P. and Golombok, S. (1981) 'Form and content in the conjoint treatment of sexual dysfunction: a controlled study', *Behaviour Research and Therapy* 19: 47–54.

Crown, S. and d'Ardenne, P. (1982) 'Symposium on sexual dysfunctions: controversies, methods and results', *British Journal of Psychiatry* 140: 70–7.

Dryden, W. (1990) *Rational-Emotive Counselling in Action*, London: Sage.

Ellis, A. (1962) *Reason and Emotion in Psychotherapy*, New York: Lyle Stuart.

—— (1975) 'The rational-emotive approach to sex therapy', *Counselling Psychologist* 5(1): 14–22.

—— (1976) *Sex and the Liberated Man*, New York: Lyle Stuart.

—— (1980) 'Treatment of erectile dysfunction', in S. R. Leiblum and L. A. Pervin (eds) *Principles and Practice of Sex Therapy*, London: Tavistock.

—— (1983) 'Does sex therapy really have a future?', *Rational Living* 18: 3–6.

Everaerd, W. and Dekker, J. (1985) 'Treatment of male sexual dysfunction: sex therapy compared with systematic desensitization and rational-emotive therapy', *Behaviour Research and Therapy* 23 (1): 13–25.

Feldman, M. P. and MacCullough, M. J. (1971) *Homosexual Behaviour: Theory and Assessment*, Oxford: Pergamon Press.

Fenichel, O. (1945) *The Psychoanalytic Theory of Neurosis*, New York: W. W. Norton.

Friedman, D. (1968) 'The treatment of impotence by brietal relaxation therapy', *Behaviour Research and Therapy* 6: 257–61.

Gagnon, J. H. and Simon, W. (1973) *Sexual Conduct: The Social Sources of Human Sexuality*, Chicago: Aldine Publishing Company.

Gersham, L. (1970) 'Case conference: a transvestite fantasy treated by thought-stopping, covert sensitization and aversive shock', *Journal of Behaviour Therapy and Experimental Psychiatry* 1: 153–61.

Golombok, S. and Rust, J. (1988) 'Diagnosis of sexual dysfunction: relationships between DSM-III (R) and the GRISS', *Sexual and Marital Therapy* 3(1): 119–24.

Harbert, T. L., Barlow, D. H., Hersen, M. and Austin, J. B. (1974) 'Measurement and modification of incestuous behavior: a case study', *Psychological Reports* 34: 79–86.

Hastings, D. W. (1963) *Impotence and Frigidity*, London: Churchill.

Hawton, K. (1982) 'Symposium on sexual dysfunction. The behavioural treatment of sexual dysfunction', *British Journal of Psychiatry* 140: 94–101.

—— (1983) 'Recent research in the treatment of sexual dysfunctions', paper presented to the meeting of the Association of Sexual and Marital Therapists, Manchester, UK.

—— (1985) *Sex Therapy: A Practical Guide*, Oxford, Oxford University Press.

Heisler, J. (1983) *Sexual Therapy in the National Marriage Guidance Council*, Rugby: National Marriage Guidance Council.

Henson, D. E. and Rubin, H. B. (1971) 'Voluntary control of eroticism', *Journal of Applied Behavior Analysis* 4: 37–44.

Hoch, Z., Safir, M. P., Peres, Y. and Shepherd, J. (1981) 'An evaluation of sexual performance: comparison between sexually dysfunctional and functional couples', *Journal of Sex and Marital Therapy* 7(3): 195–206.

Hoon, E., Hoon, P. and Wincze, J. (1976) 'An inventory for the measurement of female sexual arousal', *Archives of Sexual Behavior* 5: 291–300.

Hoon, P., Wincze, J. and Hoon, E. (1977) 'A test of reciprocal inhibition: are anxiety and sexual arousal in women mutually inhibitory?', *Journal of Abnormal Psychology* 86: 65–74.

Hughes, R. C. (1977) 'Covert sensitization treatment of exhibitionism', *Journal of Behavior Therapy and Experimental Psychiatry* 8: 171–9.

Jehu, D. (1979) *Sexual Dysfunction: A Behavioural Approach to Causation, Assessment and Treatment*, New York: John Wiley.

Kaplan, H. S. (1974) *The New Sex Therapy*, New York: Brunner/Mazel.

—— (1975) *The Illustrated Manual of Sex Therapy*, New York: Quadrangle.

—— (1979) *Disorders of Sexual Desire*, London: Balliere Tindall.

—— (1983) *The Evaluation of Sexual Disorders*, New York: Brunner/Mazel.

Kinsey, A. C., Pomeroy, W. B., Martin, C. E. and Gebhard, P. H. (1948) *Sexual Behavior in the Human Male*, Philadelphia and London: W. B. Saunders.

—— (1953) *Sexual Behavior in the Human Female*, Philadelphia and London: W. B. Saunders.

Kockott, G., Dittmar, F. and Nusselt, L. (1975) 'Systematic desensitization of erectile impotence: a controlled study', *Archives of Sexual Behavior* 4: 493–500.

Kolodny, R. C. (1981) 'Evaluating sex therapy: process and outcome at the Masters and Johnson Institute', *Journal of Sex Research* 17: 301–18.

Kowalski, R. (1985) 'Cognitive therapy for sexual problems', *British Journal of Sexual Medicine* 12: 64–6, 90–3, 131–5.

Kuriansky, J. B. and Sharpe, L. (1976) 'Guidelines for evaluating sex therapy', *Journal of Sex and Marital Therapy* 2: 303–8.

Laws, D. and Rubin, H. (1969) 'Instructional control of autonomic sexual response', *Journal of Applied Behavior Analysis* 2: 93–100.

Leiblum, S. R. and Pervin, L. A. (1980) *Principles and Practice of Sex Therapy*, London: Tavistock Publications.

Levine, S. and Agle, D. (1978) 'The effectiveness of sex therapy for chronic secondary psychological impotence', *Journal of Sex and Marital Therapy* 4: 235–58.

LoPiccolo, J. and LoPiccolo, L. (1978) *Handbook of Sex Therapy*, New York and London: Plenum.

LoPiccolo, J. and Steger, J. (1974) 'The sexual interaction inventory: a new instrument for assessment of sexual dysfunction', *Archives of Sexual Behavior* 3: 585–95.

McCarthy, B. W. (1977) 'Strategies and techniques for the reduction of sexual anxiety', *Journal of Sex and Marital Therapy* 3(4): 243–8.

—— (1984) 'Strategies and techniques for the treatment of inhibited sexual desire', *Journal of Sex and Marital Therapy* 10(2): 97–104.

McCormick, N. B. (1987) 'Sexual scripts: social and therapeutic implications', *Sexual and Marital Therapy* 2(1): 3–27.

Mahoney, M. J. (1974) *Cognition and Behavior Modification*, Cambridge Mass.: Ballinger.

Marquis, J. N. (1970) 'Orgasmic reconditioning: changing sexual object choice through controlling masturbation fantasies', *Journal of Behavior Therapy and Experimental Psychiatry* 1: 263–72.

Masters, W. H. and Johnson, V. E. (1966) *Human Sexual Response*, Boston: Little Brown & Co.

—— (1970) *Human Sexual Inadequacy*, London: J. A. Churchill.

Maultsby, M. C. (Jr.) (1975) *Help Yourself to Happiness*, New York: Institute for Rational Living.

Mears, E. (1978) 'Sexual problem clinics: an assessment of the work of 26 doctors trained by the Institute of Psychosexual Medicine', *Public Health* 92: 218–33.

Melman, A., Kaplan, D. and Redfield, J. (1984) 'Evaluation of the first 70 patients in the center for male sexual dysfunction of the Beth Israel Medical Center', *Journal of Urology* 131(1): 53–5.

Milne, D. and Cordle, C. (1984) 'Evaluating sex therapy', *British Journal of Sexual Medicine* 11: 110–14.

Morrow-Bradley, C. and Elliot, R. (1986) 'Utilisation of psychotherapy research by practising psychotherapists', *American Psychologist* 41(2): 188–97.

Munjack, D. J., Schlaks, A., Sanchez, V. C., Usigli, R., Zulueta, A. and Leonard, M. (1984) 'Rational-emotive therapy in the treatment of erectile failure: an initial study', *Journal of Sex and Marital Therapy* 10(3): 170–5.

Norton, G. R. and Jehu, D. (1984) 'The role of anxiety in sexual dysfunction: a review', *Archives of Sexual Behavior* 13: 165–83.

Pietropinto, A. (1986) 'Male contributors to female sexual dysfunction', *Medical Aspects of Human Sexuality* 20(12): 84–91.

Ramsey, G. (1943) 'The sexual development of boys', *American Journal of Psychology* 56: 217.

Rathus, S. A. (1978) 'Use of covert assertion in cognitive restructuring of sexual attitudes', *Behaviour Therapy* 9: 678.

Reynolds, B. S., Cohen, B. D., Schochet, B. V., Price, S. C. and Anderson, A. J. (1981) 'Dating skills training in the group treatment of erectile dysfunction for men without partners', *Journal of Sex and Marital Therapy* 7(3): 184–94.

Rook, K. S. and Hammen, C. L. (1977) 'A cognitive perspective on the experience of sexual arousal', *Journal of Social Issues* 33(2): 7–29.

Rust, J. and Golombok, S. (1985) 'The Golombok Rust Inventory of Sexual Satisfaction (GRISS)', *British Journal of Clinical Psychology* 24: 63–4.

Rust, J., Bennun, I., Crowe, M. and Golombok, S. (1986) 'The Golombok Rust Inventory of Marital State (GRIMS)', *Sexual and Marital Therapy* 1: 55–60.

Sarrel, D. M. and Masters, W. H. (1982) 'Sexual molestation of men by women', *Archives of Sexual Behavior* 11: 117–31.

Schiavi, R. (1976) 'Sex therapy and psychophysiological research'', *American Journal of Psychiatry* 133: 562–6.

Schultz, J. H. (1951) *Autogenic Training*, New York: Grune and Stratton.

Semans, J. H. (1956) 'Premature ejaculation: a new approach', *Southern Medical Journal* 49: 353–7.

Shaw, W. (1954) *Operative Gynaecology*, Baltimore: Williams and Wilkins.

Southern, S. (1985) 'Hypoactive sexual desire: a cognitive model. Special issue: sex education past, present and future', *Journal of Sex Education and Therapy* 11(2): 55–60.

Stoller, R. (1976) 'Sexual excitement', *Archives of General Psychiatry* 33: 899–909.

Stravynski, A. (1986) 'Indirect behavioural treatment of erectile failure and premature ejaculation in a man without a partner', *Archives of Sexual Behavior* 15 (4): 355–61.

Sue, D. W. (ed.) (1981) *Counseling the Culturally Different*, New York: Wiley.

Thyer, B. A. and Papsdorf, J. D. (1981) 'Relationship between irrationality and sexual arousability', *Psychological Reports* 48(3): 834.

Truax, C. B. and Carkhuff, R. R. (1967) *Toward Effective Counseling and Psychotherapy*, Chicago: Aldine Publishing Company.

Tullman, G. M., Gilner, F. H., Kolodny, R. C., Dornbush, R. L. and Tullman, G. D. (1981) 'The pre- and post-therapy measurement of communication skills of couples undergoing sex therapy at the Masters and Johnson Institute', *Archives of Sexual Behavior* 10: 95–109.

Valins, L. (1988) *Vaginismus: Understanding and Overcoming the Blocks to Intercourse*, Bath: Ashgrove Press.

Virag, R. (1985) 'About pharmacologically induced prolonged erection', *Lancet* i: 519–20.

Walen, S. R. (1980) 'Cognitive factors in sexual behavior', *Journal of Sex and Marital Therapy* 6(2): 87–101.

—— and Perlmutter, R. (1988) 'Cognitive-behavioral treatment of adult sexual dysfunctions from a family perspective;, in N. Epstein, S. Schlesinger and W. Dryden (eds) *Cognitive-Behavioral Approaches to Family Therapy*, New York: Brunner/Mazel.

Walen, S. R. and Roth, D. (1987) 'A cognitive approach', in J. H. Gerr and W. O'Donohue (eds) *Theories of Human Sexuality*, New York: Plenum.

Watson, J. P. and Brockman, B. (1982) 'A follow-up of couples attending a psychosexual problems clinic', *British Journal of Clinical Psychology* 21: 143–4.

Whitehead, A. and Matthews, A. (1986) 'Factors related to successful outcome in the treatment of sexually unresponsive women', *Psychological Medicine* 16(2): 373–8.

Wilcox, D. and Hager, R. (1980) 'Towards realistic expectations for orgasmic response in women', *Journal of Sex Research* 16(2): 162–79.

Wolchik, S. A., Beggs, V. E., Wincze, J. P., Sakheim, D. K., Barlow, D. H. and Mavissa-kalian, M. (1980) 'The effects of a subjective monitoring task in the measurement of genital response to erotic stimulation', *Archives of Sexual Behavior* 9: 533– 45.

Wolfe, J. and Walen, S. (1982) 'Cognitive factors in sexual behavior', in R. Grieger and I. Grieger (eds) *Cognition and Emotional Disturbance*, New York: Human Sciences Press.

Wolpe, J. (1958) *Psychotherapy by Reciprocal Inhibition*, Stamford: Stamford University Press.

—— (1978) 'Comments on "A test of reciprocal inhibition" by Hoon, Wincze and Hoon', *Journal of Abnormal Psychology* 87: 452–4.

Wright, J., Perreault, R. and Mathieu, M. (1977) 'The treatment of sexual dysfunction: a review', *Archives of General Psychiatry* 34: 881–90.

Zilbergeld, B. (1978) *Male Sexuality*, New York: Bantam Books.

—— (1980) *Men and Sex*, Glasgow: Fontana/Collins.

—— and Ellison, C. R. (1979) 'Social skills training as an adjunct in sex therapy', *Journal of Sex and Marital Therapy* 5(4): 340–50.

Zilbergeld, B. and Evans, M. (1980) 'The inadequacy of Masters and Johnson', *Psychology Today* August: 29–43.

Name index

Abrams, D. 140, 146
Abramson, L.J. 61, 66, 67
Abramson, L.Y. 11, 257, 291
Abu EI Eileh 220
Adams, A. 302, 303
Adams, S.H. 185, 186
Adesso, V. 144
Ager, A.K. 236, 240, 241, 244, 246, 249, 250, 251
Agle, D. 347
Agras, W.S. 125, 128
Alberman, E. 234
Alberti, R.E. 301
Alden, L. 260
Alexander, B. 148
Alexander, J.F. 309
Alford, G.S. 182
Allaman, J.D, 258
Allen, H.A. 182, 183
Allgeier, A.R. 318
Allon, N. 124
Alloy, L.B. 11, 62, 65, 67, 76
Allsop, S. 159, 161, 164, 166
Alston, W.P. 92
Altman, I. 341
American Psychiatric Association 27, 41, 43, 115–16, 117, 260
Anderson, B.L. 334
Andrasik, F. 275
Ansari, J.M.A. 347
Apfelbaum, B. 334
Argyle, M. 254, 255
Arkowitz, H. 265
Arnkoff, D. 15
Arnkoff, D.B. 31, 32, 50, 51, 59
Asarnow, J. R. 264
Asher, S. 264
Atkinson, D.R. 349

Averill, J.R. 104, 107
Ayllon, I. 196
Azar, S.T. 294, 298, 303, 310
Azrin, N. 160

Baddeley, A.D. 5
Baikie, E. 207, 209, 218, 220
Bailey, K. 280
Bakeman, R. 260
Baker, R. 160, 174
Baldwin, S. 233
Baltes, P.B. 204
Bancroft, J. 323, 328, 340, 344, 347
Bandura, A. 8, 9, 13, 29, 46, 47, 50, 51, 62, 69, 86, 90, 97, 101, 105, 139, 144–5, 147, 171, 255, 294, 295, 300
Barclay, L.R. 246
Barlow, D.H. 34, 42, 260, 265, 266, 328, 329, 330, 343, 349
Barnett, L.R. 300
Barrowclough, C. 215
Bass, B.A. 336, 337, 339
Baucom, D.H. 289, 290, 291, 292, 293, 296, 298, 302, 303, 306, 308, 309, 310, 311, 312
Baumeister, A.A. 262
Beach, S.R.H. 309
Bebbington, P. 79
Beck, A.T. 5, 6, 10, 15, 18, 29, 30, 31, 33, 34, 35, 39, 45, 50, 56, 58, 63, 64, 65, 67, 71, 72, 74, 75, 94, 100, 101, 120, 125, 126, 161, 209, 214, 256, 258, 262, 289, 290, 291, 297, 305, 325, 329, 330, 338
Becker, R.E. 274
Bedell, J.P. 187
Begg, A. 344
Beidel, D.C. 261
Beinhart, H. 121, 163

Subject index

ABC(D) model (in RET) 6, 320, 337–8
addiction *see* alcohol problems, drug problems
ageing *see* elderly people, problems of
aggression 86, 89; affective 90–2; and alcohol comsumption 140; cognitive models of 89–92; defining 87–8; treatment of 89; *see also* anger, violence
agoraphobia 30, 41–2
alcohol problems 138–70 *passim*; and aggression 140; assessment for 142–3; counselling model for 165; generalization process in 150–1; as an interpersonal problem 264; modelling and 144; and sexual arousal 140–1; *see also* drug problems
analogue research studies 12–13, 17
anger 86–113; Anger Control Training 100–2; – anxiety overlap 107; as a clinical problem 95–6; cognitive models of 92–5; control, and relaxation 101, 105–6; defined 88; development of 96–9; future developments 107–9; treatment of 99–107; vs. violence 88–9; *see also* aggression, violence
anorexia nervosa 119–20; diagnostic criteria 115–16; treatment 125–6
antidepressants, 71, 75
anxiety 27–55; alcohol comsumption and 146; – anger overlap 107; cognition and 29–32; development of 32–4; DSM-III-R classification 27–8; in the elderly 206, 212; evolutionary bias of 33; and expectations 34–8; future developments 47–51; neuroanatomy of 34; and schemata 35–8; sexual dysfunction and 328–9, 330, 332;

social 260–1, 265–72; three-systems model 28–9; treatment 38–47, 265–72; *see also* agoraphobia, fear, generalized anxiety disorder, obsessive-compulsive disorders, panic attacks/disorders, phobias
artificial intelligence 14
assessment: cognitive 31–2; for drug problems 142–3; for eating disorders 130; for, elderly, problems 209–11; instruments for family problems 311; for interpersonal problems 254–7 *passim*, 259–64; role-play in 259. 261; for schizophrenia 173–5
attachment 255
attributions *see* inferences

behaviour therapy: for bulimia nervosa 128; criticisms of 4; for the elderly 213–15; features of 4; historical context of 2–4; for marital/family problems 300, 301, 304, 307–10 *passim*: for mental handicap 241–6, 250; for obesity 129; for phobias 45–7 *passim*; research methods in 12–15 *passim*; for sexual problems 331–4; treatment outcome in 8
behaviourism 2, 12; vs. psychoanalysis 5; purposive, 4–5
bereavement, of the elderly 205, 206, 215–17
binge eating 163; *see also* bulimia nervosa
body-image distortion 123–4, 130–1
bulimia nervosa 120–2; diagnostic criteria 116–17; treatment 126–8

catastrophic thinking styles 30; in anorexia nervosa 120
children, aggression in 98–9, 104